MONEY AND THE EARLY GREEK MIND

How were the Greeks of the sixth century BC able to invent philosophy and tragedy? In this book Richard Seaford argues that a large part of the answer can be found in another momentous development, the invention and rapid spread of coinage, which produced the first ever thoroughly monetised society. By transforming social relations, monetisation contributed to the ideas of the universe as an impersonal system (presocratic philosophy) and of the individual alienated from his own kin and from the gods (in tragedy). Seaford argues that an important precondition for this monetisation was the Greek practice of animal sacrifice, as represented in Homeric epic, which describes a premonetary world on the point of producing money. This book combines social history, economic anthropology, numismatics and the close reading of literary, inscriptional, and philosophical texts. Questioning the origins and shaping force of Greek philosophy, this is a major book with wide appeal.

RICHARD SEAFORD is Professor of Greek Literature at the University of Exeter. He is the author of commentaries on Euripides' *Cyclops* (1984) and *Bacchae* (1996) and of *Reciprocity and Ritual: Homer and Tragedy in the Developing City-State* (1994).

MONEY AND THE EARLY GREEK MIND

Homer, Philosophy, Tragedy

RICHARD SEAFORD

CAMBRIDGE
UNIVERSITY PRESS

PUBLISHED BY THE PRESS SYNDICATE OF THE UNIVERSITY OF CAMBRIDGE
The Pitt Building, Trumpington Street, Cambridge, United Kingdom

CAMBRIDGE UNIVERSITY PRESS
The Edinburgh Building, Cambridge, CB2 2RU, UK
40 West 20th Street, New York, NY 10011–4211, USA
477 Williamstown Road, Port Melbourne, VIC 3207, Australia
Ruiz de Alarcón 13, 28014 Madrid, Spain
Dock House, The Waterfront, Cape Town 8001, South Africa

http://www.cambridge.org

First published 2004

Printed in the United Kingdom at the University Press, Cambridge

Typeface Adobe Garamond 11/12.5 pt.   *System* LaTeX 2_ε [TB]

A catalogue record for this book is available from the British Library

Library of Congress Cataloging in Publication data
Seaford, Richard.
Money and the early Greek mind: Homer, philosophy, tragedy / Richard Seaford.
p.   cm.
Includes bibliographical references (p.) and index.
ISBN 0 521 83228 4 (hardback) – ISBN 0 521 53992 7 (paperback)
1 Greek literature – History and criticism.   2 Money in literature.   3 Greek drama (Tragedy) –
History and criticism.   4 Epic poetry, Greek – History and criticism.   5 Greece – Economic
conditions – To 146 B.C.   6 Economics and literature – Greece.   7 Homer – Knowledge –
Economics.   8 Economics in literature.   9 Philosophy, Ancient.   10 Money – Greece.   I. Title.
PA3015.M64S43   2004
80.9′3553–dc22   2003055724

ISBN 0 521 83228 4 hardback
ISBN 0 521 53992 7 paperback

For Yana
Hoc non desinit incipitque semper

Contents

Preface

This book argues that the monetisation of the Greek polis in the sixth and fifth centuries BC contributed to a radical transformation in thought that is, in a sense, still with us. Academics – perhaps because they are more interested in texts than in money – have emphasised rather the role of alphabetic literacy in the radical intellectual changes of this period. They are often also emotionally invested in the autonomy of their various specialisms, an investment encouraged by the institutional division of academic labour. For most presocratic scholars, to allow that any kind of social process might illuminate their texts would threaten their control of their subject and the autonomy of 'doing philosophy'. The consequent subconscious policing of the boundaries can be simultaneously sincere and brutal. For embarking on such a fundamental question I make no apology, and hope that others will be inspired to remedy the inadequacies of my answers.

I thank all those who have over many years, in formal and informal settings, discussed with me a theme – the western genesis of money and its consequences – that seems to be of interest to everybody. Further, the book has benefited from the reading of chapters 2–8 by Jack Kroll, 2–7 by Henry Kim, 4D–5A by Robert Parker, 6 by Peter Haarer, 9 and 10 by Geoffrey Lloyd, 9–13 by Malcolm Schofield, 13B by Carl Huffman, 13C by Paul Woodruff, and the whole book by Christopher Gill and by Robin Osborne. I am also grateful for numismatic discussion to Chris Howgego and Ute Wartenberg, and to Paul Curtis for checking the references. I continue to owe much to the stimulating and collegiate atmosphere of the Department of Classics and Ancient History in the University of Exeter. Thanks go finally to my publisher for courteous efficiency and for openness to radically new ideas.

Abbreviations

ABV	J. D. Beazley, *Attic Black-Figure Vase Painting*. Oxford, 1956.
*ARV*²	J. D. Beazley, *Attic Red-Figure Vase Painting*. 2nd. ed., Oxford, 1963.
DK	*Die Fragmente der Vorsokratiker*, ed. H. Diels and W. Kranz, 6th ed. (with subsequent impressions), Berlin, 1951.
FGrH	*Die Fragmente der Griechische Historiker*, ed. F. Jacoby. Berlin and Leiden, 1923–58.
KRS	G. S. Kirk, J. E. Raven, and M. Schofield, *The Presocratic Philosophers*. 2nd ed., Cambridge, 1983.
PMG	*Poetae Melici Graeci*, ed. D. L. Page. Oxford, 1962.
RE	*Pauly's Real-Encyclopädie der Klassischen Altertumswissenschaft*. Stuttgart, 1894–1919.
*SIG*³	*Sylloge Inscriptionum Graecarum*, ed. W. Dittenberger. 3rd. ed., Leipzig, 1915–24.

Comic fragments are cited in *Poetae Comici Graeci* (Berlin), edited by R. Kassel and C. Austin. Tragic fragments are cited in the volumes of *Tragicorum Graecorum Fragmenta*, (edited by B. Snell and S. Radt, Göttingen), except for Euripides, which is cited in the old edition of A. Nauck.

Presocratics are cited in DK (see above).

Help in understanding abbreviations of ancient authors and works is to be found in the Greek–English Lexicon edited by Liddell and Scott, and of periodicals in *Année Philologique*.

CHAPTER ONE

Introduction

Money is central to our lives. But what exactly is it? A definition is surprisingly elusive. Money is, puzzlingly, both a thing and a relation. And the relation – because it is one of power that is interpersonal and unspecific, over the labour not of another but of others in general – tends to be mystified, to be disguised as a thing. Further, different kinds of thing, used in different kinds of transaction in different kinds of society, have all been called 'money': mediaeval coinage, the silver of second millennium BC Mesopotamia, large stone discs on the Pacific island of Yap, the shells circulated on the Trobriand islands, the money used in advanced industrial societies ('modern money'), and so on.

A detailed analysis of 'money' will be provided in due course (IC). I begin here with modern money, which – unlike some other kinds of money – is a mere token, without use-value or even (sometimes) physical embodiment. If imagined nevertheless – as it generally is – as a thing, intangible yet promiscuous, what sort of thing is it? Apparently a token or symbol, commanding the labour of others. But a symbol of what? Not, surely, of all or any one of the numerous goods and services that it can be exchanged for, but rather of the homogeneous, numerical *exchange-value* abstracted from – so as to embody command over – goods and services.[1] And because this value is too abstract to be embodied in money in the way that the abstraction of strength may seem embodied in a symbolic lion, we should perhaps call modern money not even a mere *symbol* but a mere *sign*, whose meaning is exhausted in its function as a means of payment or exchange.

But does not modern money have symbolic associations constituting 'meanings' in the broad sense? The pound sterling symbolises – for some – British identity. Less sublimely but more universally, according to Freudian

---

[1] I leave aside the problem of the precise relation of this value to labour.

theory money is subconsciously associated with excrement.[2] And is not money generally associated with a vague sense of well-being? But whatever the associations of modern money (conscious or unconscious, universal or specific), its central and predominant function – requiring precisely its identity in all contexts, unaffected by any incidental associations – is to embody abstract value as a general means of payment, of exchange, of the measurement and storage of value. It is precisely this absence or marginality of specific symbolic associations or meanings that arose from, and permits, its general effectiveness.

But might not symbolic associations arise from precisely this function? For what it bestows on money – permanent, unique, transcendent, mystified, all-embracing power for good or evil – may seem to associate money with the divine. The metaphor of money as god is sufficiently telling to seem somehow more than a metaphor;[3] sociologists have claimed to find sacredness attaching to modern money;[4] and in European folklore money often has magical powers.[5] But most people would firmly dissociate modern money from sacredness. As transcendent power that is set apart, money resembles the sacred, but it is antithetical to it in the worldliness of its promiscuous[6] exchangeability.[7]

The numerous forms of 'primitive money', by contrast, generally have intrinsic (if only aesthetic) value, are rarely[8] universally exchangeable, and are frequently invested with emotions and meanings that may vary according to the context of use, even within the same society. Here, to take an example almost at random, is a (somewhat lyrical) interpretation of the shells used by the Are'are people of the Solomon Islands both in exchange for other goods and in ceremonies such as the funeral.

---

[2] For bibliography see Shell 1982, 196.

[3] E.g. in Timon's 'thou visible god . . .' (*Timon of Athens* 4.3.388) or Marx 1973 (1857–8), 221 '. . . Money is therefore the god among commodities . . . It represents the divine existence of commodities, while they represent its earthly form'; 1992 (1844), 377; Simmel 1978 (1907), 236; most elaborately discussed by the early German socialist Moses Hess.

[4] Belk and Wallendorf 1990.   [5] Schöttle 1913; Weil 1980.

[6] Its almost universal exchangeability is limited by (a) some things being by common agreement (though not always in fact) put largely beyond its reach, such as national monuments, body parts, a place in heaven; (b) sentiment deriving from non-commercial relationships: e.g. a *gift* of money should not be spent on just anything; (c) some contexts in which one of the forms of money – paper, metal, cheques, credit cards, electronic transfers – is not accepted. But this does not mean that in those contexts *money* is unacceptable: the various forms (as well as bank accounts) are inherently worthless embodiments of the same abstract value and so are in principle intertransformable.

[7] For sacralisation as embodying the singularisation that is antithetical to commodification see Kopytoff 1986. For anthropological antithesis between sacred and exchangeable see Godelier 1999, 33, 35, 37, 100, 164–7.

[8] For some exceptions see Douglas 1967, 123–4.

In their circulation these moneys observe precise rules, and are, together with men, women, and children and all cultural goods, the objects of a system of exchanges which animates and reproduces indefinitely what is established in the life of this society. This implicit immortality of the society is maintained by the mortality of the people and goods which cross its path. Both the living and the dead combine in the progressive wearing out of all things, of which in the end no trace remains except these pieces of money, and the unceasing ballet that they perform. These moneys, the tangible supporters of the law, are all that remains of the ancestors: they are the all-powerful accomplices of time.[9]

The most famous example of 'primitive money' invested with social symbolism is the 'Kula' system of the Trobriand islands.[10] In so far as it is a circulating exchange of items (shells) which have very little use-value (being hardly ever used as ornaments), there is a superficial resemblance with the circulation of modern money, from which however it differs fundamentally. The shells are exchanged only for each other (and so should not perhaps be called money), having instead the role of establishing and maintaining supportive relations between the transactors, and are the object of the kind of admiration that only a lunatic would lavish on a ten euro note.

Among the Baruya of New Guinea salt is on the one hand exchanged with outsiders for all that they themselves lack, and so plays the role of money, and on the other hand, within the community, is never bartered, only given and distributed, and consumed only within the framework of the solemn rituals celebrating birth, initiation, and marriage.[11] Even where modern money enters premodern societies, the meanings with which it is invested are, it has been argued, 'quite as much a product of the cultural matrix into which it is incorporated as of the economic functions it performs as a means of exchange, unit of account, store of value, and so on. It is therefore impossible to predict its symbolic meanings from these functions alone'.[12] The significance and functioning of money can never be understood separately from the kind of transaction, and indeed the kind of society, in which it is used.[13]

Where, in all this, does ancient Greek money belong? The first people in history to use extensively something approaching modern money were,

[9] de Coppet and Zemp 1978, 116.
[10] E.g. Malinowski 1967 (1920); Hart 1986, 647–51; Godelier 1999, 78–95.
[11] Godelier 1977, 127–51.
[12] Parry and Bloch 1989, 21, on the basis of the essays contained in the volume. A striking instance not therein mentioned is discussed by Bessaignet 1970; see also Crump 1981; Dalton 1971, 167–92.
[13] Dalton 1971, 167–92.

I believe, almost certainly[14] the Greeks, whose money consisted of metal, coined and uncoined. Their coinage had all seven of the characteristics of money set out below (1C). And there is no evidence that it had different meanings in different contexts. Whatever its specific associations,[15] the collective confidence required for Greek coined money to work as currency is confidence in its equal acceptability in a wide variety of contexts.[16] There is among the Greeks evidence neither of 'special purpose money' nor of the ritual, known from some societies, of converting money from one sphere to another.[17] Indeed, the Greeks were struck by the power of the same one thing – 'wealth', 'money', or 'currency' – to do a wide variety of things.[18] In Sophocles, for instance, money is in one passage said to create friends, honours, tyranny, physical beauty, skill in speaking, enjoyment even in illness, and – most significantly – access to things both sacred and profane, and in another passage to destroy cities, drive men from their homes, transform good men into evil-doers, and cause men to know every kind of impiety.[19]

But what of the symbolic associations of ancient Greek money as a whole? As we have noted of modern money, the marginality of specific associations does not preclude a general association with the divine or the sacred. For modern money such a general association is extremely tenuous, for Greek money only slightly more substantial. Money, coined and uncoined, was stored in huge quantities in sanctuaries, and might be imagined as belonging to deity.[20] At least as early as the Classical period some Greek sanctuaries functioned as banks (4D). Coins were often stamped with an image of a deity. Money was often imagined as having a superhuman will of its own.[21]

---

[14] I leave aside the difficult problem of early Chinese 'money': cf. n. 36. For the early Near East see ch. 15.

[15] Of these the most notable is the association of a currency with its issuing polis by its emblem. See also 8B (with the vast homogeneity of the sea), 8H (with what is represented on the coin), 14A (with the soul or person), 14E (with reproduction).

[16] The fact that coinage was used in various contexts, sometimes alongside other valuable objects (esp. von Reden 1995, 195–216; 1997), does not mean – any more than it does today – that it had various symbolic associations.

[17] This is admitted by von Reden 1995, 96, who in claiming nevertheless that liturgies and *eisphora* 'can be regarded as ritual "conversions" . . .' overstretches the terms 'ritual' and 'conversion'.

[18] See the passages discussed in ch. 8, esp. 8E.   [19] Fr. 88, *Ant.* 295–301.

[20] E.g. Isocr. *Antid.* 232. Some of the coins found in temple precincts are counterfeit (e.g. in those of the Mother of the Gods in Athens); an Athenian inscription requires counterfeit coins to be made sacred to the gods: Stroud 1974.

[21] E.g. Theogn. 190; Soph. fr. 88; *Ant.* 295–301; fr. adesp. 129, 341; Eur. *Hec.* 865; 14A. Wealth (Ploutos) was a minor deity who in the Aristophanean comedy of that name has the characteristics of money, and is shown to be more powerful than Zeus.

It played a part in some religious ritual: for instance, the tribute from the allies was displayed in the procession at the Athenian City Dionysia;[22] coins were buried with the dead; and they might be dedicated, presumably not entirely without ceremony, to deity. But in these Greek ritual contexts there is no reason for believing that the money carried any symbolic meaning beyond its monetary value.[23] It has been suggested that the profane character of money in Christianity and Islam (in contrast to eastern religions) derives from the Jews, who relegated it to the status of the profane because their first encounter with it was as commercial and exogenous: 'if money is profane, it is because it is exogenous'.[24] But this is at best only a small part of the story, for Greek money was neither inherently sacred nor on the whole perceived as exogenous.[25] In Aristotle's analysis of currency,[26] which along with his disapproval of usury influenced mediaeval Christianity, there is no suggestion of exogeneity or sacredness.

In this analysis Aristotle maintains that currency was created, in the process of trade, out of something that was both useful and easy to handle (metal), defined at first by size and weight, then finally by a stamp to dispense with the need for measurement. But the *nomisma* (currency, coinage) thereby created, so far from being inherently useful, has a value that, Aristotle notes in the same passage, is merely conventional. In this uselessness Greek coins may seem to resemble both modern money and much 'primitive money' – for instance the shell money of the southern Pacific. But both comparisons require qualification.

It is true that the only use of gold and silver, from which the earliest coins were made, was – like shells but in contrast to most commodities – their aesthetic allurement (and its symbolic associations), a luxurious superfluity that both permits and encourages circulation, which may endow them with further symbolic associations. But the application of the stamp to

---

[22] Compare Callim. *H.hom.Dem.* 126–7: sacred baskets (*likna*) of gold in the procession of the mystic Demeter.

[23] The coins for the dead are imagined as paying Charon, and provide for Aristophanes a joke about the *universality* of the power of money: 8E n. 72. On precious metal in temples as monetary value see e.g. Thuc. 2.13.

[24] Crump 1981, 285, 289.

[25] Greeks attributed the invention of coinage to themselves or to the Lydians (7A), but they were themselves the first to use it en masse, and had no non-Greek words for 'money' or 'currency' or 'coinage' or for any coins. Greek money is in the sixth and fifth centuries quite different from the earlier and contemporary use of precious metal elsewhere (ch.15), but this does not prevent the Greeks from sometimes projecting the negative qualities of their own attitude to money onto barbarians (14E n. 102).

[26] *Pol.*1257ab, *EN* 1133ab, *MM* 1194a; 7D.

precious metal introduces radical change. What is unprecedented about Greek coined money is that a substance with ornamental use-value and association with immortality (2C), precious metal, was transformed by a sign into an object which, inasmuch as its conventional was generally greater than its intrinsic value, was unlikely to be melted down to make objects. Precious metal, which had exchange-value based on its ornamental use-value, was in effect deprived of this use-value by being stamped.[27] This importance of the sign guaranteeing future acceptability, together with the promiscuous exchangeability that it facilitated, wider than most 'primitive money', meant that – in contrast to much 'primitive money', and despite the beauty and symbolism of Greek coins – any other value the metal may have had (whether beauty, status, social relations, or immortality) seems to have been marginalised by the practical effectiveness of the coins as signs of monetary value. And along with this importance of the sign necessarily comes another characteristic that distinguishes coinage from all or most 'primitive money' (and from all previous objects performing money functions): if value can be added to metal merely by the addition of a sign to produce currency, then this production must be restricted: currency is issued and controlled by political authority. And yet on the other hand Greek coinage is not the *mere* token that modern money is. The intrinsic value of its precious metal helps to create confidence in its conventional value (7D). Greek coinage is located between commodity and sign, between 'primitive' and modern money.

The widespread adoption by the Greeks of this invention – substance given extra and uniform value by its sign – was of immense significance, both for the Greeks and for the other societies who under their direct or indirect influence adopted coinage, which has been in continuous and widespread use from antiquity to the present day. It was a crucial and unprecedented step towards modern money. And it was a factor, I will argue, in a crucial and unprecedented *conceptual* transformation, by which the Greeks seem closer to us than are any of the sophisticated civilisations that preceded them. Worthy of investigation therefore is what it was that enabled the Greeks to make widespread use of monetary value marked by a sign on a substance.

Aristotle simply notes the transition from metal to coinage as arising from the needs of trade (*Pol.* 1257b). But this leaves unexplained why other traders, such as the Phoenicians, did not develop their own coinage and

---

[27] Cf. Marx 1973 (1857–8), 212: '. . . symbolic money can replace the real, because material money as mere medium of exchange is itself symbolic'.

were slow to adopt the idea from the Greeks.[28] Perhaps the development
was favoured by the existence of a series of small-scale, culturally homogeneous, and independently minded political units separated from each
other by mountains and sea. But a crucial requirement for the development of what I call 'fiduciarity' – the excess of the fixed conventional value
of pieces of money over their intrinsic value[29] – is collective trust in its future acceptability. What was it that produced in the Greeks this collective
trust?

Confidence in money (general belief in its future general acceptability)
may depend on habit, which depends on confidence. This interdependence,
once established, may be enough to sustain fiduciarity, but for it to become
established something else is required. The something else may seem to be
the inherent value of the object used as money – say the ornamental value
of silver (despite the inconvenience of establishing purity and quantity).
But inherent value is not enough for fiduciarity, which requires general
belief in the future acceptability of the *conventional* value of the money in
exchange.[30] Such a belief cannot be merely self-fulfilling. A group of individuals who know nothing of each other, or who have no shared symbols,
have no basis on which the general belief can construct itself. Such a general
belief may be encouraged by an institutional guarantee ('I promise to pay
the bearer . . .') that may be symbolised by an image of authority – notably
the head of a monarch – represented on the money. But in European history
such measures have always been supported by an ancient habit of acceptance confirmed by results. And there is anyway evidence neither for such
institutional sophistication behind early Greek coins nor for such images
of secular authority on them. Neither political authority nor the market
nor habit nor results are enough to explain the Greek adoption of coinage.
The origin of the crucial habit of collective confidence in the conventional
value of money requires another kind of explanation. We must return to
the symbolic associations of money.

Symbols may organise a whole community. A flag – a mere decorated
piece of cloth – may rally an army in battle, for every soldier knows that

---

[28] Cf. (on modern money) Parry and Bloch 1989, 16: 'It is also surprising that a great many societies
failed to borrow the idea of a generalised means of exchange from more astute neighbours. One
might have expected Kapauku or Tolai ingenuity to spread like wildfire.'

[29] I say 'excess' rather than merely disparity, because were the intrinsic value higher than the conventional, the money would be used (or sold) as a commodity rather than as money (e.g. coins would
be melted down). 'Token' money I define as fiduciary money of which the material is worthless or
near-worthless.

[30] On the importance generally of networks and of information as preconditions for money see Dodd
1994.

the others too are devoted to it. We have seen instances, among the Are'are and the Baruya, of objects that combine shared symbolic value with fairly general exchange-value. In both cases the symbolic value is manifest in, or even bestowed by, ritual.[31] There are indications that among the Greeks a precondition for the initial general acceptability of coinage was its symbolic association – inherited from communal distributions in the ritual of sacrifice – with the solidarity of the community (6AB). Once this general acceptability was established, there was of course little further need for the persistence of its precondition. That is to say, the genesis and widespread adoption of coinage involved transition from the kind of social symbolism that we find in 'primitive money' to the relatively asymbolic universal effectiveness characteristic of modern money.

The connection of money with ritual is no accident. Both money and ritual mediate social relations by providing a detached, easily recognised, symbolic paradigm that depends on collective confidence and persists through everyday vicissitudes, bringing order to numerous potentially uncontrollable transactions.[32] Both of them are communicative, organising abstractions, providing a common standard for the vast variety of goods and services (money) or for ways of e.g. killing and eating an animal or uniting a man with a woman (ritual). Much the same could be said of some other symbolic systems, notably language.[33] Collective confidence in a merely human, alterable construction is required for conventional monetary value and for ritual, for *nomos* (law or convention), even for the gods. This similarity between these essential institutions is implicit in Aristophanes' *Clouds*, in which Socrates – prefiguring his pupil Pheidippides' contempt for *nomos* as a merely human construction (1421–4) – declares that 'the gods are not currency (*nomisma*) with us', to which Strepsiades replies 'What do you swear with? Iron (coins), as if in Byzantium?' (247–9). *Nomisma* is the object or consequence of *nomisdein*, which means to acknowledge by belief or practice – whether the gods (*nomisdein tous theous*) or coinage. In iron coinage, which is of very low intrinsic value, fiduciarity is especially conspicuous. To this brilliant passage I will return (7D).

---

[31] Cf. also e.g. Weil 1980, 105–41 (rites of passage), 163–4 (money of the far east passing from earth to heaven); Douglas 1967; Einzig 1966 index s.v. religious payments; Bessaignet 1970.

[32] Douglas 1970 (1966), 70: 'money is only an extreme and specialised type of ritual'.

[33] The word, like the monetary unit, stands for a vast range of items with which it has no essential connection, reducing multiplicity and tangibility to a single abstraction, as part of a symbolic system which through rule-governed circulation promotes cohesion of action. Language and money have been compared since antiquity: e.g. Kratin. fr. 239 K–A; Zeno St. fr. 81 von Arnim (ap. D.L. 7.18); Plut. *Lyc.* 19; *Mor.* 406b; Riegel 1979, 60–70; Eco 1979, 24–6; Shell 1982; Goux 1990, 96–111.

The use-value of Greek coinage is merely potential: it is unlikely to, but can, be transformed into metal objects. Modern money has no use-value, beyond the infinitesimal value of the material in which it may be embodied. But money in general originates as, and may continue to be, an object that combines use-value with convenience as money. This is the historical duality of money, as both commodity and token, corresponding to its persistent mystifying duality as both thing and interpersonal relation. The duality underlies the historical opposition, which has taken political as well as theoretical forms, between those who insist that money is, or should be tied to, something with intrinsic value (precious metal) and those who are happy with money as a mere token of value.[34] As a commodity, money enters into impersonal relations with other commodities in the marketplace. As a token, money is value created by people by means of law or of collective confidence based on shared symbolic associations. There are today two (roughly speaking) competing ways of thinking about Greek coinage: on the one hand the view, first formulated by Aristotle, that it developed out of trade (and the related view that it was the instrument of a 'disembedded' market economy), and on the other hand the view that it emerged from the redistributive activity of the polis (and the related view that it remained, despite its commercial use, imbued with civic associations in an economy still 'embedded' in non-market social practices such as reciprocity and redistribution). I have given no more than a crude summary of this controversy, for I do not intend to enter it. My concern is rather with the *complementarity* of these two aspects of Greek coined money, of its initial symbolic associations with its commercial use, of its dynamic duality as commodity and token.

B   OVERVIEW OF THE ARGUMENT

In my *Reciprocity and Ritual* (1994) I argued for the importance of the development of the polis for the understanding of (in particular) Homer and tragedy. I now take the argument further by including presocratic philosophy, and by concentrating on a central element – the advent of coined money – of the (crucial) economic dimension of that development. This will mean attempting to transcend the conventional divisions of academic labour, with all the attendant dangers. It is not just that almost no connections have ever been made between these important texts and something as fundamental as the advent of coined money, and very few even with

---

[34] Hart 1986.

the economy as a whole. The earliest 'philosophy' presents a special case. Whereas it is by now commonplace to recognise the importance – ignored by Aristotle in his *Poetics* – of the institutions and life of the polis for the understanding of tragedy, the study of philosophy, with some exceptions,[35] generally fails to recognise the limitations of Aristotle's account of earlier philosophy as produced in a historical vacuum. This is surprising, given the oddity of so many of the views of the presocratic 'philosophers'. Scholars ask the important question 'What did they mean?', but almost never the question '*Why* did they hold those extraordinary fundamental beliefs about the world?'.

Part I describes the unprecedented preconditions, absent from the ancient Near East, for the widespread adoption of coinage by the Greeks of the sixth century BC that accelerated the pervasive monetisation of the advanced city-states. Part II describes the contribution made by this monetisation to the unprecedented emergence, at the same time and in the same city-states, of metaphysics and then of tragedy. The final chapter argues that there is no evidence for pervasive monetisation in the Near East before the Greek adoption of coinage.

The earliest surviving texts in the Greek alphabet were written shortly before and concurrently with the monetisation of the city-states. Chapters 2 and 3 are concerned with the wonderfully detailed heroic world described or constructed by Homeric epic, largely premonetary but nevertheless containing signs of reaction to the increasing importance of trade and even of monetisation. In particular, Homer contains indications of the social conditions – notably the failure of centralised reciprocity (redistribution) and the idealisation of communal sacrificial distribution – that are not found in the Near East (chapters 4 and 15), and that allowed the Greek city-state, as it appears in Thucydides and Aristophanes, to be the first thoroughly monetised society in history (chapter 5). The communal sacrificial distribution was a precondition for the emergence of the communal confidence in abstract monetary value (chapter 6) embodied in the rapid development of coinage (chapter 7), resulting in the general acceptance of money, whose features as registered by the Greeks are described in chapter 8.

---

[35] For instance the work of Lloyd and Vernant, which I challenge in ch. 9. Another exception, though again with no interest in the economic, is Capizzi 1990, who rightly maintains (6) that 'no useful discussion is possible between the writer who tries to insert the word "philosopher" into a synchronic perspective, which is still made up of the culture in which the philosopher lived and breathed, and his colleague who is ready to clarify obscure points purely and simply through rereading other "philosophers"'.

In Part II I argue that the universal power bestowed by this communal confidence[36] on the abstract substance of money was in turn a precondition for the genesis and subsequent form of presocratic metaphysics, in which universal power belongs to an abstract substance which is, like money, transformed into and from everything else. Presocratic metaphysics involves (without *consisting of*) unconscious cosmological projection of the universal power and universal exchangeability of the abstract substance of money.[37]

I must here emphasise the *unconsciousness* of the process. When the Babylonians or the Greeks construct the cosmos as monarchy, or the Greeks project the principle of sacrificial distribution (*moira*) as a personified cosmic power (3A n. 27), or Anaximander projects reciprocity and justice onto the cosmic process, in no case is this a *metaphor*. Rather, cosmology is actually envisaged in terms of transcendent human institutions. Consciousness of the process of projection would undermine the process: for instance Xenophanes' revolutionary insight that men construct anthropomorphic gods in their own image means that he does not himself believe in anthropomorphic gods (13C). But this is not because he has miraculously freed himself from all unconscious projection. What has changed is that *impersonal all-powerful substance*, on its first appearance in history, has entered into his cosmic preconceptions, encouraging belief in impersonal deity. It is this new monetary projection that has distanced him from – enabling him to be conscious of – anthropomorphic projection. Unconscious cosmic projection of transcendent social institutions does not suddenly stop with the advent of money as a transcendent social institution. Moreover, there are reasons, specific to money, why it should be so projected, and why the projection should be disguised from those engaged in it (10C). Indeed, money may enter into the unconscious process of cosmic projection without itself being conceptualised as 'money', for which the Greeks do not have a precise word.[38] But none of this is inconsistent with money also being used as a metaphor for a cosmic process into which it has been unconsciously

---

[36] Requiring a collective consciousness of a different order from that required for merely inheriting, as we all have done, the established success of fiduciarity from another culture. Endogenous (ch. 7) pervasive monetisation seems to have happened only among the Greeks – perhaps also in China (I leave aside the problem of the chronology of the earliest Chinese coinage and whether it had any relationship to the Greek; cf. 10C n. 82).

[37] For a psychological and anthropological account of the mechanism of projection see Sierksma 1990 (1957), e.g. on Aristotle's concept of the divine (48–9).

[38] Any more than they do for, say, 'projection' or 'the economy' or 'ideology' or 'society' or 'class' or 'language'.

projected, as when Heraclitus says that 'all things are an exchange for fire and fire for all things, like goods for gold and gold for goods' (B90).

The unconscious cosmological projection of abstract monetary substance first occurs in early sixth-century Miletus, and continues – at least[39] until Plato – to be a factor in philosophy, which accordingly develops by interaction not only with its philosophical predecessors but also with the growth and development of abstract monetary value.

The second point to emphasise is that I neither *reduce* presocratic philosophy to money nor propose a *monocausal* explanation of it. My aims are in two respects strictly limited. The first is that what I aim to explain is not the entire cosmology of each presocratic but more specifically the genesis and form of their metaphysical preconceptions about the basic constituent of the world and its transformations. The second respect is that in this explanation I regard money as only one factor among many, albeit an important and hitherto neglected one.[40] It would therefore be simplistic to call the single principle or substance that underlies the presocratic cosmos an 'expression' or 'representation' of money. For instance the emergence of multiplicity from unity in cosmology is premonetary (in Hesiodic mythical cosmogony), but the advent of money transforms the unity into a general and increasingly abstract, impersonal (non-mythical) unity that continues to underly apparent multiplicity (11B).

In the advanced city-states coined money was used generally, but belief in the impersonal cosmos of the presocratics was almost certainly confined to an elite. Accordingly, Heraclitus and Parmenides propound general theories that they claim are not understood by humankind in general. Where are we to look for the impact of money on the mind of ordinary people? Systematic exploration of comedy, the orators, vase-painting, and so on, is beyond the scope of this study. I have concentrated rather on the influence of monetisation on (premonetary) myths as represented in Homer and tragedy: firstly on the Homeric reaction to incipient monetisation (chapters 2 and 3), secondly on characterisations of money in tragedy and other contemporary texts (chapter 8), and finally on ways in which some epic and tragic passages are shaped by preconceptions similar to those which, we will have argued, monetisation contributed to philosophical cosmology (chapter 14). One result is that the so-called 'birth of the individual' traced by others in

---

[39] The question whether ancient philosophy thereafter emancipated itself from socially determined preconceptions is a question beyond the scope of this book.

[40] Other factors are tyranny (10D), mythical cosmology, psychological and political factors (11B), mystic doctrine (12ABC), the aristocratic ideology of self-sufficiency (12BC), music (13A). Nor does my argument exclude e.g. the contemporary development of architecture (Hahn 2001).

the texts of this period is, I propose, incomprehensible without attention to monetisation.

One way of approaching the difference between the refraction of money in cosmology on the one hand and tragedy on the other is through the anthropological model of long-term and short-term transactional orders. Bloch and Parry identify in various premodern societies[41]

a similar pattern of two related but separate transactional orders; on the one hand transactions concerned with the reproduction of the long term social or cosmic order; on the other a 'sphere' of short-term transactions concerned with the arena of individual competition . . . In each case this long-term transactional order is concerned with the attempt to maintain a static and timeless order. In each, however, cultural recognition is also explicitly given to a cycle of short term changes associated with individual appropriation, competition, sensuous enjoyment, luxury and youthful vitality.

The relationship between the two orders is not simply one of opposition. Rather, continue Bloch and Parry,

What we consistently find is a series of procedures by which goods which derive from the short term cycle are converted into the long term transactional order . . . the two cycles are represented as organically essential to each other. This is because their relationship forms the basis for a symbolic resolution of the problem posed by the fact that the transcendental social and symbolic structures must both depend on, and negate, the transient individual . . . . all these systems make – indeed *have* to make – some ideological space within which individual acquisition is a legitimate and even laudable goal; but such activities are consigned to a separate sphere which is ideologically articulated with, and subordinated to, a sphere of activity concerned with the cycle of long term reproduction . . . If that which is obtained in the short-term individualistic cycle is converted to serve the reproduction of the long-term cycle, then it becomes morally positive . . . But equally there is always the other possibility – and this evokes the strongest censure – the possibility that individual involvement in the short-term cycle will become an end in itself which is no longer subordinated to the reproduction of the larger cycle; or, more horrifying still, that grasping individuals will divert the resources of the long-term cycle for their own short-term transactions . . . Both in Madagascar and in the Andes, certain forms of money are closely identified with the long-term order of exchange. Because of the instrumental uses to which money lends itself, the more familiar case however is for it to be most closely associated with the short term order . . .

This model has been applied recently to the early Greeks by Sitta von Reden and by Leslie Kurke.[42] In Homer the long-term order is represented by gift-exchange between aristocratic heroes and by offerings and sacrifices to the

---

[41] Bloch and Parry 1989, 23–30.   [42] von Reden 1995; Kurke 1999.

gods, whereas the short-term order is represented by trade. Subsequently
the introduction of coinage meant 'the acknowledgement of the polis as
an institution that controlled justice and prosperity', indicating 'a shift of
authority over social justice from the gods to the polis'.[43]

I would apply the model rather differently. I agree that in Homer gift-
exchange and sacrifice to the gods represent the long-term transactional
order. But the historical shift that produces coinage is a process in which
the model of sacrificial *distribution* acquires the permanent material embodiment (e.g. the dedication of sacrificial images and instruments) that
in Homer is confined to the prestigious aristocratic gift. The ancient tradition of communal egalitarian distribution (3A) is powerful enough to
ramify into the distribution of numerous standardised and communally
recognised pieces of metal (e.g. coins named 'obols' after roasting spits)
associated with the social solidarity of the sacrifice (6AB). But coinage is
early used by the individual for trade (7C). And so an instrument of the
short-term order (coinage used for trade) acquires some of its unique effectiveness from the long-term order (sacrifice). Athenian coins accumulated
by the humble tradesman depict the goddess who protects the polis, just as
the temple dedications, and even the gold on the statue of Athena, may be
melted down to pay the various expenses of the Peloponnesian war. To be
sure, the revolutionary fusion of the two transactional orders[44] need have
been only transient to have established the communal acceptability and
permanence (12C) of the value of the coinage, which once established may
perpetuate itself (1A). But the two complementary aspects of the fusion underlie two important developments of the period, philosophy and tragedy,
in the following way.

On the one hand the communal transcendence of monetary value, its
embodiment – derived from sacrificial distribution – of the long-term order,
underlies its unconscious projection onto the heart of the cosmic order in
presocratic metaphysics. At the apex of the long-term transactional order the
anthropomorphic deities are replaced – at least in the minds of an elite – not
so much by the polis as by the metaphysical projection of the impersonal,
unitary, abstract, transcendent, seemingly self-sufficient power of money,
a process that is first observable in Anaximander in early sixth-century

---

[43] von Reden 1995, 175.
[44] This fusion may perhaps be another respect in which ancient Greek money represents a step towards
modern money, for it is arguable that 'what has uniquely happened in capitalist ideology is . . . that
the values of the short term order have become elaborated into a theory of long term reproduction',
in the words of Bloch and Parry (1989, 29), who prefer however the view that 'Western ideology has
so emphasised the distinctiveness of the two cycles that it is then unable to imagine the mechanisms
by which they are linked.'

Miletus (probably the very first thoroughly monetised society in history) and that culminates in the metaphysics of Parmenides and Plato. But on the other hand the individual appropriation of this communal transcendence, its use for the short-term order, underlies the unprecedented individualism of the extreme man of money, the tyrant at the centre of tragedy, who by virtue of his perversion of the sacred (14DE) belongs precisely to Bloch and Parry's horrifying category of individuals who 'divert the resources of the long-term cycle for their own short-term transactions'.

Kurke focuses on the 'conflict around the civic appropriation of the long-term transactional order' (1999, 17), between 'elitist' and 'middling' traditions. She maintains that the elitist tradition, unlike the middling tradition, is hostile to coinage, which by putting precious metal into general circulation threatens the old system of ranked spheres of exchange (12C). But in general the importance of an ideological distinction between elitist and middling distinctions is difficult to sustain.[45] There is moreover no evidence for elite hostility to coinage before Plato and Aristotle,[46] and even they are interestingly ambivalent towards it (12C). To be sure, the astonishing new power of coinage is egalitarian, for it may be used by all citizens of the advanced polis and – as Aristotle points out – *equalises* the two parties to an exchange.[47] But accordingly the crucial economic division in the polis is not between aristocrats hostile to coinage and traders who welcome it, but rather between those who are imagined to be economically self-sufficient (the 'free') and those who have to work for others (12B). The introduction of abstract value embodied in coinage actually reinforces this imagined self-sufficiency, for it conveniently concentrates automatic (and so self-sufficient) power (over labour) in durable objects that are easy to transport, to store, to conceal.

It is rather in mediaeval theology that we find significant hostility to money. The unified hierarchy of the mediaeval cosmos, profoundly influenced though it is by Aristotle, is also the projection of feudal society united by Christianity but divided into a hierarchy of statuses under autocracy, a hierarchy that limits the power of money. By contrast, the advanced Greek polis of the Archaic and Classical periods is a community united not by autocracy or theological doctrine but by citizenship and the pervasive use of currency, a community within which the most significant division is between on the one hand those whom abstract monetary value elevates

---

[45] Seaford 2002. The difference in our perspectives is only partly explicable by the fact that whereas Kurke concentrates on Herodotus and lyric poetry, I concentrate on Homer, philosophy, and tragedy.
[46] Kroll 2000; Seaford 2002.   [47] 8B; *EN* 1133a17–21.

as self-sufficient, above the production and exchange of physical goods (in contrast to the modern bourgeois), and on the other those who must engage in this production or exchange. This division is projected in the metaphysical superiority of *being* (abstract, unitary, self-sufficient, unchanging) over the changeability and variety of physical appearance.

C   WHAT IS MONEY?

The terms 'wealth', 'money', and 'currency' are conceptually distinct, even though there may be much overlap in what they refer to. We tend to think of 'wealth' and 'money' as synonymous, but only because we tend to think of wealth as something measurable and exchangeable. We may for instance say 'she has a lot of money', when in fact she has very little money but a lot of wealth that can be easily transformed into money. 'Money' has expanded well beyond the coinage in which it has its etymological origin, whereas Greek *chrēmata*, which often seems to mean money, has come to that meaning from the opposite quarter, as it were: originating as 'things used', it continues to mean also 'wealth' or even just 'things' (8A). This allows *argurion*, a small piece of (coined or uncoined) silver, to acquire some of the meaning of money (to be in debt may be described as 'to owe *argurion*'). And 'wealth' (*ploutos*) or even e.g. 'silver' (*arguros*) may be used with money in mind. *Nomisma* means coinage, as currency, but also the broad sense of currency: e.g. it can refer to a paean (7D). That is to say, the Greeks have several words which can mean money (as well as other things) but no word *precisely* equivalent to our 'money', even though they certainly use what we call money. This imprecision in both English and Greek usage makes it all the more important to be precise about what I will mean by money.

And so in this section I list those characteristics the possession of which by something (x) inclines us to call x money. The dry abstraction of this analysis may cause some readers to omit it, but it will assist clarity in subsequent discussion.

Almost anything might in principle serve as money. That is to say, money is socially constructed. Indeed the so-called SCIATI principle ('social construction is all there is'), often misapplied to nature, applies much better to money. What are people doing when they construct x as money?

(1) Firstly, they are valuing x not for its power directly to meet need – for its *use-value* – but rather for its *power to meet social obligation*, obligation involved in receipt of something else (i.e. for its exchange-value) or obligation to pay tribute, compensation, etc. These two kinds of obligation are

sometimes distinguished into two different functions of money, means of exchange and means of payment, which may have distinct historical origins.[48] This characteristic of being valued for the power to meet obligation is probably[49] a *necessary* condition for x to be 'money', but is of course to be found, in a sense, in all acts of payment and exchange (whether or not we would say that money is present), and so is certainly not a *sufficient* condition. But if x is *in general* (rather than just in a particular case) valued for its power to meet obligation rather than for its use-value, this will incline us to call it money – but not if the obligation is restricted to a narrow sphere, e.g. to compensation for murder: see (4) below. If x does have this characteristic of being more generally valued for its power to meet obligation than for its use-value, then it may well of course be *acquired*, or even *stored*, for that purpose. The storage of x for the purpose of using it to meet obligations *in the future* is sometimes called a function of money ('store of value'), separate from the functions of payment and exchange.[50]

(2) Money tends to be *quantified*, by virtue of number (e.g. of cowrie shells), or of amount (e.g. of gold), or of both number and amount (e.g. coins of various weights). In such transactions as gift-exchange and ritual payment, the power of x to meet obligation may have nothing or little to do with the quantity of x. But in such cases we are less inclined to call x money than where quantity matters. In our next characteristic, on the other hand, quantity is of the essence.

(3) x may provide a *measure of value* (e.g. y and z may each be valued as worth so many units of x). This may have various benefits, such as facilitating the process of exchange or ensuring the equity of taxation. This function of money resembles the exchange function described under (1) in that x is brought into relation to each commodity *as if* it were to be exchanged for it (e.g. y is worth – would be exchanged for – two units of x, z for five units of x). This may facilitate the exchange of y or z for x, or of y for z (with no need for the presence of x). It may also facilitate the mere transfer (rather than exchange) of x or of y or of z, by allowing credit and debit to be recorded in terms of x, which thereby operates as *unit of*

---

[48] See esp. Polanyi 1977, 99, 104–5, 107, 109. To the extent that the functions are independent, the means of exchange is (he argues) the least basic: with the introduction of market exchange, payment comes to be envisaged in terms of the obligation to pay in market exchange. Another way of distinguishing money as 'medium of circulation' from money as 'means of payment' (and as means of storing wealth) is in Marx 1976 (1867), 227–40.

[49] I.e. if the *only* money function performed by x is to provide a measure of value (see (3) below), that would probably not be enough to incline us to call it money, despite Grierson 1978, 9.

[50] But cf. Grierson 1978, 9.

account or *standard of deferred payment*, functions that are assisted by the availability of writing.[51]

(4) The performance by x of one of the functions of money does not mean that it necessarily performs any of the others. It has even been argued that the four main functions of money – payment, exchange, storing wealth, measuring value – are in early communities institutionalised separately from each other.[52] Further, even within a single function its acceptability may be restricted, e.g. in 'special purpose money'. If, say, the only context in which x has the characteristic described under (1) is as a means of acquiring barley in exchange, or as payment in compensation for murder, should we call it money? The more money-functions x is able to perform, and the more widely usable it is within each money-function, the more inclined we are to call it money. *General acceptability*, in payment and exchange and as a measure of value, is therefore a characteristic of money.

(5) *Exclusive acceptability* is in principle quite separate from general acceptability. x may be generally used in all money functions without being the *only* thing used as money. Conversely, x may be the only thing used with money functions in one or more spheres, but not used at all in the others. The exclusive acceptability of x in exchange (unlike general acceptability) does not by itself incline us to call x money, for x might be *bartered* exclusively with y. Exclusive acceptability acquires special significance for the functioning of x as money only when it combines with a degree of general acceptability. With this combination x has become quite distinct from all other commodities.

Among the various qualities that tend to transform a commodity into money (notably homogeneity, divisibility, durability, portability, relative inelasticity of supply) is an existing general acceptability as money – i.e. it is more likely to be accepted as money if it can be used in further exchanges and payments.[53] There is a dynamic here by which general acceptability increases itself towards universal acceptability, and indeed towards the combination of this universal acceptability with exclusive acceptability as money in all functions and spheres.

If x has all the characteristics listed so far, i.e. it is valued and stored for power to meet obligation (in exchange and payment), is quantified, provides a measure of value, and is generally and exclusively acceptable,

---

[51] Codere 1968 argues that money is a symbolic system that acquires greater symbolic power by being integrated with other symbolic systems, namely ('in logical developmental order') a number system, an amounts system, and a writing system.
[52] Polanyi 1977, ch. 9.
[53] E.g. Anderlini and Sabourian in Humphrey and Hugh-Jones 1992, 87.

then we call it money. But we should add two further characteristics that belong especially to modern money, as well as to ancient Greek money.

(6) *Fiduciarity*, as defined in IA. Here too, as in (3), money operates as an abstraction.

(7) The *state* may be involved in issuing money, controlling it, guaranteeing it, enforcing its acceptability, and so on. For instance the state may decide to guarantee the weight and purity of pieces of metal by stamping them. Or it may decide to so guarantee merely the value. In other words, the state may either exclude the possibility of disparity between substance and appearance or make it irrelevant.

Two general observations should be made on these characteristics. Firstly, they have not been presented here as belonging to a historical process. Obviously the historical development of money has been untidy, occurring variously in various cultures, and has not necessarily been unilinear even within each culture. This does not mean that it is impossible to generalise about the history of money and to identify typical dynamics in its development. For example, the order in which I have listed the characteristics is more likely to correspond to actual historical development than some other orderings. But such generalisation is not my concern. The point is rather to have acquired tools for the analysis of historical material. For this purpose clarity about exactly which of the characteristics of money are present in x in each context (whether or not we choose to call x money) renders a single definition unnecessary. Of the characteristics listed only (1) is (probably) a necessary condition for 'money', and only (4) – an extension of (1) – is (probably) a sufficient condition. At any rate, the more of these characteristics x has, the less we hesitate to call it money.[54]

Secondly, because money is socially constructed, it may be hard to obtain the required clarity on whether a characteristic is present in x. It may be present in varying degrees, and the degree may be difficult to ascertain. As regards the crucial characteristic (1), for example, x may be valued (simultaneously or consecutively) both for its use-value and for its exchange-value. Hence a transaction may be ambiguous – between barter (e.g. metal valued for its use-value, exchanged for oil) and sale/purchase (e.g. metal valued for its exchange-value, exchanged for oil). Whether the transaction should be called barter or sale/purchase may depend at least in part on social or individual attitudes to the metal (as having exchange-value, or use-value, or both). Can money have use-value? Although the development of x as

---

[54] Or rather the less I myself would hesitate: though it owes much to Jevons, Polanyi and others, the list of seven characteristics is my own construction.

'money' may involve a gradual decrease in regard for its use-value, such regard may persist – except in the case of (6) fiduciary money, which by definition could buy a greater quantity of its material (metal, paper, etc.).

These then are the characteristics of money. What are the conditions of their possibility? Some are obvious. (2) and (3) are conditional on systems of number and amount. (4) and (6) require extensive trust. But what was it about Greek society that allowed it to be the first to adopt something like modern money, with all seven characteristics (at least sometimes and in some places), early in their recorded history? A tentative answer will emerge from what follows.

PART ONE

The genesis of coined money

CHAPTER TWO

Homeric transactions

A   FORMS OF ECONOMIC TRANSACTION IN HOMER

Before looking for money functions in Homeric society,[1] I will list the various kinds of transaction (in the broad sense) by which goods are allocated. I list them in roughly ascending order of the extent to which they approximate to trade, defined for our present purpose as *the impersonal instantaneous[2] exchange of goods equivalent in value*, so that the final category is the full embodiment of such exchange.

(1) First we register allocation by *violence*, as when Odysseus and his followers take from the city of the Ciconians 'their wives and many possessions' (*Od.* 9.41), in which no exchange is involved.

(2) *Prizes*, notably those offered by Achilles at the funeral games of Patroclus.[3] No exchange is involved, except in so far as the prize may be in return for the honour done to Achilles or Patroclus by participation in the games.

(3) *Gifts* are – depending on the context[4] – usually given rather than exchanged, although we also find statements of the expectation that a gift will be followed eventually by a gift or benefit in return.[5] As is the case in most societies, precise equivalence of value and enforceable immediacy of return have no place in the exchange of gifts.[6] Gifts may bestow prestige,[7] and may initiate and sustain alliances between powerful individuals. And

---

[1] By 'Homeric society' I mean not the actual, historical society from which the poems emerged but rather the society implicit in the poems, which is an ideological depiction of an actual society of, roughly speaking, the eighth and seventh centuries BC, though the *final shape* of the poems was probably subject to later influences: Seaford 1994a, 5–6, 145–54.

[2] The transaction (unlike in gift-exchange) is instantaneous, even though delivery of goods or money may be delayed.

[3] *Il.* 23.259–70, 653–6, 740–51, 798–802, 831–5, 851, 884–5.

[4] van Wees 1992, 228–32 distinguishes between symbols of friendship (exchanged), special requests (given), and parting-gifts (given).

[5] *Od.* 1.318; 24.284–6.   [6] E.g. Bourdieu 1977, 5–8, 171, 195–6.

[7] E.g. *Od.* 11.355–61, where Odysseus says that with gifts from Scherie he will be 'more respected and more dear' to all who see him return to Ithaca; *Il.* 9.604–5.

so for example Odysseus, given a bow by Iphitus, gives him in turn a sword and spear as 'the beginning of guest-friendship' (*Od.* 21.35), and Hector and Ajax exchange gifts in order to establish 'friendship' (*Il.* 7.302). Menelaus gives Telemachus a goblet with which to pour libations 'remembering me all your days' (*Od.* 4.592), and the point is later made general: Peisistratus tells Telemachus to wait for Menelaus' parting gifts, 'for a guest remembers all his days a man who receives him as a guest and provides friendship'.[8] It is as if, as stated by Mauss in his comparative study of the gift, 'the objects are never completely separated from the men who exchange them'.[9] And so the description of a valuable object in Homer frequently contains an account of its having once been given to its present owner (as a *xeinēion*, a gift of guest-friendship), together with the name of the donor (or succession of donors).[10]

(4) Whereas gifts create solidarity between individuals from different groups, solidarity within the group is created by *distribution* or (if centralised) *redistribution*. This is the mode of allocation obtaining within the basic economic unit, the household,[11] as well as in two prominent contexts in particular – the sharing of booty, and the sharing of meat in the animal sacrifice. As we will see in more detail (2E), in both these contexts we find not only a privileged share or leading role for the chieftain or leading men but also the principle of equal distribution among all. Redistribution involves reciprocity, in that its beneficiaries have duties (in the army, the household, etc.).[12]

(5) When redistribution attaches to a specific service, we may categorise it as *reward*, as when Agamemnon promises Teucer that in return for his prowess in battle he will, if Troy falls, give him a tripod, or a chariot with horses, or a woman (*Il.* 8.281–91), or when a reward is offered to encourage volunteers for a particular daring task.[13]

(6) When what is given is in exchange not for the dangers of military service but for loss or insult, then we call it *compensation*. Examples of such loss or insult are Agamemnon's insult to Achilles, the Trojans' theft of Helen, the murder of a kinsman, Ares' adultery with Aphrodite, Euryalus' insult to Odysseus at the Phaeacian games, the suitors' crimes against Odysseus.[14]

---

[8] *Od.* 15.52–5; cf. 1.313; see further e.g. Finley 1977, index s.v. gifts; Seaford 1994a, 13–25.
[9] Mauss 1967, 31; also e.g. Godelier 1999 (1996), 42, 45, 48.
[10] *Il.* 7.137–9; 10.261–71; 11.19–23; 23.741–8 (a prize); 24.233–4; *Od.* 4.125–33, 615–19 (= 15.115–19); 21.11–41; 24.74–5.
[11] Finley 1977, 62–3.   [12] For redistribution, and a definition of reciprocity, see 4A.
[13] *Il.* 10.211–17, 303–9. See also *Od.* 4.525–6 (two talents of gold promised by Aegisthus to his watchman); *Il.* 13.366–9 (a bride promised in return for military service); cf. *Il.* 18.507.
[14] *Il.* 1.213 (*dōra*); 19.138 (*apoina*); 3.286–7 (*timē*); 9.632–3; 13.659; 18.498 (*poinē*); *Od.* 8.318, 332 (*moichagria*), 396–415 (*dōron* – a sword); 22.55–8 (*timē* – bronze and gold).

The compensation may also take the form of reciprocal suffering, in which case we call it *revenge*.[15]

(7) The *ransom* of someone taken by force is a common theme of the *Iliad*.[16]

(8) Another example of the exchange of a person for goods is *bride-price*. When a girl is lost to her kin through marriage (like a man through murder), goods may be given to her family by the bridegroom, as when e.g. Iphidamas gives a hundred cattle, with the promise of a thousand goats and sheep.[17]

(9) Yet another example of the exchange of a person for goods is the trading[18] of someone into slavery.[19] Unlike (7) ransom, which is an exchange that liberates from possession (from slavery), this is mere exchange of possessions. And unlike (8) marriage, it creates no links. It is on the other hand less impersonal than our next category, (10) trade in things, in that here one of the items exchanged is a person, and indeed usually a person with a specific personality or identity, such as Lycaon, Eurycleia, or Eumaeus (whereas a slave who appears in any of the previous categories, e.g. as a prize at *Il.* 23.263, is anonymous).

(10) The exchange of *things*, not of people, and not to create interpersonal links but for the sake of the things. There are only three instances.[20] Euneus' ships from Lemnos bring wine to the Greek camp: 'Separately to the Atreidae . . . he gave wine, a thousand measures. And thence the flowing-haired Greeks acquired wine,[21] some with bronze, others with shining iron, others with skins, others with whole cattle, others with slaves taken in war' (*Il.* 7.467–75). A distinction is implied here between the gift (to the leaders) and barter (with the other Greeks). Secondly, Mentes (Athena in disguise), the king of the Taphians, claims to be sailing 'to men of alien language, to Temese, after bronze, and my cargo is gleaming iron' (*Od.* 1.183–4). Our

---

[15] E.g. *Il.* 1.42, 2.355–6; *Od.* 12.382: all with the verb *tinō*.

[16] 1.12–13, 20–1, 99; 2.230; 6.46–8; 10.378–80; 11.131–4; 21.42, 80; 22.50; 23.747. The person may be dead, as at 22.342, 349–52; 24.76, 137, 228–37, 237, 579, 594, 686–7.

[17] *Il.* 11.244–5; see also e.g. 22.472; *Od.* 2.53, 8.318.

[18] I will throughout use words such as 'trade', 'acquire', 'export' rather than such words as 'sell' and 'buy', as the latter kind may imply the use of money, which is not found in Homer.

[19] *Il.* 21.41, 79 – cf. 23.746–7 (Euneus acquires Lycaon from Achilles); 21.102 – cf. 22.44–5; 24.752 (Achilles exports Trojans); 21.454 (Laomedon threatens to export his hired labourers); *Od.* 1.430–1 (Laertes acquires Eurycleia); 14.115 – cf. 15.388 and 483 (Laertes acquires Eumaeus from Phoenicians); 14.202 (a 'traded' woman in Crete), 297 (a Phoenician plans to export the 'Cretan'), 452 (Eumaeus acquires Mesaulius from the Taphians); 15.429 (Taphians export a Phoenician woman); 17.250 (Melanthius threatens to export the beggar Odysseus); 20.382–3 (the suitors threaten to export Telemachus' guests to the Sicilians).

[20] *Il.* 18.291–2 refers to gifts or rewards (to allies) rather than to barter: cf. 17.225–6.

[21] The word for 'acquiring wine' (οἰνίζεσθαι) occurs elsewhere in Homer of the 'conveying out' of wine (*Il.* 8.506, 546), rather than of purchase.

third case, unlike the first two, clearly involves professional traders: Eumaeus says that when he was a child there came to his home a Phoenician ship with things for exchange, including a gold necklace.[22]

My description of these categories has implied considerable overlap between them, so that for example compensation and ransom may also be called 'gifts'. Furthermore, it is possible to think of transactions that do not fall clearly into one category rather than another. The categories are nevertheless useful both for thinking about the variety of transactions and because in fact each category does have transactions that fall entirely within it.

B   THE MARGINALITY OF TRADE AND THE ABSENCE OF MONEY

Apart from (1) violence, all the categories listed in 2A involve an element of exchange. At one extreme, prizes and gifts establish personal relations, with no suggestion of instantaneous or precisely equivalent return. As we go down the list, we move along a spectrum from the subjective to the objective, through exchanges that convey prestige and honour or embody feelings such as loyalty to friend, leader or kin, until we end with the instantaneous exchange of commodities of (presumably) equivalent value, performed for the sole purpose of acquiring the commodities. It is on this the latter end of the spectrum that we will concentrate in this section.

Some goods are more suited than others to bestow honour and prestige, to retain something of the identity of the donor, and consequently to appear towards the top rather than the bottom of our list. Such goods tend to be valuable, portable, of individual character, and imperishable – in particular therefore artefacts of precious metal or fine cloth, but also unworked precious metal, women, and chariots with horses.[23] These luxury items have a much higher value than such subsistence goods as cattle or small animals,[24] and to some extent form a separate sphere of prestige exchange as is to be found in many other societies without general purpose money.[25] They are not on the whole acquired through trade.[26] Trade in

---

[22] *Od.* 15.416, 445, 452, 460–3.

[23] Donlan 1981, 105 suggests that women and horses are included in this category partly because they produce cloth (women) and gold (horses and chariots, as prizes).

[24] Donlan 1981, 104, citing *Il.* 2.449; 6.234–6; 21.79; 23.703–5, 885; *Od.* 1.430; 22.57.

[25] Donlan 1981, 106–7; Morris 1986, 8–9; Finley 1977, 61–8; Kurke 1999, 10, 47. Van Wees 1992, 210–27 shows that the degree of non-convertibility of goods between the prestige sphere and the subsistence sphere in Homer is somewhat less than has sometimes been supposed. Comparative evidence: refs. in Morris 1986, 8 (add esp. Bohannan and Dalton 1962, 3–7; Dalton 1971, 147–9; Douglas 1967; Bohannan and Bohannan 1968; Kopytoff 1986). Cf. 8E.

[26] The possible exceptions are that (a) slave women (traded at *Od.* 1.430–1; 14.202; 15.429) occasionally occur in lists of prestige items, (b) Achilles received a silver bowl in exchange for Lycaon (but see

Homer never occurs *within* a community. It always (or almost always) involves non-Greeks.[27] Unlike other forms of exchange, it hardly ever has a function in the main narrative, but is generally confined to asides. And it has negative connotations.[28] In respect of the centrality of reciprocity and redistribution as principles of allocation, Homeric society resembles the economies of the ancient Near East (4A), however little it may do so in other respects.

Moreover, the mentions of trade in Homer are generally brief, with few details given. Because there is no mention of a means of exchange (money), all trade is presumably an exchange of goods (barter). Barter may involve three elements – the items exchanged (A and B) and an imagined item (X) that provides a measure of value. The only measure of value in Homer is provided by cattle. In most instances of Homeric trade we hear of only one item (A), generally a slave, with no X, and B left unspecified other than by some such phrase as 'with his possessions'[29] or 'a worthy price'.[30] The only exceptions are as follows. In one, again the acquisition of a slave, A and X are specified: Laertes acquired Eurycleia with his own possessions worth twenty cattle (*Od.* 1.430–1). There are two instances, both noted in 2A under (10), of the specification of both A and B: Mentes sailing to exchange iron for bronze, and Euneus exchanging wine for various items provided by the Greeks. Our final exception is the sale of Lycaon by Achilles, discussion of which we postpone to 2D.

Of interest here are the various less than heroic sub-narratives told on Ithaca. In Eumaeus' narrative of his past we hear of the Phoenician traders, 'nibblers, bringing countless delights in their black ship', who with the help of Eumaeus' Phoenician nurse (herself once traded by Taphian pirates), and with a gold necklace offered for trade as a decoy, kidnap Eumaeus and trade

---

below); (c) the items with which the Greeks acquire wine (*Il.* 7.467–75) include unworked bronze and iron – barely an exception.

[27] Notably the Phoenicians and Taphians (if the Taphians are non-Greeks; they seem at least marginal to the Greek world – as is implied perhaps by *Od.* 1.210–1; see also Bravo 1984, 104 – cf. Mele 1986, 68–9). As for Euneus, his name, and his father ('Jason'), suggest that he is Greek; on the other hand he does not belong to the heroes who fight at Troy, and Lemnos seems to have had a largely non-Greek population in the eighth and seventh centuries, and 'is not a proper part of the Achaean world in the Homeric poems': Finley 1981, 291; cf. van Wees 1992, 400 n.151. If we leave aside the Taphians and Euneus, no Greek actually exports for barter, except Achilles exporting captives as slaves: *Il.* 21.41, 79, 102; 22.44–5; 23.746–7; 24.752: cf. below.

[28] Esp. at *Od.* 8.159–70; 14.288–97; 15.415–70.   [29] *Od.* 14.115, 452; 15.483.

[30] *Od.* 15.388, 429; cf. 20.383; cf. 'an unspeakably great price' (*Od.* 14.297), an 'immense price' (*Od.* 15.452), a 'price' (*Od.* 15.463), 'much livelihood' (*Od.* 17.250). Despite its occurrence in all these passages, the word for price (*ōnos*) does not imply money: see e.g. *Il.* 21.4 (cf. 79). Interestingly, the adjectives *aspetos* ('unspeakably great') and *murios* ('immense') go with the price obtained by Phoenicians. Cf. Mele 1986, 77–8.

him into slavery (*Od.* 15.415–83). In Odysseus' story of his past as a 'Cretan' he becomes rich through plunder, then (in Egypt) through gifts, before attempting to win a cargo in conjunction with a Phoenician, who in fact plans to trade him into slavery. But the ship is wrecked, and the 'Cretan' is the sole survivor. He is entertained by the Thesprotian king, and sent off on a Thesprotian ship, whose crew then plan to trade him as a slave (*Od.* 14.199–359).

In Egypt the 'Cretan' acquires wealth by being given gifts. Similarly Menelaus, on the way back from Troy, wandered around the Near East and Africa, 'gathering much livelihood' (*Od.* 4.90). We discover specific examples of this wealth, in the form of various gifts given to Menelaus and Helen by various individuals in Egypt and Sidon.[31] Menelaus also suggests to Telemachus that they take a trip together 'through Hellas and the centre of Argos', in which their hosts will give them gifts – a tripod, or a bronze cauldron, or a pair of mules, or a golden goblet (*Od.* 15.80–5). Clearly the noble traveller might exploit the convention of gift-giving to enrich himself.

There is one further example of this phenomenon, in another fictitious narrative told on Ithaca. The disguised Odysseus explains to Penelope why Odysseus is still absent: he is in Thesprotia, and 'is bringing much good treasure, asking for it among the people' (19.272). He would have been back before, but 'thought it more profitable to go about and visit much land collecting goods; for Odysseus above all mortal men knew gains (*kerdea*) and no other mortal could rival him.' (19.283–6).[32] In the earlier fictitious narrative told about himself by Odysseus to Eumaeus the same treasure is described as consisting of 'bronze and gold and much-worked iron' (14.323–5). There has here been a significant shift in emphasis from the other references to journeys on which gifts are gathered. Firstly, the treasure is explicitly asked for.[33] Secondly, the aim is explicitly said to be gain, at which Odysseus excels. Thirdly, there is no mention of gifts, or of individual donors, as there is in the other journeys in which gifts are gathered. Rather the treasure is obtained, generally, 'among the people' and by 'visiting much land'. Fourthly, it is said of the treasure thus gathered that it would feed one man after another to the tenth generation (19.294). Here, strikingly, the treasure handed down through the generations will 'feed' them. This

---

[31] 4.125–32, 227–9, 615–19 = 15.115–19.

[32] *Kerdea* appears also in the disparaging description of the sea-trader at *Od.* 8.161–4. With 'no other mortal could rival him (. . ἐρίσσειε . . ἄλλος)' Cozzo 1988, 26–7 compares Hdt. 4.152.3 on the exceptional profit made by Sostratos the Aeginetan, 'for it is impossible for another to rival him (ἐρίσαι ἄλλον)'.

[33] The Greek used for asking for it among the people (19.273 αἰτίζων ἄνα δῆμον, and 284 ἀγυρτάζειν) is elsewhere used of begging (cf. esp. 17.222, 558).

is certainly not a mere metaphor. Treasure is transformed, by implication, into food. There is only one other example in Homer of this implied transformation.[34] It is the more striking in that there are in Homer few, if any, examples of treasure being exchanged for agricultural produce.[35] Generally treasure is stored, or given away.[36]

These four differences cohere. The fictitious expedition by the craftiest of heroes may adhere roughly to heroic decorum as a journey in which gifts are gathered, but is marked by the crafty self-enrichment of a trader's journey. In particular, it is no coincidence that treasure acquired in this unique manner is by implication a commodity transformed, also uniquely, into sustenance. The representation of Odysseus' expedition seems to embody the tension between heroic decorum and the importance of trade.

What Odysseus will bring home, in this account, is metal: bronze, gold, and iron. And indeed it may be thought that such metals, whether worked into specific objects or as bullion, were generally prized and therefore perhaps played the role of a generally acceptable means of exchange or payment. However, neither metal nor anything else in Homer plays this role. Transactions may produce 'gains'. But there is not even a case of a commodity said to be acquired in order to acquire another one, unless we count the treasure gathered by the fictitious Odysseus.[37] It might be thought that when Euneus receives various things in exchange for his wine, he will exchange rather than keep them. But nothing of the kind is even implied; and it is notable that the variety of the things received by Euneus is stressed by the only case in Homer of the word *allos* being used to introduce no fewer than five clauses in a row: they acquired the wine 'some with bronze, some with gleaming iron, some with hides, some with whole cattle, some

---

[34] The hypothetical 'eating treasure (*keimēlia*)' at *Od.* 2.75, which has however (as 14.92 = 16.315) a special point: see 2E. *Il.* 18.290–1 probably refers to the transport of Trojan *keimēlia* as gifts to persuade the Phrygians and Maeonians to fight (cf. 17.225).

[35] The possible cases are *Il.* 7.472–5, where among the items exchanged for wine are 'bronze' and 'shining iron', which may perhaps count as treasure, and *Od.* 15.416, 446, 456, 460, which imply exchange between luxury items and *biotos* (livelihood), which generally means agricultural produce (e.g. Donlan 1981, 115), although at *Od.* 4.90 it must include treasure.

[36] So Finley 1977, 61, who is however too categorical: cf. van Wees 1992, 210–27.

[37] Other passages that might be or have been suggested are as follows. (a) Euneus acquires Lycaon for goods worth 100 cattle and then ransoms him for three times the value (*Il.* 21.40–2, 79–80; 23.746–7). But profit is certainly not the point of the lines, still less that Euneus *intended* to make a profit. (b) Mentes king of the Taphians (Athena in disguise) claims to be going to Temesa after bronze, with a cargo of iron (*Od.* 1.184). But there is no reason to suppose (with Mele 1979, 67) that the iron was acquired as a means of exchange, for we cannot know whether or not the land of the Taphians was imagined as having its own iron: the poet may not have had a definite place in mind (and if he did, it was further from Ithaca than the land later called Taphious): Heubeck, West, and Hainsworth on *Od.* 1.105.

with slaves'.[38] It seems that the poetic impulse is to exclude any implication of there being a single means of exchange.

There are, as well as trade, various other categories of exchange and payment: prize, gift, reward, compensation, ransom, bride-price. Some things are used as payment in more than one category (e.g. cattle occur once in trade and once as bride-price). But in not one of the categories is the same thing paid in every instance of the category. And even a single payment is often composed of a multiplicity of things. There is nothing that comes anywhere near acquiring money functions generally enough to unite two or more of the categories. Further, given the rarity of convertibility between treasure and subsistence items, and the variety of things stored as treasure, there is nothing that we can single out as used as a store of wealth.[39] And so the only money function that we can find in Homer is the measurement of value, performed only (and rarely) by cattle.

C   GOLD AND SILVER IN HOMER

This general absence from Homer of money functions (despite numerous important transactions) might seem surprising given the centuries-old money functions performed in the ancient Near East by precious metals, especially silver (ch. 15). It is therefore worth looking further at the role of gold and silver in Homer.

Silver is less frequent in Homer than gold, is sometimes associated with deity,[40] and generally takes the form of artefacts. There are only two mentions of it in an unformed state: the suspicion of Odysseus' companions that in the bag given him by Aeolus he has gold and silver,[41] and the statement that the Trojan allies called Halizones come 'from far away, from Alybe, where is the genesis of silver'.[42] The silver artefacts are sometimes said to derive from non-Greek areas of the eastern Mediterranean.[43]

Like silver, gold in Homer generally takes the form of artefacts, which are sometimes said to derive from non-Greek areas of the eastern Mediterranean.[44] Gold is especially associated with the gods, who may themselves be called golden[45] and possess a large range of golden things that in the

---

[38] *Il.* 7.473–5. The closest I have been able to find is the threefold occurrence at *Od.* 22.257–9.
[39] Wealth in Homer is called by general terms: *olbos, ploutos, biotos, chrēmata, ktēmata.*
[40] E.g. *Il.* 1.37, 538; 5.726–9; 18.389, 413; *Od.* 4.73, 615; 6.232–3; 15.115; 22.159–60.
[41] *Od.* 10.35, 45: 2E.
[42] *Il.* 2.857. Bravo 1984, 108–10 argues that Alybe may have been the site of Trapezous on the Black Sea.
[43] *Il.* 10.438 (Thrace); *Od.* 4.125–32 (Egypt), 615–19 = 15.115–19 (Phoenicia); 9.203 (Thrace).
[44] *Il.* 2.872 (Caria); 6.236 (Lycia); 10.438–41 (Thrace); 12.297 (Lycia); *Od.* 4.126–32 (Egypt).
[45] *Il.* 3.64; 8.398; etc.

human world are not made of gold.[46] Furthermore, the golden artefacts used by mortals are frequently associated with deity either explicitly[47] or by their origin[48] or by their use in ritual[49] or by their association with immortality.[50]

The associations of gold and silver derive not only from their lustre but from not suffering corrosion: unlike other metals, they may seem immortal. For instance, the gold and silver dogs guarding the house of Alcinous are 'immortal and ageless all their days' (*Od.* 7.94).

Unformed 'gold' occurs frequently in lists of objects and substances, whether lists of gifts,[51] of prizes,[52] of booty,[53] of items stored in the house[54] or offered as compensation[55] or as ransom.[56] For example, the gifts of the Phaeacians to Odysseus consist of bronze, gold, and clothes.[57] Sometimes the gold is quantified by weight, as so many talents: for example, the gifts offered to Achilles for the body of Hector consist of various clothes, ten talents of gold (weighed), two tripods, four cauldrons, and a beautiful goblet.[58]

The passages listed so far show that silver and gold are highly prized, but contain no indications of silver or gold as valued above everything else, or as having exchange-value, or as representing wealth in general. Quite the reverse: gold occurs, with no special status, in lists of other prized things.[59] And indeed in the only cases in which there is ranking of the objects on the list – the lists of prizes in *Iliad* book 23 – the two talents of gold are *fourth*

---

[46] E.g. sandals (*Il.* 24.341; *Od.* 1.97 etc.), throne (*Il.* 1.611; *Od.* 23.244 etc.), sword (*Il.* 5.509; 15.256), tripods (*Il.* 18.375), scales (*Il.* 8.69; 22.209), cord (*Il.* 8.19, 25; 15.20), floor (*Il.* 4.2), cloud (*Il.* 13.523; 14.344 etc.), shuttle (*Od.* 5.62), reins (*Il.* 6.205).

[47] *Il.* 10.438–41; *Od.* 4.72–4; 6.232–5 (=23.159–62); 16.183–5; 19.33–4. Perhaps therefore Diomedes suspected that Glaucus was a god because he was wearing gold armour (*Il.* 6.128, 236; cf. 10.441). Association of gold with deity in the ancient Near East: Jeremias 1929, 179–81.

[48] Notably Achilles' shield (*Il.* 18.475 etc.), of which the gold is twice called 'gifts of a god': *Il.* 20.268; 21.165. See also *Il.* 22.470; *Od.* 4.616–17; 7.91–2.

[49] *Il.* 1.15, 374; 3.248; 10.294; 11.774; 23.196, 219; 24.285; *Od.* 3.41, 50, 53, 384, 425–6, 435–8, 472; 8.431–2. Cf. also *Il.* 1.246 (cf. 238–9).

[50] *Il.* 2.447–8; 5.724; 13.22; 23.92, 253; 24.795; *Od.* 7.91–4; 24.3. Cf. Hes. *Op.* 109 (cf. 113–14); Theogn. 449–52.

[51] *Od.* 4.129; 5.38; 8.393; 9.202; 13.11, 136, 368; 16.231; 23.341; 24.472.

[52] *Il.* 23.269, 751 (cf. 796), cf. 549–50.   [53] *Il.* 9.137, 365–7.   [54] *Od.* 21.10–12.

[55] *Il.* 9.122; 19.247; *Od.* 22.58.   [56] *Il.* 6.48; 10.379; 11.133; 22.50, 340; 24.232.

[57] *Od.* 5.38; 13.10–15, 368; 16.231; 23.341. At 13.10–15 the list is more detailed: there is clothing, intricately wrought gold, tripods, and cauldrons.

[58] *Il.* 24.229–34.

[59] Brown 1998, 172 notes that the poet seems to go out of his way to subordinate large amounts of gold bullion (whose purchasing power his audience would be familiar with) to the symbolic objects which substantively would be worth much less, so that 'the closest thing the Homeric epics would have to money can be shown to be regarded by the heroes as of essentially symbolic rather than substantial value'. The size of vessels as prizes at *Il.* 23.264, 268 is described in terms of capacity not weight.

prize (out of five) in the chariot race (269) and the half-talent of gold is *third* prize (out of three) in the foot-race (751).

In some other passages, however, there are indications of a special or representative status for gold. Whereas the phrase 'bronze and gold and well-wrought iron' – used (we saw) of the wealth gathered by Odysseus, and several times of the wealth available for a ransom[60] – indicates a special status for metal rather than for gold in particular, Menelaus gathering wealth in Egypt is described as 'gathering much livelihood (*biotos*) and gold' (*Od.* 3.301). Whether or not gold is mentioned because associated with Egypt,[61] it does seem in this phrase to have a special association with wealth.[62] There are other passages in which gold is mentioned along with one other item (bronze, clothing, silver).[63] But the passages in which gold may be thought to come closest to embodying wealth in general are those in which it occurs by itself. There are only seven such passages.[64] In two of them the reference is to *talents* of gold (almost certainly excluding[65] the possibility of an artefact). One of these is the presence of two talents of gold in the famous trial scene represented on Achilles' shield.[66] The other is the two talents of gold promised by the usurper Aegisthus to the watchman stationed to warn him of the return of Agamemnon (*Od.* 4.525–6).

It is significant that in these the only two instances of a specific weight of gold by itself (rather than in a list of valuable items), the gold is a *payment*. Further, the trial scene represents a way of dealing with homicide quite different from what is found in all the other Homeric cases of homicide, whether because it is chronologically later than most of Homer or because (like much else depicted on Achilles' shield) it embodies a different, non-heroic view of the world. As for the case of Aegisthus, here it is significant that the payment is for a nefarious purpose.[67] A negative connotation is also to be found in each of the other five instances of 'gold' by itself,

---

[60] *Il.* 6.48; 10.379; 11.133.   [61] Cf. *Od.* 4.126–32.

[62] It may be that '*biotos*' here stands for agricultural produce and 'gold' for treasure: Donlan 1981, 115.

[63] E.g. *Il.* 10.315; 18.289; *Od.* 1.165; 10.35, 45.

[64] Unless one adds the phrase 'Mycenae of much gold' (*Il.* 7.180; 11.46; *Od.* 3.304). I discuss below (3C) the gold used to ornament the horns of the sacrificial victim: *Il.* 10.294; *Od.* 3.384, 426, 435, 437.

[65] Despite *Od.* 9.202 (cf. 13.11). Neither the weight of the Homeric talent is known nor even whether the poet (or audience) had a specific weight in mind: see Aristot. fr. 164 R³, and in general Richardson (1993) on *Il.* 23.269. Nevertheless, because the talent signifies a *weight*, it is the closest thing in Homer (though not very close) to an abstract idea of value. And so it is interesting that (apart from the two cases of payment mentioned) talents (always of gold) occur only in the thoroughly heroic context of lists of gifts (*Il.* 9.122, 264; 19.247; 24.232; *Od.* 4.129; 8.393; 9.202; 24.274) or prizes (*Il.* 23.269, 614), never in anything like a commercial context.

[66] *Il.* 18.507. See most recently Westbrook 1992.

[67] Furthermore, the gold is called *misthos*, which almost everywhere else in Homer is pay for hired labour: Brown 1998, 167. Aegisthus also sacrificed and 'hung up many dedications, gold, and things woven' (3.274).

except one.[68] There is mention of Antimachus, 'who beyond all others had taken the gold of Alexander, glorious gifts, so that he had opposed the return of Helen to fair-haired Menelaus', and indeed had proposed that Menelaus, when he came to the Trojans as envoy, should be murdered on the spot.[69] In the underworld we see 'hateful Eriphyle, who accepted precious gold for the life of her own dear husband'.[70] Eumaeus tells how he was kidnapped by his Phoenician nurse, who gave him to some Phoenician traders in return for being taken home, and also offers to steal gold for them: 'for I will bring you gold, whatever I can lay my hand on' (*Od.* 15.448). What she eventually steals is three goblets. But the important point for our purposes is that anything will do (for the Phoenicians) *provided that it is gold*: the substance gold seems to have acquired a value greater than any other thing.[71] But its power may nevertheless be heroically dismissed, as when, in our final passage, Achilles claims that he will not return Hector's body even in exchange for gold (*Il.* 22.351).

The adjective 'precious' of the gold received by Eriphyle is *timēeis*. It derives from the noun *timē*, which in Homer could mean honour, esteem, or a penalty (or compensation), and in later Greek could also mean price. *Timēeis* is in Homer applied only to men, to gold,[72] or to gifts – in one case an unspecified 'gift' (*Od.* 1.311–12), in the others a silver bowl with edges finished in gold (*Od.* 4.614–16; 15.114–16). This means that Homeric *timēeis* is applied to no specific thing other than gold or (to a lesser extent) silver. The high value of gold is perhaps most strikingly indicated in the description of the all-golden tassels on Athena's aegis as 'each worth a hundred cattle' (*Il.* 2.449).

To conclude, gold artefacts may be aristocratic gifts and are associated with deity and immortality, but unformed gold does sometimes look like money – and as such tends to have negative associations. Similarly the only appearance of unformed silver (apart from a statement of its origin) – imagined in Aeolus' bag – causes disastrous hostility within the group.[73]

---

[68] And even this exception – the horses offered (along with other items) by Agamemnon to Achilles have won much gold (*Il.* 9.126) – has a negative connotation in that it is part of a list (described unusually *quantitatively*) of gifts *rejected* by Achilles (2D, 3B, 14C). The gold mentioned at *Il.* 2.229–31 is in fact part of a list (negatively presented by Thersites).

[69] *Il.* 11.123–5, 141–5; the great wealth of his house is defined as metal (132–3): cf. the agricultural and pastoral wealth of the worthy Tydeus (14.122–4).

[70] *Od.* 11.327; cf. 15.247.   [71] The Phoenicians also use a gold necklace as a decoy (460).

[72] *Il.* 18.475; *Od.* 8.393. Moreover, the cognate adjective *eritimos* occurs in Homer only four times – twice of gold (*Il.* 9.126, 268) and twice of the aegis (*Il.* 2.447 – described in the next line as having golden tassels; 15.361).

[73] This prefigures the dissent that will arise from the concealability of money. Similarly the only mention of writing in Homer is of 'baneful signs' on a folded tablet (*Il.* 6.168).

A measure of value occurs only six times in Homer,[74] always as cattle – of a single golden tassel on Athena's aegis (*Il.* 2.459), of the armour exchanged by Diomedes and Glaucus (*Il.* 6.235–6), of Lycaon sold as slave (*Il.* 21.79), of prizes in the games (*Il.* 23.702–5, 885), of Eurycleia sold as slave (*Od.* 1.430–1), and of the compensation proposed by a suitor to Odysseus (*Od.* 22.56–8). Only two of these (Lycaon, Eurycleia) are trade, even though it is in trade that one might expect the measure of value to be most useful and to have originated. And in only three of them do we find specified both the items exchanged (A and B) as well as the measure of value (X). These three cases, the only instances of A–B–X in Homer, deserve scrutiny.

Firstly, there is the famous exchange of gifts between Diomedes and Glaucus. Their ancestors had once exchanged gifts, a war-belt for a golden cup (*Il.* 6.219–20). When they too now clasp hands and exchange armour, despite being on opposite sides in the battle, it is like the exchange of gifts between Hector and Ajax, who after fighting exchange a war-belt with a sword, sheath and sword belt (7.299–305). But Glaucus, uniquely, attracts comment from the narrator: Zeus stole away his wits, for he exchanged with Diomedes gold armour for bronze, a hundred cattle's worth for nine cattle's worth (6.235–6). Here gift-exchange is seen from the perspective of trade, in which, in contrast to gift-exchange, numerical equivalence of value is of the essence.[75] It is a reminder that trade, despite its marginality in the Homeric narratives, was surely an important part of the world in which the narratives were produced.

Secondly, a suitor, faced with death, offers Odysseus compensation: 'for all that has been eaten and drunk in your halls, each setting upon himself a value of twenty cattle, we will pay bronze and gold' (*Od.* 22.56–8). Odysseus replies that no amount of compensation will prevent him killing the suitors.[76] So far from being an instance of trade, the equivalence is specified only to allow Odysseus, in the interest of heroic revenge, to *reject* all equivalence.

Our third instance is in this respect similar. It is though, unlike our first two cases, trade. First we hear that Achilles exported Lycaon as a slave to Euneus (*Il.* 21.40–1), then that Lycaon fetched a price worth one hundred cattle (21.79), and finally, much later, that Euneus gave to Patroclus (presumably

---

[74] Cf. though the expression 'of much . . . worth (*axion*)', of a gift (*Od.* 8.405) and a prize (*Il.* 23.562).

[75] This is not to deny that there are also other resonances in the comment: see e.g. Donlan 1989; Traill 1989. The passage may be relatively late: Seaford 1994a, 337–8.

[76] On similarities in this matter between *Il.* and *Od.* see Seaford 1994a, 65–6.

as Achilles' agent) a supremely beautiful Sidonian bowl as the price (*ōnon*)
of Lycaon (23.746–7). The bowl had once been given by the Phoenicians
to Thoas of Lemnos, and is now offered by Achilles as a prize in the games.
Despite the negative associations of trade in Homer, there is nothing demeaning about the heroes Achilles and Patroclus receiving something of
quantified value in trade, for what is relinquished is a royal prince, a son of
Priam, and what is acquired is an exquisite artefact thoroughly integrated
(as gift and prize) into the sphere of prestige exchange.[77] The only other
quantification of value (x) in Homeric trade – Eurycleia acquired for goods
worth twenty cattle – serves to distinguish a servant who will play a loyal
and important role in the story. Similarly, the quantification of the value of
Lycaon has a narrative function, as part of his desperate plea to Achilles to
spare him: when you captured me before, he says, I earned you the value
of a hundred cattle, and then I was ransomed for three times as much.

But the enhancement of Lycaon's plea is not its only function. Remarkable, after all, is that a transaction so rare in Homer (especially in the *Iliad*),
and one nowhere else performed by a Greek, namely an export with value
quantified, should have been performed, as an integral part of the main
narrative, by its sublimely heroic central figure. The explanation comes in
Achilles' *rejection* of the plea, in the interest (like Odysseus' similar rejection) of heroic revenge. The two transactions, trade and ransom, have now
merely brought Lycaon back to the knees of Achilles, who this time, in
a memorable elevation of heroic values above exchange-value, begins his
dismissal of the plea by exclaiming 'Fool, do not speak to me of ransoms,
nor argue it' (99). Lycaon had in fact concentrated less on ransom than on
the pity and respect due to a suppliant, on the fact that he and Achilles ate
together, and, in his final words, on the fact that he was not from the same
womb as Patroclus' killer, Hector. But it is the ransom that Achilles dismisses, going on to explain that before Patroclus met his fate he (Achilles)
took many Trojans alive and exported them to be traded.[78] Now though
no Trojans who met him would escape death. 'But, friend (*philos*), die you
too. Why all this clamour about it? Patroclus also is dead, who was better
by far than you are.' And there will come a time, adds Achilles, when I too –
despite my size, beauty, and parentage – shall be killed in the fighting.

A reason (implied rather than stated) for rejecting the talk of ransom is the
need to avenge Patroclus. Moreover, if Lycaon is ransomed he will outlive

---

[77] The heroic spirit of 23.741–9 is such that translators (e.g. Lattimore) mistranslate 746 Λυκάονος
ὦνον to refer to *ransom*, even though it is clear that Lycaon was sold by Achilles *into* slavery (21.41–2).

[78] 102 πέρασσα: cf. e.g. *Il.* 21.40; *Od.* 14.297. The etymology of the word contains the idea of movement.
It is usually translated 'sell', which I avoid because it may imply money.

Patroclus and Achilles, who are far better than he. One can think of the injustice of that, or of the uselessness of wealth to Achilles who will soon be dead. But it is rather the shared certainty of death that somehow makes talk of ransom foolish. The revenge against Lycaon goes beyond revenge: firstly, because it is, in contrast to the revenge against Patroclus' killer Hector, indiscriminate (indeed Achilles says he will kill all the Trojans he meets); secondly, because this lack of discrimination acquires a kind of justification, the implied notion that because such great heroes as Achilles and Patroclus must die, then all must die; thirdly, because this gruesome notion acquires in turn an unexpectedly positive dimension: it is, paradoxically, precisely in being killed in revenge that Lycaon becomes a friend (*philos*), because, as the next words ('die you too') make plain, the death is shared with Patroclus, and indeed with Achilles.[79] The trafficking that has merely brought Lycaon back to his starting point is, in the face of the shared certainty of death embraced by Achilles, foolish irrelevance. Achilles rejects gain in favour of a grim heroic solidarity. One does not sell a *philos*.

This is not the first time that Achilles has rejected an offer of goods. In book 9 he stated that no amount of wealth – not even all the wealth of Orchomenos or of Egyptian Thebes, not even gifts as many as the sand or dust – will reconcile him to Agamemnon 'until he gives back to me all the heartrending insolence' (9.387).[80] In the same speech (401–9) he insists again on the ineffectiveness of wealth: all the wealth of Troy, and of Delphi too, is not *equivalent in value* (*antaxios*) to his *psuchē* (soul or life): cattle and sheep can be plundered and tripods and horses can be obtained, whereas the *psuchē* of a man cannot be plundered or captured to come back again once it were to exchange the barrier of his teeth. Once you lose it, through a kind of exchange[81] that involves (like trade rather than gift-exchange) total and irrevocable alienation, you cannot reacquire it even by heroic force. Agamemnon describes the long list of gifts he offers Achilles: seven tripods, ten talents of gold, twenty cauldrons, twelve horses that have won gold, seven women, and (if Troy is sacked) as much gold and bronze as he likes, twenty Trojan women, and (if they return to Greece) a daughter as bride

---

[79] When Achilles does finally accept a ransom, for the dead body of Hector, it is also as a consequence of the community-in-death, now expressed in ritual that reconciles him to his enemy Priam, whom he calls *philos* (24.650): Seaford 1994a, 172–80.

[80] The debate about whether this rejection is consistent with the norms of Homeric society (e.g. Gill 1996, 143–8) has ignored the historical phenomenon of exchange-value. I return to this passage in 3B and 14C.

[81] The word used here of exchange (*ameibesthai*) elsewhere in the *Iliad* always refers to exchange of armour. In the *Odyssey* it refers to exchange, alternation, requital (and goes with the 'barrier of teeth' again at *Od.* 10.328).

and seven citadels. But for Achilles wealth is incommensurable with life, with independence, and with the honour that is the supreme value for the heroic life. It is striking that Achilles will in his words to Lycaon again reject an offer of wealth as meaningless in the face of certain death.

The 'gifts' offered by Agamemnon and Lycaon are ineffective. Moreover, in general – complains Achilles – there has been no gratitude (*charis*) for fighting. The good and the bad fighter get the same, and are held in equal honour (9.316–19). Agamemnon has not only taken Briseis but kept for himself most of the booty won by others (330–3). Reciprocity between leader and warrior, the form of centralised reciprocity known as redistribution (2A(4)), has been destroyed by the leader's selfish control of the process. The breakdown is forcefully encapsulated in the words 'hateful to me are his gifts' (9.378).

More is at stake than the relation between two individuals. Honour (*timē*) and its material manifestations as reward for bravery are conferred by the Lycians as a whole (*Il.* 12.310–21). Honour is an essentially social phenomenon. But among the Greeks before Troy it seems that the right to redistribute booty belongs only nominally to the people, in fact to the leader (2E). Agamemnon's control of the process has produced not just a rift between himself and Achilles but a generalised crisis. What Achilles complains of is a general disparity between worth (in battle) and reward. The implication is that worth should attract its equivalent in the concrete manifestations (booty) of honour (*timē*), that this general equivalence has been selfishly abolished by Agamemnon. In a sense this implication embodies the spirit of trade: one cloak is equivalent to three vases or ten drachmas, whatever the personal relations (e.g. leader and follower) between their respective owners. It illustrates how the breakdown of the interpersonal relations of reciprocity might favour the development of the impersonal equivalence inherent in trade and of a universal measure of value. Socially conferred *timē*, inherent in distributed booty, has fallen under the control of a leader (Agamemnon) who denies it to Achilles, but will in the monetised economy embody – with the depersonalised meaning 'price' – the relationship between commodity and money (10B).

This does not however mean that Homeric epic embodies the historical transition from reciprocity to trade. Indeed, we have seen in detail how it tends to marginalise or denigrate trade and monetisation. Moreover, the heroic Achilles is far from being a proponent of trade. The exchange of Lycaon for a specified price is described only in order for another such exchange to be heroically rejected by Achilles with the assertion of a personal relation of solidarity. By invoking the idea – alien to reciprocity and essential to trade – of *equivalence in value* Achilles rejects the integrative power of reciprocity, leaving himself isolated. It is an isolation that derives from the breakdown of reciprocity, but cannot be overcome by the newer kind of integration provided by trade. Achilles responds to the emphatically enumerated list of goods by insisting that no amount of goods would be 'equivalent in value to his *psuchē*'. Trade and monetisation make for the isolated autonomy of the individual (14A), who as the beneficiary of the exchange cannot himself be exchanged (whereas the *timē* and its material manifestations conferred by the Lycians *are* a fair exchange for the life of its recipient: 12.315).

This rejection by Achilles of the integrative power of goods (whether as gifts or commodities) isolates him from the community. But the impasse is in a sense resolved by a remarkable statement: told that he will be honoured like a god with gifts, he replies 'I have no need of this honour (*timē*). I think I am honoured by the *aisē* (ordinance, distribution: 3A) of Zeus' (9.607–8). True value is here separated from, no longer depends on, the material goods by which it is normally conveyed.

This separation will prove to be highly significant (14C). Let us note here merely its detachment of the subjective from the objective. Our list of material transactions in Homer moved through a spectrum from the considerable subjectivity embodied in the prize and the gift (as embodying the identity of the donor, honour, etc.) to the complete absence of such subjectivity from commodities exchanged only for their own sake. There is an asymmetry here in that whereas the prize and the gift (as well as reward, compensation, etc.) embody the subjective in the objective, the commodity is *purely* objective, untouchable by heroic subjectivity. Symmetry is introduced only by the pure heroic subjectivity of Achilles, which lies beyond all objects and their power to create equivalence, just as, at the other extreme, the objective equivalences of trade lie beyond the power of honour, loyalty, and personal identity to embody themselves in objects. Commodification, in contrast to the gift, separates out the purely subjective (isolated individual) from the purely objective (11B, 14C).

We return, finally, to our two other cases of A–B–X. First, the exchange between Diomedes and Glaucus is flawed by lack of equivalence, which turns an exchange that is (as gift-exchange) merely honourable into an act of folly. Our second case was the suitor's offer of compensation. Just as the *Iliad* is dominated by the crisis of reciprocity (redistribution) consequent on Achilles' rejection of Agamemnon's goods, so the *Odyssey* is dominated by the distortion of redistribution constituted by the suitors feasting on the wealth of the absent leader. And in both epics the resolution of the main crisis gives rise to another such crisis. For Odysseus as for Achilles, no amount of goods can be equivalent to the wrong suffered. His rejection of goods offered as compensation by the suitor produces a mass slaughter and thereby another crisis, the armed attack by the suitors' relatives. Similarly Achilles, reconciled with Agamemnon, returns to battle to avenge Patroclus, and rejects offers of goods from Lycaon and then from Hector, the latter rejection resulting in the mutilation, unacceptable to the gods, of Hector's corpse. To this theme of reciprocity in crisis I will return (2E, 4B).

In both epics the final crisis of reciprocity is helped to its resolution by orders from the gods, and in the *Iliad* (I have shown elsewhere) also by the integrative power of ritual.[82] The next step in our argument is to show that in Homer ritual also provides an ideal form of the allocation of goods, one that contrasts with both the instability of booty-distribution and the marginality of trade. I mean the ritual of animal sacrifice.

E   THE CONTRAST BETWEEN THE (RE)DISTRIBUTION OF BOOTY AND OF SACRIFICIAL MEAT

The *Iliad* begins with king Agamemnon, faced with having to return his prize (*geras*) Chryseis to her father, seeking a replacement. Achilles responds (1.122–9) that the Achaians cannot give him another prize because all the things taken as booty have been distributed, and it is unseemly for the people to gather them back again.[83] To this Agamemnon replies that either the Achaians will give him another prize worth the one lost, or he himself will go and take the prize of Achilles, or of Ajax, or of Odysseus. Achilles protests not only at the threat to strip him of the prize he has worked hard to win, given to him by the sons of the Achaians (162), but also at a general inequity: when a city is sacked, he, Achilles, does not have a prize equal to Agamemnon's, despite doing the greater part of the fighting; in the distribution Agamemnon's prize is much bigger than his (165–8). In book 9 Achilles returns to the point: from the cities he sacked he would take much booty and give it to Agamemnon, who would distribute little and keep much (330–3).

From these passages it seems that the right to redistribute belongs nominally to the people but in fact to the leader. In normal circumstances this control by the leader produces (according to Achilles) inequity, and in special circumstances it produces the crisis that dominates the *Iliad*.

---

[82] Death ritual: Seaford 1994a, 144–90.   [83] Or perhaps 'to gather them back again from the people'.

But the (re)distribution of booty is not the only form taken by (re)distribution in Homer. It also occurs in the animal sacrifice, of which there are six lengthy descriptions. Although no one description is entirely identical with another, the actions constituting each sacrifice are never related in a different order, and there is much that is identical between descriptions.

In the *Iliad* twenty rowers, and Odysseus as leader, take Chryseis on a ship back to her father Chryses, and perform a sacrifice which ends the plague that Chryses had invoked on the Greeks. Although a leading role is taken by Chryses (1.450, 462), and some functions are performed by a group of young men (463, 470), the sacrifice is performed by the whole company, who are the subject of no fewer than twenty-four plural verbs in about as many lines (448–74). The consumption, too, involves the egalitarian participation of the whole group, as is stressed by the line 'they feasted, nor was anybody's hunger denied the equal feast' (468), a formulaic sentence that reappears elsewhere in Homer six times,[84] and by the distribution of wine 'to all' (471).

The sacrifice performed by Agamemnon at *Iliad* 2.402–32 is a peaceful preliminary to the warfare that starts immediately afterwards and continues, interrupted only by ritual, throughout the *Iliad*. After Agamemnon's prayer there are twelve lines (421–32) that are almost identical with those after the prayer of Chryses (1.458–69); but the sacrificing group is rather different, not anonymous rowers but seven of the best Greeks. It is nevertheless said (even for this select band) that 'they feasted, nor was anybody's hunger denied the equal feast'. As for the other Greeks, it is briefly stated that each sacrificed individually (2.400).

The description of sacrifice in book 3 of the *Iliad* is of a special kind, being designed to enforce an oath between the hostile armies in an attempt to create peace. As may be typical of an oath-sacrifice, there is no meal.[85] Nevertheless, a distribution occurs – of the victim's hairs to the best men (274) of both sides. Whereas in general the animal sacrifice may express and confirm the solidarity of the group, this oath-sacrifice unites people from different groups.

This same power of integration is manifest also, in a different way, in those sacrifices into which are integrated strangers who arrive by chance, of which a notable example[86] is the lengthily described sacrifice at the opening

---

[84] *Il.* 1.602; 431; 7.320; 23.56; *Od.* 16.479; 19.425. 'Equal feast' occurs also at *Il.* 4.48; 9.225; 15.95; 24.69; *Od.* 8.98. See also *Od.* 20.281–2, 293–4.
[85] Seaford 1994a, 46–7.
[86] See also esp. *Il.* 11.768–80; *Od.* 7.136–8; 15.222, 257–62; Eur. *El.* 779–96; Seaford 1994a, 50–1.

of book 3 of the *Odyssey*. Athena (disguised as Mentor) and Telemachus arrive by ship at Pylos to find the Pylians sacrificing on the beach, arranged in nine groups, each of five hundred men with nine bulls (5–8). It is 'they', i.e. the people of Pylos, who are said to be performing the sacrifice. Telemachus and Athena go to the 'assembly and seats of the Pylian men' (31), where Nestor is sitting with his sons and around them companions are preparing meat. The strangers are welcomed and given shares (*moiras*) of the innards and wine. Telemachus and Athena pray to Poseidon, with Athena asking him to provide gracious recompense to all the Pylians for the wonderful hecatomb (58–9). The company then feasts: 'dividing shares, they held their communal high feast'.[87] There is in this sacrifice no role for a leader or priest, and the communal participation of the 4,500 men involved is emphasised. We then move to the house of Nestor, where there is another lengthily described sacrifice, on a much smaller scale, in which Nestor, his five sons, and the women of the extended family each play an important role.

The communal sacrifice on the beach at Pylos plays an architectural role in the narrative, as marking Telemachus' entry into the world outside Ithaca. Similarly, the last of our six lengthily described sacrifices, performed on Ithaca by the swineherd Eumaeus, marks the return of Odysseus from the world of fable to his own country (*Od.* 14.418–38). Eumaeus divides the meat of the sacrificed pig into seven portions, sets aside one for Hermes and the nymphs, distributes the others to each of his companions, and honours (*gerairen*) Odysseus with a special portion.

These descriptions of animal sacrifice occur in different kinds of context. And yet each of them combines emphasis on communality (whether of a large or small group) with traditional typicality of procedure, and with a key position in the narrative. The ancient,[88] regular, and highly ritualised slaughter and distribution of the animal ensures that everybody is given a share, that there is an 'equal feast'. Equal distribution to all and (especially) collective participation (*koinōnia*) are persistently emphasised in numerous later references to the animal sacrifice performed by groups varying in size from the household to the whole city-state or even Greeks from different city-states at Panhellenic festivals.[89] The distribution of booty, on the other

---

[87] Lattimore's translation of 66 (also of the suitors at 20.280) μοίρας δασσάμενοι δαίνυντ' ἐρικυδέα δαῖτα, in which in fact every word except the penultimate derives from a root meaning divide up.

[88] Burkert 1983.

[89] Equal distribution: see 3A n. 5. *Koinōnia*: e.g. Aesch. *Ag.* 1037–8; Ar. *Peace* 1115, 1129–31; Thuc. 3.59.2; Xen. *Hell.* 2.4.20; Pl. *Rep.* 470e; *Laws* 738d, 909de; Isocr. *Paneg.* 43; Men. *Dysk.* 560–2; Theopomp. *FGrH* 115 F213; *IG* II² 1496 (Rosivach 1994, 48–67); Burkert 1985, 55–9, 254–60; Parker 1996, 1.

hand, is inevitably irregular, dependent on uncontrolled violence, the result of special circumstances, and so likely to be relatively unritualised.[90] Certainly it is not ritualised in Homer.

Nevertheless, the (re)distribution of booty and of the sacrificial animal in Homer have a certain amount in common: they are both called by the same verb (*dateësthai*); both of them may be performed either by the chieftain[91] or the whole group;[92] and in both we find a special share (sometimes called *geras*) for the chieftain[93] as well as the receipt of an 'equal' share by everybody in the group.[94] The two forms of distribution may even, when the booty consists of animals, go closely together.[95] All the more striking, therefore, is the contrast, in the opening of the *Iliad*, between on the one hand the traditional, controlled communality of the sacrifices, in their key (concluding and initiating) positions in the narrative, and on the other hand the inequity, at the heart of the *Iliad*, that arises from the ambiguous, uncertain procedures in the distribution of booty. The same contrast is implicit in the words of Odysseus after Agamemnon's envoys have just participated in a sacrificial meal prepared by Achilles and Patroclus. He begins 'Your health, Achilles. [We are] not lacking[96] in the equal feast, either in the hut of Agamemnon son of Atreus or here now', and proceeds to describe the crisis caused by Achilles' withdrawal. The communality of eating will play a part in the reconciliations of Achilles with Agamemnon and with Priam.[97]

The contrast corresponds, roughly speaking, to the contrast mentioned earlier (2B) between two kinds of goods, on the one hand goods for subsistence, which include animals sacrificed for food, and on the other hand treasure, artefacts of precious metal or fine cloth, unworked precious metal, women, chariots with horses. Whereas the animal is sacrificed and consumed by the group, treasure (whether or not it was acquired as booty) circulates, between members of different groups, as gifts.

---

[90] A nice example of the conflict between the ordered egalitarianism of sacrificial distribution and the potentially conflictual distribution of booty occurs in the story of the Dioscuri and the sons of Aphareus falling out over the distribution of plundered cattle: Apollod. *Bibl.* 3.11.2.

[91] Sacrifice: n. 108 below. Booty: *Il.* 9.333; 11.704–5.

[92] Sacrifice: 3A. Booty: *Il.* 1.162; *Od.* 9.41–2, 549.

[93] Sacrifice: *Il.* 7.321; *Od.* 9.160, 550–1; cf. 4.66; 14.437. Booty: *Il.* 1.167; 9.333; 11.704; *Od.* 9.550–1; *geras* can also refer to other forms of conferred privilege, e.g. at *Il.* 20.182; *Od.* 7.150.

[94] Sacrifice: 2E n. 84. Booty: *Il.* 11.705; *Od.* 9.42, 549; cf. 1.118–19.

[95] *Il.* 11.703–6; *Od.* 9.548–53.

[96] ἐπιδευεῖς. The variant ἐπιδευής gives much less awkward syntax, and by referring to Achilles (as would also ἐπιδεύῃ, probably suggested by Aristarchus) makes the contrast with his treatment in the booty distribution even more obvious.

[97] 23.48 (cf. 19.179–80); 24.621–8.

When Odysseus and his companions sack the city of the Ciconians and kill the men, they share out the captured wives and possessions, so that nobody should go without an equal share (*Od.* 9.41–2). It is only later in the narrative, during the Cyclops episode, that we learn that Odysseus had received from one of the Ciconians, in return for safety for himself and his family, 'glorious gifts': seven talents of gold, a silver mixing-bowl, and twelve jars of wine (9.197–205). It is hardly surprising therefore that when Odysseus leaves the island of Aeolus with a bag containing the winds, his companions take the opportunity, while he sleeps, to open the bag, thinking that it contains gold and silver as a gift from Aeolus. The result is disastrous, but the companions' reasoning is not unconvincing: 'Odysseus', they say, 'is loved and honoured when he visits lands and cities, and is bringing home with him much fine treasure from the booty of Troy, whereas we who have gone through the same venture are returning with empty hands. And now Aeolus, with the favour of friendship, has given him these things' (10.38–44).

By contrast, the distribution of meat among Odysseus and his companions, whether from sacrifice or from hunt, is unproblematic. The descriptions of meals, with Odysseus sometimes receiving slightly more than his companions,[98] form peaceful intervals of ordered solidarity between the succession of terrifying ordeals which often also involve dissension between Odysseus and his men. And yet the exotic places in which their adventures occur are marked by the absence or abnormality of sacrifice.[99] On Calypso's island it is said that there are no sacrifices (5.101–2). Polyphemus' contempt for Zeus, his disgusting killing of Odysseus' companions, and his eating them raw, are antithetical to sacrifice. At the sacrifices of the Phaeacians the gods are (abnormally) present. And even Odysseus' companions are forced by hunger to devour, with an abnormal sacrifice, the forbidden cattle of the Sun. With this single, fatal exception, however, Odysseus and his companions eat according to civilised, Greek procedures in an exotic world in which those procedures do not obtain. At Pylos, by contrast, those procedures are displayed in magnificent detail, as well as in the humbler context of Eumaeus' dwelling on Ithaca. Where, in this range of possibilities, are we to place the feasting of the suitors?

The special circumstances on Ithaca produce feasting extensive enough to destroy the distinction between agricultural produce (especially animals) and other forms of possession, for 'it will soon smash completely the

---

[98] *Od.* 9.156–65, 548–57; 10.181–4, 468, 476–7; see also 9.231. Privileged share for Odysseus: 9.160, 550–1.

[99] For details of this argument see Vidal-Naquet 1986, 15–38.

whole household, and will destroy its livelihood (*biotos*)' (2.48–9). Now *biotos* can refer to wealth in general, as can the word *ktēmata*. But whereas *biotos* refers in particular to agricultural produce, *ktēmata* refers generally to more durable possessions and frequently to treasure.[100] And so the phrase *ktēmata dardaptousi* (they devour – like animals – the possessions: 14.92; 16.315) implies a bestial, indiscriminate devouring that will consume all the household's wealth, not just the meat.[101] The feasting is, in consequence, assimilated to, or envisaged as passing into, the distribution of Odysseus' wealth as booty. The house will be 'smashed completely'. The warnings received by Telemachus to return soon to Ithaca 'lest they eat up everything, dividing up *ktēmata*'[102] are confirmed by the Ithacan Philoetius: 'they are grown eager to divide up the *ktēmata* of the master long gone' (20.215–16). The feasting of the suitors is extensive and unruly enough to confound the opposition between distribution in the feast and the distribution of booty. Their feasting is therefore generally unaccompanied by sacrifice;[103] indeed it is in its rowdy disorder antithetical to sacrifice.[104]

The crisis of the *Iliad* is a breakdown of the form of reciprocity (Achilles' prize is in return for fighting) controlled by the leader (redistribution). At the centre of the *Odyssey* too is a crisis of redistributive reciprocity. The balance breaks down on the other side, as it were: although over the long period of the suitors' feasting the normal arrangement would be for the nobles to entertain each other, reciprocally,[105] that suitors should feast at the house of a chief is not necessarily unacceptable, and certainly not unparalleled.[106] But in the special circumstances on Ithaca, namely prolonged uncertainty as to whether Odysseus lives compounded by Penelope's indecision, the practice is unacceptably extended, resulting in an excessive, one-way transaction, the consumption of Odysseus' wealth without compensation.[107] Redistribution is in crisis in that the normal role of the chief in giving a feast to the nobles[108] is exploited, or even reversed – in the sense that his authority is subverted, rather than confirmed, by the feast.

Redistributive (centralised) reciprocity breaks down as a result of excessive appropriation by the redistributor (*Iliad*) or by the community of

---

[100] E.g. at *Od.* 14.323–4 *ktēmata* are qualified as bronze, gold, and iron.

[101] Cf. the process imagined by Telemachus: 'for me it would be better for you to eat the treasures (*keimēlia*) and cattle' (2.74–5).

[102] 3.315–16; 15.12–13.   [103] See further Saïd 1979.

[104] Another conflict at a feast, referred to at *Od.* 8.76, was significant enough to be a sign predicted by the Delphic oracle (76–82).

[105] 1.374–5; 2.139–40; as in an *eranos*: 1.225–9; Seaford 1994a, 57.

[106] Hdt. 6.126–30; Seaford 1994a, 53–6.   [107] *Nēpoinos*: 1.160; 2.142 etc.

[108] *Il.* 2.402; 7.314; 9.69–70; *Od.* 3.42, 445; 14.249–51; 15.506–7.

nobles (*Odyssey*). In the *Iliad* the distribution is of booty, in the *Odyssey* of food and wine in feasting which passes into the distribution of booty. In both cases there is a sharp contrast with the peaceful, ordered communality manifested in the lovingly described distributional procedures of the animal sacrifice, so pleasing to deity.[109]

In general traditional ritual provides stability, creating a consensual expectation of when, how, and by whom the ritual will be performed. It may represent control, predictability, and cohesion in an otherwise uncontrollable, unpredictable, and conflictual world. The consequent vital importance of ritual for society is expressed in the belief that its performance is ruthlessly demanded by the gods. In animal sacrifice, at least as it is described in Homer, the end point and (it seems) main purpose of the ritual is the equal distribution and communal eating of the meat. The power of this principle of sacrificial distribution is, as we shall see in 3A, manifest in its influence (as a model) on other forms of communal distribution, and even on the notion of fate (*moira*). Animal sacrifice, more than other rituals, impinges on the *economy*. As we have seen, in some Homeric accounts of sacrifice an individual has a leading role or privileged share, but this does not disturb the principle of communal distribution. Tension between individual appropriation and communal distribution in Homer occurs not within the animal sacrifice but rather in the narrative as a whole – both within the distribution of booty and between it and sacrificial distribution. This is because in the distribution of booty, in sharp contrast to sacrificial distribution, the heroic individualism that forms so much of the Homeric ethos has disturbed or even marginalised the principle of equal distribution.

The contrast can be pursued further. The procedure of sacrificial ritual, as of ritual in general, is defined. For instance, it is performed at certain regular intervals (e.g. annually), or as a regular accompaniment to certain actions (warfare, purification, wedding, etc.). The rights to perform a leading role or to receive an equal or special share are established by tradition (later frequently by inscribed regulation), as are the number and kind of animals to be slaughtered. In Homer the numbers are, when specified, a hundred, twelve, nine, or one.[110]

The distribution of booty, by contrast, is irregular and unpredictable, dependent on the success of uncontrollable violence. In Homer the right

---

[109] Cf. *Od.* 14.249–71: the leader of a raid first provides a sacrificial meal for his companions, who subsequently are so keen to plunder that they disobey him and come to grief.
[110] One hundred is implied by the word *hekatombē*; twelve: *Il.* 6.93; *Od.* 13.182; nine: *Il.* 6.174; *Od.* 3.8; one: *Il.* 2.402; etc.; Laum 1924, 18.

to perform a leading role and to receive an equal share are, we have seen, uncertain and ambiguous. Animal sacrifice is perhaps the most formulaic of all Homeric actions (along with arming scenes), with the recurrence of whole sequences of identical lines. But the distribution of booty is neither ritualised, nor described at length, nor described formulaically; and the single exception to these generalisations – the occurrence in three different places of the same formulaic phrase 'lest anybody should go away deprived of an equal share'[111] – refers, significantly, to the retention of the principle of universal equal distribution, a principle that is clearly contradicted by the distribution at the heart of the *Iliad*. The amount and kind of material for distribution is, again in contrast to sacrifice, unpredictable and uncontrollable, dependent on what has been looted and what has been made available for distribution. Moreover, the kind of items that would be looted might be much more valuable, and much more variable in value, than animals: the armour of Glaucus is worth a hundred cattle (*Il.* 6.236), and so too apparently is the Sidonian bowl given as the price of Lycaon (2D), whereas a skilled woman is worth four cattle (*Il.* 23.705) and a cauldron one (*Il.* 23.885).[112]

Furthermore, whereas the sacrifice is in essence the act of a group, and if on a large scale inevitably a public, visible event, the distribution of booty may become a series of one-to-one transactions between the leader and all or some of his followers,[113] and therefore relatively invisible. In the animal sacrifice there persists the ancient necessity of collective participation in the killing and eating of the animal.[114] Moreover sacrificial animals, and the killing of them, are difficult to conceal. Treasure, by contrast, may be durable, portable, of very high value relative to its size, and easier to conceal. Odysseus' men think that he has gold and silver hidden in his leather bag. Treasure is kept in the house, out of public view,[115] emerging only (or largely) in order to create, as gifts, a series of one-to-one relationships. The items of treasure given as gifts, or as prizes, are frequently individualised, or sometimes even unique, with an individual history or of supreme quality. The silver mixing-bowl, for instance, made by the Sidonians, given to

---

[111] *Il.* 11.705; *Od.* 9.42 and 549.

[112] Sacrificed animals are often called *teléeis* or *teleios* (i.e. full-grown: Rosivach 1994, 151): *Il.* 1.66; 24.34; etc. In fourth century BC Athens the sums budgeted (in inscriptions) for sheep, goats, and piglets are, over a long period, remarkably consistent, but for cattle there is much more variety – between the extremes of forty and one hundred drachmas: Rosivach 1994, 95–6, 101–2.

[113] That indeed is the impression given by *Il.* 9.332–3 'and he (Agamemnon) remaining behind by the ships would distribute a few things and keep many things'.

[114] Burkert 1983.

[115] Even though it may still be desired by many, as is said of the stained ivory cheek-piece (for horses) stored (*keitai*) in the inner chamber (*thalamos*) of a king: *Il.* 4.143–4.

Thoas, then to Patroclus as ransom to Lycaon, then by Achilles as a prize in the funeral-games, is said to be the most beautiful in the world (*Il.* 23.741–8). Another bowl of silver and gold, given by the Sidonian king to Menelaus and by him to Telemachus, was made by Hephaestus himself.[116] Among the gifts given as ransom by Priam to Achilles is 'a goblet of surpassing loveliness that the men of Thrace had given him when he went to them with a message, a great possession' (*Il.* 24.233–5). Even the seven women offered (among much else) by Agamemnon to Achilles, skilled workers captured from Lesbos, are said to surpass other women in beauty (*Il.* 9.128–30). And so on.

To conclude, the distribution of booty in Homer is haphazard, un-ritualised, potentially invisible, and ambiguously regulated; and the booty distributed is generally treasure, which may be of extremely variable value, of unpredictable quantity, used to embody interpersonal relationships, and highly invidualised. Sacrificial distribution in Homer is, by contrast, a pub-licly visible ritual,[117] with traditionally regulated and accepted procedures, in which nobody is denied an equal share. The meat is consumed there and then. The number of victims is set, generally one hundred, twelve, nine, or one. We may moreover infer that the animals, which are never distinguished from each other, must all be pleasing to the deity and so do not fall below a certain standard. There is presumably typicality of quality as well as of quantity.

---

[116] *Od.* 4.615–19 = 15.115–19.
[117] Even as late as fourth century BC Athens private sacrifices generally had a public dimension: Rosivach 1994, 9–10.

CHAPTER THREE

Sacrifice and distribution

A HOMERIC SACRIFICE: SUBJECTIVE CONTINUITY

The Homeric ideology that marginalises the growth of trade and monetisation (2BC) does nevertheless register the fatal instability of the old centralised reciprocity (2D), and respects the tradition of communal[1] distribution embodied in animal sacrifice (2E). In the historical transition refracted in Homer it will be this model of sacrificial distribution that will eventually predominate – no longer confined, as in Homer, to the distribution of meat, but incorporating (we shall see in this chapter) the more valuable and durable goods that in Homer occupy a separate sphere of exchange and distribution.

Whence the power of this sacrificial model? There is no doubt of the economic centrality, from the beginnings of homo sapiens, of the act of killing an animal, first in the hunt, and then, relatively recently, in the sacrifice of domesticated animals. The survival of the group depends not only on power over the animal but also on an agreed mode of distributing the flesh. And yet the act of killing and eating is in itself transient. It may, despite the emotion of the dramatic killing and of the collective participation in the meal, leave no physical trace of itself. The consequent vital need for continuity may be expressed in three ways: (a) in the continuity of *deity*, who remains to demand the same form of sacrifice at regular intervals or in specific circumstances; (b) in the *subjective* continuity of the human insistence that in the future the animal be killed and distributed in the

---

[1] Both distribution of booty and animal sacrifice tend to pass into the control of a leader (see below). But whereas the distribution of booty tends to become interpersonal gift-giving (by the leader), animal sacrifice remains distribution among a group: the only recipient of the sacrificed animal as an interpersonal gift is the deity – animal sacrifices are explicitly called gifts for the gods at *Il.* 24.68–70; see also 4.48–9, 20.298–9, 22.170–2; *Od.* 1.66–7; as these passages show, the gods are imagined as reciprocating. Indeed, both treasure and the sacrificial animal in Homer are not only *distributed*, they also function as *gifts to individuals*; but whereas treasure is the characteristic gift between humans, the characteristic gift for deity is animal sacrifice.

same way; (c) in continuity of an established *object or place* (altar, shrine, temple), in which the preservation of the durable part of the animal, or of the implements of sacrifice, may be a first step.

To what extent do we find these continuities in Homer and generally in early Greek religion? (a) is relatively straightforward: animal sacrifices are made 'to' or 'for' (dative) deities, who appreciate them.[2] But the deities occupy only a marginal place in the Homeric descriptions of the ritual, for they are not actually present at the meal, and anyway feed on nectar and ambrosia rather than on meat. For (b) and (c) more detailed treatment is required.

(b) The stereotypical description of the sacrifice in Homer (2E) is a symptom of the subjective element of continuity, of the insistence that the sacrifice continue to be performed in the same way. The power of this subjective element manifests itself widely. It has been in various ways argued that the idea of sacrificial distribution exercised considerable influence on a range of Greek vocabulary, conceptions, and institutions. The beginning of civilisation is associated with the ordered distribution of food.[3] The solidarity and articulation of the polis is expressed in its animal sacrifices,[4] in which the principle of equal distribution (found in Homer: 2E) remains powerful.[5] Full citizenship and entitlement to participation in the sacrificial meal seem to be one and the same.[6] Even the division of urban space may use the terminology of dividing up an animal.[7] More specifically, the word for law or convention, *nomos*, derives from *nemein* (to distribute) and so presumably at first meant distribution,[8] then the principle of distribution. In Homer *nomos* does not occur, but *nemein* (and the compound *epinemein*) does – almost always (when in the active voice, meaning distribute) of food or drink.[9] *Nomos* first occurs in Hesiod, where of the eight occurrences two refer to sacrifice[10] and one to the eating habits of

---

[2] On the importance in Homer of repeated sacrifices to deity see e.g. *Il.* 1.40; 22.170; 24.33–4; *Od.* 1.66–7.

[3] Baudy 1983, 133, citing Dicaearchus frr. 59, 72 Wehrli and Athenaeus 12f.

[4] E.g. Baudy 1983, 156; Burkert 1985, 58–9, 256; Detienne and Vernant 1989, 13, 153.

[5] Plut. *Mor.* 644AB; Dosiad. *FGrH* 458F2; Xen. *Cyr.* 2.1.30; 2.2.2.; Sokolowski 1955, no. 39.22–5; 1969, no. 33 B15–16, 24–7; *SIG*³ 1044.42; Hiller von Gaertringen 1906, 123.6–7; Borecký 1963; Berthiaume 1982, 50–1, 62–4; *IT* 953 (wine).

[6] Schmitt Pantel 1992; Parker 1997, 13–14.

[7] Aristot. *Pol.* 1267b22–3; see further Svenbro 1982.

[8] Such masculine nouns with the accent on the stem are usually *nomina actionis*: e.g. *logos* from *legein*, *tropos* from *trepein*: Laroche 1949, 175.

[9] *Il.* 9.217, 24.626; *Od.* 7.179, 8.470, 10.357, 13.50, 14.436, 449, 15.140, 20.253.

[10] *Theog.* 417, and fr. 322 M–W, which refers to sacrifice by the polis. Cf. also Theognis 54–6; Baudy 1983, 158–9.

animals.[11] And so it seems reasonable to infer that *nomos*, to which in the classical period is attributed despotic power,[12] originated in the widespread and economically fundamental practice of distributing *meat*.[13] Cognate words for which a sacrificial origin has been inferred are *nemesis* (retribution),[14] *isonomia* (equality of political rights),[15] and even *nomisdein* (acknowledge, consider).[16]

The only three Homeric occurrences of *nemein* (meaning distribute) in which it does not refer to the distribution of food or drink are *Od.* 14.210 (of an inheritance), *Il.* 3.274 (of the victims' hair in a *sacrifice*), and *Od.* 6.188, where it is said that Zeus distributes prosperity to humankind. In this last case the varying prosperity of humankind is imagined in terms of a single distributor projected onto the cosmos. The right to distribute booty seems to belong nominally to the people but in fact to their leader (2E). There is a similar duality in the distribution of food. Food is occasionally said to be distributed by the group as a whole.[17] On the other hand wealthy individuals are said to hold feasts.[18] And food and drink are frequently distributed by the host or his henchmen.[19] In such cases the verb used for 'distribute' is generally *nemein* (or *epinemein*); whereas distribution by the group – whether of food, booty, land, or inheritance – is generally referred to by *daiesthai* (or the cognate *datëesthai*). This is pointed out by Borecký (1963) as part of a subtle argument to the effect that between Homer and the classical period there is a change in the vocabulary of sharing and equality, and that the beginnings of this change can be observed within Homer. *Nemein*, Borecký argues, belongs to the later layer, in which distribution is appropriated by a powerful individual, whereas *daiesthai* etc. belong to an earlier layer of collective distribution, as does also *moira* (the equal[20] portion distributed).

This hypothesis of a development from group to powerful individual is controversial.[21] It is however clear that the projection of distribution onto the cosmos is to be found in two antithetical forms, corresponding to the

---

[11] *Op.* 276–8. The remaining five occurrences are *Theog.* 66, 74 (by emendation), 307 (*anomon*); *Op.* 388; fr.280.14.

[12] Pi. fr. 1 69.1; Hdt. 7.104; Pl. *Prt.* 337d, *Laws* 715d.   [13] Baudy 1983, 157–61. Cf. Plut. *Mor.* 644C.

[14] Baudy 1983, 159. On *nemesis* and *nemein* s. *RE* s.v. Nemesis 2338.

[15] Baudy 1983, 159; Svenbro 1982, 955; cf. also *isomoiria* 'equality of portions' (and on *moira* below). The idea is also to be found in medical theory (Borecký 1963, 56; Svenbro 1982, 955) and in cosmology (Borecký 1963, 56; cf. Baudy 1983, 152).

[16] Baudy 1983, 159. The verb is associated with the religious sphere (*theous nomisdein*, 1A), and its first occurrence is, it seems, in the context of eating an animal: Alcaeus fr. 71 L–P.

[17] E.g. 2E n. 87.   [18] *Il.* 9.70, 19.299, 23.29; *Od.* 3.309; 4.3; 14.250–1.

[19] See the passages cited in n. 9 above.

[20] On *moira* in Homer as meaning an *equal* share see Borecký 1963, esp. 52 n. 10. On *aisa* meaning (originally) an *equal* share see Bianchi 1953, 1–10.

[21] Baudy 1983, 164 n. 137 rejects it, albeit without engaging the argument.

antithesis between distribution according to an established principle and distribution by a powerful individual: on the one hand in the *principle* of destiny, which Zeus may wish to transgress but should not, and on the other hand in Zeus himself distributing (*nemei*) prosperity (noted above) and in the gods themselves giving *moiras* to mortals (*Od.* 19.592).

The antithesis in Homer between Zeus and destiny is as follows. Poseidon resents Zeus's imperious attitude, and claims to be (*Il.* 15.209) 'with an equal portion (*isomoron*) and provided with the same share/destiny (*aisē*)'. On two occasions Zeus wants to save a warrior but does not do so because told by another deity that the warrior is long since provided with his destiny (*aisē*).[22] The original and basic sense of *aisē* (or *aisa*) is, like that of *moira*, 'part' or 'share'.[23] Poseidon is provided with the same share as Zeus. Mortals may be provided with varying shares, but in one respect, death, the share is the same for all.[24] The god of the underworld, Pluto, is *Isodaitēs*, the divider into equal portions.[25] The words *moira* and *aisē* (*aisa*), both feminine, both refer originally to the share distributed, and then to the principle of distribution, which may be contrary to the will of the powerful individual male Zeus, or subordinated to him,[26] and may itself be personified as *Aisa* or *Moira*.[27]

---

[22] *Il.* 16.441, 22.179.

[23] E.g. *Od.* 5.40; see Chantraine 1968–80 s.v. αἶσα and s.v. μοῖρα; Dietrich (1965) 339. Both *aisa* and *moira* may denote a share of sacrificial meat (LSJ s.v. αἶσα II 3; *moira*: e.g. Ar. *Peace* 1105 and frequently in inscriptions – e.g. Sokolowski 1955, nos. 37.10, 50.36; 1969, 54.7, 120.5); Leumann 1950, 281; Dietrich 1965, 12, 192. Yet another word for destiny, *heimarmenē*, comes (like *moira*) from *meiresthai*, and so means that which has been received as a portion. The word *daimōn* too seems to derive from sacrificial distribution: Baudy 1983, 164–7.

[24] Borecký 1983 argues that the original principle of equality expressed in *moira* (cf. 52 n. 10) 'was never violated in the share of death' (56).

[25] Hsch. s.v. Ἰσοδαίτης.

[26] As in the expression 'the *aisē* of Zeus' (*Il.* 9.608, 17.321, etc). Cf. *Od.* 11.292 '*moira* of god', 3.269 '*moira* of gods', and the title 'leader of *moira*' (Μοιραγέτης) applied to Zeus.

[27] E.g. *Il.* 19.87; *Od.* 7.197. See Thomson 1961a, 327–46. Much misguided effort has gone into trying to discover which of the various associations of *Moira* (or the *Moirai* (plural), or *moira*) – death, birth, fertility, etc. – is what she originally or basically represents. To the extent that this may be discovered, it can hardly be other than 'share', as suggested not only by etymology (e.g. Chantraine 1968–70 s.v. μοῖρα) but also by *moira* having that meaning (share of the sacrificial feast, of inheritance, of booty) in Homer and in later texts. The strong association with death develops from the notion that death constitutes a share (equal for everybody), with intermediate stages still visible in expressions such as '*moira* of death' (e.g. *Il.* 13.602) and 'death and *moira*' (e.g. *Il.* 17.672): i.e. the *natural* brute process of death is, by a familiar kind of operation, assimilated to the *cultural* (human-controlled) process of distribution. But e.g. Dietrich (1965) is misled by the association of *moira* with death into imagining an original *Moira* as death-goddess, and makes the absurd claim that 'Μοῖρα might well have existed as a divinity prior to the idea of μοῖρα = "share"' (13), untroubled by a whole series of facts that he himself states – that *moira* and *moros* 'derive directly from μείρομαι, "receive as one's portion"', that *moira* may mean a portion of *life* (75), that the cognate 'Mycenean moropa means "owner of a portion"' (206 n. 4), that *aisa* (fate) 'was originally used to denote a share of sacrificial meat' (11–12), and so on. His preconception that 'the Homeric share [μοῖρα] already inculcates an idea of limit, justice, and therefore cannot be assumed to have been the starting point of the comparatively more primitive Μοῖρα who was concerned with death' is in a sense the opposite of the truth (on this kind

According to Plutarch meals were once administered by *Moira* and *Lachesis* on the principle of equality (*Mor.* 644A). It is argued by Baudy[28] that the notions of *moira* and *aisa* originated specifically in the distribution of *meat*, from which it spread to distribution of other things – notably food and land. This can hardly be certain, but is (given the extreme antiquity of the ordering of the collective meal) not unlikely.[29]

The power of the subjective continuity (b) of the Greek animal sacrifice is, then, manifest in various ways: in the central importance of animal sacrifice to the polis, in important conceptions such as law and fate, and in Homer in the divine superstructure as well as in the descriptions of sacrifice, which are no more than a typical series of actions. Now it is striking that in Homer this subjective continuity is virtually the *only* form of continuity attaching to sacrifice: the Homeric sacrifice is centred on the feeding (and general participation) of the group, or even (as at Pylos) of the entire community, with barely a mention of any continuity of *object* or *place* as a context for animal sacrifice (c), and with (a) deity marginalised. Hesiod feels obliged to explain this marginalisation, why it is that the human participants receive the best parts of the animal, with the deity receiving typically the smoke rising from burning bones and fat (*Theog.* 556–7).

In these respects a sharp contrast is provided by the sacrificial meals offered to Mesopotamian deity (4B). The image of the deity, at the hub of a great temple complex, is regularly presented with food. Some humans, notably the king, may partake of the meal, which is nevertheless envisaged as a meal for the god. Aspects (a) and (c) of continuity have here acquired their fullest possible embodiment: the sacrificial meal is centred, almost exclusively, on the god, and takes place at the heart of a great temple.

B   HOMERIC SACRIFICE: THE LACK OF OBJECTIVE CONTINUITY

What has emerged from the Homeric narratives is a contradiction. Reciprocity is in crisis: the obligation of the leader to (re)distribute booty (*Iliad*)

---

of Frazerian fallacy see Douglas 1978, 27–9). It may well have been precisely the very *ancient* moral and social force of *moira* (as the socially crucial principle of distribution) that enabled its projection onto a broad canvass as *cosmic* order, fate, death, and as *general* order in the Homeric phrases κατὰ μοῖραν, ἐν μοίρῃ. The *principle* of moira (and *Moira*) did, it is true, lose its specific connection with *distribution* (except at Plut. *Mor.* 644A, and even though the shares continue to be called *moirai*), replaced perhaps by the deity sacrificed to on each occasion or (as we have seen Borecký suggesting) by the sacrificer (with strict equality of sharing surviving only in death).

[28] Baudy 1983, 163–6.

[29] Baudy's (1983) cross-cultural perspective is based on a general view of the collective meal that goes back to the beginning of the human species. One might add to Baudy's argument that of the sixteen Homeric occurrences of *moira* meaning 'portion', thirteen refer to food. However, the three Homeric occurrences of *aisa* meaning 'portion' all refer to booty.

or food and drink (*Odyssey*) produces discord, and gifts are ineffective. Sacrificial (re)distribution, by contrast, seems to embody perfect communality. And yet whereas booty and gifts are prestige objects (treasure) that may, we shall see, be prized as lasting over generations, animal sacrifice has almost no material permanence.

This contradiction has to be seen in the context of the historical developments contemporary with an especially creative phase of the long development of Homeric poetry. Excavation has shown that in the eighth century BC there occurred a sharp increase in phenomena associated with the early development of the polis in various parts of the Greek world, notably the genesis of monumental temples and a massive increase in the quantity and quality of dedications made in public sanctuaries. It has become clear that another important function of these early temples, in addition to the storage of dedicated wealth, was the sacrificial feast.[30]

These extraordinary developments of the eighth century are in Homeric epic barely reflected. The word for altar (*bōmos*) occurs seventeen times, but only ever as a brief reference. There is no *description* of an altar. Nor on the whole[31] is there mention of anything else constructed to constitute the environment of sacrifice. And of the six sacrifices that are described in detail (2E) there is mention of an altar in only one (*Il.* 1.448). There is nothing in the Homeric narrative to prevent sacrifice being represented as attached to specific places designed for sacrifice. But it is generally not so represented. The descriptions do rather emphasise the *subjective* continuity of sacrifice (3A) by reproducing the stereotypical actions involved in the killing and eating of the animal(s). Even the deity, for whom in a sense the sacrifice is performed, is marginal. Moreover, it is not only from scenes of sacrifice that religious buildings are notably absent. With the exception of the temple of Athena at Troy, which is the context for the offering of a robe, temples are in Homer mentioned but rarely and fleetingly,[32] and the same is true, as we shall see, of the dedication of objects in sanctuaries.

There are various possible attitudes to this discrepancy between Homer and the archaeology. One is to take it as a reason for dating Homer early, to the early eighth century or even before. Another is to explain it by the

---

[30] For detail of these developments see 3C below.

[31] The only exceptions are two brief mentions of animal sacrifice in a temple (*Il.* 2.549–51, 6.308–9), of which the former may be a result of Athenian editorial activity and the latter occurs in a passage that has been argued on independent grounds to be relatively late: Seaford 1994a, 183, 195, 330–8 (esp. n. 28).

[32] Apart from the instances mentioned in the immediately preceding footnote, see *Il.* 1.39, 5.446–8, 7.83; *Od.* 6.10, 7.81, 8.80, 12.346–7; Vermeule 1974, 106, 108, 132; on *Il.* 9.404 see below. This slightness cannot be attributed merely to the fact that much of the *Iliad* takes place where you would not expect to find temples (notably outside Troy).

hypothesis that Homeric epic was not created before these developments but nevertheless gave them little importance in its construction of the heroic world.[33] The need to decide between these views is not of vital importance to my overall argument. Nevertheless, I believe that Homeric epic was in the year 700 BC far from attaining its final form,[34] and therefore that Homeric epic ignores or excludes numerous contemporary developments. The two views can of course be combined (in varying proportions), in that the exclusion of some contemporary developments may be indistinguishable from loyalty to a heroic past preserved in an oral tradition that reaches back, in some respects, to a time when those realities did not yet exist.

The exclusion is to be explained, at least in part, by ideological neglect of the development of the polis. An advantage of this hypothesis of *ideological* neglect is that it is able to explain the Homeric marginalisation or exclusion of a whole number of other items too, for instance exchange-value (2BC), the god Dionysus, or patriotism.[35] It is also able to account for the fact that the tendency to exclude or marginalise is accompanied by the tendency to *devalue*. For instance, we have seen both that there is not much either of money or of commerce in Homer, *and* that what there is tends to have various negative associations. Dionysus is largely excluded from Homer, and moreover is in his main appearance pathetically ineffective (*Il.* 6.135–9). Another striking instance is provided by the practice of dedication. Wealth is accumulated in temples by this practice, which in the eighth century acquired massive proportions. And yet there are in Homer only eight mentions of the practice, as follows.

1 *Il.* 6.269–311. The dedication of a robe at the temple of Athena in Troy. Athena rejects the accompanying prayer (311).

2 *Il.* 7.81–3. Hector says that if he kills his opponent in the imminent duel, he will hang his armour at the temple of Apollo in Troy. But in the event he does not win.

3 *Il.* 8.203–4. Hera complains to Poseidon that the Greeks are dying despite bringing him gifts at Helicon and Aegae, and tells him to will (or that

---

[33] Vermeule (1974, 132, also 106, 107–8) rejects (rightly for the most part) various attempts to explain the discrepancy – by a geographical gap between Ionian epic and mainland cult, by an ideological gap between aristocratic epic and popular cult, and by a chronological gap between Homer's own time and the supposedly Mycenaean world he describes. She herself proposes instead that the answer is to be found simply in the 'laws of the poetic art', but does not attempt to specify these laws.

[34] The arguments in favour of dating Homer after 700 BC (sometimes considerably thereafter) have proliferated in recent years. For instance the year 1995 saw the appearance of three papers (Crielaard, Dickie, West), each of which argues, using material quite different from the other two, for a seventh-century Homer. See also van Wees 1994, and Seaford 1994a, 144–54, who gives earlier bibliography.

[35] Seaford 1994a, ch. 9.

he once willed)[36] their victory. But Poseidon replies that the other gods cannot defy the will of Zeus.

4 *Il.* 10.462–4. Odysseus promises to Athena the spoils taken from the corpse of Dolon, and, on his return after killing the Thracians, puts them in his ship to be prepared as a dedication for Athena (570–1).

5 *Il.* 23.141–6. Achilles refers to a lock of his own hair which had been vowed to be given, on his return home, to the river Spercheios. But this return is now precluded, and Achilles instead puts the hair into the grave of Patroclus.

6 *Od.* 3.274. Aegisthus, the seducer of Clytemnestra, vainly 'hung up (ἀνῆψεν) many dedications (*agalmata*), texiles and gold'.

7 *Od.* 8.509. The Trojans decide not to destroy the wooden horse but to 'leave it as a great dedication (*agalma*) to please the gods', with the result that the Greeks pour out of it and destroy Troy.

8 *Od.* 12.347. Odysseus' companions agree, before eating the forbidden cattle of the Sun, to build him (if they ever return to Ithaca) a temple and put in it 'many and good dedications (*agalmata*)'. But none of them lives to return to Ithaca.

Of these instances all except the first is brief. The only unproblematic one is 4, from the Doloneia, which has since antiquity been recognised as a late addition to the *Iliad*.[37] In all the other instances the dedication either does not work or does not even occur. In two cases (6 and 8) the dedication (or promise of it) accompanies a crime that, despite the (promised) dedication, dooms its perpetrator(s). In one case (5) the item promised seems, by being given elsewhere, to doom the donor; and in another (7) the item dedicated destroys its donors. The normal word for to dedicate, *anatithenai*, does not in fact occur in Homer.[38]

An instance that deserves further comment is 2. Having said that he will hang his vanquished opponent's arms at the temple of Apollo, Hector adds that he will return the corpse to the Greeks, 'so that the Greeks heap up a mound [*sēma*, literally "sign"] for him beside the broad Hellespont, and somebody of men born hereafter will say, as he sails in his benched ship over the wine-coloured sea, "this is the *sēma* of a man who died long ago, one of the best, whom glorious Hector killed." So he will speak one day, and my fame (*kleos*) will never pass away.' It is significant that Hector envisages his immortal fame as coming not through his own dedication of arms in Apollo's temple but rather through the indirect route of a grave-mound

---

[36] βούλεο could be imperative or imperfect indicative.   [37] See e.g. Kirk 1962, 310–12.
[38] It does once in Hesiod – of a positive and unproblematic dedication by Hesiod himself of a tripod to the Muses (*Op.* 656–8).

built by the Greeks for his slain opponent. This is in part explicable by the later presence of tumuli along the shores near Troy, and perhaps too by Hector's knowledge that Troy will fall (6.448). But it is also another sign of the relative marginality, in the Homeric perspective, of the practice of dedication.

Dedications in temples accumulate wealth. There is in Homer only one reference to the wealth contained in temples,[39] and here again the surprising rarity combines with devaluation. It occurs in the ninth book of the *Iliad* during Achilles' rejection of the numerous and various gifts offered by Agamemnon to induce him to return to the battle. Achilles says that not equal in value to his life (9.401) is all the wealth of Troy, or 'all that the stone threshold of the archer holds within it, of Phoebus Apollo, in rocky Pytho'. For cattle and sheep, he explains, may be robbed, and tripods and horses obtained, whereas the life of a man cannot be brought back once it has exchanged the barrier of his teeth.

This passage, with its assertion of the incommensurability of wealth with the heroic values of honour and life, may reflect reaction to the growing power of exchange-value (2D). What concerns us here is its illustration of a specific power of wealth – to obtain perpetual fame through the practice of dedication. In this speech of Achilles there are four basic values: honour, wealth, life, and perpetual fame. He knows that if he stays fighting at Troy he will lose life but win perpetual fame (412–13). But the dishonour done him by Agamemnon has disturbed this balance, with the result that he wants to go home, preserving life but losing the perpetual fame that is won by deeds of war (393–400, 415–16). The wealth offered by Agamemnon is unequal to life (401) and unequal as compensation for the dishonour (387). The point is generalised: it is not just the wealth offered by Agamemnon but wealth *in general* that is inadequate, even the wealth in Apollo's temple at Delphi. The interrelated heroic values of life, honour, and perpetual fame are thereby elevated beyond the reach of wealth. And the elevation has particular point in a world in which wealth is in fact increasing its power over the other basic values. Well before Homeric poetry reached its final form, fame could be perpetuated by the dedication of wealth in a temple: for example, the Phrygian Midas is remembered nearly three centuries after his death by Herodotus (1.14) for having dedicated at Delphi a throne that was still there for Herodotus to admire.

---

[39] Although in addition a brief indirect reference is perhaps to be found in the application of the word πίων, 'rich', to a temple at *Il.* 2.549, 5.512.

How then *is* the fame of Achilles, or of other warriors, to be preserved? One means is the tomb. Hector imagines his fame as perpetuated by a tomb (his slain opponent's). Elsewhere in Homer we find the notion that the tomb brings future fame for its occupant,[40] as well as mentions of tombs of individuals already dead.[41] In the *Odyssey* Achilles is said to have been given a tomb, on a promontory over the Hellespont, visible to sailors now and in the future (24.80–4).

And yet the Homeric epics acquired their final form after the relative decline in importance of the tomb as a recipient of goods, a decline that accompanied the massive increase in the quantity of goods dedicated in the burgeoning public sanctuaries.[42] Despite this shift, the tomb could nevertheless perpetuate the memory of its occupant – in the same way as the dedicated object could perpetuate the memory of its donor – by the newly introduced medium of *writing*. The first surviving inscribed epitaphs and dedications seem to be from the early seventh century.[43] But writing is yet another of those contemporary phenomena that are in Homer both rare and devalued. The words that Hector imagines will be spoken by a passing sailor as he sees the tomb (of Hector's slain opponent) are highly reminiscent of certain inscribed epitaphs of the late seventh and sixth centuries.[44] And yet there is no writing: the sailor is imagined as simply recognising the tomb from a distance. At the same time, in its only Homeric occurrence[45] writing appears in the worst possible light.[46] Bellerophon is given his own death-warrant: Proetus sent him from Argos to Lycia with 'baneful signs, having written them in a folded tablet, many murderous things' (*Il.* 6.168–9). The context of this episode deserves our attention. Glaucus has been asked by Diomedes who he is, and is giving an account of his ancestors stretching back to his grandfather's grandfather Sisyphus (*Il.* 6.145–211), an account that consists mainly of the vicissitudes of his grandfather Bellerophon. It is a fine example of the individual *oral* memory of past generations. In

---

[40] *Od.* 1.240, 4.584.   [41] *Il.* 2.604, 793, 814; 10.415; 11.371–2.

[42] Bibliography at Seaford 1994a, 195.

[43] Epitaphs: Jeffery 1990, 61, 131 no. 6, 317 nos. 3–4. Dedications: Jeffery 1990, 94 nos. 1 and 2 (Boeotia); Langdon 1976, 9–50 (Attica). Seventh-century verse epitaphs: Hansen 1983, nos. 132, 140, 143, 144, 165; seventh-century verse dedications: Hansen 1983, nos. 287, 326, 352, 357, 401, 402, 403.

[44] Hansen 1983, nos. 27, 112, 145. Raubitschek 1968, 6–7. Although there may well have been earlier such inscriptions (now lost), the form of expression may of course predate its embodiment in inscriptions. It seems however likely that the poet was familiar with written inscriptions and has deliberately excluded writing: this is certainly consistent with the repeated mention of *speaking* (εἴπῃσι . . . ἐρέει).

[45] I exclude the 'sign' on the lot, recognised only by its inscriber, at *Il.* 7.185–9.

[46] This is so whatever the degree of knowledge (the description implies *some* knowledge) the poet had of writing.

response to Glaucus, Diomedes recounts how his own grandfather Oineus was once host to Glaucus' grandfather Bellerophon, and how they gave each other gifts of guest-friendship. Diomedes still possesses Bellerophon's gift (218–21). Diomedes and Glaucus, a Greek from Argos and a Lycian, have inherited the relation of guest-friendship, and so, despite belonging to opposite sides in the war, they clasp hands and exchange armour. The past is perpetuated not only by the individual oral memory but also by the persistence of physical objects, *gifts* that have been exchanged in the past and continue to be exchanged. In a double contrast to these two means of perpetuating the past, the gift and individual oral memory, what Proetus sent over the Aegean to his friend the king of Lycia was not a gift but murderous writing.

Another example of individual oral memory, Nestor's reminiscence of the games at the funeral of Amaryngkeus (*Il.* 23.626–50), has as its theme an event meant (like the tomb) to perpetuate memory, and itself occurs at a funeral (of Patroclus). Indeed, Nestor has just received from Achilles the gift of a jar, which, Achilles tells him, he should 'lay away as treasure (*keimēlion*) to be a memorial (*mnēma*) of the burial of Patroclus'. *Mnēma* occurs elsewhere in Homer only twice, both times of a gift: of a robe given by Helen to Telemachus, a 'memorial of Helen's hands', and of the great bow given by Iphitus to Odysseus, stored in the house as a 'memorial of a dear guest-friend', Odysseus having given him a sword and spear 'as the beginning of a caring guest-friendship'.[47] The gift embodies the memory of its donor, and of obligation to its donor.[48] Peisistratus tell Telemachus to wait for Menelaus to bring gifts, 'for a guest remembers all his days the man who received him as a host receives a guest and gave him gifts of friendship'.[49] A special case of the gift, perpetuating political authority, is the sceptre given by the gods to Pelops and by him to subsequent generations (*Il.* 2.101–8).

The vicissitudes of Bellerophon may well, like other such self-contained memories of the distant past in Homer, have once been an independent lay that was incorporated into the Homer epic.[50] Perhaps the most important means of preserving the fame of heroes in the world of Homer is oral individual memory in the form of *song*. Just as the tomb both exists in the present (preserving the memory of past individuals) and is imagined as existing in the future (preserving the memory of Hector's deed), so too song is both sung in the present[51] and imagined as being sung in the future,

---

[47] *Od.* 15.126, 21.35, 40.   [48] E.g. *Od.* 1.309–18, 24.271–86.
[49] Lattimore's translation of *Od.* 15.54–5.   [50] See e.g. Kirk 1962, 164–6, and on *Il.* 6.168–70.
[51] E.g. Achilles singing 'the fames of men' at *Il.* 9.189.

as preserving the memory of what is happening now.[52] The Muses preserve the memory of the past (*Il.* 2.492). In the world of Homer individuals and their deeds are perpetuated to a large extent *subjectively*, through the oral memory of individuals, particularly singers. And where the perpetuation does occur through objects (tombs and gifts), the object never contains the impersonal device of writing and always seems to embody an individual: the tomb contains its occupant, and the gift is invested, as so often in pre-modern societies, with the identity of its donor.[53]

Early dedications made in sanctuaries are often the kinds of object that in Homer are interpersonal gifts.[54] The dedication in a temple is a gift, but a gift to a god. A reciprocal return may be expected.[55] But the object dedicated may also acquire a new function: such items as arms, tripods, and precious metal dedicated[56] in a temple are a means of public display that will outlive the donor. The word *agalma* refers in Homer to something in which one delights (its original meaning),[57] to a gift from person to a person,[58] and to a gift from person to a god, i.e. a dedication[59] – the meaning to which it subsequently narrows. The gift has acquired a function that is dependent not on the memory of the recipient, on the recipient preserving good will towards the donor, but rather on the communal creation and preservation of the context of display, the temple and its rituals, and on the communal and impersonal device of writing. Some of the very earliest surviving examples of writing identify dedications; and indeed some dedicatory inscriptions make the perpetuation of memory their explicit goal.[60] The word *mnēma*, memorial, which in Homer was confined to the interpersonal gift, is frequently used in inscriptions to characterise dedications.[61] Another example of the Homeric tendency to exclude perpetuation

---

[52] *Il.* 6.357–8, 9.189; *Od.* 8.73, 580, 24.200–2. None of the rich bibliography on these passages bears on my present concern.

[53] Mauss 1967, 79.

[54] Notably armour and tripods: Langdon 1985, 108–9; Seaford 1994a, 195–6.

[55] E.g. Hansen 1983, nn. 258, 275, 326 (early seventh century), 360, 426.

[56] Literally set (or attached) up high (*ana*): *anatithenai* (*anaptein*).

[57] Hsch. s.v.: 'everything in which one delights (*agalletai*)'; *Il.* 4.144 (in royal store); cf. *Od.* 3.438; 18.300.

[58] *Od.* 4.602; 18.300.   [59] *Od.* 3.274, 438; 8.509; 12.347.

[60] E.g. an early sixth-century dedication from Phocis (Hansen 1983, n. 344): 'these δρα[. . .]ς (see 6A) Phanaristos gave to Athena and Hera so that he too might have unperishing fame for ever', or in words denoting *memory* (e.g. Hansen 1983, no. 234). The famous Phrasicleia inscription (Hansen 1988, n. 24) combines reciprocity and perpetuation in a remarkable way that is appropriate for the permanence of the dedicated *korē* (maiden) statue: 'This is the monument (*sēma*) of Phrasicleia. I will be called a *korē* always (αἰεί), receiving this name from the gods instead of/in return for (ἀντί) marriage.'

[61] E.g. Hansen 1983, nn. 207, 234, 235, 304, 305, 380, 393; van Straten 1981, 76–7; Versnel 1981, 58–61.

through communal cult appears in the fact that although (as we have seen) tombs in Homer preserve memory, there are nevertheless in Homer few traces[62] of the communal cult that, performed at tombs, perpetuated[63] the memory of heroes, namely hero-cult, for which the archaeological evidence begins, on the whole, in the second half of the eighth century.[64]

To conclude, Homer tends to exclude or devalue forms of making permanent, centred around the place of sacrifice (3C), that were during the final stages of the formation of Homeric epic rapidly gaining ground: the temple, dedications, writing. Permanence in Homer is instead accorded to the embodiments of heroic individuality in gift and tomb, and to the oral commemoration embodied by heroic epic itself. And yet Homer, the product of various poets over more than one generation, is not confined within a single ideology. Central to the narratives are the traditional communality of animal sacrifice and the crises of reciprocity, both of which contributed to that development of the polis to which much else in Homer seems indifferent if not opposed.

C   SACRIFICE AND DURABLE WEALTH IN HOMER

Despite our contrast between the distribution and giving of prestige objects (treasure) on the one hand and animal sacrifice on the other, the two forms do not belong to different worlds. They involve the same people. And even in Homer they occasionally seem to interpenetrate. The perverse distribution of Odysseus' livestock by the feasting suitors as if it were booty is an example (2E). And there are two notable cases of treasure and the sacrificial animal combining as a gift to deity. Both cases concern the embellishment of the durable parts of the animal.

First, there is the *aegis*. A lasting remnant of the sacrificial victim is its *skin*, which was sometimes preserved for ritual use.[65] In Homer Zeus, Athena, and Apollo wield in battle the terrifying *aegis*, in origin (as it was generally taken to be) the skin of a goat.[66] Burkert associates it with the goat sacrificed before battle: after victory its skin was set up, along with

---

[62] They are collected by Hadzisteliou-Price 1973; see also Crielaard 1995, 271. *Il.* 2.551 (perhaps an Athenian insertion: see n. 31 above) does pick out the *continuity* of hero-cult ('as the years circle by').

[63] On the importance of this perpetuation see Seaford 1994a, 114–39.

[64] For bibliography see Seaford 1994a, 109; Crielaard 1995, 266–7.

[65] Burkert 1983, 14–15, 16, 66, 113, 115, 127, 140, 153, 166–7. In a (probably) late sixth-century narrative the young Hermes sacrifices cattle and spreads out their skins on a rock, 'and so they are still there long afterwards, a long time after these things and continually' *(h.hom.Herm.*124–6).

[66] Farnell 1895–1909, I 100; Nilsson 1967, 437; Hdt. 4.189, etc.; *aegis* means goatskin at e.g. Eur. *Cyc.* 360.

captured arms, on a stake, which came to represent the goddess Athena with her armour and *aegis*. Athena also received a special annual sacrifice of a goat on the Acropolis,[67] where it seems there was kept a sacred *aegis*.[68] In Homer the *aegis*, in the hands of Athena, is called 'valuable, ageless, immortal, from whose edges float a hundred all-golden tassels, each one carefully woven, and each worth a hundred cattle'.[69] If the conception of the *aegis* was influenced by dedicated sacrificial skins, then the details fall into place. In contrast to the animal's flesh, its skin may become a lasting dedication to the immortals, and as such it may, like the heifer's horns in Nestor's sacrifice (see below), be decorated with gold, which is associated by the Greeks with immortality (2C) and so enhances the claim of the skin to be 'ageless, immortal' as well as 'valuable'.[70] It is even said to have been given to Zeus by the 'smith' Hephaestus (*Il.* 15.309–10). The golden-fleeced lamb that bestowed the sovereignty at Argos, and was locked by Atreus in a chest, seems to have been meant for sacrifice.[71] The golden-fleeced ram that brought Phrixus to Colchis was sacrificed, and its skin set up on a tree in a grove of Ares.[72] It was said that on Samos once one Mandroboulos found a treasure, and so offered to Hera a golden sheep the first year, a silver one the second, and a bronze one the third.[73] The theme embodies the transition from one form of primary wealth (sheep) to another (gold).

Another detail that connects the *aegis* to sacrifice is the evaluation of each tassel as worth a hundred cattle. It was pointed out by Laum that the Homeric evaluation of things in terms of cattle is in numbers ('worth a hunded cattle', etc.) that correspond on the whole to the numbers of cattle sacrificed in various Homeric sacrifices.[74] Although the only Homeric measure of value, cattle are too large and cumbersome to be used as a medium of exchange, and so as a measure could not have derived from commerce. The numbers specified suggest rather that their suitability as a measure of value derives, at least in part, from the sacrifice of set numbers of cattle of standard quality (2E). In this typicality of quantity and quality sacrificial victims contrast with the individualised and highly variable value of gold and silver (2C). To Laum, who regards this typicality as a factor in

---

[67] Varro *De Re Rust.* 1.2.19–20; Burkert 1983, 152–3.

[68] *Suda* s.v. αἰγίς; *Corpus Paroem. Gr.* (Leutsch-Schneidewin) I 339.

[69] *Il.* 2.447–9. Interestingly, it creates confidence in battle (450–2): cf. 7D on the paean.

[70] *Eritimos*, which in Homer refers only to the *aegis* and to gold: 2C n. 72.

[71] Eur. *El.* 713–15; Apollod. *Epit.* 2.10–14. Apollo demanded it as a dedication (*anathēma*): *Suda* s.v. ἀνάθημα and s.v. Ἀντικλείδης.

[72] Apollod. *Bibl.* 1.83 (cf. Pausan. 9.34.5; Pi. *Pyth.* 4.68).

[73] *Corp. Paroem. Gr.* Zenobius iii.82; Greg. Cypr. iii.50. According to Aelian the lost treasure of the temple was found by a sheep (*Hist. An.* 12.40).

[74] Laum 1924, 18; 2E.

the contribution of animal sacrifice to the genesis of coined money, I will return (6A).

The second Homeric instance of the combination of sacrificial animal with treasure occurs in the third book of the *Odyssey*. Before sacrificing an unyoked heifer to Athena in his palace, Nestor sends for a goldsmith, who arrives with his various tools. Nestor gives to a smith gold, which he 'poured and worked around the horns of the heifer, so that the goddess would rejoice seeing the offering (*agalma*)' (3.437–8). Much is made of this gilding.[75] Part of the point of the emphasis may be that this sacrifice, in contrast to the large-scale sacrifice by the Pylians that precedes it, belongs to the royal household, where gold is appropriate.[76] Rather as the animal sacrifice adds the agrarian to the pastoral, by sprinkling the victim with barley,[77] so it may incorporate another, relatively new form of wealth by adding precious metal to the victim. The gilding marks the heifer (or its horns) as an *agalma*, a word that elsewhere in Homer refers to treasure – whether in store-room or as interpersonal gift or as given (dedicated) to the gods (3B).

As a lasting remnant of the animal, horns were sometimes (in Greece and elsewhere) preserved at the place of sacrifice.[78] Burkert assembles much evidence for the ancient Greek practice of making some permanent mark of the sacrificial act: the preservation of the skulls and horns of the animals, the setting up of the skin of the animal sacrificed before battle, the construction of a statue over a victim, the establishment of a tomb at a place of sacrifice.[79] Such practices, from Greece and elsewhere, are derived by Burkert from very ancient hunting practices, in which 'the gathering of bones, the raising of a shield or stretching of a skin is to be understood as an attempt at restoration' in the anxious hope that the sources of nourishment will continue to live.[80] The sacrificial place is likely to be marked in such ways before the construction of buildings at regular places of sacrifice. In Homer we find both the embellishment of the durable parts of the sacrificial

[75] See also lines 384, 425–6, 432–5.

[76] The only other sacrificial animal whose horns are (to be) gilded is the unyoked heifer promised by Diomedes to Athena (*Il.* 10.294) in return for her protection in a dangerous exploit. Odysseus' promise to dedicate to her the spoils of the very same exploit is the only unproblematic dedication in Homer (see above).

[77] *Il.* 1.449, 458; 2.421; *Od.* 14.429.

[78] van Straten 1981, 69; Burkert 1983, 6 n. 26, 14, 72, 79. It is interesting that in the *Epic of Gilgamesh* a (rare) mention of measures of weight (30 mnas of lapis lazuli, 2 mnas of gold) is in the decoration of the horns of the slain bull of heaven (Tablet VI.v, p. 82 Dalley 1991).

[79] Burkert 1983, 2, 6, 38–9, 56, 66, 140; 1985, 65, 92, 372 n. 93; van Straten 1995, 53, 139.

[80] Burkert 1983, 16, etc.

animal and the relative absence of such buildings, a combination that seems to hark back to the Dark Age.

Turning to the archaeological evidence, we find that before the eighth century BC such buildings were very rare. Most offerings to deity seem to have been sacrifices conducted either in the open[81] or at the house of a chieftain.[82] These two kinds of context are exemplified in the two lengthy descriptions of sacrifice in the third book of the *Odyssey* (one on the beach, the other at Nestor's house), in neither of which is there any mention of any kind of permanent installation.[83] Much activity of this kind, without installations or permanent management or regular dedications, will have left little or no trace,[84] though the sites of built sanctuaries are often found to contain, as their earliest layer, indications (bones, burnt deposits, sacrificial *bothroi*, etc.) of sacrifice performed before the construction of any building.[85] The earliest construction in a sanctuary is generally an altar for sacrifice.[86] Accordingly some of the earliest temples seem designed to contain cooking and feasting,[87] and this was clearly an important function of various sanctuaries in the Archaic period.[88] But this does not mean that the rapid development of monumental buildings (temples) in sanctuaries, which occurred from the beginning of the eighth century,[89] was designed primarily to accommodate feasting.[90] For it was in the same period that there occurred an enormous increase, in both quantity and quality, of the

---

[81] 'During the Dark Ages it seems that almost all worship took place in the open air, usually round a raised altar for burnt sacrifices': Coldstream 1977, 317, referring to Desborough 1972, 281. Cf. Rupp 1983, 101.

[82] Mazarakis Ainian 1988; de Polignac 1994, 7–8; Crielaard 1995, 250; Osborne 1996, 88 (Nikhoria).

[83] Cf. de Polignac 1995, 15–16; Gebhard 1993, 159. Sourvinou-Inwood 1993, 2 objects that altars on the beach do occur elsewhere in Homer (*Il.* 8.238–40, 11.806–8), and that *Od.* 3.7. θεῷ δ' ἐπὶ μηρία καίον 'implies an altar'. But description is selection, and selection is judgement about what matters: it is significant that the mass sacrifice on the beach, though there is nothing irregular or abnormal about it, is envisaged without any installation.

[84] de Polignac 1994, 10.

[85] See e.g. Coldstream 1977, 324 (Thermon); Burkert 1993, 179 (Samothrace); Gebhard 1993, 156 and Morgan 1994, 110, 113 (Isthmia); Morgan 1994, 129 (Perachora); Cole 1994, 208 (Knossos); de Polignac 1995, 17 (Kalapodi); cf. Bookidis 1993, 47 (Corinth); Sourvinou-Inwood 1993, 7 (Asine); Crielaard 1995, 250. On Delos a famous altar of Artemis consisted of goat horns. According to R. Hägg (abstract for FIEC Conference 1999) 'recent studies of the animal bones from Greek sanctuaries seem to indicate that this type of altar (or monument commemorating sacrifices performed) was more common than hitherto known'.

[86] Sourvinou-Inwood 1993, 10; de Polignac 1995, 17; Coldstream 1977, 317 (Samian Heraion), 321.

[87] See e.g. Burkert 1985, 89 (Perachora, Dreros, Thermon); Mazarakis Ainian 1988, 117–18.

[88] For recent bibliography see de Polignac 1994, 10 n. 21, to which add e.g. Bookidis 1993 and Kyrieleis 1993, 137.

[89] Coldstream 1977, 317–27; Snodgrass 1980, 33, 58–62; Crielaard 1995, 240–1; de Polignac 1995, 17; Osborne 1996, 88–9; etc.

[90] Even though there was also a big increase in the building of altars: Coldstream 1977, index s.v. Altars; Crielaard 1995, 247–9.

durable offerings made at a wide range of Greek sanctuaries,[91] and it was an important function of the temples to house the offerings.

The main categories of these offerings are vessels of various kinds[92] (notably bronze tripods),[93] human figurines,[94] animal figurines (notably of horses and bulls, but also of undomesticated creatures such as deer),[95] items of personal adornment such as pins and jewellery (especially for goddesses),[96] and (mainly after *circa* 700 BC) armour.[97]

There are three main sources of the practice of dedication. Firstly, the tomb: the context in which personal ornaments are to be found shifts, from about the end of the ninth century, from the cemetery to the sanctuary;[98] and the same is true, about a century later, of armour.[99] Secondly, it has been suggested that offerings in sanctuaries developed out of the kind of gift-giving described in Homer, for they 'partake of a consistent symbolic sytem that harkens back to the aristocratic world of Homer'.[100] In particular, the bronze tripod is both a gift (or prize) in Homer and an offering frequently found in sanctuaries; and the same can be said of the horse (in sanctuaries in the form of small figurines).

Thirdly, there is the sacrifice. The transient act of sacrifice finds permanent embodiment not just in the remnants (horns, skin, bones) of the victim, but also in various kinds of artefact. There are utensils: sacrificial axes, roasting spits, and various kinds of vessel used for libation or in the killing and cooking of an animal (notably tripod cauldrons).[101] There are animal figurines, at least some of which were no doubt envisaged as substituting for (or commemorating) animal sacrifice.[102] A study of the placing of animal

---

[91] Coldstream 1977, 338; Snodgrass 1980, 52–4; Morgan 1993, 19; de Polignac 1995, 14–15; Osborne 1996, 89, 92–8; etc.

[92] Coldstream 1977, 332; Burkert 1985, 93.

[93] Coldstream 1977, 334–8; de Polignac 1995, 26; Osborne 1996, 94, 96.

[94] Coldstream 1977, 332; Burkert 1985, 93; de Polignac 1995, 26.

[95] Coldstream 1977, 332; Burkert 1985, 93; Langdon 1987, 108–9; Morgan 1993, 21, 1994, 119–20; de Polignac 1995, 26; Osborne 1996, 94.

[96] Coldstream 1977, 333; Morgan 1993, 21, 1994, 118, 129; de Polignac 1995, 26; Osborne 1996, 92–3.

[97] Coldstream 1977, 338; de Polignac 1995, 26.

[98] Coldstream 1977, 333; de Polignac 1995, 14.

[99] Snodgrass 1980, 52–4; Morgan 1994, 127–8; de Polignac 1995, 14–15; Osborne 1996, 101, 172–3. 'Metal objects' generally: Coldstream 1977, 338.

[100] Langdon 1987, 108; cf. de Polignac 1994, 12 n. 26.

[101] E.g. Morgan 1994, 115; Coldstream 1977, 332: 'Pottery forms the largest class of finds in almost all geometric sanctuaries. Most vessels served to contain libations; after the liquid had been poured out, the pot would be left behind by the worshipper. Large trays, such as have been found at the Samian Heraion, would have contained some solid offering, such as fruit.' Of course not all utensils found in sanctuaries are necessarily offerings: Tomlinson 1992, 343–6.

[102] Coldstream 1977, 332; Cole 1994, 203–4, 207; Burkert 1985, 93, 367 n. 62 (terracotta votive bulls characteristic of very early open-air altars). This may not be true of the horses, for which, as we

and human figurines in some sixty sanctuaries (mostly from the Geometric to the Classical period) has established that overall about two thirds of the figurines were found on or around the altar, or in ash layers (often together with animal bones),[103] and infers that even the human figurines (as well as, more obviously, the animal ones) were perhaps a 'symbolic sacrifice'.[104] The dedication of sacrificial instruments and of animal figurines continues, in great numbers, well into the historical period,[105] in which we also find, beginning in the third quarter of the sixth century, dedications of visual representations of animal sacrifice and of bloodless offerings.[106] But it may be that during the very earliest period of the sanctuary, as it developed around the nucleus of the altar, dedications embodying sacrifice formed a larger proportion of all dedications than they did later: the seventh century saw a shift from the animal to the human figurine,[107] a large increase in dedications of armour,[108] and, for the first time, a clear separation between on the one hand the building designed to house the god and his treasure and on the other hand buildings designed for ritual meals.[109]

The extraordinary eighth-century development of votive offerings and of temples surely involved a radical shift in consciousness. One aspect of the change is the dissolution of the Homeric division that we have described between the transience of gifts to the gods (libation, animal sacrifice) and the durability of gifts to mortals ('treasure'). The ancient need for a lasting expression or mark of sacrifice was, before the eighth century, fulfilled mainly by the preservation of parts of sacrificed animals of which we find exotic hints in Homer (gilded horns, the *aegis*) and by the continuity of place that we find in Homeric 'altars' and in the archaeological discovery of numerous places of sacrifice marked by deposits of ash and fragments of burnt animal bone mixed with votive offerings, generally without any architectural construction.[110] The construction at these sacrificial places of

---

have seen, there is an alternative motivation; but it probably is true of the deer, which were (at least in this early period) sometimes sacrificed (Osborne 1996, 31), and whether available for sacrifice or (being wild) not, might be regarded as *appropriate* for sacrifice, especially to certain deities. It should be added that images of animals reach back early into the prehistory of humankind; Burkert 1983, 14.

[103] The deposits (in the central area of the *temenos*) of ash and burnt animal bone fragments, which have been described as 'the most common type of evidence for sacrificial activity at Geometric and early Archaic period sanctuaries', are found 'mixed with broken remains of votive offerings': Rupp 1983, 101.

[104] Alroth 1988.   [105] Rouse 1902, esp. 295–302.

[106] van Straten 1981, 83–8; 1995, 53 *et passim*.   [107] Osborne 1996, 207–8.

[108] Coldstream 1977, 338; de Polignac 1995, 26.

[109] de Polignac 1995, 18–19; Mazarakis Ainian 1988, 116, 117–18.   [110] Rupp 1983, 101.

sanctuaries and temples, which became – through dedication of gifts to the gods – stores of metal, combined the *durability* of the Homeric aristocratic interpersonal gift (treasure) with the ancient and tenacious *visibility* and *communality* of the Homeric sacrifice. And just as the Homeric interpersonal gift may elicit good will from the recipient as well as remind him 'for all his days' of the donor[111] and be retained over generations (3B), so the gift dedicated to a god in a temple may be designed to elicit his good will[112] as well as to perpetuate through its public visibility the communal memory or fame of the donor.[113] One factor in this process was the increase in the availability of metals (gold, silver, and especially bronze), which had been in short supply in the Dark Age (6B). From the vast quantity of bronze offerings in sanctuaries from 750 to 700 BC it has been inferred that 'at the time when bronze reappeared in common use in Greece, the lion's share was channeled directly into the cult places'.[114]

Another phenomenon favoured by the combination of sacrificial and durable offerings is that of *representation*.[115] As we have seen, from the eighth century the sanctuaries are full of (terracotta and bronze) figurines of sacrificial animals.[116] One may regard the motivation as economic, the figurines as *substitutes* for sacrificial animals. But this is not the whole story. The figurine is *durable*, and so may also *commemorate*. Economising cannot be the motive where marble, bronze, gold or silver goes into producing images of sacrificial animals, some of them of considerable size,[117] or where the representation is of a sacrificial cake.[118] Such objects are *functionless* (except as offerings), as are numerous other items made (it seems) to be offerings and unsuitable for any other use, such as outsize pins, outsize tripod cauldrons, and thin sheet gold.[119] The terracotta and bronze figurines

---

[111] *Od.* 8.431, 15.54; *Il.* 14.235.   [112] See n. 55 above.

[113] See nn. 60 and 61 above; note esp. Hansen 1983, no. 344 (an early sixth-century. dedication for the sake of 'imperishable fame' (*kleos aphthiton*). In Homer *aphthiton* is confined to what is *made by the gods,* with two exceptions: the miraculous vines on the Cyclops' island (*Od.* 9.133), and the imperishable glory of Achilles (*Il.* 9.413) that we discussed in 3B.

[114] Langdon 1987, 108. Given the archaeological focus on cult places, 'lion's share' may exaggerate. On the metals see Desborough 1972, 313–18.

[115] This is not to say that imitations as offerings are confined to sanctuaries. Small clay tripod cauldrons have been found in graves of the tenth and ninth centuries BC: Coldstream 1977, 334.

[116] Another interesting albeit problematic example is provided by the numerous small models of buildings found in various sanctuaries from about 800 BC onwards: Coldstream 1977, 322; Morgan 1994, 132–3; de Polignac 1995, 17. The temple may itself have been envisaged as an offering (*anathēma*): e.g. Plut. *Pericles* 12, 14.

[117] Rouse 1902, 296–301. Note also e.g. the sixth-century. BC large bull of copper, silver, and gold in the museum at Delphi, and the golden cattle dedicated by Croesus at Ephesus (Hdt. 1.92).

[118] Coldstream 1977, 332; Rouse 1902, 296.

[119] de Polignac 1995, 15; Morgan 1994, 129 'purpose-made votives including thin sheet gold and votive jewellery' at Perachora; Coldstream 1977, 335.

were from at least the early seventh century produced in large numbers from moulds.[120] The idea of mass production among the Greeks, originating in their dedication of figurines, was a precondition for coinage. We have come a long way from the uniqueness of the Homeric artefact lovingly described as the work of a famous craftsman or even of a god (2E).

I summarise and conclude. The individualistic heroic ethos of Homeric epic makes it idealise the prestige sphere of gift-exchange while neglecting and devaluing commodity-exchange, monetisation, and the practice of making permanent by communal dedication. And yet it is marked by crises of redistributive reciprocity. And the prestige objects of gift-exchange are also the objects of that divisive distribution of plunder that contrasts, in both epics, with the ordered communality of traditional sacrificial distribution.[121] The development of the polis, in Homer generally neglected, will transcend these contradictions by the synthesis of sacrificial communality with the permanence of prestige objects, and with their typicality, mass production, and substitutability (by mere symbol). We shall see that it is a synthesis favourable to the genesis of coinage (6A). But first we must make a detour to the Near East.

---

[120] Higgins 1967, 1, 25; Mattusch 1996, 1, 18–21, 37. Another early instance of mass production is of roof tiles for temples: Winter 1993, 304.

[121] A parallel prefiguration of the polis is the narrative importance of the integrative power of another kind of ritual, death ritual, sufficient to unite the bitterest enemies (Achilles and Priam): Seaford 1994a; 2D n. 82.

CHAPTER FOUR

Greece and the ancient Near East

A ECONOMIES OF THE ANCIENT NEAR EAST

I will now draw a brief contrast between Homer and the two most famous epics from ancient Mesopotamia. This is in order to qualify the recent success in discovering similarities between Homeric poetry and its Mesopotamian predecessors, and thereby to bring out the distinctiveness of Homer and of the world he describes – the distinctiveness of a society that is soon to create the unprecedented phenomenon of pervasive monetisation. For this purpose I first provide a very brief and so inevitably crude characterisation of the Mesopotamian economies, which will narrow to a focus on the important distinction between the social functions of the offering of food to deity in Mesopotamia (4C) and in Greece. By bringing out the early role of money in the Greek provision of sacrificial victims (4D), this will also contribute to the case, set out in chapter six, for regarding animal sacrifice as an important factor in the genesis of coinage.

One way into the bewildering mass of evidence for the economies of Mesopotamia (and of the whole ancient Near East) is to think of the allocation of goods and services as belonging, in principle, to the three categories that we used in our discussion of Homer (2A): reciprocity, trade, and redistribution.[1] A transaction may exhibit one of these forms, or combine elements from two or all of them: in particular, reciprocity and trade are sometimes difficult to distinguish.[2]

Reciprocity is the voluntary, non-instantaneous exchange of goods or services that is based not on (supposed) equivalence between the items

---

[1] This is influenced by, but not identical with, Polanyi's discussion of reciprocity, exchange, and redistribution: See Polanyi 1968, 148–57, 307. By 'exchange' Polanyi generally (but not always) means market exchange, and by 'trade' external (foreign) trade. I prefer to use 'trade' to refer to all kinds of trade, and 'exchange' to cover both trade and reciprocity. A good analysis on these lines is by Zaccagnini 1976, 468–93.

[2] E.g. Zaccagnini 1976, 491–3. On the transformation of reciprocity into redistribution see the work of Marshall Sahlins.

exchanged but rather on the desire to create or maintain a relationship between the parties to the exchange. But in *trade* (whether barter or with money) the transaction (if not the actual exchange of goods) is instantaneous, and the point of the exchange lies not in the relationship between the transactors but rather either in the utility of the items exchanged or, in the case of the sub-category *market trade*, in the profit made by the exchange. In our discussion of Homer we called *redistribution* a (centralised) form of reciprocity. In the elaborate state systems of Mesopotamia the centralisation has reached an extreme point: redistribution has become the enforced collection of goods and services at a central building (notably temple or palace), where they are used for the upkeep of the central institution, for redistribution among the population, and for communal functions such as storage against famine,[3] the administration of justice, and irrigation.

Neither of the boundaries within this tripartite categorisation necessarily corresponds to the boundary between *public* or *institutional* activity (notably by palace or temple) and *private* activity, in that the parties to reciprocity and to trade may be either public institutions or fairly autonomous individuals, and redistribution or something analogous to it is to be found even within the private household.

The debate on the relative importance of these three overlapping forms of allocation has centred around the work of Karl Polanyi, who regarded market exchange, in which prices are set by supply and demand, as emerging as a major principle of allocation only after the Industrial Revolution in Europe and North America: in the economies of the ancient Near East the basic principle of allocation is redistribution, with a subordinate role played by reciprocity and only a minor one by market trade.[4] Polanyi has been frequently criticised as underestimating the evidence for marketplaces and market trade. But most of the critics also allow that the economies of the ancient Near East were nevertheless basically of the redistributive type.[5]

---

[3] This function is beautifully encapsulated in Genesis 41 (the seven lean years following seven fat ones in Egypt).

[4] Polanyi 1957, 16–26; 1968, 156, 188–9, 249–60, 306–34; Humphreys 1978, 42–6, 56–7.

[5] E.g. Adams 1974, 246–8 restates some of Veenhof's (1972) criticisms of Polanyi on the international Kanish trade (15D), but allows that 'Oppenheim's (1957: 35) more cautious statement that markets were of limited and marginal importance within Babylonia proper still remains generally consistent with the textual evidence.' Cf. also esp. Oppenheim 1970. The Kanish trade is regarded as exceptional by e.g. Oppenheim 1977, 92 and Renger 1994, 164 n. 12. Polanyi is defended against Adams by Wright (in Adams 1974, 254). Adams 1984, 90–7 stresses the *co-existence* of redistribution and commercial exchange, but allows that 'a much larger part in the circulation of commodities probably was played, at least until well into the second millennium, by redistributive than by exchange processes' (93). Polanyi's position is attacked by van de Mieroop (for Ur in the Old Babylonian period), but even he denies a 'fully fledged market system'. See also Zaccagnini 1976, Oppenheim 1977; Renger 1984; Oates 1986, 25. For Egypt see 15E.

A compromise position is provided by, among others, Renger (1984), who in his study of Mesopotamia as a whole in the period *circa* 1850–1600 BC, based on legal documents, letters, and royal inscriptions, finds evidence for 'several locations or occasions which served as or had the function of a market place',[6] which he calls 'market substitutes', as well as for peddlers and vendors (mainly of prepared food). And yet 'the market, even in the restricted form of market substitutes as described above, was never more than an accessory complementing the economic processes essentially governed by the principles of redistribution and reciprocity on their respective societal levels' (114). There are detectable differences in the importance of redistribution between periods and regions. During the Ur III period (*c.* 2100–2000 BC) 'the system obviously included most of the population', whereas in the Old Babylonian period (*c.* 2000–1600 BC) 'a large part of the population was not provisioned through rations but was given its sustenance in the form of fields which guaranteed subsistence. But institutional households – temples as well as palace – also existed and maintained their dependents with rations.'[7]

The question of whether money was used in the early Near East I postpone to chapter 15.

B   HOMER AND MESOPOTAMIAN EPIC

Martin West (1997) has recently produced a detailed set of correspondences between Homer and the *Epic of Gilgamesh*. Gilgamesh has the following points in common with Achilles in the *Iliad*: each of them is the son of a goddess and a mortal king, is emotional and impulsive, appeals to his mother who then intercedes with a god (Shamash, Zeus) on his behalf, has a beloved friend (Enkidu, Patroclus) who dies despite the desire of a god to save him, laments his friend, tearing his hair and raging (or groaning) like a lion(ess) whose cubs have been caught, and then after some delay – and anxiety about worms in the body – buries him, and eventually embraces (or tries to embrace) his ghost and acquires a better understanding of death. This list can be supplemented by a number of parallels between Gilgamesh and Odysseus in the *Odyssey*, as well as by a striking parallel between Gilgamesh and Diomedes in the *Iliad*.[8]

---

[6] Similarly van de Mieroop 1992, 188–90; Veenhof 1972, 355–6, 394–7.
[7] Renger 1994, 179–80.
[8] They each wound a goddess (Ishtar, Aphrodite), who goes up to heaven and weeps before the sky god (Anu, Zeus) and Antu/Dione.

The concern of West, and generally of those who in recent years have with great success compared Greek with ancient Near Eastern material in various fields,[9] is confined to the points of correspondence, which are indeed enough to show that the Homeric narratives were, however remotely, influenced by the Mesopotamian. But given these similarities, of no less interest is a fundamental difference. Each of the Homeric epics is, when compared with the epic narratives of other cultures,[10] including the Mesopotamian, unusually centred around a crisis that is both political and economic.

In the *Epic of Gilgamesh* events are set in train by the unusually vigorous energy of the hero Gilgamesh, which causes the people of Uruk to complain to the gods, who respond by creating for Gilgamesh a companion of equal vigour, Enkidu. It is the vigorous energy of the pair that makes them fight each other, become friends, and go off to kill the monster Huwawa. The god Enlil punishes this killing by killing Enkidu, and the loss of his friend causes Gilgamesh to make his final lonely journey to the distant island where dwells Utnapishtim.

The *Iliad*, on the other hand, begins with a crisis of redistribution. Agamemnon is forced to return the captive Chryseis to her father, and so takes from Achilles his prize Briseis. It is Achilles' consequent withdrawal and subsequent return that structures the *Iliad*. So far from being set in train by the energetic activity of the young hero, like the *Epic of Gilgamesh*, the action of the *Iliad* is largely determined by his *in*activity – his withdrawal because the prize given him in the distribution of booty has been taken from him by the leader. The adventures of Odysseus in books 5–12 of the *Odyssey*, which also exhibit points of correspondence with the *Epic of Gilgamesh*, are framed by the political and economic crisis on Ithaca. In both *Iliad* and *Odyssey*, a reciprocal system has broken down under the pressure of special circumstances involving the *absence* of the central hero (2DE).

---

[9] Notably Burkert 1992; Bernal 1991.

[10] An apparent exception and instructive contrast is provided by the Nibelungenlied, which was created *c.* AD 1200 somewhere between Vienna and Passau, i.e. in a fairly monetised economy, but as the culmination of numerous earlier (some much earlier) narratives. Though silver is not infrequently mentioned, the predominant precious metal in the narrative is gold; and even the 'marks' are (when specified) of gold (pp. 51, 164 of the pages of the Penguin translation by A. T. Hatto), although the coins of *c.* AD 1200 were in fact mainly of silver. The treasure of the Niebelungs, obtained by Siegfried (27–8), passes into the hands of his widow Kriemhild, where it is regarded as a potential source of disruption by her enemy Hagen because of its power to create a following (148, also 178, 256, 263). However, Hagen throws it all into the Rhine (149). And although – inconsistently – Kriemhild later still has some of it (163–4), the issue of control over it remains of secondary importance to the issue of revenge, Kriemhild's revenge on Hagen for killing her husband Siegfried, a killing that arose ultimately from a dispute between Kriemhild and Brunnhilde not over wealth but over the relation in rank of their respective husbands. To Wagner's version, by contrast, the power of money is central.

This is not to say that Mesopotamian literature is never concerned with political crisis. The Babylonian creation epic entitled *Enuma Elish* narrates the struggle between primeval deities (Apsu and Tiamat) and the gods who come after them. After Apsu is killed, Tiamat gives birth to a group of monsters, and gives to her new husband, Quingu, leadership of the army, command of the assembly, and the Tablet of Destinies, saying 'Your utterance shall never be altered! Your word shall be law!' In response, the frightened gods in assembly choose as champion Marduk, who announces 'If indeed I am to be your champion, to defeat Tiamat and save your lives, convene the council, name a special fate . . . My own utterance shall fix fate instead of you. Whatever I create shall never be altered! The decree of my lips shall never be revoked, never changed.'[11] The gods found a princely shrine for Marduk, proclaim him sovereign over the whole universe, and invest him with sceptre, throne, and staff-of-office. He defeats Qingu's army, wrests from him the Tablet of Destinies, and then, together with the gods, arranges the present order of the world: humankind is created from the blood of Qingu to release the gods from toil, Babylon is built, the gods are assigned portions and offices, and Marduk's sovereignty is elaborately confirmed.

In this narrative events are, as in the *Epic of Gilgamesh*, set in train by the exuberant energy of youth: Tiamat and Apsu are disturbed by the dancing of their offspring. But at the centre of the narrative is the relationship between the group (of gods) and a powerful individual (Marduk): we move from anarchic conflict to the creation by the group of a monarchy for the purpose of victory in the conflict, and from there to the establishment of a permanent monarchy in which the various gods confirm the sovereignty of the king but also have their own portions and offices. In both *Gilgamesh* and the *Enuma Elish* the exuberance of youth initiates action that leads to the slaying of a monster, but in the *Enuma Elish* the action also expresses and confirms the centralisation of human and divine power in a large-scale, redistributive economy based on the central storage of, among other things, the produce of irrigational agriculture.[12] The *Enuma Elish* is recited in the Babylonian New Year ceremony, in which powerful officials come to renew their oaths of loyalty to the king and his mandate is renewed by the gods.[13] The movement of the narrative towards the necessity of the current

---

[11] The translations are by Dalley 1991, 240, 243–4.

[12] A much earlier narrative that nicely embodies the imperatives of a storage economy is the Sumerian 'Dumuzi's Wedding', in which the bride, Inanna, represents the numen of the communal storehouse for dates, which she opens for the bridegroom: Jacobsen 1976, 32–47.

[13] Frankfort 1949, 215; Dalley 1991, 231–2.

order is also an in-gathering of potentially centrifugal powers: it ends with the gods naming Marduk's fifty names, each one representing a different power or accomplishment. Central to Homeric epic, by contrast, is the *failure* of redistribution – redistribution among mortals and on a small scale. Homer, in sharp contrast to the Mesopotamian epics, is the epic of a society in transition.

C   MESOPOTAMIAN FOOD OFFERINGS

A list of common elements has been drawn up by Penglase[14] between the Old Babylonian Atrahasis epic (*c.* 1600 BC) and the story of Prometheus and Pandora told by Hesiod. One of these elements is the imposition on humankind of hard toil and sacrifice. In the Atrahasis epic humankind is actually created so as to relieve the gods of labour and provide them with food.[15] When humankind is subsequently destroyed, the gods suffer famine.[16] With this notion Penglase compares the passage of the *Homeric Hymn to Demeter* in which 'Demeter threatens destruction of the human race, and Zeus fears the loss of sacrifice which would be the result.' But what the Hymn actually says is that Demeter would have destroyed humankind with famine, 'and would have deprived those who dwell on Olympus of the glorious honour of offerings and sacrifice' (311–12), had not Zeus intervened. There is no suggestion here that the Olympians are dependent on humans for their sustenance: it is rather a matter of 'honour' (*timē*).[17] After all, the Greeks ate the good meat of the sacrifice themselves, leaving only the fatty vapour to rise in smoke to the gods, who in their consumption of nectar and ambrosia[18] are in no way dependent on humankind. The guilty responsibility for this unfair division of the sacrificial victim is projected, in the aetiological myth preserved in Hesiod (*Theog.* 535–60), onto the malefactor Prometheus, who tricked Zeus into choosing the portion that consisted of bones covered with fat. Penglase writes that 'the idea of the sacrifice as food for the gods is suggested in Prometheus' offering of a portion of the ox to Zeus at this feast'. But in fact whereas the Atrahasis epic, along with Sumerian and Babylonian literature generally,[19] tells of the human race being created in order to feed the gods, the Greek aetiological myth explains why it is mortals that eat the good meat themselves.

---

[14] Penglase 1994, 216–22.   [15] Dalley 1991, 14–15, 18.   [16] Dalley 1991, 32.

[17] The notion that without offerings from humans the gods would *starve* is found only at Ar. *Birds* 186–93, 1519–20, *Wealth* 1123, and is regarded by Dunbar (on *Birds* 186) as a 'fantastic comic development of the traditional notion that the offerings burnt on the altar were the gods' share of the feast'.

[18] E.g. Ar. *Peace* 724, 854.   [19] Lambert, W. G. 1993, 197–8.

This contrast has a socio-economic basis. Generally speaking, in Mesopotamia the massive temple owns much land, and is a centre for the collection, storage, and distribution of food,[20] vast amounts of which are regularly supplied for the god, to be consumed in fact by the other members of his household, the temple personnel.[21] Humans partake of a meal that is nevertheless envisaged as a meal for the god.[22] The food is presented to the god as one presents food to a king. During the period of its presumed consumption,[23] divine image and food are secluded by a curtain. The Assyrian kings prided themselves on partaking of the 'leftovers' from this sacrificial meal.[24] In a Sumerian aetiological myth the first animal sacrifice is performed by a king (Lugulbanda of Uruk), with the only other participants being the gods, who 'consumed the best part'.[25] Despite the aloofness of the god, his image is at the hub of a great temple complex, indeed of an entire redistributive system. The offering of food to him is an economically central practice, for it is identical with the gathering of food for storage and distribution at a centre.[26] The motor of the system is divine demand.

Given this identity of religious and economic form, it would not be surprising if, as has been suggested,[27] the neo-Assyrian and Persian royal exploitation of the wealth of the temples contributed to the decline of the old Mesopotamian religion. But even as late as Seleucid times we have a text from Uruk that 'enumerates among other offerings a daily total of 500 kg of bread, 40 sheep, 2 bulls, 1 bullock, 8 lambs, 70 birds and ducks, 4 wild boars, 3 ostrich eggs, dates, figs, raisins, and 54 containers of beer and wine'.[28] The Mesopotamian deity receives not the insubstantial smoke that ascends from the Greek sacrifice,[29] but food as eaten by humankind. Numerous terms in common use refer indiscriminately to human and to divine food.[30]

---

[20] Oppenheim 1977, 89, 95–6; 106; Oates 1986, 25–6, 44; Postgate 1992, 120–1, 125–6; Snell 1997, 18, 56, 105.

[21] Burkert 1976, 177; Oppenheim 1977, 96, 189; Postgate 1992, 120–1, 124–5; Lambert, W. G. 1993, 199–200.

[22] Hallo 1987, 7.

[23] The claim that Marduk and the other Babylonian gods really did eat the food put in front of them is attested in the apocryphal *Bel and the Dragon* (probably written *c.* 130 BC): Lambert, W. G. 1993, 200.

[24] Oppenheim 1977, 188–92.   [25] Hallo 1987; cf. n. 44.

[26] Lambert, W. G. 1993, 197–8 argues that it is a misnomer to call this 'sacrifice'. Presumably only a small proportion of the food brought to the god's household was placed before the god himself: cf. Postgate 1992, 120, 125.

[27] Snell 1997, 107–8, 131–2.   [28] Oates 1986, 175.

[29] 'Incense is the only thing totally consumed by fire in the course of Babylonian offerings' (Lambert, W. G. 1993, 194).

[30] Lambert, W. G. 1993, 197.

D   GREEK FOOD OFFERINGS: THE MONETISATION OF CULT

When thinking about offerings to the gods (as indeed about the allocation of goods and services in general) we may deploy various polarities. Are the offerings enforced or voluntary? Are they made in kind, or in things valued for their exchange-value (notably precious metal)? Do they sustain an elite or the whole community? The contribution of large quantities of goods to the household of the Mesopotamian deity seems to have been in general enforced, and in general in kind (notably food), and to combine a redistributive function with sustaining an elite.

Do we find anything comparable in Greek religion? For the late Bronze Age, yes. The Linear B tablets give us a picture of centralised control over much economic activity, recording as they do the administrative transfer of large numbers of goods and personnel, without money and with very few suggestions even of the equivalence of value between commodities that is a necessary (though insufficient) condition for trade.[31] The basic similarities with economies of the contemporary Near East have often been noted.[32] The tablets record both divine property and offerings to deity: for example one tablet[33] lists rams, a bull, cheeses, sheepskins, wheat, wine, flour and honey, all for Poseidon. The sanctuaries so documented were apparently under the control of the palace, and the transactions involving them belonged in effect to the palatial economy.[34] The collection of goods at the centre seems to have been largely to sustain the elite, perhaps also for the provision of subsistence relief to the whole kingdom.[35] There is evidence, at Thebes and Pylos, for a banquet of meat for about a thousand participants.[36] The elite might have included at least some of the temple personnel recorded in the tablets: temple-servants, priests, priestesses,[37] and numerous 'servants of the god' holding leases of land.[38] In the archaeological evidence as a whole there is some evidence for dedications of precious objects,[39]

[31] Finley 1957, 135; Halstead 1992, 57–8, who also however cites de Fidio 1982, for 'possible indirect evidence of such equivalences', and Killen 1985, 284–5 for rare references to 'buying' (only of slaves, and its precise sense uncertain); Shelmerdine 1997, 567. Of course there may also have been much economic activity independent of the palace and so not recorded in the tablets.
[32] See esp. Killen 1985, who also refers to earlier bibliography (274 n. 4).
[33] Ventris and Chadwick 1973, n. 171 (from Pylos). See further Killen 1985, 244.
[34] Chadwick 1985, 200; Killen 1985, 289; Halstead 1992, 62.
[35] Killen 1985, 253, 283–4; Halstead 1992, 73.
[36] Piteros, Olivier, and Melena 1990,; Hägg 1998, 103; Killen 1994, adds evidence from Knossos.
[37] Ventris and Chadwick 1973, n. 49, and General Index s.v. priests and priestesses.
[38] Ventris and Chadwick 1973, nos. 114, 115, 116, 119, etc.
[39] E.g. Hägg 1998, 106–11; Cf. though earlier Langdon 1987, 108: 'It can hardly be said that the Myceneans dedicated as common practice the finest objects of their society to their deities.'

but barely any for burnt-animal sacrifice.[40] The subsequent adoption by
the Greeks of burnt-animal sacrifice might have been influenced by West
Semitic practice.[41]

Moving on several centuries to our next extant texts, the Homeric epics,
we find a very different picture. In the five detailed Homeric descriptions
of sacrificial meals the source of the victim(s) receives only slight attention.
Nestor sends to the plain for an ox (*Od.* 3.421), and the swineherd Eumaeus
has no difficulty in providing a swine (*Od.* 14.414). Agamemnon 'sacrificed'
an ox and invited six Greek notables to the feast (*Il.* 2.402–7) – one of several
indications in Homer of the feast as belonging to a system of redistribution
in which the chieftain exchanges largesse for loyalty.[42] However, the fact is
that, here and generally in Homer, the emphasis is on consumption and on
the inclusiveness of the consuming group (3A). Even within the small group
invited by Agamemnon there is emphasis on equal shares for all (2.431).
Another symptom of the inclusiveness of the Homeric sacrifice is that all
three of the sacrifices described in detail in the *Odyssey* are marked by the
participation of one or more strangers.[43] Indeed it is a *topos*, in Homer
and elsewhere, that strangers arrive during a sacrifice and are invited to
participate (2E). Homer does not refer to a system of contributions from
below to support an elite.

We have seen that this egalitarian inclusiveness coexists in Homer with
the relative absence of a material context for the sacrifice (3AB). When, with
the widespread building of substantial temples from the eighth century onwards, such a context does develop, the tradition of egalitarian inclusiveness
persists (3A). This is in sharp contrast to Mesopotamia, where the temple
is a centre for the gathering of food, and the food so gathered has various destinations: to feed the deity, to feed the numerous personnel of the
temple, to be stored for future consumption, to be exchanged for other
goods required by the temple. It is the feeding of the deity that 'presents
itself as the *raison d'être* of the entire institution'.[44] In Mesopotamian myth
humankind was created to provide the deities with food (4C). The divine
demand for food is at the centre of an institution that has economic, social,
and legal functions.[45] By contrast the Greek sanctuary combines the storage
of wealth with the *communal* distribution of sacrificed meat.

The temple and its image of the god seem to have been derived by
the Greeks from their eastern neighbours.[46] However, 'for the living cult

---

[40] Burkert 1976, 178; 1985, 45; Bergquist 1988, and 1993; Hägg 1998, 100–1.
[41] Burkert 1976, 181–2; Bergquist 1988, 33; 1993, 42–3.   [42] Cf. 3A nn. 18 and 19.
[43] *Od.* 3.5–66, 419–74; 14.414–53.   [44] Oppenheim 1977, 187–8.
[45] E.g. Oppenheim 1977, 187.   [46] Burkert 1985, 88–91; Romano 1988, 133.

they were and remained more a side-show than a centre'.[47] The relative centrality of the temple housing its divine image in parts of the Near East expressed its crucial role in the collection, storage, and distribution of food. Of the numerous Mesopotamian deities each one resides in his image, which resides in his temple and may be given life by magical rites.[48] Although the Greek image of deity may be prayed to, it is not thought to live, and it was possible (for an intellectual at least) to emphasise the distinction between image and deity[49] as early as the sixth century BC.[50] It too, like the dedicated figurine, substitutes for the reality. And in Greek sacrifice the community feasted outside the temple while the image of the god remained inside and the god's portion of the sacrifice ascended heavenwards. Even in an individual offering of an animal to deity, the Greek surrenders very little – insubstantial smoke to the gods, a certain small part of the animal to the priest. A whole animal is offered only in the (occasional)[51] holocaust, or in merely symbolic form in the animal figurines offered in the temples. Just as the statue is a mere image of the god, and the temple is *as if* it were his house, so the animals he receives are generally mere images (albeit more durable than the flesh of real ones). It is in this symbolic sphere, in the dedication of durable offerings rather than in the provision of food, that the Greeks surrender much to the gods.

In our mass of evidence from classical Attica there is, again in contrast to Mesopotamia, no evidence for the public ownership of herds and flocks.[52]

---

[47] Burkert 1985, 91. This view has been challenged by Scheer 2000, but remains true for animal sacrifice, which is what concerns us here. The evidence for the image participating in animal sacrifice, gathered by Scheer (61–5), is marginal, and Scheer admits the contrast with Mesopotamia and Egypt.

[48] Oppenheim 1977, 186.

[49] By Heraclitus B5; cf. Aesch. *Eum.* 242. The emphasis will have a long history.

[50] In combining communality with the (marginal) divine image the Greeks are intermediate between Mesopotamia and Israel, which combines complete rejection of the image of deity with communal eating and the burning of part (or all) of an animal (similarly the West Semites generally, but the best evidence is from the Old Testament: Burkert 1976, 179–80; 1985, 51 and n. 46, 63–4; Bergquist 1993, 26 with bibliography; Lambert, W. G. 1993, 192; Brown 1995, 183–221). 'In Mesopotamia, the sacrificial cult was literally taken as a means of feeding the gods and specifically, beginning with the end of the third millennium, their cult statues. In Israel, where anthropomorphic conceptions and representations of the deity were proscribed, and where the worshipper already participated in the consumption of the earliest (paschal) sacrifice, the later cultic legislation explicitly provided priesthood and laity with a share of the sacrificial offerings' (Hallo 1987, 11). This may be connected with the fact that the Old Testament, in contrast to Greek sources, gives evidence of tension between food offerings characteristic of the tribe and those characteristic of the state. Anderson (1987) modifies and develops Robertson Smith's emphasis on the distinction between 'slain offerings' and 'tribute offerings': 'along with Smith we believe the manner by which sacred offerings were collected and distributed was vastly different in tribal and state polities' (23).

[51] E.g. Jameson 1988, 88.

[52] Rosivach 1994, 79. For the few slight and scattered instances of evidence for sanctuaries (outside Attica) owning animals see Isager (1992 – N.B. the discussion on pp.19–20).

Greek temple income does not consist of food en masse, which – the number of temple personnel being relatively small – is unnecessary and would be (because perishable) inconvenient. Offerings to the gods are instead for the most part *durable*: the durable parts of the animal, animal figurines, instruments of the sacrifice, votive offerings generally. A 'tithe' (*dekatē*), which may derive from the redistributive economies of the Near East,[53] might in Greece be dedicated from commercial profit, for instance in the form of a huge decorated bowl (Hdt. 4.152).

But even durable objects, in excessive numbers, may be inconvenient. The practice of *substitution*, originating in the substitution of durable for perishable offerings, is extended to the substitution of money for objects in kind (offerings to deity or portions for the priest). And so the victim's skin, to which the sanctuary frequently had a right, might be replaced by a monetary fee.[54] This money could be named after the skin, as could also money received for the sale of sacrificial skins. Another illustration of the need for cult to be monetised is provided by the *pelanos* – an offering, in particular a kind of cake. No doubt sanctuaries preferred money to a surplus of cakes, and *pelanos* comes to mean a monetary fee paid at a sanctuary.[55] Perhaps a transitional stage was the offering of clay or metal imitations of round cakes.[56] If so, then imitative (or symbolic) substitution prepared the way for monetary substitution: we pass from a cake to a non-perishable imitation of a cake, and from there to money, which – though it may still, as coinage, resemble the imitiation of a round cake[57] – has in fact left the particular use-value of the imitated cake well behind, for it has instead only the relatively general (and so abstract) quality of exchange-value. Already in the fifth century *pelanos* could refer (with an even greater degree of generality) to a *fund*.[58] In an (early Hellenistic?) Cretan inscription[59] payment is specified in staters, in triobols, and in *lebētes* – presumably coins named after sacrificial cauldrons;[60] and this

---

[53] It 'may go back to Mesopotamian bureaucracy; it makes its appearance in Israel as well, as a tribute to the monarch, the temple, the priests': Burkert in Linders and Nordquist 1987, 46.

[54] ἐς τὸ δέρμα (Sokolowski 1962, no. 41.12–15); δερματικόν.

[55] *Corpus Inscr.Delph.*1 n. 1 (late sixth or early fifth century); Sokolowski 1962, nos. 38A26 (perhaps actual cakes), 39.2 (fee in coin), 41.8 (fee in coin) (all from Delphi fifth to fourth century BC); Amandry 1950, 86–103. On cakes in Greek sacrificial regulations see Kearns 1994.

[56] Cf. 3C n. 116; Caccamo Caltabiano and Radici Colace 1992, 153.

[57] Hesychius explains the Laconian *pelanor* as a coin (τετράχαλκον).

[58] Sokolowski 1969, 5.36 (the Eleusinian first fruits decree, perhaps of the 420s); Sokolowski 1962, nos. 13.19 (the first fruits decree of 353/2 BC), 19.29–30, 35 (the Salaminians accord of 363/2 BC); Stengel 1920, 99; Ziehen in *RE* 19.250.

[59] *Inscr.Cret.* I.viii.5 (Melville Jones no. 46).

[60] Guarducci 1944–5, 174, who compares Pollux 9.61 ('ox' as festival payment is two drachmas).

semantic shift from a particular sacrificial item to the generality of money is exemplified also by the word obel/obol.[61] Sacrificial equipment itself (cauldrons, spits) might be used as a means of payment (6A). Again, the regular word for treasurer in the classical period, *tamias*, originally meant carver. The name *kōlakretai* of early Athenian financial officials seems to derive from the gathering of sacrificed thigh-bones.[62] The word *danos*, 'loan', might originally have meant the part of the sacrifice given to the priest. The meaning of *eranos* passes from communal meal to cash loan.[63]

Originally temple income probably consisted mainly of (voluntary or enforced) offerings, to which however it did not remain limited. We hear also of fines, rent, and money voted by the polis. As a site for communal sacrifice and the storage of durable communal wealth, the temple is an institution of the polis. Indeed, the growth of durable wealth in sanctuaries was an aspect of the development of the polis. The communal wealth of the polis is stored in temples (5B). And the polis may oversee the purchase of sacrificial animals.

Further evidence for the variety of temple income, and of its transformation into precious metal, is provided by the following four surviving pieces of evidence for the resourcing of temple building in the sixth century.

(1) A fragmentary inscription, of the mid-sixth century or earlier,[64] from the temple of Artemis at Ephesus, generally believed to concern the expenses of building the temple.[65] It records silver and gold 'weighed out' from various sources – 'from the polis', 'from the wood', 'from here', 'from the naval', 'from the salt', 'from the dockyards' (?), 'from the stitching' (?), 'from the salt' [again], 'from the water', 'from the garden' (?). A wide variety of sources (tax? sale? rent?) contribute either precious metal or what is transformed into precious metal. I will return to this inscription in 5A.

(2) A fragmentary inscription from the last quarter of the sixth century from Sidene on the Propontis records that a certain individual and his companions 'made the roof from (the proceeds of) the sacred domains and

---

[61] 6A. Other names of coins (or of units of value or of precious metal) for which a sacrificial origin has been claimed are ἄγκυραι, πέλεκυς, and φθοῖδες: Laum 1924, 107–9, 113–14, 124; Caccamo Caltabiano and Radici Colace 1992, 153, 175–6. The reports of early Athenian coins named after, and stamped with, the ox (βοῦς: Poll. *Onom.* 9.60–1; Plut. *Thes.* 25.3) are almost certainly late inventions.

[62] κωλ-αγρέται: Laum 1924, 53, 77; Chantraine 1968–80 s.v. κωλακρέται. Note however the form κωλοκράται in *SEG* 39.148 (331/0 BC).

[63] Millett 1991, 29 (*danos*), 155 (*eranos*).

[64] *SGDI* IV 4 no. 49; Jeffery 1990, 344 no. 53 with 339; generally dated to the mid-sixth century, but up to half a century earlier by Manganaro 1974.

[65] From Hdt. 1.92 we learn that Croesus donated the golden cattle and most of the columns.

of the skins (from sacrifices). [–]os son of Leukippos finished off the temple with his own hand'.[66]

(3) Herodotus records (2.180) that when the temple at Delphi burnt down (548 BC), the Amphictyons contracted to have it rebuilt at a cost of 300 talents, with a quarter of that sum to be provided by the Delphians, and that the Delphians went round from city to city asking for contributions, which came even from Egypt (Amasis gave a thousand talents of alum, and the Greeks in Egypt twenty mnas – i.e. of silver).

(4) Herodotus records (3.57–9) that some Samians who had fought against Polycrates exacted 'one hundred talents' from the Siphnians and then settled in Crete, founded the city of Cydonia, and built temples there (presumably with some part of the hundred talents).

These four cases suggest a wide range of sources: the temple treasury, taxes, sacred land, the sale of skins, voluntary (?) labour, exaction, voluntary contributions both in kind (from a non-Greek) and in silver. Most of these involve the mediation of precious metal; and precious metal was, at least as early as the seventh century BC, donated to temples.[67] It may be that sixth-century public sacrifices were paid for from a similar range of sources.[68]

We have seen that in the context of splendid temples with relatively few personnel, traditional food offerings to deity tended to be substituted by items with durable or even monetary value that was subsequently supplemented by precious metal money from other sources (tax, fines, rent). This wealth was stored, but also used for building and maintenance, and for communal sacrifices. How – in the absence of a large-scale redistributive economy, of a deity and his household demanding to be fed, of temple ownership and control of herds – was it possible for the Greek community to organise the communal feasts on which its solidarity depended? Even those who own no animals have a right to a portion of the feast.[69] The victims have to be of the right standard, and to arrive all at the right moment. And yet the independence of the providers of the victims has to be respected. And so the durable form naturally taken by the offerings is convenient also for use at the appropriate time to *purchase* animals of standard quality, thereby co-ordinating what would otherwise be a haphazard process. Much metallic wealth flows into and out of sanctuaries, which

---

[66] Robert and Robert 1950, 78–80; Jeffery 1990, 372 no. 50. The translation is taken from Davies 1988, 387.

[67] By the Lydian king Gyges to Delphi (Hdt. 1.14; see also e.g. 1.50 Croesus).

[68] We cannot though exclude the possibility of the direct contribution of animals, as occurs in the regulations for a festival in fourth century BC Eretria (contributions from rural communities, with mention of purchase where animals are not forthcoming): Sokolowski 1969, no. 92.26–32.

[69] At least in Athens in the fifth century, when we begin to have detailed evidence.

become centres of wealth that is durable and exchangeable. Sacrifice is an early agent of monetisation. At least as early as the classical period some Greek sanctuaries functioned as banks[70] or as places (during festivals) for tax-free trading.[71]

But the provision of sacrifice was a matter not just for the sanctuaries but also for the polis. The relationship between polis and sanctuaries in this matter is hard to disentangle. It is at any rate important that public precious metal was generally stored in sanctuaries (5B n. 42). Although we have no detailed evidence for the resourcing of animal sacrifice before the first surviving detailed inscriptions, which are it seems from the early fifth century, there was somewhat earlier almost certainly a degree both of control (if not actual resourcing from taxation) by the polis and of monetisation. Fifth-century Athenians attributed to Solon a calendar prescribing public sacrifices of specified victims to specified deities. This code, which is best known from surviving parts of a version reinscribed around the year 401 BC, very probably goes back to the sixth century BC, if not to Solon himself.[72] As Parker notes, the specification of a victim implies a cost, even where this is not explicitly stated. And 'a prime function of the sixth century code was surely to define what monies of the Athenian people were to be expended on what gods'.[73] Plutarch reports that Solon gave

(as a reward) for bringing in a wolf five drachmas, for a wolf's whelp one drachma. Demetrius of Phaleron (*FGrH* 228 F22) says that the former was the price of an ox, the latter of a sheep. For the prices that he lays down in the sixteenth *axon* are of choice sacrificial victims, and it is reasonable that they are many times higher (than the prices for ordinary animals).[74]

These prices of sacrificial victims were presumably included in Solon's sacrificial calendar and (as were penalties and rewards in Solon's laws) expressed as amounts of silver – either drachmas or, more likely, staters.[75] Significantly, it is above all in the central institution of public sacrifice that the surviving evidence shows us the state regulating monetary payments shortly *before* the introduction of coinage.

[70] Bogaert 1968, 279–304; and the fifth-century inscriptions discussed by Davies 2001. N.B. Xen. *Anab.* 5.3.4–8. This function is denied to the Mesopotamian temple by Renger 1996, 316.

[71] Sokolowski 1969, no. 92.32–5 (fourth century BC Eretria); see also 67.26–7 (fourth century BC Tegea).

[72] See the judicious examination by Parker 1996, 43–55. There is a little inscriptional evidence for the organisation of public festivals in Attica in the sixth century BC: Davies 1981, 374.

[73] Parker 1996, 52–3.

[74] Plut. *Sol.* 23.2 = F81 Ruschenbusch 1966. The *axones* were revolving wooden tablets on which Solon's laws were inscribed.

[75] 5A n. 15. See most recently Kroll 1998,; F83–6 Ruschenbusch 1966.

Plutarch reports that Solon in his legislation 'for the costs of sacrifices reckons a sheep and a drachma as equivalent to a *medimnos*' (a cereal measure).[76] This threefold equivalence has been compared to a fourth-century Attic inscription in which *medimnoi* of cereal offered to Demeter are sold, with the proceeds used to buy sacrificial victims.[77] Given that Solon divided up property classes by the criterion of number of *medimnoi* of cereal produced,[78] and that this criterion might have been associated with festival offerings,[79] his establishment of equivalences 'for the costs of sacrifices' may also have been used to translate non-cereal wealth (in drachmas or animals) into *medimnoi* for the purpose of assigning people to the property classes[80] – or even have functioned more generally as a stable equivalence conducive to further stable equivalences.

More detailed is the evidence from the fifth and fourth centuries, most of it inscriptional. The economics of cult in this period have not received the attention they deserve, though for fourth-century Attica we do have the detailed study of public sacrifices by Rosivach.[81] We find the description *dēmotelēs* ('paid for by the people') used by Herodotus (6.57) of Spartan sacrifices and by Thucydides (2.15.2) of an old Attic festival, as well as *dēmosios* ('public') of cult in Attic inscriptions.[82] Lysias' speech *Against Nikomachos* refers to large sums expended by the polis on sacrifices (30.19–20). In public sacrifices the right to consume the victim(s) belongs to all members of the community, whether all citizens of the polis or, in the case of a sacrifice by a sub-group of the polis such as the deme, then all members of the deme. How were these public distributions of meat resourced? For fifth-century Attica we have some evidence for the support of cult by taxation.[83] For fourth-century Attica Rosivach concludes that in general 'public sacrifices were performed by agents of a larger community

---

[76] Plut. *Sol.* 23.3 (= F77 Ruschenbusch); cf. F126a–c; Poll. 8.130: Horsmann 2000, 272–3.

[77] van den Oudenrijn 1952; *IG*² 1672 (Cavanaugh 1996, 13–15, 43).

[78] Or the top class only (the *pentakosiomedimnoi*), if we accept the argument of de Ste Croix (forthcoming) that only this class was defined by a quantitative assessment (produce valued in *medimnoi* of barley).

[79] Connor 1987.

[80] This is well argued by Horsmann 2000. Solon himself lists as wealth 'much silver and gold and wheat-bearing tracts of land and horses and mules' (fr. 24). Wilcken's emendation οὐσίων (properties) for θυσιῶν (sacrifices) at Plut. *Sol.* 23.3 would actually refer to the 'evaluations of properties' (so e.g. Kroll 1998, 227): but cf. van den Oudenrijn 1952; Horsmann 2000, 271.

[81] Rosivach 1994. See now also the brief but useful Davies 2001. There are also brief studies by Schlaifer (1940) and Sokolowski (1954). For the demes see also Whitehead 1986, 163–80. Two other brief recent studies not confined to Attica (mostly of post-classical material) are by Ampolo (1992) and Linders (1992).

[82] Collected by Davies 1988, 379 n. 52. See also Parker 1996, 5 n. 17.

[83] Parker 1996, 125; Schlaifer 1940.

for the benefit of that community',[84] and were funded largely by public money raised by taxation and by the rents on property owned by the god but administered by the polis.[85] The provider of the sacrifice, the community, is therefore in a sense the same as the consumer, with the provision generally made by means of money raised by the community – albeit from another perspective, taking into view the *source* of the money, an element of redistribution from rich to poor may be involved, as is claimed in the fifth century by the 'Old Oligarch'.[86]

Rent and state taxation were however not the only sources of income available to Greek sanctuaries of the classical period. As we have seen, offerings of (*inter alia*) precious metal had been made for generations. And indeed the very act of animal sacrifice implies renunciation. The sacrificer will share the animal with others. Even private sacrifices, notes Rosivach, 'frequently had a public dimension when others were invited to share the sacrificial meal'.[87] And the sacrificer will also of course offer part of the victim to deity. Now a tradition of offering may easily turn into enforced relinquishment, i.e. payment to priest or sanctuary. Inscriptions survive (the earliest from the early fifth century) that define such payments. The inscribing, regulation, and enforcement of numerous payments may attract and require the indirect or direct intervention of the state. And in certain fifth-century Attic inscriptions some have seen voluntary contributions to cult being transformed into state taxation.[88] Whatever the truth of that, a nice example of the coexistence of compulsion with voluntary offering is provided by the Eleusinian inscription (perhaps of the 420s) which *requires* the Athenians and their allies, but can only *invite* the other Greek cities, to contribute first fruits of barley and wheat to the Eleusinian goddesses 'according to ancestral tradition and the oracle from Delphi'.[89] Enforced payment may also take the form of fines, which are frequently specified in surviving inscribed cult regulations from the early fifth century onwards.[90]

[84] Rosivach 1994, 11.
[85] Rosivach 1994, 122, etc.; Schlaifer 1940; Aleshire 1994, 15. Deme sacrifices were funded by rents and interest on loans, as well as by individual contributions (voluntary or (perhaps) sometimes enforced): Rosivach 1994, 128–42; Whitehead 1986, 163–4, 171–5.
[86] [Xen.] *Ath. Pol.* 2.9; Rosivach 1994, 3.
[87] Rosivach 1994, 9, citing Men. *Dysk.* 393–418; Isaeus 1.31; Xen. *Oik.* 2.4–5.
[88] For the bibliography see Parker 1996, 125, who was sceptical.
[89] *IG* I³ 78 = Sokolowski 1969, no. 5.
[90] Fifth-century examples are Sokolowski 1969, nos. 3 (Attica 485–4 BC or earlier), 14 (Athens), 76 and 77 (Delphi), 100 (Arkesine), 108 (Paros); Sokolowski 1962, nos. 3 (Athens), 18 (Athens), 32 (Arcadia), 34 (Corinth, *c.* 475 BC), 37 (Delphi, *c.* 480–470 BC), 38 (Delphi), 50 (Delos), 113 (Axos), 128 (Aetolia), 129 (Chios).

Payment may throughout this period be in kind (e.g. the skins of the sacrificial animals). But at least as early as the early fifth century, when our inscriptional evidence patchily begins, there is also already a considerable degree of monetisation of cult payments, not only in the form of fines. Given that contributions were often of parts of the sacrificed animal, the sanctuary would avoid large surpluses either by insisting on monetary contributions instead or by selling the contributions in kind. Of inscriptions referring to these practices I will confine myself to a few examples. Early fifth-century regulations for a communal sacrifice on Andros requires each child and man to pay an Aeginetan obol per day during the burning of the corn.[91] The regulations of the Eleusinian mysteries of about 460 BC[92] specify monetary payments to the officiants by each initiand. In fifth-century regulations of the deme Paiania fees for sacrifice are paid in kind and in cash.[93] The calendar of sacrifices of the urban deme Skambonidai, apparently from shortly after the Persian wars, prescribes, among other things, the selling of an animal skin,[94] a sacrifice in which each member of the deme is to get a three(?)-obol portion, and other sacrifices in which the meat is to be sold raw.[95] The Eleusinian first-fruits decree mentioned in the previous paragraph specifies that some of the offerings of grain are to be sold, with the proceeds to be used for setting up dedications.[96] A nice example of the centrality of monetary evaluation and of purchase is provided by the prescriptions, inscribed in the late fourth century BC, for the festival of Zeus Polieus on Cos. After elaborate procedures for the selection of a sacrificial ox, it is led to the *agora*, where the owner or his representative is to proclaim: 'To the Coans I provide the ox. Let the Coans pay the price to Hestia.' The officials then immediately take an oath and value the ox. The herald announces the price. And the ox is taken to be sacrificed.[97]

What emerges throughout this period is the clarity of the dependence of cult on money[98] – money from whatever the source. This dependence can, in inscriptions, take vivid form: 'to build three granaries at Eleusis according

---

[91] Jeffrey 1990, 298, 306 n. 53.

[92] *IG* i³ 6 = Sokolowski 1962, 3; Clinton 1974, 10–13.

[93] Sokolowski 1954, 156. Other fifth-century examples of monetary cultic payments: Sokolowski 1969, nos. 12 (Athens), 178 (Attica); Sokolowski 1962, nos. 38 (Delphi), 85 (Lindos).

[94] Cf. Stengel 1920, 116–17; Burkert 1983, 7. A sanctuary might even sell dung: Sokolowski 1969, n. 67.28–30 (early fourth century BC Tegea). For a (much later) account of the purchase of sacrificial victims at a sanctuary see Aelian *Hist.An.* 10.50.

[95] *IG* i³ 244 = Sokolowski 1969, no. 10. On the sale of sacrificial meat see Berthiaume 1982, 62–70.

[96] Cavanaugh 1996, 36–9. Cf. e.g. *IG* i³ 391 (Cavanaugh 6, 126). A sanctuary buying dedications with proceeds of animal skins: Sokolowski 1955, no. 72.48–50 (third century BC).

[97] Sokolowski 1969, no. 151.

[98] Beautifully expressed at Ar. *Wealth* 137–42 (quoted 8E). A reaction against the undiscriminating power of money in this sphere is apparent perhaps in stories about punishment for the *replacement* of sacred or sacrificial animals (8B n. 17), implying the uniqueness of the animal.

to ancestral custom . . . from the money (*argurion*) of the goddesses',[99] 'to make sacrifices . . . from the money (*argurion*) from the quarry';[100] 'the purchaser of the mud . . . to give the money (*argurion*) to Neleus'.[101] The source may be remarkably remote. Alcmaeon brought back to Greece twice as much gold as he was able carry about his person from the treasury of Croesus, gold that was the source for, among other things, the Parian marble on the façade of Apollo's temple at Delphi.[102] Xenophon narrates that with money (*argurion*) from the sale of booty from his Asiatic adventures he bought land near Olympia, on which he built an altar and temple, and used a tenth part of the crops to sacrifice annually to Artemis, who provided the local people with sacrificial meat and other food.[103]

Between the economic role of the Mesopotamian and the Greek temple I have sketched a basic contrast, which nevertheless co-exists with numerous elements shared by the two. For example, the Mesopotamian temple contained durable dedications.[104] And conversely the setting of food and drink before deities imagined to be present at the feast does sometimes occur in Greek cult.[105] Martin West has recently produced a long list of features shared by Greek and Semitic (especially West Semitic) sacrifice, together with a number of Greek sacrificial terms apparently derived from Semitic ones.[106]

These similarities are of great interest, but – like the Asiatic similarities with Greek epic (4B) – should not blind us to the profound socio-economic differences.[107] The offering of food to deity by the Greek polis may, as in Mesopotamia, involve the transfer of food from producer to consumer, and the officiant (or small number of officiants) may receive a special part

---

[99] The Eleusinian first-fruits decree (*IG* I³ 78: see above n. 90), lines 10–12.

[100] Sokolowski 1962, no. 11.8 (beginning of the fourth century).

[101] *IG* I³ 84 = Sokolowski 1969, no. 14.20–2 = *SIG*³ no. 93.b (418/17 BC).

[102] Hdt. 5.62–3, 6.125.

[103] Xen. *Anab.* 5.3.4–13. Nicias was said to have funded sacrifices on Delos from the proceeds of land he purchased there for 10,000 drachmas and gave to the god: Plut. *Nic.* 3.7.

[104] Though Oppenheim 1977, 106 notes that 'income was derived primarily from invested gifts, i.e. from land donated to the temple by kings, and only secondarily from occasional dedications of the spoils of war, precious objects, and, above all, prisoners of war'.

[105] Burkert 1985, 107 calls the presence of deity at a meal 'the exception'. Jameson 1994 presents rather more widespread evidence, but the amount of food presented to deity is relatively small (relative both to the amount consumed by the humans and to the amount presented to Mesopotamian deities).

[106] West 1997, 38–42.

[107] West's concern, as of others in this field, is in general confined to listing and explaining certain correspondences of detail in language, literature, and so on. He wrily observes that, though he would have no objection to a book pointing out the *differences*, he would not promise to read it (viii). Differences are, of course, infinite, so that not even West could list them all. But it is precisely the demonstrated similarities in certain areas that should invite and make possible an understanding of *significant* difference in those areas, which may then require a socio-economic perspective.

or parts of the animal. But in terms of the three polarities we deployed earlier in this section to characterise Mesopotamia and late Bronze Age Greece, we find that in the Greek polis two of them have been reversed: public food-offerings for the gods involve on the whole the intermediary of money, and are not made in order to sustain an elite, though they may be publicly enforced. What is distinctive about the polis is the *indirectness*, the economic *marginality,* and the *communality* of the process.

These three characteristics cohere. With some exceptions,[108] the offerings brought to the deity in public sacrifices come *indirectly*, by means of money, whether the money comes from the temple's own property (treasure, land, etc.) or is raised by the polis through taxation. Between offerings and deity come both the impersonal intermediary of money and the legislative and executive machinery of the polis. Money of course may act as an intermediary in the allocation of food not just in public sacrifices but generally in the life of the polis.[109] In Aristophanes the citizen eats a meal at the Panathenaea (*Clouds* 386), but also takes coins to the market to buy barley meal (*Eccles.* 818–19). Some of the functions of the Mesopotamian temple may be performed in other societies by money, which can both allocate food and store value for times of shortage. Greek temples on the whole neither store food nor organise its large-scale production, but they may contain a large store of value in the form of precious metal.[110] The Greek public sacrifice provides much meat,[111] but is, in relation to the activities of the Mesopotamian temple, *marginal* to the economy as a whole.[112] Moreover, within the public sacrifice the Greek deity is in turn, we have seen, relatively marginal not only to the *acquisition* of the food but also to its communal *consumption* outside the temple. Accordingly, the public offering may seem to be primarily a *communal* and inclusive feast, as can be seen as early as Homer. The community – especially the polis, but also

---

[108] E.g. the rent from the temple estates in Heraclea at the beginning of the third century BC were paid in *barley*: Ampolo 1992; a few temples owning their own animals: n. 52 above.

[109] An illuminating exception is provided the Spartans, whose failure to produce their own coinage (until the third century BC) is to be connected both with the collective consumption of food brought by each Spartiate from his own farm (Plut. *Lyc.* 12; Dicaearchus fr. 72 W) – i.e. without the mediation of money that we have seen to be so important to Athenian public sacrifice – and with the lack of a large urban centre and of public funds in Sparta (Thuc. 1.80.4; Aristot. *Pol.* 1271b11). The development of a central store of durable wealth (money) was in Sparta precluded by the conservatism of the tradition of redistribution. Accordingly, and despite their political significance, the Spartans had no large urban centre (Thuc. 1.10.2) and no interest in philosophy or tragedy (cf. chs. 9–14 below). They seem to have been reluctant to use (Delphic) temple funds for warfare (Thuc. 4.118.3), a principle not shared by monetised naval states such as Athens: Davies 2001, 125.

[110] Even where grain was contributed to a temple, it might be sold, as in the Eleusinian decree discussed above (n. 96).

[111] Rosivach 1994, 67.   [112] E.g. Jameson 1988, 105–6.

a sub-section such as the deme – performs some of the social, economic, and legal functions that in Mesopotamia were performed by the temple, and it finances public sacrifice so as to provide a feast not for an elite but for itself. A consequence of this combination of indirectness, marginality, and communality is a tendency towards the symbolic. The role of the god is not to demand food for the centre, for himself and his household, but rather to require a human feast, whose vital political importance is as a symbolic expression of communality, participation, *koinōnia*.[113] For Aristotle, writing in the thoroughly monetised polis, what permits *koinōnia* of equals (*qua* transactors) is – by enabling commensurability of goods – currency (*nomisma*).[114]

---

[113] Parker 1996, 1–3.   [114] *EN* 1133a17–19, 1133b16–19.

CHAPTER FIVE

Greek money

From the role of sacrifice in monetisation we now proceed to Greek money in general. It will be convenient to postpone discussion of coinage, a particular form of money, to the next chapter, even though this will mean first pursuing money into the Classical period (5B) before returning to the late seventh or early sixth century (the time of the earliest coins). The distinction between coinage and unstamped precious metal – a distinction that we take for granted – was in the earliest phase of coinage not (so far as we know) linguistically expressed. Words in sixth-century texts that may refer to coins ('stater' and 'drachma') may also refer to units of weight.[1] Such ambiguous references will be included in the broad category of money, i.e. in this chapter. Bullion, which performed money functions for the Greeks before the invention of coinage, continued to do so long after the widespread adoption of coinage. Among the Greeks money was precious metal (and occasionally bronze or iron) – or rather two precious metals (silver and sometimes gold) united by an exchange ratio – coined or uncoined.

A   THE EARLIEST GREEK MONEY

When do the Greeks first use money? It cannot be detected in Bronze Age Greece (4D). Nor is there any trace of money in Hesiod, in whose *Works and Days*, where the economic theme provided plenty of opportunity to mention money, wealth is in fact conceived of largely as the contents of a barn.[2]

It is also, on a reasonably narrow definition of money, largely absent from Homeric epic, which does nevertheless contain suggestions of it (2BC).

---

[1] It is only in texts of the second half of the fifth century (Hdt., Thuc., Aristoph., etc.) that we can be sure that certain words refer to coins.

[2] *Op.* 30–2, 300–1, 307, 374, 411, 476. 'Goods (*chrēmata*) are life/soul (*psuchē*) for wretched mortals' (686), on the risks of sea-trade, may signify an exclusive devotion (beyond anything in Homer) to acquiring wealth, but does not suggest *money*.

Notably, there is evidence for precious metal as a *store of value* in the passage in which Odysseus is said to have gathered possessions on his journeys, 'gold and bronze and much-worked iron', that would feed one man after another to the tenth generation.[3] Similarly, when Herodotus (1.24) tells of Arion returning after a concert tour of Magna Graecia where he had gathered enough *chrēmata* to invite the murderous interest of the sailors, by *chrēmata* he probably means precious metal money.

From the seventh century, the fragments of Archilochus contain no certain reference to money, but several of them do perhaps imply it.[4] An early example of money as a *means of payment* is the Lesbian Alcaeus' remark that 'the Lydians, indignant at our (or 'their') misfortunes, gave us two thousand staters, if we could enter the holy city, although they had never had benefit from us, nor knew us'.[5] It is very likely that Alcaeus reached adulthood before 600 BC, but we do not know when he died.[6] From the fifth century onwards the 'stater' is generally a coin, but could also be a unit of weight. We do not know, at this early date,[7] whether Alcaeus' 'staters' are coins or units of weight (or standardised but unstamped pieces). In favour of coinage is their Lydian source (7A), the fact that such a large sum[8] is not expressed in mnas or talents, and also perhaps the fact that no metal is specified. On the other hand, whether the 'staters' were coins or not, it seems unlikely that at this early date stamped metal was distinguished by its own noun from unstamped. It is unclear whether the money was offered to fund the action or as a reward for its achievement. In either case, the poem seems to exemplify the military power of money.[9] Significantly, Alcaeus is struck by the power of the money to (as we might put it) transcend reciprocity in its mobilisation of people well beyond the acquaintance of the donors.

The elegiac verse collected under the name of Theognis seems to contain material from the late seventh century to the early fifth. Some of it

---

[3] *Od.* 14.323–5; cf.19.293–4; see 2B.

[4] Fr. 5 (shield as replaceable commodity), 19 (not caring about the tyrant Gyges' much gold), 34 (payment), 93a (gold, private gain creating public harm), 124b (contribution to the cost (*timos*) of wine), 302 (*chrēmata* difficult to retain).

[5] Fr. 69 L–P. Staters seem to be mentioned also in another fragment, too slight to reveal the context (63 Voigt): χε]λίοις στάτ[ηρας.

[6] Page 1955, 149–61.

[7] The next mentions of staters are from the same area – (a) in the inscription (mentioned below) from mid-sixth-century Chios; (b) in the Ephesian inscription *SGDI* VI 4 n. 49 (4D), in which the staters are probably units of weight; (c) by Hipponax the sixth-century poet of Ephesus: frr. 32 and 105 West.

[8] Breglia 1974, 7–8.

[9] 6E. Presumably *forcible* entry into the city (of unknown identity) is meant (with ἐς πόλιν ἔλθην Page 1955, 227 compares *Il.* 12.301).

(esp. 19–254) seems very likely to be by Theognis himself, whom ancient commentators dated to the middle of the sixth century, although West argues for the second half of the seventh.[10] The power of money as a threat to traditional values is frequent in lines 19–254 and elsewhere in the *Theognidea* (8D); and in lines 77–8 it is said that a loyal man is worth his weight in gold and silver. In the poetry of Solon, which probably belongs to the early sixth century, the first two items in the list of what constitutes wealth (fr. 24) are gold and silver. In contrast to Homer (2C), precious metal is coming to stand unequivocally for wealth. But the first unequivocal evidence for money (apart perhaps from the Alcaeus passage, and the roughly contemporary earliest surviving coins: 7B) seems to be provided by the *legislation* of Solon.

Homeric epic is the product of a society that is not only in process of developing the polis but also about to become the first society in history to be pervasively monetised. His narratives combine the conflict arising from successive crises of reciprocity (2D) with the striking communality of animal sacrifice (2E). Accordingly, the polis develops by – among other things – establishing centralised means of resolving crises in reciprocity and building itself around the communality of animal sacrifice. And it is in these two areas of early polis activity in particular that we find, in the laws of Solon, our earliest evidence for money (probably *c*. 593 BC).

The communality of animal sacrifice has an inherent tendency to be monetised (4D) and is of concern to the polis. And so Solon's sacrificial calendar set prices, it seems, to be paid for victims in public sacrifices (4D). The other main area[11] in which the Solonian legislation specified monetary sums was compensation for injuries. Of the extant Solonian laws, five[12] mention compensation (or fines) in drachmas.[13] These drachmas are presumably not coins, which were almost certainly as yet unknown in Athens. They may have been weights of uncoined silver.[14] But

---

[10] West 1974, 65–71. Lane Fox 2000, 37–40 argues for 600–550 BC.

[11] Other Homeric forms of payment, the reward and the athletic prize (2A), also appear in laws attributed to Solon, again expressed now in 'drachmas', although the law on athletic prizes is unlikely to be authentic: F92 (from those regarded by Ruschenbusch as genuine) and 143a. The rewards were for the capture of wolves and their offspring.

[12] F26, 30, 32, 33, 65 Ruschenbusch 1966. See further 7C. Note also F36, which mentions a (variable) fine expressed as the value (*axion*) of property. Although certainty is impossible, all these are among those regarded as authentic by Ruschenbusch (see also Rhodes 1981, 133), and two of them (F36, 65) are said to be from the Axones. The laws of Draco had specified compensation (or a fine) of twenty cattle's worth (Poll. 9.61 ἀποτίνειν εἰκοσάβοιον).

[13] That the 'drachmas' are silver is not made explicit, but suggested by the importance of silver in the Solonian economy ([Aristot.] *Ath. Pol.* 8.3; Lys. 10.18: n. 25 below) and among the Greeks' eastern neighbours, as well as by the imminence of the introduction of silver coinage into Athens.

[14] Kroll 1998. Clearly the development within the polis of a uniform system of weights and measures is an important precondition for the monetary use of uniform weights of precious metal: see

more likely is that the original laws specified 'staters', replaced later by 'drachmas'.[15]

Important to the Homeric narratives is rejection of the offer of compensation, notably Achilles' rejection of Agamemnon's, and Odysseus' rejection of the suitors'. Given that the judicial trial will be a central institution of the polis, it is significant that the only judicial trial in Homer (among the non-heroic scenes represented on the shield of Achilles) probably concerns the issue of whether the relatives of a murder victim should accept the compensation offered, and that it is also only one of two Homeric instances in which a specific amount of gold occurs by itself (not in a list).[16] Social peace requires general agreement both on the principle and on the amount of compensation for injury (notably murder),[17] which becomes therefore a major concern of the developing polis.

For this the evidence is not confined to Solon. It is precisely the definition of penalties that is particularly remembered in traditions about the earliest lawgivers generally, notably the very earliest of them, Zaleukos of Epizephyrian Locri, probably of about the mid-seventh century,[18] who was said by the fourth-century BC historian Ephorus[19] to have defined penalties in the laws in order that the same offences should have the same penalties, whereas previously judges had imposed different penalties for the same offences. The 'precision' that Aristotle ascribes to the laws of another legendary legislator, Charondas of Katane (late sixth century?), may well have involved precision of penalties.[20] We know of early laws also from inscriptions. From Crete we have sixth-century inscriptions (and two perhaps of the late seventh) that specify penalties in cauldrons and tripods:[21] here we

---

Crawford 1982, 5–10, who follows J. M. Keynes in regarding the invention of coinage as in consequence a relatively banal next step (a false inference, in my view). A recent survey of Greek pre-coinage weight standards is by Kroll 2001a.

[15] 7D; Mørkholm 1982; Haarer 2000, 1.182–3.

[16] 2C; *Il.* 18.497–508 (esp. 499–500). The passage has been variously interpreted, most recently by Westbrook 1992. 508 seems to say that the gold will be given to a judge. I suggest that this is an insertion, or uncomprehending adaptation, and the gold was originally the compensation.

[17] For Homer see 2A (6). In a comparative study Grierson (1978) concludes that 'where societies have developed the notion of money as a general measure of value, it will, I believe, most often be found that a system of legal compensation for personal injuries, at once inviting mutual comparison and affecting every member of the community, lay behind them' (19).

[18] Adcock 1927, 101; Mühl 1928, 457–61; Dunbabin 1948, 68–75; Hölkeskamp 1999, 188 is sceptical.

[19] 70 F139 *FGrH*.

[20] *Pol.* 1274b8 (cf. 1297a22); cf. Herondas *Mim.* 2.46–8; accepted even by the sceptical Hölkeskamp 1999, 135. D. S. 13.35.4 attributes minuteness of detail concerning penalties to Diocles of Syracuse (an earlier lawgiver). Note also Pittacus of Mytilene (*c.* 650–570 BC) prescribing a greater penalty for an offence when committed drunk (Aristot. *Pol.* 1274b18–22). See in general Gagarin 1986, 64–5. Cf. also Hdt. 3.52.1: Periander, tyrant of Corinth *c.* 627–587 BC, announces a quantitative penalty (ζημίην . . . ὅσην δὴ εἶπας) to be paid to Apollo.

[21] Van Effenterre and Ruzé 1994–5, 1 nos. 12, 82, 11 nos. 11, 22, 38, 92.

have the state imposing uniformity, but the objects paid still belong to the Homeric world of prestigious *agalmata* (as well as having a sacrificial role), and are hardly practical as money. 'Staters', i.e. units of precious metal (if not coins), are required to be paid (it is unclear whether as fine or as deposit) by an inscribed law from mid-sixth-century Chios.[22] A legal inscription from Eretria of about 525 BC, which will be discussed in 7D, mentions an officially required payment in staters and payment of a fine or compensation in 'acceptable things/wealth' – probably currency.[23] A fragmentary inscription apparently from Leontini of *circa* 525 BC seems to refer to sums of money, perhaps fines.[24] Then there are numerous inscriptions from the end of the sixth century onwards, in Crete and elsewhere, in which penalties (and other kinds of payment) are specified in staters, drachmas, or mnas.[25]

In this legislation we can perceive a social process making for the development of money. Take the Solonian laws in particular, about which we have the most detail. Firstly, it seems that different kinds of payment are required to be made in the same medium (silver). This may encourage the use of silver as a *general means of payment*.[26] Secondly, the same kind of offence has always the same penalty, the various kinds of offence all have precise penalties in the same easily quantifiable units (of silver), and all this is independent of the quality, status, or will of offender, victim, or judge – the price inheres in the offence, as it were.[27] This means that along with the *definition* of compensation come *quantitative precision, uniformity*, and *depersonalisation* – a process manifest also in Solon's division of the citizen body into categories according to precise quantities of income in kind rather than by descent.[28] Further, all such penalties, being paid in amounts

[22] Van Effenterre and Ruzé 1994, I no. 62. The 'staters' in the contemporary inscription *SGDI* IV 4. n. 49 (4D) are probably units of weight: Manganaro 1974, 72.
[23] χρέματα δόκιμα. Here again, as in all early inscriptions, it is uncertain whether or not the reference is specifically to *coins*.
[24] *SEG* 4.64; Jeffery 1990, 242.
[25] Early instances are Van Effenterre and Ruzé 1994–5, I nos. 4, 15, 16, 23, 24, 29, 48, 59, 84, 85, 108, II no. 17. For staters, drachmas, and mnas as measures of value see I nos. 6, 7, 19, 36. Early instances of *obeloi* apparently with a monetary value are I nos. 25, 96 (Attic = *IG* I³ 4), II 1 (Attic, = *IG* I³ 2–3), 62.
[26] Cf. n. 13 above. A basic use of silver in the economy of Solonian Athens is suggested by a phrase quoted at Lysias 10.18 from one of the 'ancient laws of Solon', 'Money (*argurion*, literally small silver) to be *stasimon* (weighed out?) at whatever rate the lender may choose', which implies that lending at interest might take the form of weighing out silver: Kroll 1998, 228–9; cf. Schaps 2001.
[27] This principle is eventually made explicit at Aristot. *EN* 1132a2–7.
[28] Or perhaps the wealthiest category only: 4D. He did not go so far as to define these quantities by their monetary equivalents, preferring perhaps to anchor them in the traditional and visible practice of festival offerings: Connor 1987.

of silver, belong to the same mathematical scale as things of quite different kinds – state rewards and the values of various sacrificial animals. Silver is becoming a *general measure of value*.

Note also the crucial role of the *state* in this process. Some of the laws specify penalties to be paid both to the injured party and 'to the public' (treasury)[29] – the former, which is the historically earlier kind of payment, is compensation, whereas the latter is a fine. Like the temple, the state exacts contributions and fines, keeps the money in a public treasury, and spends it (notably on buying sacrificial animals). The Aristotelian *Constitution of the Athenians* reports (8.3) that in the laws of Solon no longer in use it is frequently written that 'the *naukraroi* are to exact' and 'to spend out of the naukraric silver'.[30] Stores of precious metal had existed in sanctuaries from the eighth century (3B). But the first evidence for precious metal stored by the state, and indeed for the purpose of payments, is in the Solonian legislation. It seems that silver has also become a *means of storing value*. And so the Solonian laws provide some evidence for silver performing all four money functions (1C), albeit not for performing all four functions *generally* and *exclusively*. However, because the polis is an interlocking system of communal practices, institutions, and beliefs, we may conjecture that polis laws specifying monetary payments provided the communal authority required for the communal confidence in (the future acceptability of) money that was in turn required for its adoption as a general and eventually exclusive means of payment and exchange.

If, as seems likely, coinage spread in Greek Asia Minor from the late seventh or early sixth century and in the mainland from about the middle of the sixth century (7B), then from the evidence so far assembled we may infer that precious metal was used as money before the advent of coinage. This is what we might have expected *a priori*: the very rapid development of precious metal coinage seems to presuppose an existing familiarity with precious metal money.[31] Solon's observation that the desire for *chrēmata* is

---

[29] F32, 33, 36, 65 Ruschenbusch 1966.

[30] The *naukraroi* were officials whose power over Athens even before the time of Solon emerges from Hdt. 5.71.

[31] In this I agree with Kroll (2001a) not Schaps (2001). Kim 2001, 15–20 discusses, as considerations in favour of pre-coinage silver money, uncoined pieces of silver – some very small – found along with coins in early hoards, and the high level of sophistication apparent already in early coin-weighing systems, especially at weights of under a gram. The rarity of pre-coinage discoveries of Hacksilber in Greek lands (in contrast to the Near East) is convincingly explained by Kroll 1998, 229–30 and 2000. Unstamped pieces of electrum do in fact occur with coins in the famous hoard (pre-mid-sixth century) at Ephesus (7B), and in another sixth-century hoard, 'discovered very probably in Ionia', in Tel Aviv (Le Rider 2001, 36). See also Furtwängler 1986, 156 on finds from eighth century BC Knossos (gold and silver) and Eretria (gold) of *c.* 700 BC.

unlimited suggests that the *chrēmata* is money (8F). It was this new unlimit that created the severe crisis of indebtedness that he was appointed to resolve.

What is an *ethical* problem in the *Theognidea* – the power of money to displace all other values – takes an almost *metaphysical* form in the saying of Pythermus (sixth century, from Teos near Ephesus) that 'the things other than gold were after all nothing'.[32] Certainly metaphysical in its implication is the famous statement of Heraclitus of Ephesus that 'all things are an exchange (*antamoibē*) for fire and fire for all things just as goods (*chrēmata*) are for gold and gold for goods',[33] for gold here as a *universal means of exchange*[34] is a model for the cosmic role of fire, which is for Heraclitus constitutive of the cosmos in some sense as well as being the agent of transformation within it (12A). Illustrating the actual role of gold in Ephesus, probably not long before the birth of Heraclitus, is our fragmentary inscription (4D) from the temple of Artemis. It records silver and gold 'weighed out' from a wide variety of commodities or activities (the polis, the wood, the salt, etc.). A variety is reduced to a single thing, precious metal.[35] It is true that the metal is twofold, silver and gold. But one section of the inscription seems to express, in mnas of pure gold, the combined total of the mnas of silver and gold listed.[36] If so, everything – even the silver – is reduced in a sense to (pure) gold. Still in Ephesus, we find the late sixth-century Hipponax reproaching Zeus for not giving him gold and silver, and complaining that the god Wealth '. . . for he is very blind, has never come to my house and said "Hipponax, I give you thirty mnas of

---

[32] *PMG* 910. The date in the sixth century (if not before) comes from the fact that the saying was quoted either by Hipponax of Ephesus or by Ananios (see Ananios fr. 2 West), both sixth-century poets.

[33] Fr. 90 DK. Musti (1980–1) argues that *chrēmata* here means coins (as opposed to gold bullion). But (a) *chrēmata* cannot mean coins as opposed to bullion, especially so early (Musti refers to the Eretrian inscription I discuss in 7D – but if this does refer to coinage, it is by virtue of the qualification *dokima*); (b) *antamoibē* means exchange not (as required by Musti's idea) transformation; (c) Musti's idea is inconsistent with Heraclitus' emphasis on universality ('all things'); (d) the evidence for the transformation by Greeks of Greek coinage into bullion is at best sparse (7D – unsurprisingly, given that coinage was generally worth more than bullion), and could not conceivably have been the continuous process that Musti implies. *Pace* Vannicelli (1985), Hdt. 3.90–6 does not imply that Darius constantly transformed coin into bullion, as his tribute was most unlikely to be in coins.

[34] In Heraclitus' lifetime electrum (called 'gold') coinage was being replaced by silver coinage. 'The final manifestation of electrum coinage in Ionia proper' (Kraay 1976, 30) was a series of staters on the 'Milesian-Lydian' standard (used by Ephesus) with obverse types from various cities, that has been connected with the Ionian revolt (500–494 BC). Presumably Heraclitus chose to say 'gold' rather than 'silver' in part for its associations (notably with immortality: 2C). Gold bullion continued to have exchange-value after the decline of electrum coinage.

[35] Even earlier is *SEG* 12.391 (early sixth century), which lists as dedications to Hera a golden Gorgo, a silver Siren, and an iron lamp, 'all (worth) two hundred Samian staters with the stone'.

[36] With a silver-to-gold ratio of 14.5 to 1: Manganaro 1974, 63.

silver and many other things"'.[37] This is an early reflection of the apparently impersonal arbitrariness of the distribution of money: impersonal money is, if imagined in terms of the old interpersonal gift-giving, blind – like Wealth in Aristophanes' *Wealth*.

Finally, in Herodotus' picture of the sixth century, precious metal is able to pay for the multifarious goods and skills required to build a magnificent temple, or a magnificent wall, to pay a doctor, obtain an Olympic victory in the chariot race, buy whole islands, hire mercenaries, win wars, or even seem enough whereby to 'rule the whole of Greece'.[38]

The Greeks probably inherited at least some of the money functions of precious metal from the ancient Near East (chapter 15). But it was only among the Greeks that it performed (already in the sixth century) all four functions with the degree of generality that allows us to call it money. It is also significant that in so far as Homer indicates an economy divided into separate spheres of exchange, with precious metal in the sphere of prestige goods (2B), then already in the sixth century this had in some areas been transcended by precious metal money – some of it in the form of tiny coins of small value (7C) – as a universal means of exchange.[39]

B   MONEY IN THE FIFTH CENTURY

We know more about Greek money in the fifth century than in the sixth. This is partly because of the increased importance of money (especially in the form of coinage), and partly because of the survival of more substantial texts. In particular, works of historiography, comedy, and oratory illuminate in detail, from the perspectives peculiar to each genre, the workings of money. I will confine myself to a small selection of this evidence from texts of the fifth century (though straying occasionally into the very early fourth) so as to consider in turn our four functions of money – storage of wealth, means of payment, means of exchange, and measure of value.

(a) The most striking example of precious metal as a *store of wealth* is provided by the speeches attributed by Thucydides to Pericles and to the Spartan king Archidamus at the beginning of the Peloponnesian war. Pericles encourages the Athenians by listing their financial resources: 'from

---

[37] Frr. 36, 38. Cf also fr. 32.

[38] Hdt. 1.61 (see also [Aristot.] *Ath. Pol.* 15.2), 64, 154, 163; 2.180; 3.45, 54, 59, 122–3, 131; 6.125. Cf. also Hdt. 3.143 (all Maiandrios wants to keep is six talents and a priesthood), and Thuc. 1.13 on the importance of *chrēmata* in the time of the tyrants.

[39] Early (post-Homeric) spheres or 'institutions' using money (dowries, fines, prizes, etc.) are analysed by von Reden 1997. As Howgego 1995, 14–15 notes, what is significant, and requires explanation, is that the same medium of exchange came to be used in all these spheres.

the allies an average of six hundred talents annual tribute for the polis (besides the other income), six thousand talents of coined silver kept on the Acropolis, as well as uncoined silver and gold in private and public dedications and all the sacred vessels used in processions and in contests and the Persian spoils and all that sort of thing – not less than five hundred talents' (2.13.3–5). He adds 'no small sum of money from the other temples', and forty talents weight of refined gold on the statue of Athena (only for an emergency, and to be restored if removed).

In order to be militarily effective the wealth has to have been (publicly) *stored*: 'it is reserves (*periousiai*) rather than violent exactions that sustain wars', observes Pericles.[40] The Athenians' public surplus of precious metal is, despite the variety of its forms and its traditional protection by the temple, entirely liquid – as Pericles notes of Athena's statue.[41]

Most or all of this money (coined and uncoined) was to be found in *sanctuaries*.[42] It is claimed in Aristophanes that the Athenians will continue to fight 'so long as they have that boundless money with the goddess' (*Lysistrata* 174). Thucydides also reports emphasis on the military potential of the treasures in the sanctuaries of Olympia, Delphi, and Selinous.[43] Two generations earlier Hecataeus had advised the Ionians, in revolt from Persia, to use the temple treasure at Branchidae to gain control of the sea (Hdt. 5.36). The crucial concentration of monetary wealth generally in the sanctuaries of the city-states, at the disposal of the community,[44] can be related to the earlier developments described in chapters 3 and 4: the growth of durable wealth at the place of the communal sacrificial meal resulted eventually in considerable communal wealth in the form of precious metal stored in sanctuaries.[45]

Our second, quite different example of money as a store of wealth is also provided by Pericles, who was said[46] to have decided that the easiest and most precise way of running his household was to sell all his annual

---

[40] 1.141 (cf. *periousia* in 2.13). The point is that soldiers on campaign cannot afford absence from their homes and expenditure from their private resources, and moreover will risk their bodies more than their money because they feel more likely to lose the latter (1.141). The difficulty of raising money from individuals is admitted by the Spartan king Archidamus (1.80). On money in Thuc. see Kallet–Marx 1993.

[41] Athenian minting of temple treasure: 6B n. 53.

[42] Gomme ad Thuc. 2.13.3 ἐν τῇ ἀκροπόλει; and esp. Meiggs and Lewis 1988, no. 58; Harris 1995.

[43] It is the money in the sanctuaries of Delphi and Olympia that gives the Corinthians the hope of tempting away Athens' foreign sailors (1.121, 143; cf. 4.118.3; for Selinous see 6.20.4).

[44] Ampolo 1990.

[45] This may be a factor behind the idea that all wealth belongs to the gods (Eur. *Phoen.* 555–7).

[46] Plut. *Per.* 16.

crops as a whole, and then to buy from the marketplace each thing that was needed, with the result that every expense and receipt involved number and measure. Presumably then Pericles kept a large store of silver in his house. The text implies that this lack of abundant supplies in kind was unusual in a wealthy household (perhaps Pericles was applying his economic statecraft to his own household, or needed cash to win political favour). On the other hand, by the time of the pseudo-Aristotelian *Oeconomica* I (late fourth century BC) the Attic household economy is distinguished from the Persian and the Laconian: in Attica they sell their produce and buy what they want, and so in the smaller houses have no need of a storehouse (1344b31). According to Lysias, Pericles' contemporary Nicias was thought to have almost a hundred talents in his house.[47] And Lysias himself claims to have been robbed of three talents of silver, four hundred cyzicenes (staters), a hundred darics, and four silver cups – all kept in a chest in his bedroom.[48] It was fear of loss in the unstable conditions of early sixth-century Ionia that made a Milesian turn half his property (*ousia*) into silver and deposit it with a Spartan (Hdt. 6.86). The prudent practice of burying coins has given us hoards from as early as the sixth century, and is attributed by Aristophanes to 'the ancestors'.[49]

(b) The emphasis on the vital military importance of precious metal implies its power to perform the broad range of *payments* (and exchanges) that warfare involves. A crucial form of military expenditure was the use of coinage to pay soldiers and sailors.[50] Already in the sixth century Peisistratus, we are reliably informed, in the obtaining of tyranny at Athens used silver to hire troops.[51] The consequent need to make uniform payments of small pieces of silver acceptable to numerous individuals might well have been a crucial factor in the decision to mint coins.[52] We are also reliably informed that Peisistratus used silver to *consolidate* his tyranny (Hdt. 1.64). This suggests that convenience of coinage in payments by a central administration was not confined to military pay. Peisistratus may well also have

---

[47] Cf. Plut. *Nic.* 4.2: he had most of his property in money (*argurion*). Nicias' son when dying claimed that he was not leaving any silver and gold *Lys.* 19.47).

[48] 12.10–11; see also 19.22; Ar. *Wealth* 808–9. Eupolis fr. 162 refers to robbery of gold and silver from a house. The word ἀργυροθήκη (silver/money chest) first appears in Diocles fr.15 K–A.

[49] *Birds* 599–602; see further 14E n. 95.

[50] E.g. Thuc. 3.17; 5.47; 6.31; 7.27; 8.29, 45.

[51] [Aristot.] *Ath. Pol.* 15.2: he went to the area around Mt Pangaios [where there were rich silver ores], 'from where having acquired money (χρηματισάμενος) and hired soldiers . . .'; see also Hdt. 1.61, 64.

[52] 7B. At Athens the production of fractions began with the earliest minting of coins: Kim 1994, 41–2; 2001, 12–13.

paid in coinage the workers on his building programme and the expenses of state sacrifices.[53] In the fifth century Athens made payments in coinage for building work, for large amounts of sacrificial meat distributed *gratis* in state festivals,[54] as well as for military, political, and judicial service. The importance of these payments is illustrated by their frequent mention in Aristophanes.[55] There were pensions for the disabled,[56] and distributions (at least in the fourth century) of precious metal from the so-called theoric fund.[57] In archaic Siphnos resources of silver were distributed annually to the citizens, and such distribution, from the silver mines at Laurium, was proposed in Athens in 483 BC. Another collective distribution at Athens was of the lead and bronze stamped *sumbola*, embodying for citizens the right to jury-pay, seating, and so on.[58]

These distributions may well derive, at least in part, from the same powerful tradition of communal sacrifice[59] that we have seen behind the storage of precious metal in communal sanctuaries and indeed as a factor in the development of Greek money, a tradition powerful enough (chapters 3 and 4) to persist from the vital ancient practice of sacrificial distribution at a communal centre into the storage and distribution of the relatively new kind of wealth (precious metal).[60] This need for *uniform* payment of large numbers of people derives from ancient tradition, and yet may have been an important factor in the revolutionary invention of coinage. The ancient

---

[53] Thuc. 6.54.5; Rutter 1981, 2; Martin 1996, 272–3. On tyrants and building projects see Aristot. *Pol.* 1313b.

[54] E.g. 5,114 drachmas were spent on the hekatomb at the Greater Panathenaea of 410/9 BC (*IG*³ 375.7). See further 3D.

[55] E.g. *Acharnians* 66, *Clouds* 863–4, *Wasps* 607, 609, 690, 1121, *Knights* 51, 255, 798, 800, 1350–3, *Eccles.* 186, 292, 305b, 380, 392. Cf. Plut. *Per.* 12.4 on 'almost the entire polis . . . receiving wages' under Pericles; [Aristot.] *Ath. Pol.* 24; see Rutter 1981, and for bibliography see Burke 1992, 215–18. Military pay by the Athenian democracy began at some time between the Persian and the Peloponnesian wars: Pritchett 1971, 7–14. For state pay in other city-states see de Ste Croix 1975 and 1981, 289–90, 602–3; Gauthier 1993, 232 n. 3.

[56] Lysias devotes an entire speech (24) to supporting a claim for a state disability allowance of a single obol per day; cf. [Aristot.] *Ath. Pol.* 49.4.

[57] Apart from the pension for the disabled, none of all this is poor relief, but rather for all citizens. A general account is Buchanan 1962; theoric fund: Parker 1996, 220. The aim of Xenophon's proposed economic reforms is to supply every Athenian with adequate public maintenance (*Poroi* 4.33).

[58] Rhodes 1981, 711–12, 731; Kroll 1993, 24.

[59] Plutarch (*Mor.* 556F–557A) reports the tradition that Aesop came to Delphi with some gold from Croesus intending to make a magnificent sacrifice to the god and to distribute four mnas to each of the Delphians. For inscriptional and later literary evidence for similar distributions see Latte 1948.

[60] This persistence is implicit in Aristophanes' joke at *Knights* 255 φράτερες τριωβόλου, 'brethren of the three-obol', which implies the kind of solidarity expressed in the sacrifice performed by the ancient institution of the phratry: e.g. Lambert S. 1993, 205–22. For the treasurers of Athena making distributions of money to Athenian citizens in the fifth century see Rhodes 1981, 355.

tradition is given a new and powerfully effective form by the invention of coinage.

When observing the evidence for this ancient tradition in Homer we distinguished between two forms of distribution among the group, one performed by the group itself, the other by a powerful or wealthy individual (3A). The former form persists into historical Athens in the democratic distributions just described, the latter in the payments by Peisistratus and then, with democracy, in the funding by wealthy individuals of liturgies as well as in the largesse exemplified by the open house kept by Cimon. It is significant that Pericles was said[61] to have introduced jury-pay in demagogic rivalry with Cimon's use of his great personal ('tyrannical') wealth in patronage. The use of personal wealth to obtain political power had reached an extreme form in tyranny at Athens and elsewhere. But at Athens at least the form was extreme enough to contain the means of its reversal. Peisistratus' control of the communal activities of warfare, building, and sacrifice was according to Thucydides (6.54.5) enabled by his imposition of a 5 per cent income tax. Presumably not only the communal *expenditure* but also the uniform *contributions* thereto were greatly facilitated by the associated processes of the centralisation of the polis and its pervasion by small uniform pieces of monetary value (coins). The development of centralised taxation (in coinage) out of individual liturgies is indicated by a report[62] that Peisistratus' successor Hippias set, for whoever was about to perform a liturgy, a *timēma* (evaluation, payment, fine), and told him to pay it (if willing) and be enrolled among those who had performed liturgies. But this centralised use of coinage both for expenditure (notably uniform mass payments) and for contributions (liturgies, taxes)[63] must have facilitated – after the fall of the tyranny – the control of the financial system by the democracy, which was thereby able to distance such crucial institutions as the military and the law courts from the influence of personal patronage.[64] Another form of payment made in coinage, in classical Athens, was rent.[65] Whereas in the Near-Eastern temple and palace economies the circulation of goods (contribution, storage, redistribution) had been enforced by a personal central authority (deity, king), in the Greek polis it was achieved

---

[61] In a tradition preserved at [Aristot.] *Ath. Pol.* 27.3.

[62] [Aristot.] *Oecon.* II (1347a10–14), probably written in the last quarter of the fourth century by a student of the Lyceum: van Groningen and Wartelle 1968, xiii. The passage is given some credence by Wilson 2000, 15. See also Polyaenus 3.10.14.

[63] Martin 1996.

[64] Even though speakers frequently refer to their liturgies so as to gain favour with the jury: Millett 1998.

[65] 3D; Davies 1984, 54–5.

(in the urban centres at least) by the impersonal intermediary of small pieces of stamped metal.[66]

(c) Old Comedy allows us to see the use of coinage for a wide range of everyday *exchanges* – for small amounts of food,[67] for sex,[68] for a signet-ring,[69] to pay the fuller,[70] and so on[71] – what Plato will call 'coinage (*nomisma*) for daily exchange'.[72] It is a joke that someone in Athens from outside the Greek world, a Scythian, does not have a drachma to pay for sex.[73] Coins are carried in purse[74] or mouth.[75] And small change is needed, what is called 'cut up money' (*argurion . . . kekermatismenon*) by Aristophanes (fr. 215), who also even uses the word *akermatia*, 'lack of small change' (fr. 14). A coin or token of especially low value, probably of bronze, is the *kollubon* or *kollubos* (7D). The widespread power of low-value coins is made into a joke in Dionysus' reaction to the two-obol fare payable to Charon: 'what great power the two obols have everywhere'.[76]

(d) If something operates as a general means of payment and exchange, as we have seen metal to do in the fifth century, then it can hardly fail to operate also as a general *measure of value*. Aristotle can say that currency (*nomisma*) 'measures everything', and defines *chrēmata* as 'all things of which the value is measured by currency (*nomisma*)'.[77] Rather than accumulate examples, I note two respects in which the monetary measurement of value takes a relatively advanced form. The first is the (inevitable) tendency to overall monetary valuation of an accumulation of various items (exemplified already in the sixth century by the list from the temple at

---

[66] Cf. Martin 1996, 268–9, 276. This does not of course mean that the polis did not keep account of income and expenditure.

[67] Ar. *Acharnians* 960–2, *Peace* 254, *Frogs* 561, *Eccles.* 815–22.

[68] Ar. *Thesm.* 1195–7, *Frogs* 148, *Wealth* 154, Eupolis fr. 247.

[69] Ar. *Thesm.* 425.   [70] Ar. *Wasps* 1128.

[71] A survey of money in Aristophanes is Burelli 1973. On the prices of various containers in a group of inscriptions of 414/3 BC see Amyx 1958, 275–310. This evidence is mainly for urban life. To what extent had money penetrated the Attic countryside? Ar. *Acharnians* 33–6 implies the absence of trade there (though cf. *Peace* 1202). Osborne (1991) argues, on the basis of mainly fourth-century evidence, for the need of wealthy landowners to sell their produce for cash, to pay for, dowries, liturgies, funerals, taxes, and so on (obligations already there in the fifth century). See also Humphreys 1978, 173; Cohen 1992, 6; Meiggs and Lewis 1988, 146–7. The problem is of secondary concern to my overall argument, which is about *urban* culture.

[72] *Laws* 742a. For the universality of money as a means of exchange made explicit (as earlier by Heraclitus) see e.g. *Laws* 849e.

[73] Ar. *Thesm.* 1195–7.   [74] Ar. *Knights* 1197.   [75] Ar. *Wasps* 609, 791, *Birds* 503, *Eccles.* 818.

[76] Ar. *Frogs* 141 (there is an allusion to the *diobeleia* – the two-obol dole). Cf. Trygaios' chance of eternal mystic bliss depending on three drachmas for a sacrificial pig (Ar. *Peace* 375–6; cf. *Eccles.* 412–13). An inscription dated to before 460 BC specifies obol-payments to be made by Eleusinian initiands (*IG* I³ 6).

[77] *EN* 1133a21, 1133b22 (cf. 1133b15); 1119b27.

Ephesus, 4D): Athens' income from empire,[78] a meal for an army,[79] a man's entire property,[80] the cargo of a ship, the cost of bringing up children, or the cost of all the radishes, onions, and garlic consumed by the builders of the Great Pyramid,[81] and so on. Such evaluation is, like everything else in this section, something that we take for granted, but is not to be found (say) accompanying the numerous lists of valuable objects in Homer.[82] The second respect is the tendency to describe the quantity or quality of a thing in terms of money: the moon with its light saves people a drachma per month in torches; someone knocks over ten obols' worth of loaves; the council is won over with an obol's worth of coriander; meat is distributed in half-obol portions; someone is to get a 'twenty mna banquet'; someone is 'worth a talent'; and so on.[83]

As well as performing our four functions, money in the fifth century, at least in Athens, possessed the three further features that we noted (1C) as characteristic of modern money. One was the role of the *state* in its issue and acceptability: although not all states issued coins, coins were issued by the state, which is also sometimes seen enforcing their acceptability (7D). Another was *exclusive* (as well as general) acceptability as money: in the Greek city-states there was on the whole nothing other than metal (coined or uncoined) that was used as money.[84] The third was what I call *fiduciarity* (defined in 1A): that this was from the beginning an important feature of Greek coinage will be shown in 7D.

---

[78] Ar. *Wasps* 656–60.   [79] Hdt. 7.118.

[80] E.g. Lys. 3.24: 'he valued his entire property at 250 drachmas' (also 17.7; 19.40, 46–7).

[81] Lys. 32.25; 32.20, 29; Hdt. 2.125.

[82] Though at *Od.* 1.431 Laertes gives for Eurycleia 'things worth 20 oxen' (what the things are is not stated).

[83] Ar. *Clouds* 612, *Wasps* 1391, *Knights* 681–2, *Frogs* 554; Lysias fr. 19; Crates fr. 36 (ταλαντιαῖος: cf. the adjective δραχμιαῖος, 'worth a drachma', at Ar. fr. 438).

[84] This does not of course mean that all exchanges involved money. The extent of barter is (now as then) difficult to measure. Note barter, in special circumstances, at Ar. *Acharnians* 811–17, 895–905; and n. 71 above.

CHAPTER SIX

The preconditions of coinage

A SACRIFICIAL SPITS

The Greeks themselves were aware that their coin of low value the obol (*obolos*) took its name from the spit (*obelos*), and that 'drachma' meant originally a handful of (six) spits.[1] Six obol *coins* do not make a handful. As we shall see, it is almost certain that 'drachma' can refer to spits in sixth-century inscriptions; and 'handfuls of spits' (*obeliskōn drachmai*) are recorded in an early fourth century BC temple inventory.[2] In early inscriptions the coin is refered to *obelos*, to be generally replaced later by *obolos*.[3]

This apparent transition from roasting spits to coins was, along with other terms that seem to embody the transition from the sacrificial to the financial (4D), adduced by Laum as part of an argument to the effect that animal sacrifice was an important factor in the genesis of coinage. The public sanctuary becomes, with the development of substitutes (such as figurines) for animal victims, a centre of exchange. And the communal distribution of sacrificial meat – to warrior, priest, prize-winner, etc. – is, he argues, the earliest form of polis finance. Of Laum's complex argument I can here give only this brief summary. Although he did in various details go too far, his basic insight has on the whole suffered neglect rather than refutation.[4] In the course of my overall argument I modify and develop it in line with my overall concern with the distinctiveness of Greek culture.

A consideration that was not yet fully available to Laum is the discovery of numerous actual iron spits from tombs and sanctuaries in various

---

[1] Aristot. *Sicyon.Const.* fr. 481, 580 Rose ap. Pollux 9.77. *ARV*[2] 554.82 shows a bundle of six identical spits filling the grasp of a hand, though other paintings show four or five (Haarer 2000, 1.137).

[2] From Chorsiai in Boeotia: Melville Jones 1993, no. 39; Tomlinson 1980, 221–3.

[3] Threatte 1980, 215; Haarer 2000, 1.144. It is not impossible that the earliest occurrence of *obelos* meaning a coin is from mid sixth-century Attica: 7B n. 40.

[4] The most effectively critical review known to me is Blinkenberg 1926. Recent interest is manifest in a conference on Laum published as Parise 1997.

parts of the Greek world.[5] I limit myself to a few examples. First, in the
Argive Heraion was discovered a bundle of iron spits, now estimated as
approximately a hundred in number, along with a heavy iron bar that, with
its disk-like bulge at one end, seems to have been made in the form of an
(oversize) spit.[6] The likelihood that the spits were a dedication is confirmed
by their being bound together and fixed into a lead disc. Their date can be
made no more precise than the period *c.* 690 to *c.* 550 BC.[7] Second, from
Perachora there survive on a stele the initial words of a verse inscription,
apparently from the first half of the sixth century: 'A drachma, I, Hera of
the white [arms . . .'.[8] 'Drachma' refers to a set of spits, for the stele had
cuttings for clamps, probably for holding spits in a vertical position. Third,
another inscription (now lost) of about the same period, from near Delphi,
refers to the dedication of *dra*[. . .]*s* to Athena and Hera by Phanaristos 'so
that he too might have immortal fame'. The supplement *dra*[*chma*]*s*[9] has
been challenged, but is supported by the drawing of the base, which has
on it a small round hole, well suited for holding spits.[10] We may compare
the report of Herodotus (2.135) that you could still see a tenth part of the
chrēmata (money/wealth) of the courtesan Rhodopis (mid-sixth century)
dedicated at Delphi in the form of iron spits.[11]

Neither these examples nor any of the other finds of spits demonstrate
that spits had any monetary function. The large iron bar found in the
Argive Heraion, spit-like but too large to function as a spit, may have been
a (large denomination) monetary unit.[12] There is a tendency for the spits,
especially those found in tombs, to occur in groups (or multiples) of six,[13]
prefiguring perhaps six obols to a drachma, but there are also sets of spits in
other numbers.[14] Inscriptional evidence for payment in spits is very slight

---

[5] There are recent (brief) discussions of the spits by von Reden 1997, 159–60 and Tandy 1997, 159–61.
By far the best and most comprehensive account is by Haarer (2000), who also discusses recent
finds, e.g. a large number of miniature spits found in sixth-century tombs at Sindos in Macedonia.
Strøm (1992) is to be treated with caution.

[6] See esp. Courbin 1983; Strøm 1992, 45.   [7] Haarer 2000, 1.82.

[8] Hansen 1983, no. 354: Δραχμὰ ἐγὼ Ἥρα λευκ[ώλενε . . .; Haarer 2000, 1.93; Jeffery 1990, 121–3.

[9] I.e. δρα[χμα]ς· Raubitschek 1950; in fact he less cautiously prints δρα[χμ]ας.

[10] Strøm 1992, 49. And note the reconstruction by Haarer 2000, 1.94–6. Cf. Hansen 1983, no. 344: he
does not mention the hole and reads δραϝεός.

[11] 8c. For spits dedicated at Delphi see also Epicharmus fr. 79 Kaibel.

[12] So Kroll 2001a. It has been imagined to be a standard weight, but Kroll points out that 'certifiable
Greek weights are normally square or have some other compact shape'.

[13] Strøm 1992; Haarer 2000, 1.54–5, cf. also 156 (inscriptions); Lo Porto 1987; Courbin 1959, 218
calculated that the Argive Heraion dedication contained maximum 96 spits (i.e. 16 drachmai), but
cf. Haarer 2000, 1.86. As for the reason for six, Courbin (1983), refers to the Greek use of the
duodecimal system, Strøm (1992), to the practice of groups of six people dining together.

[14] Note esp. the five spits found together at Paestum, corresponding it seems to the Homeric
pempōbolon: Kron 1971, 131–44.

and confined to Crete.[15] No more helpful is the ancient view that spits were once used as money or its precursors,[16] for it may have been instigated by the etymology of obol.

But are there reasons for believing that iron spits were the kind of objects that could function as money, or at least perform one or more money functions to some extent? The answer to this question is an emphatic yes, which when taken together with the etymology of obol and drachma makes it almost certain that the spits played a role in the development of Greek money.[17]

The characteristics that qualify iron spits to perform money functions are *portability, countability, durability*, economic *value* that is neither too great nor too small, *standardisation* of shape and size, *mass production*, the kind of familiarity that creates *communal confidence*, and *substitutability* for other objects.[18] Of these the first three, which all inhere in the spits themselves, require no further discussion. The other five are conferred by social context.

As for the *value* of the spits, Courbin (1959) calculated that if an iron spit of the size found in the Argive Heraion was equal in value to the Aeginetan obol, this implies that iron was less valuable than silver in the ratio 1:2,000. Haarer has discovered errors in Courbin's calculation, and would prefer a ratio of 1: 922–1078.[19] But 'even these numbers', claims Haarer, 'would be much too high. Near-Eastern textual evidence of the Neo-Babylonian

---

[15] Melville Jones 1993, nn. 44 and 45, which may indicate spits as fines.

[16] (a) Plut. *Lys.* 17 iron spits used early as coinage. (b) Pollux 7.105 iron spits as the currency of the Spartans and Byzantines; cf. the cessation of finds of iron spits in the Spartan sanctuary of Artemis Orthia in the early third century BC, about the time Sparta first minted its own coins: Hodkinson 2000, 162. (c) Plut. *Fab. Max.* 27 illustrates the 'poverty' of Epaminondas by the report that his only possession at death was an iron spit. (d) Heraclides Pont. (fr. 152 Wehrli) ap. *Et. Magn., Et.Orionis* s.v. ὀβελίσκος; also Melville Jones 1993, nos. 27–9: king Pheidon of Argos, when he minted the first coins, withdrew the spits and dedicated them to Hera at Argos. This has been connected by modern scholars with the spits found dedicated in the Argive Heraion.

[17] Haarer 2000, 1.187 concludes that 'we do not exclude the possibility or probability that [spits] belonged to the wide and varied repertoire of goods which do seem to have functioned as precoinage money in its broadest sense', but also suggests (181–6) that coins were named after *obeloi* and *drachmai* as a result of the *visual analogy* supplied by bundles of six spits. The analogy would however be neither likely to suggest itself nor effective in aiding memory, for (as Haarer himself notes) six was not the only typical number of spits in a bundle; whereas (on the view I favour) in deciding on the definitive value of a drachma coin one of the typical numbers of spits had to be chosen (and the number six had advantages). If *merely* a visual analogy was required, more familiar and more uniform would be e.g. the hand and its fingers. Haarer adds that spits were suggested perhaps because the rectilinear punchmark on some early coins may have been made by a spit-like tool, but recognises the difficulties in this view (e.g. the rectilinear punchmark is not confined to the obol).

[18] In deciding what qualifies an object to perform money functions, we can observe the large range of monetary substances and objects (including instruments) that have been so used in various societies world-wide: Quiggin 1963; Einzig 1966.

[19] The ratio given in a much later discussion of the old Spartan iron currency at Plut. *Mor.* 226D is 1:1,200 (assuming that he means the Aeginetan obol), dismissed by Haarer 2000, 1.168.

period (612–547 BC) indicates that in Babylon silver was exchanged for iron at ratios of 1:831, 1:573, and even as much as 1:229. In Lebanon the rate was 1:361, and in a place almost certainly identified as Cyprus it stood at 1:240.' He finds confirmation for this conclusion in a mid-fourth century inscription from Delphi, which preserves the minimum and maximum prices for iron, giving iron–silver ratios of 1:435 and 1:100.[20]

This is however not enough to exclude the possibility that at some point in time and place an iron spit was equivalent in value to a silver obol. And this equivalence, even if it obtained only briefly and in a limited area, could have been the basis for the transfer of the names *obelos* and *drachma* to specific weights or pieces of silver, which would have retained these names whatever the subsequent history of the iron–silver ratio. Haarer's point does not take account of the likelihood that the supply of silver among the Greeks increased greatly in the sixth century (6B), and that this increase might have been much greater than any decrease in the value of iron. And so all later evidence – for instance the Delphic inscription adduced by Haarer from the fourth century, when silver had become very common – is irrelevant.[21] In Homer silver is rare, especially as bullion (2C), whereas in the Neo-Babylonian texts, which Haarer uses for comparison, it is extremely common (15F). If the names *obelos* and *drachma* were transferred to coins when coins were first used in mainland Greece (say Aegina in 575 BC), then we cannot know that at that time and place an iron spit was not roughly equivalent in value to a silver obol. And it is not inconceivable that, even earlier, the names were transferred to amounts or pieces of silver (obol and drachma also mean weights), from which they were subsequently inherited by coins. Iron was of the right order of value to embody monetary value in spit form. That is to say, spits could be produced in large numbers, but not *too* cheaply – until the increasing supply of iron, resulting in a decrease in its value in relation to most commodities (though not necessarily silver), probably became a factor in its loss of money functions to the much more valuable and so much less bulky silver.

Next, *standardisation* of shape and size. Spits may of course vary in weight. They have, unsurprisingly, been found in different sizes at different periods and from different areas, although some evidence of a standard size has been claimed for the Argolid.[22] They are easier to carry than unformed lumps, and no less easy to weigh. But it is possible that rough conformity

---

[20] Haarer 2000, 1.86–92, cf. 157.
[21] The price of a sheep in Solon's laws was reported to be one drachma (4D), whereas the price of a sheep in sacrificial calendars of the first half of the fourth century is from twelve to fifteen drachmas.
[22] Strøm (1992, 42, with further references) claims that three separate tombs in Argos of the late eighth century BC have each produced spits of the same length (1.65m); but cf. Haarer 2000, 1.54–5; II.56.

to a roughly standard size was sufficient to inspire confidence in their value without weighing,[23] rather as the mark on the coin was to do later. This is where our sixth characteristic, familiarity creating *communal confidence*, is important. Iron was used for various artefacts, and spits would be familiar to all from the sacrificial meals, which were often on a large scale, requiring a multiplicity of spits.[24] And we would expect all the spits used in a sacrificial meal to be of the same size. This expectation is confirmed by vase-paintings, which sometimes show identical spits in use[25] and sometimes bundles of (four, five, or six) identical spits being carried in one hand.[26] Given that spitted portions of the sacrificed meat, or sometimes no doubt the spits themselves,[27] were distributed, the natural tendency to standard size (whether of spits or of tea cups) would have been reinforced by the powerful tradition, manifest even in the aristocratic Homeric epic, of equal portions of the sacrificed meat (2E, 3A). Standardisation – in large-scale sacrifices such as those of deme, phratry, and polis – has a vital social meaning familiar to all.

This sacrificial context also confers *mass production, communal confidence*, and *substitutability*. The importance of communal participation ensured that (even allowing for the use of wooden spits) standard iron spits were produced in large numbers, perhaps within the sanctuaries.[28] And the religious significance of the sacrifice – the emotional dramatisation of the collective contact with deity, the solemn respect for others inherent in the ordered distribution – invests the implements of sacrifice, including

---

[23] Especially as the form of the spits 'necessitated that metal of good quality in terms of its ability to be forged was used for their manufacture' (Haarer 2000, 1.231, 197–200).

[24] 'Spits' (plural) are a regular feature of the Homeric sacrifice. The Homeric *pempōbolon* may be a collection of five spits rather than (as often supposed) a fork (Kron 1971, 131–44), but anyway occurs in Homer in the plural.

[25] E.g. on the Caere Hydria (525–500 BC) discussed and reproduced by Durand 1989; see also Haarer 2000, II. Figs. 5.A1, A.2, C.2, E.1, E.7, G.3, and others in his catalogue (II.59–76); van Straten 1995, 118, 130–6, 144–53. Cf. the chorus implied by the play title 'Similar Ones or Spit-carriers' ("Ομοιοι ἢ 'Οβελιαφόροι) by the middle comedy poet Ephippus.

[26] Haarer 2000, 1.137; II.71–3; 2. Figs 5. J6, J9, K1. He notes that bundles of spits have also been unearthed. Of the large number of spits (*circa* 100: 96?) found set at one end in lead to form a bundle dedicated in the Argive Heraion it seems that no single one has survived complete (Haarer 2000, 1.83–5, who concludes that 'all that may be said of the length of spits from the bundle is that they measured more than 142cm but less than 168cm'). They had handles of three different shapes, but this would not preclude the identical length that we might expect of a bundle. The South cemetery Area tomb 1 at Argos contained six spits, of which only two are intact, but these two are each 162 cm (Haarer 2000, II.56).

[27] Some vase-painting shows meat on spits being carried, presumably for distribution after, or elsewhere than, the sacrifice itself: Haarer 2000, 1.134. Meat served on the spit: *Od.* 14.77.

[28] Strøm 1992; Haarer 2000, 1.118–19 is rightly sceptical. Metal-working is archaeologically attested at a number of Greek sanctuaries from the late Geometric period onwards: Risberg 1992.

the spit, with communal symbolic value.[29] That is why spits are significant enough to transcend their context of use (the sacrificial meal), to be dedicated in sanctuaries and placed in tombs.

The communality and equality of sacrificial distribution remained crucial to the cohesion of the polis, and its social significance was powerful enough to have influenced basic conceptions such as law and fate (3A). But the wealth so distributed, meat, is not durable enough to be money.[30] Much more suitable are the standardised spits on which the meat is roasted. In order to account for the significance of a mere instrument, the spit, we must refer again to our earlier discussion (3C) of the tendency of the transitory act of sacrifice to find permanent embodiment in the setting up (dedication) of durable objects associated with it – the skull of the animal,[31] the cauldron, the spit, an image of the animal, and so on. The dedicatory inscription ('of Olympian Zeus') on a spit found at Olympia expresses not its metal value, which is very small, but the importance of the ritual in which an animal was sacrificed to Zeus and its meat fleetingly carried by the spit.[32] Spits have been found in various sanctuaries, in some cases from the Classical period, though 'their main period of functioning in large quantities seems to be the seventh century, perhaps beginning in the late eighth century or around 700 BC and lasting until some time in the first half of the 6th century',[33] that is to say precisely in the period leading up to the introduction of coinage into mainland Greece.

Sacrificial instruments dedicated are not merely of durable material. They also, whether regularly used in the traditional and persistent ritual or dedicated in the temple, embody *permanence* (3C). It is the prospect of permanent value that inspires the communal confidence needed for currency. Moreover they are, as dedications, not only permanent embodiments of, but also in a sense substitutions for, the animal that is sacrificed to deity but eaten by humans (3C, 4D). This paradoxical combination of permanence with *substitutability* is a precondition for currency. Substitutability is in general not exhausted in a single replacement: if a spit can be substituted for the distributed meat, or a counter for a chess piece, then so can

---

[29] Einzig in his survey of 'primitive money' produces numerous examples of the importance of religious belief and religious practice for the establishment of a currency (1966, 369–76).

[30] Although cattle sometimes serve as a measure of value (in numbers characteristic of sacrifice) in Homer (3C).

[31] Not far from the altar of Hera at Samos were buried, *c.* 600 BC, three spits together with the skull of an ox (*boukranion*): Furtwängler 1980, 97–8.

[32] Furtwängler 1980, 95. Haarer 2000, II.23 reports a view that it may not be a spit but the leg of a tripod.

[33] Strøm 1992, 47; Kron 1971, 133; Haarer 2000, I.70–2; II.44.

another symbol for the spit or counter.[34] Spits are both associated with the distributed meat and possessed of the various characteristics required for currency.[35] Their communal standardisation of shape and size provides a link between the practice of sacrifice and the communal standardisation of metal pieces that is a precondition of coinage.

All this, together with the independent etymological evidence (obol and drachma) and the sacrificial origin of other financial terms (4D), make it extremely likely that iron spits did at some time, somewhere, perform one or more of the functions of money (means of payment and exchange, measure and store of value), even if they were never a *general* means of payment and exchange.[36] They may have been prized simultaneously for their sacrificial use, as prestige objects, and for their monetary function or functions.[37]

An interesting analogy to monetary spits comes from Olbia, where according to Herodotus (4.79) the Scythian king Skyles was initiated into the mysteries of Dionysus. A number of rectangular bone plates or tablets have been discovered, some in a sanctuary area, others in residential areas. Three of them, from the fifth century BC, bear inscriptions referring to Dionysus, and one of these also has the letters OPΦIK (orphic). It has been plausibly suggested that 'the little bone tablets scattered about the town were membership tokens, bone slices symbolising participation in common sacrifices'.[38] If so, then I would add that, in relation to the transitory sacrifice, the victim's bones, sliced into pieces of roughly standard size[39] and distributed to the participants, embody *permanence*.[40] The plates show signs of use over a long period.[41] And the plate with the Dionysiac-Orphic

---

[34] This is I think the answer to what Haarer 2000, 1.160 calls an insoluble enigma: a statue base from the sanctuary of Apollo Ptoieus in Boeotia is inscribed (mid sixth century) 'I am the *obelos* of Protanios . . .' ([Π]ροτανίο ἐμὶ ὀβελός γα). It has been suggested that the statue was made from spit metal, or had the same value as a spit (Lazzarini 1979). But the point is that *obelos* was so typical an individual portion or individual dedication that it could refer, in a context of substitutability, to something else individually dedicated.

[35] Another sacrificial utensil, less suitable than the spit, that might have been used as a means of payment (in Crete) was the cauldron: Melville Jones 1993, nos. 42, 46; see further Laum 1924, 119–24; Kraay 1976, 314–15.

[36] There is no definite evidence to resolve the debate (e.g. Furtwängler 1980; Courbin 1983; Strøm 1992) about whether the various unearthed spits are 'premonetary' or 'protomonetary' or neither.

[37] Cf. the tokens called *méreaux* given to mediaeval clergymen for participation in the mass, which were passed on to laymen, looked like coins and were used in exchange: Shell 1982, 42–3.

[38] West 1983, 17–18, for whom I also rely for my description of the tablets.

[39] West 1983, 17 describes them as 'roughly rectangular . . . about five to seven cm. in length'. They may belong to widely different periods.

[40] Cf. knucklebones (*astragaloi*), which are associated with sacrifice, found in tombs and temples, used to obtain prophecies, and depicted on some of the earliest Athenian coins: Kurke 1999, 288–95. They were also sacred objects of the Dionysiac mysteries: Kern 1922, frr. 31, 34.

[41] Vinogradov 1991, 77.

inscription also has the words BIOΣ ΘANATOΣ BIOΣ (life death life): after the death and dismemberment of the sacrificial animal, which may seem to embody the death of the mystic initiand,[42] the durability of the bone may seem to embody the permanence of the happy fate of the mystic initiand as member of the *thiasos*.[43] Similarly, the only other inscriptions of mystic formulae surviving from the Classical period, some of which are remarkably similar despite being from (tombs from) different parts of the Greek world, are of gold, presumably for its association with immortality (2C, 12C). Iron rings were given to the initiates into the mysteries at Samothrace.[44] At Olbia the standard pieces of bone from the dismembered animal are dispersed among the participants, but each embodies permanent belonging to the same whole. So too coins are dispersed among the community, but each embodies permanent communally agreed value. The function of coinage, as of sacrifice, was – according to Aristotle – *koinōnia*, communality.[45]

The argument that sacrificial spits were forerunners of coinage requires there to be at least one credible account of the transition, to which we now turn our attention.

B   FROM SPIT TO COIN

We do not know what money functions were performed by spits, or to what extent. And so we do not know how exactly obols and drachmas inherited their names from spits. If spits had been used as a medium of payment and exchange, then precious metal may have gradually replaced them as a more convenient medium. If so, then *obelos* and *drachma* were adopted for weights of metal equivalent (at some point in time and place) in value to one or six spits (six being a typical set of spits, albeit not the only one), and then inherited by coins of the same weight; or conceivably they were adopted directly for the coins.[46] The change would have been motivated, at least in part, by the increasing availability and cheapness both of iron,[47] which

---

[42] Seaford 1994a, 282–3.

[43] For the permanent mystic happiness (*eudaimonia*) of the *thiasos* see e.g. Aristophanes' *Frogs*; Seaford 1996, 157, 221.

[44] Cole 1984, 30, 115; iron plated with gold: Pliny *NH* 33.1.23; ring commemorating mystic release: Seaford 1986a, 24–5; magnetised iron rings as image for collective enthusiasm: Pl. *Ion* 533d; Lucret. 6.1044.

[45] 14A; sacrifice: 2E n. 89.

[46] The latter possibility would mean that the weights specified as drachmas in Solon's laws were originally specified in 'staters', replaced later by 'drachmas': 5A n. 15.

[47] On the gradual decline in the value of iron see most recently Haarer 2000, 1.118, 120, etc., who also argues that 'iron retains considerable value at least as far as the eighth century' (202).

thereby became too bulky to use as money, and of precious metal, which thereby became useable even in everyday transactions, albeit in very small pieces which required new names less cumbersome than those – e. g. 'one ninety-sixth' (of a stater) – used in the eastern Aegean. These new names were conveniently supplied for the small pieces of silver by the *obelos* and *drachma* that they were replacing. We are familiar with the transfer of the name of something (e.g. 'floppy' disc) to its rather different replacement. In the case of money an extra reason for continuity is the need for confidence in identity of value. The new names probably originated in the area of the Saronic gulf,[48] at sufficient distance from the oriental influence on Greek monetary schematisation manifest in the stater, mna, and talent (7A). But the structural connection between sacrificial distribution and monetisation was surely a feature of all the advanced Greek city-states.

A link in this connection was the sanctuary. To provide communal sacrifice, the sanctuary must attract contributions (figurines, dedications, fees, fines, etc.), which take durable form (3C, 4D) – not least because mass contributions of animals or animal parts would produce for the sanctuary an excess of (perishable) meat. Better to have precious metal, which may itself however accumulate in excess, especially if supplemented from collective sources such as booty, or mines – as in Attica at Laurium, 'the rock, with silver under it, of divine Athena' (Eur. *Cyc.* 294). The protection by deities of their wealth, together with strong walls, secured the store of precious metal that, like the sacrificial victim, was dedicated to deity so as to belong to the community. This well-defined security of communal precious metal would be the natural – or even necessary – basis for distributions of it among the citizens such as we hear of on Siphnos in the sixth century[49] and proposed at Athens from the Laurium silver early in the fifth.[50] We have suggested (5B) that the impetus to such distributions among the citizens (i.e. the sacrificing group: 3A n. 6) derived at least in part from the ancient and powerfully persistent notion (3A) of the universal right to a share of sacrificial meat, carried over into pieces of metal that, just like the meat, would have to be in small pieces of standard size and quality, acceptably equal for all. For the (citizen) army the distribution of meat, with which

---

[48] Kroll 2001a argues that 'the obol/drachma division of the stater spread from being originally confined to a small group of silver coinages – Aeginetan, Corinthian, and Attic – from cities concentrated around the Saronic Gulf.'

[49] Hdt. 5.17; 6.46–7; 7.112; 3.57.

[50] Hdt. 7.144; [Aristot.] *Ath. Pol.* 22.7 (with Rhodes 1981 ad loc.). In the event it was used instead to construct ships. Note the metaphor at Hdt. 9.7 'thus is this distributed unadulterated (ἀκίβδηλον νέμεται) by us to the Greeks' (i.e. we have remained loyal to the Greeks).

it was content in Homer, is no longer enough. This quasi-sacrificial distribution of temple wealth would form the natural basis also for payment of soldiers or sailors from elsewhere (mercenaries)[51] and for state services (temple building, jury-pay, service in the fleet, etc.). The *use* of temple treasure[52] generally required its transformation into coinage.[53] This could occur whether or not the spit had been used as money, and even whether or not a spit was equal in value to a silver obol. The name *obelos*, which we have seen could refer even to a dedicated statue,[54] would naturally be adopted for the new, nameless piece of silver that was distributed en masse in the way that meat on an *obelos* had been distributed en masse. This adoption would have to happen only once for the name to catch on.

In Homer there are indications of money functions being performed by precious metal (2BC), which may indeed have performed them from the eighth century onwards, albeit only for large-scale transactions, beyond the reach of the rank and file. The increasing availability of iron may have allowed the extension of money – in the form of iron spits, that were distinctively Greek[55] – to relatively small-scale transactions conducted not only by the wealthy.[56] This would introduce a radical difference into the world described by Homer. On this basis a further radical difference was created by the subsequent advent of silver *obeloi*, representing a fusion of the two spheres into which the Homeric economy is, roughly speaking, divided: on the one hand the aristocratic circulation of prestige objects (treasure, sometimes of precious metal) – as interpersonal gifts or sometimes ransom or prizes – stored temporarily or permanently in private houses, and on the other hand the egalitarian sacrificial distribution of meat that integrates a group or community.

The division may seem transcended in Homer by the principle of the egalitarian distribution of booty, which includes some treasure. But the unpredictability of booty and its distribution, and the Homeric representation of its distribution as in fact inequitable, contrast sharply with the positive Homeric representation of sacrifice (2E). The fusion of the

---

[51] 5B n. 43; 7C.

[52] It might be used even by an individual, the tyrant, with characteristic impiety consolidating his power by taking over temple wealth (14DE). Similarly in Homer a leader might appropriate ('provide') the communal sacrifice (3A nn. 18 and 19; 4D).

[53] E.g. the transformation of the Delphic treasure by the Phocians in the mid fourth century BC into coins spent on mercenaries and bribery: D.S. 16.33.2, 36.1, 56.5–7. In the Peloponnesian war the Athenians minted gold coins from temple treasure: Philoch. 328 *FGrH* F141; Figueira 1998, 517–19. The Arcadians minted temple treasure of Olympia 364 BC: Kraay 1976, 106.

[54] 6A n. 34.   [55] Haarer 2000, I. 191–6 (as opposed to bidents, tridents, etc).

[56] For the view that in general the increased availability of iron tools meant democratisation and decentralisiation of economic power see e.g. Mann 1986, 184–8, 196–7, 223.

spheres that would be represented by the distribution of treasure among the rank and file or by the accumulation of treasure at the place of communal sacrifice is resisted, or at least excluded, by Homer: the resentment of Odysseus' companions at what they imagine to be his gifts of precious metal (from Aeolus) produces disaster (2E); temples with their dedications are mentioned rarely and negatively (3B); in urging various reasons on the Greek army for continuing to fight at Troy (*Iliad* 2) neither Odysseus nor Nestor nor Agamemnon includes booty; and so on. And yet even as early as the formative period of Homeric poetry in the eighth century precisely this transcendence was beginning to assume massive dimensions in the growth of sanctuaries and durable dedications at places of communal sacrifice (3BC).

The unprecedented storage of durable, valuable objects at a place of egalitarian, communal distribution had two consequences in particular. Firstly, large-scale distribution and (voluntary or enforced) contribution at the sanctuary, the concentration of numerous people, animals, and durable goods under the protection of deity – all this was likely to favour the development of various kinds of exchange,[57] perhaps even with barbarians.[58] Secondly, the nature of the distribution and contribution – combining as it did communality, standardisation, substitution by durable symbol, and mass-production (3C) – contributed to its early monetisation, and perhaps to monetisation in general (4D).

As currency precious metal has advantages over iron. It is rarer and more valuable, and so can embody monetary value in pieces that are smaller, more easily concealable and portable than spits. Its aesthetic appeal and resistance to deterioration, underlying its Homeric association with immortality, are both advantages over iron. On the other hand a small piece of precious metal is of less certain value than a much larger iron spit, unless the precious metal is both tested for purity and weighed. Iron spits, like 'utensil money' generally, might have had the advantage (over precious metal bullion) of immediate acceptability, being fairly large objects of roughly standard size (a little more or less iron would not matter much), endowed by sacrificial ritual with communal familiarity and communal respect for their equal value (6A). Such availability was obtained for precious metal (electrum,[59] then silver) by marking pieces of it, as a guarantee not so

---

[57] On early sanctuaries as contexts for exchange see de Polignac 1994, 5; Morgan 1993, 21.

[58] Suggested by the discovery, in certain early sanctuaries, of numerous objects from distant places, including many from various parts of the Near East: Strøm 1992, 50; de Polignac 1994, 6–7; Osborne 1996, 93–5.

[59] An alloy of gold and silver that the Greeks called 'white gold': e.g. Hdt. 1.50.2; cf. Soph. *Phil.* 394, *Ant.* 1037–8; Strabo 13.4.5.

much of weight and quality as of *future* acceptability. But this solution had not occurred in centuries of the use of precious metal for money functions in the Ancient Near East.

Even if the very first coins were made by the Lydians (7A), it was the Greeks who first made pervasive everyday use of them, in small denominations (obol and drachma) as well as large ones. This use arose out of the synthesis of Near-Eastern with Greek practice. On the one hand coinage is *substance*, precious metal, such as had been used for money functions for centuries in the Near East. But on the other hand it is given immediate acceptability by its form (mark), which makes it a specific *object*, as iron in the form of a spit is an object.[60] The level of technology required for making coins had long existed in the Near East no less than the money functions of metal. What was new, among the Greeks, was rather the synthesis of this ability and these functions with the social centrality of sacrificial communality. The collective confidence in the guarantee of future conventional value bestowed by the standard stamp on pieces of precious metal (regardless of small variations in quantity and quality) arises – at least in part – from the entry of precious metal into the communal sacrificial distributions in which each individual citizen has the right to (ownership of) a standard portion of communally sacrificed meat, just as most citizens in a polis like Athens own a plot of land.[61] Both ingredients are crucial: individual ownership bestows independence on the citizen, and communal ritual provides general familiarity with the objects distributed and confidence in their equal value. The naming of low-value coins of everyday use 'obol' and 'drachma' marks the continuity between two forms of confidence – in sacrificial spit and stamp – in the standardisation of value.

Such socially central sacrificial communality was unknown in the redistributive economies of Egypt and Mesopotamia, where accordingly money functions were performed by mere substances (silver, barley, copper, etc.).[62] Just as entitlement to participation in the Greek sacrificial meal comes to embody participation in the polis as a citizen (3A), so the inheritance of sacrificial distribution in generating collective confidence is reinforced, and then replaced, by the mark stamped on the metal by the polis. The polis, controlling communal sacrifices and the temple treasuries that had developed out of the sacrifices, stamps on the metal distributed a symbol that

---

[60] Σίγλος, the Greek term for a Persian coin, derives from the Semitic *seqel* (weigh), but could also mean a ring: Caccamo Caltabiano and Radici Colace 1992, 39.
[61] Osborne 1985, 142. On the vocabulary shared by the distribution of sacrificial meat and of land see 3A.
[62] See chapter 15.

transcends the particularity of specific treasuries and sacrificing groups, establishes the value of the metal, and enhances the identity of the polis among both its own citizens and outsiders. Certification by the state is one of the ways in which coinage is quite different from anything that had performed money functions in the past.

I cannot, despite the important consequences of what I have called the fusion of the Homeric spheres of treasure and sacrificial distribution, enter here into the causes of this transformation – a vast historical question bound up with the development of communal institutions that was part of the emergence of the polis. But I will dwell briefly on the increase in access to supplies of precious metal that I have already mentioned as a factor. It seems that the early seventh century saw the beginning of (or at least a considerable increase in) the exploitation of the precious metal of the Tmolus area in Lydia, and in particular of the electrum washed down in huge amounts by the river Pactolus. The consequent vast metallic wealth is reflected in the Greek myth of the Phrygian king Midas[63] and in Greek texts from the time of Gyges, who ruled Lydia circa 680–652 BC.[64] It was from this Lydian electrum that the first coins (Lydian and Greek) were made. The existence of a vast supply of electrum may have been a precondition for the genesis of coinage, but was not a precondition for its continued existence. From about the middle of the sixth century electrum was generally replaced as the material of Greek coinage by gold and much more widely by silver, in part perhaps as a result of the discovery of how to separate electrum into silver and gold,[65] but also as a result of increasing supplies of silver from Greek lands and elsewhere.[66] Herodotus mentions silver mines

---

[63] The myth, which ends in Midas washing off his unwanted gift into the Pactolus, is influenced by the historical Midas, under whose rule (c. 738–696 BC) Phrygia was a major power; Seaford 1994a, 224.

[64] Archilochus fr. 19 ('Gyges of much gold').

[65] The cementation process, separating silver from gold, seems to have come to fruition just before or during the reign of Croesus: Ramage and Craddock 2000. Croesus sent both alloyed and refined gold to Delphi: Hdt. 1.50.

[66] Initially supplies of silver in the Aegean may have increased along with the improvement of communications and the general increase of wealth after the Greek Dark Age. In the seventh century it seems that the amount of silver in the lands of the Assyrian empire had been increased by new supplies brought by the Phoenicians from the Aegean and from further west, and this traffic may have resulted in increased availability of silver in the Aegean: Kroll 1998, 230; Sherratt and Sherratt 1993; Stos-Gale 2001; Kim 2001, 16. The Phokaians were said to have received enough money (*chrēmata*) from the king of Tartessos to build a large wall around their town: Hdt.1.163 (cf. 4.152). Cf. Treister 1996, 24–7, 30–1, 151–2, 177. Forbes 1950, 190–2 lists twenty-six places in Asia Minor with deposits of silver. The silver deposits in the territory of Sybaris may well have been worked in antiquity: Kraay 1976, 325. Silver may have come also from from Illyria and the Black Sea: Boardman 1980, 226; Drews 1976, 26–31. Cf. 3c.

on the island of Siphnos,[67] in the northern Aegean, and at Laurium in Attica.[68]

C   FROM SEAL TO COIN

The use of seals to make impressions on clay is very ancient.[69] Their earliest discernible functions, which acquire clarity with the survival of numerous seals and seal-marks from Mesopotamia of the fourth millennium BC, were to symbolise goods, and to protect them by sealing the fastenings of doors and containers.[70] An early use was also surely to mark possession.[71] Later, with the development of writing, seals were used for receipts, contracts, instructions, letters, and treaties.[72] A general function of sealing, common to many if not all of its specific functions, is the imagined extension of the power or authority of a person or persons[73] to a location or event at which they are not (or no longer) physically present, whether it be a container, a storeroom, a written agreement,[74] a transaction such as the transfer of goods, an action required by central authority, and so on.[75]

This imagined extension of personal power or authority was surely not imagined in merely formal terms, like the modern signature. In interpreting dream omens the Assyrians associated seals with offspring. On this association it has been remarked that 'the fact that cylinder-seals, because of their function as well as their highly individualised form, are likely to be considered not only as identifying marks but also as "carriers" of the individuality

---

[67] 3.57: he says that the Siphnians were consequently at the height of their prosperity (*c.* 525 BC) and the richest of the islanders.

[68] 5.7, 23; 6.46; 7.112, 144. Chemical and isotopic analysis of 112 coins from fourteen mints, mainly from the Asyut hoard, indicates Laurium and Siphnos as the two chief sources, with very little indication of Spanish silver: Gale, Gentner, and Wagner 1980.

[69] The first evidence of systematic use is from northern Iraq in the sixth millennium BC: Pittman 1995, 1591.

[70] E.g. Pittman 1995, 1591–2; Collon 1987, 113; Steinkeller 1977, 4. For Egypt see Williams 1977, 138; James 1997.

[71] Collon 1987, 113; cf. e.g. Larsen 1977, 95; James 1997, 34.

[72] Pittman 1995, 1599; Collon 1987, 113; Winter 1987, 81–2; Steinkeller 1977, 42–5, and various other contributions in Gibson and Biggs 1977. For Egypt see also James 1997, 37–9.

[73] According to Collon 1987, 113 the earliest seals do not seem to have been 'personal' but 'administrative'. 'It was only in the latter part of the early Dynastic period (3000–2334 BC) that seals inscribed with personal names appear and can be said to belong to individuals. From then on the choice of design and material probably reflects the personal preference of the owner . . .' According to Larsen 1977, 100 all known old Assyrian seals 'were owned by individuals and there is no evidence anywhere to indicate that corporate entities, private firms or families, or political organs had seals'.

[74] On the function of seals in written agreements see esp. Renger 1977.

[75] '. . . common purpose of the seal impression seems to have been to signal to any viewer that a certain person as an individual or member of a group was present at a certain act, be it as witness, as overseer, or as controller . . .': Nissen 1977, 19.

of the person who wears and uses them tends naturally to foster their association with children, especially sons whose function is to extend the personal existence of the father beyond the natural limitations'.[76] Accordingly, seals might be inherited within families, including royal families, and indeed might be important vehicles for the transmission of royal power.[77] The notion of the seal embodying personal identity may also underlie the placing of seals in tombs,[78] and the great importance attached to the *loss* of seals.[79] A Neo-Assyrian text associates the material of a seal with the fate of its owner.[80] The embodiment of personal identity or power in seals is a form of magic. Fixed on the fastenings of containers and storehouses, they might mark ownership and prevent (or at least expose) tampering. Such protective power, indistinguishable from magical power, might also extend to other functions such as the protection of the wearer of the seal.[81]

The embodiment of power in the seal might be imagined as achieved by the representation on it of ritual, or of the gods. An interesting example of the transference of personal power is provided by the 'royal presentation' seals of the Mesopotamian Ur III period (2112–2004 BC), which depict an individual being introduced into the presence of the king. The individual is frequently accompanied by an interceding goddess. The representation of the seated king is similar to, but also differentiated from, the representation of seated deities in other scenes. Most of these seals are also inscribed with the personal name, patronym, and office of an individual. It has been persuasively argued that the depictions and the inscriptions should be taken together, and that the seals represent the concrete manifestation of the seal-owners' authority to exercise their high office within the Ur III bureaucracy,[82] as well as legitimating the authority of the king 'both to grant the particular seal and office, and, by implication, to exercise his divinely-sanctioned rule in the first place'.[83] The personal power embodied in the seal is in this case actually represented, on the seal itself, as passing from king (or deity) to the high official who owns the seal.[84] The ultimate

[76] Oppenheim 1956, 277; cf. Steiner 1994, 114–15; *Song of Solomon* 8.6 Bridegroom to Bride: 'Set me as a seal upon thy breast.'

[77] E.g. Larsen 1977, 98; Cassin 1960, 748–50.

[78] Pittman 1995, 1597; Rathje 1997; Larsen 1977, 98. For Egypt see e.g. Johnson 1977; Williams 1977, 131; James 1997.

[79] Steinkeller 1977, 48–9; Hallo 1977; Cassin 1960, 745.

[80] Hematite means one fate, lapis lazuli another, and so on: Pittman 1995, 1594.

[81] E.g. Collon 1997, 19–20; 1987, 119. For Egypt see e.g. James 1997.

[82] There is a 'marked absence' of such seals designating the owner as a *merchant*: Winter 1987, 79.

[83] Winter 1987.

[84] For seals marking the status or authority of officials see further e.g. Pittman 1995. For Egypt see Johnson 1977, 142–3; James 1997, 34. For an Egyptian official being handed his seal of office see James 1997, 37. On the relation in general of seal designs to function see Collon 1997, 16–17.

source of personal power is divine. The gods own seals, and may use them to decide the fate of humankind.[85]

Marks on coins are, like seal-marks, distinctive authenticating impressions, reproducible as numerous instances from a single source (the seal, the die). Some of the earliest coin-marks are, like seal-marks, on one surface only, and there are some similarities between seal-devices and coin-devices.[86] That the devices on some of the earliest coins may have been personal is indicated in particular by an early electrum stater on which a stag is accompanied by the words 'I am the sign (*sēma*) of Phanes.'[87] The lion, which appears on some early electrum coins, was associated with the kings of Lydia.[88] And one of the legends that accompanies the lion on some coins may conceivably represent the name of the Lydian king Alyattes.[89] These considerations suggest that the idea of stamping coins may have derived from the use of the stamp-seal to make circular impressions.[90] The emblem of the Lydian king (or of some other powerful person), which conveyed his authority through his seal, might also have been stamped on pieces of metal so as to authenticate their value.[91] The first marks on coins may have acquired their authority from their association with the ancient power of the seal-mark. Laum, while maintaining this association, attempts also to associate early coin-marks generally with the divine sphere and in particular with offerings to the gods.[92] But this is a complex issue that cannot be pursued here.

The transition from the seal as a means of power to precious metal money, and then to coinage, is embodied in the mythical stories told of Gyges and Midas, both historical potentates out of whom the Greeks fashioned mythical figures.[93] Gyges was imagined to be a Lydian shepherd who discovers a subterranean bronze horse containing a corpse from whose hand he takes a gold ring, and discovers that when he turns its seal inwards (i.e. so that it cannot be seen) he too becomes invisible. This he uses to acquire the

---

[85] Pittman 1995, 1597–8.

[86] Spier 1990, 110–13; Balmuth 1980, 25; Macdonald 1905, 44–52. For an Athenian coin actually used as a seal at Persepolis in the early fifth century BC see Starr 1976.

[87] Kraay 1976, 3, 6, 23. But cf. Howgego 1995, 4. *Sēma* could also refer to a seal: an Archaic Greek scarab is inscribed 'This is the *sēma* of Thersis, do not open me' (Boardman 1997, 79); cf. Soph. *Trach.* 614–15.

[88] E.g. Spier 1990, 118.

[89] Kraay 1976, 24; Le Rider 2001, 56–8 sets out various possibilities. Update on similar finds: Spier 1998, 331–3.

[90] Balmuth 1971, 2 calls the stamping of coins a 'translation from' the use of seals, but does not argue in detail. For stamp seals in the seventh century BC see Collon 1997, 15.

[91] The seal of the grand Khan was used establish the authority of token (paper) money, in Marco Polo's *Travels*.

[92] Laum 1924, 140–50.

[93] Ure 1922, 148; Shell 1978, ch. 1; Steiner 1994, 159–63; Seaford 1994a, 225.

Lydian kingship.[94] The story expresses features we have already noted of the seal in the ancient Near East – its embodiment of the identity of its owner (when it is invisible, so is Gyges), its consignment to the tomb, its magical power, and its importance in the transmission of royal power. Its power to make its wearer invisible expresses the invisibility of the magical power embodied in it, in particular the invisible power of the king (i.e. even where he is not personally present) to enforce his will throughout his kingdom. The Median king Deiokes was said to have consolidated his power by being invisible to his subjects, and to see king Gyges was a crime.[95] But the power embodied in the seal enables Gyges to *usurp* power. Indeed, he is for the Greeks the prototype of the tyrant.[96] And he is, like the Greek tyrants, wealthy in precious metal. As early as the mid-seventh century Archilochus refers in the same breath to Gyges' 'tyranny' and to his 'much gold',[97] and 'Gygean' gold and silver was on display at Delphi (Hdt. 1.14). Association of the coin-mark with the ancient power of the seal-mark may be reflected in the detail that Gyges' seal-ring was said to have brought him much wealth.[98] King Midas too was famous for his gold, which could also be seen at Delphi, and he too had a ring that made him invisible, as well as a Greek wife who was among those said to have been the first to mint coinage.[99] Even the invisibility of Deiokes was obtained by concentric walls of which the innermost was of gold. As oriental potentates Gyges and Midas exercise power through the seal, but also exercise it through the medium of the precious metal that was especially abundant in their realms, a medium that resembles the seal-mark in embodying power that does not require the physical presence of the ruler.

Despite the similarities between seal-mark and coin-mark, and the likelihood that the former was a model for the latter, the two are essentially different in social function. The seal-mark, as we have seen, typically signifies ownership, power, or authority by seeming to embody a person, by somehow attaching the person to what is sealed. This is so even when there is a certain standardisation of seals, as in the elaborate bureaucracy of the Ur III period, in which the seals 'serve at once as markers of the unity of the system and of an individual's place within the system'.[100] The coin-mark

---

[94] Pl. *Rep.* 359e–360b (σφενδόνη, which is the part of the ring that contains the seal).

[95] Hdt. 1.98–9; Xanthos ap. Nik. Dam. 90 *FGrH* F47.11.

[96] Seaford 1994a, 231. The word τύραννος may be of Lydian origin.

[97] Fr. 19: the tyranny is invisible ('away from my eyes'), but in Plato Gyges is powerful precisely through his invisibility; 10D n. 112.

[98] Anon. in Aristot. *Art. Rhet.* Comm. 256.

[99] Hdt. 1.14; Hcld. Pont. ap. Aristot. fr. 611.37 Rose; Poll. *Onom.* 9.83; Plin. *NH* 33.48; 7A, 14D.

[100] Winter 1987, 92. See also Nissen 1977, 19–20.

on the other hand does not attach the coin to any person (except for a few of the very first coins). Almost the only persons represented or evoked by the coin-marks of the Greek city-states in the Archaic and Classical periods were deities or legendary heroes.[101] And even after coins came to be stamped with the heads of rulers, they were of course nevertheless entirely owned and controlled by whoever possessed them – a contradiction exploited by 'Render unto Caesar that which is Caesar's'. If there is technological continuity between seal-mark and coin-mark, then the mark has turned into its opposite: so far from attaching the coin to a person, it facilitates its promiscuous passage from the ownership of one person to the ownership of another. Whereas seal-marks seem to embody the power of the owner of the seal, coin-marks create no imagined attachment between the coins and their source. And so the transition from the seal to money (coined or uncoined) as a means of power, embodied in the figure of Gyges, facilitates the tyrannical usurpation of power by a newcomer – first exemplified for the Greeks by Gyges himself. Being (unlike the seal) impersonal, money (and its source) can be controlled by anyone.[102]

How can it be that, whereas seal-marks embody attachment to the owner of the seal, coin-marks embody no such attachment to their source (the die)? It is not just that the die does not belong to an individual. The crucial point is that coin-marks, unlike seal-marks, relate to the material on which they are impressed (metal, not clay). They authenticate the metal as possessing a certain value. And they do so not by transmitting power (magical or otherwise) to the piece of metal, but by imposing on it a form that recognisably assigns it to a distinct category of things, the category of authentic coins. The seal-mark may function as a sign (of ownership, receipt of goods, etc.), but only by embodying the identity or power or authority of its owner. It signifies by substitution (of person by his seal-mark). The coin-mark, on the other hand, operates in effect as a mere sign, not embodying personal or divine power but itself embodied (as pure form) in the metal that it thereby transforms from mere substance to something else, an authentic coin. This is not to say that the coin-mark could not evoke powerful associations (with a polis, a deity, a ritual, etc.), or that these associations were unimportant in establishing the acceptability of the coins so marked. But once established, it is the recognisability of (say) the

---

[101] It seems that the first portraits of living rulers on Greek coins were of the *Persian* satraps Tissaphernes and Pharnabazos at the end of the fifth and beginning of the fourth centuries: Kraay 1976, 74, 258, 281. Cf.13A n. 9 (Pythagoras on coin?).

[102] Theognis, who deplores the indiscrimate power of money (8D), sets a personal 'seal' on his poetry (19).

head of Athena on a coin, not the embodiment of her power, that sustains the general habit of its acceptability.

But if a mere sign, what is a coin-mark a sign of? Not – we have said – of its source (person, die). Nor of the quality or purity of its metal, for the electrum of which the earliest coins are made is variable in its proportions of gold and silver, though the size of the coins is remarkably regular, with the result that the coins are of variable intrinsic value. And indeed the disparity between intrinsic and conventional value is a general feature of Greek coinage (7D). If then the sign is a sign of value, but not of the intrinsic value of the metal it marks, is it simply a sign of purely abstract value, like the number printed on a banknote? No, because for instance Athenian two-drachma coins and Athenian four-drachma coins bear the same sign. Although the coin-marks render irrelevant variations in the quality and weight of metal pieces that look the same, thereby transforming them from pieces of a natural substance into specific things, each of exactly the same value, the things (coins) are not mere tokens. Unless they were composed of (roughly) the right amount of valuable metal, they would not inspire the necessary confidence. They remain, to a certain extent, amounts of substance. What is required is the *combination* of substance (valuable metal) with form (the mark). The coin has no use-value: it is the physical embodiment of abstract, homogeneous value – exactly two drachmas. Implicit in this semi-abstraction is *ideal substance* which, not the actual substance of the coin but signified by the coin-mark, belongs to a new kind of reality, concrete and visible (being metal) and yet (because distinct from the actual metal) abstract and invisible.

This gives Greek coinage (and its successors) a special place in the world-wide history of money. Things that have performed money functions may be classified as natural substances (salt, iron, etc.), natural things (shells, cattle, etc.), or artefacts (axes, cloth, paper, etc.). Such things may or may not have use-value – though they generally do, if only as ornaments. But where an artefact can be so easily produced that it is of small inherent value, such as paper, it can become money only by the imposition of a sign. And indeed paper is an especially convenient form of token money. What distinguishes coinage from all the other things known to me that have performed money functions is that on the one hand, unlike most such things, it bears a sign, and on the other hand, unlike all other such things that do bear a sign (such as paper), it is also inherently valuable.

Another ruler whose legend embodies a reaction to the transition from seal to coin is a Greek, Polycrates. In order to avoid the resentment of the gods, he throws into the sea his most valued possession – his seal-ring – only for it to be returned to him in the belly of a fish. The supreme value of the seal reflects the power of the oriental potentate, and yet Polycrates inhabits a world in which power is obtained by means of precious metal money (Hdt. 3.122–3). In such a world the sacrifice of a single talismanic object has lost its efficacy. Polycrates' seal-ring is returned to him by the sea, which in its unlimited homogeneity seems to express the unlimited homogeneous power of money to replace all things.[103]

Polycrates' tyranny coincided with the early rapid spread of coinage in the Aegean, and he himself minted coins.[104] The ruler's seal may have been early connected in the popular imagination with coinage, and, as we have seen, may even have been used, in a combination of the two kinds of power, to mark metal on the way to the invention of coinage. By controlling the die or dies by which coins are produced, the tyrant may make a profit from the disparity between the conventional value of the coins and their value as bullion. And yet the power of precious metal, coined or uncoined, depends on its general acceptability in payment and exchange. Power passes from the ruler's *identity embodied in* the seal-mark to the *substance valorised by* the coin-mark, a substance over which the ruler can exercise only limited control (14A, 14E). Both the seal-mark and the coin-mark embody the invisible – the seal-mark the invisible presence of the ruler, but the coin-mark the invisible ideal value of the metal.

The detail of the transformation of seal-mark into something as fundamentally different as the coin-mark has been lost. An example of how such a paradoxical transition may have occurred would be as follows.[105] A Lydian potentate wishes to use the military skills of Greeks who are outside his political control. But these Greeks are not the subjects of a redistributive monarchy; they are relatively free individuals, who must be given gifts.[106] Fortunately, our potentate has enough electrum to give each of them a piece. Every piece is stamped with his own device (e.g. the royal lion of Lydia) – for two reasons, both stemming from the novelty of mass distribution of prestige gifts: firstly, in order to impress a crucial reminder of its source on what would otherwise be a strangely impersonal gift, and secondly in order to neutralise, by his authority, the variety in the proportions of gold and silver in the electrum (7D). The first motive is to preserve, in new conditions, the traditional personal association of gift with donor. But the material needs of the numerous Greek soldiers are more important to them than the contrived personal link with the potentate. And so the

---

[103] 8B; 8F; Seaford 1998a, 126–7.   [104] Hdt. 3.56: Kraay 1976, 30, 36.
[105] The case for mercenaries as an important factor in the genesis of coinage was first made by Cook 1958. For early Greek mercenaries employed in the Near East see Parke 1933, 1–6. For the early Lydian employment of mercenaries, probably Greeks, see Parke 1933, 4–5 (add Hdt. 1.154).
[106] Nik. Dam. 90 *FGrH* F47(9) τοῖς δὲ δῶρα διδοὺς ἐπικούρους ἐποιεῖτο (Gyges).

authoritative typicality of the mark survives as an impersonal guarantee of future acceptability.[107]

D   SEALS, COINAGE, WRITING

The first impressions on clay were made to imitate, represent, or symbolise goods, with an 'accounting' or 'administrative' function – to control the storage and movement of the goods. Out of this practice (sealing) there developed, in fourth-millennium Mesopotamia, writing, which continued the 'accounting' function, but also acquired other functions, and became detached from the *particularity* of sealing in two respects in particular. First, whereas a seal-mark can only be reproduced by the same specific seal, a piece of 'writing' can be reproduced by any pen. Second, whereas the seal-mark embodies in some sense the power or identity of its owner, the early development of writing is, roughly speaking, from the pictographic and ideographic to the phonographic (reference through the intermediary of sound), thereby becoming relatively detached from the thing represented. The end point of this development is the alphabet, in which a sufficiently full range of phonological differences is represented by the minimum necessary number of components.

A similar detachment from specific association occurs in the transition from seal-mark to coin-mark. Seal-marks, like the pictograms (and ideograms) they give rise to, may seem to embody something of what each one refers to, whereas the much fewer coin-marks and alphabetic letters are deployed too promiscuously for such specific embodiment. Coinage and the alphabet each constitute a system of all-embracing equivalence or reference that is, through deployment of an intermediary (value, sound), reduced to a minimum of components (the types and sizes of coins, letters). And they are each radical developments of Near-Eastern practice that have their first widespread use among the Greeks,[108] and will be united, in a sense, in the *logos* of Heraclitus, which combines the meanings of verbal and monetary account (12B). Among the causes of this parallel simplifying reduction of symbols may be popular pressure for access to powerful symbols. Despite their crucial link with their specific source, coins are

---

[107] Renger 1995, 310 explains the Babylonian failure to invent coinage, and to use it for at least two centuries after its invention, by the usefulness of coinage for *impersonal* transactions; 'closed communities, as represented by the Babylonian upper layer, do not need it'.

[108] The question might be pursued of an analogy in the uniquely Greek development of ancient Near-Eastern visual art – from the image as symbol embodying its object (i.e. what is felt to be important about the object) to the image as a collection of signs representing the reality of the object through the intermediary of appearance (perspective, shade, etc.).

mass-produced, among the first mass-produced objects in history, along
with and preceded by the dedicated figurines that were durable relics of the
sacrifice (3C) and probably also by the sacrifical spits (6A).

The storage and movement of goods in the redistributive economies of
the ancient Near East (4A) were controlled in part by means of seals and
writing, under a regime of centralised directives rather than market trade.
As a result, surviving written documents often take the form of *lists* of
various kinds of goods.

In redistribution systems such as those centered in the Mesopotamian palaces and
temples, officials recorded incoming taxes, tributes, and the yield of the royal or
priestly domain and workshops as well as the distribution of materials and rations
to craftsmen and workers. This type of recording, strictly formalised and acutely
co-ordinated, is very much in evidence in Mesopotamia and wherever, under
Mesopotamian influence, officials in similar economic situations have resorted to
writing on clay.[109]

The visual counterpart of these lists is the theme of a procession of individuals bearing various offerings that is to be found in various kinds of
Near-Eastern art, from the magnificent 'Uruk vase' from Warka to the no
less magnificent reliefs created for Darius' palace two and a half thousand
years later at Persepolis.[110] Presumably it is this feature of the economy
that, together with the demands of scribal training, is reflected also in the
numerous lists of words (e.g. the names of trees) that are attested from very
early on and become an important feature of Mesopotamian scribal production.[111] These lists have been related to a general feature of Mesopotamian
civilisation – 'much the same process of growth by accretion, the same
preference for additive elaboration and amplification (rather than structural changes) which we can observe in Mesopotamian legal practices, in
the evolution of the votive inscriptions, in the layout of a temple, to mention some few examples'.[112] But surely the fundamental instance of the list
in Mesopotamian society was the list of goods that was so essential to the
working of the economy and that itself provided constant opportunity for
'additive elaboration and amplification (rather than structural changes)'.
The centrality of listing to redistributive economies tended to produce a
specific form of cognition, a specific form of representing the world.[113]

---

[109] Oppenheim 1977, 230.   [110] Illustrated at Frankfort 1970, 26, 373.
[111] Oppenheim 1977, 246–9. It may accordingly indirectly give rise also to other kinds of Mesopotamian
list (of events, of astronomical data, of signs, etc.).
[112] Oppenheim 1977, 248–9.
[113] Oppenheim 1977, 244–9. The effects of the written list in producing forms of cognition that are
less likely to be produced in illiterate cultures are explored by Goody 1977, 74–111.

The economic effect of the coin-mark, on the other hand, was, by spreading rapidly throughout the Greek city-states in the sixth century BC, to facilitate the development of a monetary economy[114] in which goods and services are allocated not so much by enforced contribution and redistribution as by market trade, more specifically by numerous acts of decentralised exchange – decentralised in that they do not belong to a bureaucratically controlled redistributive system. The element that tends to unite these otherwise discrete acts of exchange is not bureaucratic control but the use in each of them of the same general-purpose *money*, which in the form of coinage does depend on the central authority of the polis. But in its dependence on authority the validity of the coin-mark is, as we have seen, quite unlike the validity of the seal-mark. The coin-mark, because it does not embody power from its source but refers rather to the value embodied in its metal, disperses unqualified economic power into the pocket of the ordinary citizen. Along with a new kind of economy emerges a new kind of signification. Among the Greeks seals retained the functions of protection and personal identification, but were of far less importance than in Mesopotamia.[115]

The creative period of Homeric epic occurred before this development. The world refracted by Homeric epic, very different though it was from the bureaucratic structure of the Mesopotamian redistributive economies, was nevertheless, as we have seen (2AB), marked by redistribution and reciprocity rather than by money and market trade. There is in the narrative an important place for lists of goods, as gifts – an example is the list of goods whose rejection by Achilles constitutes a crisis of reciprocity. If the redistributive economies of Mesopotamia tended to favour a specific form of representing the world, how was the post-Homeric representation of the world affected by the rapid transition to a monetary economy? Before attempting an answer, we must first explore further the genesis and features of coined money.

[114] This is not to deny a period of Greek silver money before coinage: 5A n. 31.
[115] For a summary of the archaeological evidence see Boardman 1997, 74–5, 78, 80. In Hdt. and Thuc. the only Greeks to have seals are the tyrant Polycrates (Hdt. 3.41–2), and king Pausanias writing to the Persian king (Thuc. 1.132.5). Cf. Hdt. 1.195.6 (in Babylonia everyone has a seal); 2.38, 121 (Egyptians); 3.128 (the effectiveness of the Persian king's seal); 7.69.6 (Ethiopians); Thuc. 1.129.6 (Persian king). In the royal myths of tragedy seals are used for personal recognition (8C) and to seal stores and letters (Aesch. *Suppl.* 947 refers with contempt to the Egyptian practice of sealing documents). In Aristophanes seals seem (when not associated with sexuality) to be associated with the wealthy (*Clouds* 332 (?), *Eccles.* 632).

CHAPTER SEVEN

The earliest coinage

A   WHO INVENTED COINAGE?

Our conclusion that Greek coinage represents a synthesis of Near-Eastern and Greek practice now requires more precision. The influence of the ancient Near East on numerous elements of early Greek culture has long been recognised; and the exploration of this influence has in recent years accelerated (4B). It seems likely that, as in so many other areas, so too in the area of money the Greeks were influenced by their eastern neighbours, some of whom had been employing silver for various money uses since the third millennium BC (chapter 15). This is reflected in the Greek adoption of the Semitic word *mna* to refer to a weight (or unit of account) equal to one hundred drachmas or one sixtieth of a talent. The Mesopotamian *manā* is one sixtieth of a larger unit.[1]

Balmuth has argued that coinage was not so much an *invention* as a *development*, consisting in the combination of two functions that had existed for centuries in the ancient Near East, the metal piece as a means of payment with the seal mark as a means of identification.[2] Further, it seems that the Greeks themselves, in the earliest extant statements about the invention of coinage, attributed it not to themselves but to eastern neighbours, the Lydians. According to Pollux (9.83) Xenophanes of Colophon (sixth century BC) maintained that coinage was invented by the Lydians; and Herodotus (1.94) wrote that the Lydians 'were the first, of men whom we know of, to have minted and used coinage of gold and silver'. This tradition, though not necessarily reliable,[3] is consistent with fact that the earliest surviving coins are of electrum, of which Lydia possessed the natural sources. In

---

[1] West 1997, 24.   [2] Balmuth 1971, 1975, 1979, 1980.
[3] Kraay 1976, 313 observes that the Pollux notice 'may be no more than an incomplete repetition of Herodotus' note that the Lydians were the first to mint pure gold and silver (as opposed to electrum)'. Herodotus is probably not referring to electrum, which apparently was called λευκὸς χρυσὸς ('white gold', Hdt. 1.50) or ἤλεκτρον. The Greeks sometimes associate (the negative consequences of) precious metal money with barbarians: 14E n. 102.

particular, the famous early coin hoard buried underneath the mid sixth-century Artemision at Ephesus contains Lydian as well as Greek coins, all made of electrum (7B). The later tradition that the first coins were issued by Pheidon of Argos is untrustworthy.

It is on the other hand significant that none of the various Greek traditions regards coinage as an ancient invention of Mesopotamia, Syria, or Egypt. The Greeks attributed it either to themselves or to their neighbours the Lydians.[4] And indeed in this respect too the traditions cohere with archaeology, for the vast amount of pre-sixth-century material (including numerous texts) discovered from the Near East has produced surprisingly little indication of the use of standardised pieces of metal for payment, and even less, if any at all, for the use of marks or inscriptions to guarantee the quality or weight of metal pieces (15B).

The Greek use of coinage represents not the development of earlier practice, as Balmuth claims, but rather something radically new. The coin-mark is in function essentially different from the seal-mark (6C). The novelty of coinage consists of four closely interrelated features. First, the coins were issued by (and their acceptance sometimes enforced by) the state, which guaranteed their value by its mark, so that they were counted[5] rather than having to be weighed. Second, their conventional value was generally higher than their value as metal (7D). Third, coins were not one of a number of commodities, but rather a special kind of thing, of use *only* for their monetary value (because they were generally worth more than their metal, it made no sense to melt them down). Fourth, Greek coins have been found in vast numbers. Coinage spread rapidly throughout the Greek city-states and was convenient enough to be used for a very wide range of transactions – including transactions of low value, which were greatly facilitated by the acceptance of tiny pieces of precious metal without testing or weighing and subsequently by coinage in bronze, which has very little intrinsic value. In all the mountainous evidence for economic transactions in the ancient Near East there is not the slightest indication of any of these characteristics until the invention of coinage in western Asia Minor. Greek coinage is closer to modern money than it is to anything in the ancient Near East.

This distinctiveness of Greek coinage, and in particular its use in low-value transactions, is reflected also in its terminology. As we have seen, the Greeks derived their large weights (mnas and talents) from the Semites, and used them also as units of account. But their words for *coins*, which were of relatively low value and had no Near-Eastern equivalent, are mainly *Greek*

---

[4] Ephorus 70 *FGrH* F115; Hcld.Pont. fr. 152 Wehrli.   [5] E.g. Le Rider 1989, 163.

words for *things*. With the equivalence of a hundred drachmas to one mna, the two systems – Greek coinage and Semitic weights – coalesce.[6]

The obol was the basic unit on which higher weights (or values) such as the drachma, didrachm, and so on were constructed. But among the Greeks in the eastern Aegean the basic unit was a relatively high-value coin, the stater, with smaller coins being subdivisions of it – 'thirds', 'sixths', and so on down to the ninety-sixth.[7] And so the stater is intermediate between the ancient Near East and mainstream Greek practice, not only geographically but also in the sense that on the one hand the word means 'weigher' and refers to a coin of fairly high value,[8] but on the other hand, a coin, it does *not* have to be weighed at every transaction, and is part of a system that includes coins of low value.

Given that the Greeks were the first people to use coinage in this way, what are we to make of the tradition that it was in fact invented by the Lydians? The apparent contradiction is diminished by a number of considerations. Firstly, at the time of the birth of coinage (probably towards the end of the seventh century, 7B) Lydia seems to have been subject to considerable Greek cultural influence. Pottery found at Sardis is influenced by Greek fashions probably as early as the eighth century, and Greek vases are imported regularly in the seventh.[9] It seems that the Lydian alphabet was adapted from the Greek at some time in the seventh century BC.[10] And Greek influence in various respects is detectable at least from the early sixth.[11] The large mixing-bowl sent to Delphi early in his reign by the Lydian king Alyattes (*c*. 610–560 BC) was made by a Greek craftsman, as was the one sent by his successor Croesus (Hdt.1.25, 51). The same weight standard[12] was used for Lydian coins and the coins of the Greek city-states of southern Asia Minor. It may not be too far from the truth to suggest that in the invention of coinage the Lydians contributed the material (electrum),

---

[6] 6B; See most recently Kroll 2001a.   [7] For this contrast see Kraay 1976, 316.

[8] For a possible Near-Eastern origin for the Euboic stater standard see Kroll 2001a; also Kraay 1976, 316; Caccamo Caltabiano and Radici Colace 1992, 138–9.

[9] Hanfmann 1978, 28; Boardman 1980, 95; Mellink 1991, 646; Hanfmann 1983, 79, 80, 89, 98. According to a recent survey of Corinthian pottery in Sardis, it 'increased significantly' in the years *c*. 720–680 and 'reached its peak' during the reigns of Ardys and Alyattes (*c*. 645–560): Snyder Schaeffer, Ramage, and Greenewalt 1997, 3.

[10] The earliest surviving text in the Lydian alphabet is from the early sixth century: Masson 1991, 669–71; cf. Hanfmann 1983, 88. Greek writing appears on a Lydian bowl of *c*. 570–550 BC: Hanfmann 1983, 89.

[11] Hanfmann 1978, 29; Boardman 1980, 97–9; Hanfmann 1983, 71, 74, 98 (buildings); Hanfmann and Ramage 1978, 17 (sculpture); Mellink in Boardman et al. 1991, 650 (architectural decoration); cf. Sappho fr. 96 L–P; Nik. Damasc. 90 *FGrH* F62 (song), F63 and Aelian *VH* 3.26 (marriage), and Radet 1893, 289 *et passim*.

[12] The so-called 'Milesian', though such terms for weight standards have no ancient authority.

whereas the dominant culture was Greek. The maritime Greek neighbours of Lydia were numerous, enterprising, without their own supplies of precious metal, and (at least before the time of Croesus) largely politically independent. The Lydian kings were probably happy to give some of their massive surplus of electrum[13] to these Greeks in exchange for goods and services, for the Greek art found in Lydia, for the use of Greek ports, Greek trading ships, and Greek mercenaries. In this way, though the first coins were of Lydian electrum and may have been of Lydian issue, it was among the Greeks that coinage first *circulated widely*. Many of the earliest surviving coins are from Greek areas.[14]

Payment of mercenaries (6c) would require numerous pieces of standard weight, but also, given the varying intrinsic value of pieces of electrum of the same weight (7D), marks on the pieces to guarantee a standard value. It is even conceivable that it was Greek mercenaries who insisted on such a mark. When the idea had proved effective, it was transferred to coins of gold, silver, or indeed eventually bronze – metals more generally available in Greek lands (6B). After the initiating impetus provided by the vast supply of Lydian electrum, the institution of coinage was rapidly taken much further by the Greeks than by anybody else – and this too suggests a role for the Greeks in its genesis. The combination, in this genesis, of Pactolus electrum, Lydian monarchy, and the Greek polis may be reflected in the Greek traditions about who invented coinage: the Lydians, the Greeks, or the Greek wife of king Midas, Demodoke, daughter of the ruler of Cyme.[15]

The third people to issue coins were the Persians. Their conquest of western Asia Minor in 545 BC did not seriously disrupt the issue of Lydian and Greek coinage in the area under their control. But towards the end of the sixth century they replaced Lydian-type coinage by making their own gold (darics) and silver (sigloi) coins.[16] By this time the peculiar dynamic of Greek coinage (involving, as described above, the interrelation of state guarantee, conventional value, low-value denominations, widespread use, and general acceptability) was in full swing across the Greek world.

---

[13] Sardis was dominated by the palace, and the processing of gold was controlled by the king (Hanfmann 1983, 76, 85). According to its excavator, 'the nearly total lack of gold or silver coins in the excavated commercial-industrial areas of Sardis suggests that they were concentrated in the hands of the king and possibly wealthy merchants' (Hanfmann 1983, 77; cf. 73, 83; 246 n. 87). No such coins have been found since (information I owe to Laura Gadbery).

[14] All early electrum coins are from western Asia Minor and neighbouring islands, except for a hoard from Gordion in Phrygia, which was at the time closely associated with Lydia: Le Rider 2001, 43, 47.

[15] See n. 4; Demodoke: Pollux 9.83; Arist. fr. 611.37 Rose; cf. 6c n. 99.

[16] Kraay 1976, 31–2.

In the words of Kraay, coinage 'was and for some time remained an essentially Greek phenomenon, which non-Greek peoples such as the Etruscans, Phoenicians, Carthaginians, and Egyptians were slow to adopt', with the Persians providing 'only a partial exception'.[17] Persian coins were relatively high in metal value, and used in a much narrower range of transactions.[18] Sigloi did not circulate outside western Anatolia, the area of the earlier Lydian coinage: elsewhere in the Persian empire they are found only rarely, and were treated as bullion. Darics were too valuable to have much circulation anywhere, although they 'were obviously welcome everywhere as a source of gold, whether to serve as a store of private wealth or to be converted into jewelry and sacred offerings'.[19]

B WHEN WAS COINAGE INVENTED?

About a century ago were discovered, in and around the 'Central Basis' under the Ephesian Artemision, numerous Greek and Lydian coins, all of electrum, and almost all on the same weight standard (ranging from half a stater to a ninety-sixth). They seem to represent various stages in the genesis of coinage, from unmarked pieces of standard weights (not really coins)[20] to full coins.[21] They must have been buried before the temple was built in the mid-sixth century.[22] But how long before that were the coins made? The various answers to this question have been influenced by a number of factors: the dating of numerous other artefacts found along with the

---

[17] Kraay 1976, 317. As partial exceptions one may add other peoples producing coinage in proximity or interaction with the Greeks: (a) the Lycian and Karian coins produced under the Persian empire; (b) the large denomination coins produced by the Macedonian tribes in the late sixth and early fifth centuries, presumably from the local ores of Mt Pangaios, probably intended for foreign use, perhaps as tribute to the Persian empire: Kraay 1976, 139–41; (c) fifth-century Thracian occasional issues, perhaps minted by their Greek neighbours: Kraay 1976, 147–8. Kraay notes (325) that 'apart from during a few decades in the late sixth and early fifth century, the northern Greek tribes must normally have disposed of most of their silver in the form of bullion rather than coin. The fact that it was only in the Greek coastal cities that bullion was converted into coin serves to emphasise the close connection of coinage with Greek city life'.

[18] See e.g. Naster 1970, who concludes that 'one is almost led to believe that for the Achaemenids and their higher administration darics and sigloi remained ingots of good metal in practical sizes rather than coins in the proper sense' (604); similarly Le Rider 2001, 166–7, 170–3, 174 (most of the Empire did not know the use of coinage); Caccamo Caltabiano and Radici Colace 1992, 41 n. 51, 100 n. 84, 126–7 (on *eudokimos*), 138. Persian coins also differ from Greek coins of our period by seeming to evoke the authority of the king, whom they depict.

[19] Kraay 1976, 33–4. Greek perception of the exceptional purity of Darius' gold coins: Hdt. 4.166.

[20] As well as typeless pieces with an incuse square on the reverse (some with striations on the obverse).

[21] Though cf. Price 1983; and one typeless piece has been struck with the same stamp as a piece with a type (lion) on the other side: Karwiese 1991, 9–10.

[22] This archaeological dating coheres with Hdt. 1.92 (Croesus (*c.* 560–546 BC) donated most of the columns).

coins,[23] the dating of a jar in which nineteen of the coins were found,[24] the artistic qualities of these and other electrum coins and whether their variety implies much chronological development,[25] the very little known from other contexts of electrum coins,[26] and the dating of the first silver coinage.[27] One problem has only recently been solved: according to the excavators, the context in which the coins were found does not after all (contrary to the view of earlier excavators) provide a *terminus ante quem* for their burial any earlier than the mid-sixth century.[28] On the other hand, recent excavations at the temple have provided an earlier *terminus ante quem* for coinage by unearthing other coins that must have been deposited at around 600 BC – this is the earliest dateable archaeological context we have for coinage.[29] We can at present be no more precise than to say that the very earliest development of coinage probably occurred towards the end of the seventh century.[30]

The earliest known electrum coins were Lydian and Greek.[31] The only Greeks to mint electrum were those who lived relatively close to the Lydian source of electrum, in Asia Minor or the neighbouring islands. From about the mid-sixth century electrum coinage disappears from Lydia and from most of those Greek cities that had used it, to be replaced in Lydia by gold and silver coinage and in most of the Greek cities by silver coinage. Before this shift, had the advanced Greek cities of the mainland, such as Aegina, Athens, and Corinth, already been minting silver? The problem of the chronology of the earliest Greek silver coins resembles that of the earliest electrum. The number of cities minting silver coins before 480 BC seems to be very large.[32] We have a *terminus ante quem* provided by coins (from Aegina, Abdera, Cyprus) placed in the foundation deposits of the Apadana at Persepolis in about 515 BC.[33] And before being destroyed in 510 BC Sybaris in Southern Italy had surely already produced much of its coinage, the volume and stylistic development of which 'suggest that it can hardly have lasted for less than several decades'.[34] The decision on how much

---

[23] Jacobsthal 1951.   [24] Williams 1991–3.   [25] Weidauer 1975; cf. e.g. Karwiese 1985, 127–8.

[26] E.g. Isik (1992) on a hoard from Clazomenae, about the genuineness of which serious doubts have been raised.

[27] Price argued that his downdating of the first silver coinage implies a downdating also of electrum coinage: Price and Waggoner 1975, 122–3, 139. But cf. Spier 1998, 334.

[28] Bammer and Muss 1996, 89; Karwiese 1995, 118–19.

[29] Bammer and Muss 1996, 89; Karwiese 1995, 135.

[30] For earlier dating see esp. Weidauer 1975 and Kagan 1982; for late dating see esp. Price 1983. An impossibly late dating is proposed by Vickers 1985.

[31] Kraay 1976, 20–30; Karwiese 1995, 117–28.   [32] They are listed by Osborne 1996, 253–5.

[33] Even this date is however not entirely certain: Howgego 1995, 141 n. 1; to his refs. add Root 1988.

[34] Kraay 1976, 163.

further back from these *termini ante quos* to extend the coinage depends largely on the co-existence of coins from various cities in hoards (some with *termini ante quos*), combined with complex arguments concerning stylistic development. The claim that the coinage of Athens, Corinth, and Aegina could not have begun before *c.* 550 BC[35] is too confident,[36] especially for Aegina, which as well as being at that time a centre of trade was associated by a later Greek tradition with the first coins.[37] But neither, it must be admitted, are there good reasons for a much earlier date.[38] And it is tempting to associate the beginning of coinage in Attica with Peisistratus' use of precious metal, shortly after the middle of the century, to consolidate his tyranny (5B, 14D).

Besides the discovery of actual coins, there are two other kinds of evidence for the date of the earliest coinage. One of these – direct statements by ancient authors – is of little use. In particular, the tradition attributing the first issue of coins to Pheidon of Argos is untrustworthy, even for Greece;[39] and anyway Pheidon cannot be dated with any confidence. The remaining kind of evidence – the early mention of coins in literary texts and inscriptions – is also unreliable, in that the words that may refer to coins may also refer to units of weight. The mentions of 'staters' in early literary texts and inscribed laws have accordingly been discussed in 5A under the broader category of money, along with the 'drachmas' in the laws of Solon. We should perhaps be less sceptical about the 'drachmas' in inscriptions of around 500 BC (from Olympia, Athens, Delphi, Knossos).[40]

C WHY WAS COINAGE INVENTED?

Both Plato and Aristotle thought that coinage was introduced to facilitate trade,[41] albeit thereby serving the *koinōnia* (communality) of the polis.[42]

---

[35] Price and Waggoner 1975.   [36] Note the criticisms of Holloway 1984.

[37] The tradition first surfaces in the fourth century BC: Brown 1950.

[38] Kroll and Waggoner 1984; Howgego 1995, 6. A seventh-century date was still maintained by Kagan 1982.

[39] E.g. Brown 1950; Kroll and Waggoner 1984.

[40] Van Effenterre and Ruzé 1994–5, I nos. 4, 6, 24, 72, II 17; a discussion of the earliest inscriptions that do or may mention coinage is Holle 1978, 211–22. Intriguing is a mid sixth-century Attic vase-painting inscribed ΔΥΟΒΕΛΟΚΑΙΜΕΘΙΓΕΣ, variously interpreted as δυ' ὀβέλω καὶ μὴ θίγη(ι)ς ('two obols, and hands off!'), δυ' ὀβέλω καὶ μ'ἔθιγες ('two obols and you have me'), or – more likely perhaps – with ὀβέλω meaning spits: *ABV* 136 n. 50 (with bibliography). For pre-480 BC vases with prices marked in obols see Johnston 1979, 33–5.

[41] Pl. *Rep.* 371d; Aristot. *Pol.* 1257a19–40. Aristot. *EN* 1133a19–b28 is (contrary to what is sometimes claimed) based on the same view.

[42] Pl. *Rep.* 371b; Aristot. *EN* 1133b16–18; Martin 1995, 257–62. The *Magna Moralia* states that the use of currency (*nomisma*) to facilitate exchange holds together the *koinōnia* of the polis (1194a23–5).

Demosthenes (*Timocr.* 213) attributed to Solon the view that silver coinage was invented by private individuals for their private transactions. And Ephorus (70 *FGrH* F176) reported that the first silver coinage was struck in Aegina because people there became sea-traders as a result of the poverty of the soil. Modern historians on the other hand have tended to emphasise the need of central authority to make and receive numerous uniform payments – paying mercenaries (7A) or temple-builders, for example, or receiving fines or taxes.[43]

Neither of these explanations fully satisfies, for both complex trade and uniform payments had – along with the technological ability to make coins and the use of metal (notably silver) for money functions – existed for centuries in vast areas of the Near East. What was the new factor or factors that motivated the revolutionary idea of stamping numerous pieces of metal to guarantee their value?

For its first fifty years or so coinage was made only of electrum, an alloy of gold and silver, even though it was silver that had in the Near East been the metal most used for money functions – and was found in the form of flattened but unstamped dumps along with the early electrum coins under the Artemision.[44] Unlike gold and silver, electrum varies greatly in colour and intrinsic value, depending on the proportions it contains of gold and silver, proportions not easily discernible with any precision.[45] The consequent problems surrounding the use, whether for exchange or uniform payments, of the abundant electrum available to the Lydians could best be solved, it has been argued, by adapting the idea of the seal to stamping pieces of metal so as to guarantee that they would (whatever their colour or intrinsic worth) be accepted back by the issuer at a certain value.[46] Given that private individuals were unlikely to be in a position to issue such a

---

Aristotle's account is central to the claim by Will (1954; 1955; 1975) that coinage originated as a means of distributive justice in the polis. Though this has a certain plausibility, and may be thought to converge with my argument in chapters 3 and 4, there is hardly any real evidence to connect the earliest coinage with a *political policy* of distributive justice: e.g. Will's view that in some cities coinage was adopted by the tyrant to facilitate the redistribution of the confiscated property of the rich is no more than a guess. And even if we accept that in *EN* Aristotle thinks of currency as 'l' instrument d' évaluation d' une justice sociale rétributive, destiné a maintenir la réciprocité des rapports social sur le plan de la justice' (Will 1955, 8), he does think of this as occurring within *exchange.*

[43] Kraay 1976, 320–3; Rutter 1981; Martin 1996. There is no real evidence for 'civic pride' as a factor: Martin 1996; cf. Le Rider 2001, 240–1.

[44] Robinson 1951, 166–7, nos.1 and 48.

[45] Wallace 1987, 390–2 considers, and rules out, specific gravity, the touchstone, and cementation: cf. Le Rider 2001, 89–91.

[46] Notable (and different) versions of this idea are Holloway (1978) and Wallace (1987).

guarantee, most of the electrum coins were issued by the state – as indeed is suggested by the earliest coin types.[47] The stamp then seems to have been a guarantee not of weight, which being fairly regular helped to impart uniformity of value,[48] but rather of redeemability or conventional value. It was probably in the second quarter of the sixth century[49] that cementation, a heating process that separated gold from silver, came to fruition in Sardis, and thereafter coins were generally issued in silver rather than in electrum.[50]

The electrum found in the rivers of ancient Lydia had a silver content of circa 10 per cent to 30 per cent.[51] For the making of the coins this natural alloy was, metallurgical analysis has shown, at least sometimes diluted by the addition of silver. Eight chemically analysed 'royal' Lydian coins have a silver content of between 42 per cent and 46 per cent.[52] Despite the small sample, this homogenisation of the value of electrum coins counts against the explanation just given of the practice of stamping. And the low gold content of coins whose conventional value seems to have been based on a higher gold content[53] may seem to support another explanation – that the disparity between conventional and intrinsic value was designed to make a profit for the minting authority.[54] On the other hand, suspicion of electrum content may have impeded its monetisation even where its intrinsic value had been made consistent. And early Greek electrum coins seem to have been less consistent than the Lydian. Along with the Lydian coins just mentioned were analysed six 'Geometric' coins (with geometric designs similar to those found in the excavations at Ephesus, and probably Ionian), which were found to vary in their silver content from 32 per cent to 62 per

---

[47] Wallace 1987, 393–4.

[48] Wallace 1987, 385–7; Hanfmann 1983, 76–7; Figueira 1998, 92–4. Wallace argues (394) that the coins were likely to have been weighed at each transaction. But weighing of the many tiny coins that were produced from the beginning would have been difficult and might have seemed not worth the trouble. Weighing is more likely for foreign trade than within the polis, as noted by Kroll 1998, 228 n.19, who argues that generally even in the archaic period (as certainly in the fourth century) silver coins were *counted* by Greeks, not weighed.

[49] 6B n. 65. Previously the awareness that electrum varied in value was based on perception of its varying gold and silver content (and indeed on the fact that it could be diluted by the addition of silver, even though there is evidence that it might be envisaged as a kind of gold – 'white gold': Hdt. 1.50; Pi. *Nem.* 7.78), not on the possibility of extracting pure gold and pure silver from it.

[50] Wallace 1987, 392: 'The ultimate solution to the unstable value of electrum was cementation. Before the discovery of that process, the solution was coinage.'

[51] Wallace 1987, 386. Other figures given are not very different.   [52] Cowell et al. 1998.

[53] The gold stater that eventually replaced the electrum stater was lighter by a proportion that implies that the electrum stater was *circa* 70 per cent gold: Le Rider 2001, 94–5; but cf. Wallace 2001.

[54] An idea pioneered by the as yet ill-informed work of Bolin 1958, recently revived by Le Rider 2001, 79–84, against whom Kroll (2001b) supports Wallace.

cent. Twenty sixth-century electrum coins categorised by Kraay as from 'uncertain cities of Ionia' were shown by analysis to have a silver content ranging from *circa* 21 per cent to *circa* 76 per cent.[55] Eighteen electrum coins from Samos, buried probably between 560 and 540 BC, vary in silver content from 18.5 per cent to 50.3 per cent.[56]

The motivation for the invention of coinage is irrecoverable, and may anyway be irrelevant to its subsequent significance. The use of the very first coinage might have been quite different from its subsequent rapid and widespread adoption, especially as the context of the former (at least partly Lydian, with coins perhaps issued by individuals) might have been very different from the context of the latter (issued by the Greek city-states). Profit for the minting authority, being possible with metals other than electrum, is insufficient as an explanation of the invention of coinage (especially if for the already hugely wealthy Lydian kings), but may – once coinage and its convenience had been established – have played a part subsequently in the Greek city-states, for instance in the transition from electrum to silver coinage, which is more detectably consistent in content than is electrum and so depends less on its stamp for acceptance. Again, even if we knew that coinage had been introduced for a specific use, say paying Greek mercenaries, it is difficult to see how payment with small pieces of precious metal (as opposed to, say, food) would be generally acceptable unless those pieces also had fairly general exchange-value in a wide area.[57] It is striking that the earliest surviving electrum coins from the various mints of western Asia Minor are dominated by only two weight standards (the Milesian in the south and Lydia, the Phokaian in the north). Early electrum coinage is a stream rather than a trickle, early silver coinage a torrent: its convenience (as small durable pieces of standardised value) must have unleashed, or at least accelerated, that self-generating dynamic by which because something reaches a degree of acceptability as payment it becomes more and more generally acceptable. The dynamic is likely to

---

[55] Kraay 1958; cf. Cowell et al. 1998, 530, 533.

[56] Nicolet-Pierre and Barrandon 1997. A list of the proportions of gold to silver in successive periods of electrum coinage from Phokaia and Mytilene is reproduced from Bodenstedt (1976), by Figueira 1998, 93–4 (the earliest Phokaian coins are typical: silver varies from 34.6 per cent to 40.8 per cent; later it reaches 55.8 per cent). For a recent overview and continuing technological advance see Keyser and Clark (2001).

[57] Conceivably the attitude of a mercenary paid in money (albeit before the introduction of coinage) is represented by Archilochus (5A n. 4), who says not only that his bread and wine depend on his spear (fr. 2) but also, in contrast to the Homeric hero, that he cares not about losing his shield in battle because he can acquire another one just as good (fr. 5). Cf. Hybrias the Cretan, *PMG* 909: 'Spear and sword are great wealth for me.'

require the authoritative guarantee of value and redeemability that only a state is able to provide;[58] and indeed coinage was almost always issued by a state. If there had been a specific use for the very first coins, it would very quickly have been transcended by this dynamic.

If this is so, and coins were early used generally for various kinds of payments (including commerce),[59] we would expect there to be coins of small as well as large value. And that is what we find. The smallest denomination of early electrum is one ninety-sixth of a stater, at 0.15g presumably as small a size as was thought convenient to manufacture and handle, but perhaps equivalent in value to one third of a goat.[60] As for silver coinage, which is much less valuable, it is now clear for various parts of the Greek world that fractions (i.e. denominations lower than a stater or a drachma) were produced in the earliest period of minting and that there were already in the sixth century very large numbers of low value coins, far more than was thought to be the case a generation ago.[61] For instance, a sixth-century hoard from Asian Ionia has 906 silver coins of which the two smallest denominations (average 0.43g and 0.21g) were struck with 394 known obverse dies, suggesting an original production of hundreds of thousands or even millions of coins.[62] Silver is no longer the mere luxury it is in Homer, but circulates throughout the citizen body.

We might also expect the self-generating dynamic unleashed by coinage to have extended to trade between different city-states, and even to the long-distance maritime trade that had expanded markedly from the last quarter of the seventh century BC.[63] Early electrum is in fact not found far outside its area of issue, perhaps because the difficulty of knowing its (highly variable) intrinsic value (7D) made it unacceptable outside the relatively small area in which there was general confidence in its face value. However, we now know that the silver coins of Corinth and Aegina (trading cities without their own supplies of silver) reached Magna Graecia by the end of the sixth century and (as well as other coinages) Egypt not long afterwards;

---

[58] The consequent acceptability of its coins may spread outside the borders of the issuing state. The many fifth-century city-states (e.g. Megara) that did not mint their own coins might use the coins of others.

[59] See Schaps 1997, 1 for a case that at Athens 'coinage, the agora, and retail trade seem to have grown up simultaneously'.

[60] If we assume that the ratio of silver to electrum was 1:10 and that Plutarch is right to say that in Solon's time in Athens a drachma was worth a goat: Kim 1994, 4.

[61] Howgego 1990, 3; Arnold-Biucchi 1992; Kim 1994; 2001; Warren 1998, 349 n. 30. Inasmuch as small coins are more expensive (relative to value) to manufacture than large ones, they might have had a greater disparity between their conventional and their bullion value.

[62] Kim 1994, 23–6, 61; 2001, 12; Howgego 1995, 7.   [63] On this expansion see e.g. Reed 1984.

and future discoveries may extend this picture.[64] Although long-distance
maritime trade continued without the use of coinage, it may nevertheless
also have been an important factor in the astonishing rapidity of the spread
of the idea of silver coinage, which is relatively uniform across the Greek
world: for instance, we have seen that Sybaris had its own coinage well
before 510 BC.

D   FIDUCIARITY[65]

Crucial for our overall argument is that, however exactly coinage was invented and first used, the stamp on the earliest coins was not a sign of
quality, and almost certainly not of quantity, but rather of redeemability –
i.e. of politically (or socially) conferred value. The coin is accepted not
merely for its intrinsic value but on trust (that it will be disposable without
loss).[66] Certainly, the quality of the material mattered in so far as it had
to be electrum (albeit in varying proportions of gold and silver). And the
quantity of the material mattered in that it might at any point be checked
for weight (and so was not clipped). Nevertheless, where the stamp signified metal with value x but the intrinsic (bullion) value of the metal was
$x + 1$ or (much more likely) $x - 1$, then generally the coin was worth x.
The invention and use of the earliest coins demanded the recognition of
the combination of, and antithesis between, sign (or form) and substance,
an antithesis in which, although the substance must have some intrinsic
value, decisive is the sign, which implies a homogeneous ideal substance
distinct from the metal in which the sign is expressed.[67] Originally it was
probably the otherwise insoluble problem of valuing electrum, a valuable
but variable mixture, that forced this antithesis into consciousness. But
once the antithesis had been established, then even after the abandonment
of electrum coinage, the possibility persisted of generally accepted disparity between the conventional and the intrinsic value of money. Was this

---

[64] Howgego (1990, 3 and 1995, 95–8) revises the sceptical account of Kraay (1976, 318–20) by means of
subsequent discoveries.
[65] For my broad definition of 'fiduciary' see 1C. 'Token' I use as a sub-category in which the
material is virtually worthless.
[66] Of course in all acceptance of money *qua* money there will be trust (in its future acceptability as
money), even where there is no disparity between intrinsic and conventional value. The disparity
increases the importance of the trust.
[67] 6C. Momentously mistaken therefore are the first two sentences of Shell 1982: 'Between the electrum
money of ancient Lydia and the electric money of contemporary America there occurred a historically
momentous change. The exchange value of the earliest coins derived wholly from the material
substance (electrum) of the ingots of which the coins were made and not from the inscriptions
stamped into these ingots.'

possibility subsequently realised? The evidence – from the coins themselves, literary texts, and inscriptions – gives us three forms of its realisation.

(a) Like early electrum, so subsequently silver might be (openly or secretly) adulterated by the issuing authority, resulting in a disparity between the conventional value of the coin and its value as bullion. Strictly speaking, conventionality is involved only if the adulteration is open, as it seems generally to have been (serious adulteration is easily detected). On the one hand the silver of Greek coins that survive from the archaic and classical periods is generally of a high level of purity. But on the other hand Demosthenes maintains (24.214) that 'many cities using silver coinage mixed with bronze and lead, even openly, are saved and suffer nothing at all as a result'. Already in the sixth century Lesbos and Cyzicus were producing coins in base silver.[68] Chemical analysis has detected 'small apparently deliberate additions of copper' to archaic silver coins from various mints.[69] The so-called light tetrobols of Alexander I of Macedon (*c.* 495–450 BC) always include a 'significant amount of base metal' with their silver, and so were presumably intended as a fiduciary coinage for circulation only within Macedonia (unlike his purer coins).[70] According to Herodotus the purest silver coinage of his day was the one once issued[71] by Aryandes, the governor of Egypt, in imitation of the purity of the gold coinage issued by his master the emperor Darius.[72] This is curious, given the scarcity of Egyptian coinage (until after the conquest of Alexander the Great). What is significant for us is that although coinage was primarily a Greek institution, the purest coins were (rightly or wrongly) supposed to have been produced by non-Greeks, who (unlike most Greeks) treated coins as bullion and so had more interest in their purity.[73]

(b) In a more extreme move than (a), coinage may be issued in base metal, which is in coin size near worthless. A number of lead coins have been identified as Samian of the sixth century BC, but these may well have been covered with electrum foil – perhaps in a desperate attempt to deceive, or even, paradoxically, to inspire a degree of confidence.[74] A late fourth century BC text[75] records various instances of base-metal coinage being issued

---

[68] Kraay 1976, 38–9, 353.   [69] Gale, Gentner, and Wagner 1980, 48.
[70] Kraay 1976, 142. Further examples and bibliography: Stroud 1974, 171–2.
[71] *Circa* 500 BC: Tuplin 1989, 77–8.
[72] Hdt. 4.166. Interestingly, Hdt. implies that this is why Darius killed him (though ostensibly for rebelling). A full discussion of the scholarship on this passage is by Tuplin 1989.
[73] E.g. Kraay 1976, 16; Figueira 1998, 31; Möller 2000, 209. In the huge early hoard from Asyut in Egypt there are many coins gashed, or even cut in two, to test quality.
[74] Kraay 1976, 30. They may have given rise to the story (disbelieved by Hdt., 3.56.2) that Polycrates once bribed the Spartans with lead coins covered with gold.
[75] [Aristot.] *Oecon.* II 1348b–1350a.

along with measures to create confidence. Dionysius the fourth-century BC
tyrant of Syracuse called an assembly which heard him praise his new tin
coinage[76] and voted (willingly or unwillingly) to accept it.[77] Timotheus
the fourth-century BC Athenian general on campaign in northern Greece
issued bronze coinage to his soldiers and at the same time took steps to create confidence in the new coinage among the traders. Some of the bronze
coins struck by Timotheus have been discovered at Olynthus.[78] The success of such fiduciary (or token) coinages, and indeed of any coinage of
which the conventional exceeds the material value, will be limited to the
area within which confidence can be created. But this limitation will also
have the advantage of requiring the money to be spent locally.[79] It was said
that traders accepted the base-metal coinage issued by Perdiccas (king of
Macedon c. 450–413 BC) to his troops, 'and since it was useless beyond the
border, they took in exchange the food produced in the country'.[80] Nor
do such devices always require autocrats to implement them: the people of
Clazomenae were said to have paid off a debt by issuing an iron coinage
which was exchanged for silver (in such a way that in the end, we are told,
nobody lost out).[81] We do not have to believe every detail of these narratives in order to recognise an element of historicity. Contemporary detail is
provided by Attic comedy. The term *kollubon* (or *kollubos*), which is found
as early as the 420s,[82] refers to a coin or token of very low value, probably of
bronze.[83] The parabasis of Aristophanes' *Frogs* (405 BC) compares the new
bronze coinage unfavourably with the older coinage (and the newer gold
coinage), which had a circulation 'among the Greeks and the barbarians
everywhere', implying that the new bronze coins had no such circulation.
And in his *Ecclesiazousai* (392 BC) a citizen remembers that 'we voted for
those bronzes', and that some time later he was about to pay for some
barley meal with bronze coins when the herald shouted that nobody was
to receive bronze any more 'for we are using silver'.[84]

---

[76] Pollux 9.79 adds that this small coin (*nomismation*) was worth four Attic drachmas instead of one;
    Caccamo Caltabiano and Radici Colace 1992, 92 with further bibliography.
[77] The story combines the empty persuasiveness of coinage and of rhetoric: cf. Zeno St. fr. 81 von
    Arnim, ap. D. L. 7.18 (rhetoric compared to coinage); Kratin. fr. 239 K–A (sophists as minting
    words like coins?).
[78] Picard 1989, 681; Kroll 1993, 25–6.
[79] Cf. Plato's desire to legislate a distinction between a local currency for everyday use and a common
    Greek currency for external use (*Laws* 741e–742b).
[80] Preserved in a late author: Polyaenus 4.10.2.   [81] [Aristot.] *Oecon.* 1348b.
[82] Ar. *Peace* 1200, fr. 3.2; Eupolis fr. 247; Pollux 9.72; etc.; cf. *kollubistēs* meaning a small money-changer.
[83] Robinson 1960, 6–7, 14; Kroll 1993, 24–5; a full recent discussion is by Figueira 1998, 497–511.
[84] Ar. *Frogs* 718–33, *Eccles.* 815–22; cf. fr. 3 (*aiolosikon*) and Kassel–Austin ad loc. The earliest surviving
    Athenian bronze coinage dates from after 350 BC, except for the special case of numerous bronze
    coins plated with silver, which are very likely to be the official issue referred to in Aristophanes:
    Kroll 1976; n. 122 below.

The base-metal coinages mentioned so far were all issued in response to specific crises such as the absence of silver. But iron coinage was regularly used already in the fifth century by Byzantium,[85] and a few iron coins of the Classical period survive from Phocis and various parts of the Peloponnese.[86] Regular bronze coinages were instituted in Southern Italy and Sicily from the middle of the fifth century[87] and in various parts of mainland Greece and the Aegean from the end of the fifth; and in the rest of the Greek world they became an accepted medium of exchange in the fourth.[88] It was a founder of the southern Italian colony Thurii (444/3 BC), one Dionysius, who urged the Athenians to adopt bronze coinage (Athen. 669d). Bronze had the advantages of being available in the absence of silver and of providing coins of very low value (without being too small) for everyday transactions. In fact the value of bronze was, at about a hundred times less than that of silver, low enough to prompt the remark that 'the principle of intrinsic worth was abandoned for bronze coins' (otherwise they would have been too big).[89] Martin Price stresses the continuity of the overvaluation of coinage against its bullion from the earliest electrum coins (of different intrinsic value but the same weight) to silver coins of poor alloy (produced perhaps to retain silver within the area of issue), from which 'it is but a short step to persuade the citizens to accept large, overvalued pieces of bronze, and from large pieces of bronze to small pieces of bronze'.[90]

(c) The silver in coins might be unadulterated, but valued more highly than the equivalent amount of bullion. For the general rule that 'coins were more valuable than the equivalent amount of bullion' Kraay gives three reasons.

---

[85] Ar. *Clouds* 247–9; Plat. Com. fr. 103; Pollux 9.78 (Strattis fr. 37); Ael. Arist. *Orat.* 46.145 Dindorf; Hodkinson 2000, 162.

[86] Hodkinson 2000, 161–2; Oeconomides 1993.

[87] The origins of bronze coinage in this area were the subject of a conference published as a Supplement to vol. 25 of *Ann. Ist. Ital. Num.* (1979). It seems to have been preceded in Sicily by cast bronze objects with monetary use: Price (1979) who also discusses the bronze dolphins and arrowheads that seem to have had monetary use, the former from Olbia, the latter (cf. 15B n. 17) notably from what was probably a Milesian settlement on Berezan – from about the mid-sixth century when dateable: Stancomb 1993.

[88] Macedonia: Kraay 1976, 145; Samos and Chios: Kraay 1976, 253; Corinth: Zervos 1986, 184; Sicyon: Warren 1998, 348–9; in general see Price 1968 and 1979; Howgego 1995, 7–8; Picard 1989, 673–87, 1996, 252–3. The picture will no doubt be expanded by future discoveries and publications: e.g. for recent discoveries and recent and forthcoming publications of bronze coinages in the Peloponnese see Warren 1998, 347–8. The issue of bronze coinage might be accompanied by a reduction in the real value of silver coinage: Picard 1989.

[89] Kraay 1976, 252. This statement will be qualified later in this section.

[90] Price 1979, 358. Fiduciarity might not have been confined to coinage: the usefulness to the polis of the distribution of quasi-monetary tokens is illustrated by the identity-tokens called *sumbola*, which because they entitled the bearer to fees for attending court or assembly seem may have acquired a kind of (small) monetary value: Ar. *Eccles.* 296; *Wealth* 278; fr. 41; Hermipp. fr. 13; Archipp. fr. 8; etc. (LSJ s.v. σύμβολον I 5); cf. Lang and Crosby 1964, 76–8.

First, an amount of labour and equipment had been expended in converting bullion into coin; in addition to that basic charge the state could use its power to exact a still higher price for its coinage; and finally, the balance of supply and demand might increase the market value of a coinage still further. All these factors no doubt varied from time to time and place to place, but their general effect will have been usually to militate against the dispersal of coin from the area in which it had been struck. Coins will have been in greatest demand in the area controlled by the minting authority; beyond that they will have been in demand in places in regular contact with the area of origin; elsewhere they will have tended to revert to the value of bullion. This seems to be the reason why there was nothing like a general interchange of coin between different parts of the Greek world . . .'[91]

Subsequent discoveries have provided more evidence of interchange than was available to Kraay, but without removing the factors he describes. The widespread dispersal of Athenian coinage was, he notes, a result of the special factor that Athens had more than sufficient silver (from Laurium, and after 450 BC from the tributary allies) for her internal needs: 'in these circumstances coin will have been slightly more valuable than bullion, and was readily exported'.[92]

It is beyond doubt that for the citizens of a polis (and for some outsiders, no doubt) the value of coinage may reside not (or not only) in its *intrinsic* value, but rather (at least to some extent) in its *socially conferred* value.[93] The latter value was conferred not only by stamping the coins with an official mark but also, it has emerged, by legislation or edict to establish the value or the acceptability or unacceptability of coin. The agent of this conferral was generally the community organised as polis, but might also be a dominant individual. In a fourth-century text[94] it is reported that

---

[91] Kraay 1976, 323. Bogaert 1968, 316 produces a comparable but more articulated scheme, in which each coin possesses three values: (a) *intrinsic*; (b) *nominal* (higher than the intrinsic), fixed by the issuing city and operative only in the area under its jurisdiction; (c) *commercial*, resulting from various factors – intrinsic value, supply and demand, reputation of the coinage, commercial relations.

[92] Xen. *Poroi* 3.2 (discussed by Le Rider 1989) reports that *argurion*, which means silver or silver coinage (or both), could be exported from Athens at a profit.

[93] For a similar recent generalisation see Figueira 1998, 237–8. Mørkholm (1982) (see also Rhodes 1981, 166–7) argues, on the basis of a disparity between two Athenian weight systems – one for coinage and one for trade – that Athenian coins were consistently 5 per cent lighter than bullion of equivalent value. This is denied by Kroll 2001b, 205, but even he states that 'we can be sure that precious metal coinages locally circulated at a premium over bullion – the premium being a result of minting costs and forced acceptance of the local specie'. Cohen 1992, 12 maintains that 'Athens made great effort to insure the full value of its money', for which the only piece of evidence he cites is the 375/4 BC currency law (Stroud 1974, 157–88 = Melville Jones 1993, no. 91), which refers to the testing of the genuine silver coins and perhaps also to the acceptance of counterfeit Athenian coins as legal tender if they had full silver value. But ensuring a certain silver content does not entail equality of intrinsic with conventional value. For the charging of a fee for the transformation of external into local currency see Le Rider 1989.

[94] [Aristot.] *Oecon.* II 1347a8, 1349b30 (see 5B n. 62). See also Polyaenus 6.9.1.

the late sixth-century Athenian tyrant Hippias made the currency of the Athenians *adokimos* (unacceptable, invalid), fixed a price, recalled it, and – when the Athenians came together for the minting of a new type – issued the same coinage; and that Dionysius of Syracuse called in the citizens' silver and made with it a new coinage in which one drachma was worth two: he was thereby able both to pay for the silver and to pay his other debts. An inscription from Eretria of *c.* 525 BC[95] refers in one section to a fine or compensation to be made in 'acceptable things/wealth' (*chrēmata dokima*), and in another section to a payment of 'ten staters' to be enforced by the archon. It is possible that *chrēmata dokima* refers to any kind of acceptable goods, with 'staters' in the other section being used merely as a standard of weight. But *dokimos* (acceptable) and *adokimos (*unacceptable) are found somewhat later of the acceptability and unacceptability of coinage: e.g. an inscription from Oropus of the early fourth century BC refers to a payment of nine obols in acceptable (*dokimos*) silver coin.[96] And so it may well be that *dokimos* in the Eretrian inscription specifies coinage, or acceptable coinage.[97] It has been objected that *chrēmata* (or singular *chrēma*) 'is not securely attested with the meaning "coinage" before Herodotus'.[98] But *c.* 525 BC is early enough in the history of coinage for there to be as yet no specific word for 'coinage' (*nomisma* meaning coinage is also not found before Herodotus). And so *chrēmata dokima* may refer periphrastically to coinage (or acceptable coinage), especially if *dokimos* had already begun to be associated with the acceptability conferred on coinage by its stamp. If so, then such early insistence by the state on payment in coinage may have helped (or even been essential) to increase its circulation.

Later inscriptions show the state enforcing the acceptability of currency within its own borders. In the Athenian currency decree of 375/4 BC, referred to above, it is prescribed that anyone who does not accept the silver coinage which the certifier has approved will have everything he has on sale that day confiscated (lines 16–18). In an inscription, probably of the fourth century

---

[95] *IG* XII 9 1273/4; *Hesperia* 1964, 381–91; Melville Jones 1993, n. 48, van Effenterre and Ruzé 1994, 1 no. 91. 5B n. 23.

[96] *IG* XII 235 = *SIG*³ 1004.22–3: ἐννεοβόλου δοκίμου ἀργυρίου. Fourth-century examples of *adokimos* of coinage are Pl. *Laws* 742a and [Aristot.] *Oecon.* II 1347a (cited above). For further examples see Volkmann 1939.

[97] It has been objected that Eretrian coinage does not predate 500 BC. But this objection does not allow for accidents of survival and for margins of error in dating coinage and inscription, and for the likelihood that non-Eretrian coinage was already in circulation in Eretria. And see Kraay 1976, 91.

[98] Cairns 1984, 149.

BC, from Olbia on the north coast of the Black Sea it is stated that 'all selling and buying is to take place in the coinage of the polis' and conditions are laid down for the exchange of foreign into local currency.[99] In a law of Gortyn, probably of the third century BC, it is prescribed that 'the bronze coinage is to be used which the city has established, and silver obols are not to be accepted. And if anyone accepts them or refuses to accept the coinage or sell produce for it, he shall pay five staters of silver.'[100] Whereas the confidence generated by the stamp and the intrinsic value of a coin might enable coinage to circulate well outside the area controlled by its issuing authority, the power of a state to *enforce* the acceptability of its coinage is of course confined to its own sphere of jurisdiction, though not necessarily to its own borders – to judge from the Athenians' comprehensive but not entirely successful attempt to enforce by decree exclusive use of its coinage (and weights and measures) throughout their empire.[101]

The shift from intrinsic to socially conferred value had a linguistic dimension. Certain words which had once denoted things, or weights, or both, came – during the development of coinage – to refer (primarily or exclusively) to coins: *statēr*, *drachmē*, *siglos*, and various others.[102] The Greeks also called coins after the things represented by the type (e.g. 'owls': 8H): it is the type that matters. The word for coinage or currency, *nomisma*, does not appear before the fifth century. It comes from *nomisdein*[103] (to acknowledge), is the object or consequence of *nomisdein*.[104] In Aristophanes' *Clouds* Socrates declares that 'the gods are not *nomisma* (currency/coinage) with us', to which Strepsiades replies 'What do you swear with? Iron (coins), as if in Byzantium?'[105] Here the paradox of currency, in which we have to trust but can alter at will, is brilliantly extended to deity[106] whose image stamped on (e.g. Athenian) coins conferred acceptability. *Nomisdein* means

---

[99] *SIG*³ 218 = Melville Jones 1993, n. 349.

[100] *Inscriptiones Creticae* IV 162 = *SIG*³ 525 = Melville Jones 1993, n. 334.

[101] At some time between *c.* 450 and 413 BC; see recently Howgego 1995, 44–6; Figueira 1998, 431–63. The decree, which was to be set up in marketplaces throughout the Athenian empire, has survived in various fragmentary inscriptions.

[102] This is treated in much detail by Caccamo Caltabiano and Radici Colace 1992: note esp. the table at 173.

[103] *Nomisdein* in turn derives from *nomos*, which could itself refer to a monetary unit: e.g. Epicharmos fr. 136–7 Kaibel; cf. Aristotle fr. 590; Laroche 1949, 234–8. *Nomos*, like money (8DE), may have all-embracing power: Pi. fr. 169.1; Hdt. 7.104; Pl. *Prt.* 337d, *Laws* 715d.

[104] Similarly, *psēphos* is a voting-pebble or vote, *psēphisdein* is to vote, and *psēphisma* is what is voted (a decree); *agōn* is a contest or conflict, but *agōnisma* (from *agōnisdesthai*) is generally what is done at an *agōn*; *sphrāgis* is a seal, *sphrāgisdein* is to seal, *sphrāgisma* is the impression produced by the seal; and so on.

[105] 247–9; for the iron coinage of Byzantium see above n. 95.

[106] Cf. also Ar. *Frogs* 890 (Euripides' gods as a 'new minting'). Woodbury 1980, 110 compares the fact that Athenian coins might be called 'maidens' (Eur. fr. 675N²; Pollux 9.75) or even 'Pallases' (Euboulus Fr. 6).

to acknowledge (by belief or practice) – whether the gods (*nomisdein tous theous*) or coinage. The earliest surviving occurrence of *nomisma* is Alcaeus fr. 382 L–P: 'truly she [Athena?] was bringing together a scattered army, inspiring them with *nomisma*'.[107] *Nomisma* here, mysterious enough to be divinely inspired, is the collective confidence, based on custom, that can unite an army. Its next[108] surviving occurrence is strikingly similar – of the paean that Aeschylus' Eteocles (*Sept.* 269) urges the women of Thebes to shriek out – the 'Greek *nomisma* of sacrificial cry, giving confidence to friends, dissolving the terror of battle'. Customary collective practice (*nomisma*), *whether coinage or in battle*, depends on and objectifies the collective confidence of the community, for whom it introduces order into potential chaos.[109]

In contrast to the ancient Near East, then, the Greeks develop a notion of (monetary) currency, and produce thoughts about it. Most famously, Aristotle emphasises that *nomisma* (currency, coinage) has a merely conventional value: it is created by agreement 'and so it is called *nomisma*, because it is not by nature but by convention (*nomos*), and it is in our power to change it and make it useless'.[110] The pseudo-Platonic *Eryxias* develops the same point by observing that the currency of one society may be useless in another: for instance the engraved stones used as currency in Ethiopia would be useless in Sparta, just as the iron that the Spartans deliberately make useless[111] and use as money has no value elsewhere.[112] And Plato himself (*Rep.* 371b) describes coinage (*nomisma*) as a 'symbol for the sake of exchange'.

These texts may seem to exaggerate. Aristotle surely does not mean only *bronze* coinage, but gold and silver coins are not intrinsically worthless, and so are in this respect quite distinct from modern token money (whether metal, paper, notional, or electronic). It is only the disparity between intrinsic and conventional value that is merely conventional.[113] And in the

---

[107] ἦ ποι σύναγ' ἄνδρων <κεκε>δάσμενον στρότον, νόμισμ' ἐπιπνέοισα (<κεκε> Lobel; νομισμένοι πνέοισα cod.: em. Perger).

[108] Unless Pi. fr. 215 Snell had *nomisma* and is earlier. Aesch. *Pers.* 859 has the unlikely variant *nomismata*.

[109] Cf. the collective confidence in battle provided by the (sacrificial, gold-tasselled) *aegis*, associated with Athena and in Homer wielded by her in battle (3c). Not entirely dissimilar is Eur. fr. 542: *nomisma* is not just gold and silver, 'but virtue too is there for all as *nomisma*, which they should use'.

[110] *EN* 1133ab; *Magn. Mor.*1194a; at *Pol.* 1257b he adds the example of Midas starving amid all his gold. An early example of the same thought is the sixth-century Ananios fr. 3 West: 'if someone were to shut in a house much gold and few figs and two or three men, he would soon realise how much better the figs are than the gold'.

[111] Cf. Plut. *Lys.* 17.1.

[112] Ps. Plat. *Eryx.* 399e–400c. Cf. Hdt. 3.23 (the Ethiopians value bronze above gold).

[113] Aristotle is not thinking of the truth that, because all economic value is conferred by desire, there is strictly speaking no such thing as intrinsic economic value.

same passage Aristotle maintains that the metal that developed into coinage was a commodity. Most Greek coins of the Archaic and Classical period are silver, and whatever the nature of the guarantee embodied in the stamp on a silver coin, clearly it was not generally *by itself* enough to create confidence (especially outside the area of issue): for otherwise the issuing authorities would not have made it a general practice to put large amounts of valuable silver, as pure as could be achieved,[114] into their coins. On the other hand coins were, despite some weight variation within the same denomination, counted rather than weighed[115] – at least for small transactions within the area using the weight standard on which the coins were minted. Under-lying Aristotle's view is the probability that even precious metal coinage was (especially as conventional value generally exceeded bullion value) not normally envisaged by Greeks as having potential use-value (i.e. as trans-formable into ornamentation).[116] Even so, it may be sensed as possessing intrinsic value, which would become important were it declared invalid as coinage. The conventional value of Greek coinage always retained some relation with its intrinsic value. Even bronze coinage, which was probably sensed as having *some* intrinsic value, had a conventional value higher than this very low intrinsic value but generally much lower than silver coins of the same size.

In other words the Greeks did not develop *token* money. Credit seems to have been widespread in fourth-century Athens, where our evidence is most plentiful; but even here relations of credit were between individual parties (persons or banks). There is no unequivocal evidence for any general clearing system between banks.[117] But whatever the extent or sophistication of transfer of money without the transfer of metal,[118] the crucial fact is that the Greeks never used anything like the bill of exchange sufficiently to allow the development into *generally* exchangeable bills, money in the form of e.g. papyrus.

---

[114] Kraay 1976, 11; Tuplin 1989, 73; Le Rider 1989, 162.

[115] Le Rider 1989, 163; Kraay 1976, 8 'In practice mints probably varied in their standards of accuracy, but apparent anomalies may be due as much to wear, corrosion or damage as to original carelessness.' Variability is emphasised by Picard 1979, 108, along with the correspondingly greater importance of the *type* as determining value; see also e.g. Caccamo Caltabiano and Radici Colace 1992, 100 n. 81.

[116] A role here may have been played by disapproval of personal luxury in the advanced Greek city-states.

[117] This is admitted even by Cohen 1992, 18, who in general argues for a much greater degree of financial sophistication in Athens than is generally recognised.

[118] For the absence of credit instruments see Millett 1991, 8 ('From the whole of classical Athens we hear of only three occasions on which arrangements were made to avoid the actual transference of cash'). Cohen 1992, 11–18 gives a different picture.

Confidence then is created by a *combination* of factors – quality, quantity, stamp, state authority. A regularised small excess of the coin's value over its bullion value, such as we have seen at Athens, would be accepted as the price paid for the general convenience, for the profit made by the state (perhaps), and most importantly – from the perspective of the recipient's individual interest – for the greater *ease of disposal* which a coin would have over a piece of unmarked bullion. The result is the paradox that even coinage of unadulterated silver (let alone bronze) may tend to become in effect fiduciary coinage: although the silver contributes to confidence, it is not envisaged as a *commodity*.[119] And so whereas we frequently hear of metal artefacts being melted down to make coins,[120] we do not hear of Greek coins being melted down by Greeks to create bullion or artefacts. The only exceptions known to me prove the rule. The making of a hydria from melted Phocian coins (Plut. *Mor.* 401F) was a deliberate reversal of the Phocians' transformation of offerings into coins. And an Athenian inscription of 100/99 BC refers to two bowls each made from drachmas of *stephanēphoros* (coinage).[121] All these are offerings to the gods, and so it is no problem that the financial value of the metal is less than was its value as coin.

Given this tendency of all coinage to become fiduciary coinage, it is not surprising that in the few cases where the excess of the silver coin's value over its bullion value was considerable, this excess was not necessarily enough to destroy confidence: special circumstances, such as a lack of silver or an authoritarian regime, might contribute to ensure that much of the work of creating confidence was done by factors other than the contents of the silver coin. In the case of base-metal coinage, even less of this work was done by the coin's contents. Regular bronze coinages were instituted only after the psychological ground had been prepared by lesser (or similar but temporary) disparities between value and content.[122]

The Greeks were the first people to use coinage on a large scale, and throughout the Archaic and Classical periods such use remained largely confined to the Greeks (7A). *Fiduciarity* (even the relatively limited amount achieved) was in this period even more exclusively Greek. Even the earliest

---

[119] To refuse to accept a coin as too worn was in late fourth-century Athens a sign of boorishness: Theophr. *Char.* 4.13.

[120] E.g. Melville-Jones 1993, nos. 96–101, 327–8, 331, 333.

[121] 100 and 70 drachmas respectively: *IG* ii² 1028, lines 29–31, 40–1 = *SIG*³ 717 = Melville Jones 1993, no. 109. Cf. Hdt. 4.81.

[122] When towards the end of the Peloponnesian war the Athenians voted to institute a bronze coinage (withdrawn some time before 392 BC), they very probably plated the bronze with silver: it seems that the emotional benefit of preserving appearances through plating outweighed the disadvantages of possible confusion with genuine silver. See Kroll 1976; n. 84 above.

Lydian coins exhibit far less variation in the proportions of gold and silver than do the Greek (7c). Greek coins were treated as bullion much more generally by non-Greeks than by Greeks.[123] We remember the distinctive inclination of Greek religion to symbolic substitution.[124] Given the considerable mutual influence in this and earlier periods between the Greeks and their Near-Eastern neighbours in matters of language, visual imagery, artefacts, myth, cult, and so on, it is important to register that this did not include the fiduciarity of money: in this respect Greek culture was quite distinct. I suspect – impossible though it is to demonstrate – that this distinctiveness owed something to the distinctiveness of Greek sacrificial distribution. Collective recognition of the symbolic value of standardised pieces distributed to all citizens is carried over from perishable meat to durable metal. Whatever the truth of that, the distinctiveness of fiduciarity was a factor in the uniquely Greek developments that will be described in the following chapters.

---

[123] N. 73 above.

[124] 4D. Another instance is the barbarian astonishment (Hdt. 8.26) that the prize at the Olympic games was not *chrēmata* (goods, money) but a crown of olive – a mere symbol.

CHAPTER EIGHT

The features of money

A WALKING ON THE TEXTILES IN AESCHYLUS' *AGAMEMNON*

The use of precious metal money in the advanced city-states was in the sixth and fifth centuries accelerated and made pervasive by the invention and rapid spread of coinage. The result was a single thing of unique status, money, that could be exchanged for, and measure the value of, numerous other things. Having in 1A described the fundamental similarity of Greek and modern money, in 1C I gave an extended *definition* of money that applies to them both. On this basis I will now describe several salient *features* of Greek money that are also features of modern money. For the Greeks of this period money had developed rapidly, and much in their continuing traditions (notably Homer) predated it. And so in the texts given below (mostly from the fifth century) they express, often in subtle ways, the features of this relatively recent phenomenon, without always explicitly stating or conceptualising them.[1] These are features that we ourselves may not register because we take money more completely for granted.

This expression of the features of money occurs especially in Athenian tragedy, which – though dramatising the largely premonetary world of epic and of myth generally – was the first genre[2] to be created in the brave new world of the widespread use of coined money (7B), and – as an increasingly complex performance at a civic festival – itself required considerable monetary expenditure.[3] After arguing in chapters 9 to 13 that

[1] For instance the paradoxical saying 'money is the man' (*chrēmat' anēr*, 8D) implies the impersonality of money without explicitly stating it.
[2] Various lyric forms would have developed in this period, but without originating in it.
[3] Lys. 21.1–5; 19.42. [Aristot.] *Oec.* II 1347a10–14 (5B n. 62) mentions the *leitourgia* of the *chorēgia* paid in money under the tyrant Hippias. The variety of expenses involved (e.g. Antiphon *Chor.* 11–13; Plut. *Mor.* 348D–349B) requires money (rather than offerings in kind), perhaps also a controlling individual, whether *chorēgos* or (originally perhaps) tyrant (on the possible importance of coinage for Peisistratus' patronage of festivals see 5B n. 53). I suspect that the power of money might have

the features of money described in this chapter help us to understand some of the preconceptions underlying presocratic philosophy, I will in chapter 14 return to tragedy in order to show how monetisation has produced comparable preconceptions in the tragic shaping of myth.

As a further preliminary I must re-emphasise the frequently ignored distinction between wealth and money discussed at the beginning of 1C. Wealth and money could in our period be transformed into each other, and so tend to be denoted by the same term. For example *chrēmata*, defined by Aristotle as 'all things of which the value is measured by currency' (5B), is variously translated 'things', 'wealth', and 'money'. It means, in the post-heroic age, both *money* and those *things* which money can measure and be transformed from and into. In this sense both the things and the money seem to belong to the same category (wealth/money). All money is wealth, but wealth is money only to the extent that it is envisaged as capable of money-functions. When tragedy compares (say) noble birth with *chrēmata* or *ploutos* (wealth) or *nomisma* (currency) or *arguros* (silver, the material of Athenian coinage) or *chrusos* (gold, the most valuable of commodities, and associated with the wealth of the heroic age), these terms all refer to aspects or forms of the same thing, the wealth/money familiar to the Athenian audience. Although there is no Greek term corresponding precisely to 'money', it is nevertheless legitimate, when the interest in precious metal is (as frequently in our period) largely or entirely in its money functions, to translate such terms as 'money'.

As a basis for this entire analysis I will take a short passage from Aeschylus' *Agamemnon*, which will as we proceed be seen to imply more and more of the characteristics of money. The textiles walked over by Agamemnon are described as 'bought-with-silver' (949 *argurōnētos*, an epithet inconceivable in the largely moneyless world of Homer), and Clytemnestra justifies this dangerously extravagant use of the textiles as follows (958–65):

The sea exists – who will dry it up? – nourishing an ever-renewed gush, equal to silver [i.e. worth its weight in silver],[4] of much purple, the dyeing of garments. The household has a supply of these things, with the grace of the gods, for us to have, king. The house does not know how to be poor. Of many garments would I have vowed the trampling, had it been prescribed at the home of an oracle for me as I devised a means of recovering this man's life.

---

contributed to the *detachment of performance from specific function* (e.g. mystic initiation, hero-cult) that permitted the tragic *synthesis* of rituals and genres (dithyramb, mystery cult, hero-cult, lament, wedding-song, and so on).

[4] Commentators compare Theopomp. *FGrH* fr. 117 (at Colophon) 'for the purple was being valued as equal in weight against silver' (i.e. as worth its weight in silver).

Comment on this passage has been interested in the danger of wasting the household's *wealth*.[5] But my interest will be in the quite distinct category of *money*.

B   MONEY IS HOMOGENEOUS

The world of epic, and of myth generally, does not contain money, but it does contain numerous precious or talismanic objects with the vivid appearance of uniqueness – a bowl made by Hephaestus,[6] the bow of Odysseus, the golden fleece, and so on. Whereas the power of the talismanic object[7] derives from its uniqueness, the power of money derives from its *homogeneity* as the embodiment of the absolute abstract equivalence between commodities imposed by exchange. And so the seal-mark, which derives its power from the uniqueness of the talismanic seal, is at the opposite pole (despite obvious similarities) from the coin-mark, which assimilates a piece of metal to all other such pieces (6C). Silver is valuable by virtue of resembling other silver, silver in general. It is true that money might be of metals other than silver (notably gold and bronze), and that there were various kinds of coin (Attic tetradrachms, Attic quarter-obols, Cyzicene staters, Persian Darics, and so on). And yet the homogeneity of ancient Greek money, as of modern, is implicit in the construction of equivalences between different forms of money.[8] It is in coinage that this homogeneity of money acquires perfection, for the stamp on a coin renders all small variations of quality and quantity irrelevant. To be sure, in much coinage the metal itself was almost pure, i.e. almost homogeneous, and this purity assisted confidence (7D). But to the extent that the value of coinage is abstract, it becomes *perfectly* homogeneous. The value of silver that had performed money functions in the Near East was, by contrast, always subject to potential or actual variation in quality.

Within the Argive royal family talismanic objects are crucial. In Homer the Argive royal power is conveyed by a sceptre once held by Zeus and transmitted down the generations (*Il.* 2.101–8). In another version, frequent in Euripides, royal power is bestowed by a golden lamb.[9] In Aeschylus' *Agamemnon*, on the other hand, and even despite the frequent references to the bitter struggle for the kingship in the earlier generation,[10] neither the

---

[5] E.g. Goldhill 1986, 11.   [6] *Od.* 4.615–19 = 15.115–19.
[7] The category is discussed by Gernet 1981, 73–111.
[8] An inscription setting out such equivalences is *IG* i³ 376 (Athenian accounts? 409/8 BC).
[9] Eur. *El.* 699–746 with Cropp ad loc., *IT* 196, *Or.* 812–13, 995–1000.
[10] *Ag.* 1095–7, 1193, 1217–22, 1242–3, 1583–1602.

lamb nor the sceptre is mentioned. How then does Aegisthus hope to exercise the power that he has, in conjunction with Clytemnestra, usurped? 'I will try to rule the citizens', he says, 'through this man's [i.e. Agamemnon's] money (*chrēmata*)'.[11] In Aeschylus the power of the royal household derives not from the talismanic object of myth, a divinely granted unique object in which alone is embodied the power to rule, but rather from its opposite – from the relatively novel power of money, with its homogeneous power to acquire and achieve. Clytemnestra, in equating the ever-renewed dye from the inexhaustible sea with the silver money by which it is bought ('equal to silver'), associates the household's endless silver money ('it does not know how to be poor') with the inexhaustible homogeneity of the sea. Similarly the story of the tyrant Polycrates throwing his seal-ring into the *sea* may express the tension between the talismanic object that derives its power from its uniqueness and the homogeneous power of money.[12]

An aspect of the homogeneity of money is to be the single thing that is the measure of, and exchangeable with, almost everything else. This promotes a sense of homogeneity among things in general. Aristotle notes that currency, by making goods commensurate, 'equalises them'.[13] In so far as things are measureable on a numerical scale to which almost all other things belong, any appearance of uniqueness will be reduced. Where things can be *replaced* by means of money, such reduction will be complete. The textiles are 'bought with silver', and may be trampled by Agamemnon because their purple dye comes in constant supply from the sea. The implication is that there is money to buy replacement textiles ('the household does not know how to be poor'). The textiles walked on by Agamemnon are in essence no different from the textiles that can so easily replace them. Early Greek experience of the power of money to make everything seem like itself, and indeed the undesirability of this universal transformation, is expressed in the myth of Midas' touch turning everything into gold.[14]

Tension, we have observed, may be felt between the singularity of certain talismanic or prized items and the homogeneity promoted by the power of money.[15] In the tragic *Rhesus* an episode from the largely moneyless world

---

[11] *Ag.* 1638–9. And it is later in the trilogy repeatedly stressed that in enacting revenge Orestes is also reacquiring control of the *chrēmata: Cho.* 135, 301, cf. 250; *Eum.* 757–8.

[12] Detail in Seaford 1998a, 125–7. The retrieval of a talismanic object or *agalma* from the sea is a theme that may precede money, but in the story of Polycrates acquires new significance.

[13] *EN* 1133b16–18; cf. Pl. *Laws* 918b.

[14] Marco Polo's first experience of paper money (in China) made him argue that the emperor had the power of a 'perfect alchemist' (quoted by Shell 1978, 13).

[15] A general study of the opposing tendencies of 'commoditisation' and 'singularisation' is Kopytoff 1986.

of Homer has been reshaped, partly under the influence of money. In the
Iliad Hector offers the horses and chariot of Achilles as a reward to elicit
a volunteer for a dangerous exploit. The volunteer, Dolon, is described
as 'a man of much gold and much bronze' (10.315). The only purpose of
this description is to prefigure his later claim, when captured and asking
to be ransomed, that 'there is inside (our house) bronze and gold and
much-wrought iron' (378–9). In the tragic version the reward (or rather
payment, *misthos*) is mentioned only *after* Dolon has volunteered. Hector
suggests various possibilities, including gold, which Dolon rejects on the
grounds that 'there is (gold) in (our) household; we do not lack livelihood'
(*Rhes.* 170). The identity here assumed between gold and livelihood (*bios*),
an identification that barely occurs in Homer (2BC), means that gold is
envisaged as money. When Hector a few lines later asks him which of the
Greeks he would like to have so as to ransom, Dolon replies 'as I said before,
there is gold in (our) house' (*Rhes.* 178). Dolon finally reveals that he wants
the horses of Achilles, which Hector grants him (even though they are
not yet captured), not without expressing his own strong desire for them,
immortal as they are, the gift of Poseidon to Peleus (*Rhes.* 184–8).[16] The
Doloneia is a relatively late addition to the *Iliad*, and the characterisation
of Dolon as 'of much gold and much bronze' – the only individual so
described in Homer – may reflect the development of money. This slight
suggestion of money has in the tragic version been made a reality: the horses
of Achilles are elevated to the status of a uniquely desirable object, more
desirable even – it is stressed – than the *money* of Dolon. In the still largely
moneyless world of Homer, on the other hand, there is no need to elevate
a unique object above the power of money.[17]

Finally, money may even seem to homogenise its *users*, in various ways.
Firstly, it facilitates the kind of commercial exchange that is disembedded
from all other relations: the only relation between the parties to such exchange is commercial, and *from the perspective of this relation* the parties are
identical to each other, for all each wants is the best possible deal. Aristotle

---

[16] As if to preclude the kind of dissent created between Ajax and Odysseus by the *arms* of Achilles,
Dolon immediately consoles Hector for the loss of the item of unique *quality* ('the finest gift of
the Trojans') by invoking *quantity*: Hector should not be envious, for there are innumerable other
things for him to enjoy (*Rhes.* 191–4).

[17] Another example of the contrast between money and the unique is the offence of Euenius buying
replacements for sacred sheep: Hdt. 9. 93–4; Seaford 1998a, I 23 n. 68; cf. the offence of Minos
in replacing a unique sacrificial bull (Apollod. *Bibl.* 3.1.3; Eur. fr. 472e23–6). Archilochus (fr. 5) is
brazenly happy to replace his abandoned shield, in which he imagines an enemy rejoicing (*agalletai*,
evoking *agalma*); contrast the replacement shield of Achilles in Homer, made by a god and decorated
with an image of the whole world: cf. n. 23 below.

observes that currency equalises not only the goods but also the *parties* to the exchange.[18] Secondly, money develops into the homogeneous aim (8D) and means (8E) of a vast range of activities by numerous individuals. Confused thereby are the social distinctions once expressed by the partial separation of spheres of exchange (5A). Thirdly, whereas the individuality of the gift (or even of the bartered object) may easily be associated with the individuality of its donor, the essential uniformity of money on the other hand carries no such association. Consider how the individuality of the young Telemachus, his insertion into a heroic network, is enhanced by the gift from his host Menelaus of a mixing-bowl made by Hephaestus and given to Menelaus by his erstwhile host Phaidimos king of the Sidonians, which Telemachus will have as a *keimēlion* (i.e. to be stored in the house);[19] and compare this with the homogeneous accumulation (and expenditure) of money. The homogeneity of money implies its *impersonality*, to which we must now turn our attention.

C   MONEY IS IMPERSONAL

The uniqueness of valuable objects in Homer (8B) facilitates permanent association with specific individuals. This is most obvious in the case of gifts: for instance Odysseus, given a great bow by Iphitus, gives him a sword and spear 'to initiate the relationship of guest-friendship' (2A). Even the sceptre that conveys royal power on Agamemnon (a 'talismanic object') seems enabled to do so both by its uniqueness and by retaining an association with its original donor Zeus.[20] Both these associated qualities of the Homeric object, its uniqueness and its embodiment of the (unique) individual, are put into reverse by money. The power of money derives not from its uniqueness, its differentiation from other precious objects, but from precisely the reverse, from adherence to a type. Hence its homogeneity. And hence also its impersonality. There is nothing about money to enable it to be associated with an individual – save the mere fact of transient possession. Note the general absence of depictions of mortals from the coins of our period, even of rulers as powerful as the Sicilian tyrants (6C).

An example of the tension between on the one hand the uniqueness of the hero and of the individual objects associated with him and on the

---

[18] *EN* 1133a17–21 using the same verb (*isasdein*) as is applied to the goods (above); 1133b4. Cf. Archytas quoted 10C.

[19] *Od.* 4.600, 613–19.

[20] Zeus gave it to Hermes, who gave it to Pelops, who left it to Thyestes, who left it to Agamemnon: *Il.* 2.101–8.

other the (homogeneous, typical) impersonality of money (in the form of coinage) occurs in the recognition scene of Euripides' *Electra*. The play resembles the *Odyssey*: in each case the hero is recognised by his scar,[21] and goes on to reacquire his kingship by violence, with minimal human aid. But in the world in which Euripides lived control over a community can no longer be obtained by a few heroic individuals. What is required is, by contrast, an *impersonal* thing, money (8E). Orestes has a price on his head (*El.* 33), and has no following because he possesses nothing (601–9). The poverty of Electra, too, contrasts with the wealth of the rulers of Argos. And yet in the end the hero Orestes does succeed, and Electra taunts the dead Aegisthus: 'you prided yourself that you were someone, strong by means of money. But money is only for short acquaintance. It is nature that is secure, not money'.[22]

Shortly before her recognition of Orestes, Electra mistakenly dismisses the tokens found by the old man at Agamemnon's tomb: a lock of hair, a footprint, and a woven cloth. The lines present a well-known problem. There must be some point to them other than criticism of the use of the tokens by earlier versions. Hair, footprint, and cloth are all invested with the personal identity of Orestes. The hair also embodies his personal relation with his father Agamemnon enacted in death ritual, and the cloth (according to the old man) his personal relation with his sister. Electra's rejection of the tokens may have various functions, such as (it has been suggested) to express her nervous reluctance to accept such wonderful news. But it may also express, like so much else in this play, a contemporary reality – the marginalisation, in a world now dominated by the impersonal homogeneity of money, of the traditional power of things that were unique because invested with personal identity or talismanic power.[23]

This interpretation is confirmed by the recognition scene itself. On first seeing the strangers, the old man says (550–1) 'they are well-born – but this is in *kibdēloi*: for many who are well-born are bad'. *Kibdēlos* means false or adulterated. The metaphor of false men as like *kibdēlos* metal occurs already in an early section of the *Theognidea* (119–24). By the time of the tragedians

---

[21] *Od.* 19.390–475; 21.217–23. Odysseus' scar was acquired in a hunt. So too was Orestes', but as he was a small child, the hunt becomes a playful chase of a fawn inside the house (or courtyard).

[22] 939–41. The gold offered by Aegisthus as a reward for killing Orestes (33) proved ineffective.

[23] To this realism the choral odes provide a counterpoint. An object invested with personal identity is Achilles' shield, to be found in the preceding choral ode (432–86), with its 'signs in the circle' terrifying in heroic battle – similar to a coin-mark in form but antithetical to it in function (on the resemblance of the shield-devices in Aesch. *Sept.* to coin-marks see Steiner 1994, 53–9). An object invested with talismanic power is the golden lamb that bestowed sovereignty in Argos and is to be found in the next choral ode (699–746). At Eur. *IT* 813–15 this golden lamb is actually depicted among the scenes woven on the cloth by which Orestes proves his identity.

it has been influenced by coinage.[24] 'O Zeus', says Medea, 'why have you provided for humankind clear signs of what gold is *kibdēlos*, but there is no natural mark (*charaktēr*) on the body of men by which to distinguish the bad?' (Eur. *Med.* 516–19). Gold can be tested (e.g. by the touchstone), but in the late fifth century the most widespread means of guaranteeing the value of precious metal was the engraved or impressed mark (*charaktēr*) on silver coinage. Men, unlike gold, cannot be easily tested, and, unlike coins, do not have a *charaktēr* on their bodies.

The old man then stares intently at the as yet unrecognised hero. 'Why', asks Orestes, 'is he staring at me as if looking at a bright mark (*charaktēr*) on silver? Is he matching me (*proseikasdei*) with someone/something?' (*El.* 558–9). As occurs elsewhere in tragedy,[25] it is as if the dramatist has coinage in mind, but does not want to commit the anachronism of naming it directly. The old man is in fact 'matching' the stranger with a specific person whom he remembers (Orestes). Now 'matches' must also make sense in terms of the immediately preceding coinage metaphor, and so implies (whether or not *proseikasdein* was a technical term for it) the matching of the mark on this particular coin with the *type* of coin-mark that guarantees genuineness,[26] for that would be the point of intense staring at the mark on the coin.[27] But this implies a process antithetical to the matching of a stranger with Orestes. The stranger, who could be anybody, is identified as a unique individual, whereas to identify a coin as genuine by 'looking at the mark' means to identify the presence of the general type to be found also in any genuine coin. Taken together with his earlier remark on 'in *kibdēlōi*', the coinage metaphor makes the old man seem to be deciding not only whether the man he is scrutinising is the individual Orestes but also whether his typifying mark, as it were, is genuine – i.e. whether he conforms to the type or is instead *kibdēlos*. He seems to be looking for the *genuiness* or *quality* that is guaranteed neither (as in heroic myth) by unique identity nor even (the old man has emphasised) by noble birth, but by adherence to an impersonal type. Given the historical significance of the polarity between the personal association of the seal-mark and the impersonality of the coin-mark (6C), it is striking that in Sophocles the recognition of Orestes is clinched by his display of a *seal*.[28] At the heart of

---

[24] Falsely stamped coin is a moral image already at Aesch. *Ag.* 780.

[25] Notably Soph. *Ant.* 295–6 (8D n. 42).

[26] That is so whether the type is merely remembered or to hand in a coin known to be genuine. For the metaphor see Aristot. *Rhet.* 1375b5, *Hist. An.* 491a20.

[27] Whether by ordinary people, or by the testers called *arguroskopoi* or *argurognōmones*.

[28] Soph. *El.* 1223; 6D n. 115.

the recognition scene is the uniqueness of the person recognised. And yet here in Euripides the metaphor works in the opposite direction.

On concluding his scrutiny the old man tells Electra to pray to get a 'dear treasure' (*El.* 565), i.e. her long-lost brother. This both sustains the money metaphor and implies that Orestes himself will be their money (or rather make up for their lack of it), that he has the nature that will (we saw) defeat the wealth of Aegisthus. Electra, still sceptical, asks 'what mark (*charaktēr*) can you see by which I will be persuaded?' The word *charaktēr* does not follow from what precedes, except in so far as it picks up the use of the same word in the coin metaphor. It also anticipates the old man's reply: 'By his brow . . .' (i.e. a scar). *Charaktēr* refers both to Orestes' distinguishing scar and to the mark on a coin. In other words, the opposition between unique personal identity and *typical* value is exquisitely embodied in their each being recognised through a *charaktēr*. The ambiguity of *charaktēr* between scar and coin-mark represents the antithesis between the ancient uniqueness of the hero (marked here by a *charaktēr*) and a world in which the impersonal power of money has not only annihilated the uniqueness of the mythical hero but also provided a metaphor for the impersonal typicality of genuine worth. The scar – unlike hair, footprint, and cloth – is effective. To explain this contrast it is not enough to say that the scar is just a better kind of token (why then is e.g. Aeschylus so different?). Rather, the advantage of using the scar as the means of recognition is that Euripides is able to weave into this recognition a sustained monetary metaphor[29] that contradicts the traditional sense of the recognition as of a unique heroic individual. In other words, even the traditional scene of personal recognition is pervaded by the new impersonal power of money.

Stripped of all personal association, money is promiscuous, capable of being exchanged with anybody for anything, indifferent to all non-monetary interpersonal relationships.[30] This impersonality is brought to its extreme by the instant and generally accepted guarantee of redeemability provided by coinage. Barter, even of goods made for the market, tends to require knowledge of co-transactors and personal trust, and so to rely on lasting (and

---

[29] The novelty of coinage, from a semiotic perspective, is that the sign (the mark) authenticates its own material (the metal). In this respect coinage differs from such authenticating signs as, say, a token carried by someone to authenticate their identity, or from a seal-mark authenticating a document (6c). Of all the traditional tokens of identification the scar is the only one that resembles in this respect the coin-mark.

[30] Cf. e.g. Simmel 1978 (1907), 227 (quoted by Parry and Bloch 1989, 6): 'The indifferent objectivity of money transactions is in insurmountable conflict with the personal character of the relationship . . . The desirable party for financial transactions is the person who is completely indifferent to us, engaged neither for us nor against us.'

sometimes ritualised) interpersonal relations and contexts of exchange,[31] whereas the guarantee provided by coinage tends to enable fleeting transactions with complete strangers.[32] Money (especially as coinage) tends to promote an indefinite network of indiscriminate exchange that transcends the defined personal relations to be found within family, within various social groupings, or within networks of gift-giving and barter. Whereas the Homeric *gift* is invested with the personality of its heroic donor, the only kind of person that *money* resembles is the prostitute.[33] For Shakespeare it is 'the common whore of mankind'.[34] The prostitute, like money, is impersonally promiscuous, transcending the restricted sexual relations required for the reproduction of the household.[35] Further, she also actually exchanges her services for money – in an exchange that is therefore uniquely symmetrical in that both its elements (coitus and money) are impersonally promiscuous. And yet one of them, coitus, is otherwise generally accompanied by a restrictive personal claim, whether that claim arises out of emotional attachment or the institution of marriage (or both). Commercial prostitution is therefore an extreme case of the homogenisation and depersonalisation (rather than just the homogeneity and impersonality) characteristic of money.

It may also have been actually facilitated by the advent of money. The greater ease of exchange and of storing wealth that came with precious metal money may have freed some prostitutes from dependence on the protection provided by specific males. Rhodopis, a freed slave who acquired much wealth/money (*chrēmata*) as a prostitute in mid-sixth century Naucratis, dedicated at Delphi a tenth of her *chrēmata* in the form of numerous iron

---

[31] E.g. Humphrey and Hugh-Jones 1992, 6–8, 61, 95 107–41 (esp. 108, 132). Dodd 1994, xxii 'In barter the key requirement for transactors is information. This mostly concerns the location and trustworthiness of co-transactors. Money dispenses with this.'; xxvi 'Even where a bartering relationship is of long standing, the information that supports the relationship remains specific to it, and can be applied elsewhere only in limited ways. For this reason, barter exchange cannot possibly be anonymous, in the way that monetary transaction invariably is.' See further 14A n. 1. The distinction between barter (and gift-exchange) and monetary transactions may perhaps be compared to Bernstein's distinction between restricted and (less context-dependent) elaborated speech codes, to which Humphreys 1978, 303–4 compares the distinction between myth and scientific thought. Barter is mentioned infrequently in Homer and described (rather than being merely mentioned) only twice (briefly) – at *Il.* 7.467–75, where it is preceded by *gifts* to the kings, and at *Od.* 15.459–65, where it is with strangers (Phoenicians) and has disastrous consequences: 2AB.

[32] For an example of money payment as less prestigious than payments in kind because it does not imply an enduring interpersonal relationships see Srinivas 1955.

[33] Simmel 1978 (1907), 376–8; Kurke 1999, 197–8; Eur. *Sciron*.   [34] *Timon of Athens* 4.3.43.

[35] In Hdt. (1.93–4) the fundamentally distinct categories of prostitution and marriage are confused by the very people who are the first to use gold and silver coinage and practise retail trade, the Lydians: their daughters earn their dowries by prostitution (and, again in inversion of Greek practice, choose their husbands): cf. 2.126. In Babylon every native woman must once in her life go to the temple of Aphrodite and copulate with any man who throws a coin into her lap (1.199): Kurke 1999.

spits (Hdt. 2.134–5). Given the source (her numerous customers) of the *chrēmata*, the spits may seem phallic (cf. Ar. *Ach.* 796), but in the context of a temple are also proto-money (6AB), thereby nicely assimilating the (personal) sexual act to the impersonal homogeneity of money. In Aristophanes it is said that whereas the baser boys gratify their lovers for money, the better ones ask for *things* instead (a horse, hunting dogs), although this is merely to mask their vice: that is to say, by avoiding money the pretence is maintained of a discriminate personal relation.[36] When there is talk of exchanging horses or maidens (emblems on coins) for a prostitute's favours in Euripides' satyr-play *Skiron*, on the other hand, this is not so much denial of the indiscriminate impersonality of money as the failure, in the ancient Dionysiac world of the satyrs, to recognise its *abstraction* (8H, 14D).

Finally, in reducing individuality to homogeneous impersonality the power of money resembles the power of death. In the *Agamemnon* Ares is a 'gold-changer of bodies', who 'sends from Troy the fired heavy bitterly-bewailed (gold-)dust to their dear ones, filling the urns with easily-placed ash in exchange for men. They lament, praising one man for his skill in battle, another for his noble death amid the slaughter' (437–47). Just as the trader[37] gives money in exchange for various things, so the warriors have all been reduced, despite their variety, to the impersonal homogeneity of ash.

D MONEY IS A UNIVERSAL AIM

Because various things are exchanged with and measurable by a single thing (money), they may appear homogeneous because *pervaded* by it. And inasmuch as the purpose of the exchanges may be monetary gain, an aspect of the pervasiveness of money may be the pervasiveness of monetary gain. Just as in Aristophanes it is forcefully maintained that all the arts and crafts have the single aim of wealth (*Wealth* 160–7), so too Aristotle will observe that some men turn all capacities such as military or medical ability into the art of making money (*Pol.* 1258a11–15). The metaphor of Ares as a trader (8c) may therefore appear to be more than just a metaphor. It may rather express the extreme or universal pervasiveness of money by implying that even the death of warriors involves monetary gain.

This idea is not as far-fetched as it seems. In the *Iliad* Agamemnon offers numerous gifts to Achilles to persuade him to return to battle. In

---

[36] *Wealth* 153–9. Socrates extends what should not be exchanged for money from sex to wisdom (8D).

[37] *Chrusamoibos* (gold-changer) occurs only here (and in Hsch.). Cf. *arguramoibos* (silver-changer) in Plato (*Pol.* 289e) of those free men who trade 'in the market-place or by travelling from city to city by sea or by land, exchanging currency (*nomisma*) for other things or currency for currency'. *Chrusamoibos* is more appropriate than *arguramoibos* to the heroic age and to a god.

rejecting this offer Achilles says that wealth cannot be equal in value to his life (*psuchē*), and describes death as a kind of (irreversible) exchange of *psuchē*.[38] The image of the trader in Aeschylus' *Agamemnon* combines these notions and takes them further. The death-as-exchange in the Aeschylean image is death in battle on behalf of the Atreidae at Troy, precisely the death rejected by the Homeric Achilles, who complains that Agamemnon takes the most and best spoils of the war for himself (1.165–8, 9.330–3). So too the Aeschylean image of dying as an exchange (of bodies for ash) seems to imply that the exchange involves gain for the Atreidae, against whom, we learn in the following lines, the Greeks direct bitter resentment (450), angry talk, and curses (456). The striking image of Ares as a trader *presiding*[39] over warfare as he changes bodies for money implies the pervasive power of money even over the traditional heroism of death in battle. In the fifth century, after all, the notion that the aim of warfare may be monetary gain is common. For instance, according to Herodotus (6.132) Miltiades was enthusiastically granted ships and men by the Athenians for an expedition because he claimed, without even saying where it was going, that it would obtain for its participants abundant gold. Another example is the Athenian attack on Sicily, which was favoured by Alcibiades as likely to increase his own wealth and by the ordinary soldiers as meaning payment during the expedition and (if successful) a permanent source of pay for the future.[40] When the soldiers with Demosthenes eventually in fact have to surrender in Sicily, Thucydides (7.82) gives us the vivid detail that they threw their silver into shields. In an anonymous tragic fragment (fr. adesp. 129) gold is said to have greater power than Ares for those at war, and to be superior even to Orphic song, because 'followed by the whole earth and sea and all-inventive Ares'.

But is the power of money so pervasive that someone would in fact be prepared to give up his *psuchē* for it? The answer, according to Creon in Sophocles' *Antigone*, is yes, for that is precisely what he accuses the guard of doing (322). Frequently emphasised is Creon's firm conviction that behind the forbidden burial of Polyneices lies the power of money,[41] 'the desire to make a profit out of *everything*' (312). This power, he claims, is responsible for a wide range of evils (295–301):

---

[38] 2D; 3B; Seaford 1998a, 128–9; cf. Eur. *Supp.* 775–7 'this is the only expenditure that you cannot obtain once it is spent – human life; whereas there are means of raising money'; *Med.* 968; *Hipp.* 964–5; Pi. *Isthm.* 1.68 'paying (τελέων) the soul to Hades' (death as payment: 2D, 14C) – cf. the preceding reference to 'invisible wealth within' (67), with 12B on the invisibility of wealth; Soph. *OT* 30.

[39] Because holding the balance (439), like Zeus in the *Iliad*: 14C.

[40] Thuc. 6.15, 24. Cf. e.g. Ar. *Wasps* 684–5; Thuc. 4.52.

[41] 221–2, 289–301, 1036–9, 1047, 1055, 1063.

No currency (*nomisma*) ever grew up among humankind as evil as money (*arguros*):[42] this lays waste even cities, this expels men from their homes, this thoroughly teaches and transform good minds of mortals to set themselves to disgraceful acts; it showed men how to practise villainies and to know every act of impiety.

Creon's emphasis here on the *psychology* of money – it is said to thoroughly teach and transform minds, and to enable us to 'know' impiety – reappears later in his intense confrontation with the seer Teiresias. Creon claims that he has 'long been traded and made into cargo' (1036) by the tribe of seers. In imagining himself as like a slave shipped off to be sold, Creon implies that he has in the past made profit (presumably unwittingly) for the corrupt seers by accepting their advice. This (mistaken) sense Creon has of having been wholly in the power of money is a little later given an explicit psychological dimension, when Creon says to Teiresias 'know that you will not purchase my mind' (1063). 'Purchase my mind' does not mean that Teiresias intends to bribe Creon, rather that for Creon to obey would be to sell his mind in the sense that it would be (indirectly, and unwittingly) in the power of the money paid to Teiresias. The implication of 1036, that the power of money may be unseen by its victims, is in 1063 made a little more explicit in the notion of purchasing (and so controlling) the *mind*.[43]

Despite Creon's protestations, there is a sense in which his mind is indeed pervaded and controlled by money. To Creon's view that all seers love money (1055) Teiresias responds that it is the characteristic of *tyrants* to love disgraceful gain. Teiresias is, as always (1094), correct: the tyrant acquires and maintains his tyranny by means of money (14E). The notion persists into what follows (1061–71).

CREON   Reveal, only speaking not for gain.

TEIRESIAS   (You say that because) I too *seem*[44] to speak thus (for gain) already[45] as far as your part is concerned (i.e. because of your own money-dominated tyrannical outlook you imagine that I too am venal).[46]

CREON   Know that you will not purchase my mind.

---

[42] Crean seems to mean not just money but specifically coinage. 'Silver' – *arguros* – (rather than gold, as at 1039) was the material of contemporary Athenian (and most Greek) coinage. *Nomisma* means something like custom, but also coinage ('currency' has a similar range), and so could hardly fail to suggest coinage here. It is as if Sophocles has coinage in mind, but does not want to commit the anachronism of locating it in the heroic age.

[43] On the similar Soph. *Trach.* 537–8 see Seaford 1998a, 133.

[44] As well as you, who however really *are* mercenary.

[45] Even before having made the revelation.

[46] 1062 οὕτω γὰρ ἤδη καὶ δοκῶ τὸ σὸν μέρος. This complex line, in which Creon is said to project his obsession with money onto others, has never been understood. My translation gives point to every word in the line, as well as to Creon's reply (1063), which – we have seen – refers to the *power of money over the mind,* as do also 1036, 298, 301. Further: Seaford 1998a.

TEIRESIAS   But know well then that there will not be many revolutions of the sun before you will have given in return a corpse from your own vital parts (i.e. Haemon), an exchange for corpses, wherefore you on the one hand have (one) of those above, having thrust it below, having lodged a soul ignominiously in a tomb (Antigone), and you on the other hand have (one) of those below,[47] a corpse dispossessed, without death ritual, impure (Polyneices).

These lines are often rightly cited as expressing the dual perversion of ritual norms that is somehow at the heart of the *Antigone*.[48] What has not been appreciated is that this involves *exchange*. The corpse of Haemon will be given in exchange for (it is thrice declared) the corpses *in the possession of* Creon.[49] Creon's perversion of death ritual is envisaged as a hideous exchange, in which he makes a profit, for he controls and possesses two corpses (where they should not be) and in return has to pay with the corpse of only one (*hena*) – that of his own son.

What this hideous exchange expresses is the extreme or universal pervasiveness of money as an aim, for it becomes the aim even of the disinterested intimacy of death ritual. In fact in Classical Athens death ritual might indeed be performed for monetary gain, as establishing closeness to a dead person whose inheritance is disputed (14E). In Aeschylus there is something similar, in Clytemnestra's use of the textiles (8F), and in the image of Ares as trader: a crucial advantage of precious metal as a medium of exchange, its ease of storage and of transport, is expressed in the description of the ash/gold-dust as 'well laid out', *euthetos*,[50] a word which also evokes the ordered laying out of the body at a funeral.[51] The potential power of money

---

[47] The mss. θεῶν is suspect, and I have omitted it from my translation (this does not affect my argument).

[48] The means of killing Antigone is death ritual: e.g. the procession to the 'tomb' clearly evokes a funeral procession (806–16, 891–4).

[49] Whether we translate ἀνθ' ὧν here 'because' (as most translators do) or 'wherefore' (its more frequent meaning), it must, as it does elsewhere, refer to exchange (LSJ cite, under the meaning 'because', this line of *Ant.* and Ar. *Wealth* 433–4, which in fact means 'you will pay the penalty *in exchange for* your attempt to banish me'. Under the meaning 'wherefore' LSJ cite *PV* 31, Soph. *OT* 264, Thuc. 6.83, *Ev. Luc.* 12.3, and Jebb cites Soph. *OC* 1295; in all these cases too (except the much later *Ev. Luc.*) it is in fact a matter of *exchange*). Hence the emphasised (by position) and repeated ἔχεις. ἔχεις . . . βαλὼν κάτω is generally translated 'you have hurled the corpse below' (so Griffith 1999, ad loc., though he agrees (ad 22) that there is 'a resultative force'). But the second (parallel) ἔχεις, having no attendant participle, strongly implies *possession*. Further: Seaford 1998a, 133–5.

[50] The ms. *euthetou* (of the ash) has been emended to *euthetous* (of the urns), unnecessarily (and the corruption would be much more likely the other way: Denniston–Page ad loc.), but this problem does not affect my point.

[51] See Thomson ad loc; Phryn. *Praep.Soph.* p. 71. 9; D.C. 40.49; *SEG* 1.449. Fraenkel's comment that this sense 'is irrelevant here, for the bodies have been cremated' misses the exquisitely bitter combination in a single word of opposites – impersonal commercial convenience and ritualised love for a dead family member. The subsequent lines in Aeschylus (cited 8C) evoke the funeral oration.

to pervert death ritual is implicit also in the questions Herodotus makes Darius ask: (of some Greeks) for how much money would they be willing to eat their dead fathers? and (of some Indians) for how much money would they be prepared to burn them?[52]

Just as the universality of money as an aim may corrupt even death ritual, so too it may be perceived as a threat to other basic values. Alcaeus, who provides our earliest evidence for the military significance of money (5A), is also said to have reported the saying of one Aristodamos that 'money is the man' (*chrēmat' anēr*). Pindar (*Isthm.* 2.11–12) adds that Aristodamos had lost his friends along with his property. In this he will be followed by, among others, the Just Man in Aristophanes' *Wealth* and *Timon of Athens*. Even the reciprocity of friendship seems to depend on money.[53] This threat to traditional values by the powerful new phenomenon of money is a constant theme of the *Theognidea*. Money has become a distinct basic value that is implicitly or explicitly compared to other basic values such as birth or virtue or justice.[54] The basic values of money and justice are obviously distinct, because money is often obtained precisely through injustice.[55] The poet recommends justice or virtue rather than money.[56] But in fact it is money that is honoured most.[57] In choosing a spouse people put money above birth and reputation.[58] For the mass of humankind the only virtue is money, compared to which self-control, knowledge, rhetoric, speed of foot are of no account, for money 'has the greatest power'.[59] As we have seen, warfare depends on money. And so do speech and action.[60] Money has a *transcendent* power, evidence and expression of which is its capacity to combine (or transform into each other) opposites (8G). In tragedy we find it said that people honour money above freedom or wisdom; or that money is in fact more powerful than words or family feeling; or even that it *should* be preferred to piety.[61] One may even be a 'slave of money'.[62]

---

[52] Hdt. 3.38; cf. also 1.187 Darius, opening a tomb in the false belief that there is money there, instead finds a message that 'if you were not insatiate of money and desiring disgraceful gain, you would not have opened the tombs of corpses' (1.187).

[53] Soph. fr. 88; Eur. *Phoen.* 402–5.

[54] The same complex of ideas is frequent in tragedy: Seaford 1998a. Already in Tyrtaeus (fr. 12) wealth 'greater than Midas'. . . is one of a series of attributes all declared to be inferior to (though not a threat to) courage in battle.

[55] Theognis 50, 86, 199–201, 225, etc.; Solon fr. 4.6, 11; 15.1.

[56] Theognis 145–6; Solon fr. 15. 3–4; cf. Sappho fr.148 L–P.   [57] Theognis 523, 1117.

[58] Theognis 183–96.   [59] Theognis 699–718.   [60] Theognis 177–8, 268.

[61] Eur. fr. 142, 327 (cf. also *HF* 669–720), *Med.* 965, fr. 324; fr. adesp. 181. It should be noted that the frequency of money in the tragic fragments is due to the interest in money of the writers who preserved them, especially the anthologist Stobaeus.

[62] Eur. *Hec.* 865. Cf. [Pl.] *Epist.* 8.355b on the importance of making money the slave (of soul and body).

On the other hand Solon himself, who was the first to point to the unlimited desire for wealth, also insists that there are limits to its desirability and its power.[63] In tragedy it is said that alongside money is needed virtue and knowledge; that money is powerless to prevent a military conflict, or against death; that it is not to be preferred to a trouble-free life, a good wife, a genuine friend, the fatherland, wisdom; that in choosing a spouse people prefer ἀξίωμα (rank, reputation) to money.[64] Sometimes the priority is expressed in terms of exchange: for genuine friendship one should give much money,[65] even an innumerable amount;[66] one would not exchange youth for any amount;[67] virtue (is the only thing that) cannot be acquired by money.[68] In Euripides' *Electra* money does not prevail (8C). When Socrates is told that he should charge a price for his valuable conversation, as he would if parting with other valuable things, he replies that just as charging for physical beauty is prostitution, so too wisdom should not be exchanged for money.[69]

E   MONEY IS A UNIVERSAL MEANS

8D concerned the pervasiveness of the *desire* for money, a pervasiveness universal enough to corrupt even death ritual. But money is also universally pervasive as a *means*, so that it is required even to enable ritual to be performed. The pervasion of religious ritual by money in both these ways, as aim and as means, is taken to a brilliant extreme in Aristophanes' *Wealth*, where wealth is said not only to be the aim of sacrifice (134) but also its precondition: it is impossible to buy victims 'unless you (Wealth) are present to give the money (*argurion*), so that single-handed you will destroy the power of Zeus, if he causes you trouble' (137–42). Even eternal bliss depends on having three drachmas – to buy a pig for sacrifice at the Eleusinian mysteries (Ar. *Peace* 375). From at least as early as the sixth century BC Greek temple building and Greek animal sacrifice required money – in contrast to the ancient Near East (4D). Greek offerings to the gods early took the form of precious metal, and later could take the form of coinage,

---

[63] Fr. 24; also fr. 15: wealth is not to be preferred to virtue, because virtue (unlike wealth) is permanent; sim. Eur. *El.* 939–41 (quoted 8C).

[64] Eur. frr. 163, 542, 1066; Aesch. *Supp.* 935, *Pers.* 842; Eur. *Alc.* 56–9, *Ion* 629–31, *Med.* 598–9, *Phoen.* 552–4, fr. 543.4–5 (a good wife the *only* thing preferable to wealth), *Or.* 1155–6, fr. 1046; fr. adesp. 130; Eur. *El.* 941, fr. 405. According to Democritus happiness is not to be found in money (68DK B171), of which one should be content with a moderate amount (B286).

[65] Eur. fr. 934.   [66] Eur. *Or.* 1156–7.   [67] Eur. *HF* 643–8.

[68] Eur. fr. 527; cf. *El.* 253, 372.   [69] Xen. *Mem.* 1.6; Ar. *Wealth* 153–9 (cited 8C).

as could fees for mystic initiation, oracles, initiation, or divine cure.[70]
Among the earliest surviving coins are those found buried in a temple, the
Ephesian Artemision (5B). In an Aristophanean fantasy the gods receive
(from a bird) the monetary equivalent of sacrificial sheep (*Birds*. 1618–25).
Coins are vital for travel[71] – even in the underworld: on the payment to
Charon the ferryman Dionysus in *Frogs* comments 'What great power the
two obols have everywhere.'[72] In Euripides' *Alcestis* Death objects to the use
of wealth to 'buy' long life (56–9). But as Agamemnon in Aeschylus walks
into the house, 'destroying wealth and silver-bought weavings' (*Ag.* 949),
Clytemnestra declares that she would have vowed the trampling of many
textiles to save Agamemnon's life had it been prescribed by an oracle. Given
that the textiles are 'bought with silver/money', it follows that the fulfilment
of the hypothetical divine (oracular) demand for the trampling of 'many
garments' (to save Agamemnon's life) would depend on this money.

From all this it emerges that money is not merely a convenient (or the
only) means of acquiring a large range of commodities and services. Rather,
it also appears to be the means of acquiring such a supreme general good
as divine good will.

Another such supreme good is political power. As we have seen, Wealth
can destroy the power of Zeus by withholding money. Zeus rules the gods
'because of money (τἀργύριον), for he has the most' (Ar. *Wealth* 131). The
tyrant Polycrates was lured to his death by the promise of enough 'money to
rule the whole of Greece', and the Athenians were aware that Peisistratus had
used money to obtain and to confirm his tyranny (14D). In Athenian tragedy
money and tyranny constantly go together.[73] The Athenians were also aware
that money had been crucial in the *overthrow* of their tyranny and so in the
creation of their democracy: they believed that the Alcmaeonids in exile at
Delphi, and in particular Cleisthenes himself, bribed the Pythia to tell any
Spartans who consulted the oracle that it was their duty to liberate Athens,
which resulted eventually in the successful expedition of king Cleomenes.[74]
Isocrates states that Cleisthenes 'persuaded the Amphictyons to lend him
some of the god's [Apollo's] money, and restored the people to power'.[75]

[70] Babelon 1943); Bogaert 1976b, 819–20. Mystic initiation: 14D n. 62.
[71] Eur. *Pho.* 984 CREON: 'The god will conduct you MENOECEUS But where am I to have money
from?' implies that for travel money is at least as important as divine support.
[72] 141; cf. 173–7; Pherecr. fr. 86; Caccamo Caltabiano and Radici Colaci 1992, 149–57. Coins for the
dead in other cultures: Schöttle 1913.
[73] Seaford 2003c.
[74] Hdt. 5. 63, 66. Thuc. 6.53 reports that the Athenians knew that it was the Spartans (and not
themselves or Harmodius) that had overthrown the tyranny.
[75] *Antidosis* 232. Similar is Dem. *Meid.* 144.

According to an Athenian text of the late fifth or early fourth century BC money is valued for its use in political power struggles.[76]

It is true that political power may seem to be obtainable in other ways, notably by rhetoric or by warfare – but each of these depends in turn on money. Rhetorical skill, it is noted even in tragedy, is taught for a fee.[77] The sophists imparted, in return for money, knowledge, virtue, and (not least through rhetoric) political power.[78] Warfare too requires money: this becomes clear in the accounts of sixth-century tyrants by Herodotus, who also tells us of Hecataeus advising the Ionians (*c.* 500 BC) of the military importance of the temple treasure at Branchidae.[79] Most vivid is the Thucydidean stress on the military importance of money in speeches by Pericles, Archidamus, and the Syracusan Hermocrates, in which money comes close to seeming the *most* important factor in warfare.[80] In Aristophanes' *Lysistrata* the women seize the Acropolis so as to deny their men access to this money and thereby to prevent them making war (173–6, 421–3, 487–9). 'The winners in wars every time', it is said in Aristophanes' *Wealth,* 'are those on whose side he (Wealth) sits down' (184–5).[81]

Human power and divine favour are not the only fundamental goods that seem to depend on money. For instance noble birth results from having wealth in the house over a long period[82] and is destroyed by poverty.[83] It is the same with health: in Sophocles it is stated that everything else is secondary to money, for although some praise health, the poor man is always sick.[84] From the numerous such passages I select three that indicate the *universal* pervasiveness of money as a means. Money (*chrēmata*) creates friends, honours, tyranny, physical beauty, wise speech, and pleasure even in disease (Soph. fr. 88). It is gold and silver 'by which war *and the other things* [my emphasis] thrive' (Thuc. 6.34.2). Wealth is 'all alone the source

---

[76] Anon. Iambl. 89 DK 4; cf. [Xen.] *Ath. Pol.* 3.3.

[77] Eur. *Hec.* 816–19; Soph. fr. 88; Ar. *Nub.* 98 (cf. 1041–2).

[78] Pl. *Prot.* 312d, 318e–319a, 349a, *Gorg.* 452de, *Men.* 91ab; Ar. *Clouds* 432 (cf. 98); etc.

[79] 5B; Hdt. 1.61, 64 (Peisistratus); 3. 122 (Polycrates); 5.36 (Hecataeus). See also Aesch. *Pers.* 238, where the context makes the Greeks' 'spring of silver' of military significance.

[80] Pericles says that the Athenians' strength comes from the money from their allies and that war is for the most part won by intelligence and by a reserve of money (2.13), and that the greatest factor is that the Spartans will be hindered by lack of money (1.142). According to Archidamus (1.83) 'warfare is not for the most part of arms, but of expense, because of which the arms are useful'. For the remark of Hermocrates see 6.34.2. See also Thuc. 1.80.3–4, 121.2, 141–3; 2.13.2–3. Cf. e.g. [Xen.] *Ath. Pol.* 3.3; [Aristot.] *Ath. Pol.* 27.3.

[81] Cf. Timotheus 790 *PMG* 'Ares is tyrant; Greece does not fear gold'; Pl. *Rep.* 422: in the ideal state money is *not* needed for warfare.

[82] Eur. fr. 22; also fr. 95; Simon. ap. Aristot. fr. 92 Rose.

[83] Eur. *El.* 38; cf. on the other hand Eur. fr. 1066 (money departs but noble birth remains).

[84] Fr. 354; similarly Eur. *El.* 428–9 (money saves from disease as well as permitting hospitality).

of all things' (Ar. *Wealth* 182). The separate spheres of exchange in the
Homeric economy, involving a degree of inconvertibility between prestige
objects and subsistence items, are inevitably merged[85] by the advent of metal
money capable, on a single scale ranging from talents to fractions of obols,
of the largest and the smallest payments – in the most various contexts (in
dowries, as fines, athletic prizes, state payments, sacred offerings, and so
on) as well as for almost all kinds of goods. 'A feast is made for laughter,
and wine maketh merry: but money answereth all things.'[86]

F   MONEY IS UNLIMITED

The previous two sections have raised the possibility that money has unlimited power. There is also a sense in which money itself (and the desire for
it) may be said to be unlimited. 'Of wealth', writes Solon, 'there is no limit
that appears to men. For those of us who have the most wealth are eager to
double it.'[87] Probably a generation or so before the introduction of coinage
into Athens, Solon is describing here, though he has no specific vocabulary
for it, the unprecedented phenomenon of *money*.[88] The unlimited desire
for – or accumulation of – wealth is not found in Homer.[89] Compare the
Homeric parting-gift (e.g. *Od.* 4.600–19) with Alcmaeon returning from
Croesus' treasury with as much gold as he could attach to his body (Hdt.
6.125). It is when precious metal acquires – along with its ease of storage,
concealment, and transport in high values – the power to obtain things
unlimited in quantity and kind, i.e. when it becomes *money*, that the desire
for it also becomes unlimited: there seems to be no natural limit to the
acquisition of it, whereas to the acquisition of, for example, tripods there is
a natural limit set by the use of tripods (to boil meat, as gifts, etc.) and by
the problem of storing them. Although not a precondition for insatiable
desire for wealth, money increases its incidence and its rationale. Money
is not only the object of unlimited desire and unlimited accumulation but
also (unlike wealth) itself unlimited in the closely related sense that, to the

---

[85] 2B n. 25, 5A; Kurke 1999, 22, 47, etc. Separate spheres of exchange merged by the advent of western
  all-purpose money (among the Tiv): Bohannan and Bohannan 1968.

[86] *Ecclesiastes* 10.19, of the early Greek period (late fourth to early third century BC).

[87] Fr. 13.71–3 West; sim. 4.11–13, 4C.2, 6.3; Theognis 596, 1158. This was no doubt a major factor
  (involving lending at interest: Lys. 10.18; 5A n. 26) in the crisis for which Solon was required to
  legislate. Cf. by contrast the relative *equilibrium* of the premonetary society described by Hesiod:
  Millett 1991, 47.

[88] There is in fact even thereafter no *precise* Greek equivalent to the word 'money': cf. 1C; 8A.

[89] In Homer the word *apereisios* (unlimited) expresses the abundance of what is in fact (sometimes
  even listed as) a limited number of goods offered as compensation (*apoina*) or wedding-gifts. Cf.
  10B n. 30.

extent that it is without use-value, its function is to be exchanged. It is of the essence of money therefore to be in permanent (unlimited) circulation (M–C–M–C–M etc.), in which any periods of storage are mere intervals. Note that for Solon it is *wealth itself* that is unlimited (because people desire to double it), just as Aristotle identifies money-making as giving rise to the notion that wealth and prosperity have no limit (*Pol.* 1256b40).

It is no coincidence that Solon, whose legislation is so prominent in the earliest evidence for money (5A), and who made the first extant statement of the unlimit of money, is also the first to believe that there is a hidden *measure* (of intelligence) that holds the limits of all things, and to recommend the principle of *moderation*.[90] Nor is it a coincidence that our earliest source for Solon, apart from his own words, is Herodotus (1.29–33), who also describes him as concerned with unlimited wealth – the unlimited wealth of Croesus, which he contrasts with the ritualised *limit* (public death ritual)[91] of the life of an Athenian man named 'Tellos' – suggestive of *telos*, whose basic sense of *limit* or *completion* qualifies it to refer to ritual. Of this collision between the unlimit of money and the limit inherent in ritual I will confine myself to one further example, in a passage we have already discussed.

On the one hand Clytemnestra encourages Agamemnon to walk on the textiles by arguing that such an act would not be in all circumstances wrong: it might be prescribed as a ritual (Aesch. *Ag.* 934 *telos*), to save Agamemnon's life (963–5), presumably of the kind that marks a limit to prosperity by an offering to deity. The excess involved in trampling infinitely replaceable (with money) textiles is made to seem less dangerous by being imagined as a ritual *telos*, with its implication of completion, of limit. But in fact the act that hypothetically might, as a *telos*, have saved Agamemnon's life, does seem, by arousing the resentment of men and gods (922–5, 937–9, 946–7), to doom him. Money has the power to do opposite things (8G).

Clytemnestra also says that the sea is inexhaustible, producing an ever-renewed gush of dye equal to silver (8A). The inexhaustibility of the supply of dye from the sea is relevant only if there is an inexhaustible supply of the money (silver) used in equal quantities (*isarguron*) to pay for it,[92] which

---

[90] The same combination of measure in the cosmos and recommended moderation in behaviour is found later in Heraclitus, whose cosmology reflects the unlimit of the circulation of money: 12A; Seaford 1994a, 226–9.

[91] Solon's second example (Cleobis and Biton) involves an even more ritualised death (in the temple of Hera during her festival): Seaford 1994a, 229–30.

[92] The (potentially alarming and relatively novel) *man-made* inexhaustibility of money is envisaged in terms of the *natural* inexhaustibility of the sea – whether through reticence or anxiety or the need for a concrete analogue for a difficult abstraction (cf. e.g. Soph. *Ant.* 1077 'silvered over' – κατηργυρωμένος – meaning bribed with silver). The unfamiliarity of an unlimited good would be

by implication therefore there is. Indeed the trampled textiles are 'bought with silver', and the house 'does not know how to be poor'. The sea, being both homogeneous and inexhaustible (unlimited),[93] evokes here both the homogeneity of money (8B) and its unlimit.[94] This unlimit is embodied in the textiles, which are therefore in this respect too antithetical to the ritual limit to prosperity imagined by Clytemnestra.

These textiles are also, it has been shown, closely associated, both verbally and visually, with the textile that Clytemnestra will soon use to trap Agamemnon in and to wrap his corpse in.[95] Of this murderous textile Clytemnestra says (1382–3)

A covering (*amphiblēstron*) without limit, like (a net) for fish,
I set around him, an evil wealth (*plouton*) of cloth.

Amphiblēstron is from the verb *amphiballō*, 'put around', which is used for dressing the corpse, and so suggests a shroud. Why is it 'without limit' (*apeiron*)? Firstly because, unlike garments worn by the living, the funerary garment was wrapped around the hands and feet of the corpse, and sometimes even the head. Secondly because it encloses, like the net, which is *apeiron* in the sense that it has no limit past which the quarry can escape.[96] From *apeiron* also flows the description 'evil wealth of cloth'. The household has an unlimited 'silver-bought' supply of cloths, in sharp contrast to the ritualised individuality of the cloth normally woven by the women within a man's household (presumably often by his wife)[97] for his corpse. We have seen that the trampled textiles might in a *telos* (ritual, limit) have saved Agamemnon's life. But in fact they embody *un*limited money, and this unlimit is then embodied in the associated textile that kills him *because it has no limit*. The notion of unlimited money is an abstraction, but the (dangerous) abstraction is expressed in the concrete instrument of Agamemnon's death, what Orestes calls the 'father-killing textile' (*Cho.* 1015). Just before this death we hear the words 'for all mortals prosperity is by nature insatiable' (*Ag.* 1331–2).

---

all the more intense if Athens was, or had been, the kind of 'peasant society' generally dominated by what Foster (1965) calls the 'image of the limited good', i.e. the idea that all desirable things in life (land, wealth, friendship, honour, etc.) exist in finite quantity and are always in short supply.

[93] Note the phrase *apeirona ponton*, 'unlimited sea', at *Il.* 1.350, *Od.* 4.510; Theognis 237. The household by contrast is *limited*.

[94] The sea is appropriate here also in the quite different respect that in this period much commercial money was made via the sea.

[95] Taplin 1978, 79–82; Seaford 1998a, 129–30.

[96] And indeed in the hands of Clytemnestra it has in effect become such a net: detail in Seaford 1984b.

[97] *Il.* 22.510–11; in the *Odyssey* Penelope does so for the widower Laertes.

Clytemnestra's bathing and wrapping of her still-living husband is perverted death ritual:[98] the normally loving act of bathing and wrapping the corpse is transformed into its hostile opposite by the unlimit associated with money. Agamemnon is killed by the cloth in which normally a woman lovingly wraps her dead husband.[99] Death ritual is a *completion*, enclosing within a traditional, reassuring order the brutality of death. The Euripidean Electra vainly calls the shroud thrown over her murdered mother an 'end (*telos*) of the great sufferings of the house'.[100] In *Agamemnon*, with death ritual as the expression of brutal violence, the enclosure is turned inside out. Along with the destruction of the economic self-sufficiency of the household[101] by money goes the perversion of its ritual. As elsewhere,[102] the unlimit of money subverts the limit inherent in death ritual.

Finally, the unlimited money was in fact embodied in the trampled textiles through their *dye* from the inexhaustible sea, the 'ever-renewed gush (*kēkis*), equal to silver, of much purple, the dyings of cloths'. Even in this particular the physical embodiment of the dangerous notion of unlimited wealth seems to turn against its owner, for the same rare word, *kēkis*, is used of the gush of blood that stained the murderous textile, 'dyed' by the sword.[103]

The unlimit of money takes brilliant form in Aristophanes' *Wealth*: not only does Wealth have power over everybody and everything, it is also distinct in that of everything else (sex, bread, music, honour, courage, soup, and so on) there is satiety, whereas if somebody gets thirteen talents he desires the more strongly to get sixteen, and if he achieves this, then he wants forty and says that life is not worth living unless he gets them.[104] So too Xenophon remarks that alone among industries silver-mining never produces excess supply: nobody ever possessed so much silver as to want no

---

[98] Seaford 1984b.   [99] See esp. Eur. *Tro.* 377–8, 390; Soph. *Ant.* 897–902.

[100] *El.* 1232; cf. *Ag.* 1107–9 . . . *telos*.

[101] The basic polarity in Aristotle's economics is between community and outsider (of which the extreme form would be between the self-sufficiency of the household and trade with non-Greeks), out of which arise the corresponding polarities self-sufficiency–trade, goods–money, limit–unlimit, moral–immoral, natural–unnatural: Seaford 2000a. All these polarities are embodied in what Clytemnestra says about the textiles. Even non-Greeks are involved if the purple dye was understood as bought from Tyre.

[102] Hdt. 1.187: Darius' 'insatiable desire for money' makes him reopen a tomb (8D n. 52); 14D.

[103] *Cho.* 1011–12. Orestes has just decided, as he addresses the cloth, that it is not so much a shroud as a net (998–9), and indeed 'the kind of net possessed by a brigand, a cheater of travellers, leading a life that deprives people of money/silver'. This puzzling detail may arise from the notion of the cloth as used to deprive the king of the unlimited money that it also embodies.

[104] 189–97. This may be inspired in part by *Il.* 13.636–9, where the insatiable desire is (the Trojans') for fighting.

more, and if he has a massive amount, he takes as much pleasure in burying as in using it (*Poroi* 4.6–7). Unlimit becomes invisibility. For Aristotle there is a natural form of acquisition that provides true, self-sufficient wealth (of household or polis) adequate for a good life. But there is also, he says, another kind called money-making (χρηματιστική), and it is because of this that there is thought to be no limit to wealth or to its acquisition (*Politics* 1256b26–1257a4). Aristotle is not referring here to greed, which can of course occur in the absence of money, but rather to a form of activity (M–C–M). The selling of commodities (or effort) for money to acquire other commodities (or effort) (C–M–C) has a limit built into its form, but M–C–M does not.[105]

We have said that in *Agamemnon* the sea, as homogeneous and unlimited, evokes the homogeneity and unlimit of money. But even the sea is concrete, and so in fact limited; whereas money may seem genuinely unlimited because it is not only homogeneous but *abstract*.[106] The desire for unlimited numerical units (purchasing power) makes more sense than the desire for an unlimited number of tripods or textiles. We noted in 8B the importance of homogeneity for creating monetary abstraction, and will say more about this abstraction in 8H.

Money is uniquely desirable (8D, 8E), and the desire is unique also in being unlimited: to the unlimited accumulation and apparently unlimited power of money there belongs the unlimited desire for it that finds frequent expression.[107] Tragedy comments on this desire both in general[108] and in particular – notably in the figure of Polymnestor in Euripides' *Hecuba*, destroyed, like Polycrates of Samos (Hdt. 3.123–5), by his passion for even more gold.[109] Given that success in warfare and political power were not only obtainable by money but also a means of obtaining still more money, unlimited desire for money might make much headway in practice. And with the development of money the aim of commerce seems to be, among the Greeks as ever since, more and more the acquisition of money – rather than of the things that can be acquired by money.

---

[105] Meikle 1996, 146: 'M is a quantity, so there is no amount of M which, once gained, allows one to say that the activity M–C–M–C–M–C–M . . . has reached its end; it is an activity without a natural terminus.'

[106] As Strepsiades observes to his creditor, the sea does not grow – unlike borrowed money (Ar. *Clouds* 1286–95).

[107] As well as the passages mentioned elsewhere in this section see Bacchyl. 1.64–7. Pl. *Rep.* 442a, *Laws* 918d; Isocr. 8.7; *P.Oxy.* 1795 ii 16–19; Max. Tyr. 7.5.

[108] E.g. Eur. *Supp.* 239 the useless wealthy are 'always passionate for more'.

[109] 775, 1002–14, 1146–8, 1206–7.

G   MONEY UNITES OPPOSITES

As an example of money being a threat to other basic values we cited Theognis' complaint that in choosing a spouse people prefer wealth to noble birth (8D). 'They honour money, and a good man marries the daughter of a bad, a bad man the daughter of a good. Wealth mixes up breeding' (190). The good is mixed with the bad (192 *esthla kakois*). A man of good repute is persuaded by wealth/money (*chrēmata*) to marry a woman of ill repute (195 *eudoxos kakodoxon*). The desire for money is powerful enough to efface the distinction between good breeding and bad. The distinction becomes irrelevant in the choice of spouse, and moreover the mingling of well-bred with ill-bred in marriage tends to efface it in reality. And so the wealth itself seems to unite the opposites, to efface the distinction ('wealth mixes up breeding'). And then there is a third way in which money transcends or undermines the distinction: as we have seen, the acquisitive power of money may be such that even good breeding may actually be the *result* of having wealth over a long period, and conversely may be destroyed by poverty.[110] Wealth makes a good man bad and a bad man good.[111] If a slave has wealth he will be honoured, despite being a slave (Eur. fr. 142). Similarly, money can make a poor speaker into a clever one and an ugly person into a beautiful one.[112] It sets the worst man among the foremost (Eur. fr. 95). We have also seen how money is associated by both Sophocles (8D) and Aeschylus (8F) with the transformation of the loving intimacy of death ritual into its opposite. And the desire for wealth may be powerful enough to transform its *desirer* into his opposite – a good man into a wrongdoer (Soph. *Ant.* 298–9).

The capacity of money to transform things into their opposite[113] – a form of money's power to homogenise (8B) – expresses its transcendent

---

[110] Eur. *El.* 38, frr. 22, 95.

[111] Theogn 383–92, 649–52, 661–6, 1118. The power of money to unite social opposites is implicit also in Kurke's analysis of the story of the Pharaoh Amasis at Hdt. 2.172: Kurke 1999, 93–6.

[112] Soph. fr. 88. With the reference to clever speaking cf. the belief in the all-powerfulness of persuasion (e.g. Eur. *Hec.* 816), than which money is here seen to be more fundamental.

[113] Famously described by Marx 1992 (1844), 375–9, citing *Timon of Athens*: 'Thus much of this will make black white, foul fair, / Wrong right, base noble, old young, coward valiant . . . Thou visible god, / that solders't close impossibilities / And makst them kiss!' Cf. *The Money God* by Lu Bao (Chinese, *c.* AD 300): 'Money is a spiritual thing. It has no rank yet is revered; it has no status yet is welcomed. Where there is money, danger will turn to peace and death will give life' (quoted by Williams 1997, 155). In an anthropological account (Burridge 1969, 45) money introduced into a premonetary economy (Melanesia) 'reveals the vice in cultivated virtues, allows no vice without some virtue, concedes an element of right in wrong-doing, finds the sin of pride in an upright fellow' – quoted by Macfarlane 1985, 72, who argues that it is this confusing power of money that underlies the disappearance of the idea of evil from modern European societies.

desirability and transcendent power. Further, as a medium of exchange money itself seems to be transformed into numerous other things, even into its opposite and vice-versa. In Aeschylus' image of Ares as 'gold-changer of bodies' the large and personal (bodies) is transformed into the small and impersonal (dust, money).

H   MONEY IS BOTH CONCRETE AND ABSTRACT

It is in coinage that the homogeneity of money acquires perfection, for the stamp on a coin renders small variations of quality and quantity irrelevant (8B). This notional homogeneity endows money with *abstraction*, for the value of every (say) tetradrachm is abstract in the sense that it is in effect a mathematical figure (four) abstracted from the varying concrete particularities of each coin. This abstraction is in Greek coinage reinforced by systematic discrepancy between the conventional value of the coin and the concrete value of its bullion (7D). Such monetary value, being distinct from the metal in which it is embodied, may seem to be *ideal* substance, and as such to be *invisible* (6C). And this appearance of invisibility may converge with the tendency of precious metal to be concealed.[114]

And yet ancient Greek coinage did not on the whole, in contrast to modern money (metal, paper, notional, electronic), become a mere token, but retained some (albeit sometimes very low) intrinsic value. The bullion value of coins was an ingredient in creating the confidence on which their conventional value depended. This combination of material and conventional value makes the coin into a unique kind of thing (7D).

Coins represent value that is abstract and homogeneous, and yet they do so by virtue of types that are concrete and distinctive (an owl, a tortoise, etc.). When in Euripides' satyr-play *Sciron* prostitutes are offered in return for coins called 'horses' and 'virgins' after the images stamped on them, the (abstract, homogeneous) power of coinage is seen – with humorous anachronism – from the old perspective of the (premonetary) exchange of specific, concrete commodities, a perspective characteristic of the Dionysiac world of the satyrs (14D). In a characteristically Aristophanean reduction of abstract to concrete, Athenian coins are imagined in the *Birds* as real owls.[115]

---

[114] E.g. Bacch. 3.13–14 'he knows how not to conceal towering wealth in black–cloaked darkness'; 12B nn. 109–11.

[115] 301, 1105–8 (they reproduce). Cf. *Wasps* 789–95, *Clouds* 1283–95; Plut. *Lys.* 16.2 (a servant in pre-coinage Sparta refers riddlingly to owls); Pollux 9.74 (the proverb 'virtue and wisdom are defeated by turtles'); Euboulos fr. 5 'Pallases'; Plut. *Ages.* 13, *Artax.* 20.6 Persian 'archers'. All this goes beyond the mere convenience of referring to coins as e.g. 'maidens', 'owls', 'turtles', which was probably common: e.g. Pollux 9.74–6.

I   MONEY IS DISTINCT FROM ALL ELSE

The power of Greek metal money to obtain so many kinds of thing, together with its ease of storage, of concealment, and of deployment, and all the qualities discussed in this chapter, set it apart from everything else. More powerful than any of the numerous activities, goods and abilities that it underlies, it concentrates onto itself the desire for all that it can obtain. And so the power and desirability of money may seem *unique*. Money is said to be the most honoured and powerful thing among men,[116] to be what they all toil for,[117] to 'enslave'[118] and 'defeat'[119] them. 'Money' may even come to stand for something like 'an especially good or desirable thing', as in such expressions as 'it is money if one is pious to god', or '(I do not want money from you). It is money if you save my life, which is the dearest thing I have'.[120] As early as Theognis we find praise of a quite different and potentially competing value, loyalty, expressed in terms of money: a loyal man is worth his weight in gold and silver (77–8). In a fragment (324) of Euripides' *Danae* it is said that the pleasure given by gold is greater than that of parents and children in each other,[121] and is like Aphrodite's look that inspires innumerable passions. Erotic passion for money re-appears elsewhere,[122] notably in the anonymous tragic fragment mentioned in 8D, which I now quote in full.

O gold, offspring of the earth, what passion (*erōta*) you kindle among humankind, mightiest of all, tyrant over all. For those at war you have greater power than Ares and enchant all things: for the trees and the mindless races of wild animals followed the Orphic songs, but you (are followed by) the whole earth and sea and all-inventive Ares.

---

[116] Eur. *Phoen.* 439–40; also *HF* 774–6, fr. 325; fr. adesp. 294.   [117] Eur. fr. 580.
[118] Eur. *Hec.* 865, *Supp.* 875–6; cf. fr. 1092.   [119] Eur. fr. 341; cf. *Ion* 629.
[120] Eur. fr. 252, *Or.* 644–5; cf. also Aesch. *Cho.* 372; Eur. *Hec.* 1229, *Tro.* 432–3.
[121] Cf. Ar. *Wasps* 606–9, *Wealth* 250–1.
[122] Eur. *Supp.* 178, 239, *Hec.* 775; fr. trag. adesp. 129. Conceivably though in such passages the word *erōs* may have lost erotic associations.

PART TWO

The making of metaphysics

CHAPTER NINE

Did politics produce philosophy?

A LAW, PUBLIC SPACE, FREE DEBATE

The fundamental transition in thought, towards what we call science and philosophy (or 'philosophical cosmology'), that occurred among the Ionian Greeks of the sixth century BC may be characterised in various ways. Examination of the complexity of the transition has produced numerous qualifications: the unevenness of its development, the presence of a form of science earlier among the Babylonians and Egyptians, the persistence of dogmatic or magical elements in seemingly rational discourse, and so on. And I am well aware that what may legitimately be included in the broad term 'philosophy' is found already in Homer and Hesiod.[1] But that some such crucial transition occurred is generally agreed. My concern is not so much to describe it in detail as with the various attempts that have been made to *explain* it. Suffice it to say that what I select[2] for explanation is the advent of the idea of the universe as an *intelligible order* subject to the *uniformity* of *impersonal* power. More specifically, central to early Greek cosmology is the counter-intuitive idea of a single substance underlying the plurality of things manifest to the senses. Inasmuch as this latter idea implies concern with reality as opposed to appearance, with what is fundamental as opposed to what is derivative, and with comprehensive as opposed to partial understanding, it is *metaphysical*.

There is agreement that such explanations must remain highly speculative, and that the transition arose from a complex combination of factors rather than from a single cause. It should also be agreed that any factor or combination of factors that is also to be found in a society that did not produce anything like the Greek transition is for that reason an unlikely

---

[1] Ethical concerns, interest in linguistic representation, etc.: e.g. Osborne 1997.

[2] My *explananda* thus defined exclude numerous other aspects attributed to the transition. There is, for instance, no mention of *rationality*, which I regard as too broad a concept (myth may of course employ a kind of reason or rationality) to be helpful in studying this period.

candidate: this argument has been successfully advanced against the factors of technological development, of wealth as permitting leisure, and of
awareness of other cultures, in none of which the Greeks of this period were
in advance of the much older civilisations of the Near East.[3] Another factor
that should, more controversially, be included in this category is alphabetic literacy,[4] which was neither invented by nor confined to the Greeks,
although they made unusually widespread use of it.

The factor that holds the field in recent discussion is the political one,
ably advocated in particular by J.-P. Vernant and G. E. R. Lloyd.[5] Vernant
focuses on the first non-mythical cosmology that we can perceive in any
detail, that of Anaximander. In the polis (in contrast to monarchy) citizens
are ruled by, and are equal with respect to, impersonal law. This equality is
also expressed spatially, in the symmetrical organisation of political space
around a single centre – *meson, hestia koinē* (common hearth) – in which the
citizens participate, 'a geometrical schema of reversible relationships governed by equilibrium and reciprocity between equals'. It is, according to
Vernant, this political conception that provides the model for Anaximander's cosmology, in which the reciprocal relations between the elements
are held in equilibrium by an egalitarian order, and space is symmetrically
organised around a centre occupied by the earth.[6]

Lloyd focuses rather, in his attempt to explain 'the emergence of philosophy and science'[7] among the Greeks, on the unprecedented *freedom
of public debate* characteristic of the polis: specifically, on the radical revisability of laws and constitution by the citizens, on their expectation and
evaluation of rational justification (evidence and argument), and on the
public contexts of competitiveness in wisdom generally, so that, for example, in the development of the notion of formal or rigorous proof, 'here
too, as in our other studies, the political and legal background plays a role
at least at the beginning of what might otherwise seem a merely intellectual
development'.[8]

---

[3] Technology: against Farrington 1961, 29–41 see Thomson 1961b, 171–2; Lloyd 1979, 235–9 (also on
wealth and awareness of other cultures).

[4] Goody and Watt 1968 (1963); against this factor see esp. Lloyd 1979, 239–4; 1987, 70–8; 1990, 37, 132.
Goody in his later statements (e.g. 1977; 1987, realising that Greek alphabetic innovation was not
after all dramatic, shifts the cognitive consequences back to the ancient Near East.

[5] Vernant 1982 (1962); 1983 (1965); Lloyd 1979; 1987; 1990. See also Vlastos 1970; Humphreys 1978,
209–41; Vidal-Naquet 1986 (1967), 249–62; Capizzi 1990.

[6] Vernant 1982 (1962), esp. 47–8, 65, 101, 107–8, 122–6; 1983 (1968), 190–211.

[7] Lloyd 1979, 226–7 calls this phrase a 'convenient shorthand' (which he notes can easily distort the
discussion) for the 'complexity and heterogeneity of the various divergent strands of early Greek
speculative thought'.

[8] Lloyd 1979, 240–64; 1987, 78–102; 1990, esp. 7–8, 63–5, 96–7, 124–5, 134, 141–2. On law (but beginning
with *Sumerian* law) and the invention of (culture-dependent) proof see Feyerabend 1999, 56–7.

This political explanation, of which I have given here only the briefest summary, clearly has something to be said for it. But it also has unacknowledged weaknesses. The first of these is historical. *When and where do we first find the relevant aspects of the polis, namely (a) the egalitarian relation of the citizens to (impersonal) law, (b) the development of public space around an egalitarian centre, and (c) freedom of public debate?* What remains of this section consists of answers to these questions.

(a) The evidence here is from Greek traditions about early laws, from early inscriptions, and from early literature. Various archaic lawgivers were regarded in Greek tradition as having introduced written laws for the polis as a whole.[9] Of these the earliest seems to have been Zaleukos of Epizephyrean Locri, probably of about the middle of the seventh century BC (5A). In Athens – to take a case where we are comparatively well informed – the written code of Solon (probably 594/3 BC) was preceded by that of Draco (*c.* 620 BC); but even before the time of Draco it seems that the *thesmothetai* ('lawgivers') publicly recorded judicial decisions (*thesmia*) and kept them for judging future disputes.[10] The earliest inscribed law that happens to have survived (and there may well have been earlier ones from elsewhere) is from about the middle of the seventh century, or perhaps somewhat later. From Dreros in Crete, it begins with the words 'the polis has thus decided', and sets limits to the authority of an official.[11]

From the considerable evidence of this kind we can infer that in various city-states the relatively recent invention of alphabetic writing was used, at least from about the middle of the seventh century, to record publicly codes of law that were impersonal both in that they were uniformly binding on all citizens and in that they were decided on by the polis – or at least, if said to have been devised by an individual, were administered not by him but by the institutions of the polis and were dependent for their authority on acceptance by the citizens who had appointed him.[12] Indeed the distance between the archaic lawgiver and the laws is expressed in the lawgiver being

---

[9] Adcock 1927; Szegedy-Maszak 1978; Gagarin 1986, 49–80; a sceptical account is by Hölkeskamp 1999.

[10] [Aristot.] *Ath. Pol.* 3.4: Rhodes 1981, 102 is sceptical, but cf. Gagarin 1981a, 1986, 51, 55–6.

[11] Van Effenterre and Ruzé 1994–5, 1 306; Meiggs and Lewis 1988, no. 2. Perhaps *SEG* 30.380 (Tiryns) is as early (Koerner 1993, no. 31). For the early inscribed laws generally see Gagarin 1986, 81–97.

[12] This is preserved in some detail in the life and poetry of Solon, who was said after his reforms to have left Athens for ten years after binding the citizens not to alter his laws for that period (Hdt. 1.29; [Aristot.] *Ath. Pol.* 7.2 ('100 years'); 11.1); cf. the Spartans' oath and Lycurgus' trick to ensure the permanence of his laws (Plut. *Lyc.* 29: see further Szegedy-Maszak 1978, 207). Solon's poems seem to urge the polis to accept his laws, presented as fair for all, a compromise between factions (frr. 5; 36.18–25; 37.9–10 West; cf. [Aristot.] *Ath Pol.* 5–12; Plut. *Sol.* 14–18). The fate of the city depends on the citizens themselves, not the gods: frr. 4.5–6, 30–1; 4c3; 11.1–2 West.

frequently a political outsider or even a foreigner, as well as in stories about the lawgivers being subjected to their own laws.[13]

Clearly the impersonal uniformity of law may be promoted by the practice of its public inscription. To what extent did it have this impersonal uniformity before the advent of this practice? Here we depend almost entirely on the poetry of Homer and Hesiod, which provides us with evidence, if we use it carefully, for the eighth century. In both poets we find groups of men giving judgement in a public open space (the *agora*).[14] Given that at this early stage no writing is involved, and the role of judges is to resolve disputes rather than generally to impose penalties on lawbreakers,[15] did they do so by applying (orally transmitted) laws, impersonal and equally binding on all?

The key word is *themistes*, which men 'judge' in the *agora*.[16] The savagery of the Cyclopes is expressed in their lack of 'council-bearing *agorai*, and *themistes*'.[17] *Themistes* are a sign of civilisation. The related word *themis* means (impersonal) established principle, and is associated explicitly with the public space of the *agora*: there is in the Greek camp a place 'where there was for them *agora* and *themis*, and altars of the gods built' (*Il.* 11.807); and Diomedes, about to speak against the 'folly' of Agamemnon, appeals to his right to do so as *themis* in *agora* (9.33). *Themistes* are not *ad hoc* judgements, but rather, as etymology suggests,[18] something like 'established norms', used in the public settlement of disputes. We do not know where they stand on the spectrum between at one extreme laws (subject inevitably to personal interpretation, but orally transmitted in roughly the same form) and at the other extreme mere norms or customs (only vaguely, variously, or briefly formulated, and so dependent on personal reformulation for their judicial application).[19] And yet they are certainly impersonal in two respects, firstly in that they are publicly applied not by a single person but by a group (with the possibility of debate on impersonal principle), and secondly in that being imagined as traditional they thereby stand in this sense at least above judges and the parties to the dispute. This separation of the norms from the judges is confirmed by the emphasis, in Homer and especially Hesiod, on the giving of 'crooked'

---

[13] Gagarin 1986, 59–60; Szegedy-Maszak 1978, 206.
[14] *Il.* 1.238; 9.154–6, 16.86; Hes. *Op.* 38–9, 220.   [15] Gagarin 1986, 19–50.
[16] *Il.* 16.387; Hes. *Theog.* 85, *Op.* 221. 'Judge' is κρίνειν or διακρίνειν.
[17] *Od.* 9.112 (cf. 215 Polyphemus knows neither *dikai* nor *themistes*; *Il.* 5.761 Ares knows no *themis*).
[18] Chantraine 1968–80, 428 (s.v. θέμις).
[19] Roth (1976) argues that the idea of benefits conferred on the judges by the Muses (Hes. *Theog.* 80–93) derives from the judges' memorisation of laws; cf. however Gagarin 1986, 25–6.

themistes by the judges, who, 'drive out justice (*dikē*)'.[20] Justice is an impersonal principle,[21] sometimes abused by the people whose task should be to impose it.

However, there are other respects in which the *themistes* may appear to be personal. Although they are in general applied by an (elite) group, we find Nestor assuring Agamemnon that 'Zeus gave you sceptre and *themistes*.'[22] This discrepancy, or rather contestation of control over *themistes*, is like that found in the Homeric distribution of food (and booty), which is controlled sometimes by the whole group affected but sometimes by a single leader (3A). This latter contradiction is reflected, we saw, in the conflict between the power of Zeus and the notion of fate, a notion that originated in the ancient principle of distribution and is sometimes personified as the goddesses Aisa and Moira. Similarly, the impersonal principle of *themis* is personified as a goddess (Themis), subordinated (more so than are Aisa and Moira) to Zeus. Although Themis 'breaks up and convenes assemblies (*agorai*) of men' (*Od.* 2.68), it is at the behest of Zeus (*Il.* 20.4) that she convenes the assembly of gods. Where the *themistes* are given an origin, it is from Zeus rather than Themis.[23] In Hesiod Zeus' control over the more ancient deity Themis is achieved by their marriage.[24] Justice (*dikē*) too is not just an impersonal principle, but personified by Hesiod as the daughter of Zeus (220, 256). At the divine level the single person (Zeus) has control, and *themis* and justice are personified under him. But at the human level *themis* and justice are impersonal principles, and *themistes* are publicly administered by groups of judges without the intervention of Zeus. It is only if the judgements turn out to be crooked that Zeus will subsequently react, in the way that he does to bad men – indiscriminately against the whole community.[25] Similarly for Solon there is a human level, and a divine level of personification: he has created the laws himself and explicitly insists on the responsibility of the citizens themselves (as opposed to the gods), but also treats as personifications Justice, Good Order, and Time as judge.[26] Themis, Justice, Good Order, Time: these are powers easily imagined as

---

[20] *Il.* 16.387–8; *Op.* 38–9, 220–1, 250, 261–2. Cf. *Od.* 14.84: the gods 'honour justice (*dikē*) and appropriate deeds of men'.

[21] Hes. *Op.* 9, 192, 278; *Od.* 14.84.

[22] *Il.* 9.98–9 (99 reappears (interpolated) at 2.206); note also 9.156 (= 298), *Od.* 11.569 (Minos sole judge in underworld), 12.439 (a 'man' as judge); Hes. *Theog.* 85 (seemingly a sole judge).

[23] *Il.* 1.238; 9.99; *Od.* 16.403.

[24] *Theog.* 135, 901 – as Zeus' second wife, the first (also to confirm his power, 892–4) being with Metis.

[25] *Il.* 16.385–8; Hes. *Op.* 258–62, cf. 238–47.

[26] 4. 4–5; 11; Justice (*Dikē*): 3.14–20; Good Order (*Eunomiē*): 4.32–9; Time (cf. even Anaximander fr. 1): 36 3.

personal, but, like other Hesiodic personifications,[27] without the deep or widespread personhood that produces cult.

In both Homer and Hesiod then there are indications of the *availability* of the notion of impersonal norms to be impartially applied by a group of judges. The notion may in fact have been, even as early as the eighth century, more available than appears in Homeric poetry, which has an ideological tendency, individualist and aristocratic, to downplay or ignore elements of the developing polis, such as the massive eighth-century increase in temple building and dedications (3B). The institutions of the polis are there in Homer, but in the background.[28] They have no effective role in the main narratives, in which conflict is resolved by the action of heroic individuals, not by judicial process, with the *themistes* appropriated for a single leader (Zeus gave 'sceptre and *themistes*' to Agamemnon). In the background, by contrast, the peaceful 'polis' represented on the shield of Achilles, for instance, consists mainly of a trial held before the people thronging the *agora*, with the 'the elders' as judges (*Il.* 18.490–508), and no mention of a single leader. All this may suggest that much Homeric ideology is a reaction against the progressive eighth-century encroachment of the polis on monarchical power. On the other hand it has been argued in detail that for the geometric period (900–720 BC) there is in fact no evidence at all for monarchy *in the poleis*, which were throughout ruled rather by groups of hereditary leaders (*basileis*).[29]

(b) The relevant characteristic of *political space* is its organisation around a centre in relation to which the citizens are equal, as opposed to the hierarchical political space of the eastern kingdoms.[30] When do we first find such political space among the Greeks? Here again, the discrepancy between Homer and eighth-century building as revealed by archaeology (see below) reminds us of the ideological tendency of the Homeric *narrative*, in which a spatial centre as just defined plays almost no role. In the Homeric *background*, however, we can detect the public importance of the *agora*, as in two passages cited above: the place where 'there was for them *agora* and *themis*, and altars of the gods built', and the trial, in the peaceful polis, held

---

[27] E.g. *Theog.* 228–9 Battles, Fights, Murders, Killings of men, Quarrels, Lies, Words, Disputes.

[28] Seaford 1994a, 1–5.

[29] Drews 1983, who accordingly maintains (7, 99) that such elements of monarchy as there are in Homer (fewer than is often supposed) derive from an earlier period (and probably from Thessaly).

[30] Vernant 1983 (1965) 'As a legal inscription at Tenos [*IG* XII 872 third century BC] puts it, in the centre is the collectivity (μέσῳ πάντες); on the outside are the individuals (χωρὶς ἕκαστος).' But Vernant omits the words παντὸς τοῦ ἀργυρίου ('of all the money') after ἕκαστος ('each man'). *The phrase is not political but about money*: it occurs three times (27, 31, 38) in a list of purchases, each time after the names of the purchasers.

in the *agora* thronged by the people. The contradiction between narrative and background is visible even within Odysseus' stay at Scherie. The hero Odysseus visits the house of the man (Alcinous) who 'rules',[31] a house different from those of the other Phaeacians (6.301–2). The background descriptions of the *polis*, however, mention wall, temple, harbour, and a paved *agora* around a fine precinct of Poseidon, but not Alcinous' house, to which Odysseus has to ask for directions (even though an 'infant' could give them) and is shown the way by the disguised Athena.[32] This narrative is in fact balanced between Alcinous' house on the one hand and on the other the *agora*, in which the people assemble for athletics, song and dance, and Alcinous calls himself (merely) one of thirteen rulers (*basilēes*) (8.390–1). As for Hesiod, he has from his peasant perspective nothing to say of urban space, except perhaps for his reference to the people (*laoi*) at trials in the *agora* (*Theog.* 84–91).

Of the features of Homeric Scherie, city wall and central temple are archaeologically attested in a number of cities by the end of the eighth century.[33] *Agorai* are much harder to find and to date. But among the patchy evidence from various places there is a fine eighth-century *agora*, laid out 'at the same time and along the same alignment as the temple of Apollo Delphinios',[34] at Dreros, the home of our earliest surviving inscribed law of the polis.

(c) Finally, *freedom of debate*. In Homer there are numerous assemblies, in many[35] of which opposed views are vigorously put, although it is generally only the notable men who speak. The right to put an opposing view is on three occasions explicitly claimed.[36] Free speech is never in fact prevented, but is on two occasions threatened: Calchas speaks only after Achilles agrees to protect him against Agamemnon, and Thersites is after his dissident speech attacked both physically and verbally by Odysseus.[37] Several of these assemblies are democratic in the limited sense that the prevailing view is said to obtain mass approval.[38] In others each of the two opposed courses is followed by part of the mass,[39] or the views of the mass are simply not stated.[40] At Ithaca it seems that anyone has the right to summon

---

[31] 6.12, cf. 197; 7.11, 23, 46.   [32] *Od.* 6.9–10, 262–7, 298–300; 7.19–49.

[33] E.g. Snodgrass 1980, 33–4, 58–62; Murray 1993, 64; Osborne 1996, 89–90.

[34] Coldstream 1977, 315, who also collects the evidence for other early *agorai*.

[35] *Il.* 1.54–305; 2.94–397; 7.345–79; 8.2–40; 9.10–79; 18.245–313; 19.45–237; *Od.* 2.6–259; 3.137–50; 24.420–66.

[36] *Il.* 9.33, 61–2; 12.211–15.

[37] *Il.* 1.76–92; 2.244–69. *Od.* 2.82–3 does not result from a threat. Threats such as that at *Il.* 12.250 are to freedom of action not of debate.

[38] *Il.* 2.270–7; 7.403–4; 8.542; 9.50–1; 18.310–13.   [39] *Od.* 3.148–50; 24.463–6.

[40] *Il.* 1.304–5; 7.379; 12.251; *Od.* 2.257–8.

an assembly.[41] But despite their prominence, Homeric assemblies tend to embody the ineffectiveness or foolishness of the mass, who contribute little to the narrative.[42] Here again there is a distinction between on the one hand the individualist, aristocratic ideology of the narrative, as for example when the mass approves of Odysseus' treatment of Thersites, and on the other hand elements of the background that may be closer to the reality of the contemporary polis.

We may conclude then from the literary and archaeological evidence that all three relevant aspects of the polis were to be found, to some extent, as early as the eighth century, and are far from having any particular association with Ionia. The first natural philosopher and cosmologist was, according to Aristotle, the Milesian Thales, who predicted the solar eclipse of 585 BC. The Milesian Anaximander was regarded in antiquity as a younger contemporary of Thales, and one report made him sixty-four in the year 547/6.[43] Does this lapse in time between the eighth century and the first non-mythical cosmology in the sixth count against the political explanation of its appearance? We do not know enough to give an answer. It is at any rate dangerous to attribute the lapse to a passage of time somehow required between the emergence of certain political forms and their eventual projection by citizens onto the cosmos. Such projection would more likely occur unreflectively out of their contested emergence, especially in what archaeology suggests was the relatively rapid development of the polis in the eighth century.

Another defence of the political explanation might be the claim that in the sixth century the Ionian poleis reached an unprecedented stage of development in the aspects that concern us. This may be so, especially perhaps in the aspect (stressed by Lloyd) of freedom of debate about the *constitution* of the polis.[44] But there is no real evidence for the supposition. Moreover, none of the early lawgivers or constitutional reformers recorded in Greek tradition has any connection with Ionia. And the earliest inscribed laws that happen to have survived are from Crete.

Lloyd provides a broadly political explanation, but also, more specifically, a *democratic* one, defending the possibility of 'connecting the emergence of Greek scientific rationality with the ideology of democracy in particular', an ideology that encourages mass participation in political debate.[45] To counter

---

[41] *Od.* 2.28–9.   [42] Seaford 1994a, 3–5.   [43] KRS 76, 101–2.

[44] Although every example given by Lloyd (1979, 242) of 'the openness of the political and constitutional situation' in various Greek states from the second half of the sixth century involves the giving of a constitution by an *individual* (and are all reported much later by Herodotus).

[45] Lloyd 1990, 60–4; 1979, 242–6, 256–7, 260–2.

the obvious objection that democracy was first introduced by Cleisthenes at Athens in 508 BC, well after the emergence of philosophical cosmology, Lloyd makes two points. The first, in which there is some force, is that in fact the reforms of Solon of the early sixth century were already democratic to some extent. The second is that the second-order questions that Lloyd regards as '*chiefly* constitutive' of philosophy and science 'only begin to be raised . . . in the epistemological debate that begins with Heraclitus (at work around 500 BC) and more especially with Parmenides (who was born between 515 and 510)'.

It is an unacknowledged difficulty for Lloyd, however, that not only is neither Heraclitus nor Parmenides Athenian, but Athens in fact produced no philosopher before Anaxagoras' pupil Archelaus, who was born in the early fifth century. When philosophy did eventually arrive in Athens, the democracy proved intolerant of it.[46] Although it is not certain that Athens was the first democracy,[47] there is nothing whatsoever to suggest that any of the cities that produced philosophers born before 500 BC (Miletus, Ephesus, Samos, Colophon, Elea) were democratic. Among the little that we do know of their politics is that Miletus in the time of Thales, and probably during the youth of Anaximander, was ruled by the (reputedly) ruthless tyrant Thrasyboulos, who may have been succeeded by the tyrants Thoas and Damasenor (10C). It is likely that Pythagoras never knew anything but tyranny on his native Samos, which he left (according to Aristoxenus) to avoid the tyranny of Polycrates.[48] Xenophanes of Colophon refers to a time there before 'hateful tyranny' (10D). Ephesus seems to have been subject to tyranny for much of the sixth century.[49] About the early political form of Elea nothing is known.

It does seem then that the cities in which philosophical cosmology arose cannot be said to have been *politically* exceptional or unprecedented, whether in the idea of impersonal law, in political space, in freedom of debate,[50] or in mass participation in politics. The respect in which they undoubtedly *were* exceptional and indeed unprecedented is the *economic*; and this is especially true of the home of the very first philosophical cosmology, Miletus (10C). The politics of the Ionian city-states may be important for

---

[46] At least to judge by the reports of the decree of Diopeithes and the prosecutions of Anaxagoras, of Socrates, and (unless fiction) of Protagoras.

[47] Meiggs and Lewis 1988, no. 8 may imply an element of democracy in Chios *circa* 575–570 BC; though cf. Thuc. 8.24.

[48] We also hear of tyranny at Samos before Polycrates: de Libero 1996, 252. The constitution of Kroton at the time of Pythagoras' arrival there was reportedly aristocratic: Minar 1942, 8.

[49] Jeffery 1976, 223.

[50] The Homeric evidence does not of course show that freedom of debate was *confined* to Ionia.

explaining the genesis of philosophical cosmology, but only if taken *together with* their economy. In particular, the Ionians were the first Greeks to use coinage, in the same period in which they produced the first philosophical cosmology. Many Greek philosophers, including Heraclitus (9B), stayed out of politics, but nobody can stay out of the economy.

The second unacknowledged problem for the political explanation arises from the style and content of the early philosophical cosmology itself. Central to Lloyd's argument is that the habit of open scrutiny, the competitive expectation of evidence and proof, of fundamental justification, and the possibility of radical revision, are all to be found both in the legal and political debate characteristic of the Greek polis and in early Greek philosophy and science, so that 'the political and legal background plays a role at least at the beginnings of what might otherwise seem a merely intellectual development'.[51] Now this case is persuasive for later philosophy (notably Plato and Aristotle) and for medicine, i.e. for the period of those *democratic* institutions that are important to Lloyd's argument. But for the sixth and early fifth centuries it does not work at all.

Let us first take *style*, in the most general sense. Not enough survives of the Milesians to help us here. Nor can we gain much in this respect from the verses of Xenophanes.[52] There remain Heraclitus, Pythagoras and early Pythagoreanism, and Parmenides.

Heraclitus' followers were said by Plato to refuse all discussion (*Tht.* 179d–180c). And it would be hard to imagine discourse further from political debate than that of Heraclitus himself, whose fragments are marked by the aphoristic obscurity and contempt for humankind that were regularly attributed to him in antiquity.[53] His riddling quality is not in fact an expression of reclusiveness, but rather one element in the presentation of his *logos* in terms of mystery cult, in which eventual revelation of the profoundly inaccessible comes only after initial puzzlement and struggle.[54] Though the truth so revealed may have political significance, the manner of its revelation[55] follows a ritual model quite antithetical to political debate.

---

[51] Lloyd 1990, 96, cf. 63–5.; also e.g. 1979, 61, 240–64; 1987, 78–80, 85–6.

[52] Xenophanes does use *argument*, and attacks Homer and Hesiod: but there is no reason to connect this with *political* debate.

[53] E.g. Guthrie 1962, 410–13.   [54] 12A n. 19; Seaford 1994a, 227–8; 11B n. 36.

[55] And publication, if we believe that story (D. L. 9.6) that Heraclitus deposited his book in the temple of Artemis.

Heraclitus was said to have refused to legislate for the Ephesians, and to have given up his hereditary 'kingship' to his brother.[56] Moreover, Heraclitus also derived some of the *content* of his cosmology from mystic doctrine (12A).

For Lloyd a key position is occupied by Parmenides, as the first to produce a sustained deductive argument.[57] But Parmenides too represents himself, in a narrative which has been shown to correspond in detail to mystery cult,[58] as travelling in a chariot 'far from the path of humankind', where it is not argument or reason but rather a goddess who reveals to him 'all things, both the steadfast heart of rounded truth and the opinions of mortals, in which there is no true belief'. The passivity of Parmenides in this experience of divine revelation is emphasised by the description of the journey, in which he is 'carried along by wise mares . . . with maidens leading the way'.[59] Even apart from this, the (far from compelling) deductive argument gives the impression of being deployed to justify an eccentrically counter-intuitive theory reached in other ways (12B). Once again, we are remote from the communal antinomies of political debate. The deductiveness apparently pioneered by Parmenides may well owe something to legal formulation[60] or even, as Lloyd emphasises, to judicial and political debate. But this cannot begin to explain the content of his philosophy. There may well be truth in the report that Parmenides provided laws for Elea,[61] but this too would tend to place him *beyond* political debate. Outsiders are, as neutral, favoured as legislators (9A). The authority of legislators often comes precisely from being beyond political conflict, or even from beyond the human sphere – from the kind of isolated religious experience that Parmenides describes in his prologue.[62] It is even possible that Parmenides, like Heraclitus, derived some of the *content* of his doctrine from mystery cult (11B, 12C).

What we know of Pythagoras and early Pythagoreanism is notoriously exiguous. Confining ourselves to the seven explicit mentions made in the

---

[56] D. L. 9.2; Antisthenes ap. D. L. 9.6; KRS 182–3.   [57] Lloyd 1979, 69.

[58] Thomson 1961b, 289–90, who lists (and documents for the mysteries) the 'knowing man' (also Burkert 1969, 5; cf. B6.4 and Kern 1922, fr. 233), chariot, unveiling, light after darkness, gates. In confirmation compare, in the subsequently discovered Hipponion gold leaf, the underworld *hodos* (road) followed by the mystic initiands with the *hodos* followed by Parmenides (also in underworld: Burkert 1969; Kingsley 1995, 54–5, 252 n. 6, 354, 392–3; 1999, 61–76) and Poseid. Pell. 705 *Suppl. Hell.* 21–2 'mystic path to Rhadamanthys'. See also Kingsley 1999, 61–4. For Orphic ideas in Parmenides see West 1983, 109. For more on the religious context of Parmenides see Kingsley 1999.

[59] B1. 4–5. The revelation is a precondition for acceptance of the subsequent counter-intuitive argument.

[60] Feyerabend 1999, 87.   [61] D. L. 9.23 (quoting Speusippus); Plut. *Mor.* 1126A; Strabo 6.1 (252).

[62] Cf. e.g. Plut. *Mor.* 543A (Zaleukos attributes *everything* in his legislation to Athena); Aristotle frr. 553 and 555 Gigon; Kingsley 1999, 204–17, 252–4. Note the role of Justice in Parmenides' mystic vision (B1.14).

sixth and fifth centuries BC, we find that five connect Pythagoras or the
Pythagoreans either with (Orphic) mystery cult or with the associated
theme of survival after death.[63] The secrecy of some Pythagorean doctrine and the silence of Pythagoreans, which are well attested from the
fourth century BC, belong to the organised group constituted by mystic
initiation.[64] When this is taken together with the extraordinary veneration
and authority attached from an early period to Pythagoras,[65] it appears
again that the contexts of communication most relevant for understanding the emergence of philosophy are quite unlike the open public debate
emphasised by Lloyd. Nor is this conclusion disturbed by the reports (first
appearing in the fourth century BC) of political activity by Pythagoras and
the early Pythagoreans. To the extent that it is possible to infer anything at
all about this political activity (13A), it seems to have been undertaken by
the enclosed group, of the kind sometimes called *hetaireia*, constituted by
mystic initiation.[66]

Next there is the relation between open political debate and the *content*
of early philosophical cosmology. The open competitiveness of medicine
favoured advance, but only because therapies varied in effectiveness. The
notion that unrestricted competition will *by itself* make for advance has a
liberal capitalist feel. But the content of early philosophical cosmology is
highly theoretical, and here freedom of debate can by itself neither explain
the choice of one content over another nor even necessarily favour advance.
Why would freedom of debate arrive at the entirely counterintuitive and
indemonstrable idea – common to the earliest philosophers – of a single
substance for all things? And did it produce a continuous advance, so
that e.g. Heraclitus' cosmology is an improvement on Anaximander's and
Parmenides' on Heraclitus'? Lloyd does accordingly explicitly prioritise style
(in the broadest sense) over content as *explanandum*.[67] But this implicitly

---

[63] Xenophanes fr. 7a West (transmigration); Ion of Chios 36 DK B2 (Orpheus), B4 (happy life after
death); Hdt. 2.81 (Orphics); 4.93–4 (ritualised return from death). The other two are Heraclitus'
attacks (B40, 129 DK) on Pythagoras' *polumathiē*. The anonymous man whose wisdom Empedocles
(B129 DK) associates with transmigration is very likely Pythagoras.

[64] Pl. *Phaedo* 62b; Aristotle fr. 192 Rose; Aristoxenus fr. 43 Wehrli; Dicaearchus ap. Porph. *VP* 19; Isocr.
Bus. 29; etc.: Burkert 1972, 178–9; Guthrie 1962, 150–3.

[65] E.g. Guthrie 1962, 148–50. The secrecy and the veneration go together in the punishment of the
early Pythagorean Hippasus either for revealing a secret of geometry or for claiming its discovery for
himself although it was Pythagoras'.

[66] Burkert 1972, 115, 119; KRS 227–8; Minar 1942, 15–35. The fourth-century tradition that calls
Pythagoreanism tyrannical (Burkert 1972, 118–19) may reflect the authoritarian nature of the
Pythagorean association.

[67] Lloyd 1990, 15: 'so far as ancient Greece is concerned, what marks out their science is not only
and not so much the content of ideas and theories about natural phenomena as the degree of

admits the serious limitation of his explanation.[68] Further, the kind of
political debate stressed by Lloyd may even have been positively inimical
to the genesis of philosophical cosmology. While we have just allowed that
free *constitutional* debate, what Lloyd calls radical political revisability, may
conceivably have been relatively new in the Ionia of Anaximander, it should
also be said that it is directly at variance with the notion of an *unchanging*
impersonal order that is at the heart of philosophical cosmology (including
Heraclitus) from the beginning.[69] Moreover, the notion of physical or
cosmological 'laws' (comparable to modern scientific laws) does not exist
in presocratic philosophy (10C).

A political explanation of the *content* of Anaximander's theory is elaborated, we saw, by Vernant, who has however to admit that the explanation
works only for the very beginnings of philosophy:

> When philosophy arose at Miletus, it was rooted in the political thought whose
> fundamental preoccupations it expressed and from which it borrowed a part of
> its vocabulary. It is true that quite soon it claimed greater independence. With
> Parmenides it took its own path; it explored a new domain and posed problems
> unique to itself.[70]

Here is paradox indeed. It is precisely when the content of philosophy
reaches, with Parmenides, the remotest possible point from observable reality that it becomes, according to Vernant, independent of the political

---

self-consciousness with which the enquiries are pursued'; 36–7 'Our aim will be to see how far this
[the political explanation] and other explanatory hypotheses can take us towards an understanding
of the distinctive features of styles of enquiry developed in ancient Greece'; 82 'it is not the content
of [Parmenides'] argument, but its form, that concerns us here'.

[68] More recently (1996, 11–15) Lloyd does attempt to relate competitiveness to content. The 'preoccupation with the simplest units to which everything else can be reduced, with what is in itself
unchanging but is itself the ground of change, with foundations' derives, at least in part, from the
perceived need to 'have a secure vantage point from which to defeat the opposition' by demonstrating
the *necessity* of the particular theory being argued for. From the fourth century axiomatic starting
points in physics, the 'foundations of all physical explanation', had the same name, *stoicheia*, as in
mathematics: 'if you could persuade people of the correctness of your view of the elements, then
much of the rest of your physical theory could be held to be secure'. Again, this may contain some
truth for the fourth century. But the concern with foundations (or rather a single foundation or
substance) that is already there in the sixth century is not for the sake of a secure foundation for
deductive argument or competitive physical explanation. Indeed the monism of the presocratics,
especially the abstract monism of Parmenides (12B), would be an odd basis to choose for a persuasive
argument of this kind (11A). The persuasiveness is rather in the idea that all things are one. It is with
Parmenides, in the fifth century, that the first deductive argument appears, but in order to *deny* any
connection between the One and physical phenomena (12B). Competing accounts of the world do
not by virtue of their competitiveness produce a concern with unchanging foundations. Something
else is required.

[69] Radical political revisability is on the other hand clearly relevant to the much later preoccupation
with the distinction between *nomos* and *phusis*.

[70] Vernant 1982, 131.

or any other model, that it ceases to project social relations. It cannot of course be the mere result of deduction (from what? why from that?). Whence then does it come? In fact there is, despite the novelty, also much continuity between the content of Parmenides' ideas and his predecessors. In rightly admitting the irrelevance of the political explanation (and failing to suggest any other) for Parmenides, Vernant inadvertently casts doubt on its adequacy for early Greek philosophy generally.

It was tentatively suggested almost fifty years ago by George Thomson that 'the Parmenidean One, together with the later idea of "substance", may be described as a reflex or projection of the substance of exchange value.'[71] Why so? Because the Parmenidean One is (among other things) pure abstraction, stripped of everything concrete, sensual, qualitative. Such a strange and unprecedented notion arises as the projection of abstract exchange value, to which the specificity of concrete, sensual, qualitative features is irrelevant. A (similar) connection between philosophy and the category of property called 'invisible being' was made independently, at about the same time, and no less tentatively, by Louis Gernet.[72]

These ideas have never received the development they deserve and require.[73] Thomson's formulation, important though it is, claims too little and too much. It claims too little because in fact the Parmenidean One is not a sudden break but the culmination of a tendency (towards abstraction of a single principle) already present in earlier Ionian cosmology (12B). Accordingly, if 'exchange value' was a factor in the construction of Parmenides' One, then it may have been a factor in the construction of earlier Ionian cosmology also. What is required is a cumulative argument, correlating the development of coined money with the development of early Greek cosmology as a whole. Thomson's formulation also claims too much, in its implication of a one-to-one relation ('a reflex or projection') between the One and 'the substance of exchange value', leaving him open to the charge of reductionism. Exchange value is an abstraction that finds

---

[71] Thomson 1961b, 301 (first ed. 1955). He has a similar analysis of Pythagoreanism (13A n. 34). Cf. Marx 1976 (1867), 163 'A commodity . . . is a very strange thing, abounding in metaphysical subtleties and theological niceties . . . transcends sensuousness'.

[72] 1981 (1956), 343–51, acknowledging Schuhl 1953, 90 n. 2. Invisible being: 12B.

[73] Their neglect is attributable to their inadequate formulation, to the division of intellectual labour, also perhaps to the illusion that they entail every element of Thomson's Marxism. The only serious attempt to refute (rather than ignore) Thomson is by Vernant (12C), who is explicit that his work on the origin of Greek philosophy (specifically its connection with freedom of debate) was directed against the French Communist Party: *Libération* 19 September 1996. A partial exception to the neglect is the (historically uninformed: e.g. cf. 7D n. 67) account by Shell (1978, 30–62) of invisibility in Plato's *Republic* and metaphorisation in Heraclitus, with brief criticism of both Thomson and Vernant.

concrete embodiment in money. The rapid development, in the lifetime of Parmenides, of a radically new kind of money (coinage), whose *only* function is to embody exchange-value, is one among a series of factors (IIB) in a process making for the Parmenidean representation of reality as the abstract One. On Parmenides we agree with Feyerabend that

the uniformity of the real World, or of Being, could be proved only if a corresponding uniformity had already entered the premises . . . Thus, the most one can say is that the arguments that tried to establish uniformity formalised a historical process; they did not initiate it.[74]

But what did initiate the historical process? Feyerabend makes no serious attempt at an answer.

---

[74] Feyerabend 1999, 15. He also states that Parmenides' '*estin* [it exists] was a premise and so it certainly was not established by the argument itself' (66), that 'Parmenides' denial of change and subdivision is already contained in the premises', and that 'being unsupported by logical reasoning the choice of the premise must be left to a different agency' (86).

CHAPTER TEN

Anaximander and Xenophanes

A THE FRAGMENT OF ANAXIMANDER

Although Anaximander is largely inaccessible behind later interpretation, this will not seriously impede us, for our focus is on almost the only text which probably contains his own words, preserved via Theophrastus in Simplicius,[1] who says that Anaximander

> said that the principle and element of existing things was *to apeiron* [the unlimited or indefinite], being the first to introduce this name of the principle. He says that it [the principle] is neither water nor any other of the so-called elements, but some other *apeiros* nature, from which all the heavens and the *kosmoi* in them come into being. And from which (things) existing things have their genesis, into these [things] also occurs their perishing, according to necessity. For they give penalty and retribution to each other for their injustice according to the disposition/assessment of time, describing it thus in rather poetical terms. It is clear that, having observed the change of the four elements into each other, he did not think fit to make any one of these the substratum, but something else besides these.[2]

The reference to poetical terms suggests that what precedes are the words of Anaximander himself, at least from 'for they give penalty . . .'. It also seems unavoidable, in the light of the fragment itself and of other reports about Anaximander, that the things giving the penalty are *opposites*, notably perhaps the hot and the cold, the dry and the wet.[3]

---

[1] Although Wildberg 1993, 195 regards it as significant that Simplicius does not here use the marginal marks with which he normally indicates quotation and paraphrase.

[2] *In Phys* 24, 13 = DK 12A9 (B1): ἀρχήν τε καὶ στοιχεῖον εἴρηκε τῶν ὄντων τὸ ἄπειρον, πρῶτος τοῦτο τοὔνομα κομίσας τῆς ἀρχῆς. λέγει δ' αὐτὴν μήτε ὕδωρ μήτε ἄλλο τι τῶν καλουμένων εἶναι στοιχείων, ἀλλ' ἑτέραν τινὰ φύσιν ἄπειρον, ἐξ ἧς ἅπαντας γίνεσθαι τοὺς οὐρανοὺς καὶ τοὺς ἐν αὐτοῖς κόσμοις. ἐξ ὧν δὲ ἡ γένεσίς ἐστι τοῖς οὖσι, καὶ τὴν φθορὰν εἰς ταῦτα γίνεσθαι κατὰ τὸ χρεών· διδόναι γὰρ αὐτὰ δίκην καὶ τίσιν ἀλλήλοις τῆς ἀδικίας κατὰ τὴν τοῦ χρόνου τάξιν, ποιητικωτέροις οὕτως ὀνόμασιν αὐτὰ λέγων. δῆλον δὲ ὅτι τὴν εἰς ἄλληλα μεταβολὴν τῶν τεττάρων στοιχείων οὗτος θεασάμενος οὐκ ἠξίωσεν ἕν τι τούτων ὑποκείμενον ποιῆσαι, ἀλλά τι ἄλλο παρὰ ταῦτα.

[3] Aristot. *Phys.* A4, 187a20; Simplicius *in Phys.* 24.21; 150. 22–5; [Plut.] *Strom.* 2; Kahn 1960, 40–1, 178–9; Guthrie 1962, 76–82; KRS 119–20, 128–30. The extent to which in general Anaximander

In the process of alternating injustice (or encroachment on each other) by the opposites nature is seen in terms of society, or rather the two are not distinguished. The importance of the reciprocal encroachment of opposites on each other in nature (summer–winter, day–night, etc.) is not distinguished from the fundamental social norm of reciprocity (damage–retribution). For Vernant the words of Anaximander reflect the 'equilibrium and reciprocity between equals' characteristic of the polis, just as the spatial symmetry of his cosmos reflects the new egalitarian spatial reality of the polis (9A). '*Monarchia* was replaced, in nature as in the city, by a rule of *isonomia*' (equality of political rights).[4]

So far so good. But the words generally agreed to be Anaximander's are in fact an explanation of what precedes, introduced by 'For . . .' (*gar*). Some critics regard the whole previous sentence as Anaximander's, some none of it, some only the words 'according to necessity' (*kata to chreōn*). The first option is perhaps more likely.[5] But even if these are not the very words of Anaximander, they are Theophrastus' paraphrase of his view – that existing things, envisaged as opposites, perish into the things from which they originate. And this in turn follows (paraphrase of) Anaximander's view of *to apeiron* as the *source* of everything. It is natural therefore to assume the 'things from which existing things have their genesis' to be the *apeiron*, into which, it is now added (*de*), existing things also *perish* according to necessity. The difficulty in this assumption is in having the plural ('things from which') refer to the singular *apeiron*. One proposed solution is that, given that the opposites pay the penalty to 'each other', the plural refers not in fact to the *apeiron* but merely to the opposites: things emerge from and perish into their opposites, and this is the mutual payment of penalties, which has nothing to do with the *apeiron*.[6] But this is to ignore the flow of what is paraphrase of Anaximander by someone (Theophrastus) who undoubtedly knew far more about him than we do.[7] Another solution to the problem of the plural has been that the *apeiron* is explicitly envisaged as a plurality, in line with Aristotle's statement that Anaximander regarded the

---

envisaged existing things as opposites (cf. the pervasiveness of opposition in Heraclitus' cosmos) is unknown.

[4] Vernant 1982, 1962), 122.

[5] KRS 118 object that the words *genesis* and *phthorā* are 'well established in Peripatetic but not (from the extant evidence) in Presocratic vocabulary', but fail even to mention the powerful counter-arguments of Kahn 1960, 172–8 on this point. Cf. on the other hand Finkelberg 1993, 250–1.

[6] Kahn 1960, 166–8, 178–83; KRS 118–19, 121–2. Cf. 10B.

[7] The point is argued by Engmann 1991, 9–11, who also argues that the perishing into (and genesis from) the *apeiron* is not (as generally assumed) of the whole cosmos but rather a continual process, linked with the continuing existence of the world.

opposites as contained in the one and separated out from it:[8] their eventual reabsorption into the *apeiron*, within which they are perfectly blended, is also their full reparation to each other for any encroachment (the opposition is cancelled).[9] A third solution has been that the plural (perhaps introduced by Theophrastus) expresses the generality of the principle.[10]

There are only a handful of other words that can be attributed to Anaximander himself. Among them is Aristotle telling us that he called the *apeiron* 'immortal and indestructible'.[11] It is also almost certain from the same passage of Aristotle that it has no beginning, and that it surrounds[12] and steers all things.[13] As stated in our passage of Simplicius, it is separate from the elements, something apart.[14] Theophrastus said that it is in eternal motion.[15] Otherwise, we do not know how Anaximander envisaged the *apeiron*, except for what is revealed by the word itself, which refers to the absence of limit (*peras, peirar*). It seems then to mean that which is, in contrast to the Homeric universe,[16] spatially unlimited, or at least immense or indefinite in extent,[17] or that which is without *internal* limits, i.e undifferentiated.[18] Both senses are appropriate: *immense* in that it surrounds and is the source of everything, and *undifferentiated* in that, given the hostilities between the opposites, for one of them to be privileged as the immense surrounding source would have meant the non-existence of the others. As Guthrie puts it,

a primitive stuff must be, so to speak, a neutral in these hostilities, and must therefore have no definite characteristics of its own. It must hold, inactive in the first place and suspended as it were in solution, the characteristics of all the future opposites which in due course were to be, in the significant word which was probably his own, 'separated off' (or 'out') from it. Here we may find, in all probability, the chief reason why he called his *archē* simply 'the *apeiron*'. There were no *perata* in it between the hot, the cold, the wet and the dry.[19]

---

[8] *Phys.* A4, 187a20. We should probably believe this, especially as it conflicts with Aristotle's hypothesis elsewhere that Anaximander's *apeiron* was an intermediate substance: Kahn 1960, 44–6; Vlastos 1970, 79–80. Cf. though Gottschalk 1965, 46–7.

[9] Vlastos 1970, 77–80, criticised by Gottschalk 1965, 45–6.

[10] '[T]he plural is presumably generic': KRS 119, who also boldly think they can maintain that Theophrastus 'mistook the proper application of Anaximander's dictum'. Alternation between singular and plural in the expression of this notion is found in Aristotle (Mcdiarmid 1970 (1953), 194, but this does not mean (*pace* Mcdiarmid) that Theophrastus is not paraphrasing Anaximander.

[11] *Phys.* Γ4, 203b13=DK B3; similarly Hipp. *Ref.* 1.6.1=DK B2.   [13] Kahn 1958.

[12] Echoed in three other passages of Aristotle: Kahn 1960, 43.

[14] *Ti allo para tauta*: Kahn 1960, 37–8; Aristot. *Phys.* Γ5, 204b22 (*para ta stoicheia* probably of Anaximander (10C n. 82).

[15] KRS 126–7, 129, who seem too sceptical about this.   [16] *Il.* 8.14–16; 14.200; 17.425.

[17] Kahn 1960, 232–3 associates the word with verbs meaning to traverse or complete (*perân, perainein*, etc.), and translates 'what cannot be traversed to the end'.

[18] Cornford 1952, 178.   [19] Guthrie 1962, 86–7.

But Guthrie also insists that

> we are not yet at a stage of thought when clear distinctions between different uses of the same word are possible . . . There is no question then of deciding in which of several senses Anaximander intended us to take his word, but only which sense was uppermost in his mind.

So too Kirk, Raven, and Schofield[20] maintain that, whether Anaximander intended it to mean primarily 'spatially indefinite' or 'that which is indefinite in kind', the other sense was also present. In favour of this one may add that immense natural expanses (of sea, land, air)[21] tend also in fact to be internally undifferentiated. But even if *apeiron* did not have this meaning, it is hard to see how it was envisaged as anything other than homogeneous.

Finally, there is the problem of whether the *apeiron* is one thing or many things. Aristotle attributes to Anaximander the view that the opposites exist in the one and are separated out from it (*Phys.* A4, 187a20). But if they pre-exist in it, how can they 'have their genesis' (as Theophrastus or Anaximander himself puts it) and how can it be one thing? It is unlikely that Anaximander concerned himself with this kind of problem.[22] The *apeiron* could not be described in Aristotelian terms, whether as completely potential prime matter or as a mixture or as intermediate between the elements. There is some inconsistency in the references and apparent references to it in Aristotle and Theophrastus as they try to make sense of it in their own terms; and Theophrastus even blames Anaximander for not saying what the *apeiron* is (12A14 DK). All we can say, and it may be all that Anaximander said, is that it is one thing,[23] with no beginning, immortal and indestructible, distinct from everything that appears, the source and destination of all things, surrounding and steering all things, in eternal motion, and unlimited (probably both externally and internally).

B   RECIPROCITY AND COMMODITY

What is the relation of all this to the model provided for Anaximander's cosmology by the polis? For Vernant it is the 'equilibrium and reciprocity between equals' in the polis that provides the model. But the process of controlled reciprocity between equal opposites in Anaximander is, we have now seen, *also* a process in which the opposites perish into and emerge from the *apeiron* or each other (or both). What, if anything, does this have to do with the polis? Vernant does not even ask the question.

---

[20] KRS 110.   [21] Sea and land are in Homer characteristically *apeirōn*.
[22] Gottschalk 1965.   [23] This has been doubted, but see e.g. Gottschalk 1965.

For an answer we must first briefly describe the historical phenomenon of reciprocity. Anthropology informs us of the often central importance of reciprocity, the voluntary requital of benefit for benefit and of harm for harm, in societies in which the state is weak or absent.[24] The society described by Homeric epic exhibits exactly this central importance of reciprocity, and in a manner sufficiently consistent (and sufficiently similar in detail) with the anthropological evidence to preclude an origin in mere poetic invention.[25] Such central importance for reciprocity in early Greek society was surely a precondition for its projection by Anaximander onto cosmology, albeit in the form of hostile reciprocity that has advanced beyond Homer inasmuch as how to control it is a central concern of the polis. To be more precise, just as in the polis citizens engaging in reciprocal hostility retain autonomy of action, albeit under the overall authority of judicial procedure (as for example at Athens in Draco's homicide law), so Anaximander's opposites actively engage in reciprocal hostility according to the 'disposition/assessment of time' in a world governed by the *apeiron.*

The advent of judicial procedure is likely to change the nature of hostile reciprocity. In Homer and other early epic a killer (except in battle) generally flees into exile; sometimes it is made explicit that this is to escape being killed in revenge by the victim's relatives, which (with one exception) never occurs.[26] Reciprocity between hostile parties is generally unlikely to be stable – given inevitable disparities of strength between kinship groups – without a central authority to impose it. In the only Homeric description of a trial there is mention of 'full compensation' for murder (*Il.* 18.499), which is nevertheless rejected, just as Achilles rejects the vast compensation offered him by Agamemnon – despite the ideal held up to him by Ajax of compensation for murder paid to the bereaved kin by the murderer, who remains in his own land (*Il.* 9.632–6). No less unstable is Homeric reciprocity of benefit, which, although it may be between equals, may also be rejected as creating dependence, and indeed is found between the group and its leader in what may also be called a system of redistribution.[27]

The first Greek law code that we know of in any detail is that of Solon of Athens, an almost exact contemporary of Anaximander. His extant laws specify compensation for theft and (in specific amounts) compensations or

---

[24] E.g. Seaford 1994a, 6 (bibliography), 13–14, 25; Gill, Postlethwaite and Seaford 1998, especially the paper by van Wees (13–49).

[25] E.g. Finley 1977; Quiller 1981; Donlan 1981–2; 1982; 1985; 1989; 1998.

[26] Seaford 1994a, 25–6; the exception is Orestes avenging his father by killing Aegisthus.

[27] 2D; Seaford 1994a, 21–2; Donlan 1998.

fines for various other offences: homicide,[28] rape of a free woman, procuring, verbal insult in certain places, verbal insult of the dead, the export of food.[29] Moreover it is precisely the definition of penalties that was particularly remembered in traditions about the other early lawgivers; and the early laws known from inscriptions are also concerned to specify penalties. Public agreement on the amount of compensation for injuries[30] is a vital means of ensuring peaceful order in the polis by preventing the *perpetuation* of conflict (5A).

The establishment of such agreement in law transforms social relations. With the monetary definition of compensation come quantitative precision, uniformity, and depersonalisation (5A). Hostility between *people*, with its potential for violence and domination, is controlled and reduced by the notion of *impersonal* quantitative equivalence between the injury and its monetary compensation, applied uniformly, irrespective of the identity of victim, offender, or judge.[31] Indeed, the judicial enforcement of equivalence between offence and monetary compensation implies the equivalence also of the hostile parties. As Aristotle will make explicit, it does not matter whether a base person has offended against a decent one or vice-versa: 'the law looks only at the harm inflicted, and treats the people involved as equals' (*EN* 1132a5).

This transformation is made possible by the combination of two preconditions. One is the vital importance of ending conflict between citizens in the increasingly urban environment of the polis. The other is the development of silver as money. Not long before the introduction of coinage,

---

[28] Ruschenbusch 1966, FII, 12, which Gagarin 1981b, 139 suggests indicates that Solon was revising or refining regulations already existing in Draco's laws (of Draco's laws Solon was said to have retained only that on homicide). The existing inscribed text of Draco's homicide law appears to integrate the two pre-existing penalties (exile and compensation, both found in Homer), with exile as the primary penalty: Gagarin 1981b, 13–17, 19, 52 (on *aidesis*; cf. also *Il.* 1.23), 138–9, 147–9. Compensation specified in Draco's legislation: Ruschenbusch 1966, F10. At some time before the fourth century BC the Athenians, though making widespread use of the monetary penalty paid to victim or state, ceased to use monetary compensation as the main means of resolving homicide: it might even arouse disapproval (Dem. 58.29), but there is no reason to suppose that it was illegal (Gagarin 1981b, 138–9; Harpocr. s.v. ὑποφόνια; in Dem. 23.28, 33 *apoinân* need not refer to blood money rather than e.g. ransom). Of early homicide laws outside Athens we know almost nothing. *SEG* 4.64 (probably Leontini), *circa* 525 BC, mentions sums of money, perhaps as penalties for homicide (Jeffrey 1990, 242).

[29] 5A; Ruschenbusch 1966, F23–5 (cf. 64), 26, 30, 32, 33. 65; cf. 36.

[30] The lack of such definition of compensation in the world of Homer is manifest in e.g. the phrase 'boundless compensation' (*apereisi' apoina*): 8F n. 89.

[31] Against my earlier statement of this view Allen 2000, 356 n. 110 objects that 'the activity in the courts remained very much a matter of determining the relations between people'. Certainly it did, but with the advantage of socially specified penalties, the novelty of which we may from our perspective underestimate.

Solonian legislation refers to a public treasury, with income and expenditure (for rewards, sacrificial animals, etc.) in amounts of silver (5A). In general the early lawgivers, including Solon, concerned themselves with commercial transactions.[32] Probably the notion of precise monetary equivalences in silver for various offences was made possible, or at least encouraged, by the widespread existence of precise monetary equivalents (in silver) for commodities. At an earlier historical stage, even Achilles' rejection of Lycaon's and Agamemnon's gifts seems to imply a heroic reaction against the power of trade to create compensatory equivalence (2D, 3B).

In 2A I categorised Homeric transactions (allocations of goods) along a spectrum from the subjective (objects embodying personal relationships such as loyalty and respect) to the objective (trade). In this spectrum the overwhelming majority of transactions were found to be of the former kind, and little trace was found of money. In Homer goods leave and enter the household not on the whole by trade but as gifts. As an anthropological category, gift-exchange has been defined as 'an exchange of inalienable things between transactors who are in a state of reciprocal dependence', as opposed to commodity-exchange (trade), which is 'an exchange of alienable things between transactors who are in a state of reciprocal independence'.[33] The inalienability of the object is to be found (albeit to a limited extent) in the Homeric gift, creating a link between the transactors by continuing to embody the identity of the donor.[34] In general, as well as specifically in Homer, concern with precise equivalence of value has no place in gift-exchange, and nor has enforceable immediacy of return – two more respects in which it is antithetical to trade.[35]

The development of trade alongside (or within)[36] the positive reciprocity of gift-exchange is also therefore the advance of the notion of precise impersonal equivalence in instantaneous exchange,[37] mediated eventually by the measure provided by money, between parties who are *qua* exchangers equal (as Aristotle noted, 8B), at the expense of interpersonal exchange relations

---

[32] Gagarin 1986, 65–6, 70–1; Solon himself as merchant: Plut. *Sol.* 1.

[33] Gregory 1982; Seaford 1994a, 13–25. In a typical sequence, this opposition (a) is found illuminating, then (b) is accused of being too neat, of ignoring the common ground between the opposed terms (e.g. Appadurai 1986, 11–13; Parry and Bloch 1989, 8–12; for Greece von Reden 1999, 61–2), and finally (c) remains valuable – as a torch not a photograph.

[34] Seaford 1994a, 13–25.   [35] E.g. Bourdieu 1977, 5–8, 171, 195–6.

[36] One of the rare cases in Homer of trade is accompanied by gift-exchange: *Il.* 7.467–75. For the charging of interest as developing out of the practice of reciprocal gift-giving see Millett 1991, 40–52, 99, 121. Aristotle sees proportionate reciprocity (*to antipeponthos, kat' analogian*) at the heart of justice in commercial exchange (*EN* 1132b33–1133b7).

[37] The early lawgiver Charondas is reported to have required goods to be delivered and paid for immediately (Theophrastus ap. Stob. 4.20.2), as if preventing the bad old habit of reciprocity.

that are unstable because always potentially asymmetrical. However, money and the growth of trade introduce a new form of instability. Equality between the parties in respect of the exchange does nothing to prevent the *unlimited* impoverishment or enrichment that had been precluded by the old assymetrical relations of positive reciprocity and redistribution.[38] It was precisely this new form of instability, in which eventually the rich enslave the poor, that Solon was appointed to resolve. 'Of wealth', he writes, 'there is no limit that appears to men' – the first of many Greek statements of money as unlimited (money itself, not just the desire for it: 8F). Solon counters the instability by his legislation, but also (in his poetry) by ethics, urging his fellow citizens to moderate their ambitions: 'put your great intention among moderate/measured things (*metrioisi*)' (fr. 4c.3). By cancelling debt Solon reinstates limits, and he even calls himself a 'boundary' (37.10).

And so the money that has pervaded the world of Solon is paradoxical. On the one hand it means that wealth (and the pursuit of wealth) has no limit, so that men accumulate money and land, enslave others, and destroy the polis.[39] But on the other hand it is precisely money, as a universal measure of value, that seems to provide universal limits, for by assigning to each commodity and to each offence a specific numerical value it allows the possibility, in each individual transaction, of agreement between equal parties according to an external measure that is definite, all-embracing, and precise (13B). What 'alone holds the limits of all things' is for Solon not a deity, but the abstract concept, unthinkable in the premonetary world of Homer,[40] of 'measure' (*metron*).[41]

Reciprocal harm and reciprocal benefit, despite being opposite in spirit, may be similar in form, in terminology, even in social function;[42] and each may threaten the polis – reciprocal harm by unstoppable conflict, reciprocal benefit by secret interpersonal power (including 'bribery').[43] With the development, under the control of the polis, both of trade using money

[38] That old structures of reciprocity and redistribution were dissolved by the unobligated wealth arising from overseas trade as early as the eighth century BC is argued by Tandy 1997; cf. though Schaps 1998.

[39] Fr. 4. It is no accident that the man chosen in the story to be unimpressed by the unlimited wealth of Croesus is Solon: 8F, 14D.

[40] Once Hesiod urges preservation of measures (*Op.* 694 *metra phulassesthai*), but this is, significantly, in the passage about *commerce*: do not, he is saying, put all your goods in the ships but leave the greater part behind. See 13C.

[41] 'The obscure measure of intelligence' that is 'very hard to understand' (fr. 16). Mysterious too is the novel power of money.

[42] In both cases the duty of return involves honour and ritual, and may confirm the identity of households or kinship groups as well as creating a network of relations between them that is important where the state is absent or weak. See Seaford 1994a, 25.

[43] Herman 1987, esp. 7, 75–81; Seaford 1994a, 193–4.

(and then coinage) and of legally defined monetary compensation for offences, these similar though opposite reciprocities converge in subjection to (or marginalisation by) the mediation of money. The ancient practice of gift-exchange embodied (even where there was expectation of eventual return) generosity, whereas commercial exchange involves – *qua* commercial exchange – no feelings between the parties, but rather, inasmuch as both parties attempt to obtain the most favourable deal, at best a kind of mutually egotistic neutrality.[44] From the opposite end, legally imposed monetary compensation for harm is designed to turn hostility into neutrality by means of monetary equivalence. Overall, the advance of trade, using money, produces a form of interaction (impersonal, instantaneous, based on precisely quantified equivalence between things) antithetical to the old relations (between people, extended in time, resistant to quantification) of reciprocity. Accordingly the central Homeric value of *timē* ('honour'), the interpersonal respect and the virtue characteristic of reciprocity (and occasionally its expression in goods),[45] subsequently acquired, by attachment to the exchanged commodity, the additional, antithetical sense 'price'.[46]

C   ANAXIMANDER AND MILETUS

Herodotus narrates the war between Miletus and the Lydian king Alyattes (*c.* 610–560 BC), in which the Lydians dominated the land and Miletus – under the (reputedly) ruthless tyrant Thrasyboulos (friend of Periander tyrant of Corinth *c.* 627–587) – dominated the sea.[47] Miletus concluded a peace with Alyattes, and indeed retained considerable independence throughout the sixth century, despite Alyattes' successor Croesus' conquest of Ionia and the Persians' subsequent (*c.* 546 BC) conquest of Croesus. Plutarch mentions two tyrannical rulers, Thoas and Damasenor (probably subsequent to Thrasyboulos), whose fall was followed by civil conflict between the Manual Strugglers (*Cheiromacha*) and the Wealthy (*Ploutis*), who were also called 'Perpetual Sailors' (*Aeinautai*).[48] The civil conflict may be the same

---

[44] In Hdt. (1.153) the Persian emperor Cyrus, presiding over a different kind of economy, calls Greek commerce in the marketplace 'cheating each other'.

[45] Seaford 1994a, 6–7, 20, 25, 206.

[46] It is no accident that the first occurrence of this sense, from the (probably) sixth-century Homeric Hymn to Demeter (132), is of the item most traded in Homer (and a *person*), namely a slave. An intermediate sense is compensation (*Il.* 3.286; *Od.* 22.57.). *Timos* meaning cost occurs already in Archilochus (fr. 124b).

[47] Hdt. 1.17–22 (ruthlessness: 5.92fg); de Libero 1996, 357, 364.

[48] Plut. Mor. 298c; Hsch. s.v. ἀειναῦται. Gorrman 2001, 112–21 is unusual in arguing that this civil conflict preceded Thrasyboulos.

as that referred to by Herodotus (5.28) as having lasted for two generations. Of what may be relevant in the politics of Anaximander's Miletus, this is all we know.

In the lifetime of Anaximander (*c.* 610–*c.* 540?) precious metal was probably more available than ever before to the Greek cities of the Aegean, whether as electrum from Lydia or silver from various areas (6B). This increased supply no doubt helped it to acquire money functions, as it seems to have done even in Solonian Athens (5A), which was well behind Miletus commercially and in the introduction of coinage. Such money functions transcended borders. The Greeks probably gave silver in return for imports from Egypt, East-Greek mercenaries in Egypt and Mesopotamia were probably paid in precious metal,[49] and Alcaeus received staters from the Lydians (5A). In this vast area of incipient monetisation a special role was played by Miletus in two respects.

Firstly, some of the very earliest (electrum) coins are Milesian, perhaps even as early as the late seventh century;[50] and from the middle of the sixth century Miletus was producing silver coins.[51] It seems that throughout all or most of the sixth century Miletus was producing coins in denominations small enough for everyday exchanges.[52] From the beginning Milesian coins were made on the same weight standard as those of the other cities of southern Ionia and of Lydia (the standard to which almost all the coins found under the Artemision belong) – a clear indication of the very earliest coined money transcending the polis, and one of the circumstances in which the first 'philosopher', the Milesian Thales, was able to recommend to the Ionians to unite to form a single state (Hdt. 1.170). Thales himself, in a tradition that goes back at least to the fourth century but may of course be fabricated, was said to have made a lot of money (*chrēmata*) by investing in all the olive presses in Miletus and Chios.[53]

The second respect in which Miletus was unusual, in fact unique, was its commerce. The city was exceptional both in possessing 'next to no arable land' and in its excellent position for communication by land and sea.[54] Anaximander was said to be the first to have drawn a map of the world. It probably showed the world as circular, with the Aegean near the middle.[55] Much of what he drew would have been known to the Milesians

[49] Alcaeus fr. 350 L–P; Boardman 1980, 50–1.
[50] Weidauer 1975, 67; Kraay 1976, 23–6; Furtwängler 1986, 156–7; cf. 7B.
[51] Pfeiler 1966; Moucharte (1984) and Becker (1988) describe a subsequent find. Milesian coins are well represented in the earliest silver hoards: Price and Waggoner 1975, 15.
[52] It was for instance one of the very earliest cities to produce fractional silver coinage: Kim 1994, 67.
[53] Aristot. *Pol.* 1259a9; cf. Plut. *Sol.* 2 Thales as trader.   [54] Möller 2000, 87–8.
[55] Kahn 1960, 81–4; KRS 104–5.

through trade.[56] In the north, they had in the generation or so before his birth established a large number of colonies in the Black Sea area,[57] and he himself was said to have led a colony there.[58] In the south, the Milesians had in the same period taken a leading part in the Greek penetration of Egypt in the latter half of the seventh century.[59] In the east, it seems very likely that, besides their links with Lydia, the Milesians from the seventh century took a leading part in the trade passing through the port of Al Mina.[60] In the West, Herodotus remarks that their ties with Sybaris (before its destruction in 510) were the closest he had known between two cities.[61] The name 'Perpetual Sailors' for the wealthy no doubt expressed the main source of their wealth, untouched by Alyattes' annual destruction of Miletus' crops (Hdt. 1.17). This ubiquitous trade would have involved the circulation of precious metal, uncoined or coined.[62] For instance, the first coins of the Milesian Black Sea foundation Pantikapaion, stamped with the Milesian lion symbol, are dated by one authority as early as the mid-sixth century BC.[63] The Milesians might have been drawn to the southern and eastern shores of the Black Sea by silver.[64] What distinguishes Miletus from most if not all other Greek city-states[65] in the time of Thales and Anaximander was not its political formation but its economy.

It is this distinction that seems to underly the story told in Herodotus (6.86) of a Milesian who, in the time of Anaximander,[66] sought security for half his property by the remarkable step of turning it into silver and depositing it with a Spartan, because, he said, Ionia is unstable and the Peloponnese stable. Whether or not the story is true, it is Miletus that stands for the convertibility, transportability, and concealability of wealth as money, which is however secure only in premonetary Sparta.

---

[56] For the vast extent of sixth-century Milesian trade see Röhlig 1933; Roebuck 1959; Gorman 2001, 47–85. For the seventh- and sixth-century export – throughout the Mediterranean and Black Sea area – of (what is now known to be) Milesian pottery see Cook and Dupont 1998, 32, 77, 170–7.

[57] Murray 1993, 104.   [58] Aelian *VH* 3.17.

[59] Möller 2000, 88, 118 n. 216, 130, 141–2, 147, 176–7, 180, 184, 187, 188; Boardman 1980, 120 and Möller 2000, 94–9 (the Milesian *temenos* of Apollo mentioned by Hdt. 2.178); Ehrhardt 1983, 87–90; Murray 1993, 229–31.

[60] Boardman 1980, 49.

[61] Hdt. 6.21; cf. Timaeus *FGrH* 566F50 Sybaris a market for Milesian textiles.

[62] Boardman 1980, 130; Murray 1993, 231, 235.   [63] Shelov 1978, 9–12.   [64] Drews 1976, 26–31.

[65] And indeed from e.g. sixth-century Carthage, which in many respects (literacy, sea-trade, republican) resembled a Greek city-state, but did not use money or produce philosophical cosmology. The paradox of Miletus as a small city perched on a rock but with vast (commercial) power is expressed in Phocylides fr. 5 (probably early sixth century), in which its good order is favourably compared to senseless Nineveh.

[66] 'Three generations' before 490 BC.

Anaximander wrote the words 'for they give penalty (*dikē*) and retribution (*tisis*) to each other for their injustice according to the assessment/ ordainment of time'. The Greek (10A n. 2) is not the language of the Ionian epic but the prose of judicial procedure.[67] In particular, 'giving' (*didonai*) does not occur in the epic with *dikē* or *tisis*, though it does occur, in the only Homeric description of a judicial procedure, of compensation.[68] This suggests that behind Anaximander's words is the practice of legally prescribed compensation such as we found (5A) in the contemporary laws of the city (Athens) called by its lawgiver 'the oldest land of Ionia' (Solon fr. 4a). This gives special point to the immediately preceding words (almost certainly Anaximander's) *kata to chreōn*, 'according to necessity': for the causal connection and emphasis on giving implied by 'for they give' (*didonai gar*) support Kahn's suggestion that the word here for necessity (*chreōn*) 'may contain a secondary allusion to retribution as a debt'.[69] The '*taxis* (assessment, ordainment) of time' is assessment of the compensation and the ordainment of its payment within a certain time-limit.[70] Just as in the cosmos the yielding of one extreme to its opposite is – within a certain time – inevitable (notably in seasonal change), so at the heart of the judicial process is the inevitability – within a certain time – of compensation of victim by transgressor. Accordingly the cosmic process is imagined in terms of the judicial assessment and ordainment (by time or Time)[71] of compensation.

Now this fragment of Anaximander is the primary exhibit for the view that in general in presocratic philosophy 'the spheres of law and justice provide important models of cosmic order'.[72] The view thus formulated obviously has some truth, but may encourage the false belief that the cosmic order was envisaged, as it is in modern science, as resulting from the existence of (scientific) *laws*, influenced by our conception of law as a comprehensive set of rules enforced by the state and canonised (notably by

---

[67] This is demonstrated by Kahn 1960, 168–9.

[68] *Il.* 18.499 *pant' apodounai*, 'to give back everything'; cf. (the only Homeric case of) murder avenged by murder as 'he paid back everything' (*Od.* 1.43 πάντ' ἀπέτισε).

[69] Kahn 1960, 180.

[70] For *taxis* meaning 'assessment' of amount (of tax etc.) see LSJ s.v. τάξις II 4 (and s.v. τάσσειν), for 'ordainment' II 3; and for the sense here of controlling the time-limit for payment see KRS 120. For the phrase (and κατὰ τὸ χρεών) as certainly Anaximander's see Kahn 1960, 169–72.

[71] To the extent that time is personified (Time is imagined as a judge by Solon, fr. 36.3), this may reflect the sense that, despite the desired impersonality of equivalence of injury with compensation, the assessment is (inevitably) in a sense personal, set by legislator or judge(s). But time is, even if personified, sufficiently abstract and lacking in personality as also to imply the appropriate impersonality.

[72] Lloyd 1979, 247, who cites other proponents of the view.

writing). Just as in the Homeric 'trial scene' depicted on Achilles' shield the 'law court' is not a state organ for the punishment of illegality but a means of arbitration between conflicting parties, so too in the judicial procedure projected onto the cosmos by Anaximander the conflict is not with the law but between two parties. It is true that in reality the *taxis* of compensation was probably set in a law code and the necessary compulsion may have been associated with law. But just as there is no *nomos* (law, convention) in Homer, even in the trial scene, but rather *dikē* (justice, judgement, compensation, penalty), so too in Anaximander's projection of judicial process onto the cosmos there is no trace of law, no 'according to law (*nomos*)' but 'giving penalty (*dikē*) and retribution/compensation', and 'according to necessity (*chreōn*, implying debt)'. For Lloyd to claim that 'Anaximander refers . . . to the *rule of law*' (his emphasis)[73] suits his privileging of politics in accounting for the first philosophy, but misleads. Moreover, in the whole of surviving presocratic philosophy the idea of a cosmological or physical law (i.e. something similar to our scientific law) does not to my knowledge occur.[74] To be sure, money goes with *nomos* (law, convention) in that firstly it depends on a general convention and secondly we do eventually find some inscribed laws regulating the use of money (7D). But generally purchase occurs according to internalised uniformity, without any consciousness of law: law is at most merely implicit, as in presocratic philosophy.

In paying the penalty (compensation), the opposites perish into each other. And on a probable interpretation their simultaneous absorption into each other is also reabsorption into the *apeiron* (10A). Against this interpretation Kahn urges that 'the idea that things make amends to one another for their mutual wrongs *by both parties ceasing to exist at the same time*, is a strange one . . . We should expect the injured party or his kinsmen to survive, in order to receive some benefit from their compensation.'[75] The response of Kahn to this misfit is to deny any connection between genesis out of and perishing into the *apeiron* on the one hand and giving each other compensation on the other. But this does unacceptable violence to the text (10A). Moreover, there is a misfit even with the interpretation that Kahn does espouse. We should in fact expect *both* parties to survive – compensation (and indeed reciprocity generally) is precisely a transaction

[73] Lloyd 1966, 213.

[74] Emped. B135 refers to a law (*nomimon*) obtaining throughout the cosmos, but it is a *moral* law. In Hclt. B114 'all the human laws are fed by the one divine (τρέφονται γὰρ πάντες οἱ ἀνθρώπειοι νόμοι ὑπὸ ἑνὸς τοῦ θείου)' the 'one divine' does not have to refer to a law, and, even if it does, it is not a cosmological or physical law: Mourelatos 1965.

[75] Kahn 1960, 195 (his emphasis).

between surviving parties.[76] And so even the perishing of one opposite into the other does not in this respect fit the model of reciprocal hostility and redress undoubtedly indicated by the words 'for they give penalty and compensation to each other for their injustice according to the assessment of time'.

To this profound misfit we might be tempted to respond that Anaximander's cosmos is not after all constructed out of social relations, that the language of compensation, injustice, and assessment is merely metaphorical and restricted in its application to only one aspect of a cosmological process that has no other relation with the polis.

However, the apparently profound misfit turns out in fact to be a complex correspondence with social process. The parties to a vendetta inflict reciprocal injury on each other while retaining their identity. But in imposing compensation for injury the polis resolves the hostility by means of a transaction based not on violence or negotiation between the hostile parties but on the fixed equivalence between the injury and the compensation. The conflict is resolved by being depersonalised, assimilated to a commercial transaction (10B). This resolution of conflict will be especially important where, in Solonian Athens as in the Miletus of Anaximander, interpersonal conflict has become generalised as civil conflict, putting at risk the survival of the polis. A relation between people must be determined by a relation between things (injury and compensation). The gift in Homer, as frequently in societies where it is economically or politically significant, may retain something of the identity of its donor: the transaction expresses a personal relation. But what is surrendered in a commercial transaction is completely and permanently separated from the person who surrenders it. The receipt of x entails the simultaneous and instantaneous loss of y, with the result that y may seem to be *transformed into* x.[77] Similarly, in the payment of legal compensation for injury what is paid is entirely lost to the payer (whether or not it is imagined as embodying his identity), and the injury is – and this is vital for the resolution of the conflict – annihilated by the payment defined by the polis.

The fragment of Anaximander, our first text to represent an impersonal universe, reflects this vital social pressure towards the impersonal. On the one hand the opposites reflect antagonists, under the control of the polis,

---

[76] The (rare) possibility of the complete destruction of one clan in a vendetta is irrelevant, for it is precluded by the law court and compensation, and would end any process of alternating compensation.

[77] Just as even we, to whom purchase is historically no novelty, may think of *transforming* goods into money or vice-versa.

'giving compensation to each other'. But they also reflect the impersonal transaction into which this interpersonal relationship must, if the polis is to survive, be resolved, a transaction in which the opposed items (injury and compensation, each closely associated with one of the opposed parties) are transformed and annihilated into each other. In this way we can make sense of the paradoxical notion, made inescapable by γάρ in the fragment (10A), that the opposites' payment of compensation to each other is also loss of their identity.

Furthermore, we can in this way also make sense of the equally difficult notion that this loss of identity occurs somehow into the *apeiron* (however this is envisaged as occurring, for instance whether at the end of the world or as part of a continual process).

The Solonian law code specifies *monetary* compensation for injuries (5A), and it is most unlikely that in this respect Miletus, more monetised at this time than Athens, lagged behind. The impersonality of the transaction is strengthened by the supreme impersonality of money. If fifty staters are paid to compensate an injury, then the money has a dual function, as means of payment and as measure of value. As means of payment the money seems to annihilate or absorb the injury. And as measure of value it seems to reconcile the hostile parties by locating the injury on an accepted impersonal scale of values to which other injuries, as well as a whole range of goods and services, also belong. By providing a universal measure money permits a universe of controlled peaceful transactions. It is surely this all-embracing power of *money* that underlies the following praise, by the fourth-century Pythagorean statesman and philosopher Archytas, of the power of *calculation* to create social concord.

The discovery of calculation (*logismos*) ended civil conflict and increased concord. For when there is calculation there is no unfair advantage, and there is equality, for it is by calculation that we come to agreement in our transactions.[78]

By means of monetary compensation the relationship between hostile parties is assimilated to a commercial transaction, drawn into the unlimited sphere of the circulation of commodities regulated by money as means of exchange and measure of value. The assimilation is facilitated by the fact that commercial exchange, in contrast to relations of positive reciprocity expressed for instance in gift exchange, is a relation of *opposition* – as in traditional hostility but in a new way: each party stands opposed to the

---

[78] 47 DK B3, generally agreed to be genuine. Cf. 13A. On the *equality* cf. Aristot. *EN* 1133a17–21 (cited 8B).

other in his attempt to get as much as possible for himself.[79] Commercial transactions are described with the same vocabulary as is the satisfaction of justice.[80]

The commercial opposition is resolved by the opposed items (say a vase and three staters) each embodying the same thing (abstract value). The money into which the vase is transformed will be used to make more pots which will be transformed, in another resolution of opposition, back into money. In monetised exchange, as in the cosmology of Anaximander, opposites originate in, and embody, a single substance into which they are reabsorbed. So too the opposition between injurer and injured is resolved by the all-embracing power of monetary value to absorb the injury.

There is in fact a multiple analogy between money and *everything* that we know (as set out at the end of 10A) of Anaximander's 'unlimited' (*apeiron*).[81]

(a) Each is unlike all other things and separate from them (for money see 81).

(b) Despite (a), each in some sense contains all things. They emerge from it and are transformed back into it. Just as the apparent contradiction of the *apeiron* being both one and many probably did not trouble Anaximander (10A), so monetary value is irreconcilably both one and many – depending on whether it is viewed as a single entity or as embodied in various goods.

---

[79] 12A. I state this of commercial exchange *qua* commercial exchange. In fact of course there may in any such exchange be factors modifying this mutual absolute egotism, just as conversely gift-exchange may be (secretly) calculatingly egotistical.

[80] Vlastos 1970, 83, who documents the widespread application of this 'pattern of thought' to physical processes.

[81] I have begun with Anaximander rather than his Milesian predecessor Thales because we know much less about Thales' cosmology (it seems that he did not leave any writings), and even Aristotle's attribution to him (as the first to hold the view) of a single substrate *underlying* (i.e. not merely originating) all things has been called into question (KRS 93–4; Algra 1999, 50–2). I do in fact regard it as likely that the cosmology of Thales is, like Anaximander's, influenced both by myth (e.g. KRS 92–4) and (especially in the idea of an impersonal, homogeneous, universally underlying – or at least originating – substance) by the development of money. This is suggested by a combination of the chronology of money at Miletus with the little that we do know of Thales' cosmology. Most of the ten characteristics shared by money and Anaximander's *apeiron* do seem to belong also to water as imagined by Thales. This is clearly true of (h), and (if we believe Aristotle) of (a), (b), and (c), and may be true of (d) – for most water in the world is in constant motion (cf. Heraclitus' doctrine that all things flow, which I argue is influenced by money: 12B) – and of (g) – given the vast expanse of sea and ocean, and the report that Thales did regard water as *apeiron* (A13 (Simplic. *Phys.* 458.23), KRS 94). It may also have embodied the apparently contradictory combination (discussed in 10D, 11B, and 12B) of impersonal and personal in (f) and (e): water is impersonal (and in Greek belief surrounded everything: KRS 10–13), but the view is attributed to Thales that 'everything is full of the gods' (Aristot. *de An.* A5, 411a7) – just as money is impersonal but ubiquitously powerful. That leaves (j), and (i): but this lack of *abstraction* in water perhaps suits Thales' place at the very beginning of its progressive development (and of the development of coinage): 12D.

(c) The *apeiron* precedes and persists beyond (the genesis and perishing of) all other things, and is 'immortal and indestructible'. For money to be accepted (whether as measure of value or as means of exchange), i.e. for it to be money, it must precede – and be envisaged by its recipient as persisting unchanged beyond – any transaction involving it, into the indefinite future. Diogenes Laertius reports that according to Anaximander 'the parts change but the whole is unchangeable' (2.1=A1 DK).

(d) The *apeiron* is not just eternal but in eternal *motion*. So too the identity of money must be maintained despite its constant movement in the circulation of commodities.

(e) The *apeiron* surrounds and steers all things. So too money, as providing a pervasive aim of transactions (8D) as well as their measure of value, may seem to regulate all such activity.

(f) Despite (e), the *apeiron* and money are each *impersonal*.[82]

(g) The *apeiron* differs from other things in being envisaged as *unlimited*. The same truth about money (8F) is first expressed by Anaximander's contemporary Solon, who saw that the unlimited individual accumulation of money enslaved poor citizens and threatened the polis.[83] Aristotle says that there are some who make what is beside the elements *apeiron* – and not one of the elements, such as air or water – so as to avoid the others being destroyed by the the one of them that is unlimited, the elements being opposed to each other (*Phys.* Γ5 204b25). Whether or not Aristotle had Anaximander in mind (he probably did),[84] the idea is analogous to the pressing political problem that unlimited monetary accumulation in the network of absolute oppositions between transactors in a monetised economy may eventually result in the enslavement of some of the transactors. But free citizens in monetised transactions are *qua* exchangers both

---

[82] According to West 1971, 77–8 'Anaximander . . . was deeply influenced by the conceptions prevailing in his time among the peoples of the east.' If these peoples did not use money in the strict sense before the Greeks did, to find among their conceptions the idea (essential to 'philosophical cosmology') of an *impersonal* universe would present a difficulty for my association of the idea with money. The passages adduced by West provide important illumination of Anaximander and, throughout his book, of early Greek philosophy generally. It is significant therefore that no single one of them, it seems to me, is evidence for the idea of an impersonal universe before Anaximander. The question of the early beginnings of coinage (and its relation to the early beginings of abstract thought) in China and Northern India presents great difficulties and cannot be discussed here. A recent statement is in Williams 1997, 111–15 (the earliest Indian coins early fourth century BC, influenced ultimately from Greece), 115 (China: miniature inscribed spades and knives used in China from the late seventh or early sixth century BC; small, round, bronze coins from the fourth century BC).

[83] Frr. 4.5–18, 13.71–3.

[84] Kahn 1960, 186–7; KRS 113–14; Simplicius in his comment on the passage (*Phys.* 479, 33) specifies Anaximander.

opposites and equals[85] – like Anaximander's elements. Just as the *apeiron* must not be one of the competing elements, so the unlimit of money must remain apart – confined to the common treasury.[86] The *apeiron*, like money, is itself unlimited but imposes limits (10A).

(h) The *apeiron* is internally undifferentiated, homogeneous. The same is true of money (8B).

(i) The *apeiron* is abstract in the sense that (although it surrounds all things and is their source) it is imperceptible. So too money is both concrete and abstract, visible and invisible (6C, 8H).

(j) If the payment of compensation to each other by the opposites is also their absorption, in equilibrium, into the *apeiron*, then the *apeiron* has the transcendent power to unite the opposites. So too we have seen that the transcendent power of money, as compensation for injury (or as the agreed price for goods), mediates between the opposed parties. And more generally, the transcendent power of money to make things as homogeneous as itself is expressed as the power to unite opposites (8G).

Given the complexity of this analogy, the question must arise of whether it is more than just analogy. The notion of the *apeiron* does not derive from observation. Where then does it come from? Was money a factor in its genesis?

The cosmos presents a spectacle of opposites (e.g. hot and cold) encroaching on each other (e.g. to produce summer and winter) within an overall balance and measure.[87] This is perceived by Anaximander in social terms. Society (the polis) depends on an overall balance and measure by which oppositions (conflict) between its citizens are contained; it is made possible because the opposites are controlled by its judicial process. In this respect the cosmos is a projection of the polis.

This *political* explanation of the genesis of philosophical cosmology contains some truth but is insufficient. It makes us expect as important a role for impersonal *law* in the presocratic cosmos as there is in modern science. But at the heart of the cosmos, for Anaximander and early Greek philosophy generally, there is not impersonal *law* but impersonal *substance*. Secondly, what is remarkable about this substance is its *combination* of the

---

[85] Aristotle has just produced his own proof that the elements, as opposites, must always be equal to each other (ἰσάζειν ἀεὶ τἀναντία). Analogously, he notes that money equalises (again ἰσάζειν) the parties to exchange (8B), whose interests (we may add) are *qua* exchangers opposed.

[86] Cf. the 'bottomless (*abusson*)' money 'with the goddess' at Ar. *Lys.* 174.

[87] On the tendency of primitive societies to see the world in terms of binary oppositions, and the question whether it is possible to detect a single (social?) opposition underlying the others, see Lloyd 1966, 27–38.

characteristics of money. Thirdly, from a different perspective, if we are forced by the extant fragment to accept that Anaximander's cosmos is in some respect a projection of social relations, then we would anyway expect – since what is unprecedented about his time and place is the rapid monetisation of social relations (e.g. of the oppositions indicated in the fragment) – precisely that this monetisation would be projected into his notion of the cosmos. How was Miletus unique? As the centre of a commercial network stretching in all directions over much of the known world, united (in a sense) by that common currency of precious metal (uncoined or coined) that increasingly provided a measure of value and means of exchange, a substrate of all commercial activity.

The hypothesis with which we conclude is that one factor in the genesis of the notion of the *apeiron*, and of philosophical cosmology in general, was money. The hypothesis is not reductionist: it does not *reduce* the *apeiron* to money. Given the difficulty of recovering the detail of Anaximander's cosmology, we cannot be precise about the roles of the various factors by which it seems to have been influenced: the mythical origin of all things by differentiation from a single substance,[88] the alternation of opposites in observable nature, the apparent boundlessness of the universe, the cycle of revenge under the control of the polis, the all-embracing circulation of money.

It seems likely that money could be a factor only by virtue of structural similarity with premonetary factors. One example is the assimilation of the alternation of opposites in nature to the interaction of opposites in revenge or commercial exchange. Another is the mythical idea of a common origin taking a new form as the *apeiron*. In this new form the common origin has acquired new characteristics – as a distinct, eternal, impersonal, all-embracing, unlimited, homogeneous, eternally moving, abstract, regulating substance, destination for all things as well as their origin.

I leave aside the problem of whether and how what is discovered in a culture-dependent way – here the uniform impersonality of the universe and the imperceptibility of what is fundamental – can exist independently of the circumstances of its discovery.[89] But it does seem that the early appeal of this model[90] cannot easily be related to such truth as it contains, for this truth was not tested by experience, and the empirical and technological

---

[88] 11B; Cornford 1952, 187–201; Finkelberg 1986; Kahn 1960, 175–6 – though cf. Engmann 1991, 5.

[89] That it can do so is called the 'separability assumption' by Feyerabend, who subjects it to a critique (1999, 131–46). For an account of the history of science as historically determined imposition (rather than discovery) see e.g. Hübner 1983.

[90] I leave aside the unanswerable question of how widely within the polis it was dispersed.

successes that it assisted came much later. Invoking rather the principle that 'the basic moves that establish [a reality] consist in asserting a certain form of life',[91] and regarding the form of life that accompanied presocratic philosophy as rapidly pervaded by coined money, we suggest that just as the socially necessary transcendence (as means of integration) of sacrificial communality and of monarchy must be projected as cosmological transcendence (e.g. Moira and Zeus), the same is true, in our period, of monetary value.

To be sure, the cosmological transcendence of monetary value conceals (unlike Moira and Zeus) its origin – because this concealment belongs already to the dynamic of its social transcendence. The integrative (socially transcendent) interpersonal power of monetary value depends both on *excluding* from itself all the empirical qualities of the things transformable into it and on *disguising* itself as indeed nevertheless a *thing* independent (unlike sacrificial communality and monarchy) of all interpersonal relations. Whereas the relations between the participants (human or divine) in the sacrifice, or between monarch and subject, are direct, money bestows apparent autonomy on human beings by being interposed between them, mediating but also (because seeming to be impersonal substance) *naturalising* and thereby concealing the power relations between them. Whereas in the sacrifice the current and future well-being of the participants seems to depend on personal relationships with each other and with deity, it is precisely on the uniform transcendent *impersonality* of monetary value that individual autonomy and prosperity and collective cohesion and prosperity seem to depend.

D XENOPHANES

To the generation after Anaximander belong three 'philosophers': Pythagoras, Anaximenes, and Xenophanes. Of the doctrines of Pythagoras himself nothing is known for certain. To Anaximenes (11B) and the later tradition of Pythagoreanism (13A) we will come in due course. Here our concern is with the first 'philosopher' of whom more than a few words survive, Xenophanes.

He was born probably *circa* 570–560 BC, left his native Colophon to wander for many years 'throughout the land of Hellas', and lived into his nineties (B8). He is reported to have said that the Lydians were the first

---

[91] Feyerabend 1999, 79; cf. 157, 201; 71 'we regard those things as real that play an important role in the kind of life we prefer'. Similarly e.g. Hübner 1983, 7–8, etc.

to strike coinage (B4). This is, if the report be correct, by far our earliest mention of coinage. His lifetime coincided with the development of powerful autocracies based on precious metal money: Croesus in Lydia, for instance, or Polycrates in Samos.[92] He refers to the 'useless' luxuries of the Colophonians 'while they were free of hateful tyranny',[93] and attacks the honour paid to athletes: their physical strength is inferior to his own intelligence, and their victories do not enrich the treasure rooms of the polis. The criterion of social worth has become contribution to the communal store of precious metal money held by the polis. In his concern for the communal money and good order (*eunomiē*) of the polis, and for moderation in behaviour,[94] Xenophanes resembles Solon.[95] He resembles him also in his emphasis on human rather than divine agency,[96] an emphasis that reflects the increasing autonomy bestowed on human beings by money (14A).

It is in the light of this concern for intelligent human responsibility for the polis and its money that we should understand Xenophanes dismissing (B1) narratives of the 'useless' violence of Titans, Giants, and Centaurs ('fictions of old'), and observing (B11 and B12) that Homer and Hesiod attributed to the gods disgraceful and illicit actions – theft, adultery, and mutual deceit. Presocratic philosophy propounds a radically new conception of deity and the world, which is sometimes combined – notably by Xenophanes and Heraclitus – with an (equally unprecedented) explicit rejection of tradition.[97] Such widespread and fundamental intellectual change cannot be explained without reference to the widespread and fundamental social change occurring at the same time in the same place. The few extant fragments of Xenophanes allow us a glimpse of his sense that radically new circumstances require attitudes antithetical to those of old. What matters now is neither the ancient violence characteristic of monsters nor the physical strength of the athlete but rather human expertise, moderation, and precious metal in the vaults of a well-ordered polis.

---

[92] D. L. 9.19 (=A1 DK) says that he encountered tyrants as seldom or as pleasantly as possible.

[93] B3.2. The 'tyranny' may be the rule of Harpagos the Mede after 546 BC. The wealthy seventh-century Lydian 'tyrant' Gyges had captured Colophon. Theopompos (115 *FGrH* 117) wrote that in ancient Colophon luxury resulted in tyranny. Aristotle (*Pol.* 1290b15) remarks on the numerous wealthy citizens of Colophon before the war with Lydia.

[94] B1.14–18; 2.19; 3.

[95] Solon fr. 4.1–10, 32, 38–9; 4c.3; 6.3–4; 16; Solon and polis money: 5A (esp. [Aristot.] *Ath. Pol.* 8.3).

[96] Even though the perspective is quite different: Xenophanes B18 'Not from the beginning did gods intimate all things to mortals, but, as they search, in time they discover better'; Solon frr. 11 and 4.1–10 (men rather than gods are responsible for disaster).

[97] Xen. B10, 11, 12 with Lesher 1992 ad loc.; Hclt. B42, 56, 57, 101, 104, A22; Lloyd 1987, 56–71; similarly Pythagoreanism: Bremmer 1999, 76.

So too the rejection of the old anthropomorphic idea of deity is (at least in part) politically motivated. He notes that humans construct gods in their own image, whereas in fact '(there is) one god greatest among gods and men,[98] not at all like mortals in body and thought'. 'All of him sees, all of him thinks, all of him hears' (B24). 'Always he remains in the same place, not moving at all, nor does it befit him to go here and there at different times' (B26). 'But without effort he shakes all things by the thought of his mind' (B25). It also seems that Xenophanes regarded his deity as self-sufficient,[99] permanently unchanging,[100] and in some sense identical with the universe.[101]

Even in this brief account of Xenophanes' deity two inconsistencies are immediately apparent. One is between the complete impersonality of deity and the retention of certain personal abilities – perception and thought (in an extreme form). The other is between on the one hand the god as one and identical with the universe and on the other hand the mention of plurality – of 'all things' (shaken by the god) and of 'gods'.[102] These inconsistencies are not to be explained away.[103] Though less blatant perhaps than may at first appear,[104] they probably inhered, in some form, in the views of Xenophanes.[105]

The *apeiron* of Anaximander is impersonal and eternal, controls all things, and is the source of all things (10A). In these respects it resembles the one god of Xenophanes. We can also detect in Anaximander something resembling the two inconsistencies inherent in Xenophanes. There was perhaps an inconsistency between the impersonality of Anaximander's

---

[98] B23 εἶς θεός, ἔν τε θεοῖσι καὶ ἀνθρώποισι μέγιστος . . . This has been variously interpreted: Lesher 1992, 96. The εἶς ('one') probably intensifies the superlative – a frequent idiom (e.g. Aesch. *Pers.* 327; Soph. *Phil.* 1344–5; Hdt. 1.93.2; Kühner–Gerth 1 28). But in contrast to such examples, the εἶς is (almost certainly) predicative (as at *Il.* 2.204–5), and in the emphatic initial position in the sentence: 'god is one . . .' or 'god is the one greatest . . .' In any case, contradiction remains between the plurality of gods and a single god whose greatness is such that he seems to occupy a category all of his own – we have the impression of an incomplete step towards monotheism.

[99] [Plut.] *Strom.* 4 (=A32 DK) is carefully vindicated as a source for this detail by Finkelberg 1990, 137–46, and seems confirmed by Eur. *HF* 1341–6: Guthrie 1962, 373.

[100] B14; A12, A28, A31–7 DK; Guthrie 1962, 377–83; Finkelberg 1990, 109–10.

[101] Aristot. *Met.* 986b18–25 (A30 DK); Guthrie 1962, 379–82; all things are one: A4 DK, A29 (Pl. *Soph.* 2542d), A31 (Theophrastus) A34–6.

[102] There is also much else in the fragments and testimonia suggestive of a plural world.

[103] Especially mistaken is the view that Xenophanes was simply misunderstood (as claiming the unity of all things – as deity) by Plato, Aristotle, and Theophrastus – despite their knowledge of Xenophanes being far superior to ours: see further Finkelberg 1990; cf. e.g. Lesher 1992, 100–2, 189–92.

[104] Finkelberg 1990, 110–13 argues for a relatively sophisticated 'Xenophanean concept of god as the single and unchangeable intelligible essence unifying the manifold'.

[105] As they do also in Aesch. fr. 70 'Zeus is aither, Zeus earth, Zeus sky, Zeus is all things and whatever is above them.'

apeiron and its 'steering' (Aristotle) of all things (A15 DK), as well as between the personal reciprocity according to which the opposites compensate each other and the impersonality of the *apeiron* into which they are thereby absorbed. Secondly, the Xenophanean combination of unity with plurality is implicit earlier in the emergence of all things from the one (unchanging?) *apeiron* and their perishing into it.

Along with these similarities between the *apeiron* of Anaximander and the god of Xenophanes there are of course significant differences. Firstly, Xenophanes' god is motionless[106] and apparently self-sufficient. Being without need, he does not have to move for any purpose,[107] and can anyway himself move all things with his mind.[108] Secondly, even if Aristotle's 'steering' does imply some personhood for Anaximander's *apeiron*, Xenophanes' god seems to be envisaged, to a much greater extent than the *apeiron*, in traditional[109] personal terms (despite his denial in B23): he shakes all things with his intelligence, and (all of him) perceives and thinks. In fact Xenophanes' combination of personal with impersonal is significantly different from Anaximander's. For Xenophanes the personal is embodied not, as it is for Anaximander, in a *relation* (of reciprocity between semi-autonomous opposites, controlled by the largely impersonal *apeiron*) but rather in the one controlling *individual* (deity).

How are we to explain the difference (or development) of conceptions between Anaximander and Xenophanes, and the peculiar combination of ideas in Xenophanes?

For both Anaximander and Xenophanes there is a single divine thing that is impersonal and yet omnipotent, eternal, and in some sense the equivalent of all things. So too money is impersonal and yet omnipotent, must pre-exist and outlive all transactions, and is the equivalent of all things. Crucial here, for understanding the conceptual shift, is the startling historical novelty of

---

[106] In sharp contrast, it seems, to the *apeiron*, which was said by Theophrastus to be in eternal motion (10A). The same polarity, reflecting the polarity within money between its constant circulation and its permanent identity of value, is found between the constantly transforming fire of Heraclitus and the motionless One of Parmenides (12B).

[107] The verb used of going (here and there) in B26 (quoted above), μετέρχεσθαι, implies purpose.

[108] Cf. Aesch. *Suppl.* 100–2 (a-propos of Zeus) 'all deity is without effort: sitting he entire carries out somehow his thought (*phronēma* – not 'intention') from where he is, from a pure throne'. Cf. Aesch. *Eum.* 650–1; fr. 70 (quoted above, n. 105).

[109] Xenophanes transforms elements of Homeric and Hesiodic deity into a radically new conception. With B23 cf. Homeric Zeus as the most powerful: *Od.* 5.4; *Il.* 2.350, 412; 3.278; etc.; Hes. *Theog.* 49, 534, 548; also *Il.* 15.80–4 (deity moves as fast as thought). With B24 cf. *Il.* 8.51–2; *Od.* 20.75; Hes. *Op.* 267. With B25 cf. *Il.* 1.528–30 (physical *nod* shakes *Olympus*, whereas in Xenophanes the *mind* shakes *all things*) – and specifically with 'without effort' cf. ῥεῖα (easily) of divine action at *Il.* 3.381; 10.556; 20.444; *Od.* 3.231. With B26 cf. the Homeric Zeus sending subordinates among mortals. With B34 cf. *Od.* 18.136–7.

power that is universal, social, and yet impersonal. In the premonetary age a king, backed up by his army and the gods, extracts (and redistributes) goods and services by power that is personal. The mystery of money is its universal *impersonal* power to extract goods and services.[110]

A factor making for impersonal power in Anaximander's conception of the universe was the encroachment of the impersonality of money on social relations at the expense of personal reciprocity, an encroachment needed to control the oppositions inherent in commercial exchange and in revenge (10B).

The Xenophanean combination of personal with impersonal differs, we have seen, in that the personal is embodied no longer in the relation of reciprocity but in one controlling individual. It is as if the power of money (in the hands of the individual) is now complete, with the personal *relationship* of autonomous reciprocity marginalised. The individual with money commands goods and services irrespective of (reciprocal) personal relations. Although money too is in fact a relation, the relation is concealed by money appearing to be a mere thing, with the result that the individual with money (and even the money itself) may seem self-sufficient – like Xenophanes' deity. The principle of voluntary reciprocity in the exchange of goods and services has been marginalised by the permeation of exchange by money, and hostile reciprocity has been marginalised by the judicial process of the polis (partly through monetary compensation). Corresponding with the establishment of money as a universal measure of value and means of payment and exchange is the emphasis in our sources, from Plato and Aristotle onwards, on Xenophanes as a pioneer of the view that all things are one.[111]

---

[110] Contrast the description by Godelier 1999 (1996), 105 of the gift-giving societies discussed by Mauss: 'In such a world, one can venture to say that "things" no longer exist, there are only persons, sometimes in the guise of human beings and sometimes in the guise of things. At the same time, the fact that human social relations (of kinship and power) must assume the shape of relations between persons, intersubjective relations, is extended to the whole universe. Nature, the entire universe, is now composed uniquely of (human or non-human) persons and of relations between these persons.'

[111] N. 103 above. It is in the light of the concealed unity of all things underlying their apparent plurality that I understand Xenophanes' 'seeming has been constructed over all things' (δόκος δ' ἐπὶ πᾶσι τέτυκται (B34. 4), with πᾶσι (all) referring not to all people but to all things (picking up the same word πάντων from two lines earlier). In the six other occurrences of the phrase ἐπὶ πᾶσι in the Archaic period it refers to people only once (*Od.* 8. 554 of placing (τίθενται) names on people). The rare δόκος could no doubt mean (like the more obviously verbal δόκησις) 'seeming' as well as 'opinion'. Just as at Hes. *Theog.* 583 beauty is breathed over everything (ἐπὶ πᾶσι – figures wrought in an artefact), Xenophanes says that 'seeming has been constructed (τέτυκται) over everything'. The first statement of a general and systematic distinction between being and seeming, with a layer of universal seeming covering the (unity of) things, is produced under the influence of monetisation.

Xenophanes' conception of the universe may then appear to represent a later stage in the rapid development of money than Anaximander's conception a generation earlier. On the other hand, Xenophanes' conception of deity seems, despite his affirmation of its impersonality, more traditional and personal than anything found in (or attributed to) Anaximander. How, if the increasing power of impersonal money was a factor in these cosmologies, are we to explain this apparent reversion to a more personal idea of deity?

The answer, were we able to provide it, would no doubt include many factors other than the economic. We may for instance infer the unconscious fusion, in the mind of Xenophanes, of the impersonal omnipotence of money with the traditional, personal idea of deity implicit in the poetic genre in which he wrote. As far as the economic factor is concerned, we should again note that although money is an (impersonal) thing, it operates only between people. It is the impersonal embodiment of interpersonal power. The Xenophanean contradiction between personal and impersonal may reflect contradiction not only between traditional personal deity and the omnipotence of impersonal money but also (overlayering this) between the personal and the impersonal within the omnipotence of money. This needs further explanation.

Any possessor of money may sense its omnipotence. But at the personal level this omnipotence is fully realised only in the figure of the tyrant, who (unlike the premonetary king) exercises absolute personal power largely through money, thereby uniting the impersonal omnipotence of money with its personal aspect: because money is omnipotent, the only person to fully implement its power is the (omnipotent) tyrant.

It seems that in favour of monotheism Xenophanes produced the argument that since god is the most powerful being there cannot be more than one such being, for if one was less powerful than another he would not be a god.[112] Whence this assumption that deity is *pre-eminent* power? Why cannot one deity have power equal to, or less than, that of another, just as we find in Homer? The principle of reciprocity implies the co-existence of autonomous powers (divine or human), such as we find to some extent in the largely pre-state, premonetary world of Homer.

Interestingly, the Homeric passage closest to expressing the omnipotence of Zeus, and the unity of the universe, envisages a golden chain by which Zeus pulls up to the sky the gods along with the earth and the sea

---

[112] A 28 DK; A 31. 3; cf. A 32. That this particular argument goes back to Theophrastus' account of Xenophanes (and so probably to Xenophanes himself) is demonstrated by Finkelberg 1990.

(*Il.* 8.9–27). This clumsy fantasy may derive from an early stage of the unification of all things by precious metal controlled by the ruler. The subsequent development of money tends to eliminate the co-existence of autonomous powers. To be sure, money seems to create a new, more individualistic kind of autonomy, free of the interpersonal demands of reciprocity, but in fact dependent on the possession (and general acceptability) of the single embodiment of power in general, impersonal money (14AB). And this dependence may appear – especially from a premonetary perspective – as loss of autonomy. Moreover, the unlimit of money may concentrate apparently unlimited power in a single individual, the tyrant. In the universe imagined by Anaximander the reciprocity of autonomous powers still has a place, albeit under the overall control of the *apeiron*. But in the world of Xenophanes co-existence of autonomous powers has in a sense been eliminated: were there two moneys, one would soon be absorbed by the other; political power, maintained and permeated by unitary money, is itself unitary – most strikingly in the figure of the tyrant. Deity is power, and so must be (at least on the model of money and political power) 'one'. The autocracy which Xenophanes knew, at Colophon and elsewhere, was not monarchy but tyranny:[113] his profoundly new idea of deity did not derive from a long lost political form.

The power of the tyrant is, to the extent that it is based on money, a mysterious combination of the personal with the impersonal. Whereas the seal embodies the identity of the ruler (6C), the universal power of money is both impersonal (embodying nobody, and independent of all specific personal relations) and invisibly ubiquitous. And yet it may bind all men and all things to the will of a single person. The tyrant may seem, through the impersonal ubiquity of money, to control all things – without moving from the centre, without effort, without (reciprocal) personal relations. In what then does his mysteriously self-sufficient power consist? It is distinct from physical force, for his control of the sanction of physical force *depends on* his control of money (used to pay soldiers); even Zeus, in Aristophanes, rules the gods only because 'he has the most money' (*Wealth* 131). It belongs rather to the other pole in the polarity between physical force and intelligence: the tyrant's invisible[114] control over the mysterious new abstraction – itself invisible – inherent in monetary value involves a new kind of

---

[113] The fact that Xenophanes calls tyranny 'hateful' (B 3.2) does not of course mean that his theology was not (unconsciously) influenced by its absolute power. On the creator of the hateful 'tyrant' Zeus in the *Prometheus Bound* the influence is conscious.

[114] This invisibility is expressed, earlier in the development of money, in the invisibility of Gyges (the first *turannos*) and of Deiokes the Mede: 6C.

intelligence. Xenophanes said that most things are inferior to mind (A1 DK), and, as we saw, explicitly rated intelligence above physical strength.[115]

This unprecedented and mysterious combination of the invisible impersonal omnipotence of money with the invisible omnipotent intelligence of a person exhibits the same peculiar system of features as, and is a factor in, Xenophanes' contradictory construction of deity, who (1) is impersonal, (2) stays in the same place, (3) without effort shakes all things by his thought, (4) is self-sufficient – that is, in significant contrast to the Homeric gods, he has no need of reciprocity – and (5) in that he is almost identified with (perceiving, thinking) invisible *mind* ('all of him sees, all of him thinks, all of him hears'), is a step on the way to the idea of homogeneous abstract being. The further development of these ideas will be a theme of subsequent chapters.

---

[115] It is against the background of the monetary power of tyranny that we should understand the picture of the 'tyrant' Zeus in the *Prometheus Bound*, which contains not only many typical features of tyranny (including isolation from all personal relations – distrust of *philoi* (his own people), violence against kin, and rejection of reciprocity: 14D) but also the polarity between intelligence and physical force: Zeus will win by the former not the latter (204–25). Cf. also Aesch. *Suppl.* 100–2 (quoted n. 108 above); *Eum.* 650–1; fr. 99. 3.

CHAPTER ELEVEN

The many and the one

A WHY MONISM?

On the earliest philosophers Aristotle writes as follows.

That of which all existing things consist and from which they first come to be and into which they finally pass away (the being, *ousia*, remaining but changing in its modifications), this they say is the element and principle (*archē*) of all existing things, and therefore they think that nothing is generated or destroyed, as this kind of being is always preserved. (*Met.* A 983b6ff.)

The first such thinker, Aristotle adds, was Thales, whose *archē* was water. Philosophical cosmology begins not from the detailed information about various materials known to artisans, but from comprehensive and abstract principles. The belief that all things are in fact *one* can be ascribed also, in various forms, to Anaximander, Anaximenes, Xenophanes, Heraclitus, and Parmenides.

It is an odd belief, especially in a polytheistic society. Why was it unanimously maintained by these philosophers? We cannot explain it merely by the 'economy and simplicity' characteristic of science or the 'drive for epistemological power over nature'.[1] Monism is sufficiently antithetical to the observed world as to incur irresolveable contradiction, even within the views of its adherents. This point is honestly faced by Michael Stokes.

There has been suggested in print no good reason for so strange a beginning in Greek philosophy. Nor does common sense afford any suggestion to alleviate its strangeness; the world around us has nothing obviously suggesting a single material.[2]

---

[1] Barnes 1982, 11; Saxonhouse 1992, 24. Neither Barnes nor Saxonhouse can begin to explain why the belief occurred when and where it did. 'Economy and simplicity' and 'the drive for epistemological power' are sufficiently broad to be *part* of the explanation, and indeed to be themselves involved in the mentality required for the spread of money, and to have both produced beliefs quite different from those of the presocratics. Note also that, if Feyerabend is right (1999, 141), 'the alleged unity and comprehensiveness of science are not a fact but a (metaphysical) assumption'.

[2] Stokes 1971, 39.

Stokes rightly rejects various explanations as inadequate. If there is 'a deep-seated tendency in the human mind to seek something that persists through change', then why did it surface specifically in the sixth century? 'No explanation is forthcoming either for its long dormancy or for this precipitate efflorescence.' Stokes does accordingly allow some explanatory power to the economic factor ('the rise of Milesian merchant classes'), which, he maintains, with a reference to Farrington,[3] 'accounts well for the abolition of personal and arbitrary divine intervention in natural processes'. But without pausing to explain *how* such abolition might occur, he continues thus.

But it would not even begin to suggest a reason why that abolition should be accompanied by the postulation of a single material for everything.

Stokes' solution is to maintain that the earliest philosophers did not after all maintain such a 'departure from common sense'. Aristotle and Theophrastus were simply mistaken in ascribing monism to them. Rather, monism was projected back onto them under the influence of Parmenides' argument that one substance could not change into another, which entails that if the universe arose from a single thing (as the Milesians undoubtedly did believe) then it must still *be* that one thing.

There are several weaknesses in this argument, of which I mention two.[4] First, so complete a rejection of the testimony of Aristotle and Theophrastus is just not credible.[5] Second, there is indeed, if our argument is correct, an explanation of the sixth-century adoption of monism – in the *monetisation* that Stokes fails to see at the heart of the economic change that he reluctantly abandons as an explanation.

As we would expect on various grounds, Parmenides' abstract monism is not the radical break that Stokes supposes but rather the culmination of tendencies beginning with the Milesians. But even if Stokes were right, the problem of the motivation of the departure from what he calls common sense would simply be brought down to Parmenides, whose doctrine of the One is at least as odd (despite his 'argumentation') as Milesian monism.

Another scholar aware that 'it is hard to find a conception that contradicts common sense so sharply as material monism does' is Finkelberg, who seeks an explanation for its unanimous adoption by the earliest 'philosophers' in

---

[3] Farrington (1961), for whom the key factor is 'the rapid development of techniques' on which the prosperity of the mercantile prosperity depended (35). But the development of techniques had been more substantial in the Near East.

[4] For others see Lloyd 1973.

[5] Despite justified suspicion of their interpretative categories. This is of course a complex matter: with Stokes' detailed exposition cf. e.g. Guthrie 1962, 40–3.

a presuppostion that he calls 'cosmogonical pantheism'. The material principle of the Milesians is divine, and the emergence of the world is the
transition of the divine substance from homogeneity (uniformity of *archē*)
to heterogeneity (multiformity of *archē*). But this involves the inconsistency that the 'all-inclusive divine nature turns out paradoxically to be one
of its own manifestations'. This internal problem motivated development:
'the only way to arrive at a consistent monist doctrine is to consider a
higher unity of the universe as its intelligible and not material quality'. The
development, beginning with Anaximander,[6] culminates in Parmenides'
non-cosmogonical pantheistic conception of the world as an unchangeable intelligible unity. 'The factor that generated this development and
predetermined its path was immanent: the early thinkers were anxious
to eliminate the fundamental contradiction inherent in their pantheistic
vision and achieve its consistent or satisfactory formulation.'[7]

   Finkelberg's theory is unique as a serious attempt to unearth the preconceptions of early cosmological monism (and not merely of the idea that all
things *originate* in one). But if cosmogonical pantheism is so basically and
obviously inconsistent, why was it so attractive to the first 'philosophers'?

B   MYTH, PSYCHOANALYSIS, POLITICS, MONEY, MYSTERY CULT

Finkelberg's reply to this question would be that cosmogonical pantheism
was inherited by the Milesians from *myth*. 'We have authentic evidence
for the existence of a pantheistic outlook in the sixth century, which lends
historical plausibility to the assumption of a pantheistic motivation for
Milesian thought.' His evidence is a single text.

Into him [Zeus] all the immortals grew, blessed gods and goddesses and rivers and
lovely springs and everything else that had come into being then; and he became
the only one. Zeus is the head, Zeus the middle, from Zeus all things are made.

This is from a few lines of an Orphic theogony quoted in the Derveni
papyrus.[8] Presumably later in the narrative Zeus recreated the gods and
the world out of himself, as was recorded in the later Stoic and Rhapsodic
versions.[9]

   West argues that the Derveni poem is an abridged version of an earlier
poem, the 'Protogonos theogony', which he dates no earlier than within a

---

[6] See also Finkelberg (1993) for argument that 'Anaximander discovered the possibility of envisaging
the higher unity of the manifold as a conceptual unity rather than a material one' (255).
[7] Finkelberg 1989, 269.
[8] Cols. XVI and XVII; West 1983, 88–9; Laks and Most 1997, 16–17; cf. Janko 2001, 25.
[9] West 1983, 90.

generation either side of 500 BC,[10] too late for the Milesians. Nevertheless, it may be that the Milesians and Xenophanes were influenced by a (lost) earlier version of the kind of pantheism found in the Derveni poem – West does argue that the Protogonos theogony was of Ionian origin. What then remains to be explained is why it was transformed (in particular, depersonalised) by the Milesians, and why the transformation occurred when and where it did.

There is another myth long recognised as standing behind philosophical cosmology. That the world was created by the separation of earth from sky is found in various places outside Greece as well as in some Greek texts, including Hesiod's *Theogony*. These myths imply (despite more or less anthropomorphism) that the world was created out of a single undifferentiated mass, an assumption shared by the Milesians. But why was cosmogony constructed thus?

One kind of answer is *psychoanalytic*. The Hesiodic narrative is a cosmic projection of the formation of the self. It begins as follows.

First of all *chaos* came into being, and then broad-breasted Earth, safe seat of all things for ever, and misty Tartarus in a recess of broad-pathed earth, and Eros . . .

The Greek *chaos* is a dark and gloomy chasm.[11] By '*chaos* came into being' Hesiod (or his source) may have meant the creation of the chasm between sky and earth, i.e. the separation of sky from earth.[12] In any case, the earliest state is envisaged as undifferentiated, whether as a dark chasm or (by implication) as sky and earth forming 'one shape'.[13] For Caldwell the order *Chaos*, Earth, Tartarus, Eros is psychoanalytically significant. Just as the earliest psychic state of the child is symbiotic, of 'undifferentiation, fusion with the mother', so the mythical world begins with undifferentiated oneness. And just as the infantile sense of self then develops by a separation (from the mother) which is also a loss, so in the myth the undifferentiated state is ended by the perception of the mother (Gaia) as separate; but she is known only at the price of being lost. Accordingly, Tartarus, next to be mentioned, is the place of loss.[14] And it is on the basis of loss that desire (Eros) comes into being. The separation of earth and sky is soon re-enacted anthropomorphically:[15] Sky hides his children in their mother Earth and prevents them from emerging, but one of them, Kronos, as his father Sky makes love to Earth (fully extended over her), castrates him with the help of his mother (154–81). Here the loss of undifferentiation goes

---

[10] West 1983, 108–10.   [11] Cf. 814; West 1966 ad 116.   [12] KRS 36–41.
[13] The phrase is from Eur. fr. 484; similarly at D. S. 1.7.1(=68 DK B5).
[14] Caldwell 1989, 132–42.   [15] KRS 34–46.

with Oedipal conflict. Subsequently Kronos fails to prevent (by swallowing them) the emergence of his own offspring, and is replaced by his son Zeus.

Another kind of explanation for the particularity of this cosmogony is *political*. The succession narrative is also about *sovereignty*. After dethroning his father (490–1) Zeus gains allies in the imminent battle with the Titans by releasing giants imprisoned by his father (501–6, 624–8) and promising the gods honours if they fight on his side. (392–6). Having defeated the Titans and the monster Typhoeus, he is urged by the gods to become king, divides up honours among them (883–5), and secures his sovereignty by swallowing his wife Mētis (886–93), whose name means 'cunning intelligence'.

The Hesiodic theogony, it is well known, was influenced (even if only indirectly) by myths known to the Babylonians, the Hurrians, the Hittites, and the Phoenicians.[16] The Babylonian *Enuma Elish* told of an original undifferentiated mass (Apsu and Tiamat mingling their waters together), of conflict between generations leading to castration of an older god, of a younger god (Marduk) appointed king so as to defeat the dragon Tiamat and her band of monsters, of his victory, his consolidation of sovereignty, and his ordering of the universe – in which the first step is to cut Tiamat into two and make the halves sky and earth. The poem was recited at the Babylonian New Year festival, in which the king has his mandate renewed by the gods. Whereas the Babylonian myth may have derived stability from the monarchy that it reflects (4B), the Greek monarchical theogony that derives from it is not sustained by the institutions of the polis. The Hesiodic cosmogony, though basically genealogical and anthropomorphic, resulting in the monarchy of Zeus, sometimes seems closer to the idea of merely physical elements (esp. 116–19) than anything in the Babylonian cosmogony from which it partly derives. And Milesian cosmogony shares preconceptions with Hesiodic cosmogony (notably separation from an original undifferentiated mass) but has abandoned the idea of *personal* (monarchical) universal power. This is not to say that the decline of monarchical ideology among the Greeks left a space for non-ideological 'rational' speculation about the cosmos. The point is rather that monarchy is replaced by other forms of universal social relation (based on, notably, reciprocity and money) that help to shape ideas of the cosmos.

The Orphic theogony mentioned earlier is influenced by the Hesiodic. Among their differences is that in the former all things are at one point

[16] Cornford 1952, 202–24; Walcot 1966; West 1966, 20–31; 1997, 270–305.

*re*united.[17] Zeus absorbs into himself all things by swallowing the creator god (before recreating them out of himself).[18] What does this mean? West compares the Egyptian god Re, who resembles in various respects the Orphic creator god Protogonos, and resembles the Orphic Zeus in producing out of his mouth gods whom he then rules over. The combination of this motif with the tradition that Zeus is one of the younger gods requires Zeus first to swallow all that has preceded him before producing it from his mouth. The idea seems then to derive from the all-embracing power of (Egyptian) monarchy. We should accordingly note that in the Babylonian *Enuma Elish* too there is movement from multiplicity to unity to (controlled) multiplicity: the gods unite behind their newly appointed king, who after victory arranges the plurality of the universe (creating stations for the gods); and the poem ends with a celebration of unified plurality in the form of a catalogue of the fifty titles of Marduk.

But what was the appeal, in the Classical period, of the bizarre and apparently primitive notion of Zeus swallowing and regurgitating all things? Swallowing is an obvious image of individual control (containment) of diversity. In Hesiod Kronos swallows his children, and to secure his monarchy Zeus swallows Mētis (cunning intelligence). The Orphic Zeus unites everything within his own body, and regurgitates it out in due order.[19] The result is diversity, unified by Zeus. Indeed, Zeus actually asks how he is to preserve both the unity of the world and its individual features.[20] Such concern makes political sense, in the establishment of (monarchical) individual control over diversity. But there was no oriental monarchy among the Greeks to sustain it. Should we then turn back to the psychoanalytic perspective?

The theme also makes sense in the establishment of the individual ego, of the unitary mind over internal fragmentation. The Derveni author cites Orphic verses in which everything is absorbed into Zeus, and comments on the phrase 'and he himself was alone' as follows.

In saying this he makes clear that Mind itself being alone is worth everything, just as if everything else were nothing. For it would not be possible for them to exist, if the things were without the Mind. And in the verse following this he said that Mind is worth everything: 'And (now) he is king of all and will be afterwards.' It is clear that Mind and king of all is the same thing.[21]

---

[17] Cf. also Musaeus 2DK A4 'all things come from one and are resolved into the same'.

[18] West 1983, 88–90, 100, 113, 218, 239–41.

[19] Kern 1922, frr. 167–9; *Pap. Derv.* Cols. XVI, XVII (Laks and Most 1997, 16–17).

[20] Kern 1922, fr. 165 'How will all things be one for me and each thing separate?

[21] Col. XVI: I reproduce the translation in Laks and Most 1997, 16–17, including the translation suggested in the footnote by Tsantsanoglou.

Having succeeded his father, and swallowed and regurgitated all things, the Orphic Zeus then copulates with his mother.[22] The creation of unified deity is here framed by the Oedipal transition. Zeus is not an infant. But in one (at least) Orphic version[23] the next king is his son the infant Dionysus, who is lured by the Titans from his throne by means of a mirror, dismembered, and eaten, but then reconstituted when the Titans are blasted with a thunderbolt. Humankind is created out of the soot deposited by smoke from the blasted Titans. Finally, for the salvation of humankind Dionysus establishes mysteries.

The narrative of Dionysus' dismemberment by the Titans is a projection of Dionysiac mystic initiation, which might itself be experienced as enacting the myth.[24] The myth dramatised in Euripides' *Bacchae* also reflects mystic initiation.[25] These myths, the ritual, and the various works of art that represent them involve – as part of the assumption of a new identity – a regression to the infantile state, delight in one's own image in a mirror, bodily fragmentation,[26] the reconstitution of bodily wholeness, and the revelation of a (veiled) erect phallus – detached from the body but restorative of new life.[27] I confine myself to suggesting briefly, as one possibility of psychoanalytic interpretation, the Lacanian theory of infantile development, in which the infant's delight in its mirror image is associated with a new sense of identity that initiates the 'mirror stage', a sense of bodily wholeness that nevertheless may never cease to be threatened by a retrospective pull towards the sense of bodily fragmentation dominant in the pre-mirror stage.[28] The phallus, indissolubly associated with absence (as if veiled), is the symbol of the loss required for the infantile passage into language.[29]

The socio-political and the psychoanalytic accounts cohere. Mythical cosmogony and mythical anthropogony are shaped by the formation of

---

[22] West 1983, 73, 88–94, 100.

[23] For source references see West 1983, 74–5. The earliest allusion to this version is either Pi. fr. 133 Snell (though cf. Seaford 1986, 8) or Hdt. 2.61: see Murray in Harrison 1927, 342–3; Burkert 1983, 225 n. 43; 1985, 297–8; West 1983, 137–75; and for Plato Riedweg 1986, 13–17.

[24] West 1983, 140–75.   [25] Seaford 1996.

[26] Just before Pentheus moves (like the infant Dionysus) from mirror to bodily fragmentation it is hinted that his fragmentation (in the hands of his mother, like an infant) will be *psychological*: 14D n. 72.

[27] Nilsson 1957. The phallus was unveiled in a *liknon*-cradle, which in the fifth-century Athenian ritual depicted on the 'Lenäenvasen' contained a mask, set up after sacrificial dismemberment: Burkert 1983, 235–7; Seaford 1994a, 264–5; 1996, 227, 248; 1998b, 145 n. 55. On the equivalence of head and phallus see Burkert 1983, 202 n. 33. Cf. Burkert 1983, 69–70; *Pap. Derv.* Col. xiii; D. S. 4.6.3–4; Clem. Alex. *Protr.* 2.19.4; Iambl. *Myst.* 1.11.

[28] For the detail of this argument see Seaford 1998b.

[29] E.g. Lemaire 1977, 82–8, 245; Benvenuto and Kennedy 1986, 130–6, 177–81, 186–95.

the kingdom and by the formation of the sovereign ego, and so centre around the emergence of the many out of the one and the reimposition of unity on the many. Among the Greeks monarchy dies out, and so mythical cosmogony is no longer sustained by kingship. And yet it continues to be sustained by preconceptions deriving from socio-political power on the one hand and ego formation[30] on the other. The socio-political power is no longer monarchical but the power of money, which, like monarchical power, is all-embracing, imposing a single, universal power on all things without destroying their diversity.

The various relations we have indicated between the one and the many, and the psychological and socio-political factors that shaped them, are surely much older than the earliest known Orphic texts. The factors are joined, in the advanced city-states of the late seventh and early sixth centuries, by a new form of socially and pyschologically transformative unity underlying the plurality of appearances, namely monetary value.

Like all representations of the cosmos, presocratic philosophy attempts to discover order and uniformity underlying apparent chaos. And like many such representations, it does so by attempting to know and explain what it cannot know and explain, and so involves projection of the familiar onto the unfamiliar. And because the search is for order and uniformity, those elements of the familiar will be projected that especially embody the order and uniformity that is abstracted from the potential chaos of experience. Many such elements – monarchy, reciprocity, ritual, etc. – involve the familiar order inherent in human control. Monetary value is in this respect different. On the one hand it is indeed a human product, and especially apt for cosmic projection because it is itself a projection or abstraction, already detached from everything else: by virtue of being abstracted from all the various commodities and monetary units in which it inheres it provides a uniform unchanging standard for numerous and various transactions and thereby imposes order and control on multifarious social relations. But on the other hand it does so by its *essential im*personality, the *necessity* of its detachment from all individuals and of its *concealment* of interpersonal relations by seeming to be an impersonal thing. Moreover, it does not bring with it the vocabulary required for separating it into a new 'economic' sphere.[31] Accordingly, though created by us, money seems – in

---

[30] Burkert 1982, 8 affirms on the basis of Mesopotamian parallels (repeating cosmogony to overcome disease and other crises) that Orphic cosmogony and anthropogony 'had its place and function in the practice of the intinerant craftsmen' in providing relief for individuals.

[31] Even the brief 'economic' passages of Aristotle are fundamentally ethical and metaphysical: Meikle 1995. There is not even a Greek word precisely equivalent to our 'money': 1c.

its circulation (as opposed to in our pocket) – to be outside human control, a mysterious force of nature that controls us. It is for instance money itself (rather than people using money) that is said to unite opposites (8G). It is this unprecedented combination of human order with extra-human power that ensures its revolutionary projection onto the cosmos.

The transcendent power of monarchy had been projected onto the cosmos. The transcendent impersonal power of money, reified as a fact of nature, is projected onto the cosmos as a powerful transcendent substance. Unlike monarchy, money is *impersonal*, and is exchanged into, and is the undifferentiated *equivalent* of, all things, each of which somehow embodies monetary value. Accordingly, Milesian cosmology differs from the Hesiodic in the *impersonality* of the all-controlling[32] primary undifferentiated principle, and in that all things in a sense *consist* of it. Anaximenes' material principle, air, *maintains its identity* throughout its transformation into other things. Anaximenes identifies the process by which this occurs – rarefaction into fire, condensation into earth, and so on: plurality (qualitative differentiation) is explained by quantitative differentiation of the single substance.[33] Further, the material principles of Anaximander and of Anaximenes, perhaps also Thales' water, are each, like money, *unlimited*.[34] A factor in these radical departures from the Hesiodic model was (in another application of our cumulative argument) the new model of money as a (controlling) universal, impersonal, and unlimited means of exchange and measure of value: all things may be transformed from and into money, but are (like things in Anaximenes) differentiated quantitatively – they embody (even if the same size) different sums.

But mythical cosmogony also continues to be shaped – as it had been in the Hesiodic narrative by which it continued to be influenced[35] – by preconceptions deriving from the formation of the ego. And so cosmogony splits into two – on the one hand *impersonal* 'philosophy', and on the other hand the bizarrely *personal* Orphic cosmogony and anthropogony that reflect to some degree the re-creation of the self in mystic initiation.

---

[32] Anaximander: A15 (= Aristot. *Met.* 203b7); Anaximenes: B2; Thales: unknown; later e.g. Hclt. B64, B66 (cf. 30, 31, 90).

[33] We may agree with Stokes 1971, 43–8 that Anaximenes might have been unclear about the nature of condensation and rarefaction, and of course we do not need to claim that he entertained a notion such as 'quantitative differentiation'. But Stokes' claim that he may have 'considered the result of condensing as applied to air to be not, as we should say, condensed air, but simply water, earth, or any other appropriate substance' is impossible: 'simply' makes no sense here, and flies in the face of the unanimous ancient tradition. See also Lloyd 1973, 245–6 for further objections to Stokes' claim.

[34] For Anaximander 10A; for Anaximenes A1, A5 (Theophrastus' account, preserved by Simplicius), A6, A7, A9, A10; for Thales A13 (Simplic. *Phys.* 458. 23), KRS 94.

[35] West 1983, index s.v. Hesiod.

However, these two opposite kinds of cosmogony do not necessarily drift entirely apart. Consider for instance the subtle fusion of monetary projection with the cosmic projection both of monarchy and of the unitary self established over internal fragmentation in the Derveni Commentator's interpretation (cited above) of the monarch Zeus' absorption of all things into himself: 'Mind itself being alone is *worth all things* [my emphasis, *pantōn axion*], just as if everything else were nothing.' Compare Pythermus' 'the things other than gold were after all nothing' (5A).

Another way in which the personal and impersonal cosmogony may stay together is in the traditional use by mystic ritual of riddling utterance to hint at the truth that will finally be revealed.[36] From this practice, it seems, develops the interpretation of cosmogonic or anthropomorphic myth as allegory, as a riddling account of physical processes.[37] An example from the Classical period is provided by the Derveni commentary in which our Orphic theogony is quoted.[38] Another example, centuries later, is the neoplatonic allegorisation of the myth of Dionysus' dismemberment as referring enigmatically to the formation both of the individual psyche and of the cosmos: both kinds of formation involve the movement from unity through fragmentation (symbolised by the dismemberment of Dionysus as he looks at himself in the mirror) to a restored unity.[39]

To the personal dimension of the largely impersonal cosmologies of the presocratics I will return in 12B. An instance appropriate to describe here is Empedocles, who was much influenced[40] by Orphic ideas. He proposed a universe composed of four physical elements, to which however he also gave the names of personal gods (Zeus, Hera, Nestis, Aidoneus). The elements are, in a constant cycle, brought together by Love and separated by Strife. When they are combined into a single undifferentiated mass – a sphere that 'rejoices in its supremely joyous solitariness' (i.e. in being all there is),[41] this is the complete supremacy of Love.[42] Bodies are at first fragmentary ('many faces without necks sprang up, arms wandered without shoulders, etc.'),[43] then (with the advance of Love) made whole.[44] Thereafter (with the advance of Strife) 'whole-natured shapes' develop into males and females, which are then (with the further advance of Strife) torn apart into separate

---

[36] 12A n. 19; *Pap. Derv.* Col. VI 6–7; Pl. *Phd.* 69C; the riddling language in the mystic formulae preserved in the gold leaves (e.g. A4 Zuntz 1971, 329); Plut. *Mor.* 389A; Demetr. *Eloc.* 101; Riedweg 1987, 90; Seaford 1981, 254–5.

[37] Seaford 1986, esp. 19–20.   [38] Obbink 1997.   [39] Seaford 1998b, 141–3.

[40] West 1983, index s.v. Empedocles; Seaford 1986, 10–12; Kingsley 1995.

[41] B26.16; B28.2.; B29.   [42] B17, 27.   [43] B57; cf. B96, 98; A72.

[44] B20. 2–5, in which συνερχόμεθα, 'we come together' (provided by the recently published Strasbourg papyrus, replacing συνερχόμενα, 'coming together') makes this '*our*' experience. But cf. Osborne 2000, 344–52.

limbs.[45] Even though mythical cosmology has here become largely impersonal (elements, sphere), it still seems – like the Orphic Zeus becoming 'alone' by absorbing everything – marked by infantile experience of self. The undifferentiated (symbiotic) state is supremely joyful, and return to it is caused by Love. On the way to and from it, bodies alternate between fragmentation and wholeness, as in the process emphasised by Lacan.[46]

The idea that wholeness of the self may come from the wholeness of what is seen in mystic initiation is implied in Plato *Phaedrus* 250b8–c6:

> They were initiated into the mysteries which it is right to call most blessed, which we celebrated *whole in ourselves* and untouched by the sufferings that awaited us in later time [i.e. after birth], with the gaze of our final initiation on *whole* and simple and untrembling and blessed apparitions in a *pure light, being ourselves pure* . . .[47]

Here the two unities desiderated by Orphic myth, of self and of external world, converge: a relationship – based perhaps on the unforgettable experience of mystic initiation – is implied between the wholeness (and purity) of what is seen in the mystic vision and the wholeness (and purity) of the self (of the mystic initiand) – as if previously fragmented.[48] Further, the other epithets for the apparitions ('simple and untrembling and blessed') are also appropriate for the initiates themselves.[49]

Secret doctrine defines and elevates the initiated group, and its riddling revelation intensifies the initiatory process. But this feature may be adapted to a new function, the unification (we noted) of mythical with impersonal cosmology. This unification (allegorisation) may be propounded by the uninitiated, but also within mystic cult itself, for the fate of the soul may be envisaged as bound up with its passage through the impersonal elements, requiring mystic cosmology.[50] Further, the mystic notion of a *concealed* fundamental truth may be adapted to – or even stimulate – the

---

[45] This has been confirmed by the Strasbourg payrus: Martin and Primavesi 1999, 55–7, 80–2, 283–5, 302–6, 346.

[46] Lacan 1977 (1966), 1–7, and bibliography cited by Seaford 1998b, 136–7.

[47] ἐτελοῦντο τῶν τελετῶν ἣν θέμις λέγειν μακαριωτάτην, ἣν ὠργιάζομεν ὁλόκληροι μὲν αὐτοὶ ὄντες καὶ ἀπαθεῖς κακῶν ὅσα ἡμᾶς ἐν ὑστέρῳ χρόνῳ ὑπέμενεν, ὁλόκληρα δὲ καὶ ἁπλᾶ καὶ ἀτρεμῆ καὶ εὐδαίμονα φάσματα μυούμενοί τε καὶ ἐποπτεύοντες ἐν αὐγῇ καθαρᾷ, καθαροὶ ὄντες . . .

[48] When someone 'comprehends what is said universally, arising from many sensations and being collected into one by reasoning', this is a recollection of the soul's prenatal vision (249b6–c1).

[49] On 'untrembling' see below. Other instances of assimilation of mystic initiates to what they experience: Pl. *Phdr.* 249c7; *Phaedo* 81a; *Symp.* 212a (immortality by means of contemplating the eternal form of beauty); Plut. fr. 178 (pure men in pure places); Proclus *Rep.* 2.108.17–20 Kroll (assimilation to the sacred symbols), 185.3 (mystic apparitions 'full of calm'); Plotin *Enn.* 6.9.11.1–7.

[50] Seaford 1986; Most 1997. Cleanthes compared the cosmos to a huge mystery hall (*SVF* 1. n. 538). On doctrines about nature in mystery cult generally see Burkert 1987, 66–88. Aristot. fr. 15 does *not* mean that mystery cult did not impart doctrine: Riedweg 1987, 8–9; cf. Clem. Alex. *Strom.* 5.71. 1: 'The great mysteries are about all things, where it is no longer left to learn, but to look on and understand nature and things as a whole.'

new cosmological idea (however counter-intuitive) of a concealed impersonal reality *underlying* appearances. Moreover, in the later evidence for
mystic ritual[51] there is revealed a *single object* (e.g. the phallus) associated
with enlightened salvation. The mysteries of Dionysus seem sometimes
to have re-enacted the original divine giving of items associated with the
thiasos (wine, musical instruments),[52] and in the mysteries at Eleusis, where
Demeter gave corn to humankind, the culminating revelation 'amid silence'
of a single ear of corn, was singled out as 'the great and most wonderful
and most perfect epoptic mystery'.[53]

This focus, at the culmination of an anxious process, on a revealed single
object bringing enlightened joy, underlies Plato's explicit description of
the progress of the philosopher as mystic initiation,[54] at the culmination
of which he suddenly sees[55] a single thing for the sake of which were all
his earlier toils (*ponoi*). Just as focus on a revealed symbol belongs to the
mystic transition to eternal happiness, so the perfection (salvation) of the
philosophical self is achieved by contemplation of that single eternal entity
in which the multiplicity of the world is consummated. It is not just the
presentation but also the content of Platonic doctrine that is here influenced
by mystery cult.[56]

Like Plato, presocratic philosophy represents itself as mystic doctrine.
Whether the Milesians did so is unknown, for we possess almost nothing of their own words. Pythagoreanism was organised as a mystic sect.
Heraclitus presented his riddling doctrine in the form of mystic revelation
(9B); and some of the content, too, of his doctrine was derived from mystic
wisdom (12A). Parmenides represents his enlightenment as a kind of mystic
ritual (9B), in which reality is revealed as one invisible unchanging eternal
sphere (B8.43 *sphairē*), an idea influenced perhaps by interpretation of the
concealed sacred sphere (*sphairē*) – revealed in mystic ritual – as a symbol
of unchanging eternity.[57] Similarly the opposite idea – that unity requires

---

[51] On the continuity of the mysteries see Seaford 1996, 40.
[52] Seaford 1984a, 41–4; see further Seaford 1986a, 25–6.
[53] Hipp. *Ref.* 5.8.39; Burkert 1983, 290; cf. the cross-cultural association of (antistructural) liminality
with cultural innovation indicated by Turner 1982, 27–8.
[54] *Symp.* 209e6, etc.; Riedweg 1987, 5–29.
[55] Note e.g. that among the earliest references to the mysteries eternal happiness is for whoever has
'*seen*' these' (*h.Hom.Dem.* 480–2), '*seen* these rites' (Soph. *fr.* 837). The mystic initiator may be called
hierophantēs, i.e. one who makes sacred things *appear*. It is the power of this idea of mystic *vision*
that explains e.g. how Plato can write here of *seeing* what is beyond the corporeal, and at *Rep.* 525
desiderate 'the sight (*thea*) of the nature of numbers' while insisting nevertheless that (in contrast to
commercial practice) they be perceived 'with the mind only', free from 'visible or tangible objects':
cf. 12c n. 130.
[56] A recent detailed argument for such influence, from a different perspective, is Schefer 2001.
[57] Feyerabend 1984, 17–22.

constant change – is according to Heraclitus embodied in the *kykeon*, a special drink drunk in mystic initiation (12B).[58] This suggestion may seem far-fetched, but is supported by various considerations,[59] notably a remarkable parallel between the mystic apparitions in the passage of Plato's *Phaedrus* just quoted, which are 'whole and simple and untrembling and blessed', and Parmenides' description of his One as (B8. 4) 'whole and of a single kind and untrembling and perfect'.[60] We even find the rare word *atremēs* (untrembling) used in the Platonic and Parmenidean passages, as well as by Parmenides of what must be learnt in the goddess' mystic instruction, the 'untrembling heart of well-rounded[61] Truth'.[62] Again like the *Phaedrus* passage, this implies a similarity between subject and object in mystic initiation ('heart' is not a metaphor).[63] Trembling (*tromos*) was a typical feature of the anxiety of mystic initiation before the transition to *hēsuchia* (calm, stillness) reflected in Euripides' *Bacchae*, which also praises 'the life of *hēsuchia*'.[64] Parmenides was said to have been led to *hēsuchia* by the Pythagorean Ameinias.[65]

To conclude, we have identified three factors in the formation of presocratic monism. Firstly Hesiodic and Orphic *myth*, in which the interplay

---

[58] Cf. the Pythagorean *tetraktys*, the abstract 'source of everflowing nature' and 'a cryptic formula, only comprehensible to the initiated': Burkert 1972, 186–7. Even the abstract (Pythagorean) conjunction of limit with unlimit in all things (13B) seems at Pl. *Phileb.* 16c represented as given by the gods as if in mystery cult, like the ear of corn displayed in the Eleusinian mysteries (Schefer 2001, 206–9). This corn seems to have symbolised continuing life (although precious metal (including golden corn: e.g. Plut. *Mor.* 402A) had replaced natural produce as the continuing wealth of temples: 4D).

[59] The *sphairē* was one of the 'symbols of (Dionysiac) initation': Clem. Alex *Protr.* 2.18 (Kern 1922, fr. 34). Johannes Lydus interpreted it as a symbol of the earth (*De Mens.* 4.51). That this kind of interpretation occurred already in the Classical period, as cosmological allegorisation in mystery cult generally certainly did, is suggested by the attribution of poems called *Sphaira* to Orpheus and Musaeus: Kern 1922, 314–15; West 1983, 33. The mystic doctrine about the afterlife called by Plato (*Men.* 81a) a *logos* given by the priests and priestesses about what they handle may refer to interpretation of secret *objects* handled: cf. the context of the same verb at *Protag.* 316d. Cf. the *sphaira* in the underworld on the classical relief at Pausan. 5 20.1–2 and on some of the Locrian reliefs (contemporary with Parmenides, whose mystic journey, like that of the initiates on the Hipponion gold leaf, is to the underworld: 9B n. 58). This Locrian *sphaira* is taken to be a symbol of the cosmic sphere by Zancani-Montuoro 1935, 215–17, comparing Plut. *Mor.* 636E; Macr. *Sat.* 7.16 8. Parmenides may have been the first to call the Earth a sphere: Burkert 1972, 304–5.

[60] Plato's Greek is quoted n. 47 above. Parmenides' is οὖλον μουνογενές τε καὶ ἀτρεμὲς ἠδὲ τέλειον (DK print ἐστι γὰρ οὐλομελές τε καὶ ἀτρεμὲς ἠδ'ἀτέλεστον; but cf. Owen in Furley and Allen 1970, 76–7; 12B n. 104).

[61] *Eukukleos*; cf. *eukuklou* of the sphere at 8.12.

[62] The correlation would be even greater were we to read the transmitted οὐλομελές (whole-limbed) in B8.4 (see n. 60; 12B). We have seen that in Empedocles too the all-embracing sphere combines object and subject.

[63] Note the mystic apparitions (*phasmata*) as 'full of calm' (*galēnēs mesta*) at Proclus *Rep.* 2.185.3.

[64] *Ba.* 389, 600, 607, 621–2, 636; Plut. fr. 178; Seaford 1996, 183, 200–1.

[65] Sotion ap. D. L. 9. 21 (DK 28A1). The obscurity of Ameinias means that this is unlikely to have been a later invention.

between diversity and unity has both a socio-political and a psychological dimension. The socio-political dimension derives from the monarchy as unifying diversity, but historically the transcendence of the monarchy is replaced in this function by the second of our factors, the impersonal power of *money*, making for a cosmology of impersonal all-underlying substance with a tendency to abstraction. The psychological dimension is manifest in the formation of the unified self in the *mysteries*, our third factor, which continues to re-enact personal myth. But the novel development of impersonal cosmology does not result in its complete separation from the tradition of mystery cult and from the mystic formation of the self. There are two factors enabling it to continue to represent itself as mystic wisdom. The first is the mystic tradition of concealing the truth in riddling utterance, which enables impersonal cosmology to represent mystic myth as riddling reference to itself. The second is a *similarity of structure* between on the one hand the concealed symbolic object of mystic revelation and on the other monetary value sublimated as the concealed single substance of impersonal cosmology. As we shall see in the next chapter, the result – detectable in Heraclitus, Parmenides, and Plato – is the unconscious fusion of ideas deriving from mystery cult with the sublimation of monetary value.[66]

It is with its momentous first widespread appearance that monetary value is projected onto the cosmos. Later the conditions in which this projection occurred will pass away. The communality embodied in large-scale animal sacrifice will disappear, or be retained only at the symbolic level as in the Christian eucharist. The economy will eventually be imagined as a self-contained process. But money will in various forms remain, and along with it, also in various forms, the western metaphysical tradition,[67] still influenced, however remotely, by the form in which, together with money, it came into being.

---

[66] For the time being I note only that the single thing revealed in the actual mysteries of Dionysus might be an (initially veiled) separated (castrated?) phallus (nn. 27–9 above), whose psychological transcendence, in Lacanian theory, as a symbol of absence-in-desire has been subjected by Goux (1990, 21–30) to a detailed analogy with the economic transcendence of gold separated off as universal equivalent.

[67] For an attempt to relate the idealism of Berkeley to the development of money in his time see Goux 1990, 107–9. Cf. Sohn-Rethel 1978; Müller 1981; Adorno 1978 (1951), 231 'Metaphysical categories are not merely an ideology concealing the social system; at the same time they express its nature, the truth about it, and in their changes are precipitated those in its most central experiences.'

CHAPTER TWELVE

Heraclitus and Parmenides

A HERACLITUS

'This world-order,[1]' says Heraclitus, 'the same for all things,[2] was not made by god or man, but always was and is and will be an ever-living fire, kindling in measures and going out in measures (*metra . . . metra*)'.[3] Another description of this balanced cycle is 'fire's turnings: first sea, and of sea the half is earth, the half *prēstēr* (lightning or fire) . . . <earth> is dispersed as sea, and is measured to the same formula (*logon*) as existed before it became earth' (B31). *Logos* here clearly means something like measure or formula, making *metra . . . metra* in B30 more specific: the quantities of earth etc. remain the same throughout (and despite) the cycle of transformation. *Logos* of quantity means quantity *expressed as an abstraction* (reckoning or measure, an *account* of quantity). It is accordingly found of a *monetary* account in the fifth century,[4] and probably had this meaning even earlier.[5]

---

[1] *Kosmos*, which occurs here first in this sense, earlier referring to *human* ordering.

[2] τὸν αὐτὸν ἁπάντων, which may be interpolated: KRS 198.

[3] B30; see also B10 '. . . from all things one and from one all things' and B50 '. . . it is wise to agree that all things are one'.

[4] With Heraclitus' 'to the same formula'(εἰς τὸν αὐτὸν λόγον) cf. esp. *IG* I³ 78.8 (423/2 BC) κατὰ τὸν αὐτὸν λόγον; 52A25; 292.2; 476.189 (all fifth century BC); Hdt. 3.142–3. By contrast arithmetical proportion is in Homer expressed in terms that are both concrete and aristocratic: it is said that if both armies were counted, and each group of ten Greeks were to have one Trojan as a wine-pourer, many groups would be left without a pourer (*Il.* 2.123–8).

[5] Cf. *logisdesthai, logismos*; Dilcher 1995, 34: 'Although this meaning is not attested before the 5th century, this is certainly only due to the poetical nature of our evidence that does not deal with such everyday business. There is good reason to assume that *logos* was the appropriate term used in trade for counting and calculating from the earliest times onwards, particularly for taxes and interest rates [cf. Burkert 1972, 439–40 on phrases such as *epitritos logos*, reckoning of one plus a third]. So *logos* is a report about financial affairs, just as one can give an account (*logon didonai*) of one's own behaviour. Calculations were thus another, though particularly suitable field for the sort of detailed exposition that the *logos* gave . . . This usage must be presupposed for several expressions well established in the fifth century where *logos* expresses worth, esteem, and importance. Tyrtaeus B12.1 proves that this is a very old meaning . . . Clearly this expression is taken from financial accounts. Then, something can be said to be worth *logos*, or to be of great or small *logos*. One can have *logos* for something or someone, i.e. pay attention or attach importance to it.' See also Theogn. 417–18; Soph. *Aj.* 477; Hclt. B39.

For Heraclitus all things occur according to the *logos* (B1). And so, given all this, his statement 'all things are an exchange (*antamoibē*) for fire and fire for all things, like goods for gold and gold for goods' (B90) has *two* points of comparison: fire resembles precious metal money as universal equivalent, but also as effecting universal transformation *according to the logos*. The compound *antamoibē* reinforces the idea (implicit in purchase) of an *exact* exchange. It is this constant universal transformation that is expressed in his famous doctrine that all things flow.[6] As the ancient Greek proverb has it, 'when there is money (*argurion*), all things run and are driven' (fr. 216).[7]

In contrast to pre-existing kinds of transaction (sacrificial distribution, redistribution, reciprocity, barter, plunder, etc.) monetary sale seems to be regulated by a necessity that is precisely quantified (1 vase = 5 drachmas) and yet not externally imposed: it is imposed not, on the whole, by tradition (especially not during the novelty of monetisation), nor by deity nor by law nor by force.[8] Where then *does* this unprecedented combination of strict necessity and total precision come from?[9] Because money seems to become the *aim* of economic activity (8D) – rather than the mere *means* that Aristotle later will insist that it should be (12B) – it seems to *drive* the circulation of goods (as well as being their universal equivalent or substrate). This directive power of money, together with its embodiment of number, may make it seem to embody the invisible, impersonal[10] necessity regulating the unified system of universal equivalence between goods and money. 'Invisible harmony is stronger than visible' (B54). Just as the circulation of goods (money-goods-money etc.) is driven by (insubstantial yet all-underlying) money according to a numerical abstraction (*logos*) that may seem embodied in the money, so cosmic circulation (fire-things-fire etc.) is driven by (insubstantial yet all-underlying) fire[11] according to the *logos*,

---

[6] A6, B91. Cf. Douglas 1967, 119: 'Money is essentially something which permeates and flows'; Marx 1973 (1857–8), 196 'To have *circulation*, what is essential is that exchange appear as a process, a fluid whole of purchases and sales. . . . As much, then, as the whole of this movement appears as a social process, and as much as the individual moments of this movement arise from the conscious will and particular purposes of individuals, so much does the totality of the process appear as an objective interrelation, which arises spontaneously from nature.' On the liquid flow of money see Simmel 1978, 495–510.

[7] Epicharmus fr. 216 Kaibel = *Anonyma Dorica* 17 (Kassel–Austin 1 248).

[8] Barter tends to be more regulated by tradition, and is less likely to involve one-to-one equivalence of commodity with abstract value: 8C, 2B (Homer).

[9] On Aristotle's grappling with this question see Meikle 1995.

[10] Hclt. B32 ('One, the only wise, wishes and does not wish to be called Zeus') may mean that this power has the attributes of Zeus (notably intelligence) without being personal.

[11] B64, B66 (cf. 30, 31, 90).

which appears to be embodied in the fire.[12] Both money (6G) and fire have the transcendent power to transform things into their opposite.

All things happen according to the *logos* (B1), and the *logos* is common to all men (B2). 'Listening not to me but to the *logos* it is wise to agree that all things are one' (B50). This conception of *logos* is influenced by the power of money to unify all goods and all men into a single abstract system. But it also includes, appropriately for such a universalist conception, the meaning of *logos* as *verbal* account. The diversity of meaning[13] is less than it seems. *Logos*, whether monetary or verbal, is a unifying abstraction that transcends individual sense data. The verbal *logos* (singular) does not cover all discourse, but shares with its verb *legein* the sense (albeit not always present) of an account that is precise and complete.[14] 'A *logos* aims at conveying something, at expounding a given subject. Its main function is to disclose it and present the matter so that it be understood.'[15] This aspect is common to monetary and verbal account, and explains their designation by the same word (*logos*, account).[16]

A verbal *logos* in which this aspect is especially important is the sacred (*hieros*) *logos* spoken in mystic ritual for the instruction[17] of the initiands. For instance, about the practice of making statues of Hermes with erect phalloi the Pelasgians told a sacred *logos*, says Herodotus, 'which things have been made clear in the mysteries on Samothrace'.[18] Now in Heraclitus' conception of *logos* the mystic *logos* is undoubtedly a crucial component. He presents his *logos* as if it were spoken in the mysteries,[19] and its content

---

[12] KRS 187–8, 199–200; Guthrie 1962, 428–32; cf. West 1971, 124–9.

[13] Characteristic of Hclt. is to regard as one the diverse meanings of what is apparently the same word, even where the diversity is far greater than that of *logos*: e.g. B48.

[14] Boeder 1959, 86, 109–11 (on early Ionian prose). In Homer *logos* occurs only twice, both times in the plural. The earliest instance in the singular is Hesiod's description (*Op.* 106) of his self-contained account (*heteron . . logon*) of how gods and mortals have the same origin (the myth of the races).

[15] Dilcher 1995, 33.

[16] Expressions of the kind 'in the *logos* of prisoners' (ἐν ἀνδραπόδων λόγῳ, Hdt. 3.125) occupy a state intermediate between verbal and enumerative *logos*: despite their concrete variety individuals are assimilated to each other as a group by being all prisoners, but the most abstract form of assimilation as a group is enumeration. In Homer *legein* means to collect or enumerate (recount), e.g. *Od.* 4.451 of *number*.

[17] This is clearly demonstrated by Riedweg 1987, 5–14.

[18] Hdt. 2.51.4; also esp. Pl. *Phd.* 62b2, *Laws*. 870d5, *Ep.* 335a3; *Symp.* 201d1 (with Riedweg 1987, 10–14); *Pap. Derv.* VII 7, XX; West 1983, 9, 13, 248. Hdt. uses 'sacred *logos*' also as a sacred account or explanation (that he does not divulge) of Egyptian ritual practice (2.62.2; 81.9 of practice shared with 'Orphics and Bacchics').

[19] Like Heraclitus', mystic discourse is riddling (9N n. 54; 11B n. 36), and cannot be understood immediately (cf. Hclt. B1): Thomson 1961b, 273–5, confirmed by the discovery of the Derveni Papyrus (Col. XX: Laks and Most 1997, 18–19). Further, the best supplement of *Pap. Derv.* Col. IV 6 (cf. VII 7) is (of Heraclitus) ὅσπερ ἴκελ[α ἱερο]λόγῳ λέγων (or [α ἱερῷ]), 'who speaking things like

resembles mystic doctrine.[20] The mystic/monetary *logos* is another element in the structural similarity between money and mystic doctrine (IIB) that facilitates their subtle synthesis in Heraclitus. Before exploring further this synthesis of the two influences, we must first be more specific about one of them – the influence of mystic doctrine.

What was the instruction imparted by the *logos* spoken in the mysteries? It seems that the *logos* would, perhaps generally, be a *myth*.[21] And yet given the riddling quality frequently attributed to mystic revelation (IIB), it is not unlikely that revelation of hidden meaning in the mystic myth, such as we find in the Derveni Papyrus,[22] occurred also in mystic ritual. The Derveni author, commenting on the Orphic poetic theogony from which we quoted in IIB, says that Orpheus meant to say 'great things in riddles. Indeed he is uttering a sacred *logos*' (Col. VII 6–7). The hidden meaning that the author finds in the myth concerns physical cosmology, so that for instance Zeus is air. Exposition of myth in mystic ritual may have involved physical cosmology.[23] Such reinterpretation would adapt mystic tradition (myth, the idea of a hidden meaning) to a newly depersonalised cosmos. Heraclitus' comparison of fire with gold in respect of universal exchange is associated by Plutarch (*Mor.* 388E–389A) with the transformations of Dionysus 'by a fated intelligence and *logos*' into the cosmological elements, to which the myth of his dismemberment is a riddling reference.

The early Orphic theogony continued with anthropogony. The Titans dismember and eat Dionysus, and are blasted by a thunderbolt. The smoke from the blast deposits soot, from which is created humankind. We have seen that this myth is in part at least as old as the fifth century, corresponds in detail to the ritual of mystic initiation, and may in some sense have been experienced by the initiands (IIB). We return to it here to explore its hidden meaning for the initiand.

First, we must mention certain well known passages of Plato, referring to (1) 'the spoken-of ancient Titanic nature' exhibited by lawless men

---

a sacred discourser (or discourse)', interpreted by Sider in Laks and Most 1997, 135 as meaning that 'Heraclitus . . . writes (prose) just like Orpheus' enigmatic sacred discourse' (Sider also notes that later writers associate the ἱερολόγος (sacred discourser) with riddling discourse, and (133) compares Col. XX 7–8 with Hclt. B17); Janko 2001. Parmenides writes 'here I end the trustworthy *logos* about truth' (B8.50).

[20] Seaford 1986; see now in great detail Schefer 2000.

[21] Pl. *Rep.* 377e6–8; Isokr. *Paneg.* 28; Plut. *Mor.* 422c; Riedweg 1987, 10–17.

[22] Obbink 1997; n. 19 above.

[23] The very obscure Gold Leaf C (Zuntz 1971, 344–54), presumably a mystic text like its companions, combines a mystic eschatological myth with concern with relations between cosmological elements: Seaford 1986, 22. Cosmogony may be imagined as ritual, e.g. in the *Rig Veda* (Hubert and Mauss 1964 (1898, 91–3) or by Pherecydes of Syros.

(*Laws* 701c); (2) the doctrine of 'those around Orpheus' that the soul is being punished for sin by imprisonment in the body;[24] (3) the *logos* told in mysteries that we humans are in a prison, from which we should not escape by suicide (*Phaedo* 62b). Plato's pupil Xenocrates explains this imprisonment as 'Titanic'.[25] As early as the sixth century BC there is reference to men and gods as descended from the Titans (*H. hom. Ap.* 336). Presumably then Plato, or at least Xenocrates, had in mind Orphic-Dionysiac mysteries in which the imprisonment of the soul in the body was explained as arising from transgression by our Titanic ancestors. This transgression was not necessarily their killing of Dionysus, it may have been their rebellion against the gods.[26] But in either case Titanic transgression provides for the initiand a genealogical explanation of the contradiction between his immortality (the Titans are immortal) and his mortal suffering.[27]

In Plato's *Symposium* the *logos* concerning erotic love (201d) given to Socrates by Diotima is carefully structured to correspond to the two main stages of mystic initiation.[28] In the first, Diotima tells of the birth of Eros: as the child of Poverty and Resource, he is a contradictory being – poor and yet resourceful, neither immortal nor mortal, between ignorance and wisdom (2013b1–e5). This story corresponds, in the structure of Diotima's instruction as mystic initiation, to the significant myth told in the ritual.[29] And like the mystic *logos* (known to Plato) of the Titanic dismemberment of Dionysus, it uses genealogy to explain contradiction within humankind between mortal and immortal.[30]

With Zeus swallowing everything and the dismembered Dionysus being reconstituted, Orphic myth enacts the victory of unity over fragmentation in both cosmos and self (11B). But the establishment of the unified identity of the mortal self is, psychoanalytic theory insists, also an irredeemable

---

[24] *Crat.* 400c; cf. *Laws.* 854b, *Ax.* 365e, *Ep.* 335a2; Aristot. fr. 60.

[25] Fr. 20. Dio Chrysostom maintains that we humans are lifelong in prison because we are of the blood of the Titans (30.10).

[26] Seaford 1986.

[27] A different form of the same contradiction is provided in the sixth century AD by Olympiodorus, who, ascribing the myth of Dionysus' dismemberment to Orpheus, finds in it the meaning that we humans are part of Dionysus, for the blasted Titans had eaten his flesh. This may well be neoplatonist theorising: so e.g. West (1983), who objects that what the Titans ate 'cannot easily be imagined to have affected the quality of the puff of smoke that stayed hanging in the air . . .' (165). Quite so, but it is then perhaps too bizarre to have been invented by the civilised Olympiodorus.

[28] 11B. N.B. 209e5–210a2 'Into these erotics, Socrates, even you might be initiated, but as for the complete revelation (*telea kai epoptika*) . . .'

[29] Riedweg 1987, 11–12.

[30] Riedweg 1987, 17 argues in detail that the dismemberment myth has probably influenced ('assoziativ mithineinspielt') the *logos* about Eros. Eros resembles in various respects Socrates – an ideal representation of humankind generally: Riedweg 1987, 14–16.

loss. Accordingly, the Orphic myth of Dionysus ends with the creation of humankind as compounded of immortality and (as punishment for their immortal ancestors' transgression) mortality. Orphic myth explains contradiction, the coexistence of opposites (many–one, mortality–immortality). Mystery cult may unite opposites[31] – implicitly in the liminal inversions involved in the rite of passage (e.g. life–death, human–animal), and explicitly as mystic doctrine: the fifth-century Olbian plates (6A) even contain, along with the inscriptions 'Orphic'[32] and 'Dio(nysus)', *abstract* oppositions, detached from myth: 'life death life', 'peace war', 'truth falsehood'.[33] This phenomenon is essential for understanding Heraclitus.[34] Presenting his doctrine as a mystic *logos*, and yet despising the mysteries as actually practised (B14, B15), he seems to take to (or beyond) its limit, and to systematise, the abstraction (from myth) of the mystic unity of opposites. His claim that 'immortals (are) mortals, mortals immmortals',[35] for instance, coheres with his account of death as a transformation of the immortal fire that inheres in the soul.[36]

In the world inhabited by Heraclitus the power of genealogy is being replaced by the power of money. Just as the previous history of an object (in gift exchanges or as originating with a god) that mattered so much in Homer is less important than its monetary value, so the destiny of a person becomes determined less by his descent, and more by the new universal network of impersonal exchanges regulated by monetary *logos*.[37] Accordingly the contradiction (notably between mortality and immortality) that in mystic doctrine is inferred from mythical genealogy is for Heraclitus inherent in universal, impersonal circulation. This systematic abstraction of contradiction, detached from myth, arises from fusion of the traditional mystic *logos* with the new monetary *logos*. The fusion is facilitated by the

---

[31] Seaford 1996, 43–4. Note also the mystic *makarismos* at Pi. fr. 137a, which associates the *end* (of life) with a god-given *beginning* (*archa*).

[32] Or 'Orphics': Zhmud (1992) argues for the reading ὀρφικοί rather than West's ὀρφικ().

[33] West 1983, 17–19. Further, Vinogradov (1991) thinks to detect on plate 3 σῶμα (body) before ψυχή (soul), but this seems doubtful. Compare the use of juxtaposed antithetical words or phrases in mystic formulae: Seaford 2003b.

[34] The striking similarity between the Olbian inscriptions and various fragments of Heraclitus (B8, 10, 50, 51, 57, 60, 61, 62, 67, 76, 77, 80, 88, 91, 103, 111, 126) arises not from the influence of Heraclitus' book on Black Sea cult, but rather from the influence of the widespread phenomenon of mystery cult on Heraclitus. And even if the Olbian cult was influenced by Heraclitus, the influence could be explained only by an existing affinity between mystic and Heraclitus' doctrine.

[35] B62; cf. B77, B88.

[36] B36 (cf. 31, 76, 90), 25, 26, 27, 63, 88 (cf. Sext. Emp. *Pyrrh. Hyp*. 3. 230), 98, 118, 136, A16.129–30; KRS 203–8; Guthrie 1962, 476–82; Seaford 1986, 14–20.

[37] Resentment of money or wealth as confusing aristocratic descent is manifest in Theognis (8DG). Genealogy is negated by the mystic formula 'I am the child of earth and starry heaven': Zuntz 1971.

similarity of the two kinds of *logoi*, each denoted by the same word, each a precise and yet comprehensive account. In B1 Heraclitus presents 'this *logos*' in terms of a *logos* heard in mystic ritual,[38] and in the next sentence writes that 'all things occur according to this *logos*'. This suggests that Heraclitus does not entirely distinguish his 'heard' verbal (as if mystic) *logos* from *logos* as the measure according to which (we saw earlier) cosmological change occurs.

Further, the two *logoi* resemble each other also in content. The contradictions that we have seen embodied in Orphic mystic theogony – between the many and the one, between mortality and immortality – are central also to Heraclitus' cosmology. His cosmos is an immortal fire, which is transformed into everything else, and so is both one and many. And this immortal fire inheres in the soul, so that death is merely one of its transformations. Just as in mystic doctrine the soul circulates through the cosmological elements,[39] so for Heraclitus the fiery soul circulates through the cosmological elements, with the death of one element as the birth of another.[40] Our two contradictions now inhere in the universal circulation of fire. This transition of the same contradictions from mystic genealogy to the universal cosmology of Heraclitus is effected by the influence of the universal circulation of money.[41] Like Heraclitean fire and the mystic soul, monetary value is a single entity that in a sense[42] persists (albeit transformed) through all exchanges. Just as the individual is mortal and yet contains in his soul the immortal fire that persists beyond the transformation that we call his death, so money contains the permanent value that persists beyond its transformation into goods. Heraclitus compares the universal exchangeability of fire with that of (immortal) gold,[43] and says of the *thumos* (anger or spirit) that 'what it desires it buys at the price of soul' (*psuchē*) (B85). Another possible factor in Heraclitus' choice of 'ever-living fire' as cosmic substance is the association of fire, in Eleusinian mystic ritual, with the continuation

---

[38] N. 19 above.

[39] IIB n. 50. It is not impossible that this mystic doctrine has itself been influenced by the circulation of money.

[40] B36, 76, 80.

[41] Even the mystic circulation of the soul may be envisaged as a form of payment (note its payment of a 'penalty': 14D n. 76), albeit for its ancient offence as a Titan: Seaford 1986.

[42] The sense may seem obscure. Heraclitus may not have had any precise notion of fire as 'substrate'. But B30, B31, B50, B67, Aristot. *De Caelo* 298b29ff., *Metaph.* 984a7 (=A5), taken together, certainly indicate persistence of some kind, *pace* Stokes 1971, 103–5.

[43] B90. Although silver may in Heraclitus' lifetime have in Ephesus become more common as coinage than electrum ('gold' to the Greeks) and gold, and was because lower in value more suited to universal exchange, he uses gold in the simile because of its supreme embodiment of immortality and purity.

of life out of death.[44] There are indications that gold, too, was associated with immortality not just in literary texts[45] but also in mystery cult.[46] And in the Eleusinian mysteries (personified) wealth was of central importance, albeit of the old agricultural kind.[47] Heraclitus belonged to the Ephesian royal family, which held the priesthood of Demeter Eleusinia (A2). Mystic symbols may embody cosmology (11B): for instance, the *kukeon*, the sacred drink of the Eleusinian mysteries, embodied for Heraclitus his cosmological principle that unity involves constant movement (B125).

And so Heraclitean fire is formed from the fusion of mystic cosmological projection of the soul with the cosmological projection of all-transforming but impersonal money. A possible factor in this fusion is the assimilation of death to the loss involved in commercial exchange that is in fact already hinted at in Homer in Achilles' speech (2D), and found in Athenian tragedy – for instance in the Aeschylean image of Ares the gold-changer (8B, 14C).

Another factor is that money, like mystic ritual and doctrine, seems to have the transcendent power to unite opposites of various kinds (6G). The unlimited power of money to transform anything into anything may seem like a transcendent power to unite opposites. Further, one of the oppositions united by money is that between the two parties to a monetary transaction. Although monetary *logos* unites all things and all men, monetary purchase involves (*qua* monetary purchase) a historically unprecedented mutual absolute egotism: each party is seen to desire his maximum advantage to a degree beyond all other kinds of transaction (such as gift-exchange).[48] The *logos* of money makes the transaction possible by uniting the opposed parties. This paradox[49] is reflected in the following words of Heraclitus.

---

[44] Pl. *Phaedr.* 250bc (with Riedweg 1987, 47–52); Plutarch fr. 178; Lactant. *Inst. Ep.* 16. 7; Himerius *Or.* 29.1; Hippol. *Ref. Omn. Haer.* 5.8.40; Clem. Alex. *Paed.* 1.26. 2; cf. e.g. Firm. Mat. *Err. Prof.* 22. Apul. *Met.* 6.2; 11.6, 23. As in the mysteries (Schefer 2000, 51–2; Seaford 1996, 195–7), Heraclitean fire takes the form of thunder and lightning (B64). As the mystic initiate may feel his soul assimilated to the sacred symbol (11B, esp. n. 49), so for Heraclitus the soul should be assimilated to fire (14B nn. 33, 34).

[45] 2C; also *PMG* 541.4, 592, 842.7; Sappho fr. 204 L–P.

[46] The famous leaves on which the mystic formulae are inscribed are of gold; also Pi. *Ol.* 2.72–4; Soph. *OC* 1050–3; Antig. Car. *Mir.* 12(141). Gold blazing like fire: Pi. *Ol.* 1.1–2.

[47] And at Pi. *Ol.* 2.55 it is associated (in an allusion to the Eleusinian mysteries) with (fire)light. Cf. Emped. B132 (implied association of wealth with light in a mystic *makarismos*).

[48] Cf. 10B; cf. 14A. This point is not affected by the possibility that gift-exchange may in fact involve egotistical calculation (of return) in the long run (e.g. Bourdieu 1977, 171). What matters for my argument is how the transaction *appears*. Monetary transactions, though sometimes embedded in lasting personal relations, nevertheless permit an increase in the convenience and number of one-off, unritualised, instantaneous exchanges which cannot conceal their mutual egotism, whereas gift-exchange and (to a lesser extent) barter (8C, 14A) are more associated with personal relations.

[49] Cf. Sohn-Rethel 1978, 42–3: 'What the commodity owners *do* in an exchange relation is practical solipsism – irrespective of what they think and say about it . . . In exchange the action is social, the mind is private.'

They do not understand how in being at variance it agrees with itself; backward-stretching *harmonia* as of bow and lyre.[50]

It must be known that war is communal (*xunos*)[51] and conflict is justice, and that all things happen according to conflict and necessity. (B80 (cf. A22))

Reciprocal hostility produces alternating injustice, and this (under the control of the state) is reflected in Anaximander (10B); but both hostile and friendly reciprocity tend to be replaced by the monetary transaction, which is, as in the Heraclitean paradox,[52] *itself simultaneously* conflict (as mutual absolute egotism) *and* communal justice (being accepted by both parties and governed by the *logos*),[53] as well as according to necessity. Further, *kata . . . chreōn* ('according to necessity') in the Heraclitus fragment,[54] like the cosmic process *kata to chreōn* in Anaximander (10C), may imply the idea of debt. The idea of cosmic necessity is in Homer associated with the ancient economic mode of sacrificial distribution (Moira: 3A), in the monetised world of Anaximander and Heraclitus with debt (*chreōn*), before becoming in Parmenides mere compulsion (B8.30 *Anangkē*). And once again, as we observed on Anaximander, the importance of *chreōn* (and *logos*), where we might have had *nomos* (law), counts against the exclusively political theories of the genesis of philosophy held by Vernant and Lloyd (9AB). Both conflict and the *logos*, which go together, are communal (*xunos*: B2, 50, 113, 114).

Aiōn (life, time) is a child at play, moving pieces in a game; sovereignty belongs to the child' (B52).

In a board game absolute conflict between two parties making alternative moves (cf. B88) with symbols is contained and defined by agreed absolute rules (independently of the will or identity of the players):[55] here again we may sense the effect of the monetary transaction on Heraclitus'

---

[50] B51; also B8, B10; Osborne 1987, 149–50.

[51] This adapts *Il.* 18.309 *xunos enualios* etc. (where the communality of war is *reciprocity* – it kills the killer, *ktaneonta katekta* – not unlike the communality in the mutual egotism of the monetary transaction); Archil. fr. 110 W. The power of genealogy is being replaced by the power of money, and 'war is the father of all things' (B53).

[52] Lloyd, being without an economic perspective (9B), is bound to be puzzled by this paradox: 'in several fragments he stresses the importance of law and custom among men, which contrasts strangely, to my mind, with the cosmological notion of the universality of War and Strife . .': 1966, 222.

[53] And so 'to god all things are fine and good and just, but men assume that some things are just and others unjust' (B102). Cf. e.g. Macfarlane 1985, 72 'it is money, markets, and market capitalism that eliminate absolute moralities. Not only is every system throughout the world equally valid, as Pascal noted, but *within* every system, whatever is, is right.'

[54] The ms. has the odd χρεώμενα.

[55] The only other occurrence of 'sovereignty' (βασιλ-) in Hclt. is of conflict (B53). D. L. 9.2–3 makes Hclt. seem to associate politics with a children's game: Kurke 1999, 268.

conception of the cosmos.[56] The fundamental idea of the *unity* of opposites, inherited by Heraclitus from mystic wisdom, becomes the rule-governed, harmonious *conflict* of opposites.

Finally, we should return briefly to the comparative perspective. The advent of literacy, it has been argued, has a profound effect on cognition generally. In particular, the practice of writing lists, so common in ancient Mesopotamia, tended to produce a conception of things in general, even the world as a whole, in terms of a list (6D). While accepting this point, I insist that the crucial factor making for this conception is the redistributive economy of ancient Mesopotamia (4A), which required those lists of *goods* that are the earliest and by far the commonest surviving documents.

I would also briefly suggest that the paratactic aggregative perspective characteristic of Homeric and Hesiodic poetry should also be understood in relation to the premonetary economy. This perspective is pervasively manifest: (a) in actual catalogues or lists (of places, gifts, generations of men, goods used in payment, etc.); (b) in the paratactic style, in which clauses (therefore often events) are loosely added, like beads on a necklace, rather than – as frequently in later Greek literature – unified by syntactical hierarchy; (c) in the aggregate of psychological events and entities envisaged in physical terms, without the transcendent unity implied by our words 'mind' or 'soul', as well as in the aggregate of corporeal entities without the transcendent (not merely aggregative) unity implied by our word 'body'.[57]

The particularity of this Homeric and Hesiodic perspective is brought out by comparison with later texts. To see the world as a mere aggregate is for Heraclitus the opposite of what is required. Hence his hostility to the 'much learning (*polumathiē*)' that 'does not teach understanding' (B40),

---

[56] Though this is far from exhausting the significance of the fragment: see Kurke 1999, 263–4; Osborne 1987, 156–8; Schefer 2000, 47–8 (mystery cult): cf. Heraclitus (A1) playing knucklebones (sacred objects of the Dionysiac mysteries) with children in the temple: cf. 6A n. 40; Schefer 2000, 73 n. 258.

[57] It is admitted even by Williams 1993, 23, in his criticism of Snell 1953, that there are in Homer no 'dualistic distinction between soul and body' and no words corresponding to the Platonic *psuchē* and our 'body'. Williams correctly insists that the Homeric individual acts, decides, has his corpse ransomed, and has 'the unity needed to have thoughts and experiences', but must stop short of claiming that there are Homeric *concepts* of 'body' and (the unified interiority of) 'soul' or 'mind'. It is this absence of concepts (or at the very least, of words) that interests me. Why are the dualistic distinction between soul and body, and the Heraclitean (on B45 and B115 see 12B) and the Platonic (comprehensive unified interiority) ideas of the soul, all inconceivable in Homer? Feyerabend 1993, 170–87 attempts to show that this is not a merely technical matter (but rather the expression of a 'coherent way of life') by pursuing Snell's analogy with visual art (175 'Archaic pictures are paratactic aggregates not hypotactic systems').

and to Homer and Hesiod: Homer fails to understand a riddle based on an invisible antithetical reality (B56; B42), and Hesiod fails to recognise the unity of day and night (B57). To understand the world is to understand its unifying principle.[58] Just as any list of goods in a monetary economy can be transformed into, or totalled up as, money according to a *logos* – for instance the items listed in the Artemis temple at Ephesus not long before the birth of Heraclitus (5A) – so for Heraclitus the world is an ever-living fire that is transformed from and into everything else according to the *logos*. Money deprives the list of its cognitive comprehensiveness, not only because it underlies and unites the aggregate without belonging to it but also because it is, unlike any list, unlimited.

Along with this fundamental distinction go several others. The unifying principle, not being merely another item in the aggregate, seems to belong to a separate kind of reality: fire we would call (although Heraclitus does not have the vocabulary) the substratum of all other things, and the *logos* (at least partially) abstract. Implicit are the systematic distinctions, which are not even implicit in Homer, between essence and appearance and between abstract and concrete.[59] These distinctions are crucial for the Heraclitean idea of the soul, which, again in complete contrast to Homer, participates in the invisible unlimit of fire and the communality of the *logos* – but this topic I postpone to the next section. Suffice it here to point to another contrast – in *style*, between the aggregative parataxis of Homer and the antithetical juxtapositions (oxymora) of Heraclitus (and of tragedy: 14DE).[60] To be sure, Heraclitus may form these juxtapositions into an aggregate, but only in order to show the basic abstract principle common to them all, for instance[61] 'God is day night, winter summer, war peace, surfeit hunger, and is transformed as fire, when it is mixed with spices, is named according to the scent of each' (B67). Here I merely report the attempt in Herodotus (1.153) to envisage from the old redistributive perspective the new kind of (monetary) transaction: king Cyrus describes the Greek practice of buying and selling in the marketplace (unknown in Persia) as 'on oath deceiving each other': the oxymoron (*omnuntes exapatōsi*) embodies the tension between the absolute conflict and the formal agreement of the monetary transaction. The novelty of the formal agreement can be understood by the Persian only in the traditional form of the oath.

[58] B10, B30, B32, B50, B89, etc.
[59] It will become more explicit in Parmenides' warning to use *logos* rather than the 'habit of much experience' and the senses (B7.4–5).
[60] See further Seaford 2003b.   [61] Similarly B88, B111, B126.

A similar cognitive shift may have contributed to the first Greek map of the world (to replace lists of places), Anaximander's,[62] and to the sixth-century Ionian invention of history: a single comprehensive account, a *logos*, replaces lists of events or of generations. This is not of course to claim that the list disappears from Greek texts. In a few such lists we may feel the influence, even if indirect or negative, of money: compare for instance the carnivalesque lists of good things in Athenian comedy, evocative of (premonetary) ancient utopia,[63] with the Socratic method of replacing a list with a definition (e.g. Pl. *Tht.* 146d). 'There is' says Socrates, 'only one right currency (*nomisma orthon*), for which we ought to exchange all these things (pleasures and pains) – intelligence. And if all our buying and selling is done for and with this, then we shall have real courage, real self-control and real justice; and true virtue as a whole is that which is accompanied by intelligence, whether or not pleasures and fears and all other such things be added or subtracted' (*Phd.* 69a).

B   THE DEVELOPMENT OF ABSTRACT BEING

Among the factors shaping the single material principle of the Milesians we identified on the one hand the formation of the unitary self out of internal fragmentation (expressed also in creation myth) and on the other the emergence of a single entity (money) uniting the multiplicity of goods (11B). The combination of these two factors is favoured by their similarity of structure. Both monetary value and the mind are abstractions, embodied and yet in a sense invisible. Indeed each is a single controlling *invisible* entity uniting the multiplicity of which it in a sense consists.

Despite this similarity, the two factors are contradictory in the respect that whereas the unitary self is personal, it is precisely the impersonality of money that makes for the Milesian depersonalisation of the cosmos. We noted in 11B various manifestations of the contradiction. Another manifestation is the contradiction we noted (10D) between the impersonality of Anaximander's *apeiron* and its 'steering' of all things. Just like monetary value and like the mind, the *apeiron* is an abstract imperceptible entity exercising unifying control over the concrete multiplicity of which it in a sense consists.[64]

That the mind (as well as money) is a factor in Anaximander's imagining of his *apeiron* is a hypothesis strengthened by the fact that with his

---

[62] KRS 104–5. Like his *apeiron*, a map of the world is an all-embracing abstraction.
[63] Wilkins 2000, 110–30.
[64] 'Hail the world's soul and mine', says Ben Jonson's Volpone to his gold.

successor Anaximenes the connection between mind and material principle becomes explicit. What seems to be the only surviving sentence of Anaximenes is 'as our soul (*psuchē*), being air, holds us together, so does *pneuma* (wind/breath) and air enclose (*periechei*) the whole cosmos'. This probably does not preserve all Anaximenes' precise wording,[65] but there is no good reason to doubt the content. *Periechei* is also used by Aristotle when he states that Anaximander's *apeiron* encloses and steers all things.

The expression of abstract being in terms of the mind continues, in various forms, with Xenophanes and Heraclitus. Xenophanes' non-anthropomorphic god is both in some sense identical with the universe and envisaged in terms of all-pervasive subjectivity: 'all of him sees, all of him thinks, all of him hears', and 'without effort he shakes all things by the thought of his mind'. If this abstract unity was thought of as in some sense underlying the concrete multipicity of the world, that perhaps is why 'seeming has been constructed over everything' (10D).

For Heraclitus the cosmos is fire, and fire directs all change according to the abstract *logos*. This controlling abstract *logos* is not immediately or easily understood.[66] Nature likes (as in mystery cult)[67] to hide itself (B123), and invisible harmony is stronger (or better) than visible (B54). The senses may be necessary for access to the *logos*,[68] but are insufficient:[69] soul (*psuchē*)[70] or mind (*nous*)[71] is also needed. We would say that what is required is reason, that the abstract *logos* is to be grasped by our mental capacity to abstract. But for Heraclitus, without such vocabulary, the invisible all-controlling *logos* is somehow present within fire, and fire and the *logos* within the (invisible all-controlling) soul.[72] 'You would not discover the boundaries of soul, even by travelling along every path: so deep a *logos* does it have'.[73] 'Of soul there is *logos* increasing itself' (B115). This unlimit of the soul

---

[65] For the indications for and against direct quotation see KRS 159; cf. Guthrie 1962, 131–2; Anaximen. A23.

[66] B1, 2, 17, 72; cf. also B19, 28, 34, 40 (with 41), 56, 57, 70, 72, 73, 78, 79, 87, 93, 95, 102, 104, 108, 110.

[67] Cf. Philo *Fug.* 179 'uninitiated in nature that loves to conceal itself' (φύσεως τῆς κρύπτεσθαι φιλούσης ἀμύητοι).

[68] B55 'The things of which there is seeing, hearing, apprehension, these I prefer.'

[69] B54 'invisible harmony is stronger (better?) than visible'; B56 'men are deceived in their knowledge of visible things . . .'; cf. B41 with B108; also perhaps B46.

[70] B107 'eyes and ears are bad witnesses for men if they have barbarian souls' (i.e. souls that do not understand their language, or the *logos*).

[71] B40, 41, 104, 114.

[72] 12A; B36, 117, 118: KRS 203–4. B117 and B118 imply that it is its fiery component that makes the soul wise.

[73] B45; cf. the tragic self at Aesch. *Supp.* 407–9. Unlimited too may be 'the one divine' (not necessarily divine *law*) of B114, for it is said to be 'as powerful as it desires and sufficient for all and more than sufficient' (I adopt the translation of Guthrie 1962, 425 and KRS 211; cf. Mourelatos 1965).

derives from being a portion of the vast cosmic fire,[74] or rather from the unlimit of the soul's circulation through the cosmological elements (12A) as fire, which is itself the projection of money unlimitedly accumulated in unlimited circulation (8F). And yet the soul, again like money, does contain measure, *logos*. Heraclitus' notion of a single all-controlling but abstract-invisible *logos*, present in world and in soul, is formed out of the mutual reinforcement between on the one hand the single all-controlling abstract-invisible *logos* of money and on the other the invisible unitary self, whose interior control over multiplicity by abstraction from sensation permits its grasp of the abstract *logos* out there in the world. Hence perhaps the possibility of the profound individualism of 'I sought myself' (B101).

The Heraclitean privileging of abstraction, which goes beyond the Milesians and Xenophanes, is itself taken further by Parmenides of Elea,[75] with the result that the epistemological division it implies, between the objects of mental abstraction and of the senses, becomes both explicit and absolute. According to Parmenides mortals have erroneously applied to what exists words of coming-to-be and perishing, being and not being, changing place and changing colour (B8.38–41). The goddess warns against using sight and hearing: 'judge rather by *logos* the contentious refutation spoken by me' (B7). The senses convey the error that what exists is multiple and changing. Really it is one, invariant in time and space (eternal, unchanging, unmoving, homogeneous), self-sufficient, limited.

The antithesis between Heraclitus and Parmenides reflects the division between the concrete multiplicity of goods and the unitary abstract value of money. Whereas Heraclitus focuses on the *relation* between concrete multiplicity and the unitary abstract *logos*, with Parmenides withdrawal from the concrete reaches the stage of focusing (in his Way of Truth) only on what is abstracted, with radical epistemological consequences. How are we to explain this opposition? In order to maintain its essential change-ability into all concrete things (circulation), money must, paradoxically, maintain unchanging unitary abstract identity. These are the opposing

---

[74] 'Probably the thought here is . . . of the soul being a representative portion of the cosmic fire – which, compared with the individual, is obviously of vast extent. Thus it could be conceived as an adulterated fragment of the surrounding cosmic fire, and so as the possessor in some degree of that fire's directive power': KRS 203–4.

[75] Elea (Velia, Hyele) was founded *c.* 540–535 BC by the Phokaians, who were among the very first Greeks to mint coinage, built their city wall with money from Tartessus, and had tried to buy the Oinoussai islands from Chios (Hdt. 1.163–7). Parmenides was born probably *c.* 515 BC. Elea began minting coins plentifully at some point before 500 BC, and produced fractional coinage (in the lifetime of Parmenides; Williams 1992, 3–9, 136–42; Kim 1994, 53), as had its parent city before it.

complementary essences by which money is constituted.[76] Heraclitus'
world is modelled on the former (permanent transformation, harmony
of opposites), Parmenides' on the latter (permanent, self-sufficient abstract
unity).[77] The abstraction of monetary value is in Parmenides intensified
by being imagined in a sphere of its own, abstracted even from circulation.
The One is entirely abstracted from the many, identity from change, abstract from concrete. The transcendence inherent in monetary value, the
effacement of its genesis in the circulation of commodities, is in Parmenides
perfected. If, as seems likely, Parmenides knew of the ideas of Heraclitus,[78]
then we can say that the tendency of each presocratic to oppose his predecessor[79] takes with Parmenides the form of a shift from one of these closely knit
opposite aspects to the other.[80] Another possible factor is that Parmenides,
who may have been born a generation after Heraclitus,[81] experienced –
with the further development of coinage – more pervasive monetary
abstraction.

But these factors are far from certain. And in fact my argument depends
neither on the relative chronology of the thinkers nor on their knowing the
ideas of other thinkers. Rather another, more promising historical factor
will emerge from discussion of the one important feature of Parmenides'
One that remains to be explained. It is *limited*.

---

[76] This complementarity may have roots in a similar fundamental complementarity of premonetary
society. Godelier 1999 (1996) explores, in the gift-giving societies analysed by Mauss, 'the relations
between the sphere of sacred things that are not exchanged and that of valuables or monies which
enter into exchanges of gifts or exchanges of commodities' (37), and maintains that the development
of money in these societies depended on the principle that 'in order for there to be movement,
exchange, there had to be things that were kept out of exchange, stable points around which the
rest – humans, goods, services – might revolve and circulate' (166–7). Both gift-giving and monetised
societies contain 'realities which are in a way withheld from exchange while at the same time enabling
exchange to take place' (29). 'Money is . . both swept along by the movement of commodities and
immobilised as a point around which all this machinery begins to revolve and whose volume and
speed it measures' (29); cf. esp. 33, 35–7, 70, 164–5.

[77] The transition from (Heraclitus' quasi-mystic doctrine of) contradiction into its opposite in
(Parmenides' mystic vision of) the self-sufficient oneness of being reappears in Plato structured
as the preliminary and final stages of mystic initiation (*Symp.*: esp. 209e5–210a2; Riedweg 1987,
5–29): whereas the preliminary stage emphasises *contradiction* (within Eros, between ugliness and
beauty, mortal and immortal, resourcefulness and neediness, and (he being a philosopher) ignorance
and wisdom), the final mystic vision is, it is emphasised, of the *unequivocally* beautiful, eternally
unchanging, incorporeal, not 'something that exists in something else', but 'it in itself, with itself,
of one form', in which other beautiful things participate – coming into being and perishing while
it remains exactly the same (211a1–b5), 'the beautiful itself, unalloyed, pure, unmixed' (211e1).

[78] Cf. below on Hclt. B91 and Parmen. B4, and n. 103.   [79] Lloyd 1987, ch. 2; 1996, 21–4.

[80] This means that the shift is, although from one opposite to another, in a sense very slight, especially
if Finkelberg (1988) is right to conclude, on the basis of B8.53–61, that the 'visualisation [of Being]
by Parmenides as cosmic Fire links it with the material principle of the current form of monism'.

[81] KRS 181–2, 240.

It is motionless within the limits of great bonds, without beginning or ceasing, since coming-to-be and perishing have wandered very far away, and true belief has thrust them off. Remaining the same in the same, it lies on its own, and fixed thus remains (or 'will remain'), for strong Necessity holds it in the bonds of limit, which keeps it in on every side, because[82] it is right that what is should not be endless; for it is not lacking – if it were, it would lack everything. (B8 26–33)

It is limited because it is unchanging (27 'since'), and because it is not lacking (33 'for') – i.e. because it is self-sufficient. But why does limitedness follow from unchangingness and self-sufficiency? Because, it has been cogently argued, the limit here (*peiras*) is not spatial, but 'the mark of *invariancy*'[83] in both time and (42–9) space. On the other hand, the spatial language seems to be more than a mere metaphor.[84]

Light on this problem is shed by realisation of the importance of money in shaping this ontology. Like Parmenides' One, monetary value is homogeneous (6B), and has to be imagined as invariant in space and time, even when not abstracted from circulation (12C). But the sublimation of monetary value *abstracted from circulation* will be not only invariant in space and time but also *self-sufficient* and *limited* – that is to say it will have, in natural combination, all four of the features that are somewhat unnaturally combined in the logic of Parmenides.

Understanding this natural combination returns us to the problem of *why* value is abstracted from circulation. The historical advance of monetary abstraction, which must throughout its circulation embodied in coinage or its imagined transformation into commodities nevertheless remain one and the same, is not enough to explain the *paradox* that monetary abstraction is separated, in the imagination, from the circulation by which it is in fact given value. *Ousia* (wealth, being) is imagined with the *qualities* of monetary value (abstract, unitary, homogeneous, unchanging) but without the (exchange) *relation* by which monetary value is constituted. The effort of imagination required for this separation is perhaps reflected in the statement that 'coming-to-be and perishing have wandered *very far away*, and true belief has *thrust* them off' (my emphasis).

The factor powerful enough to enforce this unconscious separation is likely to be *ideological*. And the likelihood is increased by the statement that

---

[82] For 'because' (rather than 'therefore') as the meaning of οὕνεκεν, as generally in Homer, see Owen 1986 (1960), 19 n. 65.

[83] Owen 1986 (1960), 20.

[84] Esp. 31 'keeps it in on every side', 42–3 'but since there is a furthest limit, it is perfected, like the bulk of a sphere well-rounded on every side'.

it is Justice (*Dikē*) who firmly holds what is, preventing it from coming to be or perishing (B8.14–16). Operative is the ideal of the economic self-sufficiency of the individual (or of the household, the economic unit to which he belongs),[85] of autonomous seclusion from the uncertainty or vulgarity of the unlimited and universal circulation of precious metal as coinage.

In his convincing argument for the importance of the concept of class in understanding ancient Greek society, de Ste Croix sees a crucial opposition between those who by virtue of their command over the labour of others were *free* to lead a civilised life (the 'propertied class') and those who had to work to maintain themselves, and he cites in illustration the remark of Aristotle that 'it is the mark of an *eleutheros* ('free man', 'gentleman') not to live for the benefit of another'.[86] Such freedom I would describe as imagined self-sufficiency, and adduce another passage of Aristotle, the beginning of his *Politics*, where he states as a general assumption (manifest also in his conception of god) that 'self-sufficiency is an end and what is best'. As exemplifying this general principle Aristotle has in mind here the polis, for the individual separated from the polis is – he has to point out – not self-sufficient. But we also find later in *Politics* the implication that the individual household should be self-sufficient (for this is natural) to the limited extent possible (1256a14–1258b6): this follows after all from his general principle.[87] Hence perhaps the ambivalence of Aristotle on coinage, as required for communality but unnatural.[88]

What I am suggesting is that fundamental to the process by which Parmenides arrives at the idea of a single, self-sufficient, impersonal (but with hints of personhood: 11B), unchanging, abstract sphere as all that exists is the ideology of economic self-sufficiency, reinforced and made abstract by the all-pervasive abstraction of money. A similar process is found in the *Timaeus*, in which the aristocratic Plato reasons thus. The creator of the universe used two fundamental principles: one is that the homogeneous is better than the unlike (33b7),[89] the other that 'being self-sufficient it would be better than lacking anything' (33d). The result is a universe that is – though personal – spherical and all there is, and so has no need of eyes and ears and organs of eating and breathing and hands and feet, with 'all that he suffers and does occurring in and by himself'. It is 'one and solitary, but

---

[85] Found in e.g. Hesiod and Aristotle: Seaford 1994a, 200–2.
[86] de Ste Croix 1981, 90, 116–17; Aristot. *Rhet.* 1367a32.
[87] See also *EN* 1097b6–16 (n. 90) below); Seaford 1994a, 201–2.
[88] *EN* 1133ab; *MM* 1194a; *Pol.* 1257b.
[89] Plato praises coinage as making homogeneous the being of things of whatever kind: *Laws.* 918a (12C).

because of its virtue able to be (or converse) with itself, needing no other, a sufficient acquaintance and friend for itself'.⁹⁰

Value separated from circulation is self-identical: the value of goods so separated is neither monetary nor as barter but inheres entirely in themselves as use-value. The economic self-sufficiency of the individual consists in the self-identity of the value of his goods. Money, on the other hand, is valuable only in payment or exchange. However, the integrative interpersonal power that is monetary value depends, we remember (10C), on disguising itself as an abstract *thing* independent of all interpersonal relations – self-identical and yet all-pervasive, and so easily imagined as present even in goods separated from circulation. As we noted a-propos of the unmoving self-sufficient deity of Xenophanes, money may, by dispensing with reciprocity, itself paradoxically seem self-sufficient (10D). Although valuable only in payment or exchange, it can paradoxically only be possessed – together with its imagined virtues of self-sufficiency, unchangingness, and abstract fundamentality – by being *withheld* from payment and exchange, as 'a mere phantom of real wealth'.⁹¹ And so idealised economic self-sufficiency may easily incorporate the imagined virtues of money.⁹²

The ideology of self-sufficiency sheds further light on the emphasised *limitedness* that Parmenides infers from unchangingness and from selfsufficiency. As we have seen, this limitedness includes, puzzlingly, the sense of a *spatial* limit. Value abstracted from (unlimited) circulation is, inasmuch as it expresses the economic self-sufficiency of the household, limited by the needs of the household. Aristotle contrasts natural wealth acquisition that belongs to household management, and that he approves of as having a limit, with the limitlessness of money-making.⁹³ And this limitedness of the household may easily be imagined as spatial, as for instance in its sublimation in Philolaus' cosmogony, in which the surrounded unlimited is drawn into the limits of a central hearth (13B). Being, for Parmenides, 'is all inviolate' (B8.48 *asulon*).⁹⁴

---

⁹⁰ (34b5–8). Aristotle (*EN* 1097b6–16) regards the complete good as self-sufficient but wonders how far the self-sufficient unit should extend (e.g. parents' parents?), and discusses the view, held by some, that happy, self-sufficient people do not need friends (1169b2–10).

⁹¹ Cf. Marx 1973 (1857–8), 234 on money: 'If I want to cling to it, it evaporates in my hand to become a mere phantom of real wealth.'

⁹² It is after all, at a banal conscious level, perfectly possible to have it both ways, to love money in itself while idealising self-sufficiency or despising trade, even though money is constituted by exchange.

⁹³ *Pol.* 1257b19–32.

⁹⁴ Cf. the conjecture ἀσινῇ 'unharmed' (Meineke) for the inept ἄστη 'towns' (cf. 27) at B1.3: cf. Aesch. *Eum.* 315 where (as at *Ag.* 1341, *Cho.* 1018) ἀσινής refers to *permanent* unharmedness. This would constitute another element of the analogy between individual and Being in Parmenides.

Abstract self-sufficiency may then be not just the *result* of imagining monetary value abstracted from circulation but also its (unconscious) *aim*. The preconception of the fullness (i.e. self-identity and self-sufficiency) of Being that – we shall see – underlies much of Parmenides' argument sublimates the desired self-sufficiency of *ousia* ('wealth' or 'Being'). And the emphatically rejected vulgar belief that something may both be (so) and not be (so) sublimates the non-self-identity of the commodity, part of whose value consists in (exchangeability with) something else.[95] Notice also the (unconvincing) reason Parmenides gives for the self-sufficiency of being: if it were not self-sufficient 'it would lack everything'.[96] So too monetary value cannot enter circulation in a limited way: in (unlimited) circulation, as a medium of universal exchange, it seems to lack *everything*. A similar argument will be applied by Anaxagoras to *mind* (*nous*): if it were mixed with anything else, it would be mixed with everything (B12).

At this point there may occur what seems a fundamental objection. Parmenides argues by means of deduction. His is indeed the first extant text to produce a sustained deductive argument. And he himself claims (B7.5) that we should judge by *logos* (of which however in this period the translation 'reason' is inadequate: 12A). His arguments are, it has been objected to me by a student of ancient philosophy, 'simple and powerful and raise profound ultimate questions about the nature of language and thought and its relation to reality'.

Much writing about Parmenides has been devoted to reconstructing and (occasionally) evaluating his process of deduction about what exists. Such writing is valuable, within its limits. But it is necessary to emphasise that I am not directly concerned with the philosophical value (or otherwise) of Parmenides. Even academic philosophers must surely admit that his odd conclusions about what exists do not arise from *pure* deduction, that *at some point* one or more preconceptions have in one way or another influenced his chain of reasoning. It is the *source of Parmenides' preconception(s)* (and those of other presocratics) that I have been investigating. Preconception may provide the starting point for the deduction (the choice of unargued premiss), or it may direct or distort the process of deduction (and so be at least partly responsible for 'fallacy'). I maintain that it is not merely

---

[95] The view that it both is and is not sounds so like Heraclitus' that he has been identified by some scholars as the object of the attack (and see below on Parmen. B4 and n. 103). But it is clearly described as the view of people in general. Heraclitus' system reflects the new monetary economy, in which people in general are engaged.

[96] B8.33, following those who delete the unmetrical *eon*.

deduction but also preconception that produces Parmenides' strange conclusions about what exists.

Let us take a summary of his chain of deduction (based largely on the admiring reconstruction by G. E. L. Owen).[97]

(a) What can be spoken and thought of *can be*, whereas 'nothing' cannot (B6.1–2).

(b) What can be spoken and thought of is not nothing (B2.7–8).

(c) What can be spoken and thought of is what *is* (B3; B6.1; B8.34–6?).

(d) There is nothing that *is* and yet is not (B6.8–9; B7.1).

(e) What *is is* fully or not at all (B8.11).

(f) What *is* can have come to be neither from what *is* (for it *is* what *is*) nor from what is not (B8.6–21).

(g) What *is* is all full of homogeneous being, it cannot *be* to different degrees at different points (B8.22–5, 33, 47–8). Nor can anything *be* beside it (for that would not belong to what *is*) (B8.36–8).

(h) What *is* (Being) is one, continuous and homogeneous (B8.5–6, 22–5).

(i) What *is* is invariant in time and space (B8).

I am not concerned with the (more or less obvious) fallacies in this chain of deduction. Parmenides' fundamental claim, with which the goddess begins her exposition and on which she repeatedly insists (B2.1–3; B8.11, 22–5, 33, 47–8) is that what *is is fully*. What he is concerned to refute is the view that what *is* also *is not* (B6.4–9, B7.1–5; B8.15–16). This latter view is exemplifed by the Milesians and Heraclitus, who maintain that everything in a sense consists of an underlying substance, so that (say) air can take the (condensed) form of earth and as such both is and is not air. Parmenides surely had this kind of cosmological view in mind, but by himself taking it to a logical extreme comes to a conclusion that is in fact opposed both to this earlier cosmology and to the views of people in general. Parmenides' argument is, to the extent that it is directed against earlier monist cosmology, not unreasonable: it is only because the argument also retains monism that it produces its strange conclusions. By treating what *is* (*to eon*, Being) as substance, and substance as what *is*, Parmenides imagines it as excluding everything else. If 'it must be completely or not at all' (B8.11), and so 'all is full of being' (B8.24), then there is no scope for plurality, diversity, movement, or change. Being is permanently everywhere.

And so Parmenides inherited the monist preconception from (while being opposed to) earlier cosmology, or perhaps (at least to some extent) arrived independently at the preconception as a result of the socio-economic

[97] Owen 1986 (1960).

development that I have sufficiently delineated. But, it may be objected, he does *argue for* what I call a preconception, in steps (a) to (e) above. It is not unusual for preconceptions to be argued for. Let us look at the argument.

It is in fact difficult to reconstruct any chain of deduction (in part because of the fragmentation of the text). But let us suppose that the scheme given above is on the right lines. It gives the appearance of initial scrupulousness, comparable to Descartes' *cogito ergo sum*: *cogito erga est quod cogito*. But the same cannot be said of the argument as a whole, for instance of the transition from (a) *can be* to (c) *is*, or of the entry of the preconception that what *is* is full of *Being* in the sense that it excludes all else.

The homogeneous oneness of all Being in time and space is in fact present already from the very beginning.[98] The transition from (a) to (h) is implicit in B4:

look equally[99] with your mind (*nous*) at absent things firmly present; for it will not cut off[100] *Being* from holding to *Being*, neither scattered everywhere in every way in order nor brought together.

In step (a) 'thought of' is *noein*.[101] In B4 this process of *noein* (i.e. with *nous*) is described: everything thinkable (i.e. all that there is) consists of continuous (and so unified) being. This continuity of Being is restated with the same vocabulary[102] at step (g). And with B4.1 'equally' (*homōs*) compare – also at step (g) – *homon* and *homōs* of the homogeneity of Being (B8.47–9).

What is the point, in B4, of characterising Being as neither scattered (*skidnamenon*) everywhere in every way (*pantēi pantos*) in order (*kata kosmon*) nor brought together? What is being ruled out is not just diversity and plurality of Being but also more specifically the combination of unity and diversity propounded by Heraclitus, who claimed (of being (*ousia*) compared to a river) 'it scatters (*skidnēsi*) and again draws together' (B91). *Pantēi pantos* and *kata kosmon* may also imply a response to the Heraclitean idea.[103]

But why can the mind not separate its objects off from each other? Surely it can. It seems that right from the beginning of the argument we have the strange preconception that the objects of thought exhibit neither diversity nor even plurality. Whence this preconception?

---

[98] B5 'It is the same to me where I begin, for there I will come back again' may refer to the circularity of the path of thought.

[99] Read ὁμῶς not ὅμως: Hölscher 1956, 385–9.

[100] Cf. 8.35.   [101] B6.1; cf. B3; B8.34; 13B n. 71.

[102] Cf. B4.2 *to eon tou eontos echesthai* with B8.23–5 . . *sunechesthai . . . eon gar eonti pelasdei* (B8.23–5).

[103] Cf. Hclt. B30, B41. For other apparent echoes of Heraclitus see Guthrie 1965, 23–4, 32.

There can be a psychological response to this question, but not a philosophical one. To be sure, one might respond that a mind capable of monist abstraction imagines continuous (and so unified) *Being*: 'absent things' as the object of *nous* ('intellect' perhaps rather than 'mind') includes invisible underlying substance. But this is to push the same question back to the origins of monism. Another response might be to start by allowing that there is one respect in which all things that can be thought of do indeed constitute a homogeneous oneness: they are all objects of the mind. We have seen that just as money imposes its own invisible controlling homogeneous oneness on the multiplicity of goods that it underlies, so the mind imposes its own invisible controlling homogeneous oneness on the multiplicity of thoughts and sensations by which it is in a sense constituted. Even 'absent things' are 'firmly present' to the mind. The Derveni commentator's interpretation of the Orphic myth of Zeus absorbing everything else and becoming alone[104] as *Nous* (Mind) – for everything else, he says, could not exist without *Nous* – shows in its phrasing the influence of the universal equivalence of money: the mind 'itself being alone is worth everything (*pantōn axion*)'. It may be significant, given the mystic formation of the unitary sense of self out of bodily fragmentation (11B), that the one word transmitted in Parmenides' description of the One which does suggest the self is *oulomeles*,[105] which denotes the *wholeness of the body* – though it is now often regarded as having replaced *oulon mounogenes* ('whole and of a single kind').[106] Compare the 'whole-natured (*oulophueis*) shapes' (B62.4) in the alternation of bodily wholeness and fragmentation described by Empedocles, for whom the supreme point of wholeness is a universe with a single mind, 'rejoicing in its supremely joyous solitariness' (11B). The origins of Parmenides' fundamental preconception are in the analogous, mutually reinforcing structures of psyche and monetary economy. What is abstracted reflects the unchanging oneness and abstract homogeneity of monetary value, but also still embodies the invisible unity of the mind (out of multiplicity) that we saw reflected in earlier cosmology. To have identified this factor in the formation of Parmenides' ontology is not to deny that the factor contributed to philosophical advance.

Material monism was suggested neither by observation of the world nor by mere deduction, and so its adoption by the Milesians requires

---

[104] 11B; with 'became alone' (Col. xvi 6 *mounos egento*) cf. *mounogenes*, variant at Parmenides B8.4 (n. 106 below).

[105] Especially as it is preceded by *atremes* (untrembling), which may be a trace of correlation (clearly found in Pl. *Phdr.*) between mystic object and initiatory self: 11B.

[106] B8.4; Owen 1986 (1960), 23–4; cf. DK ad loc.

explanation. We saw that one of the very few scholars to attempt to provide one is Finkelberg, even though his explanation is inadequate (11B). The abstract monism of Parmenides, is even less likely to be suggested by mere observation, and cannot arise from mere deduction. Aristotle (*Gen. Corr.* 325a19) says that it borders on madness. And yet here again scholars in general do not seem to think that its adoption requires explanation, and credit must go once more to Finkelberg for attempting to provide one.

The crucial difficulty of material monism is the mutual irreducibility of physical substances: a body cannot be considered as single and self-identical when it is postulated to be also the rest of things. In other words, a consistently monistic representation of reality cannot be attained on the basis of reducing the manifold to one of its components. From this it follows that in order to arrive at a truly monistic conception, the higher unity of things should be conceived as a logical and not a physical unity. In light of this, it can be suggested that Parmenides' being is a notion invented with a view to overcoming the difficulty faced by material monism: Being is the unified conception of the universe . . .[107]

For Finkelberg the factor generating Parmenidean abstract being is *immanent*, a contradiction in previous doctrine, whereas for me the most important factor is external, the development of money. Finkelberg's explanation may contain some truth, but is insufficient. We have seen that the strange notion of imperceptible, abstract being was not invented *ex nihilo* by Parmenides but developed gradually in earlier views which nevertheless basically adhered to material monism. Parmenides took this development to its extreme by stripping what exists of all qualities except what is fundamental to Anaximander's *apeiron*, Anaximenes' air, etc., namely being. He did not come up with an entirely original solution to an inherent problem, in the manner we attribute to the progress of science.[108] Further, if that was what he was doing, why did he retain monism, which was even more nonsensical in its new abstract version than in its old material one? What would be the point of solving the contradiction in material monism by means of a doctrine containing an even more glaring unresolved contradiction (between what seems and what is)?

---

[107] Finkelberg 1988, 7–8; similarly Finkelberg 1989.
[108] Similarly, Finkelberg 1989, 263 imagines that Anaximander 'was aware of the contradictory implications of a physical definition of the divine, and as a result touched upon a new notion untroubled by the contradiction', namely 'the idea of divinity as an intelligible essence coextensive with the universe'. However, 'why then did he nevertheless combine it with the vision of the divine as a changeable physical body'? Whereas my answer would refer to the combination of ideal and material in money, Finkelberg states, lamely, that 'if anything could reconcile these incompatible conceptions, it could only be Anaximander's personal vision'.

The pressure to retain monism was the same pressure that – perhaps in conjunction with the factor proposed by Finkelberg – made it abstract, namely the progressive development of the unitary abstraction of monetary value. Exchange value – an imperceptible abstraction from goods and services – acquires its own perceptible embodiment in metal money. And then, with the invention of coinage, there is disparity between the material value and the conventional value of the coins: what is perceptible is worth less than the actual (conventional) value of the coin (7D), and this implies something radically new – the paradox of an imperceptible embodiment of value. In other words, the coin embodies ideal value, mysterious, powerful, and imperceptible.[109] What is more, even the coinage itself, along with precious metal generally, is a form of wealth sufficiently condensed, durable, and manoeuvrable as to be thought of as relatively invisible.[110] The categories of 'invisible being' (*ousia aphanēs*) and 'invisible wealth' (*aphanēs ploutos*),[111] inconceivable in Homer,[112] are first found in the earliest texts to reveal the everyday working of coined money (Aristophanes and the orators).

Another attempt to explain the monism of Parmenides is by Martin West.[113] He describes Parmenides' arguments on the nature of the One as 'contrived and artificial, lending a show of logic to opinions that must have been reached in other ways'. How then were they reached? West points, uncontroversially, to the intellectual environment of his time – 'current reflections on cosmic unity, the fallibility of the senses, and the relativity of some qualities'. But this is insufficient to account for Parmenides' astonishing account of the One, and so West suggests two further factors. One is that Parmenides was influenced by certain Indian texts. However, and besides the problem of identifying the means of transmission, the similarity between the Indian ideas allegedy transmitted and the Parmenidean One is superficial.[114]

---

[109] 6C, 8H. On the association of coinage with the invisibility (e.g. Pl. *Phaedo* 79a, 80d) of Hades see 8D n. 38. Gyges finds underground the seal-ring that makes him invisible (6C).

[110] Even the precious metal wealth of a polis would be largely secluded from view in the temple. Coins were often buried: 5B, 14E n. 95.

[111] Notably the kind of property that can be hidden to avoid taxation: Gabrielson 1986n; Cohen 1992, 191–4. First occurrence: Lysias *Or.* 20.23.4; cf. e.g. Ar. *Eccl.* 601–2 'money (*argurion*) and Darics, *aphanē plouton*'.

[112] Though the reality that gave rise much later to the concept is suspected at *Od.* 10.35–47 (Aeolus' bag: 2E).

[113] West 1971, 221–6; cf. Burkert 1972, 285.

[114] West 1971, 224–5 admits that the Vedantic 'idealistic monism which holds that the multiplicity of apparent phenomena is an illusion (*maya*)' emerges 'somewhat later than Parmenides'. But he calls it 'a natural development from the characteristic doctrine of all the Upanishads: that the life breath of man, *atman*, is identical with the force that sustains the whole world, *brahman*, so that the many and separate beings merge into a single continuous one', a reality that by revealing itself causes the mortal to (as Zaehner puts it) 'realise himself as immortal, unconditioned, beyond space

West's second factor is that Parmenides had a mystical experience of the kind described by the nineteenth-century nature mystic Richard Jefferies in the words 'It is eternity now. I am in the midst of it . . . Nothing has to come: it is now. Now is eternity; now is the immortal life.'

But this cannot explain why Parmenides produced his vision when and where he did. And neither transhistorical mystic experience nor Indian ideas can explain the undoubted *impact* of Parmenidean ontology on other Greeks, which the factors we have suggested *are* historically specific enough to explain. The Parmenidean One is the culmination of earlier Greek ideas *as influenced by* the rapid and continuing monetisation – with its profound influence on the lives of all their citizens – of the Greek city-states. Mystic experience may have been one factor in this synthesis, but only as the culturally specific experience of mystery *cult* and its *doctrines* (11B, 12C).

The massive impact of Parmenides does not of course require illustration. And so I will mention just two relatively unknown facts. One is that we hear of a 'Pythagorean and Parmenidean way of life'.[115] Secondly, Eucleides of Megara (*c.* 450–380 BC) maintained that the good is one, though differently named – as God, wisdom, mind, and so on – and that things contrary to the good do not exist (D. L. 2.106). It is not surprising therefore to find him placed in the tradition of Eleatic monism (Cic. *Acad.* 2.129). Parmenides, like the presocratics generally, is concerned with ontology: uppermost in his sublimation of money is its *being* rather than its *value*. Eucleides was receptive to Eleatic monism because he too, like Parmenides, was living in a recently monetised society.[116] The unitary *value* of money, which persists through its transformation into different things, was a factor in his refocusing of monism from being onto value.[117] To Plato, who combines the two, we will come briefly in the next section.

C   IS PARMENIDEAN METAPHYSICS REALLY INFLUENCED BY MONEY?

The suggestion of a relation between exchange-value and the metaphysics of Parmenides was, we remember, suggested half a century ago and then almost

---

and time and causation'. From the texts cited by West this idea is the closest to the Parmenidean One. But it is nevertheless, apart from the simple idea of oneness, very different from Parmenides' complete separation of what *is* (one, limited, unchanging, homogeneous, spherical, unmoving, without sensual qualities, etc.) from what seems.

[115] [Cebes] *Tabula* 2.2 (Hellenistic); cf. the bravery of Zeno described at the end of 12C.

[116] Megara did not produce its own coinage before the fourth century BC (Martin 1995, 276), though Eucleides, like other Megarians, would have known the coinage of other city-states.

[117] Cf. much later Epictetus *Diss.* 3.3.5–13: the good, to be preferred to all else, is currency given by god.

entirely ignored.[118] While conscious of the limitations of the suggestion
(9B), we must now defend it against the only attempt to refute it, by
Vernant.[119]

Firstly, Vernant objects to the idea hinted at by Gernet (9B) of a connection between on the one hand the legal distinction between invisible
property (called 'invisible being', *ousia aphanēs*) and visible property (called
'visible being', *ousia phanera*) and on the other hand the importance of invisible *ousia* in philosophy. He notes that the *ousia phanera* that is land is
more real, more permanent, and more substantial than the *ousia aphanēs*
that includes money, whereas in philosophy those qualities belong to what
is invisible. But that is *our* view of money, to be found first in the empirically
minded Aristotle. Among the early Greeks there is no reason to suppose
that money was, or is, perceived as being less real, less permanent or less
substantial than land, especially as, from the archaic period onwards, the
power of money was such that even land could (even if only unusually) be
bought with (transformed into) it.[120] If any single thing may be imagined
as the *ousia* of which all else consists, it is not land but money.

Secondly, Vernant objects that the Parmenidean One is set in contrast
to a reality such as money, which not only involves multiplicity in the
same way as natural things do, but furthermore implies the principle of the
possibility of indefinite multiplication. Parmenides' being, claims Vernant,
can no more be 'turned into money' than it is subject to becoming.

It is of course true that monetary value is multiple and may be indefinitely
multiplied. It is, we have ourselves emphasised, unlimited. Moreover it has,
unlike the Parmenidean One, a material embodiment that is changeable
(physically, and in value) and exchangeable (for goods). But monetary value
does *not* 'involve multiplicity in the same way as natural things do', for it
is, being abstract, perfectly homogeneous. Each 'natural thing', even if
imagined as perfectly homogeneous internally, differs from all other things
(even if only by location). But one unit of monetary value does not differ
from another even by location, for it is abstract, an object of the mind only.
As we have seen, Parmenides says that when you look at what is absent,
but present to the mind, the mind cannot cut off what exists from holding
to what exists (B4). Here and elsewhere (B8.22–5) he only has spatial terms

---

[118] The major exception is Sohn-Rethel (1978), who incorporates it into a general theory of the relationship between commodity-exchange and intellectual abstraction. For this relationship see also
Goux 1990.

[119] Vernant 1983 (1965), 361–4.

[120] Finley 1968; Cohen 1992, 31 n. 15, 51, 65, 193 n. 13. 'Transform into money' is the single word
exargurisdein, as in *exargurisdein tēn ousian* (Dem. 5.8).

with which to project the oneness of monetary value, which is however not spatially divisible. Hence the paradox that his One is indivisible although spatial.[121] The *numerical* divisibility (plurality) of monetary value is not reflected in its *spatial* (cosmological) projection.

This oneness of monetary value must, through all its exchanges with a vast variety of goods, retain its identity. It is important for the functioning of money that monetary value be exactly the same not only in different places but also at different times. It is this unprecedentedly all-pervasive *functional* unchanging oneness, uniting in the minds of its users one place with another and present with future, that enters unconsciously into Parmenides' conception of the One.

But does monetary value remain the same over time? It is a central precondition for the acceptability of coined money that its (ideal, socially constructed) value be imagined as remaining exactly the same as it changes hands and thereafter. This fact is of crucial importance both for the functioning of the monetary economy and for our overall argument, as also is the fact that in this respect there is a sharp contrast to the goods for which it is exchanged, which may lose their value, notably through consumption, use, cost of preservation, or physical deterioration. A coin suffers none of these,[122] except for slow physical deterioration, which (unless severe) will not disqualify it from embodying the same conventional value. That is to say, the (slowly changing) material of the coin is distinct from the (unchanging) value that it embodies. This desire to privilege the unchangingness of monetary value in a world of constant change and exchange means that, when the very same vase costs four drachmas one year and five drachmas the next, even we are more inclined to say that the vase has gone up in value than that the drachma has gone down. This is so even though the value of coined money may be regarded by some, with long-term hindsight, as having altered. Aristotle will note that the value of currency, though it does change, is more stable than that of other goods (*EN* 1133b11–15). The prices of goods and services (value of money) did in fact remain on the whole much more constant in pre-Hellenistic Greece than nowadays.[123] This relative stability is consistent with the Greek tendency[124] to hoard rather than invest their money. For the institution of coined money to

---

[121] Defended, it seems, by Zeno. Later the atomists will introduce plurality alongside abstract (and yet spatial) homogeneous indivisibility.

[122] Darius wished to perpetuate his memory by gold coinage: Hdt. 4.166.

[123] See notably the summary of variations in pay (and their probable causes) in Athens from 450 to 250 BC in Loomis 1998, 240–50.

[124] Millett 1991, 169–71; Figueira 1998, 22–48.

work, belief in its (socially constructed) unchanging identity over time is required (whether or not it turns out to be mistaken), and must in the sixth century have imposed itself as precondition and consequence of the rapid spread of coinage.

The Parmenidean One projects monetary value as transcending not only multiplicity of goods but also time and place, thereby as seeming to impose, permanently and everywhere, its own homogeneity on all things. Is not this transcendence characteristic of the value not just of coinage but of money in general? To an extent, yes, for money embodies (abstract) exchange-value.[125] But the Greek invention of coinage is in three relevant respects unprecedented. Firstly, it enables money to acquire universal pervasiveness.[126] Secondly, its only use is to embody exchange-value – it is the *mere* embodiment of exchange-value. Thirdly, it embodies exchange-value in material from which the exchange-value is nevertheless – in so far as it is indicated by a sign – distinct (7D). Exchange-value acquires in money a substance, and through coined money an abstract substance. The mass-produced stamp on coinage, unlike a hieroglyph or the stone lions over the gate at Mycenae, refers to something that has a merely arbitrary relation to its material manifestation. General acceptance of this disparity is (like belief in unchangeability) required for coinage to function. Moreover, grasp of the disparity both requires the belief in unchangeability (the value of coinage must not revert to its material value) and facilitates it: the durability that was an advantage of precious metal[127] is inherited and actually *enhanced* by coinage, for even precious metal (including coinage) is subject to loss of quantity by wear and tear, whereas the conventional, purely abstract value embodied in coinage is not. The general adoption of coinage requires a general power of universalising abstraction, the ability to perceive the coin as embodying the abstraction of number that remains the same in the future, in a different place, with a different person.

As well as being ubiquitously unchangeable, the Parmenidean One is, again like the value of coinage, homogeneous (B8.22–4, 42–9) and abstract (and yet hard to envisage in other than concrete terms).[128] Whence this strange conception? The only such thing in the world of Parmenides is

---

[125] On money in general as requiring a certain level of intellectual operations see Codere 1968.
[126] Elea in the lifetime of Parmenides was among those Greek states that issued fractional coinage: n. 75 above.
[127] 2C; 12A nn. 45–6. In the closest in Homer to a mention of money (*Od.* 14.323–5) it is imagined as metal lasting for ten generations into the future: 2B, 5A n. 3.
[128] Notably, it is compared to a *sphairē* (sphere or ball) in B8.43; cf. KRS 253.

the abstract, unchanging, homogeneous oneness of the value of (concrete) coinage – that newly pervasive embodiment of social relations, of universal power, the agent of abstract equalisation on which, according to Aristotle (*EN* 1133ab), the association of the polis depends. What is there, apart from money, that is transformed into so many other things? Early in the Greek experience of money we find the idea that money is everything.[129] The idea that to be transformed into something (or everything) is to *be* that thing (or everything) is common in presocratic philosophy.

The third objection advanced by Vernant is that for Plato (a successor in metaphysics to Parmenides) 'the figure of the sophist symbolises, precisely, the man who remains on the level of non-being at the very same time as he is defined as a dealer in commercial transactions' (p. 362). Certainly sophists sell their wisdom, and for Plato embody non-being. But there is no significant connection between the two. Plato is generally averse to commerce and to sophists. His attitude to money, however, is interestingly ambivalent. Coinage, a 'symbol for the purpose of exchange' (*Rep.* 371b), does good because it renders homogeneous and commensurable the being (*ousia*) of things of whatever kind (*Laws.* 918a). What is more, Vernant's objection misses the point that value may be imagined detached from circulation (12B). Money is for Plato a model of permanent invisible value: the guardians, in the *Republic* (416e), should – in contrast to the polluting human currency (*nomisma*) of the majority of the people[130] – have divine gold and silver money (*chrusion kai argurion*) from the gods[131] always present[132] in their souls.[133] In Plato, no less than in Parmenides, sublimated money is homogeneous, permanent, self-sufficient, and invisible.

Aristotle's view of coinage as originating in trade presupposes that coinage was, originally at least, worth the precious metal of which it was composed: it is stamped to guarantee its weight. But Aristotle goes on to say that 'coinage sometimes seems to be nonsense and entirely convention, because it can be changed by its users to be worth nothing and useless for purchasing anything that is needed' (*Pol.* 1257a31–b14). The view that money is simply worth its precious metal is called by Leslie Kurke essentialism, whereas the view that ignores its metallic value and sees only its symbolic function she calls functionalism. The old system of ranked spheres of exchange, with

---

[129] Pythermus *PMG* 910 (quoted 5A), and the transformation by Midas of *everything* into gold.

[130] Cf. *Rep.* 525c: the guardians are to study arithmetic, but in order to contemplate the nature of number by pure thought, 'not for the purpose of buying or selling'. Cf. 11B n. 55.

[131] The distinction reappears in comment on Matthew 22.19–21: e.g. Ignatius *ad Magn.* 5.2 'as if there are two currencies (*nomismata*), one of god, one of the world'; cf. Epictetus quoted n.117 above.

[132] Cf. already Solon fr. 15: *chrēmata* pass from one man to another but virtue is permanent.

[133] Cf. also intelligence as the right currency (*nomisma orthon*) at Pl. *Phaedo* 69a (quoted 12A).

an aristocratic monopoly of the exchange of precious goods, is, she argues, threatened by coinage, for coinage, under the symbolic authority of the polis, puts precious metal into general circulation. And so

> a whole set of aristocratic poetic texts – those of Theognis, Simonides, Pindar, and Bacchylides – focus only and obsessively on essence, that is on the quality of metal, thereby eliding or repressing the existence of coinage altogether.[134]

I suspect however that this focus on essence, if it does express something about the artificial value of coined money, expresses as much anxious ambivalence as hostility. Coinage, like the polis that issued it, was too omnipresent to be treated with lofty disdain by aristocrats.[135] Consider rather the reaction we observed in Plato, aristocratic and contemptuous of commerce, for whom there are two opposite kinds of money – sublimated money (precious metal that is divine and permanent and lodged in the invisibility of the soul) and the money used in commerce, and even this latter mundane money has the virtue of making being (*ousia*) homogeneous. Traditionally gold and silver embodied aristocratic prestige and were associated with immortality (2C). But coinage puts them into general circulation. The response of Plato is to preserve their distinct status by locating them within the soul. The immortal value of precious metal is recuperated, secluded (like the guardians themselves) from circulation, by becoming invisible. But this invisibility is not a mere device. Plato's divine precious metal combines its traditional immortality with the socially constructed, necessarily unchanging, impersonal and invisible value of coined precious metal, located in the soul – a location which not only recuperates the traditional link between precious metal and the superior *person* but also (as we saw for the presocratics) associates its strange invisibility with the more familiar invisibility of the soul. The aristocratic essentialism of Plato resembles the essentialism of pure precious metal that Kurke sees in aristocratic poetry, but is in fact rather an essentialism of the (no less pure) *invisible value* embodied in precious metal.

Monetisation tends to marginalise reciprocity (10B), and permits an unprecedented appearance of individual autonomy, especially in the figure of the tyrant (14A, 14D). This tyrannical autonomy is one of the features of money reflected in the unprecedentedly autonomous deity of Xenophanes (10D). The tyrant's money makes him seem autonomous, independent of the demands of reciprocity. But in fact his monetary power depends on general acceptance of the socially constructed value of his money. The

---

[134] Kurke 1999, 46.   [135] For a critique of Kurke on this and other points see Seaford 2002.

money that he has in his own absolute possession has (unlike the royal treasure in the Homeric store-room, e.g. at *Il.* 4.143–4) no value except in its ability to circulate, and yet to possess it is to withhold it from circulation. And so the autonomy (imagined or real) of the tyrant, or indeed of any individual with money, requires the imagined separation of value from circulation. Socially constructed value becomes a thing, individually possessed. And so money takes on the seeming self-sufficiency of its owner.

In this way money paradoxically both permeates society, uniting everybody in the same system, and yet permits the illusion of absolute individual self-sufficiency. This illusion, the separation of value from circulation, may be reinforced by the desire, felt especially perhaps by aristocrats, to be self-sufficiently superior to the uncertainty, demeaning dependence, and vulgarity of commercial circulation. Even the realistic Aristotle attempts, with inevitable difficulty, to set an unrealistic ideal of the self-sufficient household, with all its resources provided by nature, against the undesirability of artificial and unlimited money-making.[136] There is a significant contrast here between Plato and Aristotle. Aristotle says that currency equalises things by making them commensurable, but that this is just a necessary convention, for it is impossible for things so different to be in reality commensurable (*EN* 1133ab). Plato too, as we have seen, says that currency homogenises the being of various things, but also projects monetary value as divinely present in the soul. Whereas for Aristotle, with his absorption in empirical diversity, true value separated from monetised circulation consists of goods, for Plato, with his absorption in unity, it consists of sublimated monetary value. The uniform embodiment of value-for-practice (in money) allows the notion of unitary abstract value (beyond concrete things) which, when further detached from practice by aristocratic ideology, becomes unitary value-for-thought that is in the *Republic* said to be the source of being but 'beyond being' and imagined as like money producing interest similar to itself.[137] With his metaphysical basis for social division, Plato reinforces the secluded self-sufficiency of the guardians by the *metaphysical* separation of value (divine money in their souls) from circulation. And even Aristotle recognises that *koinōnia* – association, and so the polis – depends on the abstract equalisation, effected by coinage, of commodities (*EN* 1133ab).

---

[136] Aristot. *Pol.* 1256–8; Seaford 1994a, 201–2.
[137] 509b (and *Parmen.* 141e), 506e–507a. The metaphor is playful, but skilfully combines the self-identity of value with its increase – a combination to which we will return (14E).

We have identified, as factors in the genesis of the Parmenidean One, mystery cult (11B), the historical development of monetary abstraction, reaction to Heraclitus, and the unconscious imperative to separate self-sufficient true value from the uncertain and vulgar monetary circulation of precious metal. Although this imperative was not confined to aristocrats, it may not be coincidental that the two thinkers who reflect the progress of this separation were apparently both, as was Plato, of aristocratic origin. Heraclitus, for whom permanent unity and abstract *logos* are both embodied in permanent physical circulation, was said to have resigned the 'kingship' in favour of his brother and to have been isolated from politics by his intellectual contempt for humankind.[138] Parmenides, for whom permanent abstract unity is finally explicitly separated from the transformation believed in by 'ignorant mortals . . . undiscriminating hordes' (B6), was said to have been 'of illustrious family and of wealth',[139] but also, in contrast to Heraclitus, a lawgiver (9B). Heraclitus and Parmenides each feels isolated by his abstract insight, but whereas Heraclitus turns his back on his inheritance of aristocratic politics, Parmenides engages in it – albeit in a society now inescapably unified by monetary circulation and by the tendency of money to homogenise both goods and people (8B), with the result that the aristocratic seclusion of true value resorts to the *sublimation* of omnipresent monetary value, an imagined universe of invisible true being, the Parmenidean One, completely self-sufficient (B31–3, 42), eternal (B8.2, 5–21, 27–8), perfectly homogeneous (B8.5–6, 22–5, 44–9). These projections of monetary value outdo even that unchanging purity of gold which might symbolise aristocratic quality[140] or immortality. In a tradition recorded by Plutarch it is said of the bravery of Parmenides' pupil Zeno under torture that 'he provided the word of Parmenides in the fire (i.e. for testing) like pure and genuine gold'.[141]

The economic and ideological roots of the ontologies of Parmenides and Plato should not make us forget the influence on them of mystery cult. In Plato's *Symposium* the structure of Diotima's mystic *logos* corresponds explicitly to the two main stages of mystic initiation (11B, 12A). The first stage concerns the contradiction and absence inherent in desire, whereas in the second and final stage there is revealed a single thing, beauty, the goal of all efforts, distinct from all else, absolutely beautiful rather than merely in some respects or to some people, abstract rather than corporeal, itself

---

[138] D. L. 9.6; 9.3; Guthrie 1962, 410–13.
[139] Sotion ap. D. L. 1.21 (DK. 28A1). It is of course conceivable that this is an inference from B6.
[140] Kurke 1999, 42–5, 49–54, 57–60, 141–2, 304.
[141] Plut. *Mor.* 1126D (29 DK A6; cf. A1–2, 6, 7–9).

by itself with itself of a single kind, the permanent source of beauty for all beautiful things that pass in and out of being while it remains unchanged. All this is strikingly analogous to the way in which monetary value may be imagined.[142] I would accordingly suggest that in this description the transcendent mystic object is unconsciously fused with the transcendence of monetary value (sublimated as divine money in the soul).[143] The two stages correspond to our distinction between monetary circulation and monetary value abstracted from circulation.[144] In general the *purification* that is the first stage of mystic initiation becomes from the philosophical perspective separation from the sensual.[145] The Platonic (even if not by Plato himself) *Seventh Letter* uses mystic imagery to describe sudden philosophical enlightenment as 'like light, kindled by leaping fire in the soul, now nourishes itself'.[146] This insistence on self-sufficiency seems designed to exclude the constant exchange performed by the Heraclitean fire (B90) that may also derive in part from the association of fire, in mystic ritual, with continuing life out of death (12A). Similarly, whereas Heraclitus saw his cosmology of unity in constant change embodied in the mystic *kukeon*, Parmenides may have seen his cosmology of unchanging uniformity embody in the mystic sphere (11B).

For Parmenides, on whose doctrine of the abstract eternal sphere we have suggested the influence of mystic doctrine (11B) as well as of monetary value, what remains to be described here is how he, again like Plato albeit in a different way, merges the superiority of self-sufficient monetary value with the reassuringly traditional and authoritative *structures* of mystic ritual.

For Parmenides the belief held by the 'ignorant mortals . . . undiscriminating hordes' – that something may both be (so) and not be (so)[147] sublimates the non-self-identity of the commodity, part of whose value consists in (exchangeability with) something else (12B). By virtue of this belief the hordes are going astray along a road, carried along deaf, blind,

---

[142] I have already described all these features of monetary value except that of being absolute rather than relative (e.g. not καλόν (fine) in relation to some things only: 211a). Cf. Schopenhauer 1974 (1851), I. 348 other things are only *agatha pros ti*, goods in relation to something, only relatively good. Money alone is the absolutely good thing, because it meets not merely one need *in concreto*, but needs generally *in abstracto*.

[143] Cf. *Phaedo* 69a (cited 12A).

[144] On the transcendent separation (castration) of the phallus compared to the transcendent separation of universal equivalent from circulation see 11B n. 66. The phallus might be a mystic object.

[145] Pl. *Soph.* 230c8–e1, *Phaedo* 69cd; *Rep.* 560e; Plut. Mor. 47A, 382DE (=Aristotle fr. 10 Ross); Plotin. *Enn.* 6.7.36; for other late texts (e.g. on mathematics as purifying) see Riedweg 1987, 124–9.

[146] 341c5–d2; mystic: Schefer 2001, 63–4.

[147] The view attacked is so like Heraclitus' that he has been identified by some scholars as the object of the attack. But it is clearly described as the view of people in general. See 12B n. 95.

and dazed, and the path of all is backward-turning (B6). There are in fact two other roads, one 'that it is not', the other (the only right one) 'that it is' (B2, B6.1–4, B8.1–2). This last is the road taken by Parmenides himself in his mystically described (9B) journey, and is described as 'far from the treading of humankind' (B1.27). This distinction between the right road and the wrong roads derives, I suggest, from the mystic idea of right and wrong roads in the underworld. On the way to Hades, according to Plato (*Phaedo* 108a), a guide is needed, for it has many forkings, 'to judge from the sacrifices and observances of this world'. That the mystic initiates must make a crucial choice of roads on their way to eternal happiness is confirmed by the mystic gold leaves. One of them contains the instruction to travel to the *right* (emphatic position) to the sacred meadows and groves of Persephone (A4 Zuntz). Other leaves refer to a spring which must not be drunk from (in one leaf this forbidden spring is said to be on the left, in two others on the right).[148] Rather they must drink water flowing from the lake of memory, which they will obtain by reciting a certain formula in response to questioning from its guards. The leaf from Hipponion (*c.* 400 BC) ends with the instruction to go – after drinking the water – on the sacred road which the other glorious mystic initiands and *bakchoi* are treading. No doubt the uninitiated – those who are 'being refreshed'[149] in the vicinity of the forbidden spring (Hipponion leaf 4), and those who do not know the formula – will not take the same road to eternal happiness.[150] This mystic distinction between the right and the wrong road has been adapted by Parmenides to express the distinction between himself as 'a man who knows' (B1.2), i.e. the initiate,[151] from those who travel 'knowing nothing' (B6.4). Just as it is the goddess (Persephone?) who in Parmenides insists on the distinction between the right and the wrong roads, so on two gold leaves (A2–3 Zuntz) it is Persephone who sends the initiand to his happy destination.

And yet there is an important distinction between Parmenides and the picture given by the gold leaves. Whereas the latter imply a movement of many initiands along the road to final happiness, Parmenides emphasises his individual isolation. Individual isolation could occur as a temporary phase of mystic initiation (14B). But in Parmenides it may be considered an appropriate expression of aristocratic self-sufficiency enhanced by the

---

[148] Respectively B1 Zuntz, B2 Zuntz, and the Hipponion leaf (Cole 1980).
[149] *Psuchontai*, which may connote the soul (*psuchē*) and the chill of death: cf. [Aesch.] *PV* 692–3 (cf. *Eum.* 157–61); Hclt. B36 'it is death for souls (*psuchai*) to become water'.
[150] Cf. Poseid. Pell. 705 *Suppl. Hell.* 21–2 'mystic path to Rhadamanthys'.
[151] Burkert 1969, 5.

seeming self-sufficiency of the monetary abstraction imagined as separate from universal circulation, the subjective aspect – by the mystic assimilation of subject to object – of the One that is all there is (11B). To this synthesis of mystic and monetary isolation we will return in our discussion of tragedy (14D).[152]

---

[152] As a foretaste of this discussion, consider the possible significance of Parmenides travelling in a *chariot*, as opposed to the Hipponion initiands who go on foot: in Euripides' *Bacchae* the isolated mystic initiand and man of money Pentheus (14D) imagines himself returning from Dionysiac ritual in a chariot (968; cf. 319–21), unlike all the others and against the preference of the egalitarian Dionysus (191–2; 206–9): cf. Hdt. 1.60 (tyrant Peisistratus in chariot) with Connor 1987, 42–6. Chariots occur in mystic imagery (Seaford 1994b, 279–80), but Lycurgus banned women using them on the way to Eleusis 'so that the women of the people should not be outdone by the rich' (Plut. *Mor.* 842A).

CHAPTER THIRTEEN

Pythagoreanism and Protagoras

A EARLY PYTHAGOREANISM

About the life and doctrines of Pythagoras we are told much but know little. My concern is rather with the early period (roughly 530–400 BC) of the movement that acknowledged him as its founder. Early Pythagoreanism was unusual in combining three kinds of activity. It was a cultic society, giving rise to the idea of a 'Pythagorean life'. It exercised political power.[1] And it produced an orally transmitted philosophy, at the heart of which was the idea that 'number is all'. This unique combination is I think best explained by the hypothesis that Pythagoreanism was in part a reaction to the unprecedented transformation and expansion of exchange caused by the rapid growth of coined money. A cultic society may of course be politically effective.[2] And it may have been especially attractive and effective in circumstances in which rapid monetisation had marginalised traditional forms of political combination based on reciprocity, on kinship, and on land-based cult. Crotonians with a common political interest based on money, and yet potentially isolated from each other by money (14A), broke with tradition by resorting to an initiated society centred around a puritan[3] form of life and devotion to mathematics expressed in the Pythagorean saying 'of all things the wisest is number',[4] and in the belief that everything is number – a belief favoured, as we shall see, by the rapid pervasion of the economy by coined money. The construction of the unique figure of Pythagoras – combining numerical understanding with supernatural status and power – answers to a unique transition, holding together the group by mediating between the need to master the new mathematisation of social

---

[1] Burkert 1972, 118–20.   [2] E.g. Burkert 1972, 119; Minar 1942, 15–35.
[3] Burkert 1972, 191 compares Pythagoreanism with historical Puritanism in its rejection of 'primitive' religious forms. One might further speculate on similarities in the monetary dimension of the two movements. The first to be concerned with both moderation in behaviour and the economic well-being of the polis are Solon and Xenophanes (10D).
[4] Burkert 1972, 169 n. 22.

relations and the need nevertheless to manage the obscurity surrounding the life and death of the individual newly isolated by this rapid monetisation.

Given the unreliability of our sources for the history of early Pythagoreanism, this can remain no more than a hypothesis. But it gains support from various considerations. Firstly, some of what is reported about Pythagoras himself is either unlikely to have been invented or, if invented, revealing nevertheless of the attitudes of the early Pythagoreans who invented it. It is generally accepted that in 532/1 BC (or thereabouts) Pythagoras left the tyranny of Polycrates on Samos for Southern Italy, where he spent many years in Croton. Samos at that time was monetised and technically advanced, having succeeded Miletus as the most powerful commercial centre of the Eastern Aegean.[5] In contrast to the aristocratic origins of Heraclitus and Parmenides, Pythagoras is said to have been the son of a gem-cutter.[6] And as an immigrant to a state founded two centuries earlier, he is unlikely to have belonged to the landed aristocracy. His journey to Southern Italy no doubt followed an established trade route. His contemporary at Croton the doctor Democedes, whose father had emigrated from Cnidos, was attracted by salary offers in turn to Aegina (one talent), Athens (100 mnas), and Samos (two talents) – an early example of mobility inspired by monetary payment for technical skill.[7] Pythagoras was said (wrongly of course, but significantly) to have introduced weights and measures to the Greeks.[8] He arrived in Southern Italy at about the same time as did coinage, and it has even been argued that he introduced it.[9] The oldest coins of Croton show the tripod of Apollo, with whom Pythagoras was especially associated. We are even told that he claimed[10] to have been king Midas, whose touch turning everything into gold expresses early Greek experience of money as a universal means of exchange. The story that the Locrians turned him away, because despite admiring his cleverness they had no desire to change their laws, has been connected with Locri's lack of coinage before the fourth century.[11]

---

[5] Shipley 1987, 69–99; on Polycrates and money see Seaford 2003c.
[6] D. L. 8.2 (Hdt. 4.95; Hclt. B129); or merchant: Justin 20.4.3; Iambl. *VP* 5.
[7] Hdt. 3.131; cf. *Il.*11. 514; Burkert 1972, 293; Alexis *FGrH* 539F2 (Athen. 540de) Polycrates attracts craftsmen by large payments.
[8] By Aristoxenus (cf. n. 39 below): DK 14A12 (= B24 Wehrli).
[9] By Seltman 1949, 1–21, tentatively approved by Guthrie 1962, 176–7. It is more likely (though still of course a guess) that he had something to do with the first coins of Croton, which were almost certainly not the earliest coins of Southern Italy. He was likely to have been trained in his father's trade of gem-cutting. On early Crotonian coinage see e.g. Parise 1990. A head depicted on coins of Abdera *c.* 430–420 BC probably represents Pythagoras: Burkert 1972, 110.
[10] This was probably reported by Aristotle: Ael. *VH* 4.17; Iamb. *VP* 63, 143; Burkert 1972, n. 120.
[11] Dicaearchus fr. 14 Wehrli; Guthrie 1962, 178 n. 1.

Secondly, there are the traditions about the early Pythagoreans. Prominent in these stories is political conflict at Croton (and elsewhere) towards the end of the sixth century. We are told that the Pythagoreans were opposed both by a group led by a wealthy nobleman[12] and by a champion of the lower classes who declared that the Pythagorean philosophy was a conspiracy against the common people.[13] This might be thought to support the idea of the Pythagoreans as a new commercial class opposed both by the landowning aristocracy and by the landless poor. But the accounts are hardly reliable, being probably first written down about two centuries after the event. Besides, the categories of 'commercial class' and 'landowning aristocracy' may not be helpful.[14] What is crucial is monetisation, which may pervade the sale of manufactured goods, of agricultural produce, even of land. Beyond doubt is the rapid development of coinage in huge numbers. From this we can infer the probability of new common interests (reflected perhaps in the historical tradition) created by the inevitable conflict over control of newly monetised exchanges or of the import and minting of silver.

More worthy of belief than the narratives of conflict in Croton is the frequently reported tradition that the Pythagoreans of Croton controlled numerous other Greek cities of Southern Italy.[15] This is supported by the evidence of contemporary coinage. The earliest coinage of Southern Italy had, despite the apparent absence of any evolutionary process behind its difficult incuse technique, spread very quickly, with several cities sharing a remarkable uniformity both of technique and of weight standard.[16] Then, after Croton's destruction of Sybaris in 510 BC, there appear coins that combine the symbol of Croton on the obverse with that of another city on the reverse.[17] Taken together with the good evidence that there were Pythagorean groups in the cities likely to have been controlled by Croton,[18] this suggests that any political control was inseparable from the economic relations expressed in the uniformity of coinage. That is to say, the relations between the cities was determined not so much by Crotonian military imperialism, which would have been difficult to maintain, but rather by the economic relations and common interests of those, in the

---

[12] The authenticity of this detail is defended by von Fritz 1940, 97–8.

[13] Iambl. *VP* 248 (from Aristoxenus) and 258–60 (mainly from Timaeus).

[14] As an instance of potential confusion see D. L. 8.3 (the Pythagoreans deserved the name aristocracy in its literal sense).

[15] Minar 1942, 16, 36–49.

[16] For this as indicating political and economic cohesion see e.g. Le Rider 1989, 168–71.

[17] Minar 1942, 36; Kraay 1976, 166–8, 172.

[18] The sources are discussed by Minar 1942, 27–8, 37–9.

various cities, whose wealth depended on the circulation of coinage, and who were accordingly susceptible to the spread of Pythagoreanism inspired from Croton.[19]

This is of course speculative, especially as we have no Pythagorean writing before the fragments of Philolaus (*c.* 470–390 BC), which have no political content (13B). Fortunately though the next Pythagorean writings to survive are fragments from the pen of an active politician, Archytas of Tarentum (early fourth century BC).

> The discovery of calculation (*logismos*) ended civil conflict and increased concord. For when there is calculation there is no unfair advantage, and there is equality, for it is by calculation that we come to agreement in our transactions. Because of it the poor receive from the powerful and the rich give to the needy, with both confident that through it they will have their fair share. As rod (standard) and preventer of the unjust, it stops those who know how to calculate before they commit injustice, persuading them that they will not be able to escape detection when they come up against it. Those who do not know how to calculate it prevents from committing injustice by showing them that in this (i.e. their inability to calculate) they are committing injustice.[20]

The agreement created in private dealings by numerical calculation is extended to the citizen body as a whole, overcoming the division between rich and poor, as well as, significantly, the division between those who know how to calculate and those who do not. Mathematics, ethical self-restraint, and politics are all attributed by our sources to early Pythagoreanism. The case of Archytas shows how they may have been interrelated.

Among the very few mentions of Pythagoras himself before the mid-fifth century are the monist Heraclitus' *condemnation* – of his 'learning many things' (*polumathiē*) and 'base skill' (*kakotechniē*) – and the pluralist Empedocles' *admiration* – of 'a man of surpassing knowledge, capable especially of all kinds of clever actions, who obtained the utmost wealth of understanding'.[21] This suggests a man of diverse practical activity, and – together with all the other evidence, such as it is – allows us to say that it is in early Pythagoreanism, if anywhere, that we might expect to find sublimation of the *concrete plurality* inherent in commerce and practical politics, rather than of (as in Parmenides) the separation of *unitary abstract value* from circulation.

---

[19] This hypothesis coheres well with the detail, albeit unreliable, in D. S. 12.9 (14 DK A14) that Pythagoras sided with the 'wealthiest' 500 Sybarite exiles whose 'wealth' (*ousias*, not 'land') their fellow citizens intended to communalise.

[20] DK 47B3, generally agreed to be genuine. Cf. 10C.

[21] Hclt. B129; Emped. B129 (almost certainly Pythagoras).

Of Pythagoras' own philosophical views we know nothing for certain. And so we shall be concerned only with the first ascertainable Pythagorean doctrine, which is from the fifth century BC. Our reliable evidence for it is of two kinds. The first is Aristotle, who has been shown to be by far our best witness for fifth-century Pythagoreanism, preserving as he does preplatonic traditions.[22] Secondly there are certain fragments attributed to the Pythagorean Philolaus that have been shown to be genuine.[23] I will take Aristotle and Philolaus in turn.

Aristotle in the *Metaphysics* refers to 'the so-called Pythagoreans' from the second half (and perhaps earlier) of the fifth century[24] as maintaining (as the first to study mathematics) that the principles (*archai*) of mathematics are the principles of all existing things.[25] He also refers to Pythagoreans maintaining that number is the being (*ousia*) of all things (987a19), that things exist by imitation of numbers (987b11), that numbers are the cause of the being (*ousia*) of other things (987b24), that things themselves are numbers (1090a2), that physical things come into being from numbers (1090a32).[26]

The variety of these formulations may derive from difference between various versions of the doctrine,[27] or more likely from Aristotle's attempt to express, in language influenced by the conceptual framework developed in the Academy, a presocratic doctrine that has little or no place for the incorporeal.[28] But Aristotle is our best witness for preplatonic Pythagoreanism, which certainly held the doctrine that 'everything is number' or at least something very like it.

Burkert regards Pythagorean number doctrine as an instance of number symbolism as it is known among numerous peoples (including the Greeks). Some of this symbolism, notably from the Sudan and China, is similar to Pythagorean doctrine.[29] Burkert concludes accordingly that (476–7)

---

[22] Burkert 1972.   [23] B1–7, 13, 17; Burkert 1972, 218–77; Huffman 1993.

[24] He refers to them here (985b23) as 'among and before' the thinkers he has just discussed (Democritus and Leucippus, and just before them Empedocles and Anaxagoras). Elsewhere he dates them earlier than Plato (987a29; 987b32, 1053b12, 1078b21) and than Democritus (1078b21).

[25] *Met.* 985b23–7; 1078b21.

[26] See also 1080b18; 1083b8–20; 1092b8; and in general Guthrie 1962, 229–38.

[27] In particular, Philolaus, who believed that things are *knowable* by numbers (B4), might not have believed that they *consist of* numbers. So Huffman 1993, 54–77, who takes this to invalidate Aristotle's whole account of the Pythagoreans as holding that things consist of numbers; but cf. e.g. Schibli 1996; KRS 330–1.

[28] Burkert 1972, 43–6.

[29] E.g. five is for Pythagoreanism the number of marriage, and among certain peoples of the Sudan 'plays a part in the marriage ritual': Burkert 1972, 467–9.

the notion that numbers have a 'metamathematical' significance, and that they reveal the principle of the order of the world and of human life, is not any kind of scientific or philosophical insight, but a readily comprehensible characteristic of premathematical thinking about number. Pythagorean number symbolism is therefore much older than any natural science, mathematics, or astronomy that Pythagoras or his pupils could be imagined to have practiced. It has nothing to do with science in our sense – which is to say the Greek sense – of the word; it neither presupposes this nor advances it.

So far so good. But he continues thus.

The Pythagorean doctrine that 'all is number' grows directly out of 'archetypal' number symbolism, which in one degree or another is worldwide in occurrence.

The word 'directly' raises a doubt. The comparative data provide numerous examples of the *associations* of number (e.g. 3 with male, 4 with female), of the use of significant numbers in *ritual*, and of number as a means of creating *correspondence and order* in the cosmos. To take an instance that looks strikingly similar to a Pythagorean doctrine, the Chinese express the relative height of a musical tone in terms of a series of numbers, which is also used in determining lengths of bamboo flutes. However, as Burkert himself notes (471), 'this is not a matter of physical theory, but of analogies with cosmic regularities: in the ratio 3:2 or 4:3 is expressed the relationship of Yang and Yin; the numbers that occur have a value and significance of their own'. Sophisticated though the system of correspondences is,[30] it reminds us of the formulation by Lévy-Bruhl, quoted with approval by Burkert, that in primitive cultures 'each number has its own physiognomy, a kind of mystic atmosphere, a "field of action" peculiar to itself'.[31]

None of this comes anywhere near the idea that all things *consist* of numbers. Nor have I been able to find this idea in the comparative data.[32] Indeed, for numbers to have each 'its own individual physiognomy' or 'a value and significance of their own' is hardly compatible with their being the substance from which all things are made. 'Number', claims Burkert (477)

---

[30] Burkert 1972, 471 writes of 'an amazingly delicate and complex system, which comprehends cosmos and man, nature and social order'.

[31] Lévy-Bruhl 1926 (1910), 206; Burkert 1972, 468.

[32] If the tendency of numbers to be associated with what they enumerate is a primitive feature that has persisted into Pythagoreanism, then it has done so *despite* the conceptual abstraction of number from things that is a precondition of the idea that things consist of number.

is not quantity and measurability, but order and correspondence, the articulation of life in rhythmical pattern and the perspicuous depiction of the whole as the sum of its parts. To see a 'consistently quantitative view of the world'[33] in Pythagorean number theory is a mistake.

The variety of doctrines transmitted as Pythagorean is not self-consistent. And in much of it number does indeed provide order and correspondence. But the (counter-intuitive) view that 'everything is number' is indeed a universalising quantitative view of the world. Though it may well owe much to the respect for number characteristic of number symbolism, it could not have grown 'directly' out of it.

For all things to be number, or made of number, it must be the same sort of thing as, and yet ontologically prior to, everything else. The doctrine focuses on the quantitative aspect of things to the exclusion of the qualitative, with the result that numbers seem concrete (also, perhaps, somehow abstract). Focusing on the quantitative aspect of things is what the trader does. The quality of a commodity concerns him only in so far as it affects the quantity of money that it will fetch. For him what matters about the vase is that he can buy or sell it for five drachmas. In barter, the vase may traditionally be exchanged for two sacks of grain. Or it may be exchangeable for different things – two sacks of grain or five fishes or three knives. But with the development of monetary value the vase seems to embody a *single abstraction* – five (drachmas). The association with a single number is even more likely in the case of a coin, because the value of the coin is (unlike the price of vases) unchanging, and into it enters an element of convention that separates it – up to a point – from the material value of the coin (7D). Slight damage may reduce the value of a vase, but not of a coin. Unprecedentedly in history, number seems to *inhere* in things.[34]

How else would the Pythagoreans have arrived at the strange idea that things consist of numbers? Aristotle (*Met.* 985b23ff.) says that it was because they were the first to take up mathematics, and were brought up in it, and observed many similarities between numbers and entities and things coming into being. But why did they invent mathematics and take it so

---

[33] Quoted from Frank 1923, 72.

[34] Cf. Thomson 1961b, 263–4 on Pythagoreanism: 'The basic factor, therefore, was the growth of a society organised for the production of exchange values and the consequent decay of the old relations based on the production of use values.' Perhaps because he may give an impression of abrupt dogmatism, Thomson's insight has been entirely ignored, except briefly by Guthrie 1962, 221–2, who nevertheless prefers the musical explanation (177 n. 2). I differ from Thomson in focusing on monetisation, for the rapid development of which there is clearer evidence in this period than there is for the development of production for exchange: the two often go together, but are not identical.

seriously? Unless this is mere conjecture by Aristotle, we may regard the closeness of the first mathematicians with their subject – 'brought up' (*entraphentes*) suggests a way of life – as confirming the connection with trade. Aristotle then adds that they also saw the affections of harmonies in numbers. And this, the mathematical basis of the musical scale, has often been taken to be *the* explanation of the doctrine that everything is number. Now it may well have been further confirmation (as Aristotle implies) of an idea already arrived at. But it could hardly have been the only factor, for it has as an explanation three deficiencies not shared by the monetary explanation. One is its inability to explain why it was then and there that there occurred the idea – not just the fantasy of an eccentric but the enduring doctrine of a politically important school – that things consist of numbers. Secondly, the discovery of the mathematical basis of the musical scale may perhaps seem to entail the idea that *sound* is somehow determined by, or even consists of, number – but not that *things* consist of number. Thirdly, it does not seem to entail that things *in general* consist of number, whereas monetary value does seem to permeate everything. This last point must be emphasised. To be sure, not everything in the world has monetary value. But everything that is made by man does, and much that is not. What is important is the entirely unprecedented degree of universality rapidly obtained by monetary value in the sixth century BC. In projecting the social institution of money onto nature (as they had earlier the social institutions of monarchy and reciprocity) it was inevitable that the Greeks would project the transcendent universality of the institution. It is precisely the *universality* of monetary exchange that Heraclitus explicitly compares with the cosmic universality of exchange with fire (B90).

There are various further considerations. The terms used for proportion in Pythagorean musical theory, such as *epitritos logos* (reckoning of one plus a third), are in fact taken from the language of calculating interest on loans.[35] In the fourth century BC Eudemus wrote that 'the precise knowledge of numbers' began with Phoenician commerce, and a tradition attested in late sources tells us that Pythagoras learned arithmetic from the Phoenicians,[36] whose contact with the Greeks was through trade. The fourth-century BC Tarentine Aristoxenus reports that 'Pythagoras seems to have honoured (*timan*),[37] most of all, the study of numbers, and to have advanced it in diverting it (*apagagōn*) from the use of traders, likening

---

[35] Burkert 1972, 439.   [36] Eudemus fr. 133 Wehrli; Porphyr. *VP* 6; Iambl. *VP* 158.

[37] *Timē* in Homer means 'honour', but to the commercial mind came to mean 'price'. Pythagoras may have recreated non-utilitarian 'honour' for the numbers detached from the (utilitarian) price (*timē*) that embodied them.

all things to numbers'.[38] It seems that Aristoxenus regarded Pythagoras as himself concerned with trade, for he reports that he introduced weights and measures to the Greeks.[39] Although none of this can be relied on as information about Pythagoras himself, it may derive from the reality of early Pythagoreanism,[40] and it is not easy to see why Aristoxenus (a musician and musical theorist) would simply invent it: in general mathematics would, at least by the time of Aristoxenus, seem too pure for a commercial origin.[41]

This does not mean that Pythagorean mathematics emerged directly from monetised trade. A fundamental distinction between Babylonian and Greek arithmetic is that whereas the former is based on observation, practical calculation, the solution of sometimes complicated problems, the Greeks undertake the theoretical explanation or proof[42] that goes with the separation of numbers from practice, with their ontological status as abstract entities (with interesting interrelations). This unprecedented step derives, at least in part, from the unprecedented *combination* of the impact (intensified by engagement in the all-pervasive circulation of money) of the abstract value *inherent* in all goods with, on the other hand, an ideology of self-sufficiency tending to sublimate the *separation* (most manifest in coinage) of lasting abstract value from the transitory circulation of goods. One synthesis of these opposing forces, with the separation dominant, is reflected in the ontology of Parmenides (12BC). Another, with the inherence dominant,[43] is the Pythagorean doctrine that all things are number, which combines the unchangeability and ontological fundamentality of abstract numbers with the multiplicity demanded by practical sense (and even a kind of transformation, in that e.g. one and one becomes two).[44] This

---

[38] Aristoxenus DK 58B2 = B23 Wehrli, missed by Thomson.   [39] DK 14A12 = B24 Wehrli.

[40] Although Aristoxenus 'interpreted Pythagoreanism in accordance with his own preconceptions', he also 'put himself forward as an expert in Pythagorean matters', citing in evidence his father's acquaintance with Archytas and his own with the 'last' of the Pythagoreans: Burkert 1972, 107–8; Minar 1942, 51.

[41] Pl. *Rep.* 525c is careful to distinguish the study ('with the mind only') of mathematics from its commercial use. This is quite different (*pace* Burkert 1972, 414–15) from Aristoxenus' *derivation* of arithmetic from commerce.

[42] 'But it was with single problems [the Babylonians] were concerned with, making use of certain "recipes", without any theoretical explanation or even an attempt at proof' (Burkert 1972, 401).

[43] Aristotle says that Plato agrees with the Pythagoreans in making numbers the causes of the reality of other things (*Met.* 987b24), but that he differs from them in his 'separation' of numbers from the world (987b27–31), that the Pythagoreans apply their propositions to bodies as if they consisted of numbers (1083b18), and that their units have magnitude (1080b19); see also 990a15.

[44] Similarly another product of the synthesis is abstract geometry. It was probably in the second half of the fifth century that geometry 'freed itself from its bondage to the needs of practicality' by dealing with purely theoretical problems such as squaring the circle, doubling the cube, irrationality

does not necessarily mean that Pythagorean number ontology originated as a response to Parmenides, whom it may in fact have preceded. Rather, the Pythagoreans and the aristocratic Parmenides are both influenced by monetisation, but the Pythagoreans in a manner reflecting less detachment from commerce.[45] The report in Aristoxenus suggests the *transformation* of arithmetic derived from traders,[46] prefiguring Plato's distinction between polluting human money and divine money permanently present in the soul (12C). We may even hazard the mere guess that the conflicting traditions of the source of Pythagorean number ontology – commerce and music – reflect the combination of engagement in commerce with aristocratic ideology.

B PHILOLAUS

Our other main source for fifth-century Pythagoreanism is provided by the six or seven genuine fragments of Philolaus of Croton, together with the few reliable testimonia. The first words of his book[47] were as follows.

(for practical purposes approximations will do), recognising essential insolubility and offering proof. 'Mathematical logic and deductive proof go beyond what is perceptible, and this is what carried Greek geometry far beyond its predecessors, no matter how suggestive, in the oriental cultures' (Burkert 1972, 423). It has been argued that this development was inspired by Parmenides (e.g. Burkert 1972, 424–6), who shares with it purely logical deduction in a realm separated from (or even contradicting) the senses. I would suggest rather a general tendency taking various forms. Purely logical deduction arises not, or not only, from public debate (so Lloyd: 9B n. 57), but out of the separation of the object from sense data and even from change (cf. Sohn-Rethel 1978, 68, 71). And so the apparently purely logical method pioneered by Parmenides has the same root as its unargued premise (12B). For him (but not for abstract geometry and arithmetic) the separation goes to its extreme, separated also from plurality and so (although only up to a point) from space. Burkert argues that arithmetic, not geometry, is central to the oldest substratum of Pythagorean mathematics (79, 427–65). Measurement of value and of space are of course both prehistoric; my approach implies that (Greek) transformation of the former was a factor in the development of a purely abstract conception of the latter.

[45] This is not to deny that the Pythagorean table of opposites (Aristot. *Met.* 983a22ff.), inasmuch as it has on the same side *limit, one, resting, straight*, and *good* (opposed to *unlimited, plurality*, etc.), feels somewhat Parmenidean. But Aristotle distinguishes it from the number theory by introducing it with 'Other members of this same school say . . .'. It is perhaps of Platonic origin: Burkert 1972, 51–2.

[46] The rapid flowering of theoretical mathematics from the middle of the fifth century (Netz 1999, 272–5) belongs to our theme but cannot be covered here. Netz stresses the *appeal of its form* (unlike presocratic philosophy and the mere persuasiveness of rhetoric, it was incontrovertible) and the *danger of its content* (as potentially useful in banausic activity such as mechanics or land measurement). I would add to his list of practical activities, at its head, commerce, which was especially dangerous because it was a factor in the genesis of Greek mathematics. The need to elevate mathematics over its commercial use is in Plato explicit (*Rep.* 525c). Hippocrates of Chios, who has more claim than any else to be 'in an important sense, the first mathematician' (Netz 1999, 275), was said (by Aristotle and Philoponus, 42 DK A2) to have been a merchant who took up mathematics after losing money!

[47] According to D. L. (8.85); Huffman 1993, 95–6.

Nature in the world-order was fitted together (or 'harmonised', *harmochthē*) from unlimiteds (*apeirōn*) and limiters (*perainontōn*), both the whole world-order and the things in it. (B1)

How then did cosmogony occur?

The first thing fitted together (or 'harmonised', *harmosthen*), the one, in the centre of the sphere, is called hearth. (B7)

What happened next emerges from the following account given by Aristotle (likely to derive from Philolaus)[48] of Pythagorean cosmogony.

After the one was constructed . . . immediately the closest part of the unlimited began to be drawn in and limited by the limit. (*Met.* 1091a15)

The universe is one, and from the unlimited are drawn in time and breath and the void, which always distinguishes the places of each thing.[49]

What were the things 'fitted together' or 'harmonised' to produce the original one, the hearth? The role of *harmonia* ('fitting together' or 'harmony') is to hold together limiters and unlimiteds (B6). The doxography on Philolaus, and Aristotle on the Pythagoreans, report a fire, called hearth by Philolaus, at the centre of the spherical cosmos.[50] And so presumably the hearth was a fitting together or harmonisation of fire, which is unlimited, with the bounded hearth, whose boundaries limit the fire, in the middle of the sphere, by enclosing a finite amount of it.[51] The world-order (*kosmos*) came together from pre-existing limiters and unlimiteds, which were 'quite unlike each other and so could not have been ordered if *harmonia* had not come upon them, in whatever way it came to be' (B6). In the world as it is, after the drawing in of the unlimited, existing things are either limiting, or unlimited, or both limiting and unlimited (B2).

Humans are ignorant of the eternal being of things and of nature itself, except that the 'eternal being' of limiters and unlimiteds, and *harmonia*, must have pre-existed the world-order (B6). Their pre-existence, and the formation of the world-order, remain unexplained (the coming of *harmonia* explicitly so). And yet they are fundamental to the present world-order and are projected onto its origin. They represent not the result of observation or deduction but what is required, in the mind of Philolaus, for 'world-order' (*kosmos*), for the world to be *ordered*. But there are many forms of order.

---

[48] KRS 340–1; Huffman 1993, 202–15; Huffman in Long 1999, 82–3.

[49] Fr. 201 Rose (DK 58 B30). Similarly *Phys.* 213b22.

[50] E.g. A16: 'Philolaus places fire in the middle around the centre and calls it the hearth of the universe and the house of Zeus and mother of the gods and altar, holding together, and measure (*metron*) of nature.'

[51] Something similar is argued by Huffman 1993, 42, 205.

Why, in the preconception of Philolaus, does what is fundamental take this particular form?

The creation of order, of the human domain of culture out of nature, be it washing the hands or building a temple, generally involves the imposition of (internal or external) limit on the apparently unlimited.[52] But the making of money is, as Solon and Aristotle pointed out, unlimited (6F). The thesaurisation of prestige objects in a premonetary economy is limited by practical constraints on use and storage and frequently also by the need to maintain social relations by giving. The accumulation of money, on the other hand, has no such limits. And it may destroy the limits that define social relations. The same Solon who complained that people multiply their wealth without limit was faced with a crisis consisting of the destruction of vital ancient limits on the land: the poor man, unable to repay debt, sees his land absorbed into his rich neighbour's. Money is socially disruptive, and may seem to belong to nature rather than culture; it is like the sea, which seems without internal and external limit (6B, 6F).

Money may seem unlimited internally (as homogeneous), and externally – there is no limit to the sequence of exchanges by which it is accumulated (M–C–M–C–M etc.). In the unlimited cycle of exchanges in which money stays the same while exchanged for all goods and services it may, in the hands of some individuals, increase without limit. The unlimit of money is, we argued, a factor in the unlimit of the invisible material principle of the Milesians, and in the unending circulation of Heraclitean fire. The One of Parmenides however, at a later stage in the development of monetary exchange, is, he emphasises, *limited*.

The material principles of the Milesians and of Heraclitus sublimate the unlimit of money, and the reaction of Parmenides produces a limited One that sublimates the ideal of economic self-sufficiency and the separation of value from unlimited circulation (12B). For Philolaus, as for Parmenides, being is eternal. However, in contrast to Parmenides, Philolaus, appealing to the reality of 'things in their actions',[53] maintains not only that things are plural but also that being consists of unlimiteds as well as limiters (B2, B6). The ordered combination of limiters with unlimiteds sublimates the *integration* of value with circulation. This may be described as a synthesis of Parmenides' arguments for the One as limited on the one hand with

---

[52] Philolaus himself may be not far from this insight when, maintaining that there are both limiting and unlimited things, he appeals to the evidence of 'things in their actions' (B2 . . δηλοῖ δὲ καὶ τὰ ἐν τοῖς ἔργοις; Huffman 1993, 112 rightly argues that the context suggests that ἔργα 'preserves some of its original sense as "deeds" . . .').

[53] B2; see n. 52 above.

the pluralism and unlimited material principle of Ionian cosmology on the other.[54]

Philolaus' 'hearth' is not *merely* metaphorical any more than is the description of cosmology in terms of justice (10B) or of bodily health in terms of the ἰσονομία (equal rights) of opposites.[55] In all these cases preconceptions derived from social relations help to make sense of physical reality. Onto the inexplicable beginning of the cosmos Philolaus projects the self-sufficiency of the household, 'the one', which has not yet drawn in the surrounding unlimited.[56] But this self-sufficiency is an anachronistic ideal rather than a reality, and accordingly, just as the household must participate in the unlimited circulation of money, so the cosmic hearth itself immediately draws in the unlimited by which it is surrounded.[57] We noted in fact that, even before the drawing in of the surrounding unlimited, the limiting hearth presumably contains (a finite amount of) fire, the element which for Heraclitus is the agent of unending circulation, comparable (B90) in its universal exchangeability to money. Self-sufficent unitary value is reflected, in association with the ideal of household sufficiency, in a privileged position, 'the one', at the origin of Philolaus' universe, which is nevertheless from the beginning, or perhaps almost from the beginning, permeated by the unlimited, reflecting the permeation of all households by monetary circulation.

What exactly are the unlimiteds and limiters that pre-exist and constitute Philolaus' world-order, so that existing things are either limiters or unlimiteds or both? They are plural, everywhere, and manifest (B2). They are neither simply odd and even numbers[58] nor simply shapes and stuffs.[59] Time, breath (= air?), and void are, we saw, drawn from the unlimited and so are presumably unlimiteds, and so too, we noted, is fire. On the basis of these examples Huffman characterises the unlimiteds as follows (43–4):

Each in itself defines a continuum, but none of them is defined by any set quantity or boundaries within that continuum. They could perhaps be called quantifiables in that, although an account of their own essence would make no mention of any specific quantity, each of them does admit of the imposition of boundaries from without.

---

[54] For Philolaus as belonging squarely to the presocratic tradition see Huffman 1993, 37–53. For the influence on him of Parmenides see Huffman 1993, 39, 50–3, 67–8, 72, 100, 133, 229, 295.

[55] So described by Philolaus' contemporary fellow-Crotonian Alcmaeon (B4 DK).

[56] In Pl. *Crat.* (401c) *hestia* (hearth) is equated with *ousia* (wealth, being).

[57] Already Solon, who complains about the unlimit of wealth, can say that the crisis, which is both economic and political, enters into everybody's house, leaping the fence and penetrating to the inmost chamber (fr. 4.26–9).

[58] Suggested by KRS 326; but cf. Huffman 1993, 48.

[59] Suggested by Barnes 1982, II. 85–7; but cf. Huffman 1993, 43.

As another example of an unlimited Huffman gives 'the undefined continuum of possible musical pitches', with the limiters as 'the boundaries we establish in this continuum by picking out specific pitches', and with *harmonia* also required – to produce an ordered system.

> Unlimiteds and limiters turn out to be a natural pair, as Philolaus' language suggests; the unlimiteds define a continuum without any boundaries while the limiters establish boundaries in these continuums.[60]

This account by Huffman is acceptable. Still, it is interesting that, despite the importance and frequency of limiters and unlimiteds in his system and their frequency (B1, 2, 3, 6) in his few surviving fragments, Philolaus gives barely any indication (other than the words 'limited' and 'unlimited') of what they are, a vagueness arising perhaps from his epistemological humility:[61] for the world-order to exist we know that limiters and unlimiteds and *harmonia* must have pre-existed it, but we are ignorant of the eternal being of things and of nature itself (B6). This sceptical refusal to be specific clarifies further the *preconceived* importance of Philolaus' fundamental entities.[62] He does not, in what survives of his doctrine, specify what the limiters and unlimiteds are, but can nevertheless affirm that they must have pre-existed the world-order that, along with *harmonia*, they constitute. They seem to be things present in the world, and yet, being unspecified as well as fundamental, also seem abstract. Why was the antithesis limit–unlimit, reconciled by harmony, important enough, in the mind of a fifth-century Italian Greek, to produce this extraordinary metaphysic?[63]

The *apeiron* (unlimited) of Anaximander was, we argued, unlimited internally (undifferentiated, homogeneous) and externally (infinite), and in both these respects, which may not have been distinguished from each other, it resembles money (10C). When a vase is sold for five drachmas, the price belongs, in a sense, to the abstract unlimited continuum of monetary value – an unlimited continuum in that it is homogeneous and infinitely accumulatable in unending circulation. The vase is in this vital respect (abstract monetary value) assimilated to all other commodities. And yet its monetary value is also here delimited from that unlimited continuum, is defined as five drachmas. According to Aristotle (*Pol.* 1257b22–4) currency (*nomisma*) is 'a limiting factor (*peras*)' of exchange. The phrase has been

---

[60] Huffman 1993, 44, on the basis of Philolaus B6.   [61] Huffman 1993, 40–1, 44, 47.

[62] Cf. Burkert 1972, 267: 'For Philolaus philosophical ideas and specific ideas of scientific knowledge seem to have been no more than a means of expressing and illuminating a pre-existing picture, of a world consisting of a pair of basic opposites, informed by harmony and defined by number.'

[63] For the persistence in Pythagoreanism of the fundamentality of the pair limit–unlimited see e.g. Guthrie 1962, 207, 242–6, 278, 340.

interpreted to mean that 'the price of something delimits its exchange-value'.[64] In acquiring a monetary price the vase both embodies the abstract unlimited (circulating money) and delimits it (to five drachmas). In the five-drachma vase limiter and unlimited are fitted together. Just as for Philolaus eternal being consists of limiters and unlimiteds fitted together (B6), so monetary value remains always the same throughout the limitations imposed – in all its embodiments – on its unlimit.

This does not mean that money is the only unlimited continuum. Even as a mere use-value, the vase too may be imagined as representing a combination of limiter (its shape) with unlimited (clay). A *medimnos* of barley is a quantity defined from an undefined mass. Philolaus' preconceived world-order (*kosmos*) consists of a *plurality* of limiters and unlimiteds. But this preconception is unlikely to *derive* from, though it may be reinforced by, awareness of a *medimnos* of barley or of the manufacture of a vase. A more likely source would be something that is both new and a striking instance of the coming together of the limiter and unlimited through *harmonia*. One such instance is the discovery of the numerical basis of the musical scale, which Philolaus discusses in B6. In the words of Huffman,[65]

the string and the indefinite number of pitches it can produce can be compared to the unlimited, while stops placed along it to determine specific pitches are the limiters ... but not just any set of pitches will produce a musically ordered set; such a set only results when when the unlimited continuum is limited in accordance with a *harmonia* ...

Other such instances are the commodity, and coinage, for they strikingly combine the unlimited (monetary value) with limit, abstract with concrete. As we noted of early Pythagoreanism generally, music and monetary value are not *alternative* sources for Pythagorean metaphysics, which may rather seem confirmed by its manifestation in different spheres, as well as by the manifest pleasure given by musical *harmonia*. But what distinguishes monetary value is that it is, though relatively novel, no less universal to the social process than are the justice projected onto the cosmos by Anaximander or the *isonomia* (equality of political rights) projected onto the body by Alcmaeon.

This social universality involves *harmonia*. The fitting together (*harmonia*) of limiter and unlimited in a commodity occurs for the purpose of a *transaction*: it is also *harmonia* between buyer and seller. Buyer and seller are

---

[64] By C. D. Reeve in his translation. *Nomisma* can mean a quantitative measure: Ar. *Thesm.* 348.
[65] Huffman 1993, 44–5.

in a relation of mutual absolute egotism – a historically unprecedented form of exchange (10C, 12A). How then is agreement between them possible? To put the same question differently, what determines the ratio of one vase to five drachmas? Agreement may seem imposed by numerical proportion – *logos* – that somehow inheres in money and controls the universal system of equivalence between goods and money. This system is reflected – in the doctrine of Heraclitus – in the power of 'invisible *harmonia*' and in the universal *logos* according to which opposites are united (12A). For Philolaus what allows the limiters and unlimiteds to combine in an ordered way is *harmonia* (B6). Entering into the preconceived fundamentality of *harmonia* in the world-order of Philolaus is (a) the need to reconcile with the unlimited plurality of the world the limited that Parmenides had separated from it, (b) the need for agreement between the opposed parties in exchange, and (c) the overall harmony of a society now dependent on the ubiquitous daily occurrence of this agreement in innumerable monetary transactions, an overall harmony that is – given the disruption caused (Solon makes clear) by the naturally *unlimited* accumulation of money – precisely a limiting of the unlimited. It is precisely this combination – within money – of limit (or 'measure') with unlimit that we referred to earlier, apropos of Solon, as a paradox (10B).

In uniting the opposed parties (buyer and seller) *harmonia* fits together unlimited (monetary continuum) and limiter to produce a *numerical* proportion – one vase equals five drachmas. The power of calculation (λογισμός) to achieve both agreement in contracts and social concord generally is made explicit by Philolaus' younger Pythagorean contemporary Archytas (13A), said to have been his pupil (DK 44A3). The Heraclitean *harmonia* of opposites (B51) expresses, at least in part, the agreement between the opposed parties to exchange (12A). For Philolaus too *harmonia* combines opposites, but is also closely associated with *number*. Huffman[66] concludes that he 'seems . . . to conceive of all "fitting together" of limiters and unlimiteds in terms of numerically specific relations'. Furthermore, Philolaus wrote that 'all things that are known have number. For it is not possible that anything whatsoever be understood or known without this' (B4). Number is abstract, unchanging, and for Philolaus epistemologically privileged (its presence is required for there to be knowledge). In these three aspects it is like the Parmenidean One, to which it is also however – as plural and potentially unlimited – antithetical. And so, as we noted earlier of Philolaus' fitting together of limited with unlimited, his sublimation

---

[66] 1993, 73, based on *inter alia* Philolaus B6.

of monetary value as number is a synthesis of Parmenides' sublimation of self-sufficient abstract value (abstract, unchanging, the only object of knowledge) with the pluralism and unlimit of the Ionian sublimation of monetary value unseparated from circulation.

In much presocratic philosophy the macrocosm is analogous to the microcosm in that the material principle of the cosmos resembles the soul or mind (12B). The resemblance is made explicit by Anaximenes, who compares the wind (or 'breath') enclosing the whole cosmos to the soul (as air) holding us together. Anaximenes' air (his material principle) is unlimited (11B), but we do not know whether this entered into his idea of the soul. Heraclitus maintained that 'you would not find out the boundaries of soul even by travelling along every path: so deep a *logos* does it have' (B45): the fiery soul seems unlimited, and yet contains *logos* (something like measure). Compare the remarkable statement by Solon that 'it is very difficult to apprehend the mind's invisible measure (*metron*), which alone holds the limits of all things'.[67] To the unlimited accumulation that is devastating his polis Solon finds resistance within the mind,[68] although 'holds the limits of all things' seems to connect mind with cosmos, implying a cosmic role for the mind as agent of the limitation[69] that belongs, we have noted, to the human imposition of order on (unlimited) nature, and that is antithetical also to the new unlimit of money.[70] Parmenides' view that what exists is limited seems influenced by his view that what exists is co-extensive with what can be thought.[71] Similarly, Philolaus seems to imply that in some way *knowing* involves limiting.[72]

The presocratics, then, tend to project the mind onto the macrocosm, and it seems that Philolaus projects (mental) limiting of the unlimited

---

[67] Fr. 16; cf. fr. 13.52.

[68] In fr. 4c he urges the greedy rich to set their mind in measured/moderate things (*metrioisi*).

[69] Cf. Anaxagoras B12.

[70] Hence the shockingness of Clytemnestra's metaphor for the unlimit of monetary wealth: 'the house *does not know* how to be poor' (Aesch. *Ag.* 962): 8F.

[71] Note esp. B8. 34–8: 'What can be thought and the thought that "it is" are the same [or 'The same thing is there to be thought and is why there is thought' – ταὐτὸν δ᾽ ἐστὶ νοεῖν τε καὶ οὕνεκεν ἔστι νόημα: I give the translations of Guthrie and KRS respectively]. For you will not find thought without what is, in which thinking is expressed [or 'in what has been said']. For nothing exists or will exist outside what is, since fate fettered it so as to be whole and unmoved.' Conversely, '. . . you would not know what is not, for it cannot be accomplished/completed' (B2.7). See further Huffman 1993, 122; Owen 1986 (1960); cf. 12B. The view is also expressed, in terms influenced by money, by the Derveni Commentator (11B).

[72] B3 ἀρχὰν γὰρ οὐδὲ τὸ γνωσούμενον ἐσσεῖται πάντων ἀπείρων ἐόντων. Huffman 1993, 118–20 cogently defends the translation 'there will not be anything that is going to know at all, if everything is unlimited', and compares Pl. *Theaet.* 161c–162d. Others have taken γνωσούμενον as passive ('will be known': cf. the Aristotelian belief that an unlimited object is unknowable).

onto the physical creation of the macrocosm. In his cosmogony, we saw earlier, there was an original One, a central fire, which immediately after its construction drew in – from the unlimited – time, breath, and void. This is also how he envisages the physical creation of the microcosm. The human body in the womb is composed entirely of the hot, and on being born draws in immediately the cold air outside and then emits it 'like a debt (*chreos*)' – i.e. breathes out (A27). The human being is, like the cosmos,[73] created by its body drawing in (and presumably thereby limiting) part of the surrounding invisible unlimited (air). The breathing out of this part of the unlimited air is described by Philolaus as like paying a debt (the implication, which Philolaus may have made explicit, is that breathing in is like acquiring debt). Why so? There is nothing in the *physical* process to suggest the metaphor. As with Philolaus' cosmic 'hearth', the metaphor is not a mere metaphor. The constant physical process needed for life,[74] respiration, is envisaged in terms of constant monetary exchange. Just as Philolaus' physical creation of the cosmos is modelled on the household drawing in part of the unlimited invisible monetary value by which it is surrounded, so too – at the level of the microcosm – the physical creation of the human being is modelled on his drawing in part of the unlimited invisible monetary value by which he is surrounded. It is of the essence of the human being, in thought and in action, to establish limits, and yet he is – like the individual household, whose ideal is self-sufficiency – nevertheless surrounded and penetrated by the invisible unlimit that inheres in monetised social relations. Similarly, for Heraclitus the individual soul possesses *logos* and yet partakes of the invisible unlimit of the surrounding cosmic fire (12B).

C PROTAGORAS

In Homer and Hesiod we do of course find the distinction between truth and falsehood, but no trace of the idea that the world is systematically divided between seeming and being, between what merely appears but is not real and what does not appear but is real. The first surviving suggestion of this idea is Xenophanes' view that 'seeming has been constructed over everything', which I associated with his idea that a concealed (somewhat abstract) unity of all things underlies their apparent plurality (10D, 12B): all things, beneath their covering of seeming, are in fact one. This is implied also in Heraclitus: all things are one, nature hides itself, invisible harmony is stronger (or better) than visible, and for access to the *logos* there is needed

---

[73] Huffman 1993, 213.   [74] Or perhaps one should say for the soul: see Huffman 1993, 328–31.

mind (*nous*) as well as the senses (12AB). The universal division is made systematic and explicit by Parmenides, who divides his poem between the object of knowledge and the objects of 'opinions'; and here again, as implied by Xenophanes and Heraclitus, seeming belongs to concrete plurality and being to abstract unity. In general, then, a universal distinction between seeming and being is in its earliest manifestations associated with the cosmological division between concrete plurality (seeming) and underlying abstract unity (being), and therefore – indirectly – with the monetary development that I have identified as a factor in the emergence of this cosmological division.

If the reality is that deity is one, somehow co-extensive with the universe, and non-anthropomorphic, why do mortals believe in anthropomorphic deities (mere seeming)? Because, Xenophanes says, humans construct deities in their own image (B14) – as animals would if they could (B15), and Ethiopians actually do (B16). This is the first recorded instance of deprojection or desublimation, of the subversive notion that humans unconsciously project themselves or their institutions onto the world. In this way seeming prevails over being.[75]

However, the presocratic view that abstract unity is more real than concrete plurality may be thought to be the opposite of the truth, in that concrete things are in a sense more real than any abstraction. Whence the presocratic inversion of reality? The idea of abstract unitary reality underlying the appearance of multiplicity derives in part from the fundamentality of unitary abstract value to all else. But unitary abstract value is, despite its fundamentality, in a sense unreal, real by convention only. The cosmological inversion of reality reflects the paradox that monetary value is both fundamental and in a sense unreal. Xenophanes' awareness of the mechanism of unconscious projection does not mean that he escapes doing it himself. The presocratic cosmos is, in its various forms, a projection of human institutions (especially money) onto the cosmos no less than is the Olympus of ordinary believers.

Of this unreality or artificiality of monetary value the Greeks were early aware. Midas is imagined starving amidst his gold; and the sixth-century poet Ananius (fr. 3) notes that figs are in certain circumstances preferable to gold. Money, like anthropomorphic deity (Xenophanes), is a human construction: asses prefer garbage to gold (Heraclitus B9). The artificiality of currency (*nomisma*), of which the Greeks of the Classical period were well

---

[75] Cf. e.g. Simon. 93 *PMG* 'seeming constrains even truth'; Eur. *Critias* fr. 19 (humans invented the gods to inspire fear); Hdt. 3.38.

aware (7D), might have contributed to the late fifth-century insistence[76] on the mere artificiality of *nomos* (law, convention)[77] as opposed to *phusis* (nature).[78]

Were they also aware that monetary value had been unconsciously projected onto the presocratic cosmos, that the supposed reality of this cosmos was based on a double artificiality (as monetary value and as cosmic projection)? No, partly because of the obscurity of monetary value itself, which must conceal its own origin in the reification of interpersonal relations (10C): the cosmological transcendence of abstract being has a no more transparent origin than does the social transcendence of abstract (monetary) being from which it derives. The idea that the value of coinage is, as socially constructed, the same sort of things as the gods, is implicit in a joke in Aristophanes' *Clouds* (7D). But this is still a long way from awareness of the projection of money onto the cosmos.

Somewhat closer, albeit still not very close, is the famous fragment (B1) of Protagoras (*c.* 490–420 BC):

Of all things the measure (*metron*) is humankind, of the things that are that they are (*hōs estin*) and of the things that are not that they are not.[79]

A curious feature of the huge body of interpretation[80] of this fragment is the general failure to register the oddity of *metron* ('measure'). The failure has three causes: the deceptive familiarity of the saying 'man is the measure of all things', the fact that 'measure' has in fact a broader meaning than *metron*, and Plato's (*Theaet.* 178b, 160c) interpretation of *metron* in this fragment as meaning criterion (*kritērion*) or judge (*kritēs*), in which he is followed by Aristotle and Sextus Empiricus.

We should not however accept without modification Plato's polemical interpretation. The important fact, unrecognised by the commentators, is

---

[76] The insistence will culminate in the thought and life of Diogenes the Cynic, who was told by an oracle to (metaphorically) restamp the currency: D. L. 6.71.

[77] Note also the suspicion of coinage (as sign rather than substance) implied in Aesch. *Sept.*: Amphiaraus' shield is 'all bronze' and, in contrast to the emblazoned shields of the other six attacking heroes, has no sign (*sēma*), 'for he wants not to *seem* the best but to *be* the best' (592). Given the resemblance between shield and coin (circular metal with pictorial sign: 8c n. 23), the rejection of mere seeming by Amphiaraus' blank shield seems inspired by, or at least to evoke, suspicion of coinage. This association is made by Steiner 1994, 56–7, who also points to other parallels between coins and the shields described in this drama. On similarities between devices on coins and on shields see Spier 1990.

[78] Cf. Aristotle on currency as 'called *nomisma* because it is not by nature but by convention (*nomos*)': 7D.

[79] (B1) Πάντων χρημάτων μέτρον ἐστὶν ἄνθρωπος, τῶν μὲν ὄντων ὡς ἔστιν, τῶν δὲ οὐκ ὄντων ὡς οὐκ ἔστιν.

[80] A useful overview of this body is Huss 1996.

that *metron* has that meaning nowhere else, but is always bound in some way to *quantitative limit or measure*.[81] There is no reason why Protagoras should not have used the word *kritērion* (or *kritēs*, or a synonym) if that is what he had meant, especially as the sentence he did write seems awkward, even meaningless: how can you measure all things that they are or are not, unless – taking *hōs estin* to mean 'that they are so'[82] rather than 'that they exist' – you take 'so' to refer only to the quantitative aspect of all things? But existential sense cannot in fact be excluded from 'of the things that are that they are and of the things that are not that they are not'.[83] It is understandable therefore that Plato and subsequent commentators broadened *metron* to mean *kritērion*. But we should rather try to find sense in the words Protagoras wrote.

By '*metra* of the sea' Hesiod means the limits to be observed: sail only in a certain season, do not overload your ship (*Op.* 648, 694). Even the unlimited sea is given limits, by navigation, and so there is a limit even to trade. 'Preserve limits (*metra*): fitness (*kairos*) is best in all things' (*Op.* 694). For the Pythagoreans both *metron* and *kairos* were important. In the Pythagorean *Carmen Aureum*[84] the principle '*metron* is best in all things' is associated in *spending* according to *kairos* (37–8). Because order depends on limit, everything has its *metron* or (plural) *metra*.[85] Even the sun, according to Heraclitus (B94), will not overstep its limits (*metra*). For Philolaus (13B) the creation of the world and of the things in it is a process of limiting: his central fire – described in the doxography as *metron* of nature (A16) – draws in, and thereby limits, the surrounding unlimited. He envisages the human being drawing in air at birth as an analogous process. And he also regards *knowing* as in some way involving *limiting* (13B). Does then ubiquitous limitation inhere not only (or not at all) in the ordered plurality of the world but also (or only) in the order that we impose on it by thought? The same question is suggested by Solon's reference to the 'invisible *metron* of thought that alone holds the limits of all things'.[86] Even Hesiod's '*metra* of the sea' are imposed by ourselves no less than are *metra* of wine or barley. Of Cyrus' father Cambyses it was said that, in contrast to the previous

---

[81] Arist. *Met.* 1053a31–b4 is not an exception.

[82] Or (implausibly) *hōs* to mean 'how'. On these problems see e.g. Guthrie 1969, 190.

[83] Apart from the natural meaning of the Greek (especially οὐκ ὄντων), cf. his fr. 4 'About the gods I do not know either that they exist (*hōs eisin*) or that they do not exist (*hōs ouk eisin*) or what they are like in form.'

[84] This was composed before 300 BC and may contain material from the Classical period: Thom 1995, 35–58. Cf. Pi. *Ol.* 2.53–4 (influenced by Pythagoreanism? cf. 57–83).

[85] Cf. Pi. *Pyth.* 2.34 'one should see the *metron* of everything'.

[86] Fr. 16; Similar is *Theogn.* 1172.

king of Persia, 'measure (*metron*) for him was not his soul but the law' (Xen. *Cyr.* 1.3.18): *metron* may inhere in the soul (though for Cambyses it inhered instead in the law, itself a human construction). This opposition – does *metron* belong to things themselves or is it merely imposed by the human mind? – is mediated by the doctrine of Protagoras' contemporary Diogenes of Apollonia that (B3) 'all things having *metra*' could not have occurred without *noēsis* (thinking, intelligence), which is embodied in air. Somewhat similar, from the same period, is Anaxagoras' notion that in the cosmos there is a physical substance, mind (*nous*), which ordered everything (B12). Compare also, a generation or two earlier, Heraclitus' association of *logos*, which also belongs to the soul (12B), with the balanced process of cosmic change: (B30) '. . . kindling in measures (*metra*) and going out in measures (*metra*)'.

The point of Protagoras' statement is to resolve this opposition in favour of the human mind. Diogenes was right to associate *metra* with *noēsis*, but wrong to regard *noēsis* as spread, in air, throughout the universe. *Metron* does not inhere in things, but is imposed by *human noēsis*. This interpretation solves several problems.

Firstly, it has been commented that in Protagoras' 'Of all things (*chrēmata*) the measure is (*estin*) humankind' the unnecessary *estin* seems to emphasise humankind (*anthrōpos*).[87] The point of the emphasis is, I suggest, that the *metron* that others locate among things (*chrēmata*) is, in truth, imposed by *humankind*. The interpretation 'imposed by' is allowed by the ambiguity in *metron*, which means measure but also measuring instrument, and this active meaning is inevitably evoked in the emphatic reversal produced by 'is humankind'. It is only by virtue of our thought (or action) that things have *metra*.

Secondly, there is controversy over whether 'things' is too broad a translation of *chrēmata*, given its etymological connection with *chrēsthai*, which refers to human need, use, or experience. Guthrie rejects this qualification, listing numerous instances in which *chrēma* means 'thing'.[88] But all these instances (mostly somewhat idiomatic) are of *chrēma*, singular. His only instance of the plural is a passage in which *chrēmata* is actually defined as whatever is beneficial (Xen. *Oec.* 1.8–10). By far the most common meaning of *chrēmata* is goods or money. Aristotle defines *chrēmata* as 'all things of which the value is measured by currency' (5B). The normal Greek for 'all things' is not *panta* (*ta*) *chrēmata*, which normally refers to goods or

---

[87] Schiappa 1991, 119.   [88] 1969, 191.

money,[89] but (*ta*) *panta*.[90] Why then did Protagoras add *chrēmata*? Perhaps because consciously or unconsciously he had in mind the imposition of *metra* inherent in the human creation of commodities (*chrēmata*). Another possible factor is as follows. The only known occurrence before Protagoras of *panta chrēmata* meaning all things is in Anaxagoras,[91] notably the phrase – referred to by Plato and Aristotle among others – 'all things (*panta chrēmata*) were together' (B1), of the original undifferentiated mass subsequentially differentiated into recognisable things by mind (*nous*). Inasmuch as Protagoras restores this *nous* to humankind, as it were, perhaps he was influenced by the famous words of his close contemporary Anaxagoras, whom he probably knew at Athens (they were both friends of Pericles).

Thirdly, and most importantly, my approach solves the generally unacknowledged problem of how it can make any sense to say that humankind is the μέτρον of the existence (and perhaps state) of all things. Things exist as separate things by virtue of having limits (*metra*). The creation of individual things may be seen as the differentiation of (i.e. the creation of limits within) an undifferentiated mass (e.g. Anaxagoras) or as the limitation of the unlimited (Philolaus). And so to impose *metra* on the world is also to divide it up into separate things, and in that sense to be 'the *metron* (active) of the things that are that they are (so?) and of the things that are not that they are not (so?)'. But why then does Plato interpret *metron* too broadly, as *kritērion*? Because he is providing a simplifying interpretation, for the purposes of his own polemical agenda, of words of Protagoras that in fact come close to (and may even imply) that interpretation – especially if his *estin* is taken, as some modern scholars take it, to have a more than merely existential sense. And indeed Plato does, as we shall soon see, acknowledge that it is no more than interpretation.

Fourthly, the prevailing opinion is that by *anthrōpos* Protagoras means each individual human rather than humankind in general. After all, this is how it is on the whole[92] taken by Plato, who supposes Protagoras to mean that when the same thing seems different to you and to me it *is* different for you and for me. In this Plato is followed by Aristotle,[93] and by most recent

---

89 It though does occur meaning 'all things' in Plato – in quotations of Anaxagoras (see below) or Protagoras, or, elsewhere, generally in connection with knowledge (e.g. *Crat.* 440a7, 440d2, *Euthyd.* 294d2, *Protag.* 361b1).

90 And so Protagoras' words are naturally reported with *chrēmatōn* omitted at e.g. Aristot. *Met.* 1053a36.

91 This possible connection with Anaxagoras, though not the significance here of Anaxagoras' voῦς, was noted by Gomperz 1965 (1912), 252.

92 Schiappa 1991, 120 notes that in fact when discussing the fragment both Plato and Aristotle 'alternated between the individual and generic senses of *anthropos*'.

93 Pl. *Theaet.* 151e–152a; *Crat.* 386a; Aristot. *Met.* 1062b13.

commentators. But if this unprecedented doctrine was what Protagoras had in mind, he would surely have stated it (e.g. by the word 'each' – *hekastos*). Commentators have (blinded presumably by Plato) ignored the fact that the simple *anthrōpos* in a generalisation refers to humankind.[94] However, what is true of all humankind is also true of each individual. And if, as the statement in effect claims, there is no distinction between what is and what seems to humankind in general, it appears to follow that there is no independent reality to resolve differences in what seems to different humans. That is to say, Protagoras' statement about humankind appears to imply Plato's interpretation of it. Plato alights – here again, for his own polemical agenda – on what appears to be an implication of Protagoras' doctrine rather than on what it actually states. Plato (*Theaet.* 152a) does in fact acknowledge that he is merely interpreting Protagoras' words, for after quoting them he writes 'and he means something like this,[95] that as each thing appears to me so it is for me, and as each thing appears to you, so it is for you', and adds, as the logical step between Protagoras' words and his interpretation of them, 'are not both you and I *anthrōpos*?'. This interpretation (or implication) inaugurates a new phase of epistemology, but the doctrine that implied it – Protagoras' 'subjectivist' denial of the distinction between seeming and being – did not hit the Greeks like rain from a cloudless sky. It was rather, as I have indicated, the latest twist in the development of presocratic epistemology that began with Xenophanes.

Culture, the human creation of order – whether action or thought – delimits from a continuum: a vase is delimited from the continuum of earth, the 'Athenians' from people in general. This delimitation determines ontology, decisions on what does and does not exist. This is a truth underlying Protagoras' statement.[96] But it is true of all humanity. How do we explain that it was a fifth-century Greek who first focused on human delimitation or 'measurement' as determining ontology? If we are right to have argued for the development of money as a factor in the earlier development of thought, was it not also a factor in what might be called the Protagorean epistemological revolution, especially given the continuity that we have indicated between this revolution and the thought that preceded it? If so,

---

[94] Cf. e.g. Pi. *Pyth.* 8. 96 *anthrōpos* is the dream of a shadow; Hdt. 1.32; Thuc. 3.39.5; Pl. *Rep.* 619b.

[95] οὐκοῦν οὕτως πῶς λέγει . . . In *Cratylus* (386a) Plato is less cautious. Cf. Aristot. *Met.* 1053a36–b1 'Protagoras says that *anthrōpos* is the measure of all things, as if (ὥσπερ ἂν εἰ) saying the knowing or perceiving man.'

[96] As it underlies also e.g. the idea in Pl. *Philebus* (23c–31a) of a fourfold division of everything in the world into unlimited, limit, the mixture of unlimited and limit, and mind (as the cause of the mixture).

then – to repeat a proviso that needs constant repetition – it was only one of various factors, that here include the development of rhetoric.[97]

Pricing involves both delimitation and measurement (*peras* and *metron*). It both delimits specific sums from the unlimited homogeneous continuum of monetary value (13B) and creates a universe of *chrēmata* differentiated by number, not unlike the universe imagined by the Pythagoreans. Aristotle states that currency (*nomisma*) measures all things (*panta . . . metrei*), and defines *chrēmata* as 'all things of which the value is measured (*metreitai*) by currency' (5B). 'Humankind is the *metron* of all *chrēmata*' means that we measure or limit all things,[98] thereby establishing their identity and so in a sense their existence ('of the things that are that they are . . .'). Philolaus claims that knowing involves limiting (13B) and that 'all things that are known have number. For it is not possible that anything whatsoever be understood or known without this' (B4).

The universality of currency as a *metron* constituting *chrēmata* (Aristotle) is not however enough to establish it as the factor behind Protagoras' epistemology. Universal quantifying delimitation can be performed also by measurement of space or weight. But monetary measurement has another feature that measurement of space or weight does not. As we have seen, the tradition of deprojection (e.g. animals would project gods in their own image, and they prefer garbage to gold), which in a sense culminated in Protagoras, also produced, in his lifetime, awareness that such fundamentals as deity and monetary value are socially constructed. Whereas spatial or weight measurement is human dividing up of objective reality, monetary measure is subjective. An identical vase or coin always has the same weight and spatial dimensions but may change its value. Protagoras' emphasis, I have noted, is on *humankind* (*anthrōpos*). It is the *combination*, in the monetary *metron*, of universality with manifest subjectivity that produces the idea that the universe of delimited, quantified things depends on delimiting quantification by humankind. This is not to say that Protagoras' statement is about monetary value: *metron* refers rather to any kind of quantifying delimitation. My suggestion is rather that it was the merely human projection (despite its fundamentality) of universal monetary measure that was, consciously or unconsciously, an important factor in the emergence of Protagoras' universal subjectivism. Whereas the Parmenidean One represents the sublimation of monetary value abstracted even from circulation, with a consequent absolute distinction between being and seeming, it was

---

[97] E.g. Woodruff 1999.
[98] Cf. at Pl. *Pol.* 285a the view that measurement (*metrētikē*) is about all that comes into being (*ta gignomena*); also Pl. *Phileb.* 16c; [Pl.] *Epin.* 976d.

the desublimation of monetary value, its restoration to human thought and practice, that contributed to Protagoras' subjectivist challenge to the distinction between being and seeming.

Protagoras, like the presocratics generally, projects monetary value onto the universe, but his projection is dominated by the (delimiting) *subjectivity* of monetary value – and so in a sense also *de*projects itself. This deprojection implies the possibility of individual isolation. Monetary value is created by collective assent to it, and so each of us is free to withdraw assent[99] without incurring factual error. Accordingly Plato, who by contrast recuperates the objectivity of monetary value in the soul by giving it a divine origin (12B), infers from the subjectivism of Protagoras the disturbing conclusion that there is no way of resolving differences in what seems to each of us. But this is only one of the respects in which money may lead to an appearance of individual isolation – as we shall see in the next chapter.

---

[99] As e.g. Diogenes the Cynic no doubt did (cf. n. 76 above).

CHAPTER FOURTEEN

Individualisation

A INDIVIDUALISM

Reciprocity performs the exchange of goods and services by means of lasting interpersonal attachment, in which the identity of the donor may remain associated with his gift (10B). In centralised reciprocity (redistribution) tradition and interpersonal attachment (for instance of labourer to king or to god) are still at the heart of the economy, albeit supported by custom or by fear. Barter involves some impersonality in the exchange, and some autonomy for the exchangers, but tends nevertheless to require lasting (and sometimes ritualised) personal relationships sanctioned by custom and characteristic of reciprocity.[1] The Greek animal sacrifice involves reciprocity (something in return may be expected of the deity) and redistribution (meat brought to the god is eaten by all), but also the horizontal relation of egalitarian communality between the participants: there must be equal shares for all (3A). It was this traditional, sanctified equality that we saw as a factor in that communal confidence in multiple symbols of identical value that is a prerequisite for the communal adoption of coinage. Aristotle will observe that currency (*nomisma*), by creating commensurability in exchange, makes possible communality (*koinōnia*) of equals (*qua* transactors).[2]

The result is a paradox. For its beginnings coined money owed something to (sacrificial) interpersonal solidarity, but when it became a general means of payment and exchange it must have greatly increased such

---

[1] 8C. It is easy to be misled by the creation-myth of money (out of barter) into believing that premonetary society was based on barter. In fact it has been concluded that 'barter, in the strict sense of moneyless market exchange, has never been a quantitatively important or dominant model or transaction in any past or present economic system about which we have hard information' (Dalton 1982, 185). Humphrey and Hugh-Jones (1992) see a more important role for barter, which however they regard as *contrasting* with market exchange (though distinct also from gift-exchange). In Hesiod there is description of subsistence farming and mention of local gift-exchange and local begging, but of trade (i.e. barter) only (as in Homer) as trade by sea.

[2] *EN* 1132b31–4, 1133a17–19, 1133b15–22.

impersonality and personal autonomy as were present in earlier forms of exchange. Money tends to promote the autonomy of the individual.[3] We have seen the consequences of this in the 'mutual absolute egoism' of the monetary transaction that we saw as a factor in the cosmology of Heraclitus (12A), in the ideology of monetary self-sufficiency that we saw as a factor in the abstract One of Parmenides (12BC), and in the individualistic implication of Protagoras' universal subjectivism (13C).

The individual with money, although he may find useful and desirable the personal relations of kinship and friendship (reciprocity) as well as participation in collective sacrifices (redistribution), can frequently do without them, relying instead on the impersonal power of money.[4] Even in the heroic age imagined in fifth-century tragedy, all that Menoeceus is thought to need, when suddenly told to go all alone far from his city, is money (Eur. *Phoen.* 977–85). The power of money can increase human independence even from deity: this is apparent not only in the construction of impersonal cosmology but also, for instance, in the tyrant's neglect or perversion of the sacred (14D), or in the statement of Solon that the polis is protected by Athena but the citizens *themselves* (in emphatic position), persuaded by money, wish to destroy it.[5]

Monetisation is the centralisation of social power in a single, abstract, impersonal entity. This means not that social power is impersonal, rather that it consists of human use of the impersonal power of money. The point is clarified by a return to our distinction between the Greek coin and the seal-mark widely used with a social and economic function in the ancient Near East. The embodiment of invisible personal power in the numerous seal-marks of numerous people (6c), of the animate in the inanimate, is a form of magic, and seals may for instance be worn to provide magical protection. As in magic generally, autonomous personal power is not contained within the subject but is unconsciously projected onto

---

[3] Simmel 1978 (1907); Parry and Bloch 1989, 4–6, 100–1, 179; Dalton 1971, 186; Sohn-Rethel (1978) 39–43 ('commodity exchange impels practical solipsism') Adorno 1978 (1951), 153 'What presents itself as an original entity, a monad, is only the result of a social division of the social process. Precisely as an absolute, the individual is a mere reflection of property relations. In him the fictitious claim is made that what is biologically one must logically precede the social whole, . . .'. For a theory associating the genesis of money with the advent of private property see Heinsohn and Steiger (1994). Plato *Laws* 705a believes 'that commerce and money-making breeds shiftiness and distrust in the soul, making the polis distrustful of and friendless to itself and to others'; cf. the Albanians of the Caucasus as 'frank and unmercenary, for they do not use coinage for the most part . . . but make their exchanges by barter' (Strabo 11.4.4).

[4] One of the very earliest references to money (Alcaeus. fr. 69) emphasises its independence from reciprocity and even from personal acquaintance: 5A.

[5] Fr. 4.1.4–6; cf. Xenophanes B18 (10D).

physical objects. The magical symbol is identified with the person or thing it signifies. But the value embodied in coined money, being transmitted freely between strangers, is identified neither with any person nor – being the homogeneous single equivalent and abstract transcendent signifier of *all* goods – with any specific thing. Personal power resides not in the coin, but in possession of the invisible impersonal power residing in the coin. Significance, value, enduring essence, and power all tend to be gathered into a transcendent signifier and universal equivalent, money, with the result that personal power is not extended into objects such as seals (or indeed gifts) but consists of possession of the universal impersonal power of money. This tends to enhance the boundary between the autonomous self and the impersonal world. Monetisation makes for the self-containment (and so the discovery) of the individual self, no longer dispersed into physical objects such as the seal or gift.

This development of self-containment tends to diminish the role of magic,[6] and correspondingly to increase the possibility of a sense of the distinction between the sign or symbol and its referent.[7] One such sign is that other transcendent signifier and universal equivalent, the word. Analogous to the centralisation of value in money is the gathering of signification into language, which also locates it within the subject as producer of language. More specifically, the parallel development of alphabetic writing and money as minimal systems of universal equivalence converges in the Heraclitean *logos* (6D), which means both verbal and monetary account (12A). Just as Heraclitus insists on the distinction between statues and the gods generally identified with them (B5), so his *logos* is something distinct from everything else.

All this combines to suggest that money in the modern sense, first used by the Greeks, bestows on the individual an apparent self-containment and autonomy that are historically unprecedented. They are of course merely apparent, because the power of money depends on its acceptance by others. The *impersonality* of money conceals the interpersonal power that it embodies, so that – in contrast to redistribution, reciprocity, and barter – transactions involving money may seem to involve (*qua* monetary transactions) no lasting interpersonal relationship or even no interpersonal relationship

---

[6] Both money and magic are forms of dispersed invisible power, but magic is dangerous because, being personal, it is more able than money to evade communal control. The invisible power of coins has sometimes been transformed into magic, for the most part by the desperate poor: Schöttle 1913; Weil 1980.

[7] This sense may be needed for that explicit distinction between the metaphorical and the literal associated (by Lloyd 1990, ch. 1) with the foundations of science.

at all.[8] The power of money, although it is in fact the power to command the labour of others, seems to inhere in something entirely impersonal. Accordingly the power and autonomy it bestows may seem unlimited (8F), or rather limited only by the amount of money possessed. *L'argent n'a pas de maître*. With money in his pocket any individual can, roughly speaking, acquire whatever he wants from any supplier, wherever and whenever he wants. And what he acquires by money may seem to be more fully his own than what he acquires as a gift, which – besides requiring reciprocation – may seem to be invested with the identity of the donor,[9] and more fully his own even than possessions inherited with the household, such as the land with the tombs of his ancestors. Coined money – portable, concealable,[10] durable, storable, impersonal – lends itself to individual possession. Money may accordingly inspire unlimited desire (8F), and isolate even members of the same household from each other (14E). Moreover, the individual's sense of the power that money (despite its ideality) bestows on him – both as general means of payment and (as common measure) unifying all his various possessions – may unconsciously reenact the joyful sense of incipient power he felt, as an infant, in the formation of the unitary subject out of the sense of fragmentation that may continue to threaten it. This joy finds extreme expression in Empedocles' undifferentiated universe 'rejoicing in its supremely joyful solitariness' (11B). Indeed, throughout presocratic philosophy, and in the Derveni papyrus, we found the idea, in various forms, of a single mind coextensive with the universe (11B, 12B). What we must note here is that this coextensiveness is also the most extreme personal *isolation*.

Monetary impersonality bestows personal autonomy. The former we have identified as a factor in the presocratic depersonalisation of the cosmos, which nevertheless remains to some extent shaped by, or analogous to, the idea of the mind (11B, 12B). But this is an idea of the mind that has itself been somewhat shaped by money. Money is created by the mind and, seeming to acquire autonomy, organises in various mutually reinforcing ways the shape of its creator. As uniting concrete multiplicity (of goods) under a single invisible abstraction, money provides a model not only for the cosmos but also for the unitary control of concrete multiplicity (of sensation) by

---

[8] Money may create a lasting relationship by being borrowed. But among the Greeks instruments of credit were relatively undeveloped: transactions were generally of short duration, terminated by the physical transfer of money.

[9] Mauss 1967 (1925), 79; Seaford 1994a, 13–14.

[10] Compare the tradition that in Sparta Lycurgus combated injustice by ensuring that the iron currency was such that even ten mnas would require a large space, and a waggon to carry it, and so could not enter a house secretly: Xen. *Resp. Lac.* 7.5–6; Plut. *Lyc.* 9.1–2.

the invisible mind.[11] Plato writes of 'the only true currency (*nomisma*), in return for which we should exchange all these things [pleasure, pains, fears], namely *thinking*'.[12]

The result is a complex relationship between three similarly structured entities – money, mind, and cosmos – in all three of which concrete multiplicity is united and controlled (or, in Parmenidean ontology, replaced) by a single invisible abstraction. Or alternatively, for Philolaus, the control takes the form (common to macrocosm and microcosm) of limiting the unlimited.

As universal aim (8D), universal means (8E), and uniquely the object of unlimited accumulation (8F), money provides a central object of thought and action, a single-mindedness. Besides its tendency to delimit or isolate the individual by enhancing the boundary between the personal subject and the impersonal physical world, money reduces the need for reciprocal personal relations and for direct involvement in the provision of goods, and so tends to delimit the individual unitary mind from all else save a focus on money itself. The extreme (mythical) case of this delimitation is Midas, isolated from all people and all things by his unifying power of monetary transformation. The isolation of the individual soul from all goods (whether gifts or commodities) is analogous to the (illusory) absolute separation of abstract monetary separation from all goods (12B), and is forcibly expressed in the statements of incommensurability to be discussed in 14C.

The unity bestowed on the mind by money tends to be both single-minded and self-enclosed. This self-enclosed unity is variously manifest in the tragic tyrant (14DE), in the comic miser,[13] and in the Orphic Zeus's absorption of everything into himself, interpreted by the Derveni Commentator to mean that 'Mind itself being alone is worth everything (*pantōn axion*), just as if everything else were nothing': here autocracy, the autonomous individual self established over internal fragmentation, and universal monetary equivalence, are all simultaneously projected onto the cosmos (11B, 12B). Finally, there is the individualism of presocratic philosophers

---

[11] Cf. the argument of Sohn-Rethel (1978) that the Kantian 'transcendental unity of the self-consciousness' is 'an intellectual reflection of one of the elements of the exchange abstraction, the most fundamental one of all, the form of the exchangeability of commodities underlying the unity of money and of the social synthesis' (77, cf. 7).

[12] *Phaedo* 69a (12A); he also locates divine money in the soul (12C).

[13] Various fourth-century Attic comedies were entitled *Philarguros* ('Money-lover': see *PCG* on Dioxippus fr. 4), a word which first occurred in Sophocles' *Antigone* (1055) and *Tereus* (fr. 587). A discussion of the Greek sources for Plautus' *Aulularia* is by Stockert 1983, 13–16. In Theophrastus' *Characters* characteristics of the miser occur in no fewer than five types: (9) the *anaischuntos* (shameless), (10) the *mikrologos* (petty), 18) the *apistos* (mistrustful), (22) the *aneleutheros* (servile), (30) the *aischrokerdēs* (avaricious).

themselves. Whereas in mystic initiation the individual is eventually subjected to traditional wisdom, Heraclitus and Parmenides represent their doctrine not just as a mystic revelation but as individual and innovative. Heraclitus' fragments exhibit the riddling obscurity characteristic of mystic ritual, and the isolated contempt for humankind that was attributed to him in antiquity.[14] He frequently uses 'I', as in the phrase 'I searched myself' (B101). And, like Xenophanes, he attacks other thinkers, including the venerable Homer.[15] Parmenides' mystic wisdom is obscure enough to be revealed to himself alone, setting him apart from the ignorance of mortals.[16] In Pythagoreanism, 'the first major, conscious break with traditional life attested in our historical sources',[17] we find the combination of a mystic sect with the authoritative wisdom not of a god but of a sixth-century individual (Pythagoras). The innovative intellectual individualism that characterises presocratic philosophy has no precedent in the premonetary societies of the ancient Near East.

According to Heraclitus (B72) 'that which they most have continuous intercourse with, the *logos* that administers all things, with this they are at variance (*toutōi diapherontai*), and the things that they encounter daily seem to them alien (*xena*)'. The *logos* is here personified. Marcovich in his commentary compares the description in Lysias (14.44) of someone as *tois oikeiois diaphoros*, 'at variance with his own (the members of his household)'. For Heraclitus, what men have most to do with is not their kin but the *logos*, and even with this they are, despite its communality, at variance. The things they encounter daily are, because commodities (bought from relative strangers, not made in the household or given as gifts), pervaded by the *logos*, which they do not understand (B1, B2), and so seem alien. The *logos* inheres even in the soul (*psuchē*), where it is unfathomable (B45, B115). The communal monetary *logos* penetrates, *and yet isolates*, the individual.[18]

Money informs the mind and constitutes the individual. The saying 'money is the man' means in effect 'it is money, rather than personal relations, that constitutes a man' (8D). Despite its impersonality, money may, because of its power, seem personal: it takes action.[19] There is erotic

---

[14] E.g. Guthrie 1962, 410–13.

[15] B42; 10D n. 91; Lloyd 1987, 59 –61; according to Plato among Heraclitus' followers there is no master–pupil relationship, and no one of them thinks that any of the others understands anything (*Tht.* 180bc).

[16] B1. 27, 30–2; 6. 4–9; 7. 5–6; 8. 51–2; 9N n. 8.   [17] Bremmer 1999, 76.

[18] But if *toutōi diapherontai* means that men are set at variance *with each other* by the *logos* (cf. Hclt. B10; Hdt. 7.220.4 (end)), then it expresses the mutual absolute egotism introduced into exchange by money (10B).

[19] E.g. Soph. fr. 88 (8E); Eur. *Hec.* 865, 1206–7, *Suff.* 875–6.

passion for money (81), and money reproduces itself (14E). 'Money', says
the Middle Comedy poet Timocles, 'is blood and *psuchē* (soul or life) for
mortals'.[20] Creon in *Antigone* struggles against the pervasion of his mind
by money,[21] and in reply Teiresias denies being covered with silver (1077
katērgurōmenos). The identification of people with precious metal goes back
to the myth of the races in Hesiod's *Works and Days*.[22] With the invention of
coinage, people are in various ways identified with coins,[23] notably through
the mark on the coin (*charaktēr*), which indicates a type,[24] or true worth,[25]
or both together.[26] Much later, Philo of Alexandria calls the soul 'currency'
(*nomisma*), its mark the eternal *logos* impressed by the seal of god; and the
church fathers call man 'coin of god' (*nummus dei*).[27] We are reminded
of Plato's recommendation that gold and silver currency from the gods be
always present in the soul (12C).

A coin, like a human being, is the material embodiment of an invisible
essence (value, the soul) present also in other coins or human beings. And
just as the individual unitary human soul may seem self-enclosed, separate
from the social process by which it is in fact formed, so the coin may
seem to enclose within itself the unitary invisible value that in fact depends
entirely on circulation. Indeed, monetary value is easily detached by the
imagination from circulation, as we observed on Parmenides (12B). Just as
the individual may imagine himself to be independent, self-sufficient in
money that in fact depends on exchange, so the coins he possesses seem to
contain within themselves (in the way that a cup contains wine) value that
in fact depends on their acceptability by others in exchange.

B   INDIVIDUALISM AND COMMUNALITY

We explore further here the paradox that Greek coined money promoted
individualism and yet depended for its genesis on sacrificial soldarity and
for its efficacy on communal agreement on its value (14A). The Greek
adoption of coinage was facilitated by the social structure embodied in

---

[20] Fr. 37; cf. Hes. *Op.* 686 (quoted 5A n. 2). Note also the collocation of *chrēmata* with *psuchē* and *sōma*
   (body) at Anon. Iambl. 99.5 (fifth century BC); Pl. *Rep.* 366c2, *Ep.* 7. 355b; see Kallet (1999) 229–31.
[21] 1036, 1063; cf. Soph. *Trach.* 537–8; Seaford 1998a, 132–3; 8D.
[22] On this identification generally see Kurke 1999.
[23] Ar. *Frogs* 718–37; Eur. *Sciron* fr. 675N² (15A); Plut. *Per.* 26.4 (branding prisoners with coin marks; cf.
   Hdt. 7.233; Steiner 1994, 165); Kurke 1999, 310–13 (coins and citizens both subject to civic scrutiny
   (*dokimasia*)).
[24] E.g. Hdt. 1.57, 116.
[25] So that the lack of a *charaktēr* on people may be regretted: *Med.* 519, *HF 659*.
[26] 8C on Eur. *El.* 558–9; Eur. *Hec.* 379; Kurke 1999, 321–2 on Aesch. *Supp.* 282.
[27] Ph. *Plant.* 18; *Leg. all.* 3.95; etc: Kohnke 1968; Lau 1980.

communal sacrificial distribution, in which every individual has the right
to possess a standard portion of the meat dedicated to deity. This communally recognised standardisation, when once combined with the convenient
characteristics of the iron spits on which the meat was roasted, enabled the
subsequent development of communal recognition of the embodiment of
unitary abstract value in standardised and durable (precious metal) pieces,
dispersed into the possession of numerous individuals (6AB). Animal sacrifice, with its transition from anxiety at the killing to the joy of communal
feasting, was also an important element of mystery cult. The communal
focus on sacrificial contact with deity in mystery cult at Olbia left each
participant in individual possession of a bone token that, like the iron spit,
was a durable, roughly standard-size relic of the sacrifice (6A).

Participation in mystery cult – and the decision to participate – was by
the individual rather than (as in many rituals) the group.[28] The earliest
story of Dionysiac initiation concerns the lonely desire of a Scythian king
to be initiated (Hdt. 4.79). In the *Bacchae* the experiences of Pentheus that
undoubtedly reflect mystic initiation include anxious *isolation* manifest in
systematic delusion and in resistance to advice; and the experiences of the
thiasos (chorus) during the imprisonment of their god, which again undoubtedly reflect mystic initiation, include the 'isolated desolation' of each
individual before their joy at the epiphany of the god.[29] The *thiasos*, unlike
Pentheus, experience the transition to the permanent happiness praised
in their mystic *makarismos* as involving 'merging the soul with the *thiasos*'
(72–5). We know of several mystic formulae uttered by, and others addressed
to, the individual.[30] Even in Eleusinian initiation, which was a mass event,
the initiand was at one stage veiled, and there seems to have occurred a transition from the panic of a chaotic mass of individuals to communal joy.[31]
The lonely anxiety of the initiand may have been enhanced by identification with a sacrificial victim, his subsequent incorporation by communal
participation in the sacrificial meal. The mystic transition isolates and then
unites its participants.[32] And this incorporation of the initiand into communality may involve communal focus on the transcendent revelation of,
and even perhaps the assimilation of his soul to, a secret symbol or symbols
(11B).

[28] E.g. Hdt. (8.65) says of Eleusis: 'whoever of the Athenians and other Greeks wants to is initiated';
Burkert 1987, 10–11.
[29] 609 'isolated desolation': Seaford 1996, 195–203. Cf. also Pentheus' isolation made emphatically
explicit in a passage full of mystic illusions (962–3).
[30] Notably inscribed on the gold leaves; see also Dem. 18.259–60; Clem *Protr.* 2.21.2.
[31] Plut. fr. 178; cf. Ar. *Frogs* 156–7.
[32] Seaford 1994a, 281–301. Unites: e.g. Eur. *Bacc.* 75; Pl. *Ep.* 7. 333e.

And so what we find in animal sacrifice and mystic initiation is a relationship between individual and communality that helps to explain the fusion of mystery cult with money that was a factor in the cosmology of Heraclitus (12A). The dependence of individual autonomy on communal focus that inhered in the sacrificial genesis of money is present also, in a different form, in mystery cult. In this mystic form it is able to recombine with the structure of money relations to shape Heraclitus' cosmology. He states, in a manner characteristic of mystic discourse, that men fail to understand the *logos* before they hear it and just after they have heard it (B1). The everliving fire that is the cosmos and the *logos* that it embodies are communal and present in the soul.[33] We should follow (and even assimilate our souls to) what is communal, but most men live as if they have private understanding.[34] The communal *logos* is both mystic *logos* and monetary *logos* (12A). The paradox of ignorant individualism dependent on invisible communality, inherited from the mysteries, expresses the paradox of the circulation of monetary value, which bestows autonomy on the individual only by uniting everybody into a single system.

But given this unity, *why* do people live as if they had a private understanding, in ignorance of the communality of the *logos*? The answer is implicit in our discussion of the individualism promoted by money (14A), and of Parmenides (12BC). It is because of the ease with which the individual, liberated by the possession of money, may imagine himself to be self-sufficient, may imagine monetary value as detached from circulation. Parmenides' sublimation of self-sufficient unitary value, detached (in contrast to Heraclitus) from circulation, is revealed *to him alone* – after a journey, modelled on the journey of mystic initiation (9B), 'away from the path of men' (B1.27) – and sets him apart from the ignorance of mortals.[35] Heraclitus' emphasis on the communal *logos* underlying the individualism inherent in monetary circulation is presented as divulgation of the universal truth of mystic doctrine, whereas Parmenides' individual perception of Being (value static and invisible, withdrawn from circulation) finds a natural synthesis with the opposite and complementary aspect of mystery cult – the traditional isolation of the mystic initiand, journeying into a liminal space where social norms are suspended or reversed. As later in Plato's *Symposium* (11B), the fate of the individual initiand seems assured by a kind of permanent liminality, a vision of something entirely self-sufficient and

---

[33] B2, 36 (cf. 31), 45, 50, 89 (cf. 1), 113, 114, 115; A16.   [34] B2; assimilation: B118 (cf. 77, 117).

[35] 12C; B1.30–2; 6.4–9; 7.5–6; 8.51–2. Compare another context of authority for wisdom: Hesiod is while shepherding sheep under Mt Helicon taught by the Muses (*Theog.* 22–3): they know how to speak false things and true things; but there is no emphasis on Hesiod's isolation.

eternally present. In Plato's *Phaedrus* the wholeness of the mystic vision is associated with the wholeness of the individual initiand (11B).

C   INCOMMENSURABILITY

We have investigated the contribution made by money to philosophical cosmology produced by an elite. But money was used generally. Popular reaction to the advent of money is likely to be expressed not in philosophical cosmology but in the premonetary medium of myth. Whereas earlier we looked at Homer (chapters 2 and 3) for the representation of a society about to produce money, and at tragedy (chapter 8) for reactions to money itself, here we return to these texts to ask whether they too were shaped by any of the preconceptions that monetisation contributed to philosophical cosmology.

For the Homeric Achilles the *timē* (honour) that should bind the warrior to the community no longer means anything, because it goes equally to good and bad fighters. When Phoenix tells him that the Achaeans will honour him with gifts as they would a god (*Il.* 9.603), he replies that 'I have no need of this *timē*. I think I am honoured by the *aisē* [ordinance, distribution: 3A] of Zeus' (607–8). He has *timē*, but of a superior kind, independent of any manifestation in gifts from Agamemnon or even from the community. What is conveyed by gifts is there even without the gifts. What the crisis has forced on Achilles is not only a distinction between reality (honour from Zeus) and mere appearance (the manifestations of honour from men) but also a sense of his own isolated value, detached from any material manifestation. The life that he has risked exchanging for these material manifestations is in fact *a different kind of thing* from them. No amount of wealth is equal in value (401 *antaxion*) to his own *psuchē* (soul, life), which cannot be controlled by gifts. Nor, in the logic of trade, can it be bartered or purchased. This is the closest thing in Homer or Hesiod to the comparison of basic values that, frequent later (notably in Euripides), may be encouraged by the tendency of money to create a regime of universal comparative evaluation.[36]

---

[36] An early post-Homeric instance is Xenophanes (fr. 2) privileging intelligence and the wealth of the polis over athletic abilities (10D). (Preference for one kind of *person* above all others, prefigured at *Il.* 13.729–34, occurs also at Tyrtaeus fr. 12.) Theognis complains that the thing preferred above all others is wealth (183–96, 699–718). Archilochus fr. 19 (expressing lack of desire for wealth and tyranny) was probably followed by a statement of what really matters (Plut. *Mor.* 470B). Note also Sappho 16; *PMG* 890, 988; Soph. fr. 354; Eur. *Med.* 542–4, 598–9, 965, *El.* 941, *HF* 643–8, *Ion* 629–31, *Pho.* 439–40, 552–4, *Or.* 1155–6, frr. 142, 324, 327, 405, 543, 659, 934, 1046; frr. adesp. 129, 130, 181; etc.: Seaford 1998a, 122–3.

On the one hand Achilles reacts to the breakdown of centralised reciprocity (redistribution) by expressing an attitude favourable to the development of trade and money: he implies that there should be impersonal equivalence between worth (in battle) and material reward. Or, at least, his resistance to the centralised reciprocity characteristic (in an extreme form) of the ancient Near East implies the reciprocity between *equal* individuals that (in a new form) underlies the Greek development of money. Paradoxically the heroic isolation of Achilles, quite unlike that of Gilgamesh (4B), prefigures the isolation inherent in monetary transactions. Moreover, the heroic concentration on a *single* form of worth – military worth, that both attracts and is conveyed by various material goods but is imagined by Achilles in separation from them – is analogous to the (historically incipient) idea of a single form of value, monetary value, that both attracts and inheres in various commodities but can be imagined in separation from them.

On the other hand, and precisely because he does still adhere to a heroic sense of *timē* (albeit now sublimated), Achilles may be expected to react also against the (historically increasing) impersonal power of material wealth: his vehement rejection of the gifts (reciprocity) seems also to be a rejection of the integrative power of commodities (2D).

This rejection, in combining the logic of money with aristocratic superiority to it, has two unusual (for Homer) consequences. Firstly, it induces the expression, in concrete terms, of something close to the idea of an *unlimited* amount of goods.[37] Secondly, it makes Achilles separate his own *psuchē* with its supreme value (*timē*) from the various material manifestations by which it may seem constituted but with which it is in fact incommensurable. In thus putting his soul beyond even an innumerable amount of goods, i.e. beyond all exchange-value, he prefigures both the Heraclitean unlimitedness of the soul and the sublimating separation by Parmenides and Plato of abstract being, exclusive to the isolated mind or *psuchē*, from the unlimited circulation of goods (12B). This prefiguration occurs nowhere else in Homer. Nor does the isolation of a *psuchē*, from both community and material rewards. Nor does the consequent evaluation of the *psuchē* as what most matters to a man, as something approximating to the self (12A n. 57). It is no coincidence that these conceptions, that prefigure later texts, occur in Homer only in the passage that is also unique both in its onslaught on the workings of centralised reciprocity and in its suggestion of the logic of trade and money.

---

[37] 379–85 'not even if he were to give me ten or twenty times as much . . . not even as many gifts as the sand and dust . . .'

Not even the wealth of Troy or Delphi, says Achilles, is equal in value to my *psuchē*. Cattle and sheep can be plundered and tripods and horses can be obtained, whereas the *psuchē* of a man cannot be 'plundered' or captured to come back again once it exchanges (*ameipsetai*) the barrier of his teeth (401–9). There is an implicit contrast here between heroic modes of appropriation (plunder, tripods as gifts) and the kind of 'exchange' that by virtue of meaning total and irrevocable alienation (death) resembles trade (2D). Here too Achilles seems to react against the encroachment of trade. The idea of death as commercial exchange reappears, notably in Aeschylus' image of Ares as a gold-exchanger and holder of the scales in battle. In the monetised society of fifth-century Athens this hideous exchange of incommensurables – living bodies for (gold) dust that is 'heavy' (as gold, as grief) – brings monetary gain for the Atreidae.[38] Whereas in the *Iliad* it is as 'distributor (*tamiēs*) of war' – like the monarch overseeing a redistributive economy[39] – that Zeus holds (and in one passage 'inclines') scales that decide the outcome of combat,[40] the Aeschylean Ares is, as gold-changer (*chrusamoibos*), one party to the transaction.[41]

Earlier in the *Agamemnon*, in the famous choral hymn to Zeus, Zeus himself has appeared in an image of scales (160–6):

Zeus, whoever he is, if to be called by this name is pleasing to him, thus do I address him. I am unable to liken him to anything, putting everything on the scales, except Zeus, if from my mind there is need to throw off genuinely the vain weight.

The traditional doubt about the nature of the deity addressed develops into a statement of his *incomparability* (nothing may be likened to Zeus, except Zeus), which rapidly becomes, with the image of weighing, the impossibility of *equivalence*.[42] Not even all things are enough to be equivalent, on the scales, to Zeus. If the chorus are to be rid of the weight from their mind, not even all things put on the other scale will be enough. Only Zeus will be enough, who is, because set apart from all material things, commensurable with anguish in the mind.

---

[38] 8c. Similarly, the transition to money is reflected in the ransom of Hector's body – in Homer by a list of gifts but in Aeschylus' lost *Phrygians* (*TGF* 3. fr. 365) by its equivalent weight in gold. (It has been thought since antiquity that Aeschylus was inspired by *Il.* 22.351 'to ἐρύσασθαι him with gold'. But ἐρύεσθαι means 'weigh' nowhere else (though cf. ἀντερύσασθαι at *Theogn.* 77), and is in Homer and elsewhere frequent meaning 'rescue').

[39] The scales of Zeus may derive, albeit remotely, from the Egyptian notion of the use of scales to judge the dead: *RE* xxiii. 2 s.v. Psychostasie 1439–46; Dietrich 1964.

[40] *Il.* 8.69, 16.658, 19.223–4, 22.209.   [41] Like the *arguramoibos*: 8c n. 37.

[42] οὐκ ἔχω προσείκασαι, πάντ' ἐπισταθμώμενος. The transition is facilitated by the fact that εἰκάζειν could mean to estimate quantity or weight: *PSI* 5.522; *P. Gurob* 8.14. Eur. *El.* 559 (8c) suggests that προσεικάζειν (liken) was used of scrutinising coinage: Seaford 1998a, 137.

Three factors, none of them mentioned by the commentators, contribute to this remarkable passage. One is that the events at Aulis, whose narration our passage interrupts, are poised (as on a balance) between success and disaster.[43] The second is the traditional Homeric idea of Zeus holding or inclining the scales that decide the outcome of combat. The third is a new phenomenon that influenced also Aeschylus' contemporary Parmenides, the phenomenon of abstract value that, because it is perceived by the mind, seems beyond equivalence with the material goods from which it has been abstracted. The condensed sequence of thought is to be unpacked as follows. The weight of anxiety is imagined as a weight of commodities on a scale. How to raise this weight? Even a great weight of commodities is transcended by abstract value, which may therefore – being, like the mental weight of anxiety, invisible – transcend and outweigh the great weight of anxiety, and so is projected as the transcendent controller of the deciding scales, Zeus.[44] This is the point of saying that no amount of things is equivalent to Zeus except Zeus, who, like abstract value, transcends all else, is *sui generis*. Abstract value, to which no amount of things can be equivalent, is detached from all commodities and (as in presocratic cosmology) projected onto the cosmos, though here without being depersonalised.[45]

The closest linguistic parallel to *ouk echō proseikasai* . . . ('I am unable to liken (him to anything))' is from the next play in the trilogy: *ouk echoim' an eikasai* . . . (*Cho.* 518), 'I am unable to compare/liken' (the gifts sent by Clytemnestra to the dead Agamemnon). This, which has also never been fully understood, refers again to *lack of equivalence* – here between the goods offered and the anger of the dead, as is also stated in what immediately follows: 'they (the gifts) are less than the offence; for someone having poured out (i.e. as libations) all things in exchange for one blood (i.e. one life taken) – vain is the task'. Here again, as in Achilles' speech and the hymn to Zeus, but in contrast to the bitterly ironic image of Ares the gold-changer, no amount of material goods is equivalent to a single invisible agent (a soul, a mental burden).[46]

---

[43] 159 'sing the song of woe, but may the good prevail'; see further Seaford 2003b.

[44] Similarly, Aeschylus' contemporary Heraclitus tentatively identifies 'the One, alone wise' with Zeus (B32).

[45] No less influenced by money, albeit in a different way, is Aeschylus' conception of Zeus in the *Suppliant Women* 10D n. 108; on the conception of Zeus in *PV* (whether or not by Aeschylus) as influenced by money see 10D n. 115.

[46] What has survived of the ancient tradition about Aeschylus' lost dramatisation (*Psychostasia*) of the epic (*Iliad* or *Aithiopis*) weighing of the *kēres* (fates) of opposed warriors focuses on the fact that Aeschylus substituted *souls* (*psuchai*) .

D   TRAGIC INDIVIDUALISM

Tragedy developed, Aristotle tells us, from the satyr-play-like (*satyrikon*). A common theme of satyr-play was the Dionysiac *thiasos* (Silenus and the satyrs) captive to a powerful individual.[47] It occurs also in the only surviving tragedy on a Dionysiac theme, the *Bacchae*, and had probably been more prominent in Aeschylus' Dionysiac *Lycurgeia*.[48]

Plato tells us that 'initiations performed by people imitating satyrs and silens' are 'not of the polis' (*ou politikon, Laws* 815c). Drama, on the other hand, was a creation of the polis. Satyric drama was organised by the polis and performed at its heart, and yet the chorus of animalistic satyrs remained in a sense outside, or prior to, the polis. This tension between satyrs and polis merges with the tension between the satyric *thiasos* and their captor.

The captivity theme was not invented by drama. There was an old[49] story that Silenus was once captured by Midas, according to Herodotus in Midas' garden where roses grew uncultivated.[50] Forced to reveal his wisdom, Silenus spoke 'about natural and ancient things'.[51] He called Midas 'ephemeral', and revealed that for humankind the best thing is never to have been born, the second best to die as soon as possible.[52] Dionysus, glad at the release of Silenus – or in another version Silenus himself – offered Midas the fulfilment of any wish.[53] Midas chose the power to turn all things into gold by his touch, a choice that he subsequently regretted on finding even his food as gold. For Aristotle (*Pol.* 1257b16) this indicates the merely conventional power of money: a man may starve amidst his money. We may add a psychological dimension: all things are seen in terms of money; absorption in happiness in the abstract (money) is incapacity for happiness in the concrete. Midas washed his gold-making power off into the river Pactolus, thereby endowing the river with the gold from which in fact were made the first coins. This legendary Midas arose from the historical Phrygian king Midas,[54] whose Greek wife was one of those said to have

---

[47] Seaford 1984a, 33–6.   [48] *Bacch.* 226–7, 443–8 (with Seaford 1996 ad loc.).
[49] Vase-paintings of it survive from the second quarter of the sixth century BC: *LIMC* 8.850.
[50] Hdt. 8.138; Xen. *Anab.* 1 2.13; Theopomp. *FGrH* 115F75; etc. According to Strabo (14.680) this was under Mt Bermion where Midas was said to have worked the mines.
[51] de rebus naturalibus et antiquis: Serv. *V. Ecl.* 6.13, after Theopomp., part of whose account survives (*FGrH* 115 F75 Silenus decribes two remote cities: in one there is deep wealth without agriculture, in the other so much precious metal that gold is worth less than iron).
[52] Aristot. fr. 44 Rose, ap. Plut. *Mor.* 115DE. Aristotle emphasises the popularity and antiquity of the story.
[53] Ov. *Met.* 11.100–4; Hygin. *Fab.* 191; Serv. *ad Aen.* 10.142; Max. Tyr. 11.
[54] Roller 1983. At Hdt. 8.38 they are the same.

been the first to mint coins,[55] and who impressed the Greeks by being the first foreigner to make dedications at Delphi (Hdt. 1.14).

The myth of Midas represents the reaction of the Greek mythical imagination to the novel and startling power of precious metal as universal equivalent. But why the connection with Silenus? In his animal-like nature, in speaking of 'natural and ancient things', and in his wise disdain for humankind as embodied in the human for whom all nature becomes gold, Silenus belongs to the world of nature, of use-value, outside and prior to the polis, and prior to the advent of the all-pervasive power of money. Even the roses growing uncultivated may be significant as indicating primeval Utopia.

Along with this antithesis between money and nature, this contempt for humankind estranged by money from nature, there is, in Silenus' reply, the antithesis between immortality and 'ephemeral' mortality. The identity and immortal happiness of the satyr or silen may be acquired through Dionysiac initiation,[56] and so the antithesis may reflect Silenus' disdain for the mortality of even the wealthiest uninitiated. The question 'what is best for humankind?' could easily be answered with 'money',[57] but better with the permanent happiness promised (we shall see below) by the *makarismos* uttered in the Dionysiac mysteries. The question and answer suggest mystic instruction, and so it is no surprise to find that Midas was initiated into the Dionysiac or Orphic mysteries.[58] Dionysus also *saves* Midas from monetary power (Ov. *Met.* 11.134–42). What is revealed in mystery cult shares with money a unique, transcendent desirability that in cosmology makes for their fusion (12B, 12A) but in myth sets them in opposition.

The mortality–immortality antithesis has, moreover, a special point in relation to Midas as the man of money. The interposition of money between humankind and nature has a temporal dimension. Money always embodies the deferment of the enjoyment of what it may subsequently purchase. With money used as a store of wealth, such deferment frequently extends beyond the lifetime of its owner, a process facilitated by the notion of monetary value as unchanging, permanent (12C). The accumulation of money may therefore imply forgetfulness of one's own mortality, a bogus eternity quite

---

[55] At Kyme: Pollux 9.83; Heraclides *FHG* Müller 2. 216.

[56] Seaford 1984a, 8–9.

[57] So too Croesus, thinking of his own vast wealth, asks Solon who is the happiest of men (8F). On the preference for one *kind* of thing above all others, not to be found in the premonetary world of Homer (though implicit in *Il.* 9: 2D, 4B, 14B), see 14b n. 36.

[58] Ov. *Met.* 11.93; Konon *FGrH* 26 F1; Clem. Alex. *Protr.* 2.13.1; Justin 11.7.4; Seaford 1994a, 231; 1996, 219. Aristotle comments on Silenus' reply to Midas (n. 52 above) that he meant that existence after death was better than in life.

unlike the eternity bestowed by mystic initiation. Nobody is more suitable to remind Midas of his mortality than Silenus, who combines immortality with immediacy of enjoyment, complete neglect of its deferral.

The opposition between Silenus and money is made explicit in a fragment of Pindar (157), in which Silenus says to the *aulos*-player Olympus 'ephemeral wretch, you say foolish things to me in boasting of money'. Silenus speaks probably as Olympus' *aulos* teacher, drawing a distinction between the use-value and the exchange-value of its music. I describe elsewhere[59] how the remains of satyric drama contain several passages based on the contrast between on the one hand the moneyless Dionysiac world of Silenus and the satyric *thiasos*, of immediate pleasure and the creation of culture (notably wine and musical instruments) out of nature, and on the other hand the powerful man of money, who may be their captor.[60]

The experience of Pentheus in Euripides' *Bacchae* reflects in numerous respects initiation into the Dionysiac mysteries.[61] But in attempting to suppress those mysteries Pentheus explains insubordination as motivated by monetary gain (257). This reduction of the Dionysiac to money reappears at the pivotal moment of the play, when he is asked whether he would like to see the maenads on the mountains: he replies 'very much so, and would give a vast weight of gold to do so' (812). The expression 'I would give a lot of money to . . .' is more modern than ancient.[62] Here, in the very moment of Pentheus' mental reversal, of his sudden enthusiasm for the Dionysiac, he is the anti-Dionysiac man of money, who sees even the sights of the mysteries in monetary terms. The *thiasos* of Dionysiac initiates will shortly afterwards, as Pentheus emerges dressed as a maenad, ask the question asked by Midas – what is best? – and answer it with a mystic *makarismos* in which they express preference for permanent day-to-day happiness (i.e. the kind associated with Silenus) over the transience of individual wealth, power, and victory over enemies.[63] As in Solon's advice to Croesus (8F),[64] and

---

[59] Seaford 2003a.

[60] Note also in Plato's *Symposium* Socrates as 'satyr' (215b4, 216c5–e6, etc.) rejecting Alcibiades' proposed 'exchange' (218d–219d) and despising wealth (216e1–4). This final episode seems to restore *premonetary* (satyric) immortality after the immortality (212a7) through *abstraction* described to Socrates by Diotima in terms of mystic initiation (11A, 12A, 12C). Cf. Ar. *Clouds* 223 (with schol.), where Socrates (like Silenus to Midas and Olympus) says 'O ephemeral one'. Virtue should, like a tragic tetralogy, have its share of the satyric (according to Ion of Chios at Plut. *Per.* 5.4).

[61] Seaford 1996.

[62] In tragedy money is often imagined as gold. Mystic initiation might cost money (Ar. *Peace* 374–5; *Derveni Papyrus* col. 20; Pl. *Rep.* 364be; [Dem.] 51. (*Neair.*) 21; Burkert 1983, 257 n. 1), but this cannot fully explain his expression.

[63] *Bacch.* 902–12: Seaford 1996, 219, 221–2. The transience of individual wealth contrasts with the relative permanence of the *social* construction of money (12C).

[64] Which, no less ironically, Croesus values at 'much money': Hdt. 1.86.4.

Silenus' to Midas, the limit or perfection inherent in the communal rite of passage is preferred over the individual unlimit of money.

Tragedy developed out of the animal sacrifice performed in the Dionysiac mysteries.[65] The *Bacchae*, though a late play, preserves elements of the development of drama out of mystic ritual.[66] The isolation of Pentheus reflects the (normally temporary) isolation of the mystic initiand (14B). But tragedy was also a product of the polis, and the *Bacchae* dramatises the arrival of Dionysiac cult to be performed by the polis. The isolation of the enemy of the *thiasos* is more thoroughly *political* than in satyric drama. It is the isolation not just of the resistant initiand but also of Pentheus as 'tyrant'.[67] His aggressive impermeability to good advice seems to reflect both the resistance of the initiand and the egoism of the tyrant. Wealth, power, and victory over enemies, compared unfavourably by the *thiasos* with their mystic happiness, are all *tyrannical* aspirations.

In a wide range of texts of various kinds[68] – historiography, philosophy, and tragedy – the tyrant typically values the power of money above the sacredness of cult and the ties of reciprocity and even of kinship, and indeed is prepared to violate them all for the sake of this power. Pentheus, in his preoccupation with money, his abuse of the sacred, and his isolation even from his own kin (Cadmus, Agave), is a typical tyrant. And in his coming to grief in such isolation he is a typical tyrant of tragedy.

Tragedy developed out of the Dionysiac mysteries, but was shaped also by experience of the recently monetised polis, and in particular of tyranny.[69] The tyrant, not least the recent Athenian tyrant Peisistratus,[70] is the man of money par excellence. The isolation of Pentheus – in his single-minded illusion of self-sufficiency, within the rigid boundaries of his soul, set against the subjective and objective communality of the *thiasos*[71] – derives from the isolation both of the mystic initiand and of the tyrannical man of money.

---

[65] Seaford 1994a, chs. 7 and 8.   [66] See e.g. Seaford 1996, 156.

[67] 776; Seaford 1996, 46.   [68] I discuss these in Seaford 2003c.

[69] The word *turannos* (tyrant) and its cognates occur in extant tragedy more frequently than the word *basileus* (king) and its cognates. This remains a striking fact despite the greater metrical convenience of *turann-*.

[70] Hdt. 1.61, 64; [Aristot.] *Ath. Pol.* 15.2; cf. Thuc. 6.55. 3, 57.1; Ar. *Knights* 447–9. Peisistratus may have been assisted in this by the novel institution of coinage, which may have been introduced into Athens under his rule: Kraay 1976, 58–9. His cash loans to peasants presumably created allegiance to him: Millett 1991, 51.

[71] The subjectivity of 'merging the soul with the *thiasos*' (75; 14B) has its objective counterpart in e.g. the maenads as 'a wonderful sight of good order' (693). Dionysus gives wine 'to rich and poor alike' (421–3) and wants to be worshipped 'with no distinctions between people' (209); they should be 'all mixed up together': Dem. 21.52. Further *Bacch.* 35–8, 206–9; Seaford 1996, 38, 48, 152, 170, 184–5; 1994a, 246.

Pentheus' self-sufficiency is then destroyed by a process which reflects Dionysiac initiation, except that he undergoes the real death that in (political) myth reflects the merely fictional death undergone in ritual. Given the association of money with psychological unity (11B, 12B, 14A), it is significant that the passage emphasising Pentheus' isolation also predicts his death as bodily fragmentation that is also, it is hinted, *psychological fragmentation.*[72] The same scene evokes the manifold unity of opposites characteristic[73] of the liminal phase of the mystic transition: Pentheus seems to be male and female (915), adult and baby (966–9), and (by wearing funerary dress) living and dead (857), and sees the god (disguised as a mortal) as an animal (921–2). The man of money is destroyed by the Dionysiac power to unite the opposites.

In Pentheus, as in the vision of Parmenides, the self-sufficiency of the man of money combines with the isolation of the mystic initiand. But for Heraclitus the soul has an unlimited *logos* (B45), and self-sufficiency is ignorance of the *logos*, according to which things are transformed into their opposite.[74] This opposition between the two philosophers expresses the opposition between the essence of money as communal circulation (Heraclitus) and its essence as abstract value detached from circulation (Parmenides) (12B). Tragedy, like the metaphysics of its contemporaries Heraclitus and Parmenides,[75] develops as a synthesis of mystery cult with the new world of money. But whereas Heraclitus insists that the mystic-monetary *logos* (the constant circulation of all things into their opposite) is communal, Parmenides receives a mystic revelation (of self-sufficient abstract being) for him alone. Tragedy, in exposing at a communal Dionysiac festival the tyrannical household and transforming the self-sufficient tyrant into his opposite, is in this respect Heraclitean.

The completion of the rite of passage, and especially mystic initiation, gives the individual a new identity, puts an end to his isolation, and reimposes limits within the undifferentiated confusion of basic identities (human–animal, adult–child, male–female, human–deity). And so mystery cult, with its oppositions between unlimit (expressed in the confusion of opposites) and limit and between isolation and communality, may provide a traditional model for the same oppositions in money. The

---

[72] 962–70; Kepple 1976; Seaford 1998b, 135; 11B n. 26. This fragmentation is also a *sacrifice* by the *thiasos* (Seaford 1996, 231): the fragmentation of the sacrificial victim, normally communally distributed (as proposed for Pentheus' body at 1184, 1242), here destroys the isolated opponent of the communal ritual.

[73] Seaford 1996, 43–4; 1998b, 132–5.   [74] Cf. e.g. B1 with B126.

[75] Existing scholarship on what is shared by tragedy and the presocratics is surprisingly thin. Most detailed is Rösler 1970.

delimitation of the unlimited, whether by the rite of passage or in the monetary transaction, subordinates isolation to communality.[76] Conversely, unlimit goes with the unity of opposites and with isolation, a combination that in tragedy tends to prevail over the communal limit inherent in the rite of passage (8F). Pentheus offers an unlimited (*murion*) amount of money (in contrast to the rejection of wealth and power in the *thiasos*' mystic *makarismos*), is variously transformed into his opposite, and his isolated death creates unlimited grief.[77] In Aeschylus' *Agamemnon* the textiles embodying the *unlimited* (*apeiros*) money available to the household entangle the wealthy king in a manifold unity of opposites: in trampling them he is like a 'woman' (918), a 'barbarian' (919), a 'god' (925), on his way to being trapped by a textile wielded by his wife in a perversion of death ritual – the transformation of the most intimate act (of ritual) into the most hostile (8F).

The pervasive unity of opposites in the world of Heraclitus and of Athenian tragedy, and its expression in oxymora, derive in part from mystery cult.[78] The unity of opposites is by contrast rare in the aggregative parataxis of Homer and Hesiod (12A). Of the very few oxymora in Hesiod[79] the most striking is of Semele giving birth to Dionysus *athanaton thnētē* ('a mortal to an immortal', *Theog.* 942) – a myth closely associated with death and rebirth in mystic initiation.[80] And one of the most striking of the few oxymora in Homer[81] describes the only exchange that is monetary (in the sense that the objects exchanged are both related to the same measure of value): 'gold for bronze, a hundred oxen's worth for nine oxen's worth'.[82]

In Heraclitus and sometimes in tragedy the transcendent power of money to unite opposites, to efface all distinctions between things and even between people,[83] converges with the ancient power of mystery cult to unite opposites. The opposition between intimate and enemy, typically fused by

---

[76] Money confuses opposites (8G), is unlimited (8F) and yet delimits the unlimited (13B), is isolating (14A) and yet dependent on communality (12A, 14C). The rite of passage imposes completion, is a *telos*, which can also mean *payment*. The mystic formulae inscribed on the gold leaves mentions having 'paid a penalty' (ποινὰν δ'ἀνταπέτεισα) as qualifying the initiate for happiness in the next world: A 2–3 Zuntz 1971, 4; cf. Pi. fr. 133 Snell; the Pherai gold leaf.

[77] Note esp. 1244 'immeasurable grief', which may however be corrupt or interpolated; 1360–2.

[78] Seaford 2003b.   [79] *Theog.* 585, 609, 942; *Op.* 58, 179, 318.

[80] Seaford 1996, 196–7.   [81] Seaford 2003b.

[82] *Il.* 6.236 χρύσεα χαλκείων, ἑκατόμβοι'ἐννεαβοίων. The opposition between the juxtaposed words is intensified by the implicit contrast with the numerically *equal* value that is the essence of monetary exchange. Note also early monetary oxymora at *Theogn.* 192, 195 (8G); Hdt. 1.153 (12A).

[83] 8G; 8B. This homogenisation converges also with the power of *violence* in tragedy to collapse distinctions between people, on which see Girard 1972 (1977). Cf. Eur. *HF* 655–72: life does not distinguish the good from the bad but increases only *wealth*.

money and by the tyrannical man of money,[84] is in tragedy expressed in oxymora[85] and may be fundamental to the tragic plot.[86]

E   CREON AND OEDIPUS

I suspect that in general the unprecedented tragic focus on the isolation of the individual, alienated from those closest to him, is in part an extreme reflection of the unprecedented autonomy and isolation bestowed – most prominently on the tyrant – by monetisation. But this can be no more than a hypothesis. I confine myself, in conclusion, to brief discussion of two more tragedies in which money is explicitly present, Sophocles' *Antigone* and *Oedipus Tyrannus*, not – I emphasise – so as to provide a comprehensive reading, but merely to bring out the factor of monetisation in the construction of the figures of Creon and Oedipus and the consequent common ground with presocratic philosophy.

Creon has all three of the tyrannical features described above (14D): he is much concerned with money, abuses the sacred, and comes to grief entirely isolated from his kin. In 8D we described his fear of the power of money over his own mind, and how Teiresias supports his accusation – that it is characteristic of *tyrants* to love disgraceful gain – by describing Creon's perversion of death ritual as a hideous exchange in which Creon makes a profit (8D). It is in this light that we must interpret Creon's frequent explanation of the opposition to him as motivated by monetary gain,[87] and in particular the tirade against money as responsible for various bad consequences (*Ant.* 295–301), each of which – destroying cities, driving men from their homes, making good minds do shameful things, knowing every act of impiety – is an extreme example of what he himself will suffer. With psychological subtlety, Sophocles depicts Creon – and Teiresias actually points this out[88] – *projecting* his own tyrannical desire for monetary gain onto others, rather as he projects gold onto Sardis and distant India (1037–9). He professes concern for the polis, which he claims however as his own

---

[84] E.g. Eur. *Phoen.* 439–40, 506; 8G; Seaford 2003c.

[85] 8G; Seaford 2003b; e.g. Aesch. *Sept.* 695, *Ag.* 1545, *Cho.* 44, 584; Soph. *OT* 416, 1214, 1256, *El.* 1154; Eur. *El.* 1230, *Hel.* 690, *IT* 566. The monetary oxymora in *Timon of Athens* include '. . . dear divorce / 'Twixt natural son and sire'.

[86] E.g. the identity of *philos* (one's own) with *echthros* (enemy) informs the two key elements of tragic plot as described by Aristotle, *peripeteia* and *anagnorisis*, which correspond to the two basic elements – reversal and revelation – of mystic ritual. They should happen, according to Aristotle, according to necessity or probability (*Poet.* 1452a20): for Anaximander and Heraclitus the opposites are combined not by any personal agency but 'according to necessity' (12A).

[87] 221–2, 289–303, 322, 326, 1036–56.   [88] 1062: 8D n. 46.

property (737–8). He explains insubordination as motivated by money
because money bestows autonomy (14A), the power to elude his autocracy.
Money confuses the opposites, converting – in Creon's own words – good
minds to shameful things, and showing every impiety. It is as the tyrannical
man of money that Creon abuses the sacred – profiting (Teiresias implies)
from treating the dead as living and the living as dead (8D) – and sees piety
as impiety, thereby transforming his intimates into enemies and producing
Antigone's striking oxymora 'having committed a holy crime' and 'having
by pious action obtained (the blame of) impiety'.[89] In the end the only 'gain'
(*kerdos*) for Creon is to be led away (1324–6) in isolated lamentation, his
tyrannical wealth worthless because unaccompanied by happiness (1168–
71).

The Creon both claims the economic self-sufficiency of the wealthy tyrant
(737–8) and, like Pentheus, exhibits impervious *mental* self-sufficiency,
as observed by Haemon, who accuses him (705–9) of excessive single-
mindedness, of having 'only one mentality' and of imagining that he alone
can think and has a unique soul. Despite this mental detachment, his
claim to own the polis has its *mental* correlate in the 'disease' suffered by
the polis 'from your mind' (1015), that is to say directly from his mind,
from the homogenising single-mindedness that confuses opposites. And so
Creon embodies the phenomenon that we saw making for the ontology of
Parmenides (12BC): the aristocrat, despite distancing himself from the monetised world, may project onto it his isolated, single-minded, homogenising
illusion of his own monetary self-sufficiency. But Creon is represented not
from the Parmenidean but from its opposite (Heraclitean) perspective,
which we have associated with Dionysus. And so Creon is destroyed, and
the god who is invoked by the chorus to purify the polis of its disease is
Dionysus (1140–4).

The tragic self-sufficiency of the Theban tyranny takes the extreme form
of incest. In the *Oedipus Tyrannus* the tyrant suffers – along with incest and
self-blinding – our three tyrannical characteristics of violent isolation from
kin, perversion of (wedding) ritual,[90] and preoccupation with money. He
supposes both the murder of Laius (124–5) and the accusations of Teiresias
against himself (388) to be motivated by money, suspects Creon of envy of
his 'wealth and tyranny' (380–6), and points out the importance of money
in the acquisition of tyranny (541–2), which he himself in fact acquired
through self-sufficient intelligence alone, without – he himself stresses,

---

[89] 74 ὅσια πανουργήσασα and 1324 τὴν δυσσέβειαν εὐσεβοῦσ᾽ ἐκτησάμην.
[90] Seaford 1987, 119–21.

and in contrast to similar mythical ordeals – any divine assistance (396–8). Oedipus is an autonomous man of money.

The chorus' ode on the tyrant begotten by *hubris*, which may be 'over-filled vainly with many things' (873–4), associates gain (*kerdos*) with impiety and with touching the untouchable (889–91), prefiguring perhaps Oedipus' tyrannical incest. In *Antigone* his daughter Antigone identifies her *kerdos* (462, 464) with the quasi-incestuous[91] loyalty to her own blood-kin that she sets above marriage (905–12). Buried alive by her own uncle Creon in a 'bridal chamber' (804 *thalamos*), she is compared to Danae confined underground by her own male kin in a *thalamos* as 'treasurer of the gold-flowing seed of Zeus' (948–50). The same ambiguity of *thalamos* as bridal chamber and store-room accompanies Oedipus' incest.[92] Endogamy, in Athens[93] and elsewhere, preserved wealth within the family. In tragedy endogamy is associated with blindness, darkness, and male imprisonment of female kin (sometimes underground).[94] Similarly, precious metal money may be hoarded by being 'made invisible', frequently underground.[95] Money and females should circulate, and are transmitted together,[96] but the introverted household keeps, even conceals,[97] its money and its females for itself.[98]

Moreover, money and the female may both *reproduce*, with their offspring described by the same word, *tokos*. The mysterious new phenomenon of money is imagined in the familiar terms of nature: for instance as the sea (8BF), and sexual reproduction. Paying interest on a loan,[99] which seems

---

[91] *Ant.* 73–6: Seaford 1990b, 78; 2000b, 85.

[92] *OT* 1207–10 'the same great harbour sufficed for son and father as attending the *thalamos* . . .' (cf. Aesch. *Sept.* 359).

[93] Seaford 1994a, 211 with bibliography; Cox 1998, 32–6, 210; Athenian drama: Aesch. *Supp.* 338–9; Seaford 1987, 117–18.

[94] Seaford 1990b; cf. 1990a.

[95] Apart from the numerous coin hoards found buried see Ar. *Birds* 599–602 (5B) with Dunbar ad loc.; *Wealth* 237–8 (Wealth complains of being hidden in the ground); also e.g. Antiphon 87 DK B4; Xen. *Poroi* 4.6; Dem. 27.53; Pl. *Laws* 913ab; Men. *Dys.* 812 'invisible wealth' kept buried; D. S. 2.15.2; Appian *BC* 4.73 (Rhodes). Makareus buries a stranger's gold and is punished by Dionysus with the self-destruction of his family (Aelian *VH* 13. 2).

[96] One of the commonest needs that landowners had for cash was to raise a dowry: Osborne 1991; Millett 1991, 62–3. Marriage imagined as a commercial transaction: e.g. Soph. fr. 583.7: 'we are sold'; cf. Dem. 24. 202–3 (selling a sister in marriage is disgraceful).

[97] Condemnation of concealing wealth in the house: Pi. *Isthm.* 1.67–8 (quoted 8D n. 38), *Nem.* 1.31–2.

[98] This combination is at the heart of Plautus' *Aulularia* (and presumably of its Greek model: Stockert 1983, 13–16), especially the scene in which the young man's confession of making the girl pregnant is mistaken by her father as confessing to have stolen his pot of gold (731–57). The Lydian king Candaules' concealment of his wife is completely reversed by his need for her to be admired naked (i.e. for enviability for himself), which results in him losing everything to Gyges (Hdt. 1.8–12).

[99] This first appears as a fact of life in Aristophanes, notably the *Clouds*; cf. Pi. *Ol.* 10.5–9; Millett 1991, 46.

to have developed out of the practice (recommended by Hesiod) of reciprocating a gift with a better one,[100] is greatly facilitated by the use of money (M–M¹). But in contrast to gift-exchange and barter, not only is what is given (money) itself returned, but what it produces (by *tokos*) is also homogeneous with itself. Similarly, even money used for trading (M–C–M¹) may bring to the trader a return of (homogeneous) money greater than his outlay. According to Aristotle (*Pol.* 1258b1–8) 'currency came into being for exchange, but interest (*tokos*) makes it increase. Hence its name, for offspring are similar to their parents, and *tokos* is currency the child of currency (*nomisma ek nomismatos*). And so of the modes of acquisition this is the most unnatural'. In fact the only form of reproduction that matches Aristotle's characterisation of interest – as 'currency from currency', and as unnatural – is *incest*. The monied tyrant Oedipus calls himself 'of the same family (*homogenēs*) with those from whom I was born' (1361).

This homogeneity of monetary interest is a special form of the persistent homogeneity of money (8B). In contrast to mythical cosmogony, in which our genealogically produced world – now ruled by Zeus – has superseded its genesis, the originating principle of the Milesians remains fundamental, always there, like money, to take into itself again what it has generated. This shift from myth to the impersonal occurred under the influence of monetisation (11B), which diminishes the power of genealogy (12A). Still in the world of myth, Sophocles' chorus react to Oedipus' incest with 'alas generations of men, how I calculate (*enarithmō*) you as living equal to nothing',[101] whereas in impersonal cosmology the homogenising power of money finds extreme expression in Parmenides' denial of all plurality and change.

Plato in the *Republic* describes the tyrannical type of man, who (like the tyrant himself) because he needs money is violent towards his closest kin and robs temples (574). We all, according to Plato, have the illicit desires (even for sex with our mother) of this type of man, which may emerge in sleep, but we – unlike him – are able to control or eliminate them (571b–572b). The appeal of the tragic tyrant to ordinary citizens was not just from their memory or fear of tyranny but also, we may guess, as a figure on whom they could project, in extreme form, their own conscious or unconscious desires – in imaginative self-protection against the disruptivenes of monetisation and

---

[100] Millett 1991, 40–52, 99, 121.

[101] 1187–8, followed by the impossibility of bestowing permanent happiness on any man by *makarismos* (cf. Silenus' response to Midas: 14D). Oedipus' failed *makarismos* was at his incestuous wedding, which bestowed wealth and tyranny (420–3, 1275–84 (esp. 1282–4); Seaford 1987, 119–20).

its invasion and isolation of the individual psyche.[102] The isolating, potentially absolute power of money may belong to anyone who possesses it
(14A), tending to release not only the tyrant (14D) but even the ordinary
citizen from the claims of kin,[103] of reciprocity,[104] of exogamy,[105] even of the
sacred.[106] The qualities of Oedipus (energy, decisiveness, self-confidence,
intelligence, versatility), which are those of the fifth-century Athenian citizen,[107] all centre around his autonomy.[108] Just as Creon projects monetary
greed onto others (and gold onto India), so the Athenian citizen may –
with the ambivalence characteristic of Greek attitudes to tyranny – project
onto the tragic tyrant his own potentially unlimited monetary autonomy
writ large, enviable but horrifying in its consequences.

F   CONCLUSION

My argument has been that the rapid monetisation of the Greek city-states
of the sixth century BC was an important factor in the genesis and form of
the earliest 'philosophy' and of tragedy. These are two central elements of
a development that is sometimes called the 'Greek miracle'. However, in
recent years exposure – by among others Martin Bernal – of the debts owed
by Greek culture to the sophisticated and more ancient civilisations of the
Near East has encouraged the belief that the 'miracle' is a Hellenocentric
illusion. On this important controversy I will confine myself to three points.

---

[102] Greek projection of monetary greed onto barbarians: the Phrygian Midas; the Thracian Polymnestor
(8F); Soph. fr. 587; Darius as a small trader: Hdt. 3.89. 3 with Kurke 1999, 71–3 (cf. Le Rider 2001,
83–4); Kurke 1999, 238 (Hdt. 1.199 on temple prostitution in Babylon); Hdt. 8.26. Soph. *Ant.* 1037–9
(Creon: see above).

[103] Accusation of valuing money over kinship: Lys. 32.17 (cf.5.30); Is. 9.25; cf. Xen. *Mem.* 2.3.1. Conflict
with kin over money: Is. 1.6–7; Dem. 40.1; 48.1; fratricide over money: Is. 9.17;
Cox 1998, 109–14; Millett 1991, 136; cf. Eur. *Pho.* 439–42; conflict between brothers over inheritance
goes back to the premonetary world of Hesiod, but over *moveable* property (*Op.* 36–7; cf. 618–94
advice to his brother on sea-trading). 'Invisible' wealth is easier to misappropriate than 'visible': e.g.
Lys. 19.45–50; 29.2; 32.23; Dem. 27 (esp. 26, 33, 61); 29.37; 38.7; 27.57 (= 29.49); Is. 6 (see esp. 30,
38, 43); Ar. *Eccles.* 601–2; the earliest case is Aeolus' bag in *Od.* (2E).

[104] Soph. fr. 88: 'It is *money* that finds *philoi* (friends) . . . and nobody is hostile (*echthros*) to it'; cf. e.g.
Andoc. *Or.* 4.15; Ar. *Wealth* 829–39; Eur. *Pho.* 400–5, 439–42.

[105] On wealth-preserving endogamy among ordinary citizens see n. 93 above.

[106] The abundant precious metal in temples invite 'temple-robbery': e.g. Ar. *Wealth* 358–9; cf. Soph. *Ant.*
301; fr. 88.6–7. Because performance of death ritual was evidence of qualifying for the inheritance
(Is. 2.25, 36–7; 4.7, 19, 26; 8.21–7; 9.4; Dem. 43.65), unseemly conflict between kin might break
out over the corpse (Isaeus 6.40; 8.38–9; Dem. 44.32). Rituals of betrothal and wedding involve the
transfer of cash (the dowry), and indicate legitimacy and therefore the right to inherit (e.g. Is. 8.9;
cf. 3.8, 28).

[107] Argued by Knox 1957, 67–77.

[108] Cf. praise of individual autonomy in the service of the Athens at Thuc. 1.70.6; 2.41.1–2.

First, the two volumes so far published of Martin Bernal's *Black Athena* are – whatever their reliability and impact – irrelevant to this issue, as they end with the collapse of Mycenean civilisation, several centuries before the period concerned.[109] It was obvious (long before Bernal) from Bronze-age archaeology (and the Linear B texts) that the Greek palatial economies were of a general type found also in the Near East (4B).

Second, the issue cannot be resolved without careful definitions. For instance, 'philosophy' or 'science' are terms far too broad to describe what was new in Greek thought in the sixth century BC. However, the definition that I give in the first paragraph of 9A does help to isolate a radically new conception of the world.

Third, an effect of *Black Athena* has been focus on *race* as an explanatory factor. This is politically regressive (in its encouragement of identity politics at the expense of understanding economics) and historically inane. The sixth-century transition was neither a 'miracle' nor the achievement of an inherently superior 'Greek race'. What is crucial is that the Greeks, in contrast to their Near Eastern neighbours, preserved a social formation that – in synthesis with what they had taken from those neighbours – allowed a radically new kind of society and culture. I have in chapter 4 sketched the important role played, in this process of differentiation from the Near East, by the new monetary economy. In sixth-century Greece there did indeed occur a radically new conception (not necessarily superior to what preceded it) of the world and of the individual, for which a precondition was a radical development in socio-economic formation.

However fascinating for us is the culture of premonetary Egypt and Mesopotamia, it remains irreducibly alien. The earliest Greek poetry and wisdom, on the other hand, we citizens of a thoroughly monetised society recognise as alien and yet somehow more akin to us than anything from those earlier civilisations. This is, I suggest, in part because Greek poetry and wisdom sprang from a society that was about to be – or was already – monetised. I have related this development to two unprecedented phenomena: the construction by individual 'philosophers' of impersonal cosmology, and the redeployment of the traditional resources of performance to focus, in tragedy, on the extreme isolation of the individual from the gods and from

---

[109] He does make incidental remarks such as that 'Pythagoras studied in Egypt and brought back Egyptian mathematical and religious principles' (1987, 519). Whatever the truth of this, there is nothing Egyptian about e.g. the Pythagorean metaphysics of number (13A). Subsequently (2001) he has addressed the question of 'the origins of western science', without touching on cosmology (as opposed to astronomy) or metaphysics, and without being able to show that e.g. Egyptian geometry ever went beyond the practical.

his own kin. With these preoccupations we ourselves have no difficulty in sympathising.

We have no difficulty because we live in a world in which the monetisation first observable in the early Greek polis has had, despite periods of setback, several centuries to develop. We have by now thoroughly internalised the metaphysics of money – at its crudest consisting of two beliefs: firstly the belief that money is a *thing* (rather than a social convention) and that as a thing it must, like the weather, constrain our sense of what is possible, and secondly the belief that we are primarily individual agents and only secondarily (if at all) members of a larger entity, whether defined by kinship, politics, religion, or anything else.

But this internalisation finds it hard to shake off a lingering sense of arbitrariness, of there being something indefinably unsatisfying – despite its inevitablity and the massive progress it has achieved – about the individualist reification of money and the injustice and alienation thereby produced. For those with this sense, historical understanding of the relatively recent (on the scale of human history) transition from premonetary to monetary society may be of particular interest. Such understanding requires knowledge of the development of money in the early Greek polis, as well as of the distinctiveness of the early Greek polis among contemporary societies of the Near East.

For this purpose it is fortunate that the evidence survives, in particular in the early history of Greek texts from the premonetary world of Homeric epic to the monetised world of tragedy. What I have provided is the first attempt to understand the relationship between these texts and monetisation. As such, it invites further research designed to integrate economics into the study of culture. For instance, from about 500 BC Athens became the cultural leader of the Greeks, to the extent that Greek culture of the Classical period has sometimes been thought of as entirely Athenian. What is the precise relation between this and the fact that Athens was, from about 500 BC and throughout the Classical period, the only polis to extract from within its territory extensive supplies of precious metal (the silver mines at Laurium)?

CHAPTER FIFTEEN

Appendix: was money used in the early Near East?

I must first define 'the early Near East'. By 'early' I mean the period from the beginning of writing at the end of the fourth millennium BC to the collapse of the Assyrian empire in 612 BC, which occured at about the same time as the invention of coinage in western Anatolia. By 'Near East' I refer primarily to the riverine societies of the Tigris and the Euphrates (Mesopotamia) and of the Nile (Egypt), but also to other societies of the fertile crescent (Syria and Palestine), as well as Anatolia. The evidence for the economies of these various societies is mountainous; but it is also sporadic, limited to particular places, particular periods, and particular contexts. Numerous economic activities were of course never recorded. Of the records made some have survived. Many surviving records (in particular thousands of clay tablets) have not been published, and many published records have not been subject to economic interpretation.

The economies of the early Near East were, broadly speaking, of the redistributive type (4A). Redistribution organises the flow of goods to and from centres in such a way that, although it may need to use a single measure of value,[1] none of the goods are likely to acquire a combination of our listed characteristics of money (1C) sufficient to qualify them as money. It is rather most likely to be in trade, especially market trade, that there occurs the need for a quantifiable, generally accepted means of exchange and payment (as well as measure of value), important though it is to remember that trade does not *require* money. The question of the form and importance of money in the early Near East is therefore connected to the debate over the extent and nature of market trade and private enterprise (as opposed to administered trade and redistribution).

Rather than entering this debate, I focus on the questions whether money was used and, if so, what forms it took. The answers depend not only on

---

[1] See e.g. Polanyi 1968, 167–8.

what material is selected and how it is interpreted but also on how money is *defined*. This being so, it is curious that those who present evidence for 'money' generally omit to discuss, or even indicate, what they mean by 'money', even though there is in fact no single, generally accepted definition. The resulting vacuum is filled by the unconscious tendency to assume the presence of what is familiar.[2] My aim in this chapter, therefore, is to collect and evaluate, *in the light of my account of 'money'* (1C), the best evidence so far produced for 'money'.[3]

B   DID THE EARLY NEAR EAST HAVE COINAGE?

I deal first with one of the specific forms taken by money, namely coinage. It is important to distinguish[4] between (a) metal pieces of standardised weight (and/or quality) that may have been used in payments, (b) *marked* metal pieces, that may also be of standard weight and/or quality, and may have been used in payments, and (c) coins. Coins are marked metal pieces of standardised weight and quality, but such pieces are not necessarily coins.

   (a) There is some scattered evidence, in texts or in the form of surviving objects, for what appear to be metal objects of standardised weight.[5] In particular, the Assyrian King Sennacherib (704–681 BC) refers in an inscription to the casting of shekels.[6] In a find from the Median period in Iran three silver bars belong to a weight system.[7] Rings, coils, or even cups may at times have been accepted in payment as of standardised weight.[8]

---

[2]   Powell (1996), apparently unaware of this tendency, actually maintains that the use of terms such as 'money' by cuneiformists 'to describe *silver*' demonstrates that there was money!

[3]   I do not know the languages of the early Near East, and have relied on the considerable scholarly literature that exists on the early Near Eastern economies.

[4]   Failure to do so is one of the many weaknesses of Silver 1985, 126–30, which is the only attempt known to me to collect evidence from the whole early Near East to make a case for the use of coinage. For example, he thinks to have established the existence of a Babylonian token coinage in the Neo-Babylonian and Persian periods by citing a paper (Powell 1978b) which in fact neither mentions token coinage nor provides any evidence for it. Some of Silver's wide-ranging ignorance is exposed by Renger 1994.

[5]   For recent overviews see Snell 1995 and Le Rider 2001; also Bivar 1971, 99–100; Powell 1978; Postgate 1992, 203–4; Wolff 1998, 779–80. In a recent survey of Hacksilber hoards from the ancient Near East Gitin and Golani 2001, 39 note that 'except for the three cake ingots from Zinçirli and the 83 pieces from Nush-i Jan, none of the hoards reviewed above has yet been successfully equated with standard measurements known from antiquiy. In all the other hoards, including those from Ekron, the pieces are of random weight.'

[6]   Luckenbill 1924, 109. Cf. however Bogaert 1966, 124–5. Oppenheim 1977, 87 suggests possible Lydian influence. See also the apparent mention of shekel pieces in two much earlier Ugaritic texts: Gordon 1965, 245, 250.

[7]   Bivar 1971, 106; but cf. Grierson 1978, 22–3; Le Rider 2001, 2–3, 9.

[8]   Snell 1995, 1488–90; Bogaert 1976b, 800; Powell 1978; Dayton 1974; Le Rider 2001, 4–5.

(b) There is also a small amount of scattered evidence, in texts or in the form of surviving objects, for the marking of metal pieces for purposes other than decoration. Copper ingots of about 1330 BC, some inscribed or stamped with signs, but of varying sizes and weights, have been discovered in a shipwreck off southern Turkey.[9] The Egyptian word *shaty* of the Ramessid period may conceivably have referred to an inscribed piece of silver.[10] Three silver discs from Zinçirli in Turkey have 'belonging to Bar-rakkub son of Panamuwa' in Aramaic inscribed or stamped on them. Bar-rakkub was a local ruler around 730 BC. It has been inferred from seventh-century BC texts specifying silver from the temple of Ishtar at Arbela in Assyria that pieces of silver circulated stamped by that temple as a guarantee of quality (and perhaps weight).[11] The Akkadian term *ginnu*, which occurs only in texts of the Persian period (i.e. after the early Near East as we have defined it), has been taken to mean a mark denoting the quality of silver.[12]

It is notable that this evidence[13] for standardised and/or marked pieces of metal is scattered in isolated cases over a vast area and a vast period. Moreover, some of the evidence is very weak. That the *shaty* was marked is a risky inference; the same applies to the silver of Ishtar at Arbela;[14] and in neither case has anything corresponding to the description been unearthed. Even where the marking is beyond doubt, its significance may not be what is sometimes claimed: the Bar-rakkub inscription is more likely to be a mark of property than a guarantee;[15] and the *ginnu*, if it was a mark of quality, might have functioned quite differently from the mark on a coin.[16]

(c) What distinguishes a coin from a marked, standardised piece of metal that is not a coin? A mark on a coin, whether or not it is supposed to guarantee weight and quality, endows it with a general acceptability in payment without being weighed or tested. This acceptability led very rapidly to the widespread circulation, throughout Greek lands, of pieces

---

[9] Other similar ('oxhide') ingots (but unmarked) from roughly the same period have been discovered from other parts of the eastern Mediterranean area: Bass 1967, 52–78; Zaccagnini 1976, 564–5; Snell 1995, 1490.

[10] Hayes 1973, 389; Zaccagnini 1976, 570; Silver 1985, 127.   [11] Lipinski 1979.

[12] *The Chicago Akkadian Dictionary* s.v. ginnu, 79–80. It does not necessarily denote *inferior* quality: Powell 1978, 223–4; Le Rider 2001, 29–35.

[13] I have mentioned what appears in the secondary literature as the most substantial evidence, but can not claim to be exhaustive. However, it seems unlikely that even future discoveries will affect my basic point.

[14] See e.g. Parise 1973, 385, 387–8; Renger 1995, 307–8; Le Rider 2001, 22–4.

[15] Parise 1973, 387–9; Grierson 1978, 3; Renger 1995, 308; Le Rider 2001, 27; cf. Furtwängler 1986, 157–8.

[16] Renger 1995, 309.

of low and high value issued by city-states. Numerous hoards have been discovered of Greek coins – all conforming to the pattern of a small round stamped piece of metal (usually silver)[17] – from the mid-sixth century BC onward. The Greeks attributed the invention of coinage either to themselves or to the Lydians (7A).

None of this has any parallel in the early Near East. Even were the evidence in (a) and (b) less meagre, less scattered, and more homogeneous, the fact would remain that the standardisation and/or marking of metal pieces does not *by itself* make coinage. Whereas among the Greeks coinage generally removed the need to weigh or test the metal at each transaction, in the early Near East metal used in payment was, it seems, always *weighed* rather than counted.[18] The Akkadian word for 'pay' means 'weigh out'.[19] After coins were eventually introduced from Greece, even they were weighed in payment.[20]

The invention of coinage was perhaps influenced by the forms in which precious metal circulated in the early Near East (much of the evidence cited under (a) and (b) is from the eighth century BC and later). Certainly there had for centuries been no *technological* obstacle to making coins. Nevertheless, and despite considerable financial sophistication, the Mesopotamians did not invent coinage – because they did not feel the need for it. The rapid and widespread diffusion of coinage in Greek lands indicates, as we have seen, a distinct social formation.

C   WHAT FORMS DID 'MONEY' TAKE IN EARLY MESOPOTAMIA?

My main focus will be on the period *circa* 2100–1600 BC, of which, approximately, the first century is the period of the third dynasty of Ur ('Ur III') and the remaining four centuries the 'Old Babylonian' period. This Mesopotamian half-millennium provides the most detailed evidence for economic transactions in the early Near East, and the best evidence for 'money'. As for the vast mass of material that falls outside these chronological and geographical limits, I have read the most relevant discussions of economic matters that I have been able to find, in particular concerning the

---

[17] An exception that proves the rule are the bronze arrowhead-shaped objects that appear to have functioned as money, emerging from the interaction of Greek colonists with the (archer) Scythians from around the mid-sixth century in the Black Sea area: Grottanelli and Parise 1986; Stancomb 1993; von Reden 1997, 158–9.

[18] Bogaert 1966, 125; Hayes 1973, 390; Parise 1973, 385; Zaccagnini 1976, 565; Oppenheim 1977, 87; Powell 1978, 217; von Soden 1994, 124; Snell 1995, 1491.

[19] von Soden 1994, 124.

[20] Parise 1973, 389; Oppenheim 1977, 87; Balmuth 1980, 23; Lloyd, A. B. 1983, 328; Renger 1995, 310.

texts from Ebla (25th century),[21] Nuzi (15th),[22] and Ugarit (14th–13th),[23] as well as the Old Testament.[24] All these discussions are of particular contexts or periods, and most of them deal with money only peripherally. Scholarly overviews are rare.[25] Separate sections will cover Egypt (15E) and the Neo-Assyrian and Neo-Babylonian periods of the eight to the sixth centuries BC (15F).

The commodity with the best claim to be called 'money' is, throughout much of the visible history of the early Near East, silver. Given its brilliant colour, malleability, and resistance to atmospheric oxidisation, silver was (and is) a desirable material in manufacture. And this desirability, together with its relative (but not excessive) scarcity, its divisibility, its portability, and its durability, well suited it to perform the functions of money. As well as having been unearthed in pieces that may have been used in payments (15B), silver is frequently to be found in the documents as a measure of value and as a means of payment (or exchange).

In the interpretation of these documents it is easy to be imprecise. I have already condemned the practice of identifying 'money' without clarifying what is meant by it. Further imprecision may be involved in the use of translations such as 'buy' and 'sell'. In barter, where no money is involved, we would generally use a verb such as 'exchange' for the actions of both parties, reserving 'buy' for the acquisition of commodities by transfer of

---

[21] For Pettinato 1981, 185–201 (cf. also 1991, 86) the Ebla tablets exhibit three modes of the transfer of goods between cities: barter, purchase/sale (with payment in gold and silver), and tribute (mainly silver and gold, but also other goods). The measure of value is provided by silver. Ebla has abundant silver and gold, but (within the city, presumably) 'it must not be forgotten that money was unknown in protohistoric cities. Most payments were made in kind. This most commonly meant allotments of food, but it also took the form of goods such as textiles, tools, etc.' (196). A large collection of papers on the 'economy and society' of Ebla (Waetzoldt and Hauptmann 1988) contains virtually no mention of money or silver. Cf. Archi 1988.

[22] Cross 1937; Zaccagnini 1976, 548–9 discusses payments composed of various commodities evaluated in silver; see also Zaccagnini 1979 and in *Reallexikon der Assyriologie* s.v. Markt (7.425).

[23] Schaeffer 1955, 228–9; Heltzer 1978 (prices expressed in silver and in other commodities); Stieglitz 1979.

[24] Hamburger 1962, 423–5; Einzig 1966, 211–14; Bogaert 1976b, 804–6; Snell 1995, 1494–5. Payments are made in silver (e.g. Gen. 23.16 'weighed out'), even 'pieces of silver' (e.g. Gen. 20.16), but also in various other goods (e.g. I Kings 5.1, 9.10–14; II Kings 3.4; 5.23; Deut. 14.25).

[25] The best is Renger 1995. Powell 1996 is brief and gives no definition of money. Powell 1990 is mainly about long term price fluctuations (in Babylonia). He does note that in Babylonia (a) in all eras silver (along with barley) provides a standard of value (79, 98); (b) in Ur III and the Old Babylonian period barley has replaced copper as 'cheap money' (79), and indeed 'functioned throughout most Babylonian history as the "small change" *par excellence*' (88); (c) after the gap in documentation (*circa* 1600–1400 BC) gold as well as silver functions as a standard of value (79); (d) (of the early period) 'in most transactions neither copper nor silver will have changed hands but rather commodities defined in terms of copper or silver' (82), and the same is true of gold in the Kassite period (82); (e) the Middle Assyrian period knew a system of cheap metal money (tin, bronze, lead) (86). See also Müller 1982.

money and 'sell' for the acquisition of money by transfer of commodities. But for example Foster (1977), in what he claims to be the first ever study of commercial activity in Sargonic Mesopotamia (i.e. centred roughly on the 23rd century), writes that 'commerce in the Sargonic period is best defined by recourse to contemporary terminology: *šám*, that is, buying and selling of commodities'. Whereas Foster translates *šám* as 'buy' and 'sell', we note that the two activities were, as denoted by the same word, regarded as the same. Silver, for Foster (35), was a 'commodity of exchange', and may be 'considered money in the usual sense of that word'. But we are also told, in the same breath, that 'silver could be bought and sold like any other commodity'. Further, various other commodities also perform money functions. Items might be priced in gold (32) as well as in silver (33). There is evidence that 'cash rentals from lands leased by the state to individuals were payable in silver, grain, and livestock' (34). Moreover, 'like silver, grain could be used for buying and selling, renting, could be loaned at interest or interest free, and could be exchanged for other commodities', and 'other foods like dates or flour appear in commercial records as media of exchange' (36). It is possible, to judge from the evidence provided by Foster, that silver possessed characteristics (1) and (3) of money (as set out in 1C) to a greater extent than did any of the other commodities, but this possibility certainly does not justify a distinction between silver as 'money' and everything else as mere commodities. Silver is a commodity (quantified by weight) that, like other commodities, may be used to perform money functions.[26]

Moving on to Ur III,[27] we find, in the study by Curtis and Hallo (1959), reference to 'the disconcertingly rare references to silver (money) in an economy so highly organized and so careful in its accounting procedures' (105). Given this disconcerting rareness, one might ask (as of Foster) what precisely is meant by the assumption that silver is 'money'. To be sure, commodities in the Ur III period are 'occasionally' recorded with their equivalent in silver. But 'there are also not infrequent consignments of silver, and some of these, in turn, are priced in the opposite way, that is, by their equivalent in grain or certain other commodities'. Moreover, it is concluded (112) that certain 'exchangeable commodities' served as 'substitutes for money by the side of silver'. Lambert (1963), in his study of

---

[26] Much the same picture emerges from the study by Limet (1972), of metals in the dynasty of Akkad: silver is often a measure of value without being used in payment (21–3); when it is used in payment, it is often paid along with other commodities (18, 21); it is also (naturally enough) used to make objects (7–8); and loans in silver may sometimes be repaid in barley (19).

[27] Snell (1982), is a detailed study of the period, but of merchants' accounts rather than money.

Lagash in the Ur III period, attempts to explain the rarity of silver in the documents[28] by the hypothesis that although transactions between private individuals often involved silver, barley rather than silver was used as a money of account as well as generally in transactions involving the state.

For the Old Babylonian period we are well equipped with detailed studies. Sweet (1958) is unusual in carefully defining the various functions of money. His conclusions are as follows (emphasis added). Firstly, 'silver was not owned by private individuals to any great extent and was not in common use as a *means of storing wealth*' (124). Secondly, 'the object regularly used as a *standard of value* was silver', but other objects 'were also used occasionally, the ones for which we have evidence being small cattle and barley' (156). Thirdly 'silver appears to have changed hands as a *means of payment* only in small amounts and usually only in minor transactions'. Payment could be made in a wide range of commodities, notably barley and sesame oil. (177). Fourthly, 'barter of any commodity for another was the regular practice', and so 'there is no reason to think that there existed any *money or moneys of exchange* in Mesopotamia during the Old Babylonian period' (178–9).

More recently, van de Mieroop (1992) has studied the archaeology and the texts of the city of Ur, which provide a relatively good range of evidence. Here we find silver widely used as a standard of value, for loans, and for payments of various kinds: in particular, merchants converted revenues in kind into silver for temple and palace. At the same time loans, payments to palace and temple, salaries, and rents are sometimes paid in kind, notably barley.[29] Among van de Mieroop's conclusions is that 'although we cannot speak of a cash economy yet, the role of silver as a currency can no longer be denied' (249). In support of this view he advances two considerations. One is 'the great prominence of silver loans in the documentation'. The other is more controversial – a claim that the use of silver in payments extended well beyond what is known from the documents.

In my opinion silver must have played a role as a means of payment, and it cannot have been used solely as a measure to calculate equivalences for the barter of natural products. Many possessions and products changed hands, not only between individuals but also between institutions. It could be said that the contracts simply mentioned the silver equivalences of products or of landed property, etc., to make barter possible. But such a theory does not explain why prices are expressed almost constantly in silver, not in barley, dates, fish, and the like.[30]

[28] Though among the references to silver are mentions of the working of it (80).
[29] Loans: 95, 204; payments to palace and temple: 113, 114, 243; salaries: 162; rents: 172.
[30] van de Mieroop 1992, 248; van de Mieroop 1997 does not add anything on the issue.

This inference is demonstrably false, for there are many clear examples from the ancient Near East and elsewhere of a commodity (e.g. silver) being widely used as a standard of value without being used in payments.[31] From a detailed study of Mesopotamian letters of this period Renger concludes that 'silver is the usual denominator to indicate the value of a particular item, but that 'in most cases the means of payment is not explicitly mentioned'; in some of the letters goods are exchanged (or 'given') for other goods (e.g. dates and oil for a garment); in some rents or wages are paid in kind; in some goods are given for silver; in some 'silver could be bought'; in some barley is named as the medium to buy goods.[32] In the Ur III and Old Babylonian periods, according to Powell,[33] barley functioned as 'cheap money'. More extreme is the view of Oppenheim (1970) that 'it is rather obvious from the letters and administrative documents of the Old Babylonian period that, at that time, silver as a means of exchange was hardly changing hands outside the contexts of the palace and the overland trade' (138). A study of the use of silver at Mari[34] in this period shows its use as a standard of value, as a means of various kinds of payment (along with other goods), and as a material for luxury objects given as gifts or kept in palace or temple.

Although van de Mieroop, like scholars on the earlier periods, exaggerates the role of silver as money, we can nevertheless say, on the basis of the material he provides, that in the surviving documents silver is in the Old Babylonian period predominant over all other commodities as a measure of value. But it is neither the only measure of value nor clearly predominant in any of the other money functions. Nor has it ceased to be a commodity.

A similarly limited predominance of silver is to be found in the documents concerning foreign trade in the Old Babylonian period discussed by Leemans (1960). Loans, payments, and the measure of value frequently take the form of silver, for which Leemans uses (without defining them) the words 'currency' and 'money'. Silver also sometimes takes its place alongside other commodities, for example as one of various gifts to a goddess or as one of various commodities sent to acquire copper from abroad.[35]

---

[31] Powell 1990, 82 (second-millennium BC Babylonia); Limet 1972, 22–3 (Mesopotamian dynasty of Akkad); Grierson 1978, 9–10 (Homeric society, ancient Egypt, early mediaeval Europe, etc.); Janssen 1975b, 545–50 ('money-barter' in various cultures, esp. ancient Egypt) and 1981, 66; Hayes 1973, 390; Zaccagnini 1976, 532–3, 547; etc.

[32] Renger 1984, 107–8. Renger 1995, 318 affirms that silver in this period was not a general means of exchange.

[33] 1990, 79.

[34] Kupper 1982: he calls silver 'métal monétaire', without defining 'monétaire', and despite concentrating on its use as a commodity (in luxury objects).

[35] Leemans 1960, 23, 27, 29, 36, 54.

But the most detailed evidence for Mesopotamian foreign trade in this period, and perhaps the most detailed evidence for commerce from the whole early Near East, is provided by the thousands of documents found not in Mesopotamia but at ancient Kanish, south of the river Halys in central Anatolia. These require a section to themselves.

D   THE KANISH TEXTS

These documents are the archives of a settlement of Assyrian merchants at Kanish in the period *circa* 1920–1840 BC. They relate to a trade in which, basically, silver and gold were sent from Anatolia to the merchants' home city of Ashur, where they were exchanged for tin and textiles for export back to Anatolia, to be exchanged there for silver and gold, and so on. The documents have been important for the debate concerning the nature of trade (15A). It was maintained by Polanyi[36] that what they show is 'administered trade' rather than 'market trade': profits are hardly ever explicitly mentioned and losses practically never; 'prices' are not at the centre of interest, are not fixed by supply and demand, but are rather equivalences established by the authority of custom, statute, treaty, or proclamation, and so the trade is in this respect risk-free; the merchants may pursue private transactions, but are basically public officials whose income is from commission on turnover (or grants of land) rather than from profit from price differentials.

This account was contested in a much cited study by Veenhof (1972), who argued that the Kanish merchants were not temple or palace officials but private entrepreneurs, practising not administered but market trade, and using money. Veenhof studied the material in far more detail than did Polanyi, and much of his argument is convincing. In this area (overland foreign trade) as in others (notably his denial of the existence of marketplaces) Polanyi's thesis must be modified.

But our central concern is with money. For Veenhof, as for van de Mieroop, private enterprise and money go together. Although the frequent assumption that where there is market and profit there must also be money is false,[37] we may nevertheless agree that if the Kanish merchants were not government officials acquiring metal for the state but private entrepreneurs making a profit, this makes it more *likely* that 'money' was involved. And

---

[36] 1957, 17–23.

[37] E.g. Powell 1999, 16: 'to judge by the substantial number of lines devoted to merchants and commerce – about ten per cent – in the great hymn to Shamash, the phenomenon of money and buying and selling cannot have been as uncommon as the redistribution-reciprocity theorists would have us believe'.

it is to Veenhof's credit that he aims for clarity about what 'money' means by noting Polanyi's distinction between its various uses (348).

POLANYI admits that silver functioned as standard of value and means of payment, but not, and this is most important, as 'indirect means of exchange'. The latter he defines as 'acquiring units of quantifiable objects for indirect exchange through direct exchange, in order to acquire the desired objects through a further act of exchange' (POLANYI 1968, 167–8 and 192). To give an example of 'indirect exchange': one exchanges barley for silver, to exchange this silver later on (not necessarily elsewhere) for wood (which in fact one needed), because a direct exchange of barley for wood is impossible or inconvenient.

However, he then tries to show (350) that in the Kanish documents

silver did function as 'money', not only as a standard of value and means of payment, but also as an 'indirect means of exchange'. Though the exchange between e.g. tin and silver was in one respect 'direct' (silver in Ashur was exchanged for tin; tin in Anatolia was exchanged again for silver; a third product did not necessarily intervene), it was at the same time 'indirect', because there was no direct exchange between those who sold the tin in the first place (most probably the Iranians, even though the Assyrians may have imported it from Iran into Ashur), and those who ultimately bought it: the Anatolians with their bronze industry.

This is a misunderstanding. The indispensable essence of indirect exchange (as Polanyi described it) is that there be three items (a, b, c), with the same party exchanging a for b so as to acquire c with b. But in the Anatolian trade, as Veenhof himself describes it, only two transactions are involved (tin for silver, and vice-versa): neither the Assyrians nor the Anatolians nor the Iranians are engaged in three transactions. For silver to perform the money function of being a means of indirect exchange (b), it has to be acquired (by exchange with a) in order to be exchanged for something *else* (c). The movement has to be from one commodity to money, and then to another commodity (c_1–M–c_2).

   To be sure, it may be inferred that the Assyrians acquired silver in Anatolia not only in order to exchange it for more textiles and tin, and not (or not only) for their own use, but also (as profit) in order to exchange it for other commodities, and so that silver did after all perform the money function of being a means of indirect exchange. But this does not exclude the possibility of the same function being performed by a whole number of other commodities. For instance, Veenhof himself notes that 'tin or textiles imported into Anatolia were sometimes exchanged first for copper and wool, then ultimately – probably with additional profit – converted elsewhere into silver and gold'. Here, in a sequence abstracted from a different section of the cycle of barter, the money function of being an indirect means of exchange is performed not by the silver and gold but by the copper and wool, which are acquired not in order to make tools or clothes but in order to acquire silver and gold. We should also note that the money functions of means of payment and measure of value were also sometimes played by *tin*.[38]

Barter may go beyond the simple exchange of items for the use of the two parties involved. Someone may exchange a for b, and then some of the b for c, and then some of the c for d, and so on, each time with a different person, while all the while accumulating surpluses, retaining amounts of b, c, d, etc. either for his own use for for subsequent exchange. Although b acquired in order to acquire c is thereby performing a money function, it may be that no single item in the cycle has a predominant position as money – for instance as a more generally acceptable means of exchange than the others. What evidence is there, from the Kanish texts, to establish an essential difference between silver (the difference that makes it money) and the other items with which it is exchanged in what might be called a cycle of barter?

Veenhof proposes that silver was not just an indirect means of exchange (c_1–m–c_2) but 'the starting point and the ultimate goal of the trade' (m–c–m). 'It was differentiated from *luqutum*, "merchandise", which served the purpose of procuring silver.' However, silver was 'not' after all 'an end in itself', as it was exchanged for merchandise' (m–c_1–m–c_2).

Even if we accept this account, it shows not that silver had a special status (as money) in Ashur or elsewhere, but only that these traders imported silver. We do not know whether they used their silver to acquire commodities in general (c, d, e, f, etc.), i.e. as money, or exchanged it for e and f in order to exchange e and f for g, h, i, j etc.).[39] The merchants no doubt valued the silver more for its exchange-value than for its use-value, but this by itself does not make it 'money' (the same would be true of an oil-importer's attitude to oil).

There remains, however, another way by which Veenhof claims to have established the special status of silver (as money) – through the analysis of *vocabulary*, which may in principle indeed establish its special status not

---

[38] Veenhof 1972, 230–1, 257, 259, 262, 268.

[39] Some of this silver may well have ended up, by whatever route, in the treasuries of temple or palace. Veenhof admits (350 n. 446) that 'we do not know exactly what money-lenders, investors and shareholders in enterprises did with the interest they received', and that the temples may have wanted, from their investment in the trade, 'silver and gold for the treasuries for display purposes'. Further, 'what the "state" did with its silver in income – its main sources were the taxes [on the trade], but the Assyrian kings did also partake to some extent in the trade – is unknown'.

just for international merchants but generally in Assyrian society. Although those who believe that the merchants used money might sometimes want to translate the word for silver (*kaspum*) as 'money' (like the French 'argent'), there is no other word for money in these or any other Akkadian (or Sumerian) texts.[40] However, the terms 'buy' (or 'purchase') and 'sell' imply the use of money. And so (358)

> if silver did function as money, we may use the terms 'to buy' and 'to sell' without prejudice. If on the other hand the trade was basically an exchange of goods between two parties, we have to be cautious in choosing our terminology.

He then thinks to show that in fact the use of the terms 'buy' and 'sell' (and by implication, 'money') is legitimate. In mere exchanges of goods (359–60)

> (*šimam*) *ša'amum* could be used to describe the actions of both partners in complete reciprocity. But this is not true; in the case, for example, of a slave sale only the 'buyer' of the slave can be the subject of *ša'amum*, not the 'seller'. One does not describe the transaction by stating that the 'seller' 'buys' silver, and 'pays' by giving a slave.

This inference from the asymmetry of the transactional vocabulary to the appropriateness of the translations 'buy' and 'sell' is false. The asymmetry might derive, for example, from *operational* differences in giving, say, barley or silver (which must be weighed out) on the one hand and a slave (who is not weighed) on the other: this would not by itself impart a special status (as money) to the barley or silver. And sure enough, in the next paragraph Veenhof himself states that the logogram '"to buy", *šám*, . . . is written, apparent already in the Jemdet Nasr period', by a term 'the original meaning of which would have been "to measure out quantities of barley"'. My objection here to Veenhof's case does not depend on the sense 'measure out' being still present in the words he takes to mean 'purchase' in the Kanish texts (though I do not see how he could entirely exclude it). My point is that the words he translates 'buy' and 'sell' could in fact derive from any of a number of aspects (we cannot tell what) of the transaction, in such a way that each word might be appropriate for some actions and inappropriate for others. The choice of word to describe what someone does in a transaction might be influenced not only by the operation involved (e.g. weighing) but also by context, perspective, the commodities exchanged, and so on.

I will now support this point by various considerations all drawn from Veenhof's own discussion of the material. In the phrase *šimam ša'amum*,

---

[40] Renger 1995, 282.

which Veenhof translates 'purchase', *šimam* is a form (internal accusative object, giving 'to make a purchase') of *šimum*, which is frequent elsewhere as the subject of a sentence. But *šimum* is not to be found with all commodities. It is not to be found with tin and textiles, even though they were frequently 'purchased'. 'The question of why one did not use *šimum* in connection with tin and textiles is not easy to answer', acknowledges Veenhof (373), and is forced to conclude that 'it is possible that the way in which tin and textiles were bought in some way differed from that of donkeys, harnesses, etc.' That *šimum* may refer to an operational aspect (we cannot tell what) of the transaction is suggested also by Veenhof's observation that it 'is only used when the attention is focused on the purchase situation', and never in connection with goods that have been purchased (365). Moreover (375) 'twice we meet *šimum* to denote an amount paid as hire or wages to an employer or helper' – in silver and in copper. 'One might say in both cases', writes Veenhof, 'that the services of these people have been "bought" – which may in fact be true – but a translation "payment" seems more probable'. Veenhof is also troubled by a text that he translates 'convert (after arrival of the caravan in Anatolia) my merchandise into silver and sell my donkeys'. Given that 'donkeys were normally also sold for silver after the arrival of a caravan in Anatolia', the disparity in terminology is impossible for us to explain.[41]

And so an expression translated 'purchase' is (unaccountably) not appropriate for all purchases,[42] and can also mean payments that are 'probably' not to be called purchases. Another word which, according to Veenhof, is both 'virtually synonymous' with 'purchase' and also means something else ('take, collect', of tax, debt, share in profits, etc.) – is *laqa 'um*, from which derives the noun *luqutum*, 'merchandise' (369–71). Further, despite his careful distinction between 'buy' and 'sell', Veenhof must admit that 'an expression like *ana simim ibašši* may in a special context be rendered by 'it is for sale', but primarily denotes that it is possible to buy certain goods'.[43] Finally, Veenhof notes that gold, copper, and tin might be used

---

[41] Veenhof attempts to explain the rarity of the word used here for 'to sell', but not the disparity.

[42] Another possible example: *šimam ša' amum* ('purchase') is regularly used by the Assyrians of themselves giving gold and silver for tin and textiles in Ashur, but not of the Anatolians doing the same thing in Anatolia. If the explanations of this offered by Veenhof (372) are considered insufficient, then the difference was either merely a matter of perspective or the transactions were actually different in some way unknown to us.

[43] 359. See further 379–80: having identified certain constructions which 'can be used in both situations', when an Assyrian wants to buy or sell', he notes one case where the constructions are 'in opposition'. We meet here the same basic difference, as observed in the Old Akkadian constructions used to denote "to sell" and "to buy": to give an item *ana šime kaspim* is "to sell", to give silver *ana šime* some item, is "to buy".' But *kaspim* refers to silver, and so if both these phrases refer to *exchange*, the construction is exactly the same in both!

to 'purchase' things (i.e. they all operate as money),[44] and even that tin might be used to 'purchase' silver or gold (387), even though it is logically impossible to 'buy' money.[45]

These examples are enough to throw doubt on the enthusiastic confidence with which Veenhof identifies silver in the Kanish texts with 'money'. If we agree with Veenhof (against Polanyi) that the merchants are private entrepreneurs making profit, then the Kanish texts provide us with the most detailed evidence for this kind of activity in the early Near East. But we do not find in them unequivocal evidence for money.[46] This is not to deny the importance of silver and its tendency to perform money functions, in the texts from Kanish and elsewhere. But to identify silver as 'money', simple and satisfying though it is, may make us overlook various respects in which it operates differently (and less uniformly) than our money.

Finally, we should note the possibility that silver, given its ease of transport in small amounts of high value, was more likely to be used in long distance trade than in any other context of payment.[47]

E   EGYPT

For the economy of early Egypt we do not have the numerous legal, contractual, administrative, and epistolary texts that have been found elsewhere in the early Near East (especially on clay tablets), and have to rely instead on a relatively small number of surviving relevant papyri, from various periods and contexts, together with other data such as texts and images in temples and tombs, and the special case of the ostraka from the workmen's village of Deir el-Medina. There is, here too, agreement that the economy was basically redistributive, with reciprocity and trade at the international and local level.[48] This trade (at both levels) has been characterised as 'targeted barter', in which the aim of both parties to the exchange is to acquire a commodity or service rather than to make a profit.[49] This is reflected in language: the Egyptian words for 'buy' and 'sell' are in fact better translated 'acquire' and 'give'.[50] In certain Old Kingdom tombs have been found

---

[44] Gold: 366 ('money'), 382; copper and tin: 387.
[45] Our 'buying' of foreign currency is the only apparent exception.
[46] In other words, we do not find enough of the characteristics listed in 1C.
[47] This is argued by Sweet 1958, 178–9.
[48] Janssen 1975a, 139, 184; 1975b, 559; 1979, 507–8; 1981, 67–71; Lloyd, A. B. 1983, 325–6; Renger 1984, 52–4; Bleiberg 1995, 1375–6. Kemp 1989, emphasises the room left by the redistributive system for individual demand and initiative.
[49] Bleiberg 1995, 1376–9; Janssen 1975b, 540.
[50] Bleiberg 1995, 1376–7; cf. Hayes 1973, 390: 'Any illusion regarding the existence of a true monetary system, however, is shattered when we find the dynastic Egyptian not only using silver (or gold) to 'buy' (*int*) corn, but also using corn to 'buy' silver.'

pictures with descriptive texts, which show goods being exchanged in an urban setting, with little or no clear evidence for the use of silver (or anything else functioning as money); and of those associated descriptive texts that mention the items exchanged, only a few mention 'price' or any measured or numbered equivalent.[51]

In general there appears to have been in early Egypt no price-making market.[52] But all this does not mean that the commodities exchanged could not be related to each other by being evaluated each in terms of a third commodity, which would then perform the money function of a measure of value. The ostraka from the workmen's village at Deir el-Medina, which give us a uniquely detailed picture of low level economic transactions (from the late New Kingdom), show no fewer than three commodities – silver, copper, grain – acting as standards of value (or 'units of account'), although with no special role in making payments.[53] The units are entirely concrete, in the sense that a unit of e.g. copper (a deben) is a certain *weight*.[54] And although copper and grain (not silver) were among the commodities used in exchanges, 'one cannot say that they are accepted with the intention of using them again for the same purpose'.[55] The use of silver and grain as units of account has a very long history in Egypt.[56] There is no evidence that any of the various commodities used as units of account ever acquired any of the other characteristics of money (generalised means of payment, use *only* for exchange, etc.).

F   THE NEO-ASSYRIAN AND NEO-BABYLONIAN PERIODS

After centuries of a relative lack of documents containing evidence for economic activity in Mesopotamia,[57] the eighth and seventh centuries BC see an increase. However, this material has not been subjected to the same level of detailed economic interpretation as the earlier material discussed in

---

[51] Renger 1984, 54–6.
[52] Janssen 1975b, 561; 1981, 66–7.   [53] Janssen 1975b, 547; Hayes 1973, 390.
[54] 'Weight [of scrap copper] and price, both expressed in *deben*, are hardly distinguishable from one another. In the Egyptian mind there was no difference at all, for the *deben* was not "money" ': Janssen 1975b, 541.
[55] Janssen 1975b, 547.
[56] Janssen 1975b, 546. Cf., from a different context, the use of silver and copper as a standard (unit of account) to value a list of various items exchanged for a slave girl: Gardiner 1935.
[57] For the various substances performing money functions, simultaneously or successively, in Mesopotamia of the second half of the second millennium BC, notably gold, silver, and lead, see Müller 1982; Powell 1992; Snell 1997, 73, who notes that 'the use of gold is not to be understood as a conscious shift of currencies, but in an economic system in which several commodities could serve as money, it would not have demanded a conceptual adjustment for people to use more frequently a commodity that previously was too rare to use as a money but now was more widely available'.

15C and 15D. In Assyria, according to Grayson,[58] 'the standard of exchange in business deals was silver or copper, both being used contemporaneously, but copper being more common in the eighth century and silver in the seventh century. The metal was only a standard, and did not actually change hands except in the few instances where it was the substance involved.' Legal penalties might be paid in the form of various commodities, and loans were usually but not always repaid with the type of goods loaned (generally silver or corn).[59]

As for Babylonia, the relevant texts from the period of Assyrian power have received little attention.[60] More information and analysis is available from the later, Neo-Babylonian kingdom (626–539 BC), and so although it falls largely after our period (15A), it is worth mentioning the conclusions of two recent studies. According to Dandamaev[61] silver was the normal expression of price, and was also used widely in internal trade (though not in the form of coins).[62] There was concern with its quality, and different kinds had different values.[63] Nevertheless, private individuals as well as temples were apparently able to produce silver ingots to be used as currency. Ingots were weighed in every transaction. Secondly, according to a thoughtful study by Bongenaar (1999) silver performed all four money functions, but was never a universally accepted currency. Further, 'other commodities, in particular barley, dates and wool, served to some extent as money'. The value of silver in comparison with other commodities was too high for it to develop into an everyday money. Indeed, despite this relatively widespread use of silver, which is as good evidence for money as we have seen so far, it has been claimed even for Persian (post 539 BC) Babylon that 'the most usual exchanges remain at the level of barter'.[64]

G   CONCLUSIONS

The early Near East has bequeathed us no Hesiod or Aristophanes – texts that would allow us into the world of the peasant farmer. Despite the

---

[58] In Boardman et al. 1991, 215; Postgate 1976, 16; Renger 1995, 298–300, 319. Of the numerous contracts of sale in Kwasman (1988), the vast majority mention as price an amount of silver, but copper is not infrequent, and bronze (nn. 43, 75), barley (nn. 190, 202), tin (n. 145), a horse (n. 45) and a man (n. 125) also occur. As a means of payment, silver itself is far from homogeneous, for three weight standards and various qualities are attested: Radner 1999.

[59] Postgate 1976, 19–20, 39.

[60] Brinkman in Boardman et al. 1991, 64–5.   [61] In Boardman et al. 1991, 274–5.

[62] See also Bogaert 1966, 125; Renger 1995, 300–4, 319–20 (silver as a general means of exchange).

[63] See also Oppenheim 1947.

[64] Joannès 1995, 1478; Snell 1997, 110. Workers in Persepolis were paid both in kind and (to a lesser extent) weighed-out silver: Furtwängler 1986, 155.

numerous documents concerning prices, sales, loans, and so on (with far more detail than what has survived in Greek), our overall picture of the economies of the early Near East, even of a single well-documented place and time such as Ur in the Old Babylonian period, is less comprehensive than that of Athens in the Classical period. Though numerous and detailed, the documents are of limited range. We can be sure that the economies of the early Near East were basically agrarian, and yet we have little idea of subsistence farming and rural exchange. On the whole the documents record what needs to be recorded, and so reveal very little about subsistence farming, the exchange of gifts or favours, small-scale transactions of various kinds, and practices (such as barter) that may be conducted according to custom (and so without the need for written record); they tend instead to record contracts, sales, loans, transactions involving temple or palace, and large-scale transactions of various kinds (notably international trade). This recorded sector of the economy was no doubt on the whole more sophisticated that what is unrecorded, and more likely to have involved 'money'. If money was used, we are likely to have evidence of it.

Redistribution, which was certainly a central principle of allocation in the economies of Mesopotamia and Egypt, tended to exclude the need for money from large areas of the economy.[65] There is also considerable agreement on the importance of barter in local exchange. Even Heichelheim, despite his vehement opposition to Polanyi, regards most local exchange in the early Near East as taking the form of barter, and emphasises that the texts are, in sharp contrast to the Greek and Roman, 'completely silent where money economy in small sales from the city market might have come in'.[66] It should also be noted that, again in contrast to Athens and Rome, 'the sources simply do not show substantial *and* regular shipments of staples like grain over long distances as the sole source for provisioning large cities or entire districts'.[67] Whatever the independence (or otherwise) of traders from palace or temple, and despite the sophistication of certain transactions (e.g. interest on loans),[68] payments of 'money' were likely to occur mainly in certain large-scale transactions, including long distance trade (though not of course gift-exchange) in specialised or luxury items.

We may now, in conclusion, attempt to decide to what extent each of the money characteristics listed in 1C is to be found in the early Near East. We will take them in the same order as in 1C.

---

[65] E.g. Renger 1995.   [66] Heichelheim 1958, 130–2; Renger 1984, 60–1.   [67] Renger 1994, 178.
[68] Loans are widely attested for consumption and trading purposes (but never for productive purposes): Renger 1995, 203.

(1) The characteristic of being valued in general for *power to meet obliga-tion* (in payment or exchange) rather than for use-value, is, we have seen, very difficult to determine. Foodstuffs (especially grain) are often said to have been used as money. But although foodstuffs (and many other goods) were no doubt valued *in particular contexts* for their power to meet obliga-tion, it is hard to see how they could be *generally* valued for this power *rather than* for their use-value. Even those goods (notably silver) which we know in particular contexts to have been acquired in order to acquire other goods were not necessarily *generally* valued or acquired for that purpose, for it is quite possible that they were much more frequently valued or acquired for their use-value (e.g. for luxury, or for the kind of prestige which does not depend on monetary value).[69] Even where specific cases are concerned, it may be difficult to decide (even with information better than we ever have for the early Near East) whether a transaction is barter or sale/purchase (1C), and we have experienced the difficulty in the case of the Kanish texts (15D). Further, silver is often used *alongside* other commodities in payment, and the status of 'money' has been claimed for luxury objects such as gold and silver rings and cups.[70]

(2) The commodities for which the status of money has been claimed (notably grain and metal) are easily *quantified*. This quantification seems generally to have taken the form of weighing rather than measuring or counting.

(3) A *measure of value* was provided most commonly (but not only) by silver. But silver could (and did) provide a measure of value in a transaction without being used in that transaction for payment or exchange. We also have numerous records of payments and exchanges occurring without re-course to a measure of value. And probably much unrecorded rural barter did not use any measure of value, or at least did not use precious metal as a measure of value. In contrast to our own society, in which almost every economic transaction involves the same (abstract) measure, it seems that no single measure of value had penetrated the economy to such an extent as to unite all commodities – with every commodity conceived of as occupying a place on a quantitative scale. We find it slightly odd when, for example, one royal personage complains to another that in return for two horses, which he says are worth 600 shekels of silver, he has received only 20 minas of tin.[71] Would not (we think) the disparity be better expressed on the same scale? A Sumerian mythical contest of suitors (the so-called 'Wooing of Inanna')

[69] Renger 1995, 304.
[70] E.g. Snell 1995, 1488–9; Bivar 1971, 103.   [71] Dossin 1951, 20; Zaccagnini 1976, 491.

does not (as so often in later literature) involve quantitative disparity (or parity) of wealth. It is expressed rather as a contest in gift-giving, with no trace of any measure of value: 'If he pours out for me his prime date-wine', says the shepherd, 'I pour out for the farmer my yellow milk in return,' and so on through the various contrasting products of shepherd and farmer.[72] In another Sumerian mythical dispute Wheat defeats Ewe because, in the opinion of the judge, 'whoever possesses gold, or silver, or cattle, or sheep, shall wait at the gate of him who posesses grain and thus spend his day' (proverbial wisdom, it seems). Of the two authors of the major study of this text[73] one thinks the proverb refers to grain as the basic means of exchange, whereas the other, pointing out that 'in the Old Babylonian period silver [not grain] was the all important means of payment', regards the point as being that grain is the basic means of sustenance. The former view is indeed unlikely. If accordingly we accept the latter, then the dominant commodity is dominant by virtue of its use-value, not its monetary value. In yet another Sumerian mythical dispute, copper is victorious after denigrating silver for its uselessness.[74]

(4) The degree of *general acceptability* of x in payment and exchange is difficult for us to assess, because the surviving documents never provide us with anything like a complete range of the economic transactions in a given society and period. We constantly find various commodities (in the same society and period, or even within the same transaction) used in payment and exchange; but this variety of commodities cannot be taken by itself to mean that there was no single one that was generally acceptable, for it may reflect not the various demands of the payees but rather what the payer in each case has available for payment. Although silver was in general less often used for payment or exchange than as a measure of value, it did nevertheless obtain a degree of general acceptability, but only in certain places, certain periods, and above all in certain *contexts*. In the Old Babylonian period, for example, such contexts are the external trade discussed by Leemans and the payments to temple and palace discussed by van de Mieroop; but this says nothing about the degree of acceptability of silver in rural payment and exchange (or even in urban exchange not involving temple or palace). It may indeed be legitimate to speak of separate spheres of circulation, with different commodities performing various money functions in the various spheres of the economy.[75]

---

[72] Kramer 1944, 101–3; van Dijk 1953, 65–85.
[73] Alster and Vanstiphout 1987, esp. 6 and 42 n. 19.   [74] van Dijk 1953, 58–64; Kramer 1961, 15.
[75] See e.g. Zaccagnini 1976, 545 on the early Near East as a whole: 'I beni appartengono a diversi livelli e la loro circolazione spesso avviene in circuiti che non communicano fra di loro; i beni non sono

(5) The variety of items used for payment and exchange even within the same context is of course more decisive in counting against the *exclusive acceptability* of a single item than it was in counting against (4) the general acceptability of a single item. Nevertheless, the exclusive acceptability of a single item may have occurred in certain contexts, such as in certain kinds of payment to temple or palace or in certain compensations required by law.[76] However, as we noted in 1C, this limited exclusive acceptability does not make the item money. There is no trace of the combination of exclusive with general acceptability that is significant in the development of money.

(6) There is in the early Near East no trace of *fiduciary* money, of a disparity between the conventional value of x and its value as a commodity.[77] Whatever the money functions performed by certain commodities, they remained commodities, valued also for their use-value. For example silver may have been valued in certain contexts entirely as a means of payment or exchange, but not in *all* contexts – for it was also valued aesthetically.

(7) Temple and palace hoarded silver; and the state attempted to fix prices (or 'equivalences').[78] But there is no evidence for the state issuing, enforcing the acceptability of, controlling, or guaranteeing money. At best, some of the supposed evidence for coinage may be thought to imply a role for the state, but this has turned out to be very weak evidence even for coinage (15B). There was no fiduciary money for the state to guarantee. Nor did it see fit, so far as we know, to issue units of guaranteed weight and quality.

tutti indifferentemente valutabili ciascuno in termini dell' altro.' See also Polanyi 1977, 116–18, and for Homer 2B.

[76] In the law code of Hammurabi payments are specified in silver or corn. (Numbers refer to paragraphs in Driver and Miles 1955). Silver is specified for various kinds of compensation – notably for loss of life (24, 207–14), bodily damage (198–204, 247–8), theft (259–61); for the price of surgery (215–16, 221–4), house-building (228), ship-caulking (234); as hire of craftsmen (274), boats (275–7); as divorce payment (139–40). Corn is specified as compensation for various kinds of agricultural damage or loss (44, 56–8, 255; but at 59 it is silver); as rent for corn storage (121); as the hire of a shipman (239), of agricultural labourers, animals, and equipment (242–3, 257–8, 261, 268–72). Certain clauses require that corn (or sesame, or goods) be acceptable as payment instead of silver (51, C (p. 35), M (p. 39), R (p. 41), 108).

[77] An isolated apparent exception is provided by the silver objects called *kaniktum* (medals?) given to the soldiers at Mari by Hammurabi (Le Rider 2001, 4, 19–20), but the added value might have been because they were artefacts, and there is anyway no reason to suppose that they were used as money. Book transfer and (non-circulating) credit notes are not money.

[78] E.g. Postgate 1992, 194–5, 274.

References

Adams, R. C. (1974) 'Anthropological Perspectives on Ancient Trade', *Current Anthropology* 15.3.239–58.

(1984) 'Mesopotamian Social Evolution: Old Outlooks, New Goals', in T. Earle (ed.), *On the Evolution of Complex Societies. Essays in Honor of Harry Hoijer.* ed. Malibu: Undena Publications. 79–129.

Adcock, F. E. (1927) 'Literary Tradition and Early Greek Code-makers', *Cambridge Historical Journal* 2.2.95–109.

Adorno, T. (1978) *Minima Moralia* (English transl. of 1951 original, Frankfurt am Main: Suhrkamp). London: Verso.

Alcock, S. and Osborne, R. (eds.) (1994) *Placing the Gods.* Oxford U. P.

Aleshire, S. (1994) 'Towards a Definition of "State Cult" for Ancient Athens', in Hägg (1994) 9–16.

Alexiou, M. (1974) *The Ritual Lament in Greek Tradition.* Cambridge U. P.

Algra, K. (1999) 'The Beginnings of Cosmology', in Long (1999) 45–65.

Allen, D. S. (2000) *The World of Prometheus.* Princeton U. P.

Alroth, B. (1988) 'The Positioning of Greek Votive Figurines', in Hägg, Marinatos and Nordquist (1988) 195–203.

Alster, B. and Vanstiphout, H. (1987) 'Lahar and Ashnan – Presentation and Analysis of a Sumerian Disputation', *Acta Sumerologica* 9.1–43.

Amandry, P. (1950) *La Mantique Apollinienne à Delphes.* Paris: de Boccard.

Ampolo, C. (1990) 'Fra economia, religione e politica, tesori e offerte nei santuari greci', *Scienze dell' Antichità* 4.271–9.

(1992) 'The Economics of Sanctuaries in Southern Italy and Sicily' in Linders and Alroth (1992) 25–8.

Amyx, D. A (1958) 'The Attic Stelai: Part III Vases and Other Containers; IX Price of Containers', *Hesperia* 27.163–310.

Anderson, G. A. (1987) *Sacrifices and Offerings in Ancient Israel.* Atlanta: Scholars Press.

Appadurai, A. (1986) *The Social Life of Things.* Cambridge U. P.

Archi, A. (1988) 'Prices, Workers Wages, and Maintenance at Ebla', *Altorientalische Forschungen* 15.24–9.

Arnold-Biucchi, C. (1992) 'The Beginnings of Coinage in the West: Archaic Selinous', in H. Nilsson, *Florilegium Numismaticum. Studia in honorem U. Westermark edita.* Stockholm: Svenska numismatika föringen. 13–19.

Ashton, R. and Hurter S. (eds.) (1998) *Studies in Greek Numismatics in Memory of Martin Jessop Price*. London: Spink.

Austin, M. M. and Vidal-Naquet, P. (1977) *Economic and Social History of Greece. An Introduction*. London: Batsford.

Babelon, J. (1943) 'Offrandes Monétaires à des Statues Cultuelles' *Rev. Num.* 5.7.1–9.

Balmuth, M. S. (1971) 'Remarks on the Appearance of the Earliest Coins', in D. G. Mitten, J. G. Pedley and J. A. Scott (eds.) *Studies Presented to George M. A. Hanfmann*. Mainz: von Zabern. 1–7.

(1975) 'The Critical Moment: The Transition from Currency to Coinage in the Eastern Mediterranean', *World Archaeology* 6.293–9.

(1979) 'Collection of Materials for the Study of the Origin of Coinage', *Proceedings of the IX International Congress of Numismatics*. Louvain-la-Neuve and Luxembourg. 31–5.

(1980) in M. J. Price (ed.) *Coins. An Illustrated Survey 650 BC to the Present Day*. London: Hamlyn.

(ed.) (2001) *Hacksilber to Coinage. New Insights into the History of Money in the Near East and Greece*. New York: American Numismatic Society.

Bammer, A. and Muss, U. (1996) *Das Artemision von Ephesos*. Mainz am Rhein: von Zabern.

Barnes, J. (1982) *The Presocratic Philosophers*. 2nd ed., London: Routledge.

Bass, G. (1967) *Cape Gelidonya: a Bronze Age Shipwreck*. Philadelphia: Transactions of the American Philosophial Society 57.8.

Baudy, G. (1983) 'Hierarchie oder: Die Verteilung des Fleisches', in B. Gladigow and H. G. Kippenburg (eds.) *Neue Ansätze in der Religionswissenschaft*. Munich: Kosel. 131–74.

Becker, F. (1988) 'Ein Fund von 75 Milesischen Obolen', *Schweiz. Num. Rund.* 67.5–42.

Belk, R. W. and Wallendorf, M. (1990) 'The Sacred Meanings of Money', *Journal of Economic Psychology* 11.35–67.

Benvenuto, B. and Kennedy, R. (1986) *The Works of Jacques Lacan. An Introduction*. London: Free Association.

Bergquist, B. (1988) 'The Archaeology of Sacrifice: Minoan-Mycenean Versus Greek', in Hägg, Marinatos and Nordquist (1988) 21–34.

(1993) 'Bronze Age Sacrificial *Koine* in the Eastern Mediterranean', in Quaegebeur (1993) 11–43.

Bernal, M. (1987, 1991) *Black Athena. The Afroasiatic Roots of Classical Civilisation*. 2 vols. London: Free Association.

(2001) *Black Athena Writes Back*. Duke U. P.

Berthiaume, G. (1982) *Les Rôles du Mágeiros*. Leiden: Brill.

Bessaignet, P. (1970) 'Monnaie primitive et théories monétaires', *Revue européennes de sciences sociales* 21.37–62.

Bianchi, U. (1953) *ΔIOΣ AIΣA, Destino, Uomini e Divinità nell' Epos nella Teogonie e nel Culto dei Greci*. Rome: Signorelli.

Bivar, A. D. H. (1971) 'A Hoard of Ingot-currency of the Median Period from Nush-i Jan, near Malayir', *Iran* 9.97–III.

Bleiberg, E. (1995) 'The Economy of Ancient Egypt', in Sasson (1995) III.1373–85.

Blinkenberg, C. (1926) Review of Laum (1924) in *Gnomon* 2.102–7.

Boardman, J. (1980) *The Greeks Overseas*. 2nd ed., London: Thames and Hudson.
(1997) 'Greek Seals', in Collon (1997) 74–87.

Boardman, J., Edwards, I. E. S., Hammond, N. G. L., Sollberger, E. (eds.) (1991) *The Cambridge Ancient History* (2nd ed.) III 2. Cambridge.

Bodenstedt, F. (1976) *Phökaisches Elektron-Geld von 600–326 v. Chr.* Mainz: von Zabern.

Boeder, H. (1959) 'Der frühgriechische Wortgebrauch von Logos und Aletheia', *Archiv für Begriffsgeschichte* 4.82–112 (*Akad. d. Wiss. Mainz*). Bonn: Bouvier.

Bogaert, R. (1966) *Les Origines antiques de la banque de dépôt*, Leiden: Sijthoff.
(1968) *Banques et banquiers dans les cités grecques.* Leiden: Sijthoff.
(1976a) 'L'Essai des monnaies dans l'antiquité', *Revue belge de numismatique* 122.5–34.
(1976b) 'Geld', in *Reallexikon für Antike und Christentum*. Band ix. Stuttgart: Hiersemann.

Bohannan, P. (1959) 'The Impact of Money on an African Subsistence Economy', *Journal of Economic History* 19.491–503. Reprinted in Dalton (1967).

Bohannan P. and Dalton, G. (eds.) (1962) *Markets in Africa*. Evanston: Northwestern U. P.

Bohannan, P. and L. (1968) *Tiv Economy*. London: Longman.

Bolin, S. (1958) *State and Currency in the Roman Empire to 300 AD*. Stockholm: Almquist and Wiksell.

Bongenaar, A. C. V. M. (1999) 'Money in the Neo-Babylonian Institutions', in Dercksen (1999) 159–74.

Bookidis, N. (1993) 'Ritual Dining at Corinth', in Marinatos and Hägg (1993).

Borecký, B. (1963) 'The Primitive Origin of the Greek Conception of Equality', in L. Varcl and R. F. Willetts, *Geras. Studies Presented to George Thomson on the Occasion of his 60th Birthday.* Prague: Charles University. 41–60.

Bourdieu, P. (1977) *Outline of a Theory of Practice*. Cambridge U. P.

Bravo, B. (1984) 'Commerce et noblesse en Grèce archaique. A propos d' un livre d' Alfonso Mele', *Dialogues d' Histoire Ancienne* 10. 99–160.

Breglia, L. (1961) 'I precedenti della moneta vera e propria nel bacino del Mediterraneo', *Congrès International de Numismatique I*. Rome. 5–17.
(1974) 'Gli stateri di Alceo', *Numismatica e Antichità Classiche. Quaderni Ticinesi*. Lugano. 3.7–13.

Bremmer, J. (1999) 'Rationalisation and Disenchantment in Ancient Greece', in Buxton (1999) 71–83.

Brendel, O. J. (1977) *Symbolism of the Sphere*. Leiden: Brill.

Brown, A. (1998) 'Homeric Talents and the Ethics of Exchange', *JHS* 118. 165–72.

Brown, J. P. (1995) *Israel and Hellas*. Berlin and New York: de Gruyter.

Brown, W. L. (1950) 'Pheidon's Alleged Aeginetan Coinage', *Numismatic Chronicle* 6.10. 177–204.

Buchanan, J. J. (1962) *Theorika*. New York: J. J. Augustin.

Burelli. L. (1973) 'Metafore monetali e provvedimenti finanziari in Aristofane', *Annali della Scuola Normale di Pisa* 3.3.767–87.

Burke, E. (1992) 'The Economy of Athens in the Classical Era', *TAPA* 122.199–226.

Burkert, W. (1969) 'Das Proömium des Parmenides und die Katabasis des Pythagoras', *Phronesis* 14.1–30.

(1972) *Lore and Science in Ancient Pythagoreanism*. Harvard U. P.

(1976) 'Opfertypen und Antike Gesellschaftsstruktur', in G. Stephenson (ed.) *Der Religionswandel Unserer Zeit im Spiegel der Religionswissenschaft*. Darmstadt: Wissenschaftliche Buchgesellschaft. 168–87.

(1982) 'Craft Versus Sect: The Problem of Orphics and Pythagoreans', in B. F. Meyer and E. P. Sanders (eds.) *Jewish and Christian Self-Definition*. London: SCM Press. Vol. III.1–22.

(1983) *Homo Necans* (translation of *Homo Necans*, Berlin 1972). Berkeley: University of California Press.

(1985) *Greek Religion* (translation of *Griechische Religion der archaischen und klassischen epoche*, Stuttgart 1977). Oxford: Blackwell.

(1987) *Ancient Mystery Cults*. Harvard U. P.

(1992) *The Orientalising Revolution. Near Eastern Influence on Greek Culture in the Early Archaic Age*. Harvard U. P.

(1993) 'Concordia Discors: the Literary and Archaeological Evidence at the Sanctuary of Samothrace', in Marinatos and Hägg (1993) 178–91.

Burridge, K. (1969) *New Heaven, New Earth*. Oxford: Blackwell.

Buxton, R. (ed.) (1999) *From Myth to Reason? Studies in the Development of Greek Thought*. Oxford U. P.

Caccamo Caltabiano, M. and Radici Colace, P. (1992) *Dalla Premoneta alla Moneta*. Pisa: ETS Editrice.

Cairns, F. (1984) 'ΧΡΗΜΑΤΑ ΔΟΚΙΜΑ: *IG* XII, 9, 1273 and 1274 and the Early Coinage of Eretria', *ZPE* 54.145–55.

Caldwell, R. (1989) *The Origin of the Gods*. Oxford U. P.

Capizzi, A. (1990) *The Cosmic Republic*. Amsterdam: J. C. Gieben.

Cartledge, P. (1983) '"Trade and Politics" Revisited: Archaic Greece', in Garnsey (1983) 1–15.

Cassin, E. (1960) 'Le Sceau: un fait de civilisation dans la Mésopotamie ancienne', *Annales ESC* 15.742–51.

Cavanaugh, M. B. (1996) *Eleusis and Athens*. Atlanta: Scholars Press.

Chadwick, J. (1985) 'What do we Know about Mycenean Religion?' in A. Morpurgo Davies and Y. Duhoux (eds.) *Linear B: a 1984 Survey*. Louvain-la-Neuve: Peeters. 91–202.

Chantraine, P. (1968–80) *Dictionnaire étymologique de la langue Grecque*. 2 vols. Paris: Klincksieck.

Clinton, K. (1974) *The Sacred Officials of the Eleusinian Mysteries*. Philadelphia: The American Philosophical Society.

Codere, H. (1968) 'Money-Exchange Systems and a Theory of Money', *Man* 3.557–77.

Cohen, E. E. (1992) *Athenian Economy and Society. A Banking Perspective*. Princeton U. P.

Coldstream, J. N. (1977) *Geometric Greece*. London: Methuen.

Cole, S. G. (1980) 'New Evidence for the Mysteries of Dionysos', *GRBS* 21.223–38.

(1984) *Theoi Megaloi*. Leiden: Brill.

(1994) 'Demeter in City and Countryside', in Alcock and Osborne (1994) 199–216.

Collon, D. (1987) *First Impressions. Cylinder Seals in the Ancient Near East*. London: British Museum Publications.

(ed.) (1997) *7000 Years of* Seals. London: British Museum.

Connor, W. R. (1987) 'Tribes, Festivals, and Processions: Civic Ceremonial and Political Manipulation in Archaic Greece', *JHS* 107.40–50.

Cook, R. M. (1958) 'Speculations on the Origins of Coinage', *Historia* 7.257–62.

Cook, R. M. and Dupont, P. (1998) *East Greek Pottery*. London: Routledge.

Cornford, F. M. (1952) *Principium Sapientiae*. Cambridge U. P.

Courbin, P. (1959) 'Valeur comparée du Fer et de l'Argent lors de l' introduction du monnayage', *Annales: ESC* 14.209–33.

(1983) 'Obéloi d'Argolide et d'ailleurs', in Hägg (1983) 149–56.

Cowell, M. R. et al. (1998) 'Analyses of the Lydian Electrum, Gold and Silver Coinages', in W. A. Oddy and M. R. Cowell (eds.), *Metallurgy in Numismatics 4: RNS Special Publications*. 526–38.

Cox, C. A. (1998) *Household Interests. Property, Marriage Strategies, and Family Dynamics in Ancient Athens*. Princeton U. P.

Cozzo, A. (1988) *Kerdos. Semantica, Ideologia e Società nella Grecia Antica*. Rome: Edizioni dell' Ateneo.

Crawford, M. (1982) *La moneta in Grecia e a Roma*. Rome: Laterza.

Crielaard, J. P. (1995) 'Homer, History, and Archaeology: Some Remarks on the Date of the Homeric World', in J. P. Crielaard (ed.) *Homeric Questions*. Amsterdam: J. C. Gieben.

Cross, D. (1937) *Moveable Property in the Nuzi Documents*. Yale U. P.

Crump, T. (1981) *The Phenomenon of Money*. London: Routledge.

Curtis, J. B. and Hallo, W. W. (1959) 'Money and Merchants in Ur iii', *Hebrew Union College Annual* 30. 103–39.

Dalley, S. (1991) *Myths from Mesopotamia*. Oxford U. P.

Dalton, G. (1982) 'Barter', *Journal of Economic Issues* 16.1.181–90.

(ed.) (1971) *Economic Anthropology and Development. Essays on Tribal and Peasant Economies*. New York and London: Basic Books.

Davies, J. K. (1981) *Wealth and the Power of Wealth in Classical Athens*. New York: Arno.

(2001) 'Temples, Credit, and the Circulation of Money', in Meadows and Shipton (2001) 117–28.

Dayton, J. (1974) 'Money in the Near East before Coinage', *Berytus* 23.41–52.

de Coppet, D. (1970) '1, 4, 8; 9, 7 La Monnaie: Préserve des morts et mesure du temps', *L'Homme* 10. 17–39.

(1995) 'Are'are Society: A Melanesian Socio-Cosmic Point of View', in D. de Coppet and A. Itaneau (eds.) *Cosmos and Society in Oceania*. Oxford and Washington DC: Berg. 237–74.

de Coppet, D. and Zemp, H. (1978) *Are'are. Un Peuple Mélanésien et sa musique*. Paris: Seuil.

de Fidio, P. (1982) 'Fiscalità, redistribuzione, equivalenze: per una discussione sull' economia micenea', *Studi micenei e egeo-anatolici*. Rome: GEI. 23.83–136.

de Libero, L. (1996) *Die Archaische Tyrannis*. Stuttgart: Franz Steiner Verlag.

de Polignac, F. (1994) 'Mediation, Competition, and Sovereignty', in Alcock and Osborne (1994) 3–18.

(1995) *Cults, Territory, and the Origins of the City-State* (translation by J. Lloyd of a revised version of *La Naissance de la cité grecque*, Paris 1984). University of Chicago Press.

de Ste Croix, G. E. M. (1975) 'Political Pay Outside Athens', *CQ* 25.48–52.

(1981) *The Class Struggle in the Ancient Greek World*. London: Duckworth.

(forthcoming) 'The Athenian Census Classes and the Qualifications for Cavalry and Hoplite Service', in his *New Essays in Early Greek History* (ed. F. D. Harvey and R. C. T. Parker). Oxford U. P.

Dercksen, J. G. (1999) *Trade and Finance in Ancient Mesopotamia* (*MOS Studies* 1). Istanbul: Nederlands Historisch-Archaeologisch Instituut.

Desborough, V. (1972) *The Greek Dark Ages*. London: Benn.

Detienne, M. and Vernant, J.-P. (eds.) (1989) *The Cuisine of Sacrifice Among the Greeks* (translation of *La Cuisine du sacrifice en pays grec*. Paris: Gallimard, 1979). University of Chicago Press.

Dickie, M. (1995) 'The Geography of the Homeric World', in O. Anderson and M. Dickie (eds.) *Homer's World: Fiction, Tradition, Reality*. Bergen: Norwegian Institute at Athens.

Dietrich, B. (1964) 'The Judgement of Zeus', *RhM* 107.97–125.

(1965) *Death, Fate, and the Gods*. London: the Athlone Press.

Dilcher, R. (1995) *Studies in Heraclitus*. Hildesheim, Zürich, New York: Georg Olms.

Dodd, N. (1994) *The Sociology of Money*. Cambridge: Polity Press.

Donlan, W. (1981) 'Scale, Value and Function in the Homeric Economy', *American Journal of Ancient History* 6.101–17.

(1981–2) 'Reciprocities in Homer', *Classical World* 75.137–75.

(1982) 'The Politics of Generosity in Homer', *Helios* 9.2.1–16.

(1985) 'Social Groups in Dark Age Greece', *CP* 80. 293–308.

(1989) 'The Unequal Exchange between Glaucus and Diomedes in Light of the Homeric Gift Economy', *Phoenix* 43.1–15.

(1998) 'Political Reciprocity in Dark Age Greece: Odysseus and his Hetairoi', in Gill, Postlethwaite and Seaford (1998) 51–71.

Dossin, G. (1951) *Archives Royales de Mari. Vol. 5. Lettres*. Paris: Paul Geuthner.

Douglas, M. (1967) 'Primitive Rationing', in R. Firth (ed.) *Themes in Economic Anthropology*. London: Tavistock Publications. 119–47.

(1970) *Purity and Danger. An Analysis of Concepts of Pollution and Taboo.* (First published 1966.) London: Pelican.

Drews, R. (1976) 'The Earliest Greek Settlements on the Black Sea', *JHS* 96.8–31.

(1983) *Basileus. The Evidence for Kingship in Geometric Greece.* Yale U. P.

Driver, G. R. and Miles J. C. (1955) *The Babylonian Laws. Vol. II.* Oxford U. P.

Dunbabin, T. J. (1948) *The Western Greeks.* Oxford U. P.

Durand, J.-L. (1989) 'Greek Animals: Toward a Topology of Edible Bodies', in Detienne and Vernant (1989) 87–118.

Eco, U. (1979) *A Theory of Semiotics.* Bloomington: Indiana U. P.

Ehrhardt, N. (1983) *Milet und seine Kolonien.* Frankfurt am Main: Peter Lang.

Einzig, P. (1966) *Primitive Money.* 2nd ed. Oxford: Pergamon Press.

Engmann, J. (1991) Untitled in *Phronesis* 36.1.1–25.

Farenga, V. (1985) 'La tirannide greca a la strategia numismatica', in *Mondo classico: Percorsi possibili.* Ravenna: Longo. 39–49.

Farrington, B. (1961) *Greek Science. Its Meaning for Us.* Harmondsworth: Penguin.

Feyerabend, B. (1984) 'Zur Wegmetaphorik beim Goldblättchen aus Hipponion und dem Proömium des Parmenides', *RhM* 127.1–22.

Feyerabend, P. (1993) *Against Method.* 3rd ed., London: Verso.

(1999) *The Conquest of Abundance.* University of Chicago Press.

Figueira, T. (1998) *The Power of Money. Coinage and Politics in the Athenian Empire.* Philadelphia: University of Pennsylvania Press.

Finkelberg, A. (1986) 'On the Unity of Orphic and Milesian Thought', *HTR* 79.4.321–35.

(1988) 'Parmenides: Between Material and Logical Monism', *Archiv für Geschichte der Philosophie* 70. 1–14.

(1989) 'The Milesian Monist Doctrine and the Development of Presocratic Thought', *Hermes* 117.257–70.

(1990) 'Studies in Xenophanes', *HCSP* 93.103–67.

(1993) 'Anaximander's Conception of the *Apeiron*', *Phronesis* 38.3.229–56.

Finley, M. (1957) 'The Mycenean Tablets and Economic History', *Economic History Review* 10.128–41.

(1968) 'The Alienability of Land: a Point of View'. *Eirene* 7.25–32.

(1977) *The World of Odysseus.* 2nd ed., London: Chatto and Windus.

(1981) *Economy and Society in Ancient Greece* (eds. B. D. Shaw and R. P. Saller). London: Chatto and Windus.

Florenzano, M. B. B. (2000) *Entre Reciprocidade e Mercado: A Moeda na Grécia Antiga.* Universidade de São Paulo.

Forbes, R. J. (1950) *Metallurgy in Antiquity.* Leiden: Brill.

Foster, B. R. (1977) 'Commercial Activity in Sargonic Mesopotamia', *Iraq* 39.31–44.

Foster, G. M. (1965) 'Peasant Society and the Idea of the Limited Good', *American Anthropologist* 67.293–315.

Frank, E. F. (1923) *Plato und die sogennanten Pythagoreer: Ein Kapitel aus der Geschichte des griechischen Geistes.* Halle: Niemeyer.

Frankel, S. H. (1977) *Money: Two Philosophies.* Oxford: Basil Blackwell.

Frankfort, H. (1970) *The Art and Architecture of the Ancient Orient.* 4th ed. Yale U. P.

Frankfort, H. et al. (1949) *Before Philosophy.* Harmondsworth: Penguin.

Furley, D. J. and Allen R. E. (eds.) (1970) *Studies in Presocratic Philosophy.* Vol. I. London: Routledge and Kegan Paul.

Furtwängler, A. E. (1986) 'Neue Beobachtungen zur frühesten Münzprägung', *Schweizerische Numismatische Rundschau* 65.153–65.

(1980) 'Zur Deutung der Obeloi im Lichte Samischer Neufunde', in H. A. Cahn and E. Simon (eds.) *Tainia. Roland Hampe zum 70 Geburtstag.* Mainz am Rhein: von Zabern 1980. Vol. I. 81–98.

Gabrielsen, V. (1986) 'ΦANEPA and AΦANHΣ OYΣIA' in Classical Athens', *Class. et Med.* 37.99–114.

Gagarin, M. (1981a) 'The Thesmothetai and the Earliest Athenian Tyranny Law', *TAPA* III.71–7.

(1981b) *Drakon and Early Athenian Homicide Law.* Yale U. P.

(1986) *Early Greek Law.* Berkeley: University of California Press.

Gale, N. H., Gentner, W., Wagner, G. A. (1980) 'Mineralogical and Geographical Silver Sources for Archaic Greek Coinage', *Metallurgy in Numismatics* 1.3–49.

Gardiner, A. H. (1935) 'A Lawsuit Arising from the Purchase of Two Slaves', *Journal of Egyptian Archaeology* 21.140–6.

Garnsey, P. et al. (eds.) (1983) *Trade in the Ancient Economy.* London: Chatto and Windus / The Hogarth Press.

Gauthier, P. (1993) 'Sur L' Institution de l'assemblée à Athènes (*Ath. Pol.* 41.3)', in M. Piérart (ed.) *Aristote et Athènes.* Paris: de Boccard. 231–50.

Gebhard, E. (1993) 'The Evolution of a Panhellenic Sanctuary: From Archaeology Towards History at Isthmia', in Marinatos and Hägg (1993) 154–77.

Gernet, L. (1981) *The Anthropology of Ancient Greece* (transl. by J. Hamilton and B. Nagy of *Anthropologie de la Grèce antique*, Paris 1968). Baltimore: Johns Hopkins U. P.

Gibson, M. and Biggs, R. D. (eds.) (1977) *Seals and Sealing in the Ancient Near East* (*Bibliotheca Mesopotamica* vol. 6). Malibu: Undena Publications.

Gill, C. J. (1996) *Personality in Greek Epic, Tragedy, and Philosophy.* Oxford U. P.

Gill, C. J., Postlethwaite, N., Seaford, R. (eds.) (1998) *Reciprocity in Ancient Greece.* Oxford U. P.

Girard, R. (1977) *Violence and the Sacred* (translation of *La Violence et le Sacré*, Paris 1972). Baltimore: Johns Hopkins U. P.

Gitin, S. and Golani, A. (2001) 'The Tel Migne-Ekron Silver Hoards: the Assyrian and Phoenician Connections', in Balmuth (2001) 27–48.

Godelier, M. (1977) *Perspectives in Marxist Anthropology.* Cambridge U. P.

(1999) *The Enigma of the Gift* (translation of *L' Énigme du don*, Libraire Arthème Fayard, 1996). Cambridge: Polity Press.

Goldhill, S. (1986) *Reading Greek Tragedy.* Cambridge U. P.

Gomperz H. (1965) *Sophistik und Rhetorik* (repr. of first ed. of 1912). Darmstadt: Wissenschaftliche Buchgesellschaft.

Goody, J. (1977) *The Domestication of the Savage Mind*. Cambridge U. P.
(1987) *The Interface Between the Written and the Oral*. Cambridge U. P.
Goody, J. and Watt, I. (1968) 'The Consequences of Literacy', in J. Goody (ed.) *Literacy in Traditional Societies*. Cambridge U. P. 27–68 (repr. from *Comparative Studies in Society and History* 3 (1963) 304–45).
Gordon, C. (1965) *Ugaritic Textbook*. Analecta orientalia 38. Rome.
Gorman, V. (2001) *Miletos, the Ornament of Lydia*. University of Michigan Press.
Gottschalk, H. B. (1965) 'Anaximander's Apeiron', *Phronesis* 10.37–53.
Goux, J.-J. (1990) *Symbolic Economics after Marx and Freud*. Cornell U. P.
Graf, F. (1998) *Ansichten Griechischer Rituale. Geburtstag-Symposium für Walter Burkert*. Stuttgart and Leipzig: Teubner.
Gregory, C. A. (1982) *Gifts and Commodities*. London: Academic Press.
Grierson, P. (1978) 'The Origins of Money', *Research in Economic Anthropology* 1.1–35.
Griffith, M. (1999) *Sophocles Antigone*. Cambridge U. P.
Grottanelli, C. and Parise, N. (1986) 'Nozione Astratta e Nozione Preferenziale del Valore alla Frontiere fra Greci e Sciti', *Dial. d. Arch.* 4.1.133–7.
(eds.) (1988) *Sacrificio e Società nel Mondo Antico*. Rome and Bari: Laterza.
Guarducci, M. (1944–5) 'Tripodi, Lebeti, Oboli', *Riv. d. Fil.* 22–3.171–80.
Guthrie, W. K. C., *A History of Greek Philosophy*. Volume I (1962), II (1965), III (1969). Cambridge U. P.
Haarer, P. (2000) "Ὀβελοί and Iron in Archaic Greece', 2 vols., D. Phil. thesis, Oxford.
Hadzisteliou-Price, T. (1973) 'Hero-cult and Homer', *Historia* 22.129–44.
Hägg, R. (ed.) (1983) *The Greek Renaissance of the Eighth Century BC: Tradition and Innovation*. Stockholm: Paul Astroms.
(ed.) (1994) *Ancient Greek Cult Practice from the Epigraphical Evidence*. Stockholm: Paul Astroms.
(1998) 'Ritual in Mycenean Greece', in Graf (1998) 99–113.
Hägg, R., Marinatos, N., Nordquist, G. (1988) *Early Greek Cult Practice*. Stockholm: Paul Astroms Verlag.
Hahn, R. (2001) *Anaximander and the Architects*. Albany: State University of New York Press.
Hallo, W. (1977) 'Seals Lost and Found', in Gibson and Biggs (1977) 55–60.
(1987) 'The Origins of Sacrificial Cult: New Evidence from Mesopotamia and Israel', in P. D. Miller Jr. et al. (eds.) *Ancient Israelite Religion. Essays in Honor of Frank Moore Cross*. Philadelphia: Fortress Press. 3–13.
Halstead, P. (1992) 'The Mycenean Palatial Economy: Making the Most of the Gaps in the Evidence', *PCPhS* 38.57–86.
Hamburger, H. (1962) 'Money', in G. Buttrick et al. (eds.) *Interpreter's Dictionary of the Bible*. III.423–35. New York: Abingdon Press.
Hanfmann, G. M. A. (1978) 'Lydian Relations with Ionia and Persia', in E. Akurgal (ed.), *Proceedings of the Xth International Congress of Classical Archaeology*. Ankara: Türk Tarih Kurumu. 25–35.

Hanfmann, G. A. and Ramage, N. H. (1978) *Sculpture from Sardis: the Finds through 1975*. Harvard U. P.

Hanfmann, G. M. A. (1983) *Sardis from Prehistoric to Roman Times*. Harvard U. P.

Hangard, J. (1963) *Monetaire en Daarmee Verwante Metaforen*. Diss. Groningen: J. B. Walters.

Hansen, P. (1983) *Carmina Epigraphica Graeca*. Berlin and New York: de Gruyter.

Harris, D. (1995) *The Treasures of the Parthenon and Erechtheion*. Oxford U. P.

Harrison, J. (1927) *Themis*. 2nd ed., Cambridge U. P.

Hart, K. (1986) 'Heads or Tails? Two sides of the Coin', *Man* 21.637–56.

Hayes, W. C. (1973) in *The Cambridge Ancient History* II. i (3rd. ed.) 313–416.

Heichelheim, F. (1958) *An Ancient Economic History from the Paleolithic Age to the Migrations of the Germanic, Slav and Arabic Nations*. Vol. I. Leiden: Sijthoff.

Heinsohn, G. and Steiger, O. (1994) 'A Private Property Theory of Credit, Interest, and Money', *Economies et Sociétes. Série MP* 9.9–24.

Heltzer, M. (1978) *Goods, Prices, and the Organisation of Trade in Ugarit*. Wiesbaden: Reichert.

Herman, G. (1987) *Ritualised Friendship and the Greek City*. Cambridge U. P.

Higgins, R. A. (1967) *Greek Terracottas*. London: Methuen.

Hiller von Gaertringen, F. (1906) *Inschriften von Priene*. Berlin: Reimer.

Hodkinson, S. (2000) *Property and Wealth in Classical Sparta*. London: Duckworth, with the Classical Press of Wales.

Hölkeskamp, K.-J. (1999) *Schiedsrichter, Gesetzgeber und Gesetzgebung im Archaischen Griechenland. (Historia Einzelschrift* 131). Stuttgart: Franz Steiner.

Holle, B. F. (1978) 'Historical Considerations on the Origins and the Spread of Coinage in the Archaic Age'. Diss.: University of Michigan.

Holloway, R. R. (1978) 'La ricerca attuale sull' origine della moneta', *Rivista italiana di numismatica e scienze affini* 80. 7–14.

(1984) 'The Date of the First Greek Coins: Some Arguments from Style and Hoards', *Revue belge de numismatique et de sillographie* 130. 5–18.

Hölscher, U. (1956) 'Grammatisches zu Parmenides', *Hermes* 84.385–97.

Horsmann, G. (2000) 'Athens Weg zur eigenen währung: der Zusammenhang der metrologischen Reform Solons mit der Timokratischen', *Historia* 49.259–77.

Howgego, C. J. (1995) *Ancient History from Coins*. London: Routledge.

(1990) 'Why did Ancient States Strike Coins?', *Num. Chron.* 150.1–25.

Hubert, H. and Mauss, M. (1964) *Sacrifice; Its Nature and Function*. London: Cohen and West (translation of 'Essai sur la Nature et Fonction du Sacrifice', *L' Année Sociologique* for 1898).

Hübner, K. (1983) *Critique of Scientific Reason*. University of Chicago Press.

Huffman, C. A. (1993) *Philolaos of Croton*. Cambridge U. P.

Humphrey, C. and Hugh-Jones, S. (eds.) (1992) *Barter, Exchange and Value: An Anthropological Approach*. Cambridge U. P.

Humphreys, S. C. (1978) *Anthropology and the Greeks*. London: Routledge.

Huss, B. (1996) 'Der Homo-Mensura-Satz des Protagoras', *Gymnasium* 103.229–57.

Isager, S. (1992) 'Sacred Animals in Classical and Hellenistic Greece', in Linders and Alroth (1992) 15–20.

Isik, E. (1992) *Elektronstatere aus Klazomenai. Der Schatzfund von 1989 (Saarbrücker Studien zur Archäologie und Alten Geschichte, Band 5)*. Saarbrücker Druckerei und Verlag.

Jacobsen, T. (1976) *The Treasures of Darkness*. Yale U. P.

Jacobstahl, P. (1951) 'The Date of the Ephesian Foundation Deposit', *JHS* 71.85–95.

James, T. G. H. (1997) 'Ancient Egyptian Seals', in Collon (1997) 31–46.

Jameson, M. H. (1988) 'Sacrifice and Animal Husbandry in Classical Greece', in C. R. Whittaker (ed.) *Pastoral Economies in Classical Antiquity*. Cambridge Philological Society Suppl. Vol. 14.87–119.

(1994) 'Theoxenia', in Hägg (1994) 35–57.

Janko, R. (2001) 'The Derveni papyrus (Diagoras of Melos, *Apopyrgizontes Logoi?*), A New Translation', *CP* 96.1.1–32.

Janssen, J. J. (1975a) 'Prolegomena to the Study of Egypt's Economic History During the New Kingdom', *Studien zur altägyptischen Kultur*. 3.128–85.

(1975b) *Commodity Prices from the Ramessid Period*. Leiden: Brill.

(1979) in Lipinski (1979) 505–15.

(1981) 'Die Struktur der pharaonischen Wirtschaft', *Göttinger Miszellen* 48.59–77.

Jeffery, L. H. (1976) *Archaic Greece*. London: Ernest Benn.

(1990) *The Local Scripts of Archaic Greece*. 2nd ed., Oxford U. P.

Jeremias, A. (1929) *Handbuch der altorientalischen Geisteskultur*. Berlin: de Gruyter.

Joannès, F. (1995) 'Private Commerce and Banking in Achaemenid Babylon', in Sasson (1995) III.1475–85.

Johnson, J. H. (1977) 'Private Name Seals of the Middle Kingdom', in Gibson and Biggs (1977) 141–5.

Johnston, A. W. (1979) *Trade Marks on Greek Vases*. Warminster: Aris and Phillips.

Kagan, D. (1982) 'The Dates of the Earliest Coins', *AJA* 86.343–60.

Kahn, C. (1958) 'Anaximander and the Arguments Concerning the ἄπειρον at Phys. 203b4–15', in *Festschrift Ernst Kapp*. Hamburg: von Schröder. 19–29.

(1960) *Anaximander and the Origins of Greek Cosmology*. New York: Columbia U. P.

Kallet, L. (1999) 'The Diseased Body Politic, Athenian Public Finance, and the Massacre at Mykalessos (Thucydides 7.27–29)', *AJP* 120.223–44.

Kallet-Marx, L. (1993) *Money, Expense, and Naval Power in Thucydides' History 1–5.24*. Oxford U. P.

Karwiese, S. (1991) 'The Artemisium Coin Hoard and the First Coins of Ephesus', *Revue belge de numismatique et de sillographie*. 137.1–28.

(1995) *Die Munzprägung von Ephesos. Vol. I Die Anfänge: die ältesten Prägungen und der Beginn der Münzprägung überhaupt*. Wien, Köln, Weimar: Böhlau Verlag.

Kearns, E. (1994) 'Cakes in Greek Sacrifice Regulations', in Hägg (1994) 65–70.

Kemp, B. J. (1989) *Ancient Egypt. Anatomy of a Civilisation*. London: Routledge.

Kepple, L. (1976) 'The Broken Victim: Euripides *Bacchae* 969–70', *HSCP* 80.107–9.

Kern, O. (1922) *Orphicorum Fragmenta*. Berlin: Weidmann.

Keyser, P. T. and Clark, D. D. (2001) 'Analyzing and Interpreting the Metallurgy of Early Electrum Coins', in Balmuth (2001) 105–17.

Killen, J. T. (1985) 'The Linear B Tablets and the Mycenean Economy', in A. Morpurgo Davies and Y. Duhoux (eds.) *Linear B: a 1984 Survey* (Louvain-la-Neuve: Peeters). 241–305.

Killen, J. T. (1994) 'Thebes Sealings, Knossos Tablets and Mycenean State Banquets', *BICS* 39.67–84.

Kim, H. (1994) Greek Fractional Silver Coinage: A Reassessment of the 'Inception, Development, Prevalence, and Functions of Small Change during the Late Archaic and Early Classical Periods' M. Phil. thesis, University of Oxford.

(2001) 'Archaic Coinage as Evidence for the use of Money', in Meadows and Shipton (2001) 7–21.

Kingsley, P. (1995) *Ancient Philosophy, Mystery, and Magic. Empedocles and the Pythagorean Tradition*. Oxford U. P.

(1999) *In the Dark Places of Wisdom*. London: Duckworth.

Kirk, G. S. (1962) *The Songs of Homer*. Cambridge U. P.

Kirk, G. S., Raven, J. E., Schofield, M. (1983) *The Presocratic Philosophers*. 2nd ed. Cambridge U. P.

Kiyonaga, S. (1973) 'The Date of the Beginning of Coinage in Asia Minor', *Revue suisse de numismatique* 52.5–16.

Knox, B. M. W. (1957) *Oedipus at Thebes*. New Haven: Yale University Press.

Koerner, W. (1993) *Inschriftliche Gesetztexte der Frühen Griechischen Polis* (ed. K. Hallof). Köln, Weimar, Wien: Böhlau Verlag.

Kohnke, F. W. (1968) 'Das Bild der Echten Münze bei Philon von Alexandria', *Hermes* 96.583–9.

Kopytoff, I. (1986) 'The Cultural Biography of Things: Commoditization as Process', in Appadurai (1986) 64–91.

Kraay, C. (1958) 'The Composition of Electrum Coinage', *Archaeometry* 1.21–3.

(1964) 'Hoards, Small Change and the Origins of Coinage', *JHS* 84.76–91.

(1976) *Archaic and Classical Greek Coins*. London: Methuen.

Kramer, S. N. (1944) *Sumerian Mythology*. Philadelphia: the American Philosophical Society.

(1961) *Sumerische Literarische Texte aus Nippur*. Vol. I. Berlin: Akademie Verlag.

Kroll, J. H. (1976) 'Aristophanes' πονηρὰ χαλκία: A Reply', *GRBS* 17.328–41.

(1993) *The Athenian Agora. Volume XXVI The Greek Coins*. Princeton, N. J.: The American School of Classical Studies at Athens.

(1998) 'Silver in Solon's Laws', in Ashton and Hurter (1998) 225–32.

(2000) Review of Kurke (1999), *CJ* 96.1.85–90.

(2001a) 'Observations on Monetary Instruments in pre-Coinage Greece' in Balmuth (2001) 77–91.

(2001b) Review of Le Rider (2001), in *Swiss Numismatic Review* 80.199–206.

Kroll, J. H. and Waggoner, N. M. (1984) 'Dating the Earliest Coins of Athens, Corinth and Aegina', *AJA* 88.325–40.

Kron, U. (1971) 'Zum Hypogäum von Paestum', *JdAI* 86.117–48.

Kupper, J.-R. (1982) 'L'Usage de l'argent à Mari', in G. van Driel, Th. J. H. Krispijn, M. Stul and K. R. Veenhof (eds.) *Zikir sumim: Assyriological Studies Presented to F. R. Kraus on the Occasion of his Seventieth Birthday*. Leiden: Brill. 163–72.

Kurke, L. (1995) 'Herodotus and the Language of Metals', *Helios* 22.36–64.

(1999) *Coins, Bodies, Games, and Gold*. Princeton U. P.

Kwasman, T. (1988) *Neo-Assyrian Legal Documents in the Kouyunjik Collection of the British Museum*. Rome: Editrice Pontificio Istituto Biblico.

Kyrieleis, H. (1993) 'The Heraion at Samos', in Marinatos and Hägg (1993) 125–53.

Lacan, J. (1977) *Écrits. A Selection* (transl of *Écrits*, Editions du Seuil, 1966). London: Routledge.

Lacroix, L. (1958) 'Les "blasons des villes grecques"', *Études d'Achéologie Classique*. I (1955–6. Nancy). Paris: de Boccard.

Laks, A. and Most, G. W. (1997) *Studies on the Derveni Papyrus*. Oxford U. P.

Lambert, M. (1963) 'L'Usage de l'argent-métal à Lagash sous la IIIe dynastie d'Ur', *Revue d'Assyriologie* 57.79–92.

Lambert, S. D. L. (1993) *The Phratries of Attica*. University of Michigan Press.

Lambert, W. G. (1993) 'Donations of Food and Drink to the Gods in Ancient Mesopotamia', in Quaegebeur (1993) 191–201.

Lane Fox, R. (2000) 'Theognis: an Alternative to Democracy', in R. Brock and S. Hodkinson (eds.) *Alternatives to Athens*. Oxford U. P. 35–51.

Lang, M. and Crosby, M. (1964) *The Athenian Agora, X, Weights, Measures and Tokens*. Princeton N. J.: American School of Classical Studies.

Langdon, S. (1987) 'Gift Exchange in the Geometric Sanctuaries', in Linders and Nordquist (1987) 107–13.

Laroche, E. (1949) *Histoire de la Racine NEM – en Grec Ancien*. Paris: Klinksieck.

Larsen, M. T. (1977) 'Seal Use in the Old Assyrian Period', in Gibson and Biggs (1977) 89–105.

Latte, K. (1948) 'Kollektivbesitz und Staatsschatz in Griechenland', *Nachrichten der Akademie der Wissenschaft in Göttingen aus den Jahren 1945/8.Phil. -hist. Klasse*. 1946/7.64–75 (= Latte (1968) 294–312).

(1968) *Kleine Schriften*. Munich: C. H. Beck.

Lau, D. (1980) 'Nummi Dei Sumus', *Wiener Studien* 93.192–228.

Laum, B. (1924) *Heiliges Geld*. Tübingen: Mohr.

Lazzarini, L. (1979) 'ΟΒΕΛΟΣ in una dedica arcaica della beozia', *Annali dell' Istituto Italiano di Numismatica* 26.153–60.

Le Rider, G. (1989) 'À propos d' un Passage des *Poroi* de Xenophon', in G. Le Rider et al. (eds.) *Numismatic Studies in Memory of C. M. Kraay and O. Mørkholm. Louvain-la-Neuve: Numismatica Lovaniensa* 10. 159–72.

(2001) *La Naissance de la Monnaie*. Paris: Presses Universitaires de France.

Leemans, W. F. (1960) *Foreign Trade in the Old Babylonian Period*. Leiden: Brill.

Lesher, J. H. (1992) *Xenophanes of Colophon*. Toronto: University of Toronto Press.

Leumann, M. (1950) *Homerische Wörter*. Basel: Reinhardt.

Lévy-Bruhl, L. (1926) *How Natives Think*. London: Allen and Unwin (transl. by L. A. Clare of *Les Fonctions Mentales dans les Sociétés Inférieures*, Paris 1910).

Limet, H. (1972) 'Les Métaux à l' Epoque d' Agadé', *Journal of the Economic and Social History of the Orient* 15.3–34.

Linders, T. (1992) 'Sacred Finances: Some Observations', in Linders and Alroth (1992) 9–13.

Linders, T. and Alroth, B. (1992) *Economics of Cult in the Ancient Greek World*. Uppsala: Acta Universitatis Upsaliensis.

Linders, T. and Nordquist, G. (eds.) (1987) *Gifts to the Gods*. Uppsala: Acta Universitatis Upsaliensis.

Lipinski, E. (ed.) (1979) *State and Temple Economy in the Ancient Near East*. Leuven.

Lloyd, A. B. (1983) 'The Late Period', in B. G. Trigger et al. (eds.) *Ancient Egypt. A Social History*. Cambridge U. P.

Lloyd, G. E. R. (1966) *Polarity and Analogy*. Cambridge U. P.

(1973) Review of Stokes (1971), *JHS* 93.244–8.

(1979) *Magic, Reason, and Experience*. Cambridge U. P.

(1983) *Science, Folklore and Ideology*. Cambridge U. P.

(1987) *The Revolutions of Wisdom*. Cambridge U. P.

(1990) *Demystifying Mentalities*. Cambridge U. P.

(1996) *Adversaries and Authorities. Investigations into Ancient Greek and Chinese Science*. Cambridge U. P.

Lo Porto, F. G. (1987) 'Due Iscrizioni Votive Arcaiche dai Dintorni di Taranto', *Parola del Passato* 232.40–50.

Long, A. A. (ed.) (1999) *The Cambridge Companion to Early Greek Philosophy*. Cambridge U. P.

Loomis, W. T. (1998) *Wages, Welfare Costs and Inflation in Classical Athens*. University of Michigan Press.

Luckenbill, D. D. (1924) *The Annals of Sennacherib*. University of Chicago Press.

Macdonald, G. (1905) *Coin Types*. Glasgow: Maclehose.

Macfarlane, A. (1985) 'The Root of All Evil', in D. Parkin (ed.) *The Anthropology of Evil*. Oxford: Blackwell. 57–76.

Malinowski, B. (1967) 'Kula: The Circulating Exchange of Valuables in the Archipelagoes of Eastern New Guinea', in Dalton (1967) 171–84 (repr. from *Man* 51 (1920) 97–105).

Manganaro, G. (1974) '*SGDI* iv, 4 n. 49 (*DGE* 707) e il bimetallismo monetale di Creso', *Epigraphica. Rivista Italiana di Epigrafia* (Faenza). 36.57–77.

Mann, M. (1986) *The Sources of Social Power*. Vol. 1. Cambridge U. P.

Marinatos, N. and Hägg, R. (eds.) (1993) *Greek Sanctuaries. New Approaches*. London and New York: Routledge.

Martin, A. and Primavesi, O. (1999) *L' Empedocle de Strasbourg (P. Strasb. gr. Inv. 1665–1666). Introduction, édition et commentaire*. Berlin, New York: de Gruyter.

Martin, T. R. (1995) 'Coins, Mints, and the Polis', in M. H. Hansen (ed.) *Sources for the Ancient Greek City-State*. Copenhagen: Munksgaard. 257–91.

(1996) 'Why did the Greek Polis Originally Need Coins?', *Historia* 45.257–83.

Marx, K. (1973) *Grundrisse* (translation by Martin Nicolaus of *Grundrisse der Kritik der Politischen Ökonomie* of 1857–8). Harmondsworth: Penguin.

(1976) *Capital Volume* I (translation by B. Fowkes of *Das Kapital*, 1867). London: Penguin.

(1992) *Economic and Philosophical Manuscripts* (written in 1844), in *Early Writings* (translated by R. Livingstone). Harmondsworth: Penguin.

Masson, O. (1991) Chapter 34b of *The Cambridge Ancient History* III. 2 (second ed.). Cambridge U. P.

Mattusch, C. (1996) *Classical Bronzes. The Art and Craft of Greek and Roman Statuary.* Cornell U. P.

Mauss, M. (1967) *The Gift* (translated by I. Cunnison of *Essai sur le don, forme archaique de l' échange* (1925)). London: Cohen and West.

Mazarakis Ainian, A. J. (1988) 'Early Greek Temples: Their Origin and Function', in Hägg, Marinatos and Nordquist (1988) 105–19.

Mcdiarmid, J. B. (1970) 'Theophrastus on the Presocratic Causes', in Furley and Allen (1970) 178–238.

Meadows, A. and Shipton, K. (2001) *Money and its Uses.* Oxford U. P.

Meiggs, R. and Lewis, D. M. (1988) *A Selection of Greek Historical Inscriptions.* 2nd ed. Oxford U. P.

Meikle, S. (1995) *Aristotle's Economic Thought.* Oxford U. P.

(1996) 'Aristotle on Business', *CQ* 46.138–51.

Mele, A. (1979) *Il Commercio Greco Arcaico. Praxis ed Emporie.* Naples: Institut français de Naples.

(1986) 'Pirateria, Commercio e Aristocrazia: Replica a Benedetto Bravo', *Dial. d'Hist. Anc.* 12.67–109.

Melitz, J. (1970) 'The Polanyi School of Anthropology on Money', *American Anthropologist* 72.1020–40.

Mellink, M. (1991) Chapter 34a of *The Cambridge Ancient History* III. 2 (second ed.). Cambridge U. P.

Melville Jones, J. R. (1993) *Testimonia Numaria.* London: Spink.

Millett, P. (1991) *Lending and Borrowing in Classical Athens.* Cambridge U. P.

(1998) 'The Rhetoric of Reciprocity in Classical Athens', in Gill, Postlethwaite, and Seaford (1998) 227–53.

Minar, E. L. (1942) *Early Pythagorean Politics.* Baltimore: Waverly Press.

Möller, A. (2000) *Naukratis: Trade in Archaic Greece.* Oxford U. P.

Morgan, C. (1989) *Athletes and Oracles: The Transformation of Olympia and Delphi in the Eighth Century BC.* Cambridge U. P.

(1993) 'The Origins of Panhellenism', in Marinatos and Hägg (1993) 188–44.

(1994) 'The Evolution of a Sacral "Landscape": Isthmia, Perachora, and the Early Corinthian State', in Alcock and Osborne (1994) 105–42.

Mørkholm, O. (1982) 'Some Reflections on the Production and Use of Coinage in Ancient Greece', *Historia* 31.290–305.

Morris, I. (1986) 'Gift and Commodity in Archaic Greece', in *Man* 21.1.1–17.

Most, G. W. (1997) 'The Fire next Time. Cosmology, Allegoresis, and Salvation in the Deveni Papyrus', *JHS* 107.117–35.

Moucharte, G. (1984) 'À propos d' une découverte de monnaies de Milet', *Rev. Belge de Numism.* 130.19–35.

Mourelatos, A. (1965) 'Heraclitus fr. 114', *AJP* 86.258–6.

Mühl, M. (1928) 'Die Gesetze des Zaleukos und Charondas', *Klio* 22.105–24, 432–63.

Müller, M. (1982) 'Gold, Silber, und Blei als Wertmesser in Mesopotamien während der zweiten Hälfte des 2. Jahrtausends vor u. Z', in J. N. Postgate (ed.) *Societies and Languages of the Ancient Near East: Studies in Honour of I. M. Diakonoff.* Warminster: Aris and Phillips. 270–8.

Müller, R. W. (1981) *Geld und Geist.* Frankfurt and New York: Campus Verlag.

Musti, D. (1980–1) 'χρήματα nel frammento 90 D–K di Eraclito. Merci o monete?', *Annali dell' istituto Italiano di Numismatica* 1980–1. 9–22.

Murray, O. (1993) *Early Greece* 2nd ed., London: Fontana Press.

Naster, P. (1979) 'Les Monnayages satrapaux, provinciaux et régionaux dans l' empire Perse face au numéraire officiel des Achéménides', in Lipinski (1979) 597–604.

Netz, R. (1999) *The Shaping of Deduction in Greek Mathematics.* Cambridge U. P.

Nicolet-Pierre, H. and Barrandon, J.-N. (1997) 'Monnaies d' *Electrum* Archaïques. Le Trésor de Samos de 1984 (*IGCH* 1158) Conservé à Paris', *Rev. Num.* for 1997, 121–35.

Nilsson, M. P. (1957) *The Dionysiac Mysteries of the Hellenistic and Roman Age.* Lund: Gleerup (reprinted 1975: New York: Arno).

(1967) *Geschichte der Griechischen Religion.* Vol. 1.3rd ed. Munich: C. H. Beck.

Nissen, H. J. (1977) 'Aspects of the Development of Early Cylinder Seals', in Gibson and Biggs (1977) 15–24.

Oates, J. (1986) *Babylon* (2nd ed.). London: Thames and Hudson.

Obbink, D. (1997) 'Cosmology as Initiation', in Laks and Most (1997) 39–54.

Oeconomides, M. (1993) '"Iron Coins": A Numismatic Challenge', *Rivista Italiana di Numismatica e Scienze Affini* 95.75–8.

Oppenheim, A. L. (1947) 'A Fiscal Practice of the Ancient Near East', *Journal of Near Eastern Studies* 6.116–20.

(1956) *The Interpretation of Dreams in the Ancient Near East, with a Translation of an Assyrian Dream-Book.* Philadelphia: Transactions of the American Philosophical Society 46.3.

(1970) 'Trade in the Ancient Near East'. *V International Congress of Economic History.* Leningrad.

(1977) *Ancient Mesopotamia. Portrait of a Dead Civilisation.* 2nd ed. University of Chicago Press.

Osborne, C. (1987) *Rethinking Early Greek Philosophy. Hippolytus of Rome and the Presocratics.* London: Duckworth.

(2000) 'Rummaging in the Recycling Bins of Upper Egypt', *Oxford Studies in Ancient Philosophy.* Oxford U. P. 18.329–56.

Osborne, R. (1985) *Demos. The Discovery of Classical Attika.* Cambridge. U. P.

(1991) 'Pride and Prejudice, Sense and Subsistence: Exchange and Society in the Greek City', in J. Rich and A. Wallace-Hadrill (eds.) *City and Country in the Ancient World*, London: Routledge. 119–46.

(1996) *Greece in the Making. 1200–479 BC*. London: Routledge.

(1997) 'The Polis and its Culture', ch. 1 of C. C. W. Taylor (ed.) *Routledge History of Philosophy Vol. 1: From the Beginning to Plato*. London: Routledge.

Owen, G. E. L. (1986) 'Eleatic Questions', reprinted from *CQ* 10 (1960) 84–102, in *Logic, Science and Dialectic*. London: Duckworth.

Page, D. L. (1955) *Sappho and Alcaeus*. Oxford U. P.

Parise, N. (1973) 'Intorno alle riflessioni di Miriam Balmouth sugli inizi della monetazione', *Dialoghi di Archeologia* 7.382–91.

(1979) 'Per un' introduzione allo studio dei segni premonetari nella Grecia arcaica', *Annali dell' Istituto Italiano di Numismatica*. Rome. 26.51–74.

(1984) 'Rilievi inattuali su segni premonetari e nascita della moneta in Grecia', *Studi Storici. Rivista Trimestrale dell' Ist. Gramsci* (Ed. riuniti). 25.55–8.

(1988) 'Sacrificio e misura del valore nella Grecia antica', in Grottanelli and Parise (1988) 253–65 (slightly revised version of a paper with the same title in *Studi Storici. Rivista Trimestrale dell' Ist. Gramsci*. (Ed. riuniti) 25 (1984) 913–23).

(1989) 'Fra Assiri e Greci: Dall' argento di Ishtar alla moneta', *Dialoghi di Archeologia* 5.2.37–9.

(1990) 'Moneta e Società in Magna Graeca. L'esempio di Crotone', in *Crise et Transformation des Sociétés Archaiques de l'Italie Antique au Ve Siècle Av. J-C*. Collection de l' École Française de Rome 137.299–306.

(1997) *Bernhard Laum. Origine della Moneta e teoria del Sacrificio*. Rome: Istituto Italiano di Numismatica.

Parke, H. W. (1933) *Greek Mercenary Soldiers*. Oxford U. P.

Parker, R. C. T. (1996) *Athenian Religion. A History.* Oxford U. P.

(1997) *Cleomenes on the Acropolis*. Inaugural Lecture. Oxford U. P.

Parry, J. and Bloch, M. (1989) *Money and the Morality of Exchange*. Cambridge U. P.

Penglase, C. (1994) *Greek Myths and Mesopotamia*. London: Routledge.

Pettinato, G. (1981) *The Archives of Ebla* (translation of *Ebla. Un impero inciso nell' argila*. Milan, 1979). New York: Doubleday.

Pettinato, G. (1991) Ebla. *A New Look at History* (translation of *Ebla: Nuovi orizzonti della storia*. Milan 1986). Baltimore: Johns Hopkins.

Pfeiler, B. (1966) 'Die Silberprägung von Milet im 6. Jahrhundert v. Chr.', *Revue Suisse de Numismatique* 45.1–25.

Picard, O. (1978) 'Les Origines du monnayage en Grèce', *Histoire* 6.13–20.

(1979) 'La "Fiduciarité" des monnaies métalliques en Grèce', *Bulletin de la société française de Numismatique* 34.604–9.

(1989) 'Innovations monétaire dans la Grèce du IVe siècle', *Comptes Rendus de l'Académie des Inscriptions et Belles-lettres*. 673–87.

(1996) 'Monnaie et Démocratie à Athènes', in M. Sakellariou (ed.) *Démocratie Athénienne et Culture*. Athens: Ἀκαδημία Ἀθηνῶν.

Piteros, Chr., Olivier, J.-P., Melena, J.-L. (1990) 'Les Inscriptions de linéaire B des nodules de Thèbes (1982): la fouille, les documents, les possibilités d' interprétation', *BCH* 114.103–84.

Pittman, H. (1995) 'Cylinder Seals and Scarabs in the Ancient Near East', in Sasson (1995) III.1589–1603.

Polanyi, K. (1968) *Primitive, Archaic, and Modern Economies* (ed. G. Dalton). New York: Doubleday.

(1977) *The Livelihood of Man*. New York: the Academic Press.

Polanyi, K. et al. (eds.) (1957) *Trade and Market in the Early Empires*. Glencoe, Illinois: the Free Press.

Postgate, J. N. (1976) *Fifty Neo-Assyrian Legal Texts*. Warminster: Aris and Phillips.

(1992) *Early Mesopotamia. Society and Economy at the Dawn of History*. London: Routledge.

Powell, M. A. (1978) 'A Contribution to the History of Money in Mesopotamia Prior to the Invention of Coinage', in *Festschrift Matous* (*Assyriologica* 5 (publ. 1981)).

(1990) 'Identification and Interpretation of Long Term Price Fluctuations in Babylonia: More on the History of Money in Mesopotamia', *Altorientalische Forschungen* 17.76–99.

(1996) 'Money in Mesopotamia', *Journal of the Economic and Social History of the Orient* 39.3.224–42.

(1999) 'Monies, Motives, and Methods in Babylonian Economics', in Dercksen (1999) 5–23.

Price, M. J. (1968) 'Early Greek Bronze Coinage', in C. M. Kraay and G. K. Jenkins (eds.) *Essays in Greek Coinage Presented to Stanley Robinson*. Oxford U. P. 90–104.

(1979) 'The Function of Early Greek Bronze Coinage', *Le Origini della Monetazione di bronzo in Sicilia e in Magna Graeca. Atti del VI Convegno del Centro Internazionale di Studi Numismatici: Napoli 17–22 Aprile 1977. Rome: Supplement to AnnIstItNum*. 25.351–65.

(1983) 'Thoughts on the Beginnings of Coinage', in C. Brooke et al. (eds.) *Studies in Numismatic Method Presented to Philip Grierson*. Cambridge U. P. 1–10.

Price, M. J. and Waggoner, N. M. (1975) *Archaic Greek Coinage: The Asyut Hoard*. London: Vecchi.

Quaegebeur, J. (ed.) (1993) *Ritual and Sacrifice in the Ancient Near East*. Leuven: Peeters Press.

Quiggin, A. H. (1963) *A Survey of Primitive Money* (reprint of 1949 edition). New York: AMS Press.

Quiller, B. (1981) 'The Dynamics of the Homeric Society', *SO* 56.109–55.

Radet, G. (1893) *La Lydie et le Monde Grec au temps des Mermnades*. Paris (reprinted 1967, Bretschneider: Rome). Paris: Thorin.

Radner, K. (1999) 'Money in the Neo-Assyrian Empire', in Decksen (1999) 127–39.

Ramage, A. and Craddock, P. (2000) *King Croesus' Gold. Excavations at Sardis and the History of Gold Refining*. London: British Museum Press.

Rathje, W. L. (1977) 'New Tricks for Old Seals: a Progress Report', in Gibson and Biggs (1977) 265–32.

Raubitschek, A. E. (1950) 'Another Drachma Dedication', *YCS* 11.295–60.

(1968) 'Das Denkmal-Epigram', in O. Reverdin (ed.) *L' Épigramme Grecque* in *Entretiens sur L 'Antiquité.* Vol. 14.1–36.

Redfield, J. M. (1986) 'The Development of the Market in Archaic Greece', in B. L. Anderson and A. J. H. Latham (eds.) *The Market in History*, London: Croom Helm. 29–58.

Reed, C. M. (1984) 'Maritime Traders in the Archaic Greek World', *The Ancient World* 10.31–43.

Renger, J. (1977) 'Legal Aspects of Sealing in Ancient Mesopotamia', in Gibson and Biggs (1977) 75–88.

(1984) in Archi, A. (ed.), *Circulation of Goods in Non-palatial Context in the Ancient Near East* (*Incunabula Graeca* 82). Rome.

(1994) 'On Economic Structures in Ancient Mesopotamia', *Orientalia* 63.157–208. Rome.

(1995) 'Subsistenzproduktion und redistributive Palastwirtscaft: Wo bleibt die Nische für die Verwendung der Geld im alten Mesopotamien?', in Schelkle and Nitsch (1995) 271–34.

Rhodes, P. J. (1981) *A Commentary on the Aristotelian Athenaion Politeia.* Oxford U. P.

Richardson, N. J. (1993) *The Iliad: A Commentary. Volume VI: Books 21–24.* Cambridge U. P.

Riedweg, C. (1987) *Mysterienterminologie bei Platon, Philon und Klemens von Alexandrien.* Berlin and New York: de Gruyter.

Riegel, K. F. (1979) *Foundations of Dialectical Psychology.* New York: the Academic Press.

Risberg, C. (1992) 'Metal-Working in Greek Sanctuaries', in Linders and Alroth (1992) 33–40.

Robert, J. and Robert, L. (1950) *Hellenica 9. Inscriptions et reliefs d' Asie Mineure.* Paris: Adrien-Maisonneuve.

Robinson, E. S. G. (1960) 'Some Problems in the Later Fifth Century Coinage at Athens', *Museum Notes* (American Numismatic Society) 9.1–15.

Robinson, E. S. G. (1951) 'Coins from the Ephesian Artemision Reconsidered', *JHS* 71.156–67.

Roebuck, C. (1959) *Ionian Trade and Colonisation.* New York: Archaeological Institute of America.

Röhlig, J. (1933) 'Der Handel von Milet'. Diss. Hamburg.

Roller, L. E. (1983) 'The Legend of Midas', *Class. Ant.* 2.299–313.

Romano, I. (1988) 'Early Greek Cult Images and Cult Practices', in Hägg, Marinatos, and Nordquist (1998) 127–34.

Root, M. C. (1988) 'Evidence from Persepolis for the Dating of Persian and Archaic Greek Coinage', *Num. Chron.* 148.1–12.

Rosivach, V. J. (1994) *The System of Public Sacrifice in Fourth-Century Athens.* Atlanta, Georgia: Scholars Press.

Rösler, W. (1970) *Reflexe vorsokratischen Denkens bei Aischylos*. Meisenheim am Glan: Anton Hain.

Roth, C. P. (1976) 'The Kings and the Muses in Hesiod's Theogony', *TAPA* 106. 331–8.

Rouse, W. H. D. (1902) *Greek Votive Offerings*. Cambridge U. P.

Rupp, D. W. (1983) 'Reflections on the Development of Altars in the Eighth Century BC', in Hägg (1983) 101–7.

Ruschenbusch, E. (1966) ΣΟΛΩΝΟΣ ΝΟΜΟΙ. Wiesbaden: Franz Steiner Verlag.

Rutter, K. (1981) 'Early Coinage and the Influence of the Athenian State', in B. Cunliffe (ed.), *Coinage and Society in Britain and Gaul: Some Current Problems*. London: Council for British Archaeology. 1–9.

Saïd, S. (1979) 'Les Crimes des Prétendants, la Maison d' Ulysse et les Festend de l' Odyssée', in S. Saïd, F. Desbordes, J. Bouffartigue, and A. Moreau (eds.) *Études de littérature ancienne*. 9–50. Paris: Presses de l' école normale superièure.

Sasson, J. M. (ed.) (1995) *Civilisations of the Ancient Near East*. 4 vols. New York: Scribner's.

Saxonhouse, A. W. (1992) *Fear of Diversity: The Birth of Political Science in Ancient Greek Thought*. University of Chicago Press.

Schaeffer, C. (1955) *Le Palais Royal d' Ugarit*. Vol. III. Paris: Klincksieck.

Schaps, D. M. (1997) 'The Monetisation of the Marketplace in Athens', in J. Andreau et al. (eds.) *Prix et Formation des Prix dans les Économies Antiques*. Saint-Bertrand-de-Comminges: *Entretiens d' Archéologie et d' Histoire* III.91–104.

(1998) Review of Tandy (1997), in *Bryn Mawr Classical Review* 11.1 (electronic).

(2001) 'The Conceptual Prehistory of Money and its Impact on the Greek Economy', in Balmuth (2001) 93–103.

Scheer, T. J. (2000) *Die Gottheit und Ihr Bild*. (*Zetemata* 105). München: C. H. Beck.

Schefer, C. (2000) '"Nur für Eingeweihte!" Heraklit und die Mysterien', *Antike und Abendland* 46.46–75.

(2001) *Platons unsagbare Erfahrung. Ein anderer Zugang zu Platon*. Basel: Schwabe.

Schelkle, W. and Nitsch, M. (1995) *Rätsel Geld*. Marburg: Metropolis.

Schiappa, E. (1991) *Protagoras and Logos*. Columbia: University of South Carolina Press.

Schibli, H. (1996) 'On "The One" in Philolaos, Fragment 7*', *CQ* 46.114–30.

Schlaifer, R. (1940) 'Notes on Athenian Public Cults', *HSCP* 51.233–60.

Schmitt Pantel, P. (1992) *La Cité au banquet*. Collection de l'école française de Rome 157. Rome and Paris.

Schopenhauer, A. (1974) *Parerga and Paralipomena* (translation by E. F. J. Payne from German of 1851). 2 vols. Oxford U. P.

Schöttle, G. (1913) 'Geld und Münze im Volksaberglauben', *Archiv für Kutkurgeschichte* 11.320–62.

Schuhl, P.-M. (1953) 'Adela', in *Homo* 1.86–93.

Seaford, R. (1981) 'Dionysiac Drama and the Dionysiac Mysteries', *CQ* 31.252–75.
  (1984a) *Euripides Cyclops*. Oxford U. P.
  (1984b) 'The Last Bath of Agamemnon', *CQ* 34.247–54.
  (1986a) 'Immortality, Salvation and the Elements', in *Harvard Studies in Classical Philology* 90.1–26.
  (1986b) 'Wedding Ritual and Textual Criticism in *Sophocles' Women of Trachis*', *Hermes* 114.50–9.
  (1987) 'The Tragic Wedding', *JHS* 107.106–30.
  (1990a) 'The Structural Problems of Marriage in Euripides', in A. Powell (ed.) *Euripides, Women and Sexuality*. London: Routledge.
  (1990b) 'The Imprisonment of Women in Greek Tragedy', *JHS* 110.76–90.
  (1994a) *Reciprocity and Ritual. Homer and Tragedy in the Developing City-State*. Oxford U. P.
  (1994b) 'Sophokles and the Mysteries', *Hermes* 122.275–88.
  (1996) *Euripides Bacchae*. Warminster: Aris and Phillips.
  (1998a) 'Tragic Money', *JHS* 108.119–39.
  (1998b) 'In the Mirror of Dionysos', in S. Blundell and M. Williamson (eds.) *The Sacred and the Feminine*. London: Routledge. 128–46.
  (2000a) 'Aristotelian Economics and Athenian Tragedy', *New Literary History* 31.2.269–76.
  (2000b) 'Reply to a Critic', *Mnemosyne* 53.1.83–7.
  (2002) 'Reading Money. Leslie Kurke on the Politics of Meaning in Archaic Greece', *Arion* 3rd series 9.3.45–65.
  (2003a) 'Money and the Dionysiac', *Arion* 11.2.1–19.
  (2003b) 'Aeschylus and the Unity of Opposites', *JHS* 123.141–63.
  (2003c) 'Tragic Tyranny', in K. Morgan (ed.) *Popular Tyranny*. Univ. of Texas Press. 95–116.
Seltman, C. (1949) 'The Problem of the First Italiote Coins', *Num. Chron.* 6.9.1–21.
Shell, M. (1978) *The Economy of Literature*. Baltimore: Johns Hopkins U. P.
  (1982) *Money, Language and Thought*. Baltimore: Johns Hopkins U. P.
Shelmerdine, C. (1997) 'Review of Aegean Prehistory VI: The Palatial Bronze Age of the Southern and Central Greek mainland', *AJA* 101.537–85.
Shelov, D. B. (1978) *Coinage of the Bosporus. VI–II Centuries BC*. B. A. R. International Series 46.
Sherratt, E. S. and Sherratt, A. (1993) 'The Growth of the Mediterranean Economy in the Early First Millennium BC', *World Archaeology* 24 (3).361–78.
Shipley, G. (1987) *A History of Samos 800–188 BC*. Oxford U. P.
Silver, M. (1985) *Economic Structures of the Ancient Near East*. London: Croom Helm.
Simmel, G. (1978) *The Philosophy of Money* (Translation of *Die Philosophie des Geldes*. 2nd ed., Leipzig, 1907). London: Routledge and Kegan Paul.
Skiersma, F. (1990) *Projection and Religion, an Anthropological and Psychological Account of the Phenomenon of Projection* (Translation of *de religieuse projectie*, 2nd ed., 1957). Ann Arbor: UMI.

Snell, B. (1953) *The Discovery of the Mind in Greek Philosophy and Literature* (translation *of Die Entdecking des Geistes*. Hamburg 1948). Harvard U. P.

Snell, D. C. (1982) *Ledgers and Prices: Early Mesopotamian Merchant Accounts*. Yale U. P.

(1995) 'Methods of Exchange and Coinage in Western Asia', in Sasson (1995) III.1487–97.

(1997) *Life in the Ancient Near East*. Yale U. P.

Snodgrass, A. (1980) *Archaic Greece*. London, Melbourne, Toronto: J. M. Dent.

Snyder Schaeffer, J., Ramage, N. H., Greenewalt, C. H. (1997) *The Corinthian, Attic, and Laconian Pottery from Sardis*. Harvard U. P.

Sohn-Rethel, A. (1978) *Intellectual and Manual Labour*. London: Macmillan.

Sokolowski, F. (1954) 'Fees and Taxes in the Greek Cults', *Harvard Theological Review* 47.153–64.

(1955) *Lois Sacrées de l'Asie Mineure*. Paris: de Boccard.

(1962) *Lois Sacrées des Cités Grecques*. Supplément. Paris: de Boccard.

(1969) *Lois Sacrées des Cités Grecques*. Paris: de Boccard.

Sourvinou-Inwood, C. (1993) 'Early Sanctuaries, the Eighth Century, and Ritual Space', in Marinatos and Hägg (1993) 1–17.

Spier, J. (1990) 'Emblems in Archaic Greece', *BICS* 37.107–29.

(1998) 'Notes on Early Electrum Coinage and a Die-linked Issue from Lydia', in Ashton and Hurter (1998) 327–34.

Srinivas, M. N. (1955) 'The Social System of a Mysore Village', in M. Marriott (ed.) *Village India*. Washington D. C.: *American Anthropological Association Memoir* 83.1–35.

Stancomb, W. (1993) 'Arrowheads, Dolphins and Cast Coins in the Black Sea Region', *Classical Numismatic Review* 18 (3) 5.

Starr, C. G. 'A Sixth-century Athenian Tetradrachm Used to Seal a Clay Tablet from Persepolis', *Num. Chron.* 136.219–22.

Steiner, D. T (1994) *The Tyrant's Writ*. Princeton U. P.

Steinkeller, P. (1977) 'Seal Practice in the Ur III Period', in Gibson and Biggs (1977) 41–53.

Stengel, P. (1920) *Die Griechische Kultusaltertümer*. 3rd ed. Munich: C. H. Beck.

Stieglitz, R. (1979) 'Commodity Prices at Ugarit', *Journal of the American Oriental Society* 99.15–23.

Stockert, W. (1983) *Plautus Aulularia*. Stuttgart: Teubner.

Stokes, M. (1971) *One and Many in Presocratic Philosophy*. Harvard U. P.

Stos-Gale, Z. A. (2001) 'The Impact of the Natural Sciences on Studies of Hacksilber and Early Silver Coinage', in Balmuth (2001) 53–76.

Strøm, I. (1992) 'Obeloi of Pre- or Proto-Monetary Value in the Greek Sanctuaries', in Linders and Alroth (1992) 41–51.

Stroud, R. S. (1974) 'An Athenian Law on Silver Coinage', *Hesperia* 43.157–88.

Svenbro, J. (1982) 'A Mégara Hyblaea: le Corps Géometrique', *Annales ESC* 37.953–64.

Sweet, R. F. G. (1958) 'On Prices, Moneys, and Money Uses in the Old Babylonian Period'. Diss., University of Chicago.

Szegedy-Maszak, A. (1978) 'Legends of the Greek Lawgivers', *GRBS* 19.199–209.

Tandy, D. W. (1997) *Warriors into Traders: The Power of the Market in Early Greece.* Berkeley: University of California Press.

Taplin, O. (1978) *Greek Tragedy in Action.* London: Methuen.

Thom, J. C. (1995) *The Pythagorean Golden Verses.* Leiden: Brill.

Thomson, G. (1932) *Aeschylus, The Prometheus Bound.* Cambridge U. P.

    (1953) 'From Religion to Philosophy', *JHS* 73.77–83.

    (1961a) *The Prehistoric Aegean.* London: Lawrence and Wishart.

    (1961b) *The First Philosophers.* 2nd ed. London: Lawrence and Wishart.

Threatte, L. (1980) *The Grammar of Attic Inscriptions.* Vol. 1. Berlin: de Gruyter.

Tomlinson, R. A. (1980) 'Two Notes on Possible Hestiatoria', *BSA* 75.221–8.

    (1992) 'Perachora', in O. Reverdin and B. Grange (eds.), *Le Sanctuaire grecque.* Geneva: Fondation Hardt. 321–51.

Traill, D. (1989) 'Gold Armor for Bronze and Homer's Use of Compensatory *Time*', *Classical Philology* 84.301–5.

Treister, M. Y. (1996) *The Role of Metals in Ancient Greek History.* Leiden: Brill.

Tsantanoglou, K. and Parassoglou, G. M. (1987) 'Two Gold Lamellae from Thessaly', *Hellenika* 38.3–16.

Tuplin, C. J. (1989) 'The Coinage of Aryandes', *REA* 91.61–83.

Turner, V. (1982) *From Ritual to Theatre. The Human Seriousness of Play.* New York: PAJ Publications.

Ure, P. N. (1922) *The Origin of Tyranny.* Cambridge U. P.

van de Mieroop, M. (1992) *Society and Enterprise in Old Babylonian Ur.* Berlin: Berliner Beiträge zum Vorderen Orient Bd. 12.

    (1997) *The Ancient Mesopotamian City.* Oxford U. P.

van den Oudenrijn, C. M. A. (1952) 'Solon's System of Property-Classes Once More', *Mnemosyne* 5.19–27.

van Dijk, J. J. A. (1953) *La Sagesse Suméro-Accadienne.* Leiden: Brill.

van Effenterre, H. and Ruzé, F. (1994–5) *Nomima. Receuil d' inscriptions politiques et juridiques de l' archaisme grec.* Rome. 2 vols.

van Groningen, B. A. and Wartelle, A. (eds.) (1968) *Aristote. Économique.* Paris: Budé.

van Straten, F. T. (1981) 'Gifts for the Gods', in H. S. Versnel (ed.) *Faith, Hope and Worship.* Leiden: Brill. 65–151.

    (1995) *Hiera Kala. Images of Animal Sacrifice in Archaic and Classical Greece.* Leiden: Brill.

van Wees, H. (1992) *Status Warriors.* Amsterdam: J. C. Gieben.

    (1994) 'The Homeric World of War: The *Iliad* and the Hoplite Phalanx (II)', *G&R* 41.131–55.

Vannicelli, P. (1985) 'Dal χρυσός ai χρήματα. Eraclito 90 D–K ed Erodoto 3.96.2', *Rivista di Filologia e di Istruzione Classica* 113.397–404.

Veenhof, K. R. (1972) *Aspects of Old Assyrian Trade and its Terminology.* Leiden: Brill.

Ventris, M. and Chadwick, J. (1973) *Documents in Mycenean Greek.* 2nd ed. Cambridge U. P.

Vermeule, E. (1974) *Götterkult* (*Archaeologia Homerica* Band III Kap. v). Göttingen: Vandenhoeck and Ruprecht.

Vernant, J.-P. (1982) *The Origins of Greek Thought* (translation of *Les Origines de la pensée grecque*, Presses Universitaires de France, 1962). London: Methuen.

(1983) *Myth and Thought in Ancient Greece* (translation of *Mythe et pensée chez les Grecs*, Paris 1965). London: Routledge and Kegan Paul.

Versnel, H. S. (1981) 'Religious Mentality in Ancient Prayer', in H. S. Versnel (ed.) *Faith, Hope and Worship*, Leiden: Brill. 1–64.

Vickers, M. (1985) 'Early Greek Coinage: A Reassessment', *Num. Chron.* 145.108–28.

Vidal-Naquet, P. (1986) *The Black Hunter* (translation of *Le Chasseur Noir*, Paris 1981). Baltimore: Johns Hopkins U. P.

Vinogradov, J. (1991) 'Zur sachlichen und geschichtlichen Deutung der Orphiker-Plättchen von Olbia', in *Orphisme et Orphée. En l' honneur de Jean Rudhardt*. Geneva: Droz. 77–86 (reprinted in J. Vinogradov, *Pontische Studien* (Mainz: Philipp von Zabern, 1997) 242–9).

Vlastos, G. (1970) 'Equality and Justice in Early Greek Cosmologies', in Furley and Allen (1970) 56–91.

Volkmann, H. (1939) 'ΔΟΚΙΜΑ ΧΡΗΜΑΤΑ', *Hermes* 74.99–102.

von Fritz, K. (1940) *Pythagorean Politics in Southern Italy*. New York: Columbia U. P.

von Reden, S. (1995) *Exchange in Ancient Greece*. London: Duckworth.

(1997) 'Money, Law and Exchange: Coinage in the Greek Polis', *JHS* 117.154–76.

(1999) 'Reevaluating Gernet. Value and Greek Myth', in Buxton (1999) 51–70.

von Soden, W. (1994) *The Ancient Orient*. Leominster: Gracewing.

Waetzoldt, H. and Hauptmann, H. (1988) *Wirtschaft und Gesellschaft von Ebla*. Akten der internationalen Tagungen. Heidelberger Orientalverlag.

Walcot, P. (1966) *Hesiod and the Ancient Near East*. Cardiff: Wales U. P.

Wallace, R. W. (1987) 'The Origin of Electrum Coinage', *AJA* 91.3.385–97.

(1989) 'The Production and Exchange of Early Anatolian Electrum Coinage', *REA* 91.87–95.

(2001) 'Remarks on the Value and Standards of Early Electrum Coins', in Balmuth (2001) 127–34.

Warren, J. (1998) 'Updating (and Downdating) the Autonomous Bronze Coinage of Sikyon', in Ashton and Hurter (1998) 347–61.

Weidauer, L. (1975) *Probleme der frühen Elektronprägung, Fribourg: Office du livre, Typos: Monographien zur antiken Numismatik*, 1. Fribourg: Office du Livre.

Weil, A. (1980) *Les Pouvoirs cachés de la monnaie*. Paris: Fayard.

West, M. L. (1966) *Hesiod Theogony*. Oxford U. P.

(1971) *Early Greek Philosophy and the Orient*. Oxford U. P.

(1974) *Studies in Greek Elegy and Iambus*. Berlin and New York: de Gruyter.

(1983) *The Orphic Poems*. Oxford U. P.

(1995) 'The Date of the Iliad', *Mus. Helv.* 52.203–19.

(1997) *The East Face of Helicon. West Asiatic Elements in Greek Poetry and Myth*. Oxford U. P.

Westbrook, R. (1992) 'The Trial Scene in the *Iliad*', *Harvard Studies in Classical Philology* 94.53–76.

Whitehead, D. (1986) *The Demes of Attica*. Princeton U. P.

Wildberg, C. (1993) 'Simplicius und das Zitat. Zur Überlieferung des Anführungszeichens', in F. Berger et al. (eds.) *Symbolae Berolineses fur Dieter Harlfinger*. Amsterdam: Hakkert. 187–99.

Wilkins, J. (2000) *The Boastful Chef. The Discourse of Food in Ancient Greek Comedy*. Oxford U. P.

Will, E. (1954) 'De l'Aspect éthique des origines grecques de la monnaie', *Revue historique* 212.209–31.

(1955) 'Réflexions et hypothèses sur les origines de la monnaie', *Revue de numismatique* 17.5–23.

(1975) 'Fonctions de la monnaie dans les cités grecques de l'époque classique', in *Numismatique antique, problèmes et methodes*. Nancy and Louvain.

Williams, B. (1977) 'Aspects of Sealing and Glyptic in Egypt before the New Kingdom', in Gibson and Biggs (1977) 135–40.

Williams, B. (1993) *Shame and Necessity*. Berkeley: University of California Press.

Williams, D. J. R. (1991–3) 'The "Pot-hoard" Pot from the Archaic Artemision at Ephesus', *BICS* 38.98–104.

Williams, J. (ed.) (1997) *Money. A History*. British Museum Press.

Williams, R. T. (1992) *The Silver Coinage of Velia*. London: Royal Numismatic Society. Special Publications n. 25.

Wilson, P. (2000) *The Athenian Institution of the Khoregia*. Cambridge U. P.

Winter, I. J. (1987) 'Legitimation of Authority Through Image and Legend', in M. Gibson and R. D. Biggs (eds.), *The Organisation of Power. Aspects of Bureaucracy in the Ancient Near East (Studies in Ancient Oriental Civilisation 46)*. Chicago: The Oriental Institute. 69–116.

Winter, Nancy A. (1993) *Greek Architectural Terracottas. From the Prehistoric Period to the End of the Archaic Period*. Oxford U. P.

Wolff, S. R. (1998) 'Archaology in Israel', *AJA* 102.757–802.

Woodbury, L. (1980) 'Strepsiades' Understanding: Five Notes on the Clouds', *Phoenix* 34.108–27.

Woodruff, P. (1999) 'Rhetoric and Relativism: Protagoras and Gorgias', in Long (1999) 290–310.

Zaccagnini, C. (1976) 'La Circolazione dei beni', in S. Moscati et al. (eds.), *L'Alba della Civiltà*. Turin. Vol. II 425–582.

(1979) 'The Price of the Fields at Nuzi', *Journal of the Economic and Social History of the Orient* 22.1–31.

Zancani-Montuoro, P. (1935) 'Il Giudizio di Persephone in un pinakion Locrese', *Archivio Storico per la Calabria e la Lucania* 5.195–218.

Zervos, O. (1986) 'Coins Excavated at Corinth 1978–1980', *Hesperia* 55.183–205.

Zhmud, L. (1992) 'Orphism and Graffiti from Olbia', *Hermes* 120.159–68.

Zuntz, G. (1971) *Persephone*. Oxford U. P.

Index